CT / WeB / £16·00

Civil Liberties:
Cases and Materials

Civil Liberties:
Cases and Materials

S. H. Bailey
MA, LLB (Cantab)
Lecturer in Law at the
University of Nottingham

D. J. Harris
LLM, PhD (Lond)
Senior Lecturer in Law at the
University of Nottingham

B. L. Jones
MA, LLB (Cantab)
Lecturer in Law at the
University of Nottingham

London
Butterworths
1980

England London	Butterworth & Co (Publishers) Ltd 88 Kingsway, WC2B 6AB
Australia Sydney	Butterworths Pty Ltd 586 Pacific Highway, Chatswood, NSW 2067 Also at Melbourne, Brisbane, Adelaide and Perth
Canada Toronto	Butterworth & Co (Canada) Ltd 2265 Midland Avenue, Scarborough, M1P 4S1
New Zealand Wellington	Butterworths of New Zealand Ltd 77–85 Customhouse Quay
South Africa Durban	Butterworth & Co (South Africa) (Pty) Ltd 152–154 Gale Street
USA Boston	Butterworth (Publishers) Inc 10 Tower Office Park, Woburn, Mass. 01801

| ISBN Casebound | 0 406 55481 | 1 |
| Limp | 0 406 55480 | 3 |

Reproduced from copy supplied, printed in Great Britain
by Billing & Sons Limited, Guildford, London, Oxford, Worcester
Bound by Mansell (Bookbinders) Ltd., Witham, Essex

Preface

In recent years, more attention has been paid to the law of civil liberties in law teaching (and elsewhere) than used to be the case. This appears likely to prove a continuing phenomenon, resulting in part from the current debate on the question whether the United Kingdom should enact a Bill of Rights and the now substantial jurisprudence of the Strasbourg authorities applying the European Convention on Human Rights to cases coming from this country. As to the former, Lord Wade's Bill of Rights Bill has been given a Third Reading by the House of Lords. Although the Lord Chancellor has indicated that the chances of the bill being adopted this session are only those of "an icicle in June", the vagaries of British weather are such that it is not impossible that some form of Bill of Rights will be adopted in the next few years. Certainly the chances of this happening are greater now than they have been before. In any event, the law of civil liberties now plays a prominent part in many constitutional law courses and the number of separate courses on civil liberties is increasing. In these circumstances, it would seem appropriate to publish a collection of cases and materials on the subject. Hopefully, this will serve the needs of those studying the law of civil liberties as already taught, particularly as it is a subject that calls for the reading of a lot of materials other than cases which are not always readily available and which a student may find convenient to have assembled in one place. Such a publication may also encourage the teaching of more civil liberties courses. One problem with teaching the law of civil liberties in constitutional law (quite apart from that of finding room in the syllabus) is that the latter is usually a first year course and the former, which cuts across a number of traditional teaching boundaries, requires a knowledge of concepts normally taught in second and third year courses.

The book concentrates, in the terminology of the UN Covenants on Human Rights, on *civil* liberties (rights); there is only occasional and incidental coverage of economic and social rights. A choice has to be made for reasons of space and rights within the latter categories tend to be dealt with in labour and welfare law courses rather than in constitutional or civil liberties ones. The book emphasises the basic civil liberties, although room has been found for prisoners' rights as an example of an area in which the law of civil liberties is in the process of change. We have tried to show how the law works in practice as well as what it is. In this respect particularly, we would like to acknowledge the debt that anyone writing on the law of civil liberties owes to Street's *Freedom, the Individual and the Law*. Our aim has been to cover the legal position in England and Wales. We have used the situation in Northern Ireland as an example of the law of civil liberties in an emergency. Reference has been made to the position in Scotland, the United States and the Commonwealth countries where this provides an instructive comparison. There is also a section on the European Convention on Human Rights, and Strasbourg cases originating from the UK have been included or referred to elsewhere when relevant.

We wish to acknowledge the assistance given to us in providing information by a number of Government departments and other institutions. These include the Home Office, the Department of the Environment, the Attorney General's Office, the Press Council, the BBC, the IBA and the Metropolitan Police. We also wish to thank the following for permitting the publication of extracts from materials in respect of which they hold the copyright: HMSO; the Incorporated Council of Law Reporting; the All England Reports; Penguin Books Ltd; Times Publishing Co. Ltd; the Press Council; Sweet and Maxwell; Eclipse Publishing Ltd; New Society; West Publishing Co. Ltd; the Council of Europe; the European Communities; the BBC; the University of Toronto Law Journal. Finally, we would like to thank the publishers for preparing the index and tables and for generally being so helpful.

The manuscript was delivered to the publishers on 1 November 1979 and seeks to be up-to-date at that time. It has proved possible to make some alterations that take account of developments that have occurred since then. Our impression is that the law of civil liberties is an area of the law in which, more than in most, the type never sets.

S. H. Bailey
D. J. Harris
B. L. Jones

April 2 1980

Contents

Chapter 3
Public order

Chapter 4
Freedom of expression: censorship and obscenity

Chapter 5
Freedom of expression: contempt of court

Chapter 6
Freedom of expression: national security

Chapter 7
The right to privacy

Chapter 8
Freedom of religion

Chapter 9
Freedom from racial discrimination

Chapter 10
Prisoners' rights

Table of statutes

References in this Table to "*Statutes*" are to Halsbury's Statutes of England (Third Edition) showing the volume and page at which the annotated text of the Act will be found. Page references printed in bold type indicate where the Act is set out in part or in full.

List of cases

Cases are listed under the name of the accused whenever the usual method of citation would cause them to be preceded by the abbreviation "R v" signifying that the prosecution was undertaken by the Crown.

CHAPTER 1

The method of protecting civil liberties in English law

1 The present method

Legislation on Human Rights: A Discussion Document (Home Office 1976, paras. 2.01–05)

Our arrangements for the protection of human rights are different from those of most other countries. The differences are related to differences in our constitutional traditions. Although our present constitution may be regarded as deriving in part from the revolution settlement of 1688–89, consolidated by the Union of 1707, we, unlike our European neighbours and many Commonwealth countries, do not owe our present system of government either to a revolution or to a struggle for independence. The United Kingdom—

(a) has an omnicompetent Parliament, with absolute power to enact any law and change any previous law; the courts in England and Wales have not, since the seventeenth century, recognised even in theory any higher legal order by reference to which Acts of Parliament could be held void; in Scotland the courts, while reserving the right to treat an Act as void for breaching a fundamental term of the Treaty of Union [see *MacCormick v Lord Advocate* 1953 SC 396], have made it clear that they foresee no likely circumstances in which they would do so;

(b) unlike other modern democracies, has no written constitution;

(c) unlike countries in the civil law tradition, makes no fundamental distinction, as regards rights or remedies, between 'public law' governing the actions of the State and its agents, and 'private law' regulating the relationships of private citizens with one another; nor have we a coherent system of administrative law applied by specialised tribunals or courts and with its own appropriate remedies;

(d) has not generally codified its law, and our courts adopt a relatively narrow and literal approach to the interpretation of statutes;

(e) unlike the majority of EEC countries and the United States, does not, by ratifying a treaty or convention, make it automatically part of the domestic law (nor do we normally give effect to such an international agreement by incorporating the agreement itself into our law).

In other countries the rights of the citizen are usually (though not universally) to be found enunciated in general terms in a Bill of Rights or other constitutional document. The effectiveness of such instruments varies greatly. A Bill of Rights is not an automatic guarantee of liberty; its efficacy depends on the integrity of the institutions which apply it, and ultimately on the determination of the people that it should be maintained. The United Kingdom as such has no Bill of Rights of this kind. The Bill of Rights of 1688, though more concerned with the relationship between the English Parliament and the Crown, did contain some important safeguards for personal liberty—as did the Claim of Right of 1689, its Scottish equivalent. Among the provisions common to both the Bill of Rights and the Claim of Right are declarations that excessive bail is illegal and that it is the right of subjects to petition the Crown without incurring penalties. But the protection given by these instruments to the rights and liberties of the citizen is much narrower than the constitutional guarantees now afforded in many other democratic countries.

The effect of the United Kingdom system of law is to provide, through the development of the common law and by express statutory enactment, a diversity of specific rights with their accompanying remedies. Thus, to secure the individual's right to freedom from unlawful or arbitrary detention, our law provides specific and detailed remedies such as habeas corpus and the action for false imprisonment. The rights which have been afforded in this way are for the most part negative rights to be protected from interference from others, rather than positive rights to behave in a particular way. Those rights which have emerged in the common law can always be modified by Parliament. Parliament's role is all-pervasive—potentially, at least. It continually adapts existing rights and remedies and provides new ones, and no doubt this process would continue even if a comprehensive Bill of Rights were enacted.

The legal remedies provided for interference with the citizen's rights have in recent times been overlaid by procedures which are designed to afford not so much remedies in the strict sense of the term as facilities for obtaining independent and impartial scrutiny of action by public bodies about which an individual believes he has cause for complaint, even though the action may have been within the body's legal powers. For example, the actions of central government departments are open to scrutiny by the Parliamentary Commissioner for Administration; and complaints about the administration of the National Health Service are investigated by the Health Service Commissioners.

NOTES

1. On the method of protecting civil liberties in the UK and/or the question of the introduction of a Bill of Rights, see T. C. Daintith, (1968) 1 H Rts Rev 275; S. A. de Smith, *Constitutional and Administrative Law* (3rd edn., 1977) pp. 439–43; J. Fawcett, (1976) 1 H Rts J 57; Lord Hailsham, *The Dilemma of Democracy* (1978) Chap. 26; J. Jaconelli, [1976] PL 226; A. Lester, *Democracy and Individual Rights* (1968); A. Lester (1976–77) 125 U Penn LR 336; Lord Lloyd (1976) 39 MLR 121; F. A. Mann (1972) 122 NLJ 289 and (1978) 94 LQR 512; G. Marshall, *Constitutional Theory* (1971), Chap. VI, and [1976] PL 109; A. J. M. Milne (1977) 40 MLR 389; Lord Scarman, *English Law—The New Dimension* (1974), pp. 10–20, 76–88; S. Silkin, (1977) 28 NILQ 3; F. Stacey, *A New Bill of Rights for Britain* (1973); H. Street, *Freedom, the Individual and the Law* (4th edn., 1977), Chap. 13; P. Wallington and J. McBride, *Civil Liberties and a Bill of Rights* (1976); D. C. M. Yardley, [1975] PL 197; M. Zander, *A Bill of Rights?* 2nd edn., 1979) and J. Jaconelli, *Enacting a Bill of Rights* (1980).

2. As the Discussion Document states, most countries protect civil liberties by means of a Bill of Rights. Lord Lloyd (1976) 39 MLR 121, 122–3 defines a Bill of Rights as a 'constitutional code of human rights' that is binding in law, is (inevitably) generally worded and has the following other key characteristics:

'(a) The code should be given some sort of over-riding authority over other laws.
(b) Power should be vested in the judiciary (whether generally or by way of a Constitutional or Supreme Court) to interpret the rights set forth in the Bill of Rights and to determine judicially their proper scope, extent and limits, and their relationship inter se.
(c) The judiciary will possess the power to declare legislation invalid which it holds to be repugnant to the rights guaranteed in the Bill of Rights.'

3. A power of judicial review over legislation was claimed by Coke CJ in *Dr Bonham's* Case (1610) 8 Co Rep 114a, 118: 'When an Act of Parliament is against common right and reason, or repugnant, or impossible to be performed, the common law will control it, and adjudge such act to be void.' Had this claim been pressed and accepted, the resulting power could have been used to protect civil liberties in much the same way as a Bill of Rights does without any formal enactment. But it proved only to be rhetoric; no statute has ever been overturned on the basis of it. The current position was stated by Lord Reid in *British Railways Board v Pickin* [1974] AC 765, 782, HL:

'The idea that a court is entitled to disregard a provision in an Act of Parliament on any ground must seem strange and startling to anyone with any knowledge of the history and law of our constitution.... In earlier times many learned lawyers seem to have believed that an Act of Parliament could be disregarded in so far as it was contrary to the law of God or the law of nature or natural justice, but since the supremacy of Parliament was finally demonstrated by the Revolution of 1688 any such idea has become obsolete.'

In Oppenheimer v Cattermole [1976] AC 249, HL, the question was whether English courts should recognise a nazi law that deprived German Jews resident abroad of their nationality and confiscated their property. A majority of the House of Lords took the view that the law was 'so grave an infringment of human rights that the courts of this country ought to refuse to recognise it as a law at all' (Lord Cross at 278). Mann ((1978) 94 LQR 512, 513–4) refers to the case and notes that 'for more than 300 years England has been spared the necessity of facing' the question of the legality of such laws *within its own legal system.* He suggests that were it to arise 'English judges could no doubt find a legally convincing reason for reverting to the tradition of the fundamental law' and that the 'real question would be whether, in the condition which has been assumed, they would have the strength of character to search for it.'

4. Although subject to Parliament, the courts still have an important role to play in the protection of civil liberties by the interpretation of statutes, the review of administrative action and the development of the common law. As far as the interpretation of statutes is concerned, the courts have developed certain presumptions that help. The presumption against the taking of property without compensation (*Central Control Board (Liquor Traffic) v Cannon Brewery Co Ltd* [1919] AC 744 at 752, HL, per Lord Atkinson) is an example. So are the presumptions against the retrospective effect of legislation (*Ward v British Oak Insurance Co Ltd* [1932] 1 KB 392, CA) and against interference with the liberty of the subject, although the latter does not apply in wartime (*R v Halliday* [1917] AC 260, HL). The presumption that legislation complies with international law (*Collco Dealings v IRC* [1962] AC 1, HL) is important in that the UK is bound by a number of international human rights treaties, including the European Convention on Human Rights (ECHR), see below, p. 17. A determined court may also do a lot by way of interpretation of a statute that it considers infringes civil liberties (see the direction to the jury in *R v Bourne* [1939] 1 KB 687, CCC, interpreting Offences against the Person Act 1861, s. 58 – an abortion, or women's rights, case). A court's attitude to the interpretation of ambiguous provisions in legislation aimed positively at protecting civil liberties can also be crucial. Consider, for example, the interpretation given to doubtful provisions in the Race Relations Acts 1965–76, below, Chap. 9.

5. The courts have a well established power of judicial review of administrative action taken by national or local or other government authorities. This is undoubtedly so where the action is based upon *statutory* powers. In *Laker Airways Ltd v Department of Trade* [1977] QB 643 at 706, CA, Lord Denning MR, stated obiter that the courts can also examine the use of *prerogative* powers 'so as to see that they are not used improperly or mistakenly'. Cases such as *Padfield v Minister of Agriculture, Fisheries and Food* [1968] AC 997, HL, and *Secretary of State for Education and Science v Metropolitan Borough of Tameside* [1977] AC 1014, HL, show how useful the power of judicial review can be to control ultra vires action. Action that is taken properly within the discretion given by a statute or a prerogative power is not open to challenge in court and, as in the case of the Prison Act 1952, below, Chap. 10, the discretion that is given to the authorities may be very wide. Even if action is ultra vires, there is also the problem of finding an available remedy, although the new 'application for judicial review' is of help (see below, p. 34).

6. The judges have a long and proud tradition of protecting civil liberties at common law against encroachment by the executive. *Entick v Carrington,* below, p. 74, is a classic example. But although cases of this sort may still occur, some judges are less open to persuasion than others. It is a common complaint that the courts generally are not inclined to develop the law on a grand scale, at least in the field of civil liberties. Commenting upon the failure of the courts to develop a law of privacy in the way that the American courts have, Street (*Freedom, The Individual and the Law*, (4th edn., 1977), p. 264) states:

'But there is no spirit of adventure or progress, either in judges or counsel, in England today. Today's English judges are not the innovators that some of their distinguished predecessors were; in the hands of modern judges the common law has lost its capacity to expand. They have not been helped by counsel. Cases are argued and tried by a narrow circle of men who seldom look beyond the decided cases for guidance. The entire development of the American law of privacy can be traced to an article in a law periodical published by Harvard Law School. It is inconceivable that the views of an academic journal would exercise similar influence in Britain. This inward- and backward-looking attitude of the English Bar serves only to increase the likelihood that the courts will fail to make the law fit the needs of the time.'

Later in the same book he writes (p. 316):

'Our judges may be relied on to defend strenuously some kinds of freedom. Their emotions will be aroused where personal freedom is menaced by some politically unimportant area of the executive: a case of unlawful arrest by a policeman, for example. Their integrity is, of course, beyond criticism. Yet there are obvious limitations to what they can be expected to do in moulding the law of civil liberties. Two factors stand in their way: their reluctance to have clashes with senior members of the Government, their desire not to have a repetition of the nineteenth-century strife between Parliament and the courts; and secondly, their unwillingness to immerse themselves in problems of policy, which of course loom large in many of the issues examined here.'

Does the refusal of Sir Robert Megarry VC to 'legislate in a new field' in *Malone v Metropolitan Police Comr* below, at p. 328, support these criticisms? Might the reluctance of the courts (but see now *Ex parte St Germain* below, p. 430) to review prison administration and their failure to develop a means of dealing with racial discrimination at common law be other examples? (But was it ever *argued* before a court that racial discrimination might be a tort?) Are Lord Denning MR's 'right to work' judgment in *Nagle v Feilden* [1966] 2 QB 633, CA, and his 'judicial legislation' on police seizure of evidence (in favour of law and order, not privacy) in *Ghani v Jones* below, p. 94, examples going the other way? And what about Ungoed-Thomas J's willingness to lead the law of breach of confidence into the unknown in *Argyll v Argyll* below, p. 318? Do the materials in this book support the suggestion that the courts might be better at protecting some kinds of rights than others? Might it be relevant whether the protection needed is against the state or against a private institution or person?

R v Chief Immigration Officer, ex parte Salamat Bibi [1976] 1 WLR 979, [1976] 3 All ER 843, Court of Appeal

The case concerned the application by immigration officers of Immigration Rules made under the Immigration Act 1971. It was argued for the applicant (a person seeking admission to the United Kingdom as the wife of a Commonwealth citizen already in the United Kingdom) that the Rules should be interpreted and applied by immigration officers in accordance with the right to family life in Article 8, ECHR. The following extract concerns this point only.

Lord Denning MR.: The position as I understand it is that if there is any ambiguity in our statutes, or uncertainty in our law, then these courts can look to the Convention as an aid to clear up the ambiguity and uncertainty, seeking always to bring them into harmony with it. Furthermore, when Parliament is enacting a statute, or the Secretary of State is framing rules, the courts will assume that they had regard to the provisions of the Convention, and intended to make the enactment accord with the Convention: and will interpret them accordingly. But I would dispute altogether that the Convention is part of our law. Treaties and declarations do not become part of our law until they are made law by Parliament. I desire, however, to amend one of the statements I made in the *Bhajan Singh* case [1976] QB 198 at 207. I said then that the immigration officers ought to bear in mind the principles stated in the Convention. I think that would be asking too much of the immigration officers. They cannot be expected to know or to apply the Convention. They must go simply by the immigration rules laid down by the Secretary of State, and not by the Convention.

I may also add this. The Convention is drafted in a style very different from the way which we are used to in legislation. It contains wide general statements of principle. They are apt to lead to much difficulty in application: because they give rise to much uncertainty. They are not the sort of thing which we can easily digest. Article 8 is an example. It is so wide as to be incapable of practical application. So it is much better for us to stick to our own statutes and principles, and only look to the Convention for guidance in case of doubt.

Roskill LJ: In *R v Secretary of State for the Home Department, ex parte Phansopkar* [1976] QB 606 and again in *Pan-American World Airways Inc v Department of Trade* [1976] 1 Lloyd's Rep 257, Scarman LJ, who was a member of the court on both occasions, as was Lord Denning MR and Lawton LJ, went, if I may most respectfully say so, rather further in this connection than did the other two members of the court. Scarman LJ, after a reference to Magna Carta, said [1976] QB 606 at 626:

'This hallowed principle of our law is now reinforced by the European Convention on Human Rights to which it is now the duty of our public authorities in administering the law, including the Immigration Act 1971, and of our courts in interpreting and applying the law, including the Act, to have regard: . . .'

With respect, that dictum was obiter. I venture to think it is somewhat too wide . . . . In his judgment in the *Pan-Am* case [1976] 1 Lloyd's Rep 257 a few days later, Scarman LJ . . . said at p. 261:

'Such a Convention'—and there he was referring to the Convention on Human Rights— 'especially a multilateral one, should then be considered by courts even though no statute expressly or impliedly incorporates it into our law.'

There again with great respect I think the matter is somewhat too widely expressed. Lord Denning MR has already said that perhaps he too went somewhat too far in the *Bhajan Singh* case in [1976] QB 198 at 207. I most respectfully agree with that view.

Geoffrey Lane LJ delivered a concurring judgment.

Appeal dismissed.

NOTES

1. Lord Denning MR had said in *Birdi v Secretary of State for Home Affairs* (unreported, but referred to in *R v Secretary of State for Home Affairs, ex parte Bhajan Singh* [1976] QB 198, CA) that if an Act of Parliament contradicted the European Convention 'I might be inclined to hold it invalid'. Lord Denning recanted on this in *Ex parte Bhajan Singh*.

2. In *Waddington v Miah* [1974] 1 WLR 683, HL, Lord Reid, speaking for the whole House of Lords, said at p. 694 (when considering whether an offence created under the Immigration Act 1971 was intended to operate retrospectively) that in view of the Universal Declaration of Human Rights (Article 11) and the ECHR (Article 7) 'it is hardly credible that any government department would promote or that Parliament would pass retrospective criminal legislation.' For casenotes, see A. Drzemczewski, (1976) 92 LQR 33 and P. Wallington, (1974) CLJ 9. See similarly, *R v Deery* [1977] Crim LR 550, NI Ct Cr App (penalty for crime not to apply retroactively because of ECHR Article 7 and the presumption of compliance with international law). See also *R v Greater London Council ex parte Burgess* [1978] ICR 991, DC (ECHR not to prevail over clear words of statute). In *R v McCormick* [1977] NI 105, McGonigal LJ interpreted wording in a statute which he took to have been borrowed from the ECHR in accordance with the meaning given to it at Strasbourg.

3. Did Lord Denning have the common law in mind when he referred to 'uncertainty in our law'? In *Cassell & Co Ltd v Broome* [1972] AC 1027, HL, Lord Kilbrandon said at p. 1133:

' . . . since all commercial publication is undertaken for profit, one must be watchful against holding the profit motive to be sufficient to justify punitive damages: to do so would be seriously to hamper what must be regarded, at least since the European Convention [on Human Rights] was ratified, as a constitutional right to free speech.'

See also Lord Scarman in *R v Lemon* [1979] AC 617, and in *Ahmad v Inner London Education Authority* below, p. 353, who argues for the use of the ECHR in developing the common law. And see the reference to the ECHR by Forbes J in *Hubbard v Pitt* [1976] QB 142. Sir Robert Megarry VC does not think that it can be used to fill a gap where Parliament has not legislated: *Malone v Metropolitan Police Comr*, below, p. 328. The ECHR was referred to as a guide in considering a public policy argument in *Blathwayt v Baron Cawley* below, p. 359. See also *Maynard v Osmond* [1977] QB 240, CA per Lord Denning; *R v Wells Street Stipendiary Magistrate, ex parte Deakin* [1979] 2 WLR 665 at 667, HL, per Lord Diplock; *Associated Newspapers Group Ltd v Wade* [1979] 1 WLR 697 at 706–7, CA; and UKAPE v ACAS [1979] ICR 303 at 316–7, CA.

4. On the vagueness of the wording of the ECHR, see also Lord Denning in *Ahmad v Inner London Education Authority* below, p. 353, and Sir Douglas Frank QC, in *Ostreicher v Secretary of State for the Environment* below, p. 358. Is *all* of the ECHR very generally phrased? Are Articles 5 and 6 any more generally drafted than many UK statutes? And are the courts not used to applying such broad concepts as 'public policy' and 'public interest' at common law?

5. Despite the references that the courts have made to the ECHR, there has been no case yet in which the ECHR has been crucial to a decision.

6. Potentially, European Community law could have a considerable impact upon the protection of civil liberties in UK law. In addition to certain enacted provisions of European Community law (e.g. Article 48, EEC Treaty, on freedom of movement within the Communities for workers), the European Court of Justice at Luxembourg stated in the Case 4/73 *Nold v EC Commission* [1974] ECR 491 at 508:

' . . . fundamental rights form an integral part of the general principles of law, the observance of which it [the court] ensures. In safeguarding these rights, the Court is bound to draw inspiration from constitutional traditions common to the Member States and it cannot therefore uphold measures which are incompatible with fundamental rights recognised and protected by the Constitutions of those States.

Similarly, international treaties for the protection of human rights on which Member States have collaborated or of which they are signatories, can supply guidelines which should be followed within the framework of Community law.'

The indirect reference to, inter alia, the ECHR was followed by an express reference to it by the court in case 36/75; *Rutili v Ministry of Interior of French Republic* [1975] ECR 1219, 1232 in support of (although without being crucial to) its reasoning. Cf. *Prais v EC Council* below, p. 356. See A. Drzemczewski, (1977) 2 H Rts Rev 69 and Hilf, in F.G. Jacobs, (ed.), *European Law and the Individual* (1976) Chap. 8. See also the 1977 Joint Declaration by the European Parliament, the Council and the Commission of the EC on Human Rights, OJ 1977 C 103/1, 27 April 1977. The Commission of the EC has since proposed that the EC should itself become a party to the ECHR. Commission Memorandum, *Accession of the Communities to the ECHR*, Bulletin of the EC, Supplement 2/79. See Economides and Weiler, (1979) 42 MLR 683. Would it be open to a British court to regard the European Communities Act 1972, s. 2, which imports common market law, as incorporating the ECHR by a sidewind? Would it be open to the European Court of Justice to rule on a British case referred to it under Article 177, EEC Treaty by reference to the ECHR? See L. Collins, *European Community Law in the UK* (2nd edn., 1980) p. 6; and see *Allgemeine Gold und Silberscheideanstalt v Comrs of Customs and Excise* [1978] 2 CMLR 292, Donaldson J.

2 A bill of rights?

Bill of Rights: a Discussion Paper. Standing Advisory Commission on Human Rights, March 1976, paras. 10 and 11 (Reprinted in the Commission's *The Protection of Human Rights by law in Northern Ireland*, Cmnd. 7009)

On the one hand it may be argued that:
(1) It is complacent to assume that there is no need for new legal safeguards in Northern Ireland or indeed elsewhere in the United Kingdom. The existing legislative and common law safeguards against abuse of power are less comprehensive and effective than in many advanced democratic countries. . . .
(2) A Bill of Rights would remove certain fundamental values out of the reach of temporary political majorities, governments and officials and into the realm of legal principles applied by the courts. This would not be undemocratic because the exercise of political power in a democracy should not be beyond criticism or restraint.
(3) A Bill of Rights would be especially important in the context of the devolution of the present powers of Central Government in maintaining the national framework of law and order, and guaranteeing the basic rights of citizens throughout United Kingdom.
(4) A Bill of Rights would encourage a more actively and socially responsive judicial role in protecting basic rights and freedoms; it would alter the method of judicial law-making, so as to enable the courts to recognise the fundamental importance of certain values and the relationship between them.
(5) The European Convention contains a minimum Bill of Rights for Council of Europe countries and is also being used as a source of guidance about common standards within the European Community in relation to human rights questions arising under the EEC Treaty. The enactment of a Bill of Rights in this country would enable the United Kingdom to be manifestly in conformity with its international obligations and would also enable the citizen to obtain redress from United Kingdom courts without needing, except in the last resort, to have recourse to the European Commission in Strasbourg.
(6) A Bill of Rights would not necessarily hamper strong, effective and democratic government because it could recognise that interference with certain rights would be justifiable if they were necessary in a democratic society, for example, in the interests of national security, public safety or the economic well-being of the country, for the prevention of disorder or crime, for the protection of health or morals, or for the protection of the rights and freedoms of others.
(7) The generality of a Bill of Rights makes it possible for the interpretation of such a document to evolve in accordance with changing social values and needs. This process of giving fresh meaning to basic human rights—and the obligations which flow from them—from generation to generation is valuable for its own sake, as a means of educating public opinion, and as a rallying point in the State for all who care deeply for the ideals of freedom.
(8) A Bill of Rights would not be a substitute for more specific statutory safeguards against specific abuses (e.g. anti-discrimination legislation or the Parliamentary Commissioner for

Administration). It would supplement and strengthen those safeguards where they were incomplete. . . .

On the other hand it may be argued that:

(1) Because of the general nature of Bills of Rights and the increased powers of judicial law-making which they require, the scope and effect of such documents is uncertain and unpredictable.

(2) A Bill of Rights would create expectations which could not be satisfied in practice. It would be regarded as a panacea for all grievances whereas its real value (if any) would be only a limited one. It would be least effective when it was most needed: i.e. to protect fundamental rights and freedoms against powerful currents of intolerance, passion, usurpation and tyranny.

(3) A Bill of Rights might be interpreted by the courts in a manner which would hamper strong, effective or progressive government, and the role of the courts would result in important public issues being discussed and resolved in legal or constitutional terms rather than in moral or political terms. It would risk compromising the necessary independence and impartiality of the judiciary by requiring the judges to work in a more political arena.

(4) Most Bills of Rights stem from a constitutional settlement following revolution, rebellion, liberation or the peaceful attainment of independence. It would be difficult and perhaps divisive to seek to obtain a sufficient degree of political consensus about the nature and scope of a Bill of Rights in present circumstances.

(5) Human Rights are at least as well protected in the United Kingdom as in countries which have Bills of Rights since they are adequately safeguarded by traditional methods, i.e., legislative measures to deal with specific problems, combined with the unwritten but effective constitutional conventions; the sense of responsibility and fair dealing in legislators and administrators; the influence of a free press and the force of public opinion; the independence of the judiciary in upholding the rule of law; and free and secret elections.

(6) The United Kingdom differs from many advanced democratic countries in lacking (a) a written constitution, (b) a system of public law, and (c) a codified legal system. A Bill of Rights involves features of all three of these distinctive characteristics of other legal systems. It would therefore represent a fundamental departure from the existing legal tradition.

(7) A Bill of Rights which did not (i) contain a modern definition of the rights and freedoms relevant to the particular circumstances obtaining whether in the United Kingdom in general or in Northern Ireland in particular, (ii) have priority over other laws, (iii) create legally enforceable rights and (iv) apply to violations of human rights by private individuals and organisations as well as by public authorities would not satisfy some prominent supporters of such a measure. On the other hand a Bill of Rights which did have these characteristics would be unlikely to obtain widespread public support.

(8) A Bill of Rights would create wasteful duplication in relation to existing statutory safeguards for human rights and would generate unnecessary litigation.

NOTES

1. The Standing Advisory Commission on Human Rights is an independent body in Northern Ireland established to advise 'the Secretary of State on the adequacy and effectiveness of the law for the time being in force in preventing discrimination on the grounds of religious belief or political opinion and in providing redress for persons aggrieved . . .' (Northern Ireland Constitution Act 1973, s. 20(1)(a)). Although the Advisory Commission's paper is directed towards the question of a Bill of Rights in Northern Ireland, the arguments included in this extract apply to the United Kingdom as a whole.

2. A number of attempts have been made in the last decade or so to have Parliament enact a Bill of Rights. For a full record, see P. Wallington and J. McBride, *Civil Liberties and a Bill of Rights* (1976), p. 146. Early drafts modelled on the 1960 Canadian Bill of Rights (see, for example, Lord Arran's Bill in 1970) have given way to proposals for the incorporation of the ECHR into UK law. The most recent is Lord Wade's Bill (below), which is now pending. Its introduction in 1977 (after a previous introduction and debate in 1976) led to the appointment of a House of Lords Select Committee. The Committee was divided 6 to 5 in favour of a Bill of Rights; it was unanimously of the opinion that any Bill that was introduced should incorporate the ECHR (*Report of the Select Committee on a Bill of Rights* (1977–78) HL 176).

3. The powers that the courts have under the present system to control the executive and the legislature to protect civil liberties have been considered above, pp. 3–4. What the courts cannot do is refuse to apply legislation which they find to be clearly worded. In *Burmah Oil Co v Lord Advocate* [1965] AC 75, HL, it was held that the Crown was obliged in law to pay compensation to the company for the destruction of its assets in Burma during the Second World War to prevent them falling into the hands of the Japanese. While the case was pending, the Government indicated that if necessary it would change the law retroactively to defeat the claim (705 HL Deb 3 February 1965 col 1102). When the House of Lords held against it, the Government enacted the War Damage Act 1965 which overturned the decision and did so retrospectively. One remedy in such a case is for Members of Parliament to object, but the party system limits its value. Lord McNair and others opposed the War Damage Bill unsuccessfully on the grounds, inter alia, that it threatened the independence of the judiciary; was retrospective in its effect; and took away acquired rights, i.e. those resulting from court decisions (264 HL Deb 25 March 1965 col 730ff).

4. Judges already have to rule on party political matters and other matters of social policy. See, e.g., the *Tameside* case [1977] AC 1014, (comprehensive schooling), *Grunwick Processing Laboratories Ltd v Advisory Conciliation Arbitration Service* [1978] AC 655, HL (trade union rights), and *Charter v Race Relations Board*, below, p. 382 (race relations). A power to review legislation would inevitably increase the courts' participation in such matters, and under Lord Wade's Bill, give them the last word on such questions as whether the Immigration Act 1971 results in 'degrading treatment' of black applicants for admission (Article 3, ECHR); whether the Community Land Act 1975 is consistent with the right to property (Article 1, First Protocol, ECHR); and whether capital punishment is 'inhuman punishment' (Article 3, ECHR). Cf. Lloyd, (1976) 39 MLR 121. Although most cases arising under a Bill of Rights will not raise such large issues, some would. In the US, the Supreme Court, despite its discretion not to hear cases (by refusing certiorari) and the doctrine by which it refuses to rule on 'political questions' (such as the constitutionality of the Vietnam War), is constantly a focal point and arbiter in questions of great political and social moment. Between 1934 and 1936, it held 16 social welfare laws properly passed by Congress in implementation of President Roosevelt's 'new deal' policy to be unconstitutional as infringements of 'freedom of contract' between employers and employees. A conservative majority of the Court did this on the basis of 'an economic theory [of *laissez faire*, or government non-intervention] which a large part of the country does not entertain' (Holmes J, dissenting, in *Lochner v New York* (1905) 198 US 46). President Roosevelt sought to overcome the problem by an unsuccessful plan to increase the size of the Court (his 'court-packing' plan). It was resolved eventually by a change in the court's composition by retirement, etc. More recently, the Supreme Court has declared racial segregation to be unconstitutional (*Brown v Board of Education* (1954) 347 US 483) and set guidelines for capital punishment statutes (*Gregg v Georgia* (1976) 428 US 153).

Should the courts, whose members must necessarily be difficult to dismiss, be given a political and social role on this scale? Should issues of the sort mentioned above be resolved through the ballot box instead? (Note that Lord Wade's Bill would allow this in that Parliament would be free to legislate contrary to the Bill of Rights by *express or clear* provision to this effect.) Or should persons taking decisions on civil liberties (particularly those of minority groups and the unpopular) be free from the 'tyranny of the majority'? Does the experience of the judicial review of administrative action (judicial review 'writ small') which the courts now engage in, offer a guide? Might some civil liberties be more appropriate for protection through the courts by a Bill of Rights than others? In particular, is the distinction between (1) civil and political rights and (2) economic, social and cultural rights relevant? See Wallington and McBride, *Civil Liberties and a Bill of Rights* (1976) pp. 11–12. Fawcett ((1976) 73 Guardian Gaz 171) comments:

> 'Here it may be asked whether there should not be limits to judicial intervention in social policy; not, as is sometimes suggested, because the judiciary is too conservative or is socially insensitive – suggestions that have little contemporary justification – but because social policy rests upon consent and process and not upon unitary decision, however logical. Is it wise to allow a constitutional court to declare unconstitutional, by six votes to two, the provision of a statute enacted by a substantial majority in the national parliament and based on a long inquiry and report of an experienced and representative commission? This happened in the Federal Republic of Germany on the question of abortion, and is the subject of an application now before the European Commission of Human Rights.'

Does his reasoning apply equally to the powers of the European Court of Human Rights?

On the argument that the judiciary is 'too conservative or is socially insensitive', which Fawcett discounts, note the following comment of Lord Milford (379 HL Deb 3 February 1977 col 996):

> 'Let us look at the composition of the Judges today; 89 per cent of this so-called upper class went to public school, 70 per cent went to Oxford or Cambridge, and only 22 per cent ever faced an election in their lives. . . . These men's lives are miles away from the ordinary people. Why should they be made the custodians of the liberties of the ordinary people, rather than Parliament . . . ?'

His speech was interrupted to remind him that there were two female High Court judges and a number of female county court judges. For other figures on social background of the judiciary, see L. Blom-Cooper and G. Drewry, *Final Appeal* (1972) Chap. VIII (of the 50 or so law lords reported on, only one had a father who 'could be described unequivocally as working class'; only one came from a redbrick university; and only one had not been to university) and J. A. G. Griffith, *The Politics of the Judiciary* (1977) Chap. 1. Wallington and McBride, *Civil Liberties and a Bill of Rights* (1976) pp. 28–29, state that 'eight of the eleven [judges] who took part in the recent case on comprehensive schools in Tameside [above, p. 9] had been educated at independent schools, and three at grammar schools' and that 'within a week of the House of Lords' decision two commentators in the press had pronounced that the decision had killed the whole idea of a Bill of Rights as far as the Labour Party was concerned.' For a critical account of the courts' interpretation of housing legislation between the Wars, see W. I. Jennings (1935–6) 49 Harv LR 421.

5. Lord Denning (369 HL Deb 25 March 1976 col 797–8) has expressed opposition to a Bill of Rights on the different ground of the effect upon judicial independence and public confidence in the courts:

> ' . . . if judges were given power to overthrow sections or Acts of Paliament, they would become political, their appointments would be based on political grounds and the reputation of our Judiciary would suffer accordingly. One has only to see, in the great Constitutions of the United States of America and of India, the conflicts which arise from time to time between the judges and the Legislature. I hope we shall not have such conflicts in this country. The independence of our judges and their reputation for impartiality depend on their obeying the will of Parliament and on their being independent. The independence of the judges is the other pillar of our Constitution.'

More recently, however, Lord Denning has spoken in favour of a Bill of Rights; *The Times*, 11 December 1979.

On the appointment of judges, an acknowledged factor in the nomination of candidates for the US Supreme Court by the President is the latter's opinion that the candidate he chooses will judge cases the right way. Note also that Supreme Court justices are by no means always appointed from the ranks of the judiciary or practising lawyers. Warren CJ was Governor of California before his appointment in 1953. 'The correlation between prior judicial experience and fitness for the functions of the Supreme Court is zero' (Justice Frankfurter (1957) 105 U Penn LR 781, 795). If judges were to be given a power of judicial review of legislation, they would undoubtedly figure in the Sunday supplements more than they do now. Law students in the US know a lot about the judicial philosophies and quite a lot about the private lives of Supreme Court justices. How many English law students could even name the members of the Appellate Committee at present, let alone place them on the political or philosophical spectrum? Note also the view that 'British judges are not at their best in developing social policy. Our tradition in this respect differs from the Americans where lawyers commonly discuss issues of wages, social benefits and education' (Mr Lyons, Minority Report, *Report of the Committee on Privacy* Cmnd. 5012, p. 211). Could this be overcome by more emphasis on social policy in legal education? Or would judges become more adept with greater experience anyway?

6. If a Bill of Rights were adopted, would British judges take up the role expected of them? Many of them? Given time? For the less than enthusiastic response of the Canadian judiciary, trained in the same parliamentary sovereignty tradition, to the power given to them by the 1960 Canadian Bill of Rights, see W. Tarnopolsky, *The Canadian Bill of Rights* (2nd revised edn., 1975) Chap. 4. On the work of the Judicial Committee in applying Bills of Rights in Commonwealth countries, see Wallington and McBride, *Civil Liberties and a Bill of Rights* (1976) pp. 32–33, who 'come away with a rather neutral impression of the talents available.'

7. Might judges be better equipped to deal with the larger questions that would arise under a Bill of Rights if they had the advantage, as in the US, of written, Brandeis briefs (named after Brandeis J of the US Supreme Court) presenting such statistical and other factual evidence as exists on the issues raised. At the moment, British cases are decided on the basis of oral pleading only. Written briefs were permitted in *Rondel v Worsley* [1967] 1 QB 443, CA but this was said by Dankwerts LJ, at 509 to be 'wholly irregular and contrary to the practice of the court and . . . should not be allowed as a precedent for future proceedings'. Or is the judicial forum in any event not a satisfactory one for legislation? Is an inquiry and a report marshalling all of the evidence followed by a bill drafted by parliamentary draftsmen better? Cf. Sir Robert Megarry VC in *Malone v Metropolitan Police Comr* below, p. 328. And is it better for Parliament to act (at least in most cases) uninfluenced by the facts of any particular case? Hard cases make bad law. But what if Parliament doesn't have the time or the inclination? The recommendations of the Select Committee on Parliamentary Privilege (Report, 1967–68 HC 34) for the reform of the law of parliamentary privilege, for example, have remained largely unimplemented. Could a judge act on the basis of the Younger Report, below, p. 334, and create, say, the recommended new tort of unlawful surveillance?

8. Documents such as the Universal Declaration of Human Rights and the

ECHR have served a useful educational and promotional role by providing convenient, positive statements of civil liberties that can be used as a point of reference and as authority in argument. See, for example, the many letters in *The Times* that rely upon these sources. Might not a legally binding national Bill of Rights have the same effect in the UK, only more so?

9. How significant is the fact that the House of Lords Select Committee (Report, p. 29) 'received no evidence that human rights are in practice better protected in countries which have a code of fundamental human rights embodied in their law than they are in the United Kingdom'? Cf. Lord Hailsham's comment (369 HL Deb 25 March 1976 col 785):

> 'Show me a nation with a Bill of Rights and I will show you a nation which has fewer actual human rights than England or Britain because the escape clauses are used, often quite ruthlessly, by the executive of the time . . . one must not exaggerate the value of the protection given by any document of this kind.'

Note, however, that Lord Hailsham supports Lord Wade's Bill; 402 HL Deb 8 November 1979 col 1063. Note also the Select Committee's further comment (Report, p. 29):

> ' . . . in any country, whatever its constitution, the existence or absence of legislation in the nature of a Bill of Rights can in practice play only a relatively minor part in the protection of human rights. What is important, above all, is a country's political climate and traditions.'

Cf. the extract from the Younger Committee Report, below, pp. 301–3. And witness the fate of some of the Bills of Rights in the constitutions of new states. Note also that the USSR Constitution protects civil and political rights.

How would you weigh the above evidence and comments against the following arguments put by Lord Scarman and Zander? Lord Scarman states (*English Law – The New Dimension* (1974) p. 15):

> 'When times are normal and fear is not stalking the land, English law sturdily protects the freedom of the individual and respects human personality. But when times are abnormally alive with fear and prejudice, the common law is at a disadvantage: it cannot resist the will, however frightened and prejudiced it may be, of Parliament. The classic illustration is, of course, Regulation 18(b) and *Liversidge v Anderson* [1942] AC 206.'

But would the same four judges who rejected Lord Atkin's very plausible interpretation of Regulation 18(b) in his dissenting opinion in *Liversidge v Anderson* have decided the case differently on the basis of a 'freedom of the person' guarantee in a Bill of Rights? Zander argues (*A Bill of Rights*? (2nd edn., 1980) pp. 87–88):

> '[A] Bill of Rights is desirable not because human rights are grossly abused in Britain, nor to provide against the danger of future tyranny. The former is untrue, the latter unlikely. The case for a Bill of Rights rests rather on the belief that it would make a distinct and valuable contribution to the *better* protection of human rights. Certainly it would not solve all problems. The extent of the contribution it could make must, in the end, depend on how it is regarded and interpreted by the judges. It would give them greater scope than exists in the ordinary common law and statute law. It would require of them a broader, more wide-ranging approach than has been customary.'

Does the UK's record at Strasbourg (below, pp. 26–32) support Zander's argument? Might a domestic Bill of Rights reduce the number of cases that are taken to Strasbourg? If so, might it be better for our international reputation (as well as more convenient for the claimant) to decide the questions raised at home? The public hearing of the *Ireland v United Kingdom* case, below, p. 191, was well attended by USSR journalists. Might a statement of legal principles in a Bill of Rights assist the courts in taking an initiative to protect civil liberties? Might it avoid the thicket of case-law that sometimes results as the common law develops. See, for example, the tangle that the law of search and seizure is in, below, pp. 70–100. From the individual's standpoint, the law of civil liberties and its remedies (which lie mostly scattered in different parts of the law of tort and crime) may seem a maze, not a mosaic. Might a Bill of Rights aimed directly at their protection and offering a tailor-made remedy encourage and facilitate his recourse to the courts?

10. If the arguments about a Bill of Rights are evenly balanced, upon whom is the burden of proof? Those who wish to preserve the status quo? Or those who seek radical change?

Griswold v Connecticut 381 US 479 (1965) US Supreme Court

The appellants were convicted under a Connecticut statute for giving advice to married persons on contraception. They challenged the constitutionality of the statute under the US Bill of Rights, which is found in the first ten amendments to the US Constitution.

Douglas J (for the court): The association of people is not mentioned in the Constitution nor in the Bill of Rights. . . .

In *NAACP v Alabama* 357 US 449 [1958] . . . we protected the 'freedom to associate and privacy in one's associations,' noting that freedom of association was a peripheral First Amendment right[1] . . . the First Amendment has a penumbra where privacy is protected from governmental intrusion. . . . The Third Amendment in its prohibition against the quartering of soldiers 'in any house' in time of peace without the consent of the owner is another facet of that privacy. The Fourth Amendment explicitly affirms the 'right of the people to be secure in their persons, houses, papers, and effects, against unreasonable searches and seizures.' The Fifth Amendment in its Self-Incrimination Clause enables the citizen to create a zone of privacy which government may not force him to surrender to his detriment. The Ninth Amendment provides: 'The enumeration in the Constitution, of certain rights, shall not be construed to deny or disparage others retained by the people' . . .

The present case, then, concerns a relationship lying within the zone of privacy created by several fundamental constitutional guarantees. And it concerns a law which, in forbidding the *use* of contraceptives rather than regulating their manufacture or sale, seeks to achieve its goals by means having a maximum destructive impact upon that relationship. Such a law cannot stand in light of the familiar principle, so often applied by this Court, that a 'governmental purpose to control or prevent activities constitutionally subject to state regulation may not be achieved by means which sweep unnecessarily broadly and thereby invade the area of protected freedoms.' *NAACP v Alabama* 377 US 288, 307 [1964]. Would we allow the police to search the sacred precincts of marital bedrooms for telltale signs of the use of contraceptives? The very idea is repulsive to the notions of privacy surrounding the marriage relationship.

We deal with a right of privacy older than the Bill of Rights—older than our political parties, older than our school system. Marriage is a coming together for better or for worse, hopefully enduring, and intimate to the degree of being sacred. It is an association that promotes a way of life, not causes; a harmony in living, not political faiths; a bilateral loyalty, not commercial or social projects. Yet it is an association for as noble a purpose as any involved in our prior decisions.

Reversed.

---

1. Ed. The First Amendment reads: Congress shall make no law respecting an establishment of religion, or prohibiting the free exercise thereof; or abridging the freedom of speech, or of the press; or the right of the people peaceably to assemble and to petition the Government for a redress of grievances.

NOTES

1. The *Griswold* case offers a good example of what a court can do with a power of judicial review of legislation (the existence of which in the US Constitution is itself a result of judicial inference: *Marbury v Madison* 1 Cranch 137 (1803) US S Ct) and the text of a Bill of Rights to work with. The Supreme Court struck down as unconstitutional a state statute on the ground that it conflicted with a constitutional right to privacy which is nowhere mentioned in the Bill of Rights and which the Court found hidden in its 'penumbra' for the first time in 1965. The Court inferred a *general* right of privacy from the guarantee in the Bill of Rights of *particular* aspects of it. Might an English court have applied the *expressio unius* rule? Cf. the way the Supreme Court, as Douglas J mentions, had earlier read freedom of association into the First Amendment. (Cf. also the way in which the European Court of Human Rights built upon the express wording of Article 6, ECHR to find a guarantee of freedom of access to the courts in the *Golder* case, below, p. 418.) Thus imaginatively derived, the US constitutional right to privacy has since been used by the Supreme Court and lower federal and state courts in many different contexts: e.g. to strike down abortion statutes (*Roe v Wade* 410 US 113 (1973) US S Ct); to protect the private possession of obscene films (*Stanley v Georgia* 394 US 557 (1969) US S Ct) and unnatural sex acts within marriage in private (*Cotner v Henry* 394 F 2d 873 (7th Cir. 1968)); and to permit long hair in school (*Breen v Kahl* 419 F 2d 1034 (7th Cir. 1969)) and marijuana (*Ravin v State* 537 P 2d 494 (1975)).
2. On judicial review in the US, see G. Hughes, in J. A. Andrews, (ed.) *Welsh Studies in Public Law* (1970) Chap. 10, R. V. Dennenberg, [1971] CLJ 134, H. J. Abraham, *Freedom and the Court* (3rd edn., 1977), and A. Cox, *The Role of the Supreme Court in American Government* (1976) Chap. 1.

3 What kind of bill of rights?

Lord Wade's Bill of Rights Bill

1. The [ECHR] . . . , together with such Protocols thereto as shall have been ratified by the Government of the United Kingdom, shall subject to any reservations thereto by the Government of the United Kingdom immediately upon the passing of this Act have the force of law, and shall be enforceable by action in the Courts of the United Kingdom.
2. In case of conflict between any laws or enactments prior to the passing of this Act and the provisions of the said Convention and such Protocols as shall have been ratified by the Government of the United Kingdom and subject to any reservations thereto, the said Convention and Protocols shall prevail.
3. In case of conflict between any enactment subsequent to the passing of this Act and the provisions of the said Convention and such Protocols as shall have been ratified by the Government of the United Kingdom and subject to any reservations thereto, such enactment passed after the passing of this Act shall be deemed to be subject to the provisions of the said Convention and Protocols and shall be so construed unless such subsequent enactment provides otherwise or does not admit of any construction compatible with the provisions of this Act.
[Section 4 provides for derogation from the ECHR in accordance with Article 15, below p. 20.]

NOTES

1. The Bill was given its Third Reading by the House of Lords on 6

December 1979. It now awaits a second reading in the House of Commons, but appears unlikely to make further progress this Session. The Lord Chancellor (Lord Hailsham) has proposed all party talks on the constitution, including the question of a Bill of Rights: 402 HL Deb 8 November 1979 Col 1064. On the earlier history of Lord Wade's Bill, see above, p. 8. The House of Lords Select Committee (Report, pp. 20–2) was unanimously of the opinion that any Bill of Rights should be one incorporating the ECHR into English law. Although the Convention text was not ideal, it existed and it would be politically difficult and time consuming to try and draft a new one. Moreover 'if we produced for ourselves a new and different formulation of fundamental rights, we should then have to cope with two codes which would exist side-by-side.' The Committee thought, however, that the Bill should allow for the reservation that the UK had made to Article 2, First Protocol (below, p. 25) and should exclude the Fourth Protocol, which the UK has not ratified.

2. A key question is whether a Bill of Rights in the form of a statute could control legislation enacted after it. The House of Lords Select Committee (Report, pp. 22–6) thought not, except as a guide to interpretation:

> 14. . . . there is no way in which a Bill of Rights could be made immune altogether from amendment or repeal by a subsequent Act. That follows from the principle of the sovereignty of Parliament which is the central feature of our constitution. . . . The usual way of entrenching provisions in countries with written constitutions is to require a special majority in the legislature, or in some cases a favourable vote in a referendum, for any Act amending or repealing, or otherwise overriding, the entrenched provision. The Committee think it is clear, however, that no such provision (e.g. a requirement for a two-thirds majority in the House of Commons for any Bill seeking to override a Bill of Rights) would be legally effective in the United Kingdom . . .
>
> 15. The only other possibility is a provision such as is contained in clause 3 of Lord Wade's Bill. . . .
>
> 16. If such a clause were effective, it would, in the Committee's view, in practice provide an important degree of entrenchment. In this regard, the Committee do not accept the view that has been expressed that, if such a clause were included in a Bill of Rights, Governments would have no hesitation in including in future Acts the necessary express formula to ensure that the Act would override the Bill of Rights. . . .
>
> 17. The Committee have, however, felt unable to accept the assumption . . . that a Bill of Rights could protect itself from being overridden by implication. It is contrary to the principle of Parliamentary sovereignty as it has hitherto been understood in the United Kingdom. Under that principle, Parliament cannot bind itself as to the future and a later Act must always prevail over an earlier one if it is inconsistent with it, whether the inconsistency is express or implied. The Committee are aware that some legal writers have advanced the view that the principle of Parliamentary sovereignty does not preclude Parliament from laying down a binding requirement as to the manner or form of subsequent Acts of a particular kind. . . . If this view prevailed in the courts, a provision like clause 3 of Lord Wade's Bill would be efficacious in that it does no more than lay down the form in which a subsequent Act has to be framed if it is to override a Bill of Rights. The Committee are not, however, persuaded that the view is sound.
>
> 23. It follows from the foregoing that the Committee conclude that the main scope for a Bill of Rights would be to operate on our existing law. The most that such a Bill could do would be to include an interpretation provision which ensured that the Bill of Rights was always taken into account in the construction of later Acts . . .

When considered by the Committee, clause 3 had read:

> 'In case of conflict between any enactment subsequent to the passing of this Act and the provisions of the said Convention and Protocols, the said Convention and Protocols shall prevail unless subsequent enactment shall explicitly state otherwise.'

As re-drafted in 1979 (above, p. 14), ambiguous later legislation would be interpreted consistently with the ECHR, but clearly-worded legislation would prevail over it.

3. On the nature of Parliamentary sovereignty and the differing views on the question whether Parliament can bind itself by statute as to how it legislates in future, see H. W. R. Wade (Lord Wade's cousin) [1955] CLJ 172 (Parliament cannot bind itself as to the manner and form of legislation) and R. F. V. Heuston, *Essays in Constitutional Law* (2nd edn., 1964) Chap. 1 (Parliament can do so). There are Commonwealth cases in which a special voting or referendum requirement has been held to be binding upon a legislature (e.g. *A-G for New South Wales v Trethowan* [1932] AC 526, PC (referendum)), but the Select Committee (para. 14) clearly prefers H. W. R. Wade's view that these can be distinguished. An English case which supports the Committee's opinion on the effect of the first version of clause 3 is *Ellen Street Estates v Minister of Health* [1934] 1 KB 590, CA. But if, as H. W. R. Wade suggests, the doctrine of Parliamentary sovereignty is not only a rule of common law, but an 'ultimate political fact' which can be changed by a 'revolution' recognised by the courts, would it not be open for the courts to decide that a 'revolution' (albeit a markedly bloodless one) had occurred by an expression of the will of the people through the medium of a parliamentary statute? (On this basis, Parliament, speaking for the people, could go further than Lord Wade's Bill and enact that future legislation could not avoid the Bill of Rights even by express enactment.) Or would a referendum be necessary or sufficient? Or, in the absence of a civil war, are we bound by parliamentary sovereignty in its present form for ever? Cf. the unresolved question arising out of our entry into the European Communities, viz. whether the effect of s.2 of the European Communities Act 1972 is that British courts may not recognise any future law enacted by Westminster that is contrary to EC law. See Collins, European Community Law in the UK (2nd edn.) pp. 19–28.

4. Would Lord Wade's Bill have prevented the enactment of the War Damage Act?

5. How good a Bill of Rights is the ECHR for internal UK purposes? Does it cover all the civil and political rights one would like to see protected? To what extent does it protect against racial discrimination? (But note that, as in the US, a Bill of Rights can be supplemented by ordinary legislation such as the Race Relations Act 1976.) Note (1) that it represents what West European states as a whole were prepared to be legally bound by 30 years ago and (2) that it was drafted hurriedly in French as well as English and has obscurities, ambiguities and errors that reflect this. (But then statutes that come from Parliament are not always perfect.) Would the ECHR be incorporated 'bag and baggage' (i.e. with the gloss put upon it by the Strasbourg authorities) or would the British courts be free to start again in their interpretation of the ECHR for UK purposes? The former approach has the disadvantage that the European Commission and Court of Human Rights (on each of which the UK has only one national) have to interpret the Convention for Western Europe as a whole. (Cf. the problem the Federal US Supreme Court has when interpreting the US Bill of Rights for the several states.) See, for example, the accommodation of the civil law systems of criminal prosecution in the *Wemhoff* case, Eur Court HR, Series A, Vol 7, Judgment of 27 June 1968 and the *Neumeister* case, Eur Court HR, Series A, Vol 8. Cf. D. J. Harris (1970) 44 BYIL 87. See also the *Tyrer* case, below, in which the British judge was outvoted on the question of judicial corporal punishment by judges from countries with different traditions. And see the different approach to contempt of court adopted by the European Court of Human Rights in the *Sunday Times* case, below, p. 261, applying Article 10, ECHR (protection of freedom of speech subject to narrowly construed exceptions, including the interest in the proper administration of justice) to that adopted by the House of Lords in the case

applying the common law (weighing the interests in freedom of speech and the administration of justice equally). The latter approach (starting again) would allow the courts to take account of UK political and social traditions (and blindspots?) but would run a greater risk of court decisions being reversed at Strasbourg.

4 The European Convention on Human Rights

As well as being relevant to the interpretation of statutes and the development of the common law by British courts, the ECHR also provides a remedy of its own at Strasbourg for 'victims' of a breach of the Convention by the UK. If a Bill of Rights were to be enacted in the UK, this international law remedy would continue in parallel with the remedy that would exist in the British courts. A sizeable number of cases have been taken to Strasbourg against the UK, some of which have been successful. The following commentary on the ECHR concentrates upon the nature and effectiveness of the remedy provided; although some cases interpreting the rights protected are discussed, the substance of the guarantee which the ECHR provides is considered mostly in later chapters as it affects particular rights in English law.

The Convention was drafted under the auspices of the Council of Europe, an international organisation composed of 21 West European states which was formed in 1949 as the result of the first post-war attempt at unifying Europe. The impetus for the Convention came from the need to define more closely the obligations of members of the Council concerning 'human rights', and, more generally, from the wish to provide a bulwark against communism and to prevent a recurrence of conditions which Europe had then recently witnessed. It was believed that the Convention would serve as an alarm that would bring violations of human rights to the attention of the international community in time for it to take action to suppress them. In practice, this function of the Convention, which imagines large-scale violations of human rights, has largely remained dormant. The Convention has instead been used primarily to raise questions of isolated weaknesses in legal systems that basically conform to its requirements and which are representative of the 'common heritage of political traditions, ideals, freedom and the rule of law' to which the Preamble to the Convention refers. Most commonly such questions have concerned the administration of criminal justice, although the impact of the Convention in other areas is increasingly being explored. The Convention is concerned mainly with civil and political rights. Economic, social and cultural rights are protected by a later treaty – the European Social Charter 1961 (see below, p. 32).

The Convention entered into force on 3 September 1953. There are 20 parties. They are Austria, Belgium, Cyprus, Denmark, France, F.R.G., Greece, Iceland, Ireland, Italy, Luxembourg, Malta, the Netherlands, Norway, Portugal, Spain, Sweden, Switzerland, Turkey and the UK. Liechtenstein is the only member of the Council not party to the Convention.

On the ECHR generally, see R. Beddard, *Human Rights and Europe* (1973), J. E. S. Fawcett, *The Application of the European Convention on Human Rights* (1969), F. G. Jacobs, *The European Convention on Human Rights* (1975).

European Convention on Human Rights 1950 Cmd. 8969

ARTICLE 1

The High Contracting Parties shall secure to everyone within their jurisdiction the rights and freedoms in Section 1 of this Convention [Articles 2 to 18].

ARTICLE 2

1. Everyone's right to life shall be protected by law. No one shall be deprived of his life intentionally save in the execution of a sentence of a court following his conviction of a crime for which this penalty is provided by law.
2. Deprivation of life shall not be regarded as inflicted in contravention of this Article when it results from the use of force which is no more than absolutely necessary:
    (a) in defence of any person from unlawful violence;
    (b) in order to effect a lawful arrest or to prevent the escape of a person lawfully detained;
    (c) in action lawfully taken for the purpose of quelling a riot or insurrection.

ARTICLE 3

No one shall be subjected to torture or to inhuman or degrading treatment or punishment.

ARTICLE 4

1. No one shall be held in slavery or servitude.
2. No one shall be required to perform forced or compulsory labour.
3. For the purpose of this Article the term 'forced or compulsory labour' shall not include:
    (a) any work required to be done in the ordinary course of detention imposed according to the provisions of Article 5 of this Convention or during conditional release from such detention;
    (b) any service of a military character or, in case of conscientious objectors in countries where they are recognised, service exacted instead of compulsory military service;
    (c) any service exacted in case of an emergency or calamity threatening the life or well-being of the community;
    (d) any work or service which forms part of normal civic obligations.

ARTICLE 5

1. Everyone has the right to liberty and security of person. No one shall be deprived of his liberty save in the following cases and in accordance with a procedure prescribed by law:
    (a) the lawful detention of a person after conviction by a competent court;
    (b) the lawful arrest or detention of a person for non-compliance with the lawful order of a court or in order to secure the fulfilment of any obligation prescribed by law;
    (c) the lawful arrest or detention of a person effected for the purpose of bringing him before the competent legal authority on reasonable suspicion of having committed an offence or when it is reasonably considered necessary to prevent his committing an offence or fleeing after having done so;
    (d) the detention of a minor by lawful order for the purpose of educational supervision or his lawful detention for the purpose of bringing him before the competent legal authority;
    (e) the lawful detention of persons for the prevention of the spreading of infectious diseases, of persons of unsound mind, alcoholics or drug addicts or vagrants;
    (f) the lawful arrest or detention of a person to prevent his effecting an unauthorised entry into the country or of a person against whom action is being taken with a view to deportation or extradition.
2. Everyone who is arrested shall be informed promptly, in a language which he understands, of the reasons for his arrest and of any charge against him.
3. Everyone arrested or detained in accordance with the provisions of paragraph 1(c) of this Article shall be brought promptly before a judge or other officer authorised by law to exercise judicial power and shall be entitled to trial within a reasonable time or to release pending trial. Release may be conditional by guarantees to appear for trial.
4. Everyone who is deprived of his liberty by arrest or detention shall be entitled to take

proceedings by which the lawfulness of his detention shall be decided speedily by a court and his release ordered if the detention is not lawful.

5. Everyone who has been the victim of arrest or detention in contravention of the provisions of this Article shall have an enforceable right to compensation.

ARTICLE 6

1. In the determination of his civil rights and obligation or of any criminal charge against him, everyone is entitled to a fair and public hearing within a reasonable time by an independent and impartial tribunal established by law. Judgment shall be pronounced publicly but the press and public may be excluded from all or part of the trial in the interest of morals, public order or national security in a democratic society, where the interests of juveniles or the protection of the private life of the parties so require, or to the extent strictly necessary in the opinion of the court in special circumstances where publicity would prejudice the interests of justice.

2. Everyone charged with a criminal offence shall be presumed innocent until proved guilty according to law.

3. Everyone charged with a criminal offence has the following minimum rights:

(a) to be informed promptly, in a language which he understands and in detail, of the nature and cause of the accusation against him;

(b) to have adequate time and facilities for the preparation of his defence;

(c) to defend himself in person or through legal assistance of his own choosing or, if he has not sufficient means to pay for legal assistance, to be given it free when the interests of justice so require;

(d) to examine or have examined witnesses against him and to obtain the attendance and examination of witnesses on his behalf under the same conditions as witnesses against him;

(e) to have the free assistance of an interpreter if he cannot understand or speak the language used in court.

ARTICLE 7

1. No one shall be held guilty of any criminal offence on account of any act or omission which did not constitute a criminal offence under national or international law at the time when it was committed. Nor shall a heavier penalty be imposed than the one that was applicable at the time the criminal offence was committed.

2. This Article shall not prejudice the trial and punishment of any person for any act or omission which at the time when it was committed, was criminal according to the general principles of law recognised by civilised nations.

ARTICLE 8

1. Everyone has the right to respect for his private and family life, his home and his correspondence.

2. There shall be no interference by a public authority with the exercise of this right except such as is in accordance with the law and is necessary in a democratic society in the interests of national security, public safety or the economic well-being of the country, for the prevention of disorder or crime, for the protection of health or morals, or for the protection of the rights and freedom of others.

ARTICLE 9

1. Everyone has the right to freedom of thought, conscience and religion; this right includes freedom to change his religion or belief and freedom, either alone or in community with others and in public or private, to manifest his religion or belief, in worship, teaching, practice and observance.

2. Freedom to manifest one's religion or beliefs shall be subject only to such limitations as are prescribed by law and are necessary in a democratic society in the interests of public safety, for the protection of public order, health or morals, or for the protection of the rights and freedoms of others.

ARTICLE 10

1. Everyone has the right to freedom of expression. This right shall include freedom to hold opinions and to receive and impart information and ideas without interference by public authority and regardless of frontiers. This Article shall not prevent States from requiring the licensing of broadcasting, television or cinema enterprises.
2. The exercise of these freedoms, since it carries with it duties and responsibilities, may be subject to such formalities, conditions, restrictions or penalties as are prescribed by law and are necessary in a democratic society, in the interests of national security, territorial integrity or public safety, for the prevention of disorder or crime, for the protection of health or morals, for the protection of the reputation or rights of others, for preventing the disclosure of information received in confidence, or for maintaining the authority and impartiality of the judiciary.

ARTICLE 11

1. Everyone has the right to freedom of peaceful assembly and to freedom of association with others, including the right to form and to join trade unions for the protection of his interests.
2. No restrictions shall be placed on the exercise of these rights other than such as are prescribed by law and are necessary in a democratic society in the interests of national security or public safety, for the prevention of disorder or crime, for the protection of health or morals or for the protection of the rights and freedoms of others. This Article shall not prevent the imposition of lawful restrictions on the exercise of these rights by members of the armed forces, of the police or of the administration of the State.

ARTICLE 12

Men and women of marriageable age have the right to marry and to found a family, according to the national laws governing the exercise of this right.

ARTICLE 13

Everyone whose rights and freedoms as set forth in this Convention are violated shall have an effective remedy before a national authority notwithstanding that the violation has been committed by persons acting in an official capacity.

ARTICLE 14

The enjoyment of the rights and freedoms set forth in this Convention shall be secured without discrimination on any ground such as sex, race, colour, language, religion, political or other opinion, national or social origin, association with a national minority, property, birth or other status.

ARTICLE 15

1. In time of war or other public emergency threatening the life of the nation any High Contracting Party may take measures derogating from its obligations under this Convention to the extent strictly required by the exigencies of the situation, provided that such measures are not inconsistent with its other obligations under international law.
2. No derogation from Article 2, except in respect of deaths resulting from lawful acts of war, or from Articles 3, 4 (paragraph 1) and 7 shall be made under this provision.
3. Any High Contracting Party availing itself of this right of derogation shall keep the Secretary-General of the Council of Europe fully informed of the measures which it has taken and the reasons therefor. It shall also inform the Secretary-General of the Council of Europe when such measures have ceased to operate and the provisions of the Convention are again fully executed.

ARTICLE 16

Nothing in Articles 10, 11 and 14 shall be regarded as preventing the High Contracting Parties from imposing restrictions on the political activity of aliens.

ARTICLE 17

Nothing in this Convention may be interpreted as implying for any State, group or person any right to engage in any activity or perform any act aimed at the destruction of any of the rights and freedoms set forth herein or at their limitation to a greater extent than is provided for in the Convention.

ARTICLE 18

The restrictions permitted under this Convention to the said rights and freedoms shall not be applied for any purpose other than those for which they have been prescribed.

ARTICLE 19

To ensure the observance of the engagements undertaken by the High Contracting Parties in the present Convention, there shall be set up:–
    (a) a European Commission of Human Rights, hereinafter referred to as 'the Commission';
    (b) a European Court of Human Rights, hereinafter referred to as 'the Court'.

ARTICLE 20

The Commission shall consist of a number of members equal to that of the High Contracting Parties. No two members of the Commission may be nationals of the same State[2].

ARTICLE 23

The members of the Commission shall sit on the Commission in their individual capacity.

ARTICLE 24

Any High Contracting Party may refer to the Commission, through the Secretary-General of the Council of Europe, any alleged breach of the provisions of the Convention by another High Contracting Party.

ARTICLE 25

1. The Commission may receive petitions addressed to the Secretary-General of the Council of Europe from any person, non-governmental organisation or group of individuals claiming to be the victim of a violation by one of the High Contracting Parties of the rights set forth in this Convention, provided that the High Contracting Party against which the complaint has been lodged has declared that it recognises the competence of the Commission to receive such petitions. Those of the High Contracting Parties who have made such a declaration undertake not to hinder in any way the effective exercise of this right.
2. Such declarations may be made for a specific period. . . .

ARTICLE 26

The Commission may only deal with the matter after all domestic remedies have been

---

2. Ed. There are no qualifications for membership, although almost all members are lawyers. The British member (and President) is Professor J. E. S. Fawcett. Members are independent; they do not represent their national governments.

exhausted, according to the generally recognised rules of international law, and within a period of six months from the date on which the final decision was taken.

ARTICLE 27

1. The Commission shall not deal with any petition submitted under Article 25 which:
(a) is anonymous; or
(b) is substantially the same as a matter which has already been examined by the Commission or has already been submitted to another procedure of international investigation or settlement and if it contains no relevant new information.
2. The Commission shall consider inadmissible any petition submitted under Article 25 which it considers incompatible with the provisions of the present Convention, manifestly ill-founded, or an abuse of the right of petition.
3. The Commission shall reject any petition referred to it which it considers inadmissible under Article 26.

ARTICLE 28

In the event of the Commission accepting a petition referred to it:
(a) it shall, with a view to ascertaining the facts, undertake, together with the representatives of the parties, an examination of the petition and, if need be, an investigation, for the effective conduct of which the States concerned shall furnish all necessary facilities, after an exchange of views with the Commission;
(b) it shall place itself at the disposal of the parties concerned with a view to securing a friendly settlement of the matter on the basis of respect for Human Rights as defined in this Convention.

ARTICLE 29[3]

After it has accepted a petition submitted under Article 25, the Commission may nevertheless decide unanimously to reject the petition if, in the course of its examination, it finds that the existence of one of the grounds for non-acceptance provided for in Article 27 has been established.
In such a case, the decision shall be communicated to the parties.

ARTICLE 30[3]

If the Commission succeeds in effecting a friendly settlement in accordance with Article 28, it shall draw up a Report which shall be sent to the States concerned, to the Committee of Ministers and to the Secretary-General of the Council of Europe for publication. This Report shall be confined to a brief statement of the facts and of the solution reached.

ARTICLE 31

1. If a solution is not reached, the Commission shall draw up a Report on the facts and state its opinion as to whether the facts found disclose a breach by the State concerned of its obligations under the Convention. The opinions of all the members of the Commission on this point may be stated in the Report.
2. The Report shall be transmitted to the Committee of Ministers. It shall also be transmitted to the States concerned, who shall not be at liberty to publish it.
3. In transmitting the Report to the Committee of Ministers the Commission may make such. proposals as it thinks fit.

ARTICLE 32

1. If the question is not referred to the Court in accordance with Article 48 of this Convention within a period of three months from the date of the transmission of the Report to the

---

3. Ed. As amended by the Third Protocol to the Convention, Cmnd. 4552, which came into force on 21 September 1970, for all parties to the Convention.

Committee of Ministers, the Committee of Ministers shall decide by a majority of two-thirds of the members entitled to sit on the Committee whether there has been a violation of the Convention.

2. In the affirmative case the Committee of Ministers shall prescribe a period during which the High Contracting Party concerned must take the measures required by the decision of the Committee of Ministers.

3. If the High Contracting Party concerned has not taken satisfactory measures within the prescribed period, the Committee of Ministers shall decide by the majority provided for in paragraph 1 above what effect shall be given to its original decision and shall publish the Report.

4. The High Contracting Parties undertake to regard as binding on them any decision which the Committee of Ministers may take in application of the preceding paragraph.

ARTICLE 33

The Commission shall meet *in camera*.

ARTICLE 34[4]

Subject to the provisions of Article 29 the Commission shall take its decision by a majority of the Members present and voting.

ARTICLE 38

The European Court of Human Rights shall consist of a number of judges equal to that of the Members of the Council of Europe. No two judges may be nationals of the same State[5].

ARTICLE 43

For the consideration of each case brought before it the Court shall consist of a Chamber composed of seven judges. There shall sit as an *ex officio* member of the Chamber the judge who is a national of any state party concerned, or, if there is none, a person of its choice who shall sit in the capacity of judge; the names of the other judges shall be chosen by lot by the President before the opening of the case.

ARTICLE 44

Only the High Contracting Parties and the Commission shall have the right to bring a case before the court.

ARTICLE 45[6]

The jurisdiction of the Court shall extend to all cases concerning the interpretation and application of the present Convention which the High Contracting Parties or the Commission shall refer to it in accordance with Article 48.

ARTICLE 46

1. Any of the High Contracting Parties may at any time declare that it recognises as compulsory ipso facto and without special agreement the jurisdiction of the Court in all matters concerning the interpretation and application of the present Convention.

---

4. Ed. As amended by the Third Protocol, see footnote 3, above.

5. Ed. The British judge is Sir Gerald Fitzmaurice, formerly a judge of the International Court of Justice and Legal Adviser to the Foreign Office. Judges are, of course, independent; they do not represent their national governments.

6. Ed. Under the Second Protocol to the Convention, Cmnd. 4551, the Court also has jurisdiction to give advisory opinions. The Protocol came into force on 21 September 1970. It is binding on all parties to the Convention except France and Spain.

2. The declaration referred to above may be made unconditionally or on condition of reciprocity on the part of several or certain other High Contracting Parties or for a specified period.

ARTICLE 47

The Court may only deal with a case after the Commission has acknowledged the failure of efforts for a friendly settlement and within the period of three months provided for in Article 32.

ARTICLE 48

The following may bring a case before the Court, provided that the High Contracting Party concerned, if there is only one, or the High Contracting Parties concerned, if there is more than one, are subject to the compulsory jurisdiction of the Court or, failing that, with the consent of the High Contracting Party concerned, if there is only one, or of the High Contracting Parties concerned if there is more than one:
 (a) the Commission;
 (b) a High Contracting Party whose national is alleged to be a victim;
 (c) a High Contracting Party which referred the case to the Commission;
 (d) a High Contracting Party against which the complaint has been lodged.

ARTICLE 50

If the Court finds that a decision or a measure taken by a legal authority or any other authority of a High Contracting Party is completely or partially in conflict with the obligations arising from the present Convention, and if the internal law of the said Party allows only partial reparation to be made for the consequences of this decision or measure, the decision of the Court shall, if necessary, afford just satisfaction to the injured party.

ARTICLE 53

The High Contracting Parties undertake to abide by the decision of the Court in any case to which they are parties.

ARTICLE 54

The judgment of the Court shall be transmitted to the Committee of Ministers which shall supervise its execution.

ARTICLE 57[7]

On receipt of a request from the Secretary-General of the Council of Europe any High Contracting Party shall furnish an explanation of the manner in which its internal law ensures the effective implementation of any of the provisions of this Convention.

ARTICLE 60

Nothing in this Convention shall be construed as limiting or derogating from any of the

---

7. Ed. In practice, this provision has not proved important. In 1964, the Secretary-General called for reports from the contracting parties on the implementation of the Convention. The reports have been published in CE Doc H (66) 9 and addenda to it. They are mostly very short. For the UK report, see addenda 2 and 5 rev. In 1970, the Secretary-General called for information from all of the contracting parties on the implementation of Article 5 (5) of the Convention in particular. For replies, see CE Doc H (72) 2. In 1975, information was called for on Articles 8, 9, 10 and 11. For replies, see CE Doc H (76) 15. The Secretary-General has no express power to comment on information received under Art. 57 and cannot take a case to the European Commission of Human Rights.

human rights and fundamental freedoms which may be ensured under the laws of any High Contracting Party or under any other agreement to which it is a Party.

ARTICLE 63

1. Any State may at the time of its ratification or at any time thereafter declare by notification addressed to the Secretary-General of the Council of Europe that the present Convention shall extend to all or any of the territories for whose international relations it is responsible.
2. The provisions of this Convention shall be applied in such territories with due regard, however, to local requirements.
3. Any State which has made a declaration in accordance with paragraph 1 of this Article may at any time thereafter declare on behalf of one or more of the territories to which the declaration relates that it accepts the competence of the Commission to receive petitions from individuals, non-governmental organisations or groups of individuals in accordance with Article 25 of the present Convention[8].

First Protocol to the Convention 1952[9] Cmd. 9221

ARTICLE I

Every natural or legal person is entitled to the peaceful enjoyment of his possessions. No one shall be deprived of his possessions except in the public interest and subject to the conditions provided for by law and by the general principles of international law.
The preceding provisions shall not, however, in any way impair the right of a State to enforce such laws as it deems necessary to control the use of property in accordance with the general interest or to secure the payment of taxes or other contributions or penalties.

ARTICLE II[10]

No person shall be denied the right to education. In the exercise of any functions which it assumes in relation to education and to teaching, the State shall respect the right of parents to ensure such education and teaching in conformity with their own religious and philosophical convictions.

ARTICLE III

The High Contracting Parties undertake to hold free elections at reasonable intervals by secret ballot, under conditions which will ensure the free expression of the opinion of the people in the choice of the legislature.

---

8. Ed. The UK declaration under Article 63 applies to 22 territories for the international relations of which it is responsible, including Bermuda, British Honduras, Brunei, the Channel Islands, the Falkland Islands, Gibraltar, and the Isle of Man. Hong Kong is not included. The right to petition under Article 25 exists for *most* of the listed territories, including the Isle of Man. The list of territories covered has decreased as new states have achieved independence.
9. Ed. All 20 parties to the Convention except Spain and Switzerland are parties to the Protocol, which entered into force on 18 May 1954.
10. Ed. The UK has made the following reservation to Article II:
  '. . . in view of certain provisions of the Education Acts in force in the United Kingdom, the principle affirmed in the second sentence of Article 2 is accepted by the United Kingdom only so far it is compatible with the provision of efficient instruction and training, and the avoidance of unreasonable public expenditure.'

Fourth Protocol to the Convention 1963[11] Cmnd. 2309

ARTICLE 1

No-one shall be deprived of his liberty merely on the ground of inability to fulfil a contractual obligation.

ARTICLE 2

1. Everyone lawfully within the territory of a state shall, within that territory, have the right to liberty of movement and freedom to choose his residence.
2. Everyone shall be free to leave any country, including his own.
3. No restrictions shall be placed on the exercise of these rights other than such as are in accordance with law and are necessary in a democratic society in the interests of national security or public safety, for the maintenance of *ordre public*, for the prevention of crime, for the protection of health or morals, or for the protection of the rights and freedoms of others.
4. The rights set forth in paragraph 1 may also be subject, in particular areas, to restrictions imposed in accordance with law and justified by the public interest in a democratic society.

ARTICLE 3

1. No-one shall be expelled, by means either of an individual or of a collective measure, from the territory of the State of which he is a national.
2. No-one shall be deprived of the right to enter the territory of the State of which he is a national.

ARTICLE 4

Collective expulsion of aliens is prohibited.

NOTES

1. Apart from the very limited system of reports under Article 57, the ECHR is enforced by means of *state* and *individual* applications (Articles 24, 25), which go in the first place to the European Commission of Human Rights at Strasbourg (Articles 19 et seq.). There have been 13 *state* applications, of which four have concerned the UK, all as the defendant. In 1956–57, two cases (see 2 YBECHR 174 (1958–9)) were brought by Greece against the United Kingdom concerning British action in Cyprus during the emergency situation there. After the settlement of the Cyprus Question in 1959, they were terminated by agreement between the parties and with the consent of the Committee of Ministers of the Council of Europe without final decisions being reached. For the two applications brought by Ireland against the UK about Northern Ireland, see below, p. 191. Although, for political reasons, *state* applications will always be less numerous than *individual* applications, they are potentially more useful in two respects: (1) they may concern a violation of rights defined in the Convention even though there has, at the same time, been no 'victim' of it and (2) they may concern *any* provision of the Convention, whether one guaranteeing a right or not. They are also not subject to Article 27.

2. 14 Parties have accepted the right of *individuals* to bring claims against them under Article 25, including the UK. The UK declaration (Cmnd.

---

11. Ed. The Protocol entered into force on 2 May 1968. There are 11 contracting parties. The UK is not a party.

2894) was made on 14 January 1966. It only applies to violations occurring as of that date. It has been renewed and now applies for five years from 14 January 1976 (Cmnd. 6978). Only 'victims' may bring claims, but this term has been interpreted widely. Aliens and British nationals may bring claims against the UK Government. What has yet to be fully resolved is the extent to which a state is liable for violations of the guaranteed rights by *private* persons (on the basis that it should have acted to provide a remedy in its law). The question is relevant, for example, to press intrusion upon privacy (Article 8) and trade union rights (Article 11). The Commission may grant legal aid in appropriate cases. This may include travelling and subsistence expenses and a lawyer's fees. See Addendum to the Commission's Rules of Procedure. See generally *Bringing an Application before the European Commission of Human Rights* CE Publication, Case Law Topics No. 3.

3. In 1978, 335 individual applications were registered by the Commission. Ninety-seven of these were against the UK (74 by British nationals). In the same year, 715 applications were declared inadmissible, either without being referred to the defendant state for comment or afterwards. Fifteen applications were admitted for examination on their merits, i.e. about 2 per cent of those in respect of which decisions as to admissibility were taken. Six of the 15 were against the UK: *Caprino v United Kingdom* 21 YBECHR 285 (1978) (detention pending deportation); *Campbell v United Kingdom* (prisoners' rights); *Webster v United Kingdom* 12 DRE Comm HR 168 (1978) (closed shop agreement); *Kaplan v United Kingdom* (absence of fair hearing by Dept. of Trade); *A. 7525/76* 11 DRE Comm HR 117 (1978) (homosexuals in Northern Ireland); *A. 7907/77* (corporal punishment in schools). By the end of 1978, the Commission had registered 8448 individual applications during its history. Of the 189 admitted for examination on the merits during that time, 34 were against the UK (i.e. about 20% of those admitted as of 1966).

4. Both state and individual applications have to comply with the rules as to admissibility in Article 26. The *local remedies rule* means that an applicant must go to the courts or use any other *effective* remedy that is available within the defendant state's legal system. He must take his case to the highest available court so far as this offers some reasonable prospect of success: *Vagrancy Cases*, Eur Court HR, Series A, Vol 12, Judgment of 18 June 1971. In the UK, he should presumably (the point has not been tested at Strasbourg) seek leave to appeal to the House of Lords (with or without legal aid) unless there is a clear precedent of the House against him. Although the House of Lords may overturn its decisions, it rarely does so. It may be that if there is a clearly worded statutory provision against the applicant, he may not need to go to the courts at all. Administrative remedies such as a petition to the Home Secretary by a prisoner (*Golder v United Kingdom* 14 YBECHR 416 (1971)) or an application to the Parliamentary Commissioner must be exhausted. A petition for clemency in the exercise of the royal prerogative is not required (*A. 458/59* 3 YBECHR 222 (1960)). Local remedies need not be exhausted in the case of a state application where the allegation is that a law is contrary to the ECHR *in abstracto* or that an administrative practice (as opposed to an isolated breach) has been developed by a state's officials that is in breach of the ECHR. It was because such practices existed that the victims concerned did not have to exhaust the remedies available in the Northern Irish courts before the Irish Government could bring its state application in *Ireland v United Kingdom* below, p. 191. In *Donnelly v United Kingdom* 16 YBECHR 212 (1973), the Commission held (again in the Northern Ireland context) that an individual applicant need not exhaust local remedies where the breach of which he claims to be a victim results from an administrative practice.

The *6 months rule* is tempered somewhat by the rule in the *Ringeisen* case, Eur Court HR, Series A, Vol 13, Judgment of 16 July 1971, by which an application may be lodged before the final stage in the exhaustion of local remedies is over, although it must be completed before the decision as to admissibility is taken. The Commission has developed the idea of a 'continuing violation', which also helps: see *De Becker* case 2 YBECHR 215 (1968) (deprivation of freedom of speech for life).

5. Individual applications have also to comply with Article 27. An application will be rejected as 'incompatible with . . . the Convention', inter alia, if it does not raise a question of the violation of the Convention as a matter of law, i.e. if the facts do not bring the case within the scope of a right as defined in the Convention. It will be rejected as 'manifestly ill-founded' if a right as defined in the Convention is in issue but the facts show no evidence of a breach of it (i.e. no prima facie case). The decision to reject an application is final. This being so, and the final word as to the interpretation of the Convention resting with the Court, not the Commission, there is a strong case for arguing that the Commission should be reluctant to reject an application on a ground that involves its interpretation of the meaning of the guarantee.

6. The fact-finding inquiry required by Article 28 into applications admitted for examination on the merits is conducted by the Commission on the basis of written and oral pleadings by the parties and may involve an on-the-spot visit for which the government concerned is obliged to provide the necessary facilities. Members of the Commission visited Broadmoor in a case concerning conditions there. By the end of 1978, the Commission had obtained a friendly settlement in twelve cases, including three against the UK: the *Alam and Khan* case, Report of the E Comm HR, 17 December 1968 (Commonwealth immigrant case: UK undertook to admit and pay air fare), the *Knetchl* case, below p. 422, and the *Amekrane* case, below, p. 31. It has completed its proceedings and laid its report before the Committee of Ministers in over 60 cases. Thirty-one of these have been referred to the Court and have been decided or are pending. The Court has so far found violations of the Convention in 15 cases, including four against the UK: the *Golder* case, below, p. 418; *Ireland v United Kingdom* below, p. 191; the *Tyrer* case, below, p. 30, and the *Sunday Times* case, below, p. 261. The UK was found not liable in the fifth case against it—the *Handyside* case, below, p. 222—to have reached the Court. The UK made a declaration under Article 46 accepting the Court's jurisdiction in 1966 (Cmnd. 2894); the declaration has been renewed and now applies for five years from 14 January 1976 (Cmnd. 6978).

7. The question of the applicant's standing in proceedings brought before the Court was raised in the *Lawless* case, Eur Court HR, Series A, Vol. 1 Judgment of 14 November 1960. There, after confirming that the individual applicant could not initiate proceedings or plead his case before it, the Court stated that 'it is in the interests of the proper administration of justice that the Court should have knowledge of and, if need be, take into consideration, the Applicant's point of view' since the proceedings were 'upon issues which concern' him. These views, the Court said, would become known to the Court through the Commission's report. In addition, the Commission, which does have standing before the Court, 'as defender of the public interest, is entitled of its own accord, even if it does not share

them, to make known the Applicant's views to the Court as a means of throwing light on the points at issue.'

The Court could also hear the Applicant as a witness and 'as part of the enquiry, may invite the Commission, *ex officio*, or authorise the Commission at its request, to submit the Applicant's observations on the Report or on any specific point arising in the course of the debates.'

In 1971, in the *Vagrancy* cases, Eur Court HR, Series A, Vol. 12, Judgment of 18 November 1970, the Court, over the objection of Belgium, the defendant state, permitted the applicant's lawyer, at the request of and under the control of the Commission, to make a short statement on some questions of fact which the Commission thought would help the Court. Should the applicant, who has full and equal standing with the defendant state before the Commission (and is called a 'party' in Article 28, Convention), be relegated to the sidelines before the Court?

8. The Court's judgment, which is binding (Article 53), is normally declaratory. If the Court finds that a breach of the ECHR has occurred, this brings into operation the defendant state's obligation in international law to make reparation. Exceptionally, the Court may award 'just satisfaction', which will invariably be monetary compensation, to the 'injured party' (Article 50). Compensation has been awarded in several cases, none concerning the UK. The implementation of the Court's judgments is supervised by the Committee of Ministers (Article 54). The Court's judgments have been complied with in every case so far. For the steps taken by the British Government to bring its law and practice into line with the ECHR after the *Golder* and *Tyrer* cases, see below, pp. 421 and 30. The draft legislation on contempt of court now under consideration takes the *Sunday Times* case (below, p. 261) into account.

9. If a case is not referred to the Court for a final decision, it is decided by the Committee of Ministers by a two-thirds majority vote (Article 32). This was provided for because states were not prepared to accept a Convention in which every case might finally be decided by a court. There is no judicial hearing of the evidence. The Committee consists of the Foreign Ministers of the member states of the Council of Europe or their deputies. It has the Commission's report on the case before it and hears the comments of the defendant state, which is allowed to vote. The existence of alternative bodies competent to take a final decision in a case is not in the interests of the development of a consistent jurisprudence interpreting the Convention. The unsatisfactory nature of an arrangement whereby a case may be determined by the Committee of Ministers was illustrated in the *Huber* case, 14 YBECHR 572 (1971) (Decn. Admiss.). There, the Committee rejected (CM Resolution DH (75)2) an eight to two majority opinion by the Commission that Austria had detained the applicant contrary to Article 5(3). This was done after a discussion of the case in which, in accordance with the usual procedure, the Austrian representative explained his state's defence and in the absence of any hearing of the Commission or applicant. For the Committee to reject in these circumstances the considered and independent judgment of a clear majority of the Commission, arrived at after a full hearing of the facts and legal arguments of the parties, is scarcely what one would hope for in the administration of a human rights guarantee that protects the right to a fair trial. Cf. note **14**.

10. Proceedings at Strasbourg are slow. In the *Golder* case, nearly five years elapsed between the registration of the application and the ruling of the European Court of Human Rights. By this time, the applicant had been released from prison. Such a time scale is common for cases that stay the course. There are inevitable delays in an international, multilingual procedure with so many stages administered by a part-time Commission and Court. The problem is particularly acute in cases where time is of the essence (see the *Amekrane* case, below, p.31). The Commission has no power to issue an interlocutory injunction.

It is true, of course, that under the Convention as finally conceived, the primary purpose of state and individual applications is not to offer an international remedy for individual victims of violations of the Convention but to bring to light violations of an *inter-state* guarantee. Individuals are expected to benefit generally, through the containment of municipal law that that guarantee is aimed at achieving, rather than as individual claimants in particular cases. The result is still that the Convention is less useful than it might otherwise be for the individual victim.

11. Nonetheless, the Strasbourg system of applications is a valuable adjunct to the possibilities provided under UK law for the protection of civil liberties, particularly in the absence of a Bill of Rights. The numbers of applications to Strasbourg would clearly decrease if, in the exhaustion of local remedies, one had first to go to a British court which would, under Lord Wade's proposal, apply the ECHR. The *Golder, Sunday Times* and certain other Strasbourg cases against the UK are discussed in the following Chapters where appropriate. Three other cases which show the widely differing areas in which the Strasbourg remedy can have some impact are discussed in the following notes.

12. *The Tyrer* case, Eur Court HR, Series A, Vol 26, Judgment of 25 April 1978. The applicant was a UK citizen resident in the Isle of Man. In 1972, when aged fifteen, he was sentenced by a juvenile court to three strokes of the birch for an assault occasioning actual bodily harm contrary to Manx law. A sentence of corporal punishment may be imposed on males for certain offences under Manx law; it ceased to be a permissible sentence in England, Wales and Scotland in 1968. The ECHR extends to the Isle of Man as a result of a declaration made by the United Kingdom Government under Article 63. The applicant complained that the birching he was given was contrary to Article 3. Although the applicant sought to withdraw his application after it had been admitted for consideration on the merits, the Commission refused to permit this because it raised issues of a general character affecting the operation of the Convention. In its report on the case, the Commission expressed the opinion, by fourteen votes to one, that the punishment was 'degrading' contrary to Article 3 and referred the case to the Court. Confirming the Commission's opinion, the Court held, by six votes to one (Judge Sir Gerald Fitzmaurice dissenting), that the punishment was 'degrading'. The Court stated that for a punishment to be 'degrading', the humiliation or debasement must be more than that which exists in the case of generally accepted forms of punishment imposed by courts for criminal offences. In the case of corporal punishment, factors that made it 'degrading' were the institutionalised use of physical violence by one human being against another and the assault upon a person's dignity and physical integrity that this involved. The fact that, in this case, punishment was administered to the bare posterior of the applicant aggravated its degrading character but was not crucial to the decision. The Court emphasised that it was not relevant that the birch was thought to be an effective deterrent in the Isle of Man; a punishment contrary to Article 3 was not permitted however effective it might be. The Court also rejected an argument based upon the 'local requirements' of the Isle of Man (Article 63, ECHR). No further birching case is likely to arise. The United

Kingdom has notified the Committee of Ministers of the Council of Europe that it has informed the Manx Government that, in its view, such judicial corporal punishment as can be imposed in the Isle of Man is in breach of the Convention as a result of the Court's judgment. The judgment has been brought to the attention of those who can under Manx law pass a sentence of corporal punishment by the Chief Justice of the Isle of Man. He has informed them that judicial corporal punishment is contrary to the Convention. See CE Press Release B (78) 50. This action has been accepted by the Committee of Ministers as fulfilling the obligations that the United Kingdom has arising out of the judgment: CM Resolution (78) 39. The Tynwald has since proposed to the Home Office that a 'reservation' be made to the Convention or that the convention be denounced in respect of the Isle of Man. It does not want to repeal the birching law.

13. *The Amekrane* case, 16 YBECHR 356 (1973) (Decn. Admiss.). Report of the Commission adopted 19 July 1974. Mohamed Amekrane, a Moroccan national and a Lieutenant-Colonel in the Moroccan Air Force, was a party to a plot to kill King Hassan of Morocco and to overthrow his government. When the plot failed, Amekrane fled, on 16 August 1972, from Morocco to Gibraltar where he requested political asylum. The request was refused and he was declared a prohibited immigrant. The Moroccan Government asked for his return and on 17 August 1972 Amekrane was handed over to its representatives at Gibraltar airport whence he was flown back to Morocco on a Moroccan Air Force plane. On his return, Amekrane was interrogated, tried and sentenced to death by military tribunal. He was executed by firing squad on 15 January 1973.

An application was made to Strasbourg on 16 December 1972 in the name of Amekrane, his wife and his two children in which a violation *inter alia* of Article 3 of the Convention was alleged. It was claimed that the first applicant had been subjected to 'inhuman treatment' because he was returned to Morocco when it was known that he would be prosecuted there for a political offence and sentenced to death if convicted. The application was given precedence by the Commission and declared admissible on 11 October 1973. In July 1974 a 'friendly settlement' in the sense of Article 28 was reached with the assistance of the Commission by which the United Kingdom agreed to pay the applicants £37,500 in full and final settlement of their claims. The payment was made *ex gratia* and was understood by the United Kingdom as not implying any admission by it that the Convention had been violated.

The case is a remarkable one both because it is the first in which an application against the United Kingdom from an overseas territory has been declared admissible and because of the amount of compensation paid by the United Kingdom. £37,500 is by far the largest sum that a state has agreed to pay as part of a 'friendly settlement'. But then, as *The Times* said, the whole affair was 'a sad episode from which the government of the time emerged with little credit and some justified opprobrium.' (*The Times*, 14 August 1974, editorial). There was no extradition treaty between Morocco and the United Kingdom and the case would appear to have been one of extradition in the guise of the application of the immigration laws. Cf. the case of Dr. Soblen in 1963, as to which see P. O'Higgins, (1964) 17 **MLR** 521 and C. Thornberry, (1962) 12 ICLQ 414. The haste with which the matter had been dealt with effectively prevented Amekrane from questioning in the courts in Gibraltar the legality of his return. Might the need to maintain good relations with Morocco because of the dispute with Spain about Gibraltar have been a factor in the case?

14. *The East African Asians* cases, 13 YBECHR 928 (1970) and 30 CDE Comm HR 127 (1970) (Decns. Admiss.). In 1970 the Commission admitted for consideration on the merits inter alia under Article 3 the cases of thirty-one United Kingdom citizens or British protected persons who had been resident in Kenya or Uganda and who had been refused entry into the United Kingdom. In its decision as to admissibility, the Commission stated that 'quite apart from any consideration of Article 14, discrimination based on race could, in certain circumstances, of itself amount to degrading treatment within the meaning of Article 3.' In its report on the merits of the case in 1973, the Commission expressed the opinion by eight votes to three that Article 3 had been violated in the case of the twenty-five applicants who were United Kingdom citizens. After much delay, and after all thirty-one applicants in the case had been admitted to the United Kingdom, the Committee of Ministers decided in 1977 that 'no further action' was called for. CM Resolution DH (77) 2. The Committee did not rule on the question whether Article 3 had been infringed.

15. The UK has other treaty obligations to protect human rights. In particular, it is a party to the International Covenant on Civil and Political Rights 1966, Cmnd. 6702; the International Covenant on Economic, Social and Cultural Rights 1966, Cmnd. 6702; the International Convention on the Elimination of all Forms of Racial Discrimination 1966, Cmnd. 4108; and the European Social Charter 1961 (on economic and social rights), Cmnd. 2643. Although the first of these has an Optional Protocol, Cmnd. 3220, allowing a right of individual petition, the UK is not a party to it. The UK has accepted the right of other *states* parties to the Civil and Political Rights Covenant to bring cases against it, but this procedure has not yet been accepted by sufficient states to enter into force. In any event, individual and state petitions under the Covenant cannot lead to any legally binding decisions against a defaulting state. The Racial Discrimination Convention has a compulsory system of state petitions and an optional system of individual petitions (not in force and not accepted by the UK). The Covenant on Economic, Social and Cultural Rights and the European Social Charter do not provide for state or individual petitions. There are reporting systems for the enforcement of all four treaties. See E. Schwelb, (1968) 62 AJIL 827 and (1968) 1 H Rts Jo 363; L. B. Sohn (1968) 62 AJIL 909; N. Lerner, *The UN Convention on the Elimination of all Forms of Racial Discrimination* (1970).

CHAPTER 2

Police powers

1 Introduction

The materials in this chapter illustrate the powers and duties of the police in the enforcement of the criminal law. The present law satisfies nobody. It is far too complex, contained in a miscellany of, often archaic, statutes and cases. Problems which are difficult enough as examination questions are trickier still for the 'policeman on the beat' who will often have to act without prolonged deliberation. If the rules are known their precise meaning may be uncertain. And when their meaning is clear their content is often unsatisfactory. Many powers of the police are of unduly wide scope and yet, at the same time, the police do not possess certain powers which many would regard as necessary to the performance of their tasks. And when the law is reasonably clear and its content reasonably satisfactory there may be difficulties in ensuring compliance with those rules. Police officers perform their duties subject to the possibilities of prosecution, civil claim and internal disciplinary action if they exceed their powers. Yet for most of those with whom they deal the opportunity to prosecute or sue (notwithstanding possible punitive damages – see *Cassell & Co Ltd v Broome* [1972] AC 1027 HL) may be of little practical value, and, despite new arrangements, there still exists a division of opinion as to the way in which complaints against the police are handled. Moreover, with the exception of the rules about confessions, the judges have declined to use the rules about admissibility of evidence as a method of 'policing' the police.

In the past a large amount of police work has relied on the cooperation and consent of citizens together with a certain amount of 'bluff' as to the extent of police powers. With cooperation and consent apparently diminishing and a greater awareness of people as to their 'rights' the need grows for a thorough review and reform of the law of police powers. A Royal Commission was set up in 1977 with the following terms of reference:

'To examine, having regard to the interests of the community of bringing offenders to justice and to the rights and liberties of persons suspected or accused of crime and taking into account also the need for the efficient and economical use of resources, whether changes are needed in England and Wales in

(a) the powers and duties of the police in respect of the investigation of criminal offences and the rights and duties of suspects and accused persons including the means by which these are secured;

(b) the process of and responsibility for the prosecution of criminal offences,

and (c) such other features of criminal procedure and evidence as relate to the above and to make recommendations'.

At the outset the much-quoted words of an earlier Royal Commission should perhaps be borne in mind:

' . . . Criminals are often not the least intelligent members of the population, and their detection cannot for the most part be achieved without the exercise of patient and laborious investigation combined with prompt and energetic action. No responsible person would suggest that the police should be unnecessarily hampered in the performance of the essential duty of bringing criminals to justice. The difficulty is to ensure that in the performance of this duty no arbitrary attitude or excess of zeal on the part of the police should interfere with the proper rights or liberties of the individual citizen. We do not suggest that any system could be devised which would ensure that in all cases the balance should be evenly held between the interests of justice on the one hand and the rights and liberties of the subject on the other. Every system is dependent upon the individuals who are called upon to administer it, and it is inevitable that in any large organisation there should be occasional lapses of conduct . . . Moreover a system is not to be judged by the happenings in a few isolated cases of a sensational nature which are apt to attract more than their fair share of publicity, but by the general results obtained over a long period . . .' (*Royal Commission on Police Powers and Procedures*, 1928–9, Cmd. 3297)

Issues as to the *legality* (as distinct from the propriety) of police action may arise in a number of contexts. We give here some examples of the situations which are most likely to occur.

(1) Actions in Tort

A citizen may sue a police officer for trespass to the person (assault; false imprisonment) trespass to goods or trespass to land, and the officer may seek to establish the defence that he had lawful authority for his action. Conversely, a police officer may wish to sue a citizen for assaulting him. A citizen may sue to recover property in the possession of the police (or may apply to a Magistrates' Court for its return under the Police (Property) Act 1897).

(2) Criminal Prosecutions

A citizen who resists police action may find himself prosecuted for assault on or obstruction of the police in the execution of their duty (below, pp. 36–37). He may wish to establish that the police action was unlawful and that the resistance was as a consequence lawful. Conversely, a citizen may bring a prosecution against the police officer for assault or false imprisonment.

(3) Applications for Judicial Review

A citizen may challenge executive action on the ground that it is ultra vires (and on certain other grounds) by making an 'application for judicial review' to the Queen's Bench Divisional Court under RSC Order 53. A variety of remedies may be sought including, for example, certiorari (to quash a warrant: see *Inland Revenue Commrs v Rossminster* below, p.77) or a declaration (that a seizure of property is unlawful: ibid.). Proceedings for habeas corpus may be brought under RSC Order 54 (to challenge the legality of personal detention).

2 Police questioning

Asking questions is central to the task of detecting and investigating crime. Questions need to be put to a variety of persons (e.g. suspects, witnesses) at various stages of investigation (e.g. when there is general suspicion that an offence may have been committed; when suspicion begins to point to a particular individual; when the police believe an individual to have committed an offence and seek an admission of guilt). The law regulates questioning in a number of ways. In this and the following section we consider whether it imposes any obligation to answer police questions or otherwise assist the police and whether any power of detention for questioning exists. The Judges' Rules and the admissibility in evidence of involuntary confessions will be considered later (below, pp.104–108 and 115–117).

Rice v Connolly [1966] 2 QB 414, [1966] 2 All ER 649, [1966] 3 WLR 17, 130 JP 322, Queen's Bench Divisional Court

Police officers patrolling late at night in an area where a number of breaking offences had just been committed observed Rice loitering about the streets. The officers asked him where he was going to, where he had come from and for his name and address. Rice gave only his surname and the name of the street on which he said he lived. The officers asked Rice to accompany them to a nearby police-box so that this information could be checked. Rice refused to move unless arrested. The officers obliged. Rice appealed against conviction under section 51(3) of the Police Act 1964 (below, p.36).

Lord Parker CJ: What the prosecution have to prove is that there was an obstructing of a constable; that the constable was at the time acting in the execution of his duty and that the person obstructing did so wilfully. To carry the matter a little further, it is in my view clear that 'obstruct' under section 51 (3) of the Police Act, 1964, is the doing of any act which makes it more difficult for the police to carry out their duty. That description of obstructing I take from *Hinchcliffe v Sheldon* [1955] 1 WLR 1207. It is also in my judgment clear that it is part of the obligations and duties of a police constable to take all steps which appear to him necessary for keeping the peace, for preventing crime or for protecting property from criminal injury. There is no exhaustive definition of the powers and obligations of the police, but they are at least those, and they would further include the duty to detect crime and to bring an offender to justice.

Pausing there, it seems to me quite clear that the defendant was making it more difficult for the police to carry out their duties, and that the police at the time and throughout were acting in accordance with their duties. The only remaining ingredient, and the one upon which in my judgment this case revolves, is whether the obstructing of which the defendant was guilty was a wilful obstruction. 'Wilful' in this context not only in my judgment means 'intentional' but something which is done without lawful excuse, and that indeed is conceded by Mr Skinner, who appears for the prosecution in this case. Accordingly, the sole question here is whether the defendant had a lawful excuse for refusing to answer the questions put to him. In my judgment he had. It seems to me quite clear that though every citizen has a moral duty or, if you like, a social duty to assist the police, there is no legal duty to that effect, and indeed the whole basis of the common law is the right of the individual to refuse to answer questions put to him by persons in authority, and to refuse to accompany those in authority to any particular place; short, of course, of arrest.

In my judgment there is all the difference in the world between deliberately telling a false story—something which on no view a citizen has a right to do—and preserving silence or refusing to answer—something which he has every right to do . . .

Marshall J: I agree. In order to uphold this conviction it appears to me that one has to assent to the proposition that where a citizen is acting merely within his legal rights, he is thereby committing a criminal offence. Nor can I see that the manner in which he does it can make any difference whatsoever, and for the reasons given by my Lord I agree that this appeal should be allowed.

James J Also for the reasons given by the Lord Chief Justice, I agree that this appeal should be allowed. For my own part, I would only add this, that I would not go so far as to say that there may not be circumstances in which the manner of a person together with his silence could amount to an obstruction within the section; whether it does remains to be decided in any case that happens hereafter, not in this case, in which it has not been argued.
Appeal allowed.

Police Act 1964

51. (1) Any person who assaults a constable in the execution of his duty, or a person assisting a constable in the execution of his duty, shall be guilty of an offence and liable [on summary conviction to imprisonment for a term not exceeding six months or to a fine not exceeding £1,000 or to both].
(2) (*omitted*)
(3) Any person who resists or wilfully obstructs a constable in the execution of his duty, or a person assisting a constable in the execution of his duty shall be guilty of an offence and liable on summary conviction to imprisonment for a term not exceeding one month or to a fine not exceeding [£200], or to both.

NOTES

1. Section 51 re-enacted earlier provisions. The penalties were increased by the Criminal Law Act 1977 ss. 30 and 31, Schs. 1 and 6. The Act also removed the right to claim trial by jury under s. 51(1).
2. *Rice v Connolly* requires the courts to draw a distinction between certain acts of obstruction which s. 51(3) prohibits and other acts of obstruction which remain lawful notwithstanding the apparent terms of the subsection.

In accomplishing this task the Courts have sometimes distinguished between active and passive obstruction. In *Dibble v Ingleton* [1972] 1 QB 480, DC, in order to frustrate the administration of a breathalyser test, the defendant drank from a bottle of whisky. He was convicted under s. 51(3) of the Police Act 1964 and appealed. Giving the judgment of the Divisional Court, Bridge J said, at p. 488:

' . . . I would draw a clear distinction between a refusal to act, on the one hand, and the doing of some positive act on the other. In a case, as in *Rice v Connolly* [1966] 2 QB 414 where the obstruction alleged consists of a refusal by the defendant to do the act which the police constable had asked him to do—to give information, it might be, or to give assistance to the police constable—one can see readily the soundness of the principle . . . that such a refusal to act cannot amount to a wilful obstruction under section 51 unless the law imposes upon the person concerned some obligation in the circumstances to act in the manner requested by the police officer.

On the other hand, I can see no basis in principle or in any authority which has been cited for saying that where the obstruction consists of a positive act, it must be unlawful independently of its operation as an obstruction of a police constable under section 51. If the act relied upon as an obstruction had to be shown to be an offence independently of its effect as an obstruction it is difficult to see what use there would be in the provisions of section 51 of the Police Act 1964.

In my judgment the act of the defendant in drinking whisky when he did with the object and effect of frustrating the procedure under sections 2 and 3 of the Road Safety Act 1967 was a wilful obstruction of Police Constable Tully.'

However, although obstructive inaction is more likely to be excused by the courts than obstructive action, this is not always so. For example in *Johnson v Phillips* [1975] 3 All ER 682 in order to allow the passage of an ambulance a police officer ordered the defendant to reverse the 'wrong way' down a one-way street. The defendant's refusal to do so was held to constitute an obstruction of the officer within s. 51 (3).

3. A person's motive for acting in a way which in fact obstructs the police may also be important. In *Wilmott v Atack* [1977] 1 QB 498, DC the defendant intervened between police officers struggling to make an arrest and the person they were arresting. The defendant's purpose in so doing was to try to resolve the situation more peacefully. In fact his actions merely hindered the police in making the arrest. Allowing on appeal against conviction under Police Act 1964 s. 51(3) Croom Johnson J said, at p. 503:

' . . . The point which is taken is that the phrase "wilfully obstructs" means that it is not enough that there should be an intention merely to do something which happens to result in there being an obstruction, but that it is also necessary that it should import some form of hostility towards the police . . .

The question is then: is it necessary for there to have been an intention for the acts of the defendant to have been to make it more difficult for the police to carry out their duties rather than, as appears to have been found by the Crown Court here, an intention on his part to make it more easy . . . ?

One turns at this point to *Betts v Stevens* [1910] 1 KB 1, which was a case arising out of the warnings given once upon a time by A.A. patrol men to those who were exceeding the speed limit of the existence of nearby police trap. Darling J dealing with the question of intention said at p.8:

"The gist of the offence to my mind lies in the intention with which the thing is done. In my judgment in *Bastable v Little* [1907] 1 KB 59 I used these words: 'In my opinion it is quite easy to distinguish the cases where a warning is given with the object of preventing the commission of a crime from the cases in which the crime is being committed and the warning is given in order that the commission of the crime may be suspended while there is a danger of detection.' I desire to repeat those words. Here I think it is perfectly plain upon the facts found by the magistrates in this case that the object of Betts' intervention was that the offence . . . should be . . . desisted from merely whilst there was a danger of the police detecting it . . . and that therefore he was obstructing the police in their duty . . ."

Then comes an important passage:

"He did that wilfully in order to obstruct them in their duty, and not in order to assist them in their performance of their duty nor in order to prevent a motorist upon the road from committing an offence."

The point is clearly taken by Darling J in that case.

It is suggested that if any other construction than the one which the defendant is urging were to be placed upon the words 'wilfully obstructs' . . . the effect would be that any well meaning bystander, who saw the police for example having difficulty making an arrest and went to try to help him, would find, if he should unfortunately be the unwitting cause of the criminal escaping through his intervention, that he had himself committed a criminal offence.'

The appeal was allowed and the conviction quashed.

4. See further on the Police Act 1964, s. 51, Smith and Hogan, *Criminal Law* (4th edn., 1978) pp. 361–368; K. Lidstone (1976) Crim LR 617; U. Ross (1977) Crim LR 187; the following cases below: *Kenlin v Gardiner* (p. 39), *Ludlow v Burgess* (p. 40), *Donelly v Jackman* (p. 40), *Squires v Botwright* (p. 41), *R v Inwood* (p. 54), *Gelberg v Miller* (p. 57), *Bailey v Wilson* (p. 67), *Davis v Lisle* (p. 68), *McArdle v Wallace (No 2)* (p. 69), *R v Waterfield* (p. 90), *Duncan v Jones* (p. 172), *Piddington v Bates* (p. 175); and the 14th Report of the Criminal Law Revision Committee on Offences against the Person (1980) Cmnd. 7844.

Prevention of Terrorism (Temporary Provisions) Act 1976

11. Information about acts of terrorism:
(1) If a person who has information which he knows or believes might be of material assistance –
   (a) in preventing an act of terrorism to which this section applies, or
   (b) in securing the apprehension, prosecution or conviction of any person for an offence involving the commission, preparation or instigation of an act of terrorism to which this section applies,
fails without reasonable excuse to disclose that information as soon as reasonably practicable –
   (i) in England and Wales, to a constable,
   (ii) in Scotland, to a constable or the procurator fiscal, or
   (iii) in Northern Ireland, to a constable or a member of Her Majesty's forces,
he shall be guilty of an offence.

NOTES

1. The maximum penalty on summary conviction is a term of imprisonment not exceeding six months or a fine not exceeding £1,000 or both (s.11(2) and the Criminal Law Act 1977, s.28(2)). On indictment the maximum penalty is five years imprisonment or an unlimited fine, or both.
2. Section 11 applies only to acts of terrorism occurring in the United Kingdom and connected with Northern Irish affairs (s.10(5)). Terrorism is defined as 'the use of violence for political ends, and includes any use of violence for the purpose of putting the public or any section of the public in fear' (s.14(1)). By s.14(3) 'any reference in a provision of this Act to a person's having been concerned in the commission, preparation or instigation of acts of terrorism shall be taken to be a reference to his having been so concerned at any time, whether before or after the coming into force of that provision'.
3. Section 11 had no counterpart in the Prevention of Terrorism (Temporary Provisions) Act 1974. It was a controversial backbench amendment to the 1976 Bill. The *Shackleton Report* (1978) Cmnd. 7324 on the operation of the 1974 and 1976 Acts commented:

'66. . . . It was argued by some that the nature of terrorist activity was such that the citizen should be placed under the strongest possible obligation to disclose any information he might have to the police. On the other hand, there were those who saw in section 11 an unwelcome step towards a society where people were expected to inform under fear of prosecution. It is generally accepted that a suspected or accused person should not have to incriminate himself and it has been argued that section 11 is not consistent with this principle. It has also been argued that there is a distinction between suspicion and sure knowledge, and that where a person merely suspects that someone may be involved in terrorism but has no certain knowledge, he might understandably be wary of implicating someone who might be quite innocent.
   67. These are theoretical objections: more specifically, it has been claimed that the police use section 11 to bring pressure to bear on a person in detention by threatening him that, unless he gives certain information, he will be charged under the section. . . . The distinction between explaining the provisions of section 11 dispassionately to a person in custody and using it as a threat during the questioning may be a fine one indeed, particularly in circumstances where the person detained may already feel himself to be under some pressure . . .
   68. The circumstances of the security situation in Northern Ireland where so much of the

success of the security forces depends upon there being a flow of information from the local community, perhaps suggests that section 11 may, by comparison with Great Britain, have a larger part to play.

132. There are genuine doubts about its implications in principle and about the way it might be used in the course of interviewing someone. It has, in any case, been little used in Great Britain, and the obvious difficulties of proof may be a factor in this respect. On the other hand, it has been more extensively used in the different circumstances of Northern Ireland, and the Royal Ulster Constabulary left me in no doubt about its value to them.

133. Section 11 was not thought necessary in 1974. It has an unpleasant ring about it in terms of civil liberties. I recommend therefore that it be allowed to lapse forthwith. No doubt the Government will wish to consider whether the needs of the security situation in Northern Ireland are such that its continuation there could be justified.'

The Home Secretary (Mr. Whitelaw) stated in 1980: 'I have . . . considered whether section 11 could be dropped. I have consulted the police, who are firmly of the view that section 11 is still an important weapon in the struggle against terrorism. The fact is that a total of 13 charges have been brought under section 11 since it came into force in 1976, 12 of them in January 1979. Having considered the matter very carefully, I have concluded that section 11 should be retained.' (980 HC Deb 4 March 1980 col 409)

See also B. Rose-Smith, 'Police Powers and Terrorism Legislation' in P. Hain (ed.), *Policing the Police*, Vol.1 (1979) pp. 142–4 and C. Scorer (NCCL) *The Prevention of Terrorism Acts 1974 and 1976*. For powers of arrest and detention in relation to this offence, see below, p. 43.

4. See also the Official Secrets Act 1920, s.6 (below, p. 275) and the Northern Ireland (Emergency Provisions) Act 1978, below, p. 183.

3 Detention for questioning

Kenlin v Gardiner [1967] 2 QB 510, [1967] 2 WLR 129, [1966] 3 All ER 931, 131 JP 191, 110 Sol Jo 848, Queen's Bench Divisional Court

Two boys were visiting homes of members of their school rugby team to remind them of a forthcoming match. Two plain-clothed police officers became suspicious of the boys' behaviour. One approached the boys and asked them what they were doing. He stated that he was a policeman and showed his warrant card but this information did not register in the minds of the boys. One boy tried to run away but was restrained by the officer. The boy, not realising the restrainer was a police officer, struck the officer and escaped. Further struggle ensued. The boys were charged under section 51(1) Police Act 1964. They appealed against conviction.

Winn LJ: . . . [W]as this officer entitled in law to take hold of the first boy by the arm . . . ?
. . . I feel myself compelled to say that the answer to that question must be in the negative. This officer might or might not in the particular circumstances have possessed a power to arrest these boys. I leave that question open, saying no more than that I feel some doubt whether he would have had a power of arrest: but on the assumption that he had a power to arrest, it is to my mind perfectly plain that neither of these officers purported to arrest either of these boys. What was done was not done as an integral step in the process of arresting, but was done in order to secure an opportunity, by detaining the boys from escape, to put to them or to either of them the question which was regarded as the test question to satisfy the officers whether or not it would be right in the circumstances, and having regard to the answer obtained from that question, if any, to arrest them.

I regret to say that I think there was a technical assault by the police officer . . . .
Widgery J and **Lord Parker CJ** agreed.
Appeal allowed.

NOTES

1. In *Ludlow v Burgess* [1971] Crim LR 238, DC, a police constable believed that whilst boarding a bus he had been deliberately kicked on the shin by the defendant. The defendant, using foul language, claimed the kick to have been accidental. The constable told the defendant not to use such language and as the defendant began to walk away the officer put his hand on the defendant's shoulder to detain him for further conversation and inquiries. At this the defendant struggled and kicked the constable. The defendant was convicted by the justices of assaulting the officer in the execution of his duty contrary to Police Act 1964, s.51(1). The Divisional Court, allowing the defendant's appeal, held that the detention of a man against his will without arresting him was an unlawful act and a serious interference with a citizen's liberty. Since such detention was an unlawful act it was not an act done in execution of the constable's duty.

2. If an officer is found to have exceeded his legal powers no prosecution under s.51 can succeed. In cases where an officer may have exceeded his powers but nevertheless the force used by the defendant in self-defence seems out of proportion to the injury he has suffered, the police should instead bring a charge of common assault or some other offence against the person. Such a charge can be substituted even up to the point where it is apparent that the magistrates must acquit under s.51 – see *Lawrence v Same* [1968] 2 QB 93, 99 per Lord Parker CJ and (1976) 140 JPN 331. Such charges are not conditioned on the lawfulness of the police action. The liability of the defendant will depend on the reasonableness in the circumstances of the force used by him in self-defence. See the Criminal Law Act 1967, s.3 (below, p.59).

Donnelly v Jackman [1970] 1 WLR 562, [1970] 1 All ER 987, (1969)114 Sol Jo 130, 54 Cr App Rep 229, Queen's Bench Divisional Court

A police officer saw the defendant walking along a pavement and approached him to make enquiries of him about an offence which the officer believed he might have committed. The defendant repeatedly ignored requests that he should stop. The officer tapped the defendant on the shoulder. The defendant tapped the officer on the chest saying, 'Now we are even copper'. The officer again touched the defendant's shoulder intending to stop him, whereupon the defendant turned and struck the officer with some force. The defendant was charged under section 51(1) of the Police Act 1964. He appealed against conviction.

Talbot J . . . The main point taken by Mr. Purchas [counsel for the defendant]is that the result of what the officer did was such that he was not acting in the execution of his duty. He had, argued Mr. Purchas, no right to stop the defendant or any other person other than by arrest. In support of his argument he cited several authorities in which officers whilst, it is alleged, acting in the execution of their duties had been assaulted, in which the court had found that in fact they were not acting in the execution of their duties. The first one was *Davis v Lisle* [1936] 2 KB 434. . . . [see below p.68].

That seems to me a very different case from the present one which we are considering. There the police officer had gone so far as to make himself a trespasser. The other authority quoted by Mr. Purchas was that of *Kenlin v Gardiner* [1967] 2 QB 510. . . . [see above p. 39]. There again the facts of that case are vastly different from those that we are considering, because there each officer had been taking hold of one of the boys and had in fact detained him.

Turning to the facts of this matter, it is not very clear what precisely the justices meant or found when they said the officer touched the defendant on the shoulder, but whatever it was they really did mean, it seems clear to me that they must have felt it was a minimal matter by the way they treated this matter and the result of the case. When one considers the problem:

was this officer acting in the course of his duty, one ought to bear in mind that it is not every trivial interference with a citizen's liberty that amounts to a course of conduct sufficient to take the officer out of the course of his duties. The facts that the magistrates found in this case do not justify the view that the police officer was not acting in the execution of his duty when he went up to the defendant and wanted to speak to him. Therefore the assault was rightly found to be an assault upon his officer whilst acting in the execution of his duty, and I would dismiss this appeal.

Ashworth J and **Lord Parker C J** agreed.

Appeal dismissed.

NOTES

1. See further J. M. Evans (1970) 33 MLR 438 and D. Lanham [1974] Crim LR 288. For a New Zealand decision approving, obiter, the approach taken in *Donnelly* see *Pounder v Police* [1971] NZLR 1080.

2. In *Squires v Botwright* [1972] RTR 462, DC, a plain-clothed police officer saw a woman driving carelessly. He followed her into the driveway of a house, told her that he was a police officer and that he had seen her commit a moving traffic offence and asked her to wait until a uniformed officer arrived. She refused to wait and tried to push past him. He stood in her way and asked her for her name and address and driving licence. She refused to give this information and assaulted the officer. She was charged under s.51(1) of the Police Act 1964 and the question arose whether the officer was acting in the execution of his duty in blocking the driver's way to her house while he sought her name and address and licence. The Divisional Court noted that s.228 of the Road Traffic Act 1960 (now s.164 Road Traffic Act 1972) authorised an arrest where there was a refusal to provide such name, address and licence. The court interpreted the legislative provisions as implicitly authorising the detention of a person in order to make a request for a person's name, address and licence the failure to comply with which request brought the power of arrest under s.228 into operation. Accordingly, the officer's conduct had not taken him outside the execution of his duty.

R v Brown (1976) 64 Cr App Rep 231, [1977] RTR 160, [1977] Crim LR 2, Court of Appeal

Police officers decided to stop a car being driven by the defendant to warn the driver about his speed. The defendant tried to avoid being stopped. When he did stop he ran away from the officers who chased him and brought him down with a tackle. Returning him to the police van the officers noted a smell of alcohol on the defendant's breath. The defendant repeatedly refused to supply a specimen of breath and was arrested for failing to provide a specimen under section 8(5) of the Road Traffic Act 1972. The defendant was convicted of driving with a blood-alcohol concentration above the prescribed limit contrary to section 6(1) of the 1972 Act. He appealed against conviction on the ground, inter alia, that he had not been 'arrested under section 8(5) of the 1972 Act' (a condition precedent to conviction) because he was already under arrest at that time.

Shaw LJ read the judgment of the court (Stephenson and Shaw LJJ and Park J):
. . . The broad ground on which this application was based was that the whole of that procedure was nugatory and ineffectual, because the applicant had not been lawfully arrested under the provisions of section 8 of the Road Traffic Act 1972. Counsel for the applicant put this proposition in two ways. The first was that the arrest of the applicant was effected at the moment that he was seized on the pavement. From then on, so the argument went, he was in police custody and therefore under arrest. Up to that time neither Constable Dunkin, as the

ostensible arresting officer, nor Constable Haslett had suspected that the applicant had alcohol in his body. They first entertained that suspicion after they had got him into the van, by which stage in the history, he had already been arrested. His failure to comply with the requirement then made for a specimen of breath could not, in that situation, authorise the police officers to arrest him under section 8 (5) of the Act. If he was not so arrested, what ensued at the Chelsea police station was also without any legal sanction and could not found any proceeding against the applicant. . . .

A primary question, therefore, is whether the applicant was under arrest when he was taken from where he had been seized on the pavement to the police van. His counsel relied on the judgment in an Irish case *Dunne v Clinton* [1930] IR 366, where the plaintiff claimed damages for false imprisonment and trespass. There the defendant, who was the chief superintendent of the Civil Guard in Country Kerry, contended that the plaintiff had not been arrested on any charge but was only detained while police inquiries went forward. In the course of his judgment Hanna J said (at p. 372): "The first question that arises is whether this detention is something different from arrest or imprisonment. In law there can be no half-way house between the liberty of the subject, unfettered by restraint, and an arrest. If a person under suspicion voluntarily agrees to go to a police station to be questioned, his liberty is not interfered with, as he can change his mind at any time. If, having been examined, he is asked, and voluntarily agrees, to remain in the barracks until some investigation is made, he is still a free subject, and can leave at any time. But a practice has grown up of 'detention,' as distinct from arrest. It is, in effect, keeping a suspect in custody . . . without making any charge against him."

Two aspects of this call for comment. The first is that the learned judge describes detention as "keeping a person in custody . . . without making any charge against him." The second is that the actual antithesis which the defendant unsuccessfully sought to assert was between detention on the one hand and imprisonment (not "arrest" as such) on the other.

When Hanna J went on to say (ibid. at p. 372) that as in his opinion "there could be no such thing as notional liberty. This so-called detention amounts to arrest and the suspect has in law been arrested and in custody during the period of his detention," he was really equating detention with imprisonment, irrespective of whether there had been a formal arrest or not.

When *Spicer v Holt* (1976) 63 Cr App R 270 reached the House of Lords, Viscount Dilhorne said at p. 277 in the course of his speech that ' "Arrest" is an ordinary English word . . . Whether or not a person had been arrested depended not on the legality of the arrest but on whether he had been deprived of his liberty to go where he pleased.'

This is not, however, to say that while every arrest involves a deprivation of liberty the converse is necessarily true. It patently is not. Arrest can only be effected in the exercise of an asserted authority. If a person is put under restraint arbitrarily or for some expedient motive, he is of course imprisoned. In a wide and inexact sense he may be said to be under arrest if the restraint is exercised by a police officer; but it may be neither a purported nor an actual arrest and the officer concerned may have to answer for his conduct in a court of law. . . .

Was the answer in the present case concluded, as the applicant contends, by the undisputed evidence of his seizure and removal to the police van? In the view of this Court it was not. The officers concerned reacted to what they regarded as suspicious conduct by imprisoning him for so long as might be necessary to confirm their general suspicions or to show them to be unfounded. In the first event they could then arrest him upon a specific charge; in the second event they would be bound to release him. In either case, they may have rendered themselves liable to pay damages for trespass and false imprisonment as in *Dunne v Clinton* (supra).

In the second event the erstwhile suspect would be free, after a temporary interruption for a shorter or longer space of time, to resume whatever lawful activity he had been engaged in before the intrusion of the police on his liberty of action.

The judge at the trial directed the jury in the following terms: 'What is meant by being 'under arrest'? A person may be under arrest even though the word 'arrest' has not been used. It is really a matter of degree as to what was intended and what was the physical position. Conversely, even though a person may be restrained and forcibly restrained, it does not necessarily follow he is under arrest. The officers have drawn a distinction in this case, it is up to you to say whether you think it is a valid distinction or.not, between detaining and arresting. They told you that the applicant was not arrested until after the question of the breath test arose. They were detaining him because they wanted to ask him about his driving and the implication is that if he had given a proper explanation and there had been no offence for which he could be arrested, then they would have let him go. You have to consider the question of time and the question of degree, how long it was he was detained as opposed to being arrested, if he was not arrested at that time, and it is for you to say whether he was in fact actually arrested within the true meaning of the word.'

In the light of what has been said earlier in this judgment it appears to this Court that this direction was entirely correct.

Appeal dismissed.

NOTES

1. Note the difference between the above report of *R v Brown* and that contained in [1977] RTR 160 where Shaw LJ is reported as possibly suggesting that detention for questioning might not render the police liable to damages if the questioning was followed by an arrest on a specific charge. The report extracted above, which makes clear that whatever the outcome of the questioning such detention is unlawful, is to be preferred. See D. Clark and D. Feldman [1979] Crim LR 702. For earlier discussion of *R v Brown* see M. Zander (1977) NLJ 352, 379; D. Telling [1978] Crim LR 320; K. Lidstone [1978] Crim LR 332. Note also *R v Hatton* [1978] Crim LR 95 CA.

2. For further judicial denials of the existence of any power at common law to detain for questioning see *R v Lemsatef* [1977] 1 WLR 812, CA per Lawtor LJ at p. 816 and *R v Houghton and Franciosy* [1979] Crim LR. 383, CA. In evidence to the Royal Commission on Criminal Procedure the Metropolitan Police Commissioner expressly denied the existence of any such power (*Written Evidence of Commissioner of Police of the Metropolis*, Part I (1978) para. 3.1). Note however his recommendations regarding powers to detain arrested persons (see below, at p. 000).

3. The Thomson Committee on *Criminal Procedure in Scotland* (1975) Cmnd. 6218, recommended that Scottish police be given a power of 'on the street' detention to seek explanation of suspicious behaviour, to take the name and address of the detainee and to search the detainee's outer clothing or baggage for stolen goods, tools of the crime or weapons. The detention should not however last longer than was necessary for these purposes (para. 3.18). For the Committee's recommendations regarding detention at police stations see paras. 3.22–3.27 and below, p. 63. See the Criminal Justice (Scotland) Bill 1980.

4. See further A. Ashworth [1976] Crim LR 594 (comparison of proposals of the Thomson Committee, the Australian Law Reform Commission and the American Law Institute).

5. Section 66 of the Metropolitan Police Act 1839, below, p. 92, has been held to authorise the detention for questioning of a person suspected to be in possession of stolen goods: *Daniel v Morrison* (1979) 70 Cr App Rep 142.

Prevention of Terrorism (Temporary Provisions) Act 1976

12. Powers of arrest and detention
(1) A constable may arrest without warrant a person whom he reasonably suspects to be—
    (*a*) a person guilty of an offence under section 1, 9, 10 or 11 of this Act;
    (*b*) a person who is or has been concerned in the commission, preparation or instigation of acts of terrorism;
    (*c*) a person subject to an exclusion order.
(2) A person arrested under this section shall not be detained in right of the arrest for more than 48 hours after his arrest; but the Secretary of State may, in any particular case, extend the period of 48 hours by a further period not exceeding 5 days.
(3) The following provisions (requirement to bring arrested person before a court after his arrest) shall not apply to a person detained in right of the arrest.
The said provisions are—
    Section 38 of the Magistrates' Courts Act 1952, ...

NOTE

The offences referred to in s. 12(1) (a) are offences in connection with certain proscribed organisations (s. 1), offences in relation to exclusion orders made under Part II of the Act (s.9), contributing towards acts of terrorism (s.10) and failing to disclose information regarding acts of terrorism (s.11). See pp. 130, 133, 131 and 38.

Review of the Operation of the Prevention of Terrorism (Temporary Provisions) Acts 1974 and 1976 by the Rt. Hon. Lord Shackleton (Cmnd. 7324, 1978)

70. The powers in section 12 differ from those otherwise available in three respects. First, the police do not need to have a specific offence in mind when making an arrest. Secondly, they are not required to bring the arrested person to court as soon as practicable. Thirdly, they have authority to detain that person for a specified length of time. Without powers such as those in section 12, the police could not arrest a person whom they suspected of being involved in terrorism but whom they could not link with a specific offence; and if there is no power to arrest, there is no power to detain to allow a period of questioning about suspected involvement in terrorism. The argument in favour of section 12 is that the problems presented by suspected terrorists require extraordinary powers which would not be thought necessary or justifiable for the prevention and detection of other kinds of crime . . .

71. . . . where the police receive information that a person is concerned in terrorism, be it past incidents or terrorist attacks either imminent or planned for the future . . . there may be little or no information to connect that person with a specific offence, such as would justify arrest under the normal provisions of the law, but the police may consider, after careful assessment of the information, that it has such serious implications for the detection either of past offences or of offences in preparation, and such potential consequences in terms of death and serious injury, that immediate action to detain the person concerned is necessary.

72. . . . section 12 provides powers of detention as well as powers of arrest, and it is argued that the problems presented by terrorists are such as to justify a period of detention possibly for several days. The police have found that many of those they detain under the Act adopt an attitude during interview which is quite different from that of most other suspected criminals; some of them, for example, show an indifference to their own personal future and a refusal to co-operate in any way. This may lead the police to the belief that they are dealing with a person trained in techniques of countering interrogation, which both strengthens the suspicion that he may be a terrorist and makes the task of the police in interviewing him more difficult. It is, of course, possible that a person may have other grounds, innocent and entirely unrelated to terrorism, for refusing to answer questions, but it is argued that the police have the training and experience necessary for this distinction to be made. In some cases, the person may refuse to give any personal details about himself, including even his name, so that the police may have to start from negligible information. There have been cases where false names have been given so as to deceive the police and delay their enquiries. . . .

73. Faced with such difficulties, the police follow certain routine procedures. They may take fingerprints and photographs, or carry out swabbing of hands or clothes for traces of explosives. Fingerprints have to be matched against existing records in case they relate to prints outstanding from earlier terrorist incidents, bomb factories or safe houses. Photographs have likewise to be matched against existing material. The results of forensic science analysis have to be obtained. All this takes time.

74. Whether the identity of the suspect is known or not, the police have to make extensive checks of their records to see whether there is any information further suggesting involvement in terrorism. Associates have to be established and addresses verified. The results of the interviews with the person detained have to be evaluated as they become available: a single remark may prompt a whole new line of enquiry. This is time-consuming, but it is the basis of routine police-work, and it enables the police to build up a comprehensive picture of the person detained.

75. Other police forces throughout the United Kingdom, including the Royal Ulster Constabulary, may have to be consulted. I.R.A. terrorists operate in small groups, but each group may be active in several different areas of the country. The police have ample evidence of this. The links between the various centres of activity, especially as regards supplies of money or explosives, need to be carefully checked. The person detained may come to be connected, by fingerprint check or otherwise, with a terrorist incident in a different area of the country. These are factors which arise far more acutely and far more frequently in connection with terrorism than with other serious crime.

76. The results of these enquiries, as they come in, may, of course, establish quite early on that the person detained is not involved in terrorism, in which case he would be released (of 960 people detained in Great Britain under section 12, 682 were released within 48 hours); . . . But in many cases the enquiries may take several days and would involve an extension of detention, . . . The outcome of these enquiries may be a charge. Where the evidence is insufficient for a charge, however, the police may consider the possibility of applying for an exclusion order . . . and there has to be time for proper preparation and consideration of the case by the police and by the Secretary of State. . . .

78. If the police wish to apply for an extension of detention, . . . [they] submit a report in writing to the Home Office, whose officials advise the Minister of State and the Secretary of State. Where time is exceptionally short, a senior police officer explains the background to the Secretary of State in person . . .

79. The period of further detention is specified in all cases and may, if circumstances warrant it, be less than five days. For example, the police may be awaiting the results of forensic science tests which they know will shortly become available, and in such a case the extension would initially be restricted to the time thought necessary for this. A restricted period of detention has been authorised in 12 cases.

80. No extensions of detention have been refused in Great Britain, and there has been only one refusal in Northern Ireland. This is a point to which attention has been drawn by critics of the Act. It is argued that police officers dealing with these cases have developed considerable expertise and are well able to judge the circumstances in which an extension is likely to be justified. They assume that applications for extensions of detention which were thin or badly prepared would not be granted . . .

83. Fears have been expressed that the police use the opportunity afforded by section 12 to compile information about people's political beliefs and associations. Here it is important to recognise that terrorism has a political dimension, as its definition in section 14 of the Act implies. Questioning about political views may serve a valid purpose (if, for example, it establishes that a person is dedicated to the use of violence to gain a political objective). Furthermore, the police cannot assume that because a person is connected with a non-violent political organisation he has no connections with terrorist groups. It is quite possible that he may be using the one as cover for the other.

84. Another criticism relates to allegations that the police frequently use the powers of detention for the purpose of gathering intelligence in cases where they have no intention of charging a person or applying for an exclusion order. Supporters of this argument point to the small number of charges following detention under the Act in Great Britain. The primary purpose of the Act is to prevent acts of terrorism, and for this reason the police are bound to follow up any information or suspicion about involvement in terrorism although, of course, it must in every case be sufficient to justify the arrest. The difficulty for the police is that when their questioning starts they do not know the extent to which the suspect may be involved in terrorism. It is easy to argue that, if the enquiries lead nowhere, the intial grounds for detention were inadequate. But this ignores both the preventive nature of the legislation in its widest aspects and the response the police have to make to information suggesting involvement in terrorism . . .

136. The conclusion I have come to from my study is that the powers of arrest and detention in section 12, including the extended detention, are regrettably necessary if the police are to be enabled adequately to prevent acts of terrorism of the kind we have experienced . . .

NOTE

See also B. Rose-Smith, 'Police Powers and Terrorism Legislation', in P. Hain (ed.) *Policing the Police* Vol 1 (1979) pp. 131–158; C. Scorer (NCCL) *The Prevention of Terrorism Acts 1974 and 1976*. Cf. the Northern Ireland (Emergency Provisions) Act 1978, ss. 11 and 18 (1), below p. 183.

4 Arrest

(a) POWERS OF ARREST

(i) Arrest warrants.

Below are set out the more important statutory provisions governing the issue and execution of warrants for arrest. For further information see D. A. Thomas [1962] Crim LR 520, 597; L. Leigh, *Police Powers in England and Wales* (1975) pp. 73–82.

Magistrates' Courts Act 1952

1. Issue of summons to accused or warrant for his arrest
(1) Upon an information being laid before a justice of the peace for any county that any person has, or is suspected of having, committed an offence, the justice may, ...
    (a) issue a summons directed to that person requiring him to appear before a magistrates' court for the county to answer to the information; or
    (b) issue a warrant to arrest that person and bring him before a magistrates' court . . .
93. Warrant endorsed for bail[1]
(1) A justice of the peace on issuing a warrant for the arrest of any person may grant him bail by endorsing the warrant for bail, that is to say, by endorsing the warrant with a direction in accordance with subsection (2) below.
(2) A direction for bail endorsed on a warrant under subsection (1) above shall—
    (*a*) in the case of bail in criminal proceedings, state that the person arrested is to be released on bail subject to a duty to appear before such magistrates' court and at such time as may be specified in the endorsement;
    (*b*) . . . .
and the endorsement shall fix the amounts in which any sureties . . . are to be bound.
(3) Where a warrant has been endorsed for bail under subsection (1) above, then, on the person referred to in the warrant being taken to a police station on arrest under the warrant, the officer in charge of the police station shall (subject to his approving any surety tendered in compliance with the endorsement) release him from custody as directed in the endorsement.
102. Warrants
(1) A warrant of arrest issued by a justice of the peace shall remain in force until it is executed or withdrawn.
(2) A warrant of arrest . . . or search warrant issued by a justice of the peace may be executed anywhere in England and Wales by any person to whom it is directed or by any constable acting within his police area.
(3) (*repealed*)
(4) A warrant to arrest a person charged with an offence may be executed by a constable notwithstanding that it is not in his possession at the time; but the warrant shall, on the demand of the person arrested, be shown to him as soon as practicable.

Criminal Justice Act 1967

24. Process for minor offences
(1) A warrant for the arrest of any person who has attained the age of 17 shall not be issued under section 1 of the Magistrates' Courts Act 1952 . . . unless –
    (a) the offence to which the warrant relates is an indictable offence or is punishable with imprisonment; or
    (b) the address of the defendant is not sufficiently established for a summons to be served on him.

---

1. Section 93 is set out as substituted by the Bail Act 1976 s. 12, Sch. 2 para. 24.

(ii) Arrest without warrant under the Criminal Law Act 1967.

Criminal Law Act 1967

2. Arrest without warrant

(1) The powers of summary arrest conferred by the following subsections shall apply to offences for which the sentence is fixed by law or for which a person (not previously convicted) may under or by virtue of any enactment be sentenced to imprisonment for a term of five years [or might be so sentenced but for the restrictions imposed by section 29 of the Criminal Law Act 1977] and to attempts to commit any such offence; and in this Act, including any amendment made by this Act in any other enactment, 'arrestable offence' means any such offence or attempt. [The said restrictions are those which apply where, in pursuance of subsection (2) of section 23 of the said Act of 1977 (certain offences to be tried summarily if value involved is small) a magistrates' court summarily convicts a person of a scheduled offence within the meaning of the said section 23].

(2) Any person may arrest without warrant anyone who is, or whom he, with reasonable cause, suspects to be, in the act of committing an arrestable offence.

(3) Where an arrestable offence has been committed, any person may arrest without warrant anyone who is, or whom he, with reasonable cause, suspects to be, guilty of the offence.

(4) Where a constable, with reasonable cause, suspects that an arrestable offence has been committed, he may arrest without warrant anyone whom he, with reasonable cause, suspects to be guilty of the offence.

(5) A constable may arrest without warrant any person who is, or whom he, with reasonable cause, suspects to be, about to commit an arrestable offence.

(6) For the purpose of arresting a person under any power conferred by this section a constable may enter (if need be, by force) and search any place where that person is or where the constable, with reasonable cause, suspects him to be.

(7) This section shall not prejudice any power of arrest conferred by law apart from this section.

NOTES

1. The words in square brackets in s. 2(1) were added by the Criminal Law Act 1977, Sch. 12. The only 'scheduled offences' at present are those of destroying or damaging property contrary to the Criminal Damage Act 1971, s. 1 and associated inchoate offences (see Sch. 4).

2. The concept 'arrestable offence' includes most serious offences. For example, it includes murder, manslaughter, wounding with intent to do grievous bodily harm, unlawful wounding, criminal damage, robbery, burglary, blackmail, theft, handling stolen goods and obtaining a pecuniary advantage by deception. The reference to offences for which the penalty is fixed by law relates to murder (Murder (Abolition of Death Penalty) Act 1965 s.1(1)), treason (Treason Act 1814 s.1) and piracy with violence (Piracy Act 1837, s. 2).

3. Sections 2(3) and 2(4) preserve a distinction that existed at common law in respect of the powers of constables and private individuals to arrest for felony. In *Walters v W. H. Smith & Son Ltd* [1914] 1 KB 595 the defendants reasonably suspected that Walters had stolen books from a station bookstall. At Walters' trial the jury acquitted him, believing his statements that he had intended to pay for the books. Accordingly no crime had been committed in respect of the books. Walters sued the defendants, inter alia, for false imprisonment in having arrested him for an offence that had not been committed. Sir Rufus Isaacs CJ giving judgment for the Court of Appeal held that to justify the arrest a private individual had to show not only reasonable suspicion but also that the offence for which the arrested person was given into custody had in fact been committed, albeit by somebody else. In its Seventh Report (Cmnd. 2695 (1965)) the Criminal Law Revision Committee commented:

'14. We gave serious consideration to recommending the abolition of the rule that, in order to justify an arrest on reasonable suspicion that an offence has been committed, a private person, unlike a constable, must prove that the offence was in fact committed by somebody. We recognise that there is a substantial case for abolishing the distinction. First, it seems anomalous that a private person should be liable for wrongful arrest, if he arrests a person on suspicion that an offence has been committed, merely because the suspicion (however reasonable) turns out to be wrong, whereas the reasonableness of the suspicion is a defence in the case of arrest by a constable. Secondly, it is argued that in *Walters's* case . . . the Court of Appeal, in affirming the existence of the distinction, accepted too uncritically statements to the same effect in Hale and Hawkins, without considering the question fully as one of principle; in that case however Sir Rufus Isaacs LCJ said (p. 606) that he was "convinced on consideration that it [the rule] is based on sound principle" and that, in the interests of the liberty of the subject, a person who arrested another without getting a warrant should have to take the risk of its turning out, contrary to appearance, that no felony had been committed. Thirdly, it is pointed out that the existence of the distinction may be a trap to a private person who is careful instead of precipitate about deciding whether to arrest a person. If, for example, a store detective saw a person apparently shoplifting, he could arrest him under clause 2(2) on the ground that he had reasonable cause to suspect him of being in the act of committing an arrestable offence, and he would not be liable for unlawful arrest even if it turned out that he was wrong; but if he preferred out of caution to invite the other to the office to give him an opportunity of clearing himself, and then arrested him on being satisfied that he was guilty, the detective would be liable if this turned out to be wrong.
15. But the majority of the committee . . . . are not in favour of recommending that the distinction should be abolished. They doubt whether it would be desirable, or acceptable to public opinion, to increase the powers of arrest enjoyed by private persons; and they think that there is a strong argument in policy that a private person should, if it is at all doubtful whether the offence was committed, put the matter in the hands of the police or, as Sir Rufus Isaacs LCJ said, take the risk of liability if he acts on his own responsibility.'

In evidence to the Royal Commission on Criminal Procedure the Metropolitan Police Commissioner recommended the abolition of this distinction between the powers of constables and others. Private individuals should receive the same protection as that afforded constables under s. 2(4). (*Written Evidence of Commissioner of Police of the Metropolis*, Part I (1978) para. 2.10)
4. A person who would be entitled to arrest a person on reasonable suspicion of an arrestable offence is apparently still protected by s. 2 if he arrests without reasonable grounds for suspicion (e.g. on a mere 'hunch'), if it turns out that the arrested person has committed, is committing or is about to commit such an offence. See ss. 2(2), (3), (5).
5. In proposing s. 2(5) the Criminal Law Revision Committee stated:

16. There is some authority that any person may arrest without warrant anybody whom he reasonably suspects of being about to commit a felony. It seems to us enough to confer a corresponding power on constables in relation to arrestable offences. The provision is in clause 2(5). If the arrest is made before the person in question has committed or attempted to commit the arrestable offence, the constable will be able to bring him before a magistrates' court with a view to his being bound over to keep the peace and, if necessary, provide sureties. Alternatively the constable could release him, when the danger of the arrestable offence being committed or attempted has passed, on the analogy of the power of a constable to detain a person temporarily in order to prevent the commission of a felony or breach of the peace.

(iii) Arrest without warrant under other Acts

Many statutes confer powers of arrest without warrant in relation to particular offences which they create. For lists of such provisions see J. D. Devlin, *Police Procedure, Administration and Organisation* (1966), p. 305,

L. H. Leigh, *Police Powers in England and Wales* (1975) Appendix II, *Home Office Evidence to the Royal Commission on Criminal Procedure Memorandum No. III* (1978) Appendix D. Note the following important examples of such powers of arrest without warrant: Highways Act 1959, section 121(2) (wilful obstruction of the highway, below, p. 138); Public Order Act 1936 section 7(3) (wearing unlawful uniforms, carrying offensive weapon, insulting etc. words or conduct likely to cause a breach of the peace, see below, p. 151); Prevention of Crime Act 1953, section 1(3) (carrying offensive weapon); Public Meeting Act 1908, section 1(3) (disorderly conduct at public meeting, see below, p. 167); Misuse of Drugs Act 1971, section 24; Firearms Act 1968, section 50.

The conditions subject to which such powers of arrest may be exercised vary widely. Some are exercisable only where a person is 'found committing' the particular offence, others where a person is 'reasonably suspected' to be committing or of having committed that offence. Others still are exercisable only where the name and address of the person is not known and/or it is believed that unless arrested he will abscond. See e.g. *Christie v Leachinsky* (below, p. 55). Some of the powers of arrest without warrant are of broad scope. Note for example the terms of the Prevention of Offences Act 1851, section 11 – 'It shall be lawful for any person whatsoever to apprehend any person who shall be found committing any indictable offence in the night and to convey him or deliver him to some constable or other peace officer, . . .' and, as an example of a local power of broad scope available to the Metropolitan Police, the Metropolitan Police Act 1839, section 64: 'It shall be lawful for any constable . . . to take into custody without a warrant, all loose, idle and disorderly persons whom he shall find disturbing the public peace, or whom he shall have good cause to suspect of having committed or being about to commit any [offence] or breach of the peace, and all persons whom he shall find between sunset and the hour of eight in the morning lying or loitering in any highway, yard, or other place, and not giving a satisfactory account of themselves'.

Vagrancy Act 1824

4. . . . every suspected person or reputed thief, frequenting any river, canal or navigable stream, dock, or basin, or any quay, wharf, or warehouse near or adjoining thereto, or any street, highway, or avenue leading thereto, or any place of public resort, or any avenue leading thereto, or any street [or any highway or any place adjacent to a street or highway] with intent to commit [an arrestable offence] . . . ; shall be deemed a rogue and vagabond . . .

6. It shall be lawful for any person whatsoever to apprehend any person who shall be found offending against this Act, and forthwith to take and convey him or her before some justice of the peace, to be dealt with in such manner as is herein-before directed, or to deliver him or her to any constable or other peace officer of the place where he or she shall have been apprehended, to be so taken and conveyed as aforesaid . . .

NOTES

1. The words in brackets were substituted by the Prevention of Crimes Act 1871, s.15 and the Criminal Law Act 1967, Sch. 2 para. 2(1), respectively.
2. The Penal Servitude Act 1891, s. 7 extends s. 4 above to 'suspected persons

or reputed thiefs loitering about' (as distinct from frequenting) the places mentioned in s.4 with intent to commit an arrestable offence.

The maximum penalty for being found to be a 'rogue and vagabond' is a fine of £200 or three months imprisonment after summary trial. On a subsequent conviction the 'rogue and vagabond' may be committed to the Crown Court where he may be sentenced to a maximum of one year's imprisonment as an 'incorrigible rogue'. (Magistrates' Courts Act 1952, s.27(3), as amended by the Vagrancy Act 1824, ss.5, 10 and the Criminal Law Act 1977, s.32(2).)

3. This offence and power of arrest have been the subject of much criticism. In particular it is alleged that the provisions are used over-readily in respect of young black people. See for example C. Demuth, *'Sus' a report on the Vagrancy Act 1824* (Runnymede Trust (1978)); *The Police against Black People*, (Institute of Race Relations (1978)), though note the criticism of such allegations in the *Annual Report of the Commissioner of Police of the Metropolis for 1978*, Cmnd. 7580, p. 6. See also *Race, Crime and Arrests-* Home Office Research Study No 58 (1979). For figures for vagrancy arrests in the Metropolitan Police District between 1975–9 classified according to the ethnic appearance of the arrested person see 1979–80 HC 418 ii pp. 41–5. Note also the evidence given to the Home Affairs Committee of the House of Commons during February 1980: 1979–80 HC 418 i–vi.

A Home Office *Working Party on Vagrancy and Street Offences* (*Working Paper*, 1974; *Report*, 1976) concluded that 'an offence on the lines of the existing offence . . . is still necessary to deal with behaviour which falls short of any other criminal offence or of an attempt to commit an offence, but which the public interest requires to be punishable'. (*Working Paper* para. 202). The Working Party proposed a new offence similar in scope to the existing offence.

(iv) Arrest without warrant in respect of breach of the peace

At common law any person may arrest without warrant any persons found committing a breach of the peace. If the breach has taken place and peace has returned, this power of arrest only exists if a renewed breach of the peace is reasonably anticipated. Whether a power of arrest exists in relation to a reasonably anticipated breach of the peace where no prior breach of the peace has taken place has recently been doubted – see *R v Podger* [1979] Crim LR 524 (Crown Ct). However, the better view of the authorities would seem to be that a power of arrest does exist in such a situation. See commentary at p. 526.

The meaning of 'breach of the peace' has never been very precisely defined. The concept extends beyond general public disorder (e.g. riots, unlawful assemblies) to include any conduct which involves harm or threat of harm to the person. Accordingly the power of arrest is a wide one. Where persons are found fighting all may lawfully be arrested to restore the peace even though it may ultimately appear that not all have committed any offence—some of them having acted purely in self-defence (*Timothy v Simpson* (1835) 1 CrM & R 757).

Note however that danger to the person is an essential requirement of a breach of the peace. Mere disorderliness or unruliness not giving rise to fear of personal harm will not suffice. Nor does noisiness alone constitute a breach of the peace. See further G. Williams [1954] Crim LR 572; L. H. Leigh, *Police Powers in England and Wales* (1975) pp. 84–6

(v) The concept of reasonable suspicion.

Dumbell v Roberts [1947] 1 All ER 326, 113 LJKB 185, 170 LT 227, 108 JP 139, 60 TLR 111, Court of Appeal

Scott LJ: . . . the constable shall before arresting satisfy himself that there do in fact exist reasonable grounds for suspicion of guilt. That requirement is very limited. The police are not called upon before acting to have anything like a prima facie case for convicting . . . the duty of the police . . . is, no doubt, to be quick to see the possibility of crime, but equally they ought to be anxious to avoid mistaking the innocent for the guilty.

. . . [The police are] required to be observant, receptive and open-minded and to notice any relevant circumstance which points either way, either to innocence or guilt. They may have to act on the spur of the moment and have no time to reflect and be bound, therefore, to arrest to prevent escape; but where there is no danger of the person who has ex hypothesi aroused their suspicion . . . [escaping] . . . they should make all presently practicable enquiries from persons present or immediately accessible who are likely to be able to answer their enquiries. I am not suggesting a duty on the police to try to prove innocence; that is not their function; but they should act on the assumption that their prima facie suspicion may be ill-founded. . . .

Hussien v Chong Fook Kam [1970] AC 942, [1969] 3 All ER 1626, [1970] 2 WLR 441, Privy Council

Lord Devlin: . . . Suspicion in its ordinary meaning is a state of conjecture or surmise where proof is lacking: 'I suspect but I cannot prove.' Suspicion arises at or near the starting-point of an investigation of which the obtaining of prima facie proof is the end. When such proof has been obtained, the police case is complete; it is ready for trial and passes on to its next stage. It is indeed desirable as a general rule that an arrest should not be made until the case is complete. But if arrest before that were forbidden, it could seriously hamper the police. To give power to arrest on reasonable suspicion does not mean that it is always or even ordinarily to be exercised. It means that there is an executive discretion. In the exercise of it many factors have to be considered besides the strength of the case. The possibility of escape, the prevention of further crime and the obstruction of police inquiries are examples of those factors . . .

. . . There is another distinction between reasonable suspicion and prima facie proof. Prima facie proof consists of admissible evidence. Suspicion can take into account matters that could not be put in evidence at all. There is a discussion about the relevance of previous convictions in the judgment of Lord Wright in *McArdle v Egan* (1934) 150 LT 412. Suspicion can take into account also matters which, though admissible, could not form part of a prima facie case. Thus the fact that the accused has given a false alibi does not obviate the need for prima facie proof of his presence at the scene of the crime; it will become of considerable importance in the trial when such proof as there is is being weighed perhaps against a second alibi; it would undoubtedly be a very suspicious circumstance . . .

Report of Advisory Committee on Drug Dependence: Powers of Arrest and Search in Relation to Drugs Offences (Home Office 1970)

111. . . . The main cause for anxiety among witnesses who claimed to speak for a substantial minority of young people was that in this field of enforcement against dangerous drugs 'reasonable grounds' are too often founded on the appearance and not the action of the individual; that the police are apt to single out young persons with unconventional hair styles, strange dress, beads and the rest of it, and that those who follow these fashions find themselves at special risk. Many illegal drug-takers have an unconventional appearance, as those on the side of the law are swift to stress; most are young. It does not follow that a majority of young people of unconventional appearance nowadays abuse drugs. Nor does it follow that the factor of 'appearance' about which principal disquiet has been expressed will be long-lasting.

While it remains in issue, however, we are unanimous in accepting, and we think the police should accept, that hair style and unusual dress should not themselves or together constitute sufficient ground for action. Liberty of the subject must extend to the right to adopt idiosyncratic life styles without exciting police attention and 'reasonable grounds' to search. More positive factors must enter a policeman's decision to stop and search, for example, where a person is leaving premises associated with drug abuse, or is seen to make a transaction or is known to the police. In short, appearances cannot always be discounted but they should be a subsidiary and not a principal part of reasonable grounds to stop and search . . .

Could 'reasonable grounds' be positively defined?

123. Our second approach was to examine 'reasonable grounds' with a view to imposing some additional safeguards. Criteria which amount to 'reasonable grounds' have never been defined. It is not easy to define them. The present unwritten code which is familiar to every police officer, but much less familiar to the public, might be said roughly to include:
(1) the demeanour of the suspect; (2) the gait and manner of the suspect; (3) any knowledge the officer may have of the suspect's character or background; (4) whether the suspect is carrying anything, and the nature of what he is carrying; (5) the mode of his dress, bulges in his clothing, and particularly when these factors are considered in the light of all the surrounding circumstances; (6) the time of observation; (7) any remarks or conversation which he makes to any other person which might be overheard by an officer; (8) the street or the area involved; (9) information from a third party, who may in given circumstances be known or unknown; (10) any connection between that person and any other person whose conduct at that time is reasonably suspect; (11) the suspect's apparent connection with any overt criminal activity.
To any such list must be added the essential fund of common sense, training and experience which every police officer is deemed to possess in some measure and without the exercise of which he may find himself in trouble with his superior officers. It is this crucial element which makes a statutory definition of 'reasonable grounds' so difficult. We are unanimously of opinion that it is impossible to draft any such definition in positive terms.

Could 'reasonable grounds' be defined by exclusion? The minority view in favour

124. This leaves open the question whether it would be an advantage to effect some definition of reasonable grounds by exclusion. Professor Williams at the request of the Sub-committee drafted the following for consideration . . .
'The following circumstances shall not be sufficient in themselves, whether alone or in conjunction with each other, to establish reasonable grounds of suspicion for the purpose of subsection (1) above.
(a) That the person searched appeared to be the kind of person who is frequently found in possession of drugs.
(b) That he was carrying any article, other than an article commonly associated with the possession of drugs.
(c) That he was found in a locality where drugs were frequently possessed.
(d) That he was found in a public place at night or in the early morning.'
This proposal would not wholly exclude the four grounds from consideration, but it would require them to be used only as secondary factors, supporting other grounds of suspicion. The effect of the proposals, if it were implemented by statute, would be that a police officer who searched a person merely because he was young, dressed unconventionally, carrying a case and out late at night, would be acting illegally . . . Perhaps the most important effect of the proposal would be that it would enter into the instructions given to the police and so would be likely to have a restraining effect upon police searches. . . .

The majority view against

126. The rest of us find this proposal open to serious objection and do not support it. We do not believe that it is any more practicable to define negative than positive grounds for suspicion, simply because the factors influencing a police officer's judgement cannot be reduced to simple formulae. No comparable provision has been brought to our notice as having measurable effect. We fear that a provision of the kind suggested would complicate the drugs law and its enforcement, without offering any more assured basis than the present provision for redress against wrongful exercise of powers by an irresponsible police officer intent on evading the restrictions.

Dress and hair style should be excluded as sole grounds for suspicion: the Sub-committee's unanimous view

127. For the reasons we have stated earlier . . . those of us who object to statutory limitation

are prepared to say as strongly as the minority who favour it that dress and hair style should never in themselves or together constitute reasonable grounds to stop and search. We recommend that this principle should become standard police practice. . . .

NOTE

The Fourth Amendment of the US Constitution provides that:

'The right of the people to be secure in their persons, houses, papers, and effects, against unreasonable searches and seizures, shall not be violated, and no warrants shall issue but upon probable cause, supported by oath or affirmation, and particularly describing the place to be searched, and the persons or things to be seized.'

In addition it has been held that those arrests and searches which may be made without a warrant must also be based on the equivalent of 'probable cause' (*Draper v US* 358 US 307 (1959)). In contrast to the position in England, the issue of 'probable cause' (or 'reasonable cause') has received much attention from the courts (see J. L. Lambert, [1973] PL 283)

In *Carroll v US* 267 US 132 (1925), the police searched a car and seized a quantity of liquor. The Supreme Court held that they had probable cause to justify a warrantless search: 'the facts and circumstances within their knowledge, and of which they had reasonably trustworthy information, were sufficient in themselves to warrant a man of reasonable caution in the belief that intoxicating liquor' was in the car (Taft CJ at p. 162). Probable cause may be based on hearsay and a police record (*Brinegar v US* 338 US 160 (1949)). It may be based on information from an informant, provided that there are underlying circumstances showing reason to believe that the informant is a credible person and showing the basis of the conclusions reached by the informant (*Aguilar v Texas*, 378 US 108 (1964)), or provided that the information is corroborated (*Spinelli v US* 393 US 410 (1969)).

(vi) Reform

In evidence to the Royal Commission on Criminal Procedure, the Metropolitan Police Commissioner made the following recommendations in respect of police powers of arrest: the power in the Criminal Law Act 1967, section 2 to apply to all imprisonable offences; the retention of existing powers of arrest contained in statutes other than the Criminal Law Act 1967, section 2, even where they relate to non-imprisonable offences; retention of powers to arrest in respect of breaches of the peace and power to arrest in respect of all offences where the name and address of the suspect is unknown or where that given is believed to be false (*Written Evidence of Commissioner of Police of the Metropolis* (1978), Part I para. 2.7).

(b) EFFECTING A LAWFUL ARREST

(i) Notification of the fact of arrest.

Alderson v Booth [1969] 2 QB 216, [1969] 2 All ER 271, [1969] 2 WLR 1252, 133 JP 346, 113 Sol Jo 268, 53 Cr App Rep 301 Queen's Bench Divisional Court

Following a 'positive' breathalyser test a police constable said to the defendant: 'I shall have to ask you to come to the police station for further tests.' The defendant accompanied the constable to a police station. At his trial the defendant defended charges of driving with an excess of alcohol in his blood by claiming that he had not been arrested by the constable (a lawful arrest having been made being a condition precedent to conviction under the drink and drive legislation). He was acquitted and the prosecution appealed.

Lord Parker CJ . . . the narrow point here was whether the justices were right in holding, as they did, that there never had been an arrest.

In their opinion, which is clearly partly opinion and partly finding of fact, they say: 'We were of opinion that when the respondent accompanied the constable to the police station it was not made clear to him either physically or by word of mouth that he was under compulsion. We consider that compulsion is a necessary element of arrest, and we therefore did not regard the respondent as a person who had been arrested.'

. . . I for my part have little doubt that, just looking at the words used here, 'I shall have to ask you to come to the police station for further tests,' they were in their context words of command which one would think would bring home to a defendant that he was under compulsion. But the justices here had the evidence not only of the police constable but of the defendant, and they were not satisfied, having heard him, that it had been brought home unequivocally to him that he was under compulsion. I confess it surprised me that he was believed but believed he was when he said or conveyed that he was not going to the police station because he thought he was under compulsion, but was going purely voluntarily. It seems to me that this is so much a question of fact for the justices that, surprising as this decision is, I feel that this court cannot interfere.

I would only say this, that if what I have said is correct in law, it is advisable that police officers should use some very clear words to bring home to a person that he is under compulsion. It certainly must not be left in the state that a defendant can go into the witness-box and merely say 'I did not think I was under compulsion.' If difficulties for the future are to be avoided, it seems to me that by far and away the simplest thing is for a police officer to say 'I arrest you.' If the defendant goes to the police station after hearing those words, it seems to me that he simply could not be believed if he thereafter said 'I did not think there was any compulsion, I was only going voluntarily.'

Accordingly, I would dismiss this appeal.

Blain and Donaldson JJ agreed.

Appeal dismissed.

R v Inwood [1973] 1 WLR 647, [1973] 2 All ER 645, 107 Sol Jo 303 [1973] LR 290, 57 Cr App Rep 529, Court of Appeal

Inwood went voluntarily to a police station to be interviewed. After a while he was told he was going to be charged with an offence and he was cautioned. He was searched, fingerprinted and other pre-charging formalities were completed. At this point Inwood asked when he could leave the police station. He was told he would be released when the police had finished their inquiries. At this Inwood tried to leave the building and on being restrained a scuffle took place. He was subsequently charged under the Police Act 1964 s.51(1), above, p.36. The prosecution had to show that he was under arrest at the time he attempted to leave the building, thereby permitting reasonable force to be used to restrain him. (Criminal Law Act 1967, s.3 below, p. 59).

Stephenson LJ read the judgement of the court (**Stephenson** and **Orr LJJ** and **Caulfield J**) . . . This court does not wish to say and cannot conclude as a matter of law that it had been made clear to the defendant that he had been arrested. We are of the opinion that . . . this is a question of fact. It all depends on the circumstances of any particular case whether in fact it has been shown that a man has been arrested, and the court considers it unwise to say that there should be any particular formula followed. No formula will suit every case and it may well be that different procedures might have to be followed with different persons depending on their age, ethnic origin, knowledge of English, intellectual qualities, physical or mental disabilities. There is no magic formula; only the obligation to make it plain to the suspect by what is said and done that he is no longer a free man. However, what we think is clear is that it is a question of fact, not of law, and it must be left to the jury to decide whether a person has

been arrested or not, at least where there is a real dispute as to the question whether the defendant understood that he was being arrested . . .
Conviction quashed.

NOTE

See also *Wheatley v Lodge* [1971] 1 All ER 173, DC – failure of police successfully to communicate fact of arrest to a deaf person. The failure was held not to render the arrest unlawful since the mistake in not appreciating that the person was arrested was deaf was a reasonable one. As soon as the police had become aware of his deafness they had proceeded by means of written notices.

(ii) The rule in Christie v Leachinsky: notification of reasons for arrest.

Christie v Leachinsky [1947] AC 573, [1947] 1 All ER 567, [1947] LJR 757, 176 LT 443, 111 JP 224, 63 TLR 231, 45 LGR 201, House of Lords

Police officers arrested Leachinsky at his warehouse in Liverpool. They told him he was being arrested for 'unlawful possession' of certain cloth. This was an offence under the Liverpool Corporation Act 1921. The power of arrest contained in the Act in respect of this offence only authorised the arrest of offenders whose name and address was not known. The officers knew Leachinsky's name and address. In defence to Leachinsky's action for false imprisonment the officers argued unsuccessfully that since they had also suspected Leachinsky of having 'stolen or feloniously received' the cloth the arrest was lawful by virtue of their common law powers to arrest for felony.

Viscount Simon: . . . The question to be determined is therefore whether, when a policeman arrests X. without a warrant, on reasonable suspicion that he has committed a given felony, but gives X. no notice that he is arrested on suspicion of such felony, he is acting within the law. . . .
In the Court of Appeal Scott LJ strongly insisted that it was a false imprisonment. Arrest, he pointed out was the first step in a criminal proceeding against a suspected person on a charge which was intended to be judicially investigated. If the arrest was authorized by magisterial warrant, or if proceedings were instituted by the issue of a summons, it is clear law that the warrant or summons must specify the offence. . . . Moreover, the warrant must be founded on information in writing and on oath and, except where a particular statute provides otherwise, the information and the warrant must particularize the offence charged. The famous case of *Entick v Carrington* (1765), 19 State Tr 1029, dealing with the illegality of 'general warrants' is an illustration of the principle. Again, when an arrest is made on warrant, the warrant in normal cases has to be read to the person arrested. All this is for the obvious purpose of securing that a citizen who is prima facie entitled to personal freedom should know why for the time being his personal freedom is interfered with. Scott LJ argued that if the law circumscribed the issue of warrants for arrest in this way it could hardly be that a policeman acting without a warrant was entitled to make an arrest without stating the charge on which the arrest was made . . . .
The above citations and others . . . seem to me to establish the following propositions. (1) If a policeman arrests without warrant upon reasonable suspicion of felony, or of other crime of a sort which does not require a warrant, he must in ordinary circumstances inform the person arrested of the true ground of arrest. He is not entitled to keep the reason to himself or to give a reason which is not the true reason. In other words a citizen is entitled to know on what charge or on suspicion of what crime he is seized. (2) If the citizen is not so informed but is nevertheless seized, the policeman, apart from certain exceptions, is liable for false imprisonment. (3) The requirement that the person arrested should be informed of the reason why he is seized naturally does not exist if the circumstances are such that he must know the general nature of the alleged offence for which he is detained. (4) The requirement that he

should be so informed does not mean that technical or precise language need be used. The matter is a matter of substance, and turns on the elementary proposition that in this country a person is, prima facie, entitled to his freedom and is only required to submit to restraints on his freedom if he knows in substance the reason why it is claimed that this restraint should be imposed. (5) The person arrested cannot complain that he has not been supplied with the above information as and when he should be, if he himself produces the situation which makes it practically impossible to inform him, e.g., by immediate counter-attack or by running away. There may well be other exceptions to the general rule in addition to those I have indicated, and the above propositions are not intended to constitute a formal or complete code, but to indicate the general principles of our law on a very important matter. These principles equally apply to a private person who arrests on suspicion. . . . No one, I think, would approve a situation in which when the person arrested asked for the reason, the policeman replied 'that has nothing to do with you: come along with me.' . . .

. . . And there are practical considerations, as well as theory, to support the view I take. If the charge on suspicion of which the man is arrested is then and there made known to him, he has the opportunity of giving an explanation of any misunderstanding or of calling attention to other persons for whom he may have been mistaken, with the result that further inquiries may save him from the consequences of false accusation. . . .

Lord Simonds: . . . .It is to be remembered that the right of the constable in or out of uniform is, except for a circumstance irrelevant to the present discussion, the same as that of every other citizen. Is citizen A. bound to submit unresistingly to arrest by citizen B. in ignorance of the charge made against him? I think, my Lords, that cannot be the law of England. Blind, unquestioning obedience is the law of tyrants and of slaves: it does not yet flourish on English soil . . . it is a condition of lawful arrest that the man arrested should be entitled to know why he is arrested. . . .

If, then, this is . . . the fundamental rule, what qualification if any must be imposed upon it? . . . an arrest does not become wrongful merely because the constable arrests a man for one felony, say murder, and he is subsequently charged with another felony, say manslaughter. . . . It is clear that the constable has not been guilty of an illegal arrest, if he reasonably suspected that murder had been done. Again, I think it is clear that there is no need for the constable to explain the reason of arrest, if the arrested man is caught red-handed and the crime is patent to high Heaven. Nor, obviously, is explanation a necessary prelude to arrest where it is important to secure a possibly violent criminal. Nor again, can it be wrongful to arrest and detain a man upon a charge, of which he is reasonably suspected, with a view to further investigation of a second charge upon which information is incomplete. In all such matters a wide measure of discretion must be left to those whose duty it is to preserve the peace and bring criminals to justice. These and similar considerations lead me to the view that it is not an essential condition of lawful arrest that the constable should at the time of arrest formulate any charge at all, much less the charge which may ultimately be found in the indictment. But this, and this only, is the qualification which I would impose upon the general proposition. It leaves untouched the principle, which lies at the heart of the matter, that the arrested man is entitled to be told what is the act for which he is arrested. The 'charge' ultimately made will depend upon the view taken by the law of his act. In ninety-nine cases out of a hundred the same words may be used to define the charge or describe the act, nor is any technical precision necessary: for instance, if the act constituting the crime is the killing of another man, it will be immaterial that the arrest is for murder and at a later hour the charge of manslaughter is substituted. The arrested man is left in no doubt that the arrest is for that killing. This is I think, the fundamental principle, viz., that a man is entitled to know what . . . are 'the facts which are said to constitute a crime on his part' . . .

Lords Thankerton, DuParcq and **MacMillan** agreed.

NOTE

The rule in *Christie v Leachinsky* assists an arrested person in correcting any erroneous suspicion his arrestor may have of him and prevents lawful arrests being made unless the arrestor is prepared to state the offence or conduct in respect of which the arrest is made. The rule will often not give the person arrested sufficient information to assess the lawfulness of the arrest. Knowledge of his own innocence may be insufficient. When arrest on 'reasonable suspicion' is permitted, the reasonableness of the arrestor's suspicion will be crucial. *Christie* does not require the arrestor to disclose the grounds for his suspicion. See G. Williams [1954] Crim LR 16.

Gelberg v Miller [1961] 1 WLR 153, [1961] 1 All ER 291, 125 JP 123, Queen's Bench Divisional Court

The appellant parked his car outside a restaurant in London while he had a meal. Police officers asked him to move the car. He refused, preferring to finish his meal first. On being told that the police would remove the car themselves he removed the rotor arm from the carburettor. He also refused to give his name and address or show his driving licence and certificate of insurance. He was arrested by one of the officers. The officer said he was arresting the appellant for 'obstructing him in the execution of his duty by refusing to move his car and refusing his name and address'. The appellant was charged under a forerunner of section 51(3) of the Police Act 1964.

Lord Parker CJ: . . . The Attorney-General . . . has appeared and has told the court that he feels unable to contend that a constable is entitled to arrest somebody for obstructing him in the course of his duty . . . unless the circumstances show that a breach of the peace or an apprehended breach of the peace is involved, meaning by that some affray or violence or possibly disturbance. He does say, however, and has contended, that on the facts of this case there was a power of arrest under section 54 of the Metropolitan Police Act 1839. That section, so far as it is material, provides: 'Every person shall be liable to a penalty of not more than forty shillings, who, within the limits of the metropolitan police district, shall, in any thoroughfare or public place, commit any of the following offences; (that is to say) . . . (6) Every person . . . who by means of any cart, carriage, sledge, truck, or barrow, or any horse or other animal, shall wilfully interrupt any public crossing, or wilfully cause any obstruction in any thoroughfare.' The section at the end goes on to say: 'and it shall be lawful for any constable belonging to the metropolitan police force to take into custody, without warrant, any person who shall commit any such offence within view of any such constable.'

 . . . Accordingly, prima facie, there was a power to arrest under section 54 in this case.

The matter, however, does not end there, because it has always been the law of this country that a person on his arrest is entitled to know what I may loosely call the 'reason why.' As Lord Simonds said in *Christie v Leachinsky*. . . .

[Lord Parker CJ quoted from passages from Lord Simonds', speech extracted above at p. 56 and continued:]

 . . . the mere fact that in this case the charge ultimately brought was not a charge under section 54 of the Metropolitan Police Act 1839, is neither here nor there. The question is: Did the appellant know or was he told the alleged facts which would make him guilty of that offence? In this case, it is true, the respondent said to him that he, the respondent, was arresting the appellant for obstructing him in the execution of his duty, and there was no power of arrest . . . in respect of the misdemeanour of obstructing a police officer in the execution of his duty. However, the exact words which appear in the case are these: 'he told him he was going to arrest him for obstructing him in the execution of his duty by refusing to move his car and refusing his name and address.' To my mind it is clear that, by saying that he was arresting him for refusing to move his motor-car, he was informing the appellant of a fact which, in all the circumstances, amounted to a wilful obstruction of the thoroughfare by leaving his car in that position. It seems to me to matter not that the respondent also coupled with that the refusal to give his name and address or the allegation of obstructing him in the execution of his duty. May I test it in this way supposing the respondent had said nothing but had just arrested him, could it really be said that the appellant did not know all the facts constituting an alleged wilful obstruction of the thoroughfare without having that particular charge made against him at the time? In my judgment, what the appellant knew and what he was told was ample to fulfil the obligation as to what should be done at the time of an arrest without warrant.

Streatfield, Slade, Ashworth and **Elwes JJ** agreed

Appeal dismissed.

NOTES

1. If the words used in *Gelberg* were sufficient indication of the reason for the arrest why were the words used in *Christie v Leachinsky* itself insufficient?

2. In *R v Telfer* [1976] Crim LR 562 (Crown Ct) a police officer knew that the police wanted to interview the defendant in connection with a burglary. The officer encountered the defendant and when the defendant refused voluntarily to accompany the officer to the police station the officer arrested him 'on suspicion of burglary'. At the time of the arrest the officer did not know which particular burglary the defendant was suspected of having committed. The officer could have ascertained these details fairly speedily had he asked his headquarters. Instead he had merely sought confirmation that the defendant was wanted. The arrest was held unlawful. A person arrested was entitled to be told the particular burglary of which he was suspected and on the facts such information could quite easily have been given to him. Would the obligation of the officer have been less if the information had been less readily available?

3. *Gelberg* highlights the absence of a specific power of arrest without warrant in respect of offences under s.51 of the Police Act 1964. In respect of s.51(1) the 'assault' will constitute a breach of the peace and so a power of contemporaneous arrest will exist. In respect of offences under s.51(3), if the obstruction does not involve an actual or apprehended breach of the peace no power of arrest exists. The police do not seem to have been much aware of this. See the arrests made in, for example, *Tynan v Balmer* [1967] 1 QB 91, DC; *Stunt v Bolton* [1972] RTR 435, DC; *Johnson v Phillips* [1975] 3 All ER 682, DC; *Wershof v Metropolitan Police Comr* [1978] 3 All ER 540 QB. Note also Moriarty, *Police Law* (23rd edn. 1976) p. 18 (unqualified statement that a constable may arrest without warrant a person who obstructs him in the execution of his duty).

In *Wershof v Metropolitan Police Comr*, May J stated at p. 550: 'a police constable may only arrest without a warrant anyone who wilfully obstructs him in the execution of his duty if the nature of that obstruction is such that he actually causes, or is likely to cause, a breach of the peace or is calculated to prevent the lawful arrest or detention of another'. This proposition forms part of the *ratio* of May J's judgment. The authorities cited for the proposition about arrest for conduct calculated to prevent the lawful arrest or detention of another were *Levy v Edwards* (1823) 1 C & P 40 and *White v Edmunds* (1791) Peake 123.

R v Kulynycz [1971] 1 QB 367, [1970] 3 WLR 1029, 114 Sol Jo 785, [1970] 3 All ER 881, 55 Cr App Rep 34, Court of Appeal

Lord Parker CJ gave the judgment of the court (**Lord Parker CJ, Phillimore LJ** and **Ashworth J**):

. . . It has not been easy to ascertain the true facts of the case, but it does appear that the defendant was reasonably suspected—nobody has challenged that—of what one may call drug offences in King's Lynn. As the court understands it, though carrying on his activities in Cambridge, he was supplying people or pushing drugs in King's Lynn, and accordingly the King's Lynn police asked the Cambridge police to arrest him and hand him over. As a result a Police Constable Crane at 4.25 p.m. on 6 August 1969, found the defendant in the market place at Cambridge and he arrested him, using some such words as that a warrant had been issued for his arrest at King's Lynn on suspicion of offences committed there. It is said, and in the opinion of this court rightly said, that that arrest was an unlawful arrest. . . .

Mr Cheatle [counsel for the defendant] points out that the only matter conveyed to the defendant on arrest was on suspicion of offences committed in King's Lynn, no identification of the nature of the offences or, as the court prefers to put it, of the act constituting an offence or offences.

Mr Cheatle further points out that the information moreover was wrong because as it turned out a warrant had not been issued. No doubt Police Constable Crane was sent off merely to bring the defendant to the police station, and did not know whether or not a warrant had been issued, and did not know the exact nature of the acts constituting the alleged offences.

Seven minutes later the defendant was in the police station and there he was seen by Police Constable Welham, a member of the Drug Squad stationed at Cambridge. The defendant having been brought into the station, he said to the defendant: 'You have been brought to the police station as a result of a request from the King's Lynn police in connection with possible drug offences.' The defendant was cautioned and he replied: 'I know the score. I am saying nothing. I shall be out of here within 24 hours.' It is to be observed there that Police Constable Welham was more specific in that he referred not merely to offences generally, but to possible drug offences.

Shortly after that, on that same evening there arrived from Norfolk Police Constable Elliott, who had come to take charge of the defendant and take him back to King's Lynn. He said: 'We are police officers from King's Lynn. You have been arrested on suspicion of handling stolen drugs and we are taking you back to King's Lynn for questioning.' The answer he received was: 'You can't prove a thing against me. You realise you can only hold me for 24 hours.' There the information given to the defendant becomes still more specific because it not only deals with drug offences but sets out the particular kind of drug offences that the police in Norfolk reasonably suspected the defendant of having committed, namely, handling stolen drugs.

Moving on fairly quickly from there, he was brought to King's Lynn; he was there charged with handling stolen drugs and when the matter came before the committing justices the charge was a charge not of handling stolen drugs but of unauthorised possession of drugs . . . and the place alleged was not King's Lynn in fact but 'Cambridge or elsewhere.' It was on that charge that the examining justices committed him to Norfolk Quarter Sessions.

When the matter got to the drafting of an indictment, it took the form of three counts alleging unauthorised possession of drugs at different dates and instead of 'at Cambridge or elsewhere,' they were all alleged as possession 'at Cambridge'. . . .

One asks oneself at what stage, if at all, did he become in lawful custody. On that point the court is quite clearly of opinion that when he was in the police station at Cambridge informed in sufficient detail by Police Constable Welham and then Police Constable Elliott, he was thereafter in lawful custody.

Mr Cheatle says that before he could become in lawful custody he would have to be free, he would have to leave the police station and be re-arrested. The court is quite unable to accept that contention. We are satisfied that when in the police station shortly after arrest he was told all that he was entitled to know . . . that then at any rate he was detained in lawful custody. . . .

Two other matters fall to be mentioned. Mr Cheatle has relied strongly on the fact that Police Constable Crane, who quite clearly did not know what the position was, referred to the fact that a warrant had been issued, And Mr Cheatle says that that wrong statement was, as it were, never cured and covered everything which happened thereafter. The court is quite unable to accept that. While the arrested person is entitled to know, as Lord Simonds said, the act giving rise to the arrest, he is not entitled to know whether it was by warrant or as a result of arrest on reasonable suspicion.

NOTE

The lawfulness of Kulynycz's detention was relevant to the question whether Norfolk Quarter Sessions could exercise jurisdiction by virtue of the Criminal Justice Act 1925, s.11(1) (See now the Courts Act 1971).

(iii) Use of force

Criminal Law Act 1967

3. Use of force in making arrest, etc.
(1) A person may use such force as is reasonable in the circumstances in the prevention of crime, or in effecting or assisting in the lawful arrest of offenders or suspected offenders or of persons unlawfully at large.
(2) Subsection (1) above shall replace the rules of the common law on the question when force used for a purpose mentioned in the subsection is justified by that purpose.

NOTES

1. This section authorises the use of reasonable force in the making of an arrest. It also authorises the use of reasonable force to resist an unlawful arrest, such force constituting force used in 'the prevention of crime'.

2. 'Reasonable force' presumably will not exceed the minimum necessary to make or resist an arrest. However, it may well be that the minimum force necessary to make or resist arrest will exceed what is reasonable. For example, a person unlawfully arrested (e.g. because no power of arrest exists in connection with the offence for which the arrest was made) might be regarded by a court as using unreasonable force in using even a small amount of force in trying to escape if in the circumstances it was likely that the mistake could be pointed out to superior officers and the arrested person be released within a brief period.

3. See further Smith and Hogan, *Criminal Law* (4th edn. 1978) pp. 328–330; G. Williams, *Textbook of Criminal Law* (1978) pp. 440–445; *R v Fennell* [1971] 1 QB 428, CA; Attorney-General for Northern Ireland's Reference (No. 1 of 1975), below, p. 198; *R v Jones* [1978] 3 All ER 1098 CA; *Allen v Metropolitan Police Comr* (1980) *The Times* 25 March (£1,115 damages awarded in respect of the unreasonable use of force by police officers effecting a lawful arrest).

(c) DISPOSITION AFTER ARREST

John Lewis & Co Ltd v Tims [1952] A C 676, 96 Sol Jo 342,[1952] 1 WLR 1132, [1952] 1 All ER 1203, 116 JP 275, House of Lords

Mrs Tims and her daughter were arrested for shoplifting by store detectives employed by the appellant firm. After being arrested they were taken to the office of the chief store detective. They were detained there until the chief detective and a manager arrived to give instructions whether to bring proceedings. They were handed into police custody within an hour of arrest. Mrs Tims claimed damages for false imprisonment. She alleged that the detectives were obliged to give her into the custody of the police immediately upon arrest.

Lord Porter: . . . There remains only the question, therefore, whether the appellants were rightly mulcted in damages for false imprisonment because their servants did not take the respondent immediately before a magistrate, but brought her back to a part of the premises of John Lewis & Co Ltd.

It was maintained on her behalf that though an arrest might originally be justified, yet it became wrongful if the person accused was not taken forthwith before a justice of the peace. The appellants admitted that they could not detain her for an unreasonable time before handing her over to a constable or a gaoler, or bringing her before a justice, but contended that their obligation was only to act within a reasonable time and that an immediate and direct journey to the magistrate's court was not required. Of the three courses which the respondent asserted were open to them, commitment to prison may today be neglected: the accused would not be received nor the prison available. The choice lies between an immediate bringing before a magistrate or possibly handing over to a police officer and the like course taken within a reasonable time.

. . . if the latter is the true obligation and if the appellants' representative was justified in bringing back the respondent to John Lewis & Co Ltd's premises in order to get the advice of a manager and to obtain, if he thought fit, his authority to prosecute, there is no ground for saying that the time taken was unreasonable. But it is said on behalf of the respondent that it is not enough for the arrester to bring the person whom he has arrested before a justice or the police within a reasonable time: such a person must be brought before them 'immediately' or 'forthwith.' If not, the arrest is wrongful.

The Court of Appeal has found the appellants liable on this short ground, and on this short ground only . . .

Before I analyse the . . . principles which lie behind the problem presented to your Lordships it is, I think, expedient to set out the grounds on which the appellants justify their action. It is undesirable, they say, that their detectives, who must of necessity be subordinate officials, should be entrusted with the final decision whether a prosecution should take place or not. Such a decision should only rest with a senior and responsible officer and after he has heard any explanation which the accused person has to offer. Indeed, it is in the interest of the person arrested that, however conclusive the evidence should appear against him, he should have the opportunity of stating what he has to say and that in a proper case he should avoid the publicity of a public trial. The complaint here is not that the appellants acted unreasonably or harshly or detained the respondent for an unnecessarily long time, but only that it is the law and expedient in the interests of the public generally that the supposed criminal should be brought before the court as speedily as possible and afforded the opportunity of applying for and being granted bail. . . .

The question throughout should be: Has the arrester brought the arrested person to a place where his alleged offence can be dealt with as speedily as is reasonably possible? But all the circumstances in the case must be taken into consideration in deciding whether this requirement is complied with. A direct route and a rapid progress are no doubt matters for consideration, but they are not the only matters.

Those who arrest must be persuaded of the guilt of the accused; they cannot bolster up their assurance or the strength of the case by seeking further evidence and detaining the man arrested meanwhile or taking him to some spot where they can or may find further evidence. But there are advantages in refusing to give private detectives a free hand and leaving the determination of whether to prosecute or not to a superior official. Whether there is evidence that the steps taken were unreasonable or the delay too great is a matter for the judge. Whether, if there be such evidence, the delay was in fact too great is for the jury . . .

I would allow the appeal.

Lords Oaksey, Morton, Reid and **Cohen** agreed.

Dallison v Caffery [1965] 1 QB 348, [1964] 3 WLR 385, [1964] 2 All ER 610, 128 JP 379, Court of Appeal

Dallison was suspected of stealing money from an office in Dunstable. He was apprehended at about 11.15 a.m. in Clapton (34 miles from Dunstable) and the Dunstable police were informed. At about 3.00 p.m. the officers from Dunstable arrived at Clapton. They cautioned Dallison and told him he was going to be taken back to Dunstable in connection with the offence. Dallison offered an alibi. Instead of taking Dallison back to Dunstable immediately the police took Dallison to 40, Millfields Road, the house at which he alleged he was working at the time the theft took place, and sought to check out his alibi. The information gained was inconclusive. Next, the officers conducted, with Dallison's permission, a search of his home. Nothing incriminating was discovered. At about 5.30 p.m. the officers left with Dallison for Dunstable, arriving at about 6.30 p.m. Dallison sued the police, inter alia, for false imprisonment.

Lord Denning MR: . . . *The taking of Dallison round London.* Mr. Jukes [counsel for Dallison] next said that, ... it was not lawful for Detective Constable Caffery to take Dallison to 40, Millfields Road and not to take him straight back to the police station at Dunstable. This raises an interesting point as to the power of the police in regard to a man whom they have in custody. Mr. Jukes says that a constable has no more power than a private person. I cannot agree with this. So far as *arrest* is concerned, a constable has long had more power than a private person. If a constable makes an arrest without a warrant, he can justify it on the ground that he had reasonable cause for supecting that the accused had committed a felony. He does not have to go further (as a private person has to do) and prove that a felony has in fact been committed. So far as *custody* is concerned, a constable also has extra powers. If a *private person* arrests a man on suspicion of having committed a felony, he cannot take the man round the town seeking evidence against him: see *Hall v Booth (1834) 3 Nev. & MKB 316.* The private person must, as soon as he reasonably can, hand the man over to a constable or take him to the police station or take him before a magistrate; but so long as he does so within a reasonable time, he is not to be criticised because he holds the man for a while to consider the position: see *John Lewis & Co Ltd v Tims.* [above p. 60] A *constable*, however, has a greater power. When a constable has taken into custody a person reasonably suspected of felony, he can do what is reasonable to investigate the matter, and to see whether the suspicions are supported or not by further evidence. He can, for instance, take the person suspected to his own house to see whether any of the stolen property is there; else it may be removed and valuable evidence lost. He can take the person suspected to the place where he says he was working, for there he may find persons to confirm or refute his alibi. The constable can put him up on an identification parade to see if he is picked out by the witnesses. So long as such measures are taken reasonably, they are an important adjunct to the administration of justice. By which I mean, of course, justice not only to the man himself but also to the community at large. The measures must, however, be reasonable. In *Wright v Court* (1825), 4 B & C 596, a constable held a man for three days without taking him before a magistrate. The constable pleaded that he did so in order to enable the private prosecutor to collect his evidence. That was plainly unreasonable and the constable's plea was overruled. In this case it is plain to me that the measures taken were reasonable. Indeed, Dallison himself willingly co-operated in all that was done. He cannot complain of it as a false imprisonment. I hold, therefore, that the judge was right in rejecting the claim of false imprisonment.

Diplock LJ: . . . In my view, the only question (and it was one for the judge, not for the jury) was whether the defendant acted reasonably. It cannot be credibly suggested that Dallison would have been brought before a magistrates' court or bailed by the police at Dunstable one moment earlier if he had been taken direct to Dunstable. This, of course, is a relevant consideration. Seeing that he was protesting his innocence, it was in Dallison's own interest, and it was, in part at least, at his request, that he was taken to his place of work to see if his alibi was verifiable, for had it been credibly confirmed, he would have been released. He suffered no harm by being taken to his own house, and it was in his own interest, if he was innocent, that the search of his house, which he knew would have negative results, should take place without delay and in his presence . . .

Danckwerts LJ agreed with the judgment of **Lord Denning** MR.

Magistrates' Courts Act 1952

38. Bail on arrest without warrant
(1) On a person's being taken into custody for an offence without a warrant, a police officer not below the rank of inspector, or the police officer in charge of the police station to which the person is brought, may, and, if it will not be practicable to bring him before a magistrates' court within twenty-four hours after his being taken into custody, shall, inquire into the case and, unless the offence appears to the officer to be a serious one, [grant him bail . . . subject to a duty to appear before a magistrates' court at such time and place as the officer appoints].
(2) Where, on a person's being taken into custody for an offence without a warrant, it appears to any such officer as aforesaid that the inquiry into the case cannot be completed forthwith, he may [grant him bail . . . subject to a duty to appear at such a police station and at such time as the officer appoints] unless he previously receives a notice in writing from the officer in charge of that police station that his attendance is not required; . . . .
(3) (*Repealed*)
(4) Where a person is taken into custody for an offence without a warrant and is retained in custody, he shall be brought before a magistrates' court as soon as practicable.

NOTES

1. The words in square brackets were substituted by the Bail Act 1976, Sch. 2 paras. 18 and 20.
2. Before a person can be brought before a magistrates' court he must have been charged with an offence or offences. In the case of a person arrested on 'reasonable suspicion' (e.g. under the Criminal Law Act 1967, s.2) it may be that evidence justifying charging the arrested person is not immediately available. The Magistrates' Courts Act, s.38(4) requires the police to proceed as quickly as 'practicable' first in converting their 'reasonable suspicion' into a prima facie case against the arrested person justifying charging him, and then in bringing him before the magistrates. In the case of 'serious' offences (whatever that may mean), where the obligation to

release on bail under s.38(1) does not apply, no maximum time limit for such police custody is prescribed.

When a suspect has been arrested and is being detained in police custody proceedings for habeas corpus place the onus on the police to satisfy the judge hearing the application that the obligation under s.38(4) is being complied with. Perhaps more importantly the threat of such proceedings may secure either the release of a suspect or his being promptly charged and brought before the magistrates. See further Gifford and O'Connor (1979) LAG Bulletin 182; R. Sharpe, *Habeas Corpus* (1976) pp. 127–8.

In evidence to the Royal Commission on Criminal Procedure the Metropolitan Police Commissioner recommended that if a person arrested by the police and held in custody for a continuous period of 72 hours had not been charged he should have to be released from that custody unless prior to the expiration of that period an order authorising further detention for a period not exceeding 72 hours was obtained from a magistrate. The magistrate would exercise his discretion to release the suspect or authorise his further police custody after having been informed of such matters as the grounds of suspicion leading to the arrest, the progress made and expected in the investigation and the reason why charges had not yet been preferred. Further applications for 72 hour extensions should be permitted. (*Written Evidence of Commissioner of Police of the Metropolis*, Part I, (1978) Para. 3.15–3.19) Note that this recommendation was not intended to diminish obligations.under the Magistrates' Courts Act 1952, s.38(4), but rather to regulate more closely the cases when it is not 'practicable' to charge a person and take him before the magistrates within 72 hours of arrest. The period of 72 hours after which the magisterial check would operate may seem unduly long. Compare the Metropolitan Police Commissioner's proposals with the recommendations of the Thomson Committee (1975) Cmnd. 6218 that Scottish police should be required to release a person arrested on suspicion if charges were not brought within 6 hours of the arrest (para. 3.25), and see the Criminal Justice (Scotland) Bill 1980.

3. See also *R v McGregor* (below, p. 117) and *R v Houghton and Franciosy* [1979] Crim LR 383, CA.

4. What are the legal consequences of a failure to comply with s. 38.

5 Entry

The usual way in which police officers and other public officials obtain entry to premises is by invitation, express or implied. Without such an invitation, they must point to lawful authority to enter, which may be conferred by the common law[2], by a statutory power to enter without warrant, (e.g. to effect an arrest under section 2 of the Criminal Law Act 1967[3]), or by a warrant authorising an arrest[4], search[5], or entry for some other purpose (e.g. to read a gas meter[6]). An unlawful entry may be met by the use of reasonable force, and may be the subject of an action for damages, although the former is likely to be risky (both physically and legally) and the latter fraught with practical difficulties.

---

2. E. g. *Thomas v Sawkins*, below, p. 64.
3. Criminal Law Act 1967, s. 2(6), above, p. 47.
4. Above, p. 46.
5. Below, pp. 70–84, 97–99.
6. Rights of Entry (Gas and Electricity Boards) Act 1954.

Thomas v Sawkins [1935] 2 KB 249, 104 LJ KB 572, 153 LT 419, 99 JP 295, 51 TLR 514, 33 LGR 330, 30 Cox CC, King's Bench Divisional Court

Case stated by Glamorgan (Newcastle and Ogmore) justices.

On 17 August 1934 a public meeting was held at the Large Hall of the Caerau Library to protest against the Incitement to Disaffection Bill then before Parliament and to demand the dismissal of the chief constable of the county of Glamorgan, at which meeting between 500 and 700 people were present. The principal speaker was to be Alun Thomas (the appellant). He had previously addressed meetings at Nantymoel (9 August), Caerau (14 August) and Maesteg (15 August). He had lodged a written complaint against the refusal of police officers to leave the Nantymoel meeting, had threatened physically to eject the police if they attended the meeting on 17 August, and had stated at the Maesteg meeting: 'If it were not for the presence of these people' – pointing to police officers – 'I could tell you a hell of a lot more.'

The Library Hall was hired by one Fred Thomas, and the public were invited to attend, free of charge. The meeting was convened (among others) by Fred Thomas and Alun Thomas. Sergeant Sawkins (the respondent), together with Inspector Parry and Sergeant Lawrence, was refused admission by Fred Thomas. Nevertheless, the three officers entered the hall and sat on the front row. They also refused to leave on two occasions when requested to do so by Alun Thomas. Alun Thomas then stated that the police officers would be ejected, and he laid his hand on Inspector Parry to eject him. Sergeant Sawkins thereupon pushed Alun Thomas's arm and hand from Parry, saying: 'I won't allow you to interfere with my superior officer.' About thirty other police officers entered with batons drawn, and no further attempt was made to eject the police. In attempting to remove Parry, Alun Thomas used no more force than was reasonably necessary for that purpose, and Sawkins used no more force than was reasonably necessary (assuming that he and Parry had a right to be there) to protect Parry and to prevent him from being ejected.

The respondent did not allege that any criminal offence was committed. There was no breach of the peace or disorder at any time.

Alun Thomas preferred an information against Sergeant Sawkins alleging that Sawkins had committed assault and battery contrary to section 42 of the Offences against the Person Act 1861. He claimed that the police officers were trespassers. If that was correct, he would be entitled to use reasonable force to eject them, and forcible resistance by the police officers would be illegal. The justices concluded (33 LGR at 333):

'Upon the above facts and evidence given before us we were and are of the opinion that the respondent and other police officers had reasonable grounds for believing that if they were not present at the meeting seditious speeches would be made and/or incitements to violence and/or breaches of the peace would take place and that they were entitled to enter and remain in the said hall and meeting.'

They dismissed the information. Alun Thomas appealed. It was argued, inter alia, on behalf of Sawkins that:

'The respondent was entitled to be present at the meeting. A constable by his oath swears to cause the peace to be preserved and to prevent the commission of all offences. Where, therefore, the police have reasonable grounds for believing that an offence may be committed or a breach of the peace occur, they have a right to enter private premises to prevent the commission of the offence or the occurrence of the breach of the peace. If that were not so, it would be extremely difficult for the police to exercise their powers of watch and ward and their duty of preventive justice.' ([1935] 2 KB at 253).

Lord Hewart CJ: It is apparent that the conclusion of the justices in this case consisted of two parts. One part was a conclusion of fact that the respondent and the police officers who accompanied him believed that certain things might happen at the meeting which was then about to be held. There were ample materials on which the justices could come to that conclusion. The second part of the justices' finding is no less manifestly an expression of opinion. Finding the facts as they do, and drawing from those facts the inference which they draw, they go on to say that the officers were entitled to enter and to remain on the premises on which the meeting was being held.

Against that determination, it is said that it is an unheard-of proposition of law, and that in the books no case is to be found which goes the length of deciding, that, where an offence is expected to be committed, as distinct from the case of an offence being or having been committed, there is any right in the police to enter on private premises and to remain there against the will of those who, as hirers or otherwise, are for the time being in possession of the premises. When, however, I look at the passages which have been cited from Blackstone's Commentaries, vol. i., p. 356, and from the judgments in *Humphries v Connor* (1864) 17 Ir CLR 1 [below, p. 168] and *O'Kelly v Harvey* (1883) 14 LR Ir 105 [below p. 170] and certain observations of Avory J in *Lansbury v Riley* [1914] 3 KB 229 at 236, 237, I think that there is quite sufficient ground for the proposition that it is part of the preventive power, and, therefore, part of the preventive duty, of the police, in cases where there are such reasonable grounds of apprehension as the justices have found here, to enter and remain on private premises. It goes without saying that the powers and duties of the police are directed, not to the interests of the police, but to the protection and welfare of the public.

It was urged in one part of the argument of Sir Stafford Cripps that what the police did here amounted to a trespass. It seems somewhat remarkable to speak of trespass when members of the public who happen to be police officers attend, after a public invitation, a public meeting which is to discuss as one part of its business the dismissal of the chief constable of the county. It is elementary that a good defence to an action for trespass is to show that the act complained of was done by authority of law, or by leave and licence.

I am not at all prepared to accept the doctrine that it is only where an offence has been, or is being, committed, that the police are entitled to enter and remain on private premises. On the contrary, it seems to me that a police officer has ex virtute officii full right so to act when he has reasonable ground for believing that an offence is imminent or is likely to be committed.

I think, therefore, that the justices were right and that this appeal should be dismissed.

Avory J   I am of the same opinion. I think that it is very material in this particular case to observe that the meeting was described as a public meeting, that it was extensively advertised, and that the public were invited to attend. There can be no doubt that the police officers who attended the meeting were members of the public and were included in that sense in the invitation to attend. It is true that those who had hired the hall for the meeting might withdraw their invitation from any particular individual who was likely to commit a breach of the peace or some other offence, but it is quite a different proposition to say that they might withdraw the invitation from police officers who might be there for the express purpose of preventing a breach of the peace or the commission of an offence.

With regard to the general question regarding the right of the police to attend the meeting notwithstanding the opposition of the promoters, I cannot help thinking that that right follows from the description of the powers of a constable which Sir Stafford Cripps relies on in Stone's Justices' Manual, 1935, p. 208, where it is said that when a constable hears an affray in a house he may break in to suppress it and may, in pursuit of an affrayer, break in to arrest him. If he can do that, I cannot doubt that he has a right to break in to prevent an affray which he has reasonable cause to suspect may take place on private premises. In other words, it comes within his duty, as laid down by Blackstone (Commentaries, vol. i., p. 356), to keep the King's peace and to keep watch and ward. In my view, the right was correctly expressed in *R (Feehan) v Queen's County JJ* (1882) 10 LR Ir 294 at 301 where Fitzgerald J said: 'The foundation of the jurisdiction [to bind persons to be of good behaviour] is very remote, and probably existed prior to the statute of 1360–61; but whatever its foundation may be, or by whatever language conveyed, we are bound to regard and expound it by the light of immemorial practice and of decision, and especially of direct modern decisions. It may be described as a branch of preventive justice, in the exercise of which magistrates are invested with large judicial discretionary powers, for the maintenance of order and the preservation of the public peace.' That passage was expressly approved in *Lansbury v Riley* [1914] 3 KB 229 at 236 and the statement of the law which it contains was adopted by Lord Alverstone CJ in *Wise v Dunning* [1902] 1 KB 167 at 175; *R v Queen's County JJ* is there referred to sub nom *R v Cork JJ* (1882) 15 Cox CC 149. In principle I think that there is no distinction between the duty of a police constable to prevent a breach of the peace and the power of a magistrate to bind persons over to be of good behaviour to prevent a breach of the peace.

I am not impressed by the fact that many statutes have expressly given to police constables in certain circumstances the right to break open or to force an entrance into private premises. Those have all been cases in which a breach of the peace was not necessarily involved and it, therefore, required express statutory authority to empower the police to enter. In my opinion, no express statutory authority is necessary where the police have reasonable grounds to apprehend a breach of the peace, and in the present case I am satisfied that the justices had before them material on which they could properly hold that the police officers in question had reasonable grounds for believing that, if they were not present, seditious speeches would be made and/or that a breach of the peace would take place. To prevent any such offence or a breach of the peace the police were entitled to enter and to remain on the premises, and I agree that this appeal should be dismissed.

Lawrence J: As my Lord has pointed out, our judgment proceeds on the particular facts of this case, and on those facts I agree with the conclusion. I will only add that I am unable to follow the distinction which Sir Stafford Cripps has drawn between the present matter and the cases which have been cited. If a constable in the execution of his duty to preserve the peace is entitled to commit an assault, it appears to me that he is equally entitled to commit a trespass.

Appeal dismissed.

NOTES

1. Background information not available from the law reports is given in D. G. T. Williams, *Keeping the Peace* (1967) pp. 142–149. The case was adversely criticised by A. L. Goodhart in (1936–8) CLJ 22.

2. What is the *ratio decidendi* of the judgment of Lord Hewart CJ? Is it the *ratio decidendi* of the case?

3. Where Lord Hewart states that a police officer may enter and remain on private premises 'when he has reasonable ground for believing that an offence is imminent or is likely to be committed', do you think that the point he was considering was (a) the *point of time* at which the police may intervene, or (b) the nature of the *offence* which has to be anticipated, or (c) both? Does Lord Hewart's judgment amount to an endorsement of the argument of counsel for Sawkins?

4. Could Alun Thomas have been convicted of the offences of assaulting or obstructing a police officer in the execution of his duty? (cf. *Duncan v Jones* [1936] 1 KB 218, below, p. 172).

5. In principle, the occupier of land may grant or refuse permission (a 'licence') to someone seeking to go on to the land according to his own wishes, unless that other has a right to enter conferred by law. A gratuitous licence may be revoked at any time provided that reasonable notice is given (Megarry and Wade, *The Law of Real Property*, 4th edn. (1975) p. 777). A licensee must be given reasonable time to depart before his continued presence on the land constitutes trespass (*Robson v Hallett* [1967] 2 QB 939, [1967] 2 All ER 407 below, p. 69); unless he makes it clear that he will not leave voluntarily (*Davis v Lisle* [1936] 2 KB 434, below, p. 68).

Apart from the situation where there is a right to remain conferred by law, a licence will only be irrevocable where (a) it is protected by estoppel or equity; (b) the licence is coupled with a proprietary interest in other property; or (c) (in some circumstances) where the licence is granted by contract (see *Megarry and Wade*, pp. 778–782). In view of this, would it be correct to say that the person who hired the hall could *only* 'withdraw their invitation from any particular individual who was likely to commit a breach of the peace or some other offence'? (cf. Avory J). How is the position of the organiser of a *public* meeting different from that of a *private* meeting? Is it not simply the difference between a meeting to which there is a general invitation to the public, and one to which specific invitations are given? Can the fact that a meeting is 'public' limit the power of the *occupier* to refuse entry or to eject, as distinct from marking the limit of the right of the *police* to enter private premises in anticipation of the commission of offences? Is a First Division football match with an attendance of 50,000 a public or private meeting? What about a match attended by a few hundred spectators? Or by an old man and a dog? Is a private dinner party a 'private meeting'? Cf. the Public Order Act 1936, s. 9, below p. 151.

6. Consider the situation where a police officer purchases a ticket to attend a public meeting. What is the position if he attends in plain clothes, knowing that the organiser would not have sold him a ticket had they known his true identity? (Cf. *Said v Butt* [1920] 3 KB 497; *Cheshire and Fifoot's Law of Contract* (9th edn 1976) pp. 228–235, 237).

7. Consider the statement of Lawrence J that if a constable is 'entitled to commit an assault, . . . he is equally entitled to commit a trespass' in the light of section 3 of the Criminal Law Act 1967 (above, p. 59).

8. What is the position where a police officer has no legal right of entry but obtains permission to enter premises:

(a) by concealing the fact that he is a police officer in circumstances where he knows that a policeman would not be admitted;

or (b) by a false representation of fact (e.g. 'I thought I saw a burglar');

or (c) by a false representation of law (e.g. 'I have a legal power to enter')

or (d) by acquiescing in the self deception of the occupier (e.g. 'You've a right to come in so I suppose I'd better let you').

9. The judges rely on analogies (a) with the power of police and magistrates to commit acts which would otherwise constitute assaults where this is necessary in the last resort to preserve the peace, (below pp. 168–172) and (b) with the preventive power of magistrates to bind people over to keep the peace or be of good behaviour, (below pp. 176–177). How apt are these analogies? (See Goodhart, (1936–8) 6 CLJ 22, 25–29).

10. In *Handcock v Baker* (1800) 2 Bos & P 260, the defendants were held entitled to break into a house where they had reasonable cause to believe that the occupier was about to kill his wife.

11. In *Bailey v Wilson* [1968] Crim LR 617, (appeal to quarter sessions) a police officer having been informed of a domestic disturbance at a private house, walked through the open gateway and up the garden path. He heard a woman screaming, but this stopped when he knocked on the door. Up to this point, he was held to have had an implied licence to go to the door. B, the occupier, required him to leave, and attacked him when he did not. It was held that the officer had no reasonable cause to suspect that an arrestable offence had been committed, as distinct from common assault, and accordingly could not rely on section 2 (6) of the Criminal Law Act 1967. He had no legal right to enter or remain on the premises merely to make enquiries. Once he refused to leave, he was a trespasser and was not acting in the execution of his duty. B could not therefore be convicted of assaulting a constable contrary to the Police Act 1964 s. 51(1). Is a wide interpretation of *Thomas v Sawkins* consistent with this decision?

12. In *McGowan v Chief Constable of Kingston upon Hull* [1968] Crim LR 34, the Divisional Court held that police officers were entitled to enter and remain in a private house where they feared there would be a breach of the peace arising out of a domestic quarrel. *Thomas v Sawkins* was not mentioned in the report, but was presumably the relevant authority. See above, pp. 50–51 on the concept of a 'breach of the peace'.

13. Before *Thomas v Sawkins*, it was generally accepted that the police had no power to enter meetings on private premises unless they had reason to believe that a breach of the peace was actually taking place. This was stated to be the position by the *Departmental Committee on the Duties of the Police with respect to the Preservation of Order at Public Meetings* (Cd. 4673,

1909, p. 6), and by the Home Secretary, Sir John Gilmour, in a debate arising out of the Fascist meeting at Olympia on 7 June 1934 where there was considerable violence (290 HC Deb 14 June 1934 col 1968). Cf. *Robson v Hallett*, below p. 69.

14. A constable may enter premises in fresh pursuit of a person who has committed a breach of the peace within his view (see *R v Walker* (1854) Dears CC 358; *R v Marsden* (1868) LR 1 CCR 131), or of a person who has escaped from lawful custody (see *Genner v Sparkes* (1704) 1 Salk 79; Hawkins PC II Chap. XIV, s. 9). There is also common law authority for the proposition that a constable, having a warrant of arrest, after demanding and being refused admittance, may break open doors to effect an arrest (*Foster's Crown Cases* 136, 320 *Burdett v Abbot* (1811) 14 East 1). As regards arrests without warrant there are powers of entry in relation to breaches of the peace (*Thomas v Sawkins*) and arrests for 'arrestable offences' under the Criminal Law Act 1967, s. 2 (s. 2(6), above p. 47). There is no general power of entry in relation to other warrantless arrests, (see *R v McKenzie and Davies* [1979] Crim LR 164, Bristol Cr Ct: no power of entry to effect arrest under the Street Offences Act 1959, s. 1) although legislation conferring a specific arrest power may also authorise entry.

15. Contrary to expectations which might be engendered by *Thomas v Sawkins* D. G. T. Williams has noted 'the apparent determination of the police to avoid wherever possible any entanglement in the protests and demonstrations taking place on private property' ([1970] CLJ 96, 116). This was particularly marked in relation to sit ins at universities in the late 1960s. Cf. *R v Dythan* [1979] QB 422, CA(CD), where a constable was convicted of the common law misdemeanour of misconduct of a public officer in that he failed to fulfil his duty to preserve the peace. He had witnessed a man being beaten and kicked to death outside a club, but had taken no steps to intervene.

Davis v Lisle [1936] 2 KB 434, [1936] 2 All ER 213, 105 LJ KB 593, 155 LT 23, 52 TLR 475, 34 LGR 253, 30 Cox CC 412, King's Bench Divisional Court

Sidney Davis was the member of a firm which occupied a railway arch as a garage. Two police officers entered the garage to make inquiries as to the person responsible for obstructing the highway with a lorry, which lorry had subsequently been moved into the garage. D, using abusive and obscene language, told them to get out. L was in the act of producing his warrant card when D struck him in the chest and stomach with his fist, damaging his tunic. D was convicted by justices of (1) assaulting a police officer in the execution of his duty contrary to the Metropolitan Police Act 1839, s. 18; (2) obstructing an officer in the execution of his duty contrary to the Prevention of Crimes Amendment Act 1885, s.2; and (3) maliciously damaging a serge tunic (by tearing it), to the amount of 7s 6d. D appealed unsuccessfully to quarter sessions, and then appealed to the Divisional Court by case stated.

Lord Hewart CJ: The point which is raised here with regard to the appellant's first two convictions is whether the officers were at the material time acting in the execution of their duty. In my opinion, they were not, and there are no grounds on which they can be held to have been so acting. The only ground which is put forward in support of the contention that they were so acting seems to me to be quite beside the point. I feel a difficulty in envisaging the legal proposition that because the police officers had witnessed an offence being committed on the highway they were acting in the execution of their duty in entering and remaining on private premises because the offenders then were on those premises. Admittedly, the officers had no warrant entitling them to search the premises. It is one thing to say that the officers were at liberty to enter this garage to make an inquiry, but quite a different thing to say that they were entitled to remain when, not without emphasis, the appellant had said: 'Get outside. You cannot come here without a search warrant.' From that moment on, while the officers remained where they were, it seems to me that they were trespassers and it is quite clear that the act which the respondent was doing immediately before the assault complained of was tantamount to putting forward a claim as of right to remain where he was. The respondent was in the act of producing his warrant card. That was after the emphatic order to 'get out' had been made. Mr. Raphael, with his usual candour, has admitted that, if the finding in the case that the respondent was in the act of producing his warrant card is fairly to be construed as meaning that he was asserting his right to remain on the premises, it is not possible to contend that at that moment the respondent was acting in the execution of his duty. I think it is quite clear that the act of producing his warrant card constituted the making of such a claim. I cannot think that there is any ambiguity about it . . . .

In my opinion, it is not possible to maintain the conclusion that at the material time the respondent was acting in the execution of his duty as a constable. But that conclusion by no means disposes of everything contained in this case. It does not dispose of the question whether the assault which was in fact committed was justified. We have not the materials before us which would enable us to determine that question. Nor was the appellant prosecuted for assault. He was prosecuted for assaulting and obstructing a police officer in the execution of his duty. Furthermore, the conclusion to which I have come does not affect the third conviction—that of damaging a tunic by 'wilfully and maliciously tearing' it. On that part of the case no question arises whether at that moment the officer was acting in the execution of his duty and I see no reason why we should interfere with that conviction . . . .

Du Parcq and **Goddard JJ** delivered concurring judgments.

Appeal allowed as to first two convictions.

NOTES

1. The officers in this case were not entering in order to *prevent* crime, but to *investigate*. Cf. *Thomas v Sawkins*, above, p. 64.
2. In this case, the officers asserted a right to remain. Otherwise, persons requested to leave must be given reasonable time to depart. In *Robson v Hallett* [1967] 2 QB 939, a police sergeant was told to leave a private house where he was making enquiries. He at once turned and walked towards the front door but was then jumped on. Two constables went to his aid from the front path. The Divisional Court held that the sergeant had not become a trespasser the instant he was told to depart. Lord Parker CJ stated (at 952–953):

'When a licence is revoked as a result of which something has to be done by the licensee, a reasonable time must be implied in which he can do so, in this case to get off the premises; no doubt it will be very short time, but he was doing here his best to leave the premises.'

The constables were lawfully in the front garden, as they, like any other members of the public, had implied leave and licence to walk up to the front door, and that implied licence had never been revoked (see below, p. 308). They were acting in the execution of their duty in assisting the sergeant and avoiding any further breach of the peace. Lord Parker stated obiter at 953 that 'even if they had been outside the gate, it seems to me that they would have abundant right to come onto private property in those circumstances'. Diplock LJ said of the constables (at 954) that

'once a breach of the peace was taking place under their eyes, they had not only an independent right but a duty to go and stop it, and it matters not from that moment onwards whether they started off on their journey to stop it from outside the premises . . . or . . . inside . . . '

Another example of a premature attack is *Kay v Hibbert* [1977] Crim LR 226, DC.
3. In *McArdle v Wallace* (No. 2) (1964) 108 Sol Jo 483, DC, a police

constable entered a yard to inquire about some property in an adjoining passageway. The occupier's son told him to leave, and struck him when he did not. The magistrates found as a fact that the son had the implied authority of the father to ask the constable to leave. The Divisional Court held that the son was rightly acquitted of the charge of assaulting a police officer in the execution of his duty (see above, p. 36) 'albeit the constable did not know' of the implied authority.

6 Search and seizure; the case law before *Ghani v Jones*

In this section we look generally at the law of search and seizure. Various aspects of the law have been affected by the decision of the Court of Appeal in *Ghani v Jones*, which is considered separately in the next section.

(a) SEARCH WARRANTS

There are over 50 statutes which authorise entry to and search of premises by the police for various limited purposes. Normally, a warrant has to be obtained in advance from a justice of the peace. In some cases, prior authorisation from a senior police officer is sufficient. (The instances where there is a power to stop and search persons without a warrant are considered below in Section (c). A list is given in the *Home Office Evidence to the Royal Commission on Criminal Procedure, Memorandum No. III* (1978). (See also L. Leigh, *Police Powers in England and Wales* (1975) Appendix III and B. Harris, *Warrants of Search and Entry* (1973)).

The checks on the exercise of powers under warrant are (1) that in most cases the person seeking the warrant must swear an information on oath; (2) that the magistrate issuing the warrant must exercise a judicial discretion; and (3) that the action taken must fall within the limit of the warrant, or the extensions to those limits which have been accepted by the courts.

(i) Powers to issue search warrants

There is no general power whereby justices, or indeed any court or judge, may grant a search warrant in respect of any offence. There are a number of specific statutory powers, with differing limitations as to the geographical area for which a warrant may be granted by a particular court, the persons who may execute the warrant, the period within which it must be executed and the items which may be seized. For examples, see section 26 of the Theft Act 1968 (below, p. 84) and section 23(3) of the Misuse of Drugs Act 1971 (below). See also the Magistrates' Courts Act 1952, s. 102(2), above, p. 46.

Misuse of Drugs Act 1971

23. Powers to search and obtain evidence
(1) A constable or other person authorised in that behalf by a general or special order of the Secretary of State shall, for the purposes of the execution of this Act, have power to enter the premises of a person carrying on business as a producer or supplier of any controlled drugs and to demand the production of, and to inspect, any books or documents relating to dealings in any such drugs and to inspect any stocks of any such drugs.
(2) (*Given below at p. 93*)
(3) If a justice of the peace . . . is satisfied by information on oath that there is reasonable ground for suspecting—
  (a) that any controlled drugs are, in contravention of this Act or of any regulations made thereunder, in the possession of a person on any premises; or
  (b) that a document directly or indirectly relating to, or connected with, a transaction or

dealing which was, or an intended transaction or dealing which would if carried out be, an offence under this Act, or in the case of a transaction or dealing carried out or intended to be carried out in a place outside the United Kingdom, an offence against the provisions of a corresponding law in force in that place, is in the possession of a person on any premises, he may grant a warrant authorising any constable acting for the police area in which the premises are situated at any time or times within one month from the date of the warrant, to enter, if need be by force, the premises named in the warrant, and to search the premises and any persons found therein and, if there is reasonable ground for suspecting that an offence under this Act has been committed in relation to any controlled drugs found on the premises or in the possession of any such persons, or that a document so found is such a document as is mentioned in paragraph (b) above, to seize and detain those drugs or that document, as the case may be . . . .

(5) (*Omitted*)

NOTES

1. Section 23(3) expressly empowers a justice to issue a warrant authorising the search of *persons* found on the premises specified. In *King v R* [1969] 1 AC 304, the Privy Council held that the search of persons by virtue of a warrant granted under similar Jamaican legislation was not lawful unless the *warrant* expressly authorised such a search. Per Lord Hodson at 311–2:

> 'In a South African case, on consideration of a statutory provision as to the issue of warrants to search premises, persons not being mentioned, it was held at first instance that a search warrant covered persons as well as premises where premises only were mentioned since to hold the opposite would lead to the defeat of the objects of search warrants because persons on the premises would only have to take material documents and conceal them on their persons and defeat the objects of the search.
>
> This decision was reversed on appeal by the Transvaal Provincial Division in *Seccombe* v A-G [1919] TPD 270. Their Lordships see no reason to take a different view of the act in question here which by referring to persons as well as premises strengthens the argument that if a warrant is to cover persons it must say so in terms.'

[The South African Criminal Procedure Act 51 of 1977, s. 21 (2) now provides that a search warrant shall authorise a police official, inter alia, 'to enter and search any premises identified in the warrant and to search any person found on or at such premises'].

Not all statutory provisions as to search warrants mention search of persons found on premises. Examples of those that do include the power are the Incitement to Disaffection Act 1934, s. 2, below p. 296, the Official Secrets Act 1911, s. 9 (1), below p. 274 the Prevention of Terrorism (Temporary Provisions) Act 1976, Sch. 3, part II, para. 4, and the Public Order Act 1936, s.2 (5), below p. 129. Examples of provisions relating to serious offences where there is no such express mention include the Criminal Damage Act 1971, s.6(1), the Obscene Publications Act 1959, s.3, and the Offences against the Person Act 1861, s.65. Some provisions authorise the 'arrest and search' of persons found on the premises (e.g. Betting, Gaming, and Lotteries Act 1963, s. 51, Gaming Act 1968, ss. 43(4), and 8(5)). Is it proper to assume that these different formulations have been adopted deliberately by Parliament, so as to deny the police power to search persons under a warrant unless both the relevant statutory provisions and the warrant authorise such search?

2. Some statutes expressly authorise the use of force if the need arises (e.g. Public Order Act 1936, s.2(5), below, p. 129). There is probably a power at common law to use force to execute any search warrant provided admittance has been demanded and refused (see *Launock v Brown* (1819) 2 B & Ald 592).

3. In *Re Laporte and R* (1972) 29 DLR (3d) 651, Hugessen J of the Quebec

Court of Queen's Bench held that there was no jurisdiction arising from the Canadian Criminal Code or elsewhere for a Justice to issue a warrant to search the interior of a living human body. A warrant to search L's body (by a surgical operation to be performed by qualified doctors), for bullets alleged to have been fired by police officers, was quashed by certiorari. A living body was not within the phrase 'building, receptacle or place' in respect of which search warrants might be issued under s. 443 of the Criminal Code.

4. In *R v Atkinson* [1976] Crim LR 307, the Court of Appeal held that a warrant obtained under s. 23 (4) for the search of 'Flat 45' in certain premises could not justify the search of Flat 30, even though the police bona fide believed that A's flat was Flat 45. However, misspellings or trivial errors in the description of premises would not necessarily invalidate a warrant.

5. In some Commonwealth jurisdictions, there are general powers for magistrates to issue search warrants in relation to any offence. An example is s. 10 of the Australian Federal Crimes Act 1914–1966. See further: *R v Tillet, ex parte Newton* (1969) 14 FLR 10; D. C. Pearce (1970) 44 ALJ 467; E. Campbell and H. Whitmore, *Freedom in Australia*, (2nd ed., 1973) pp. 63–65. Cf. the Summary Proceedings Act 1957 (NZ) s. 198 (warrants may be issued in respect of any offence punishable by imprisonment) and the Canadian Criminal Code, s.443.

6. A warrant under the Obscene Publications Act 1959, s.3(1), below, p. 227, may be used only once: *R v Adams* [1980] 1 All ER 473, CA.

The case of Lady Diana Cooper 760 HC Deb Col 826 ff (Adjournment Debate)

At midnight on 19 February 1968, four police officers went to the home of Lady Diana Cooper and executed a warrant to search for drugs. The police had acted on an anonymous telephone call. The matter was raised in the House of Commons by Mr Norman St. John-Stevas. He complained that the conduct of the police in acting on the call, and making no attempt to check it was an 'intolerable practice.... If this is allowed to go un-challenged, then an Englishman's home, far from being his castle, is reduced to the status of a wigwam.' He also pointed out that the safeguard of the intervention of a magistrate was 'nullified if magistrates do not inform themselves fully of the grounds of which the police are seeking to act or if, having informed themselves, they are not prepared to exercise their discretion about what constitutes reasonable suspicion.'

The Under-Secretary of State for the Home Department (Mr Dick Taverne):
The first thing to say about this incident is that a serious mistake was made by the police in acting upon an anonymous telephone call in the way they did. When the facts came before senior officers, the mistake was immediately admitted and an apology offered without delay...

It is right to remind the House of the importance of the drugs problem and of the importance of dealing with illegal trafficking, particularly when there is an allegation about heroin. The police know that drugs have been introduced into legitimate consignments of goods and luggage and recovered when the container has been landed. They also know that supplies move rapidly and that bulk is soon broken down and distributed. It is therefore desirable to act quickly when information is received, so it must first be said in defence of the police that they have always to balance the need for quick action against the need to check the reliability of information. This is often a difficult matter of judgment and, although general guidance can help about which I will say more later, no hard and fast rules can be laid down, as each case presents individual problems and there is no substitute for the wisdom and experience of the individual officer.

When one comes to information from an anonymous source, one has a particular difficulty.

Recently, there has been an increasing amount of information about drugs coming from members of the public. Much of it has turned out to be true; some has no foundation and seems to be motivated by spite, malice or mental unbalance on the part of the informer. Obviously the police cannot ignore anonymous information, and it would be much preferable if information always came from impeccable and respectable sources, but that is not always so.

Anonymous information must clearly be treated with especial care, and the sort of steps that can be taken to check information will depend on the circumstances, but they can include observation of the premises to assess the likelihood of the allegation and the need for speedy action, searches in various indices at Scotland Yard—and it is fair to say of the police officer concerned that he made a search, but it is not altogether surprising that nothing was found in this case—and contact with local informants to see whether additional information is available or whether such information as has been received can be verified.

In this case, there was no attempt to find corroborative evidence. The officer concerned, felt, wrongly, that the overriding need was to act quickly, and he should not have acted in the way that he did. He should have checked his information in the ways that I have indicated. If he had, the incident would never have occurred.

As the hon. Member for Chelmsford has pointed out, the ultimate authority for the issue of a warrant rests with the magistrate, but he has to rely on the information and, to an extent, on the judgment of the officer applying for the warrant. Certainly the Commissioner of Police regards it as a police responsibility not to apply for a warrant without first taking all reasonable steps to check the reliability of the information on which the application is based. The Commissioner regrets that insufficient steps were taken in this case to check the reliability of the information on the basis of which the warrant was applied for, and that the magistrate was asked to issue a warrant.

In another place, a discussion took place on the action of the magistrate in granting the warrant. Inquiries have been made about the practice of magistrates and it has been pointed out that, from the magistrate's point of view, what he does when he grants a warrant on a police statement is merely what he is expected to do in many other cases in which applications are made ex parte. He is relying on sworn evidence from a source which he has no reason to suspect. But the mistake in this case was that the application by the police officer gave no indication that the source which he said he believed to be reliable was an anonymous one . . .

Mr St. John-Stevas: Surely there must be some duty on a magistrate to make a judiciary [sic] inquiry and to assess the evidence in some way. If that is not the practice of magistrates, the inclusion by Parliament of the intervention of a magistrate is a pure formality and of no effect.

Mr Taverne: The magistrate has to satisfy himself that the person making the application is a person whose word can be believed. If he has no reason to believe the person making the application, he should not grant a warrant. In many cases, with the many inquiries which come, particularly to Bow Street—this is not a matter for the Home Office, but we have information about this from the magistrates—the magistrates look at what is stated on the form, they look at the person before them, and, as with other ex parte applications, if they have no reason to disbelieve what is stated there, and it gives grounds for action, they grant a warrant . . .

It is therefore important that this incident should be drawn to the attention of chief officers, and that the practice in all cases should be to check anonymous information. If this is done, the magistrates can be re-assured in relying on the word of police officers, as they should normally be entitled to do.

NOTES

1. In the light of Mr. Taverne's description of the attitude of magistrates to the grant of warrant, how far is it justifiable to regard their intervention as a 'pure formality'?

2. Following this case guidance was issued as set out in paragraph 40 of the *Home Office Evidence to the Royal Commission on Criminal Procedure, Memorandum No. III*:

'40. The decision whether or not to issue a warrant is a matter for the magistrate concerned. The Lord Chancellor has advised those responsible for the training of Justices of the Peace that:
    a. it is the duty of a magistrate before issuing a search warrant to satisfy himself that it is in all the circumstances right to issue the warrant;
    b. a magistrate may question the person swearing the information to this end; and

c. although a police officer who applies for a warrant should not be expected to identify his informant, the magistrate may wish to know whether the informant is known to the officer, and whether it has been possible to make further enquiries to verify the information and, if so, with what result.

Chief officers of police have been informed that this advice has been given, and the need to take all reasonable steps to check the reliability of information received, before applying for a search warrant, has been stressed in guidance issued by the Home Office (Consolidated Circular to the Police on Crime and Kindred Matters at paragraphs 4.1 and 4.2 in the 1977 Edition.'

3. The issue of search warrants for drugs was considered in the Report by the Advisory Committee on Drug Dependence on *Powers of Arrest and Search in relation to Drugs Offences* (HMSO 1970):

'146. In contrast to the criticisms made of the stop and search powers the evidence we received in regard to search warrants for drugs did not suggest serious misgiving about the manner in which the law was being interpreted or the statutory powers were being invoked. There is, of course, some risk of abuses occurring because the machinery for search warrants cannot be operated without certain arbitrary judgements. The information on which a police officer may be prepared to swear to certain suspicions on oath is not necessarily of a kind which would be accepted in criminal proceedings and a magistrate cannot apply the same strictness of judgement as in court proceedings. If a warrant is applied for and issued in good faith, an innocent person whose premises are searched has no remedy at civil law; if the warrant were applied for maliciously or without reasonable cause, he could find this very difficult to prove. On one view, therefore, it could be argued that the procedure lends itself to "rubber-stamping" of irresponsible police applications and the execution with impunity of warrants obtained without proper cause. We are satisfied, however, that strong factors operate the other way. Most people regard police intrusion into private premises as a very serious infringement of civil liberty and would be ready to complain if police searches were made or thought to be made without reasonable justification. We are sure that magistrates and police officers of all ranks know this and are fully alive both to the risk of individual complaint and to the public concern likely to be aroused by any ill considered use of the statutory powers. For the individual police officer and magistrate concerned the rarity of the need to seek or issue a warrant, the technicalities of the law, the necessity to verify jurisdiction, and the risks of complaint are influences towards caution, applying as strongly to cases under the drugs law as to cases under any of the other statutes providing for search of private premises.'

The committee did not think that further guidance was necessary than that issued after the Cooper case.

4. Most of the English cases on search warrants concern the legality of warrants of a particular kind or the ambit of the powers granted by a warrant. Very few concern the question whether on the facts of a particular case a magistrate should have issued a warrant. In *Wyatt v White* (1860) 5 H & N 371, the defendant saw some sacks partly covered with a tarpaulin. Some had his mark on them, and others the mark cut away. He was told that the sacks were about to be shipped by the plaintiff for the manufacture of paper. He laid an information that he had reason to suspect and did suspect that some of his sacks had been stolen and were then in the possession of the plaintiff. The magistrate issued a warrant to search for the goods. The Court of Exchequer held that these facts constituted reasonable and probable cause and accordingly the plaintiff's action for malicious prosecution failed. Compare the position in relation to arrest (above pp. 51–53).

(ii) The legality of general warrants

Entick v Carrington (1765) 19 State Tr 1030, 2 Wils 275, 95 ER 807, Court of Common Pleas Lord Camden CJ

On 6 November 1762, the Earl of Halifax, one of the principal secretaries of state, issued a warrant to four King's messengers (Nathan Carrington,

James Watson, Thomas Ardran and Robert Blackmore) 'to make strict and diligent search for John Entick, the author, or one concerned in writing of several weekly very seditious papers, intitled the Monitor, or British Free holder . . . ; and him, having found you are to seize and apprehend, and to bring, together with his books and papers, in safe custody before me to be examined . . . .' The messengers entered E's house, the outer door being open, apprehended him, and searched for his books and papers in several rooms and in one bureau, one writing desk and several drawers. Where necessary these were broken open. They seized some books and papers and read others, remaining for about four hours. They then took E and the items seized to Lovel Stanhope, law-clerk to the secretaries of state. E was released on 17 November. He subsequently brought an action in trespass against the messengers. The jury gave a special verdict and assessed the damages at £300. The defendants argued that their acts were done in obedience to a lawful warrant.

Lord Camden CJ . . . :[I]f this point should be determined in favour of the jurisdiction, the secret cabinets and bureaus of every subject in this kingdom will be thrown open to the search and inspection of a messenger, whenever the secretary of state shall think fit to charge, or even to suspect, a person to be the author, printer, or publisher of a seditious libel.

This power so assumed by the secretary of state is an execution upon all the party's papers, in the first instance. His house is rifled; his most valuable secrets are taken out of his possession, before the paper for which he is charged is found to be criminal by any competent jurisdiction, and before he is convicted either of writing, publishing, or being concerned in the paper. This power, so claimed by the secretary of state, is not supported by one single citation from any law book extant. . . .

The arguments, which the defendants' counsel have thought fit to urge in support of this practice, are of this kind.

That such warrants have issued frequently since the Revolution, which practice has been found by the special verdict; . . . .

That the case of the warrants bears a resemblance to the case of search for stolen goods.

They say too, that they have been executed without resistance upon many printers, booksellers, and authors, who have quietly submitted to the authority; that no action hath hitherto been brought to try the right; and that although they have been often read upon the returns of Habeas Corpus, yet no court of justice has ever declared them illegal.

And it is further insisted, that this power is essential to government, and the only means of quieting clamours and sedition . . . .

If it is law, it will be found in our books. If it is not to be found there, it is not law.

The great end, for which men entered into society, was to secure their property. That right is preserved sacred and incommunicable in all instances, where it has not been taken away or abridged by some public law for the good of the whole. The cases where this right of property is set aside by positive law, are various. Distresses, executions, forfeitures, taxes, &c. are all of this description; wherein every man by common consent gives up that right, for the sake of justice and the general good. By the laws of England, every invasion of private property, be it ever so minute, is a trespass. No man can set his foot upon my ground without my licence, but he is liable to an action, though the damage be nothing; which is proved by every declaration in trespass, where the defendant is called upon to answer for bruising the grass and even treading upon the soil. If he admits the fact, he is bound to shew by way of justification, that some positive law has empowered or excused him. The justification is submitted to the judges, who are to look into the books; and if such a justification can be maintained by the text of the statute law, or by the principles of common law. If no such excuse can be found or produced, the silence of the books is an authority against the defendant, and the plaintiff must have judgment.

Where is the written law that gives any magistrate such a power? I can safely answer, there is none, and therefore it is too much for us without such authority to pronounce a practice legal, which would be subversive of all the comforts of society.

But though it cannot be maintained by any direct law, yet it bears a resemblance, as was urged, to the known case of search and seizure for stolen goods.

I answer, that the difference is apparent. In the one, I am permitted to seize my own goods, which are placed in the hands of a public officer, till the felon's conviction shall intitle me to restitution. In the other, the party's own property is seized before and without conviction, and he has no power to reclaim his goods, even after his innocence is cleared by acquittal.

The case of searching for stolen goods crept into the law by imperceptible practice. It is the only case of the kind that is to be met with. No less a person than my lord Coke (4 Inst. 176,) denied its legality; and therefore if the two cases resembled each other more than they do, we have no right, without an act of parliament, to adopt a new practice in the criminal law, which was never yet allowed from all antiquity.

Observe too the caution with which the law proceeds in this singular case. . . .

I come now to the practice since the Revolution, which has been strongly urged, with this emphatical addition, that an usage tolerated from the era of liberty, and continued downwards to this time through the best ages of constitution, must necessarily have a legal commencement. . . .

With respect to the practice itself, if it goes no higher, every lawyer will tell you, it is much too modern to be evidence of the common law; and if it should be added, that these warrants ought to acquire some strength by the silence of those courts, which have heard them read so often upon returns without censure or animadversion, I am able to borrow my answer to that pretence from the Court of King's-bench, which lately declared with great unanimity in the Case of General Warrants, that as no objection was taken to them upon the returns, and the matter passed *sub silentio*, the precedents were of no weight. I most heartily concur in that opinion; . . .

But still it is insisted, that there has been a general submission, and no action brought to try the right.

I answer, there has been a submission of guilt and poverty to power and the terror of punishment. But it would be strange doctrine to assert that all the people of this land are bound to acknowledge that to be universal law, which a few criminal booksellers have been afraid to dispute. . . .

It is then said, that it is necessary for the ends of government to lodge such a power with a state officer; and that it is better to prevent the publication before than to punish the offender afterwards. I answer, if the legislation be of that opinion, they will revive the Licensing Act. But if they have not done that I conceive they are not of that opinion. And with respect to the argument of state necessity, or a distinction that has been aimed at between state offences and others, the common law does not understand that kind of reasoning, nor do our books take notice of any such distinctions.

Serjeant Ashley was committed to the Tower in the 3d of Charles 1st, by the House of Lords only for asserting in argument, that there was a 'law of state' different from the common law; and the Ship-Money judges were impeached for holding, first, that state-necessity would justify the raising money without consent of parliament; and secondly, that the king was judge of that necessity.

If the king himself has no power to declare when the law ought to be violated for reason of state, I am sure we his judges have no such prerogative. . . .

[U]pon the whole we are all of opinion, that the warrant to seize and carry away the party's papers in the case of a seditious libel, is illegal and void. . . .

NOTES

1. *Entick v Carrington* was one of four leading cases which followed the publication of No. 45 of the *North Briton* (see Sir William Holdsworth *A History of English Law* (1938), Vol X pp. 659–672; George Rudé, *Wilkes and Liberty* (1962) Chap. II; Audrey Williamson, *Wilkes, A Friend to Liberty* (1974) Chap. IV). The *North Briton* was a weekly paper, of which John Wilkes was joint editor and a leading contributor. Its main purpose was to abuse and ridicule the recently appointed administration of the Earl of Bute. After No. 45 was published, the two secretaries of state, Lords Egremont and Halifax, issued a general warrant for the arrest of its 'authors, printers and publishers'. Over 45 people were arrested under this warrant, including Wilkes. The warrant was held to be illegal, and damages were awarded for trespass: see *Wilkes v Wood* (1763) 19 ST 1153; *Leach v Money* (1765) 19 ST 1002 and *Wilkes v Lord Halifax* (1769) 19 ST 1406.

2. This case is a classic illustration of the principle that any public officer must be able to point to lawful authority for actions of his which infringe the rights of others, and not merely some general conception of state necessity. It also reflects an unwillingness to 'invent' or 'discover' lawful authority, which has not been shared by some judges in more recent cases (see, for example, *Chic Fashions (West Wales) Ltd v Jones* (below p. 80) and *Ghani v Jones* [1970] 1 QB 693, CA (below p. 94). The House of Lords, however, did not regard the 'general warrant' cases as of much assistance in the *Rossminster* case (below, and see Griffiths [1980] CLJ 5).

Inland Revenue Commissioners v Rossminster Ltd [1980] 1 All ER 80, House of Lords

Section 20C of the Taxes Management Act 1970 (as substituted by the Finance Act 1976 Sch 6) provides that:

'(1) If the appropriate judicial authority is satisfied on information on oath given by an officer of the Board that—
    (a) there is reasonable ground for suspecting that an offence involving any form of fraud in connection with, or in relation to, tax has been committed and that evidence of it is to be found on premises specified in the information; and
    (b) in applying under this section; the officer acts with the approval of the Board given in relation to the particular case,
the authority may issue a warrant in writing authorising an officer of the Board to enter the premises, if necessary by force, at any time within 14 days from the time of issue of the warrant, and search them. . . .
(3) On entering the premises with a warrant under this section, the officer may seize and remove any things whatsoever found there which he has reasonable cause to believe may be required as evidence for the purposes of proceedings in respect of such an offence as is mentioned in subsection (1) above.
But this does not authorise the seizure and removal of documents in the possession of a barrister, advocate or solicitor with respect to which a claim to professional privilege could be maintained.'

'The Board' means the Board of Inland Revenue. The 'appropriate authority' is in England a circuit judge. A list of items seized must be supplied on request (s. 20C (4)).

    The Common Serjeant issued a search warrant in respect of the applicants' business premises and homes. The warrant did not specify that any particular offence was suspected, but simply recited words from s.20C (1) and (3). The officers entered the premises and seized and removed numerous files, papers and documents of all kinds.

    It was alleged that the officers did not examine the bulk of the articles before seizing them, or did not examine them in enough detail to form an opinion on their evidential value. The applicants commenced an action against the Revenue claiming, inter alia, damages for wrongful interference with goods. Subsequently they applied for judicial review of the seizure, under RSC Ord 53, and in those proceedings sought an order of certiorari to quash the warrant, a declaration that the seizure was unlawful and that the Revenue ought to return to the applicants all the articles seized, and all copies and notes taken of them. The Queen's Bench Divisional Court ([1979] 3 All ER 385) dismissed the application for judicial review. The decision was reversed by the Court of Appeal (ibid) but restored by the House of Lords.

Lord Wilberforce: . . .
    The integrity and privacy of a man's home, and of his place of business, an important human right has, since the Second World War, been eroded by a number of statutes passed by Parliament in the belief, presumably, that this right of privacy ought in some cases to be overridden by the interest which the public has in preventing evasions of the law. A formidable number of officials now have powers to enter people's premises, and to take property away, and these powers are frequently exercised, sometimes on a large scale. Many people, as well as the respondents, think that this process has gone too far; that is an issue to be debated in Parliament and in the Press.
    The courts have the duty to supervise, I would say critically, even jealously, the legality of

any purported exercise of these powers. They are the guardians of the citizens' right to privacy. But they must do this in the context of the times, ie of increasing Parliamentary intervention, and of the modern power of judicial review. In my respectful opinion appeals to 18th century precedents of arbitrary action by Secretaries of State and references to general warrants do nothing to throw light on the issue. Furthermore, while the courts may look critically at legislation which impairs the rights of citizens and should resolve any doubt in interpretation in their favour, it is no part of their duty, or power, to restrict or impede the working of legislation, even of unpopular legislation; to do so would be to weaken rather than to advance the democratic process.

It is necessary to be clear at once that Parliament, in conferring these wide powers, has introduced substantial safeguards. Those relevant to this case are three:

(1) No action can be taken under s 20C without the approval of the Board of Inland Revenue, viz two members, at least, acting personally. This Board consists of senior and responsible officials expert in the subject-matter, who must be expected to weigh carefully the issues of public interest involved.

(2) No warrant to enter can be issued except by a circuit judge, not, as is usually the case, by a magistrate. There has to be laid before him information on oath, and on this he must be satisfied that there is reasonable ground for suspecting the commission of a 'tax fraud' and that evidence of it is to be found in the premises sought to be searched. If the judge does his duty (and we must assume that the learned Common Serjeant did in the present case) he must carefully consider for himself the grounds put forward by the Revenue officer and judicially satisfy himself, in relation to each of the premises concerned, that these amount to reasonable grounds for suspecting etc. It would be quite wrong to suppose that he acts simply as a rubber stamp on the Revenue's application.

(3) The courts retain their full powers of supervision of judicial and executive action. There is nothing in s 20C which cuts these down; on the contrary, Parliament, by using such phrases as 'is satisfied' and 'has reasonable cause to believe', must be taken to accept the restraints which courts in many cases have held to be inherent in them.

The courts are concerned, in this case, only with two matters bearing on legality. First, were the warrants valid? Secondly, can the actual action taken under s 20C(3) be challenged on the ground that the officers did not have, or could not have had, reasonable cause to believe that the documents they seized might be required as evidence for the purposes of proceedings in respect of a 'tax fraud'? A third possible issue, namely that there was not before the judge sufficient material on which to be satisfied as the section requires was not pursued, nor thought sustainable by the Court of Appeal. It is not an issue now.

The two first mentioned are the only issues in the case. Three judges have decided them in favour of each side. For myself I have no doubt that the view taken by the Divisional Court on each was correct and I am willing to adopt their judgement. I add a few observations of my own.

1. I can understand very well the perplexity, and indeed indignation, of those present on the premises, when they were searched. Beyond knowing, as appears in the warrant, that the search was in connection with a 'tax fraud', they were not told what the precise nature of the fraud was, when it was committed, or by whom it was committed. In the case of a concern with numerous clients, eg a bank, without this knowledge the occupier of the premises is totally unable to protect his customers' confidential information from investigation and seizure. I cannot believe that this does not call for a fresh look by Parliament. But, on the plain words of the enactment, the officers are entitled, if they can persuade the Board and the judge, to enter and search *premises* regardless of whom they belong to: a warrant which confers this power is strictly and exactly within the Parliamentary authority, and the occupier has no answer to it. I accept that some information as regards the person(s) alleged to have committed an offence and possibly as to the approximate dates of the offences must almost certainly have been laid before the Board and the judge. But the occupier has no right to be told of this at this stage, nor has he the right to be informed of the 'reasonable grounds' of which the judge was satisfied. Both courts agree as to this: all this information is clearly protected by the public interest immunity which covers investigations into possible criminal offences. With reference to the police, Lord Reid stated this in *Conway v Rimmer* [1968] 1 All ER 874 at 889, [1968] AC 910 at 953–954 in these words:

'The police are carrying on an unending war with criminals many of whom are today highly intelligent. So it is essential that there should be no disclosure of anything which might give any useful information to those who organise criminal activities; and it would generally be wrong to require disclosure in a civil case of anything which might be material in a pending prosecution, but after a verdict has been given, or it has been decided to take no proceedings, there is not the same need for secrecy.'

The Court of Appeal took the view that the warrants were invalid because they did not sufficiently particularise the alleged offence(s). The court did not make clear exactly what particulars should have been given, and indeed I think that this cannot be done. The warrant followed the wording of the statute, 'fraud in connection with or in relation to tax', a portmanteau description which covers a number of common law offences (cheating) and statutory offences (under the Theft Act 1968 et al). To require specification at this investigatory stage would be impracticable given the complexity of 'tax frauds' and the different persons who may be involved (companies, officers of companies, accountants, tax consultants, taxpayers, wives of taxpayers etc). Moreover, particularisation, if required, would no doubt take the form of a listing of one offence and/or another or others and so would be of little help to those concerned. Finally, there would clearly be power, on principles well accepted in the common law, after entry had been made in connection with one particular offence, to seize material bearing on other offences within the portmanteau. So, particularisation, even if practicable, would not help the occupier.

I am unable, therefore, to escape the conclusion, that adherence to the statutory formula is sufficient.

The warrants, being valid, confer an authority to enter and search: see s 20C(1). This being in terms stated in the Act, I do not appreciate the relevance of an enquiry into the form of search warrants at common law (which in any case admitted of some flexibility in operation) and still less into that of warrants of arrest. There is no mystery about the word 'warrant': it simply means a document issued by a person in authority under power conferred in that behalf authorising the doing of an act which would otherwise be illegal. The person affected, of course, has the right to be satisfied that the power to issue it exists: therefore the warrant should (and did) contain a reference to that power. It would be wise to add to it a statement of satisfaction on the part of the judicial authority as to the matters on which he must be satisfied, but this is not a requirement and its absence does not go to validity. To complain of its absence in the present case when, as is admitted, no challenge can be made as to the satisfaction, in fact, of the judge, would be technical and indeed irrational. I can find no ground for holding these warrants invalid.

2. The second matter, on which the intervention of the court may be called for, arises under s 20C(3). This confers a statutory power independent of any authority in the warrant to seize and remove. Like all statutory powers conferred on executive officers it is subject to supervision by the courts exercising their classic and traditional powers of judicial review. It is undisputed that the words 'has reasonable cause to believe' are open to examination in spite of their subjective form: see *Nakkuda Ali v M F de S Jayaratne* [1951] AC 60. The existence of this reasonable cause, and of the belief founded on it, is ultimately a question of fact to be tried on evidence.

So far as regards these appeals this issue is complicated in three ways. First, it has been raised at an interlocutory stage, and at the very beginning of the investigation, on affidavit evidence. Secondly, the Revenue have refused, so far, to disclose their reasonable grounds, claiming immunity from so doing, on the grounds stated above. Thirdly, the defendants being, in effect, the Crown or Crown servants, an interlocutory injunction cannot be granted (see s 21 of the Crown Proceedings Act 1947).

The Court of Appeal sought to meet this situation by granting a declaration; and recognising, rightly in my opinion, that an interim declaration could not be granted, gave a final declaration in effect that the Revenue had exceeded their powers. I regret that I cannot agree that this was correct. It is to me apparent that there was a substantial conflict of evidence as to the manner in which the searches were carried out, the respondents broadly contending that the officers gave no real consideration to the question whether individual documents might be required as evidence, the Revenue asserting that they had detailed instructions what to look for and seize and that these were complied with. I shall not further analyse this issue which was fully and satisfactorily treated by the Divisional Court, for I am satisfied that, even if, which I doubt, there might have been enough evidence to justify the granting of interlocutory relief, this fell very far short of supporting a final declaration. I believe that the Court of Appeal was itself really of this opinion. This final declaration granted must clearly be set aside. . . .

I would wish to make it clear that the failure of the respondents at this stage is not necessarily the end of the matter. They can proceed with an action against the Revenue for, in effect, excess of power and for trespass and any aggravation can be taken into account. At some stage, which cannot be particularised now with precision but which broadly would be when criminal proceedings are over, or, within a reasonable time, are not taken, the immunity which exists at the stage of initial investigation will lapse. Then the Revenue will have to make good and specify the existence and cause of their belief that things removed might be required as evidence for the purpose of 'tax fraud' proceedings and the issue will be tried in a normal manner.

Viscount Dilhorne and **Lords Diplock** and **Scarman** delivered concurring speeches. **Lord Salmon** dissented.

(iii) The ambit of powers to seize under a warrant

Pringle v Bremner and Stirling [1867] 5 Macph (ct of Sess), 55 House of Lords

The arrival of a new minister in the parish of Dunbog caused such dissatisfaction that threatening letters were sent to him, and the bush of a cart-wheel (O.E.D.: 'The metal lining of the axle-hole of a wheel') exploded near the manse. Police officers obtained a warrant to search the premises of the pursuer (P) for pieces of the wood of which the plugs used in plugging the bush had been made, and of the fuses by means of which the bush had exploded. The officers searched the P's house, including his writing desk and drawers. They seized some papers and took them away. P claimed damages (1) for illegal search and seizure and (2) for wrongful arrest. The defenders (the police) claimed that the papers seemed to them to implicate P in the sending of the threatening letters. P was arrested and charged with sending a threatening letter. The defenders claimed that the pursuer's averments were irrelevant (i.e. assuming that his factual allegations were true, they disclosed no cause of action). This claim was upheld by the Court of Session. P appealed successfully to the House of Lords, which held (Lord Colonsay dissenting) that there was a prima facie case for the police to answer it being open to them to justify their conduct at the trial. The speeches contain dicta concerning the ambit of police powers to seize articles not mentioned in the warrant.

Lord Chelmsford LC: . . . Now, it may be said (and as the argument has been urged it may be as well to observe upon it) that the constable, having a warrant to search merely for pieces of wood and pieces of a fuse, he had no right whatever to go beyond that, to ransack the house (if I may use the expression) and to endeavour to find something which might implicate the pursuer in the charge which was preferred against him. But supposing that in a search which might have been improper originally, there were matters discovered which shewed the complicity of the pursuer in a crime, then I think the officers, I can hardly say would have been justified, but would have been excused by the result of their search. . . .

Lord Cranworth agreed with **Lord Chelmsford LC**
Lord Colonsay [dissented on the point of pleading, but continued:]

[A]s it is held that nothing that is done in this case interferes with the proposition which was contested in the Court below, – that a constable in executing a search warrant for certain articles, and finding other articles that tend to implicate the party, and taking those articles and the party himself also into custody, is only acting in the performance of what may be his duty – I think there is the less reason to regret that there should be any difference of opinion in regard to this case.
Appeal allowed.
Case remitted to the Court of Session.

Chic Fashions (West Wales) Ltd v Jones [1968] 2 QB 299, [1968] 1 All ER 229, [1968] 2 WLR 201, Court of Appeal

In 1965 and 1966, thieves stole from several shops and factories ladies' clothes of various makes, including 'Ian Peters', 'Mornessa', 'Mansfield' and 'Blanes'. The police received information that clothes of these makes were being sold at shops owned by Chic Fashions, at less than trade prices. The police obtained search warrants under section 42 of the Larceny Act 1916 which authorised searches in each shop for clothes which had recently been stolen from Ian Peters Ltd. The police who searched the Llanelli branch found no 'Ian Peters' garments, but did find other makes of clothes of the kinds which had been stolen. The labels had been removed and they were being sold at much less than the trade prices. The police thought that these were stolen and seized them. Subsequently, the police accepted that these goods had been acquired lawfully, and returned them. Chic Fashions sued the police for damages. It was agreed that none of the clothes was within the description of the search warrant, that none was stolen, that none was used in evidence on a criminal charge but that the police believed on reasonable grounds that they were stolen goods and would form material evidence in a prosecution.

Lord Denning MR: . . . The question is: were the police entitled to seize goods not mentioned in the warrant but which they believed on reasonable grounds to have been stolen?

You might have thought that this question would have been settled long ago. But, strangely enough, there is very little authority upon it. Our English law has always had great regard for the integrity of a man's home. In 1604 Lord Coke declared that "every man's house is his castle" (see *Semayne's Case* (1604) 5 Co Rep 91a and 3 Inst., cap. 73), and his aphorism has come down the centuries. It was given dramatic force by William Pitt, Earl of Chatham, when he declared that:

'The poorest man may in his cottage bid defiance to all the forces of the Crown. It may be frail—its roof may shake—the wind may blow through it—the storm may enter—the rain may enter—but the King of England cannot enter—all his force dares not cross the threshold of the ruined tenement':

see Brougham's Statesmen in the Times of George III, First Series.

Exceptions, however, have had to be made to this principle. They have been made in the public interest. No man's house is to be used as a hiding place for thieves or a receptacle for stolen goods. If there is reasonable ground for believing that there are stolen goods in the house, information can be laid before a magistrate on oath: and the magistrate can then issue a search warrant authorising a constable to enter the house and seize the goods. That case was the only exception permitted by the common law. In no other case was a constable allowed to enter and search a man's house. Even if a constable suspected that counterfeit coins were being made there, or banknotes forged, he could not at common law obtain a search warrant to enter.

[His Lordship referred to *Entick v Carrington* above, p. 74]

Since that time further exceptions have been made by statute. In a great many cases now Acts of Parliament permit magistrates to grant search warrants so as to enable the police to enter and see if a house is being used for unlawful purposes, such as coining, betting, and so forth. But with none of these are we concerned today. We have to deal with stolen goods, for which the common law always allowed a search warrant to be granted. There is, to be sure, a statute on the matter, section 42 of the Larceny Act, 1916, but, so far as concerns stolen goods, it does little more than state the common law. It says that:

'(1) If it is made to appear by information on oath before a justice of the peace that there is reasonable cause to believe that any person has in his custody or possession or on his premises any property whatsoever, with respect to which any offence against this Act has been committed, the justice may grant a warrant to search for and seize the same.'

That section deals with goods mentioned in the warrant. It does not say whether the constable can seize goods not mentioned in the warrant. To solve this question we must resort to the cases.

At one time the courts held that the constable could seize only those goods which answered the description given in the warrant. He had to make sure, at his peril, that the goods were the very goods in the warrant. If he seized other goods, not mentioned in the warrant, he was a trespasser in respect of those goods: and not only so, but he was a trespasser on the land itself, a trespasser ab initio, in accordance with the doctrine of the *Six Carpenters' Case* (1610) 8 Co Rep 146a, which held that, if a man abuse an authority given by the law, he becomes a trespasser ab initio.

If such had remained the law, no constable would be safe in executing a search warrant. The law as it then stood was a boon to receivers of stolen property and an impediment to the forces of law and order. So much so, that the judges gradually altered it. In the year 1800 they held that a constable is entitled to seize, by virtue of the warrant, any goods which he reasonably believes to be included in the warrant, even though it should turn out afterwards that his belief was mistaken. That is shown by *Price v Messenger* (1800) 2 Bos & P 158. A search warrant authorised a constable to search Price's shop for a quantity of sugar which had been "stolen from some ship or vessel lying in the River Thames." The constable entered the shop and seized some sugar there which Price was selling under prime cost, and also a bag of nails and two parcels of tea of which no satisfactory account was given. After enquiries were made, it turned out that they were not stolen, and all the goods were returned to Price. He then sued the constable for trespass. It was argued for Price that "the warrant was to seize stolen sugar, and the officers were bound at their peril to seize stolen sugar or none at all." The court rejected this argument. It was held that the constable was not liable in respect of the sugar. As to the tea and nails, the constable admitted that he was not justified in taking them because they were not mentioned in the warrant: and he suffered judgment by default in respect of them.

In 1827 the judges extended the protection of a constable further. They held that a constable is entitled to seize, by virtue of the warrant, not only the goods mentioned in the warrant, but also any other goods which are likely to furnish evidence of the *identity* of the stolen goods so as to show that they really are the goods mentioned in the warrant. This is shown by *Crozier* v *Cundey* (1827) 6 B & C 232. Cundey owned 100 lbs. of cotton copps contained in two packing cases. They were stolen from him. A search warrant authorised a constable to enter Crozier's house to search for the "100 lbs. weight of cotton copps." The warrant did not mention the packing cases. The constable found the cotton in packing cases. He seized not only the cotton but also the packing cases in which it was contained. Then Cundey told the constable that there were other things of his. Thereupon he and the constable ransacked the place looking for other things. They rummaged for half an hour and ultimately took away a tin pan and a sieve besides the cotton. There was no reason for supposing that Crozier had stolen the things. There had been previous disputes between Crozier and Cundey about property. Crozier alleged that the seizure of the packing cases, tin pan and sieve was illegal because they were not mentioned in the warrant and that the illegality related back so as to make the original entry unlawful. He sued Cundey and the constable for trespass (i) for entering the house (trespass ab initio) and (ii) for seizing the goods. . . . [T]he Court of King's Bench. . . held that the trial judge was right in rejecting the claim for the seizure of the packing cases, because they were likely to furnish evidence of the identity of the cotton copps. But they held that he ought not to have nonsuited the plaintiff in respect of the tin pan and sieve. Abbott CJ said 9 Dow & Ry KB 224 at 226.:

> 'If those articles had from their nature been likely to furnish evidence of the *identity* of the articles stolen and mentioned in the warrant, I should have been inclined to assent to Mr. Reader's argument, and to think that there might have been reasonable ground for seizing them, though not mentioned in the warrant. But it cannot be contended that the tin pan and the hair sieve were articles likely to furnish such evidence, and therefore I am of opinion that the nonsuit cannot be supported.'

Before leaving this case, it should be noticed that Crozier failed in his claim for trespass to the house (trespass ab initio). This illustrates the proposition that nowadays if a constable lawfully enters a house by virtue of a search warrant and seizes the goods mentioned in the warrant, his entry does not become unlawful simply because he unjustifiably seizes other goods. He is liable for trespass in respect of those other goods, but not for trespass to the house: see *Canadian Pacific Wine Co* v *Tuley* [1921] 2 AC 417.

In *Crozier v Cundey* (1827) 9 Dow & Ry KB 224 seizure of other goods was only allowed so as to prove the *identity* of the stolen goods. The next case goes to allow the seizure of other goods so as to prove the *guilt* of the thief or receiver.

[His Lordship referred to *Pringle v Bremner and Stirling*, above, p. 80].

Those are the only cases on search warrants. But the last extension (where a constable may seize other goods which go to prove *guilt*) is supported by the cases on warrants of arrest

[His Lordship referred to *Dillon v O'Brien and Davis*, below, p.85]

I must mention, however, *Elias v Pasmore* [1934] 2 KB 164 [see below, p. 88] Horridge J. said at 173):

> 'In my opinion the seizure of these exhibits was justified, because they were capable of being used and *were used* as evidence in this trial. If I am right in the above view, the original seizure of these exhibits, though improper at the time, would therefore be excused.'

It will be noticed that Horridge J. relied on the fact that the documents *were* used in evidence at the trial. But I cannot think that it is a necessary condition to justify their seizure. It may often happen that, on investigation, the prosecution decide not to go on with the case. The seizure must be justified at the time, irrespective of whether the case goes to trial or not. It cannot be made lawful or unlawful according to what happens afterwards.

Such are the cases. They contain no broad statement of principle: but proceed, in our English fashion, from case to case until the principle emerges. Now the time has come when we must endeavour to state it. We have to consider, on the one hand, the freedom of the individual. The security of his home is not to be broken except for the most compelling reason. On the other hand, we have to consider the interest of society at large in finding out wrongdoers and repressing crime. In these present times, with the ever-increasing wickedness there is about, honest citizens must help the police and not hinder them in their efforts to track down criminals. I look at it in this way: So far as a man's individual liberty is concerned, the law is settled concerning powers of arrest. A constable may arrest him and deprive him of his liberty, if he has reasonable grounds for believing that a felony (now an "arrestable offence") has been committed and that he is the man. I see no reason why goods should be more sacred than persons. In my opinion, when a constable enters a house by virtue of a search warrant for stolen goods, he may seize not only the goods which he reasonably believes to be covered by the warrant, but also any other goods which he believes on reasonable grounds to have been stolen and to be material evidence on a charge of stealing or receiving against the person in possession of them or anyone associated with him. Test it this way: Suppose the constable does not find the goods mentioned in the warrant but finds other goods which he reasonably believes to be stolen. Is he to quit the premises and go back to the magistrate and ask for another search warrant to cover these other goods? If he went away, I should imagine that in nine cases out of ten, by the time he came back with a warrant, these other goods would have disappeared. The true owner would not recover them. The evidence of the crime would have been lost. That would be to favour thieves and to discourage honest men. Even if it should turn out that the constable was mistaken and that the other goods were not stolen goods at all, nevertheless so long as he acted reasonably and did not retain them longer than necessary, he is protected. The lawfulness of his conduct must be judged at the time and not by what happens. afterwards. I know that at one time a man could be made a trespasser ab initio by the doctrine of relation back. But that is no longer true. The *Six Carpenters' Case* (1610) 8 Co Rep 146a was a by-product of the old forms of action. Now that they are buried, it can be interred with their bones.

In this case, on the agreed facts, the police had reasonable ground for believing the 65 items of clothing to have been stolen and to be material evidence on a criminal charge against the plaintiff company or its officers. So they seized them. On investigation they found out that they were not stolen and they returned them. On the principles I have stated they are not liable.

I would allow this appeal and give judgment to the defendant.

Diplock LJ: . . . [U]nless forced to do so by recent binding authority, I decline to accept that a police officer who is unquestionably justified at common law in arresting a person whom he has reasonable grounds to believe is guilty of receiving stolen goods, is not likewise justified in the less draconian act of seizing what he, on reasonable grounds, believes to be the stolen goods in that person's possession. The purpose of the seizure in such a case is twofold: first, that the goods may be produced as material evidence upon the prosecution of a criminal charge against the person from whom they were seized, and, secondly, that after the trial they may be restored to their rightful owner; and a similar justification exists for their detention so long as the detainor has reasonable grounds for believing that such a charge will lie and that the goods will be material evidence upon its prosecution. I leave aside the question, which does not arise in the present case, of what constitutes sufficient justification for the seizure and detention if the contemplated charge is not against the person in whose possession the goods were at the time of seizure. . . .

Neither in *Price v Messenger* (1800) 2 Bos & P 158, nor in *Crozier v Cundey* (1827) 6 B & C 232, the cases nearest in their facts to these, was the point which has been argued in this appeal taken. In the former case the defendants had suffered judgement by default in respect of the goods not described in the search warrant. In the latter, in which the facts and argument are very summarily reported, the argument appears to have been limited to the contention that the seizure of goods not mentioned in the warrant was justified if 'they might be serviceable in the investigation of the felony mentioned in the warrant.' This contention was accepted as correct, but it was found that the particular facts in the case did not support it.

The point of law in this appeal thus comes before us in 1967 untrammelled by authority. It is for us to say how in 1967 it should be answered. For my part I, like the Master of the Rolls, would answer it by allowing this appeal.

Salmon LJ: . . . On the facts of this case I would hold that the defendant has a good defence at common law. I go no further. In particular I wish to make it plain that I incline to the view that if a policeman finds property which he reasonably believes to be stolen in the possession of a person whom he has no reasonable grounds to believe is criminally implicated, the policeman has no common law right to seize the property. If, for example, a policeman is admitted to a house, and whilst there sees some silver on sideboard which he reasonably believes is stolen property but which he has no reason to suppose was dishonestly acquired by the householder, he cannot take it away without the householder's consent.

Appeal allowed.

NOTES

1. The *entry* of the police officers was authorised by the warrant. The case here concerned the legality of the *seizure* of the specific articles.
2. See case notes by J. A. Weir [1968] CLJ 193 and D. W. Pollard (1968) 31 MLR 573
3. Note the use made of this case by Lord Denning MR in *Ghani v Jones* [1970] 1 QB 693 below p. 94.
4. In relation to search for stolen goods s. 42 of the Larceny Act 1916 has been replaced by s. 26 of the Theft Act 1968:

> '**26.**–(1) If it is made to appear by information on oath before a justice of the peace that there is reasonable cause to believe that any person has in his custody or possession or on his premises any stolen goods, the justice may grant a warrant to search for and seize the same; but no warrant to search for stolen goods shall be addressed to a person other than a constable except under the authority of an enactment expressly so providing.
> (2) An officer of police not below the rank of superintendent may give a constable written authority to search any premises for stolen goods–
> (a) if the person in occupation of the premises has been convicted within the preceding five years of handling stolen goods or of any offence involving dishonesty and punishable with imprisonment; or
> (b) if a person who has been convicted within the preceding five years of handling stolen goods has within the preceding twelve months been in occupation of the premises.
> (3) Where under this section a person is authorised to search premises for stolen goods, he may enter and search the premises accordingly, and may seize any goods he believes to be stolen goods.'
> (4) (*Repealed*)
> (5) (*Omitted*).

Sub-s. (3) goes beyond the ratio decidendi of *Chic Fashions Ltd v Jones*. In principle, should sub-s. (3) be regarded as an exhaustive statement of the items that may be seized under a warrant in addition to those specified in it? Note that it does not mention items 'likely to furnish evidence of the identity of' the stolen goods (cf. *Crozier v Cundey* (1827) 6 B & C 232), or items which are merely 'evidence' (cf. *Ghani v Jones* [1970] 1 QB 693, below p. 94).
5. In the US, the seizure of items not named in the warrant is sometimes permissible.

> 'An example of the applicability of the 'plain view' doctrine is the situation in which the police have a warrant to search a given area for specific objects, and in the course of the search come across some other articles of incriminating character. . . . Where, once an otherwise lawful search is in progress, the police inadvertently come upon a piece of evidence, it would often be a needless inconvenience, and sometimes dangerous—to the evidence or to the police themselves—to require them to ignore it until they have obtained a warrant particularly describing it.'

(*Coolidge v New Hampshire*, 403 US 443 (1971) Stewart J). If the police know the location of an object and intend to seize it, a warrant must be obtained complying with the Fourth Amendment. An object can only be seized under the 'plain view' rule if there is probable cause that it constitutes the fruit, instrumentalities or evidence of crime.

(b) SEARCH AND SEIZURE ANCILLARY TO ARREST

Dillon v O'Brien and Davis (1887) 16 Cox CC 245, 20 LR Ir 300, Exchequer Division of the High Court in Ireland

The defendant police officers obtained a warrant for the arrest of John Dillon M.P. on a charge of conspiracy. They claimed that in execution of the warrant they entered the plaintiff's house (the outer door being open), and found him, with other parties to the alleged conspiracy, receiving rents from certain tenants. The conspirators had books and papers in which they were making entries of the receipt of rents.

They arrested the plaintiff, and seized bank notes and other papers for the purpose of producing them as evidence in the conspiracy prosecution. While the prosecution was pending, the plaintiff claimed damages, inter alia, for the wrongful seizure and wrongful detention of the bank notes and papers.

Palles CB: . . . Before . . . I proceed to deal with the case of a misdemeanour [such as conspiracy], it is necessary to see how the law stands in reference to greater crimes. In doing this, I desire to confine myself to the exact question which, I think, arises—that is, to a case in which the allegation is not that there was a reasonable suspicion of the plaintiff's guilt, but that he was actually guilty; that he was arrested whilst in the actual commission of the crime, that the articles taken were being at the time used in the commission of the crime; and in which their materiality as evidence is also stated as a fact, and not upon suspicion. If, then the right here claimed does not exist, even in treason and felony, it would follow that upon the arrest of a murderer caught in the act, and on the moment lawfully arrested, whilst the weapon with which the crime had been committed was in his hand, it would be illegal for the constable to detain that weapon for the purpose of evidence; so also would it be illegal for the officers of the law to take possession of poisons found in the possession of one who had caused death by poison; and, even in treason, letters from co-traitors evidencing the common treasonable design, found in the possession of a traitor, would be safe from capture upon his arrest, although from the earliest times it has been the settled and unvarying practice to seize such proofs of guilt and give them in evidence at the trial. Even were there no trace in the books of the question having been considered, this invariable practice in trials for treason and felony would prevent my affirming the plaintiff's contention. But, in truth, the point is not without authority. There are, at least, three cases in which attention was directed to the question, and in which the existence of the right was not argued, but assumed. . . .

[His Lordship referred to *Crozier v Cundey* (1827) 6 B & C 232 which is discussed by Lord Denning MR in *Chic Fashions* above, p. 80. His Lordship then discussed *R v Barnett* (1829) 3 C & P 600 and *R v Frost* (1840) 9 C & P 129 where it was held that money taken from persons arrested had to be returned unless it was material evidence.]

I, therefore, think that it is clear, and beyond doubt, that, at least in cases of treason and felony, constables (and probably also private persons) are entitled, upon a lawful arrest by them of one charged with treason or felony, to take and detain property found in his possession which will form material evidence in his prosecution for that crime and I take the only real question upon this defence as being, whether this right extends to cases of misdemeanour. No case has been cited in which the right (in reference to misdemeanour) has been judicially decided to exist, and no text book draws the distinction here attempted to be drawn. The matter must, therefore, be determined on principle. For this purpose I must first ascertain the reason of the rule as applicable to felony. . . . Its purpose and object, viz., to produce the goods in evidence in a judicial proceeding, appears to me to show that it must be derived from the interest which the State has in a person guilty (or reasonably believed to be guilty) of a crime being brought to justice . . . [T]he interest of the State in the person charged being brought to trial in due course necessarily extends, as well to the preservation of material evidence of his guilt or innocence, as to his custody for the purpose of trial. His custody is of no value if the law is powerless to prevent the abstraction or destruction of this evidence, without which a trial would be no more than an empty form. But if there be a right to production or preservation of this evidence, I cannot see how it can be enforced otherwise than by capture. If material evidences of crime are in the possession of a third party, production can be enforced by the Crown, by *subpœna duces tecum*. But no such

writ can be effective in the case of the person charged. It appears to me to be clear that this must be the origin of the right in felony; and that, being derived from the common law, it ought, *primâ facie* at least, to be deemed to exist in all cases in which that interest of the State exists. . . . This brings me to the only case relied on by the plaintiff: (*Entick v Carrington* (1765) 19 State Tr 1029, 1063–4 [above p. 74].) The question there was as to the legality of a warrant, not only to seize and apprehend the plaintiff and bring him before a Secretary of State, but also to seize his books and papers. . . . It was, of course, decided that that warrant was illegal; but the case, as a decision, is not in point here. The right here claimed is not to take all the plaintiff's papers, but those only which are evidence of his guilt; and the claim is based, not as in *Entick v Carrington* (1765) 19 State Trials 1029, upon a warrant issued upon mere suspicion, but upon an allegation of actual guilt, and a lawful apprehension of the guilty person. . . . I am satisfied that, in pronouncing that judgment, Lord Camden had not before his mind cases of seizure of evidences of guilt upon lawful apprehension, as distinguished from general warrants to seize all papers. . . . As the right to take the papers exists, I think it clear that, in some states of circumstances, there must be an ancillary right to take them by force from the plaintiff, using no unnecessary violence.
Dowse B and **Andrews J** concurred.

NOTES

1. The alleged conspiracy was the 'Plan of Campaign' – a phase in Irish land agitation led by John Dillon MP and William O'Brien MP (The O'Brien of the case name was one of the police officers). The 'Plan' was for tenants to offer to pay a portion of the rent to their landlords, and if the offer was rejected, as would usually be the case, to pay the money to trustees. Dillon, O'Brien and others acted as trustees at a series of 'rent-collections'. On 13 December 1886, Dillon was bound over to be of good behaviour on a recognisance of £1,000 with two sureties of the same amount, and the 'Plan' was declared by O'Brien J to be 'clearly, distinctly and absolutely illegal' (*The Times*, 15 December 1886). In argument, Dillon challenged the Attorney-General to put him on trial for conspiracy before a jury in any part of Ireland. The authorities obliged. The events leading to the litigation were described by W. O'Brien in *The Times* for 18 December. They took place in the rooms of the National Land League at Loughrea, where two offices were opened to receive the rents at Lord Clanricarde's estates. Dillon was downstairs, and O'Brien upstairs. O'Brien had some warning of the raid: plain clothes policemen were noticed in the offices, and a body of police were seen marching down the street. His books and papers were spirited away, leaving a blank copying book and a piece of blotting paper, which the police seized. Dillon was not so quick off the mark. The police seized about £88 out of a total received of £1,100. The prosecutions were transferred to Dublin from Loughrea, but ultimately failed. The effect was not to halt the rent collecting, but to drive it underground (see F. St. L. Lyons, (1965) Irish Historical Studies xiv, No 56 p. 313).

2. The English case law on search and seizure ancillary to arrest is sparse. In *Bessell v Wilson* (1853) 20 LT OS 233, 17 JP 52, 567, B. was awarded damages for false imprisonment against W, a JP who had exceeded his jurisdiction in issuing a warrant for B's arrest. B had declined to appear in person on a charge of infringement of copyright, but had appeared by counsel. B was searched at the police station following his arrest, in accordance with general police practice. At the close of argument on W's application to have the verdict set aside, Lord Campbell CJ made the following observations (17 JP 52):

'. . . At the conclusion of the trial of this case, I expressed my disapprobation of the manner in which the plaintiff had been searched when taken to the station house. I repeat the disapprobation which I then expressed, for there is no right in a case of this kind to inflict the indignity to which the plaintiff had been subjected. But I have been informed that an erroneous impression of what I said has gone abroad. It was supposed that I had said that there was no right in any one to search a prisoner at any time. I have not said so. It is often the duty of an officer to search a prisoner. If for instance, a man is taken in the commission of a felony, he may be searched to see whether he has any instruments of violence about him, and, in like manner, if he be taken on a charge of arson, he may be searched to see whether he has any fire-boxes or matches about his person . . . It may be highly satisfactory, and indeed necessary that the prisoner should be searched. I have never said that searching a prisoner was always a forbidden act. What I said applied to circumstances such as existed in this case. If a tradesman should be charged with an offence such as that with which the plaintiff was charged in this case, and he appeared before the magistrate by counsel and not in person, and a warrant issued against him not charging him with any crime, but merely to make him appear in person, the act of searching him was contrary to law. It is said that the search here was justified, because the person in custody might have some instrument about him with which he might make away with or injure himself, or the alderman before whom he was brought. This does not appear a satisfactory reason; it assumes that when a man is apprehended, because he has in the first instance appeared by counsel, and not in person, he will take with him the means of committing suicide or murder. This is a most absurd supposition.'

Similarly, in *Leigh v Cole* (1853) 6 Cox CC 329 at 332, Vaughan Williams J in the course of summing-up in an action for damages for assault and false imprisonment, said:

'With respect to searching a prisoner, there is no doubt that a man when in custody may so conduct himself, by reason of violence of language or conduct, that a police officer may reasonably think it prudent and right to search him, in order to ascertain whether he has any weapon with which he might do mischief to the person or commit a breach of the peace; but at the same time it is quite wrong to suppose that any general rule can be applied to such a case. Even when a man is confined for being drunk and disorderly, it is not correct to say that he must submit to the degradation of being searched, as the searching of such a person must depend upon all the circumstances of the case.'

The jury found for the defendant, a police officer who had arrested a drunk in circumstances where a breach of the peace was reasonably apprehended. Consider the view expressed by Horridge J in *Elias v Pasmore* (below) as to the ambit of the power to search on arrest, in the light of these statements. It appears to be the general practice of the police to search all arrested persons either at the time of arrest, or in the police station (see J. D. Devlin, *Police Procedure, Administration and Organization* (1966) pp. 347–349; cf. *Moriarty's Police Law* 23rd edn. (1976), p. 17.) A crown court judge has held that the police have no legal right to remove jewelry from an arrested person where there was no suggestion that it might cause injury and it had no connection with the offence for which she was arrested (*R v Naylor* [1979] Crim LR 532).

3. In *Tyler and Witt v London and South Western Rly Co* (1884) Cab & E 285, W, who claimed to be the owner of a thrashing machine (*sic*) took it from one Utting and sent it by rail to T at Maidenhead. U obtained a warrant for the arrest of W. Acting under this warrant a police constable seized the machine from the railway company and reconsigned it to Andover, where it was collected by the constable. T and W sought damages from the company for conversion. One ground given by Huddleston B for holding that there was no case to go to the jury was that 'police constables have the power to take possession of goods for the purposes of a prosecution under a personal warrant of arrest, and do not require a distress warrant for that purpose'. W was not present when the machine was first intercepted, and, although he was present in Andover when the machine was handed over to the constable, it is not stated whether he was arrested at that time. The New Zealand Court of Appeal in *Barnett and*

Grant v Campbell (1902) 21 NZLR 484 held per Cooper J at 493 that the 'right to a personal search is clearly dependent not upon the *right* to arrest, but the *fact* of arrest, and that at the time of search the person is *in custodia legis*'.

4. See further *Ghani v Jones,* below p. 94, especially p. 99 notes 7–9.

5. In the United States, it is constitutional for an arresting officer to search an arrested person in order to remove weapons or evidence (*Chimel v California* 395 US (1969)), irrespective of whether there are grounds to suspect that weapons or evidence may actually be found (*US v Robinson* 414 US 218 (1973)). Under *Chimel* the search may extend to the area within the arrested persons 'immediate control' 'construing that phrase to mean the area from within which he might gain possession of a weapon or destructible evidence' (395 US 752 at 763).

Elias v Pasmore [1934] 2 KB 164, 103 LJ KB 223, 150 LT 438, 93 JP 92, 50 TLR 196, 32 LGR 23, Horridge J

The first three of the four plaintiffs (Sidney Elias, Emrys Llewellyn George James and Wal Hannington) were lessees of 35, Great Russell Street, the headquarters of the National Unemployed Workers' Movement. On 1 November 1932, a number of police officers, including Inspector Pasmore of the Special Branch, raided the offices to execute a warrant for the arrest of H on a charge of attempting in a speech in Trafalgar Square to cause disaffection among the members of the Metropolitan Police Force, contrary to section 3 of the Police Act 1919. They arrested H, searched the offices and took away a large quantity of documents. They had no search warrant. On 8 November, H was convicted on the incitement to disaffection charge and sentenced to three months' imprisonment. In December, E was convicted of inciting L and H to commit sedition and was sentenced to two years' imprisonment. Various documents were returned on 1 November, and others on 8, 10 and 18 November, but the rest ('bundle 2(A)') were retained by the police. None of the documents in bundle 2(A) were used in the trial of H; some were used in the trial of E; and all were retained after the conclusion of the two trials. The plaintiffs claimed damages for trespass to the premises and trespass to and the conversion and detinue of the documents seized. One of the items was the copy of a letter signed 'PC' written by a police constable to the 'Worker's Weekly', which was found on H, and had been read out to the meeting in Trafalgar Square.

Horridge J: . . . I have . . . to consider how far the defendants were justified in seizing and removing the documents and goods which were in fact seized and removed. It was not contended before me that there was any general right of search or seizure, but it was submitted that in certain circumstances there was a right to seize and detain documents; but this contention, if correct, did not in any way justify the seizure and removal of the documents and goods which have already been returned, and I will deal later on in my judgment with the remedy which the plaintiffs have in respect of such seizure and removal.

The propositions put forward with regard to the removal of the remaining documents in bundle 2 (A) were: (1.) that there was a right to search the person arrested; (2.) that the police may take all articles which were in the possession or control of the person arrested and which may be or are material on a charge against him or any other person; (3.) that the police, having lawfully entered, are protected if they take documents which subsequently turn out to be relevant on a charge of a criminal nature against any person whatever; (4.) that the police are entitled to retain property taken until the conclusion of any charge on which the articles are material.

In dealing with these different propositions, I only propose to deal with the authorities which seem to me to be the most relevant to this enquiry, although others have been cited to me. (1.): As to the right to search on arrest. This right seems to be clearly established by the footnote to *Bessell v Wilson* (1853) 20 LT OS 223, 1 E & B 489 in the report in the *Law Times*, where Lord Campbell clearly lays down that this right exists, but this right does not seem to me to authorize what was done in this case, namely, to seize and take away large quantities of documents and other property found on premises occupied by persons other than the person of whom the arrest was made.

As to the second contention, I think the case of *Dillon v O'Brien* (1887) 20 LR Ir 300, at 316, clearly lays down that constables are entitled upon a lawful arrest by them of a person charged to take and detain property found in his possession which will form material evidence on his prosecution for that crime, and I think, for the reasons hereinafter stated with regard to the third contention, that that would include property which would form material evidence on the prosecution of any criminal charge. This, however, would not justify the seizure of the documents in this case with the exception of the letter signed 'PC', a copy of which was found on Hannington, and which is in the bundle 2 (A).

In support of the third contention, the Attorney-General relied on the case of *Pringle v Bremner and Stirling* [(1867) 5 Macph (Ct of Sess) 55, above, p. 80].

That case seems to me to show that in the opinion of the Lord Chancellor and Lord Colonsay, though the seizure of documents was originally wrongful, if it in fact turned out that the documents seized were documents which might be properly used in a prosecution against any one, then the seizure would become excused. This, however, is a Scotch case, and must not be taken to have been decided on the law of England, and it becomes necessary therefore to consider whether in principle the same doctrine can be applied to a seizure of documents in England. There was no direct authority cited to me in support of the proposition in English law.

In examining the case of *Dillon v O'Brien* (1887) 20 LR Ir 300, [above, p. 85] and the judgment of Palles CB, it seems to me that the principle on which he held that there was a right to detain property in the possession of the person arrested is that the interest of the State in the person charged being brought to trial in due course necessarily extends as well to the preservation of material evidence of his guilt or innocence as to his custody for the purpose of trial.

[His Lordship also referred to *Crozier v Cundey*, discussed by Lord Denning in *Chic Fashions Ltd v Jones*, above p. 80.]

It therefore seems to me that the interests of the State must excuse the seizure of documents, which seizure would otherwise be unlawful, if it appears in fact that such documents were evidence of a crime committed by any one, and that so far as the documents in this case fall into this category, the seizure of them is excused.

The documents coming within this description were all the documents contained in bundle 2 (A) which were marked as exhibits and which were used at the trial of Elias. It was admitted by counsel for the plaintiffs that these documents were capable of being evidence in the case against Elias, who was convicted of unlawfully soliciting and inciting Emrys Glunf Llewellyn and Walter Hannington to commit the crime of sedition. In my opinion the seizure of these exhibits was justified, because they were capable of being and were used as evidence in this trial. If I am right in the above view, the original seizure of these exhibits, though improper at the time would therefore be excused.

As to the fourth proposition, that the police are entitled to retain property the taking of which is excused until the conclusion of any charge on which the articles are material, Wright J says in the case of *R v Lushington. ex parte Otto* [1894] 1 QB 420 at 423: 'In this country I take it that it is undoubted law that it is within the power of, and is the duty of, constables to retain for use in Court things which may be evidences of crime, and which have come into the possession of the constables without wrong on their part. I think it is also undoubted law that when articles have once been produced in Court by witnesses it is right and necessary for the Court, or the constable in whose charge they are placed (as is generally the case), to preserve and retain them, so that they may be always available for the purposes of justice until the trial is concluded.' In this case, however, both trials of Hannington and Elias have been concluded, and I think there is no answer now to the claim for their detention after demand or for the 10*l*. claimed as damages for their detention.

The Attorney-General stated that for the purposes of this case only he did not intend to contend that the plaintiffs, because these documents were of a seditious character, could have no property in the exhibits which had been used on the charge against Elias.

As regards the claim for damages for trespass to documents and goods, I have held with regard to the letter signed 'PC', in bundle 2 (A), and also the exhibits used on the trial of Elias, that they were properly seized. The police in seizing the other documents were not actuated by any improper motives, and there is no evidence that the plaintiffs have sustained in any way any special damage, and I think in respect of this matter the sum of 20*l*. should be awarded.

There will therefore be judgment for the plaintiffs for 20*l.* damages for trespass, an order for
the return of the documents comprised in 2 (A), 10*l.* damages for detention of those
documents, and the defendants must pay the costs of the action.
Judgment for plaintiffs.

NOTES

1. The facts and counsel's arguments in this case are most fully reported in
50 TLR 196. See also E. C. S. Wade (1934) 50 LQR 354 and below, p. 298.
2. No search warrant could have been issued in these circumstances.
3. Note that the facts of this case are distinguishable from those in *Dillon v
O'Brien and Davis* on the grounds (1) that the premises searched were not
owned by the arrested person, H; (2) the documents seized did not relate to
the crime committed by H; and (3) the officers searched the premises, and
did not merely seize items which they happened to see in the course of
arresting H. Which, if any, of these grounds ought to operate as a legal
limitation on the rights of the police to search or seize?
4. Do the statements in *Pringle v Bremner and Stirling* support the
proposition that the police may seize evidence relating to a crime
committed *by anyone*? How far is it appropriate to rely on a case
concerning search under a search warrant in the context of search ancillary
to arrest?
5. The result of this case was held to be correct in *Ghani v Jones* (below p.
94), but the reasoning of Horridge J was disapproved in a number of
respects. See also note 9 at p. 100.
6. The history of the NUWM is discussed in G. Peele and C. Cook (eds.)
The Politics of Reappraisal 1918–1939, (1975), Chap. 6 (J. Stevenson);
Stevenson and Cook, *The Slump* (1977); and R. Hayburn, 'The Police and
the Hunger Marchers', *The International Review of Social History* (1973).

(c) OTHER WARRANTLESS SEARCHES AND SEIZURES

The case of *R v Waterfield and Lynn* [1964] 1 QB 164 illustrates the
limitations of police power to seize property without a warrant, although
doubts were expressed as to the correctness of that decision in *Ghani v Jones*
[1970] 1 QB 693, below p. 94.
   There are a number of statutory powers whereby the police may stop and
search persons without a warrant. These are listed in Appendix E to the
*Home Office Evidence to the Royal Commission on Criminal Procedure,
Memorandum No. III.* The most important in practice are those concerning firearms (Firearms Act 1968, sections 47(3), 49(1) and (2)), drugs
(Misuse of Drugs Act 1971, section 23(2)) and, within the metropolitan
police district, goods stolen or unlawfully obtained (Metropolitan Police
Act 1839, section 66). The latter two provisions are set out below at pp. 92
and 93.

**R v Waterfield [1964] 1 QB 164, [1963] 3 All ER 659, [1963] 3 WLR 946, 48 Cr App Rep 42,
Court of Criminal Appeal**

Two police constables, PC's Willis and Brown were told by their sergeant
that a particular parked car had been involved in a serious offence, and that
he wished to examine it. The car had in fact been in collision with a wall,
and the police wished to obtain evidence relating to a possible charge of

dangerous driving. Lynn arrived and got into the driving seat. He was told that the sergeant wished to examine the car and that it had to remain where it was. Waterfield, the owner, then arrived. He said, among other things, 'You cannot impound my car', and told L to drive it away. L reversed, coming into slight contact with Brown, and then drove the car at Willis, who was forced to jump to one side. W had said: 'Drive it at him, he will get out of the way.' L was charged inter alia with assaulting the officers in the execution of their duty, contrary to section 38 of the Offences Against the Person Act 1861, and W inter alia with counselling, procuring and commanding L to commit the assault. The jury acquitted on the charges relating to Brown, and convicted on those relating to Willis. L and W appealed to the Court of Criminal Appeal.

Ashworth J delivered the judgment of the court (**Lord Parker CJ, Ashworth** and **Hinchcliffe JJ**):

. . . The first issue raised in this appeal is whether, on the facts as summarised above, the police constables, and in particular Willis, were acting in the due execution of their duty within the meaning of section 38 of the Offences against the Person Act, 1861, . . . The two constables had been told by their sergeant that the car had been involved in a serious offence, although neither of them had any personal knowledge of the circumstances, and it is not disputed that at the time when the incidents now under consideration occurred they were engaged in preventing removal of the car; the question is, whether they were entitled to do this, at any rate without making a charge or an arrest.

In such reported cases as have involved consideration of a police constable's duties, the courts have referred to those duties in general terms and have not attempted to lay down by way of definition the scope or extent of those duties. . . .

In the judgment of this court it would be difficult, and in the present case it is unnecessary, to reduce within specific limits the general terms in which the duties of police constables have been expressed. In most cases it is probably more convenient to consider what the police constable was actually doing and in particular whether such conduct was prima facie an unlawful interference with a person's liberty or property. If so, it is then relevant to consider whether (a) such conduct falls within the general scope of any duty imposed by statute or recognised at common law and (b) whether such conduct, albeit within the general scope of such a duty, involved an unjustifiable use of powers associated with the duty.

Thus, while it is no doubt right to say in general terms that police constables have a duty to prevent crime and a duty, when crime is committed, to bring the offender to justice, it is also clear from the decided cases that when the execution of these general duties involves interference with the person or property of a private person, the powers of constables are not unlimited. To cite only one example, in *Davis v Lisle* [1936] 2 KB 434 it was held that even if a police officer had a right to enter a garage to make inquiries, he became a trespasser after the appellant had told him to leave the premises, and that he was not therefore acting thenceforward in the execution of his duty, with the result that the appellant could not be convicted of assaulting or obstructing him in the execution of his duty.

In the present case it is plain that the police constables Willis and Brown, no doubt acting in obedience to the order of their superior officer, were preventing Lynn and Waterfield taking the car away and were thereby interfering with them and with the car. It is to be noted that neither of the appellants had been charged or was under arrest and accordingly the decision in *Dillon v O'Brien and Davis* (1887) 20 LR Ir 300 does not assist the prosecution.

It was contended that the two police constables were acting in the execution of a duty to preserve for use in court evidence of a crime, and in a sense they were, but the execution of that duty did not in the view of this court authorise them to prevent removal of the car in the circumstance. In the course of argument instances were suggested where difficulty might arise if a police officer were not entitled to prevent removal of an article which had been used in the course of a crime, for example, an axe used by a murderer and thrown away by him. Such a case can be decided if and when it arises; for the purposes of the present appeal it is sufficient to say that in the view of this court the two police constables were not acting in the due execution of their duty at common law when they detained the car.

Apart, however, from the position at common law, it was contended that Police Constable Willis was acting in the execution of a duty arising under section 223 of the Road Traffic Act, 1960. That section, so far as material, provides that 'a person driving a motor vehicle on a road . . . shall stop . . . on being so required by a police constable in uniform.'

That argument, however, assuming that the car park is a road, involves considerable difficulties. In the first place its validity depends upon a construction of the section which would enable the constable not merely to require a moving vehicle to stop but to require a stationary vehicle not to move. The court finds it unnecessary to reach a conclusion on that because, in the second place, it is to be observed that the section is merely giving a power as opposed to laying down a duty. It seems to the court that it would be an invalid exercise of the power given by the section if, as here, the object of its exercise was to do something, namely, to detain a vehicle, which as already stated the constable had in the circumstances no right to do.

For these reasons appeals against the convictions in respect of the assault on Police Constable Willis must be allowed and the convictions quashed.

Appeals allowed.

NOTES

1. Convictions of L for dangerous driving and of W for inciting L to drive in a dangerous manner were upheld.
2. This case is discussed at length by P. J. Fitzgerald at [1965] Crim LR 23. Fitzgerald argues that it was not clear that the officers were committing a tort or a crime (see pp. 29–31). It has been suggested, however, that the officers may have been guilty of the offence of wilfully obstructing the highway contrary to the Highways Act 1959, s. 121 (F. J. Marshall, [1965] Crim LR 184).
3. The term 'duty' in this context may be used widely to mean 'function' (e.g. 'It is not part of a policeman's duty to entertain the general public by busking') or narrowly, in contradistinction to 'power' (e.g. 'I hold it to be the duty . . . of every chief constable to enforce the law of the land': per Lord Denning MR in *R v Metropolitan Police Comr, ex parte Blackburn* [1968] 2 QB 118 at 136). Consider the sense in which the term 'duty' is used on each occasion that it appears in Ashworth J's judgment.
4. How can the fact that s. 223 of the Road Traffic Act 1960 (now s. 159 of the Road Traffic Act 1972) gives a 'power' rather than imposes a 'duty' affect the issue whether the constables were *entitled* to act as they did?
5. As a matter of policy, is it sensible that the police should lack a power to detain property in such circumstances as these? Cf. *Ghani v Jones* [1970] 1 QB 693, below p. 94.

Metropolitan Police Act 1839

66. Constables, etc., may apprehend persons committing offences, and detain suspicious vessels, and carriages, etc.
Any person found committing any offence punishable either upon indictment or as a misdemeanor upon summary conviction, by virtue of this Act, may be taken into custody without a warrant by any constable, or may be apprehended by the owner of the property on or with respect to which the offence shall be committed, or by his servant or any person authorised by him, and may be detained until he can be delivered into the custody of a constable to be dealt with according to law; and every such constable may also stop, search and detain any vessel, boat, cart, or carriage in or upon which there shall be reason to suspect that any thing stolen or unlawfully obtained may be found, and also any person who may be reasonably suspected of having or conveying in any manner any thing stolen or unlawfully obtained; . . .

NOTES

1. Similar provisions appear in local legislation in many parts of the country (Birkenhead, Birmingham, Burnley, Hertfordshire, Liverpool, City of London, Manchester, Newcastle-upon-Tyne, Oldham, Rochdale,

St. Helens, and Salford). All such provisions outside the Metropolitan Police District will lapse under the Local Government Act 1972 (see p. 150), and if still required, will have to be re-enacted in new local or national legislation. The Home Office stated to the Royal Commission on Criminal Procedure that these powers 'are considered very helpful by the police' (*Memorandum No. III* p. 30 (1978)). The Metropolitan Police Commissioner has suggested that this provision should apply throughout the country (Evidence to the Royal Commission, Part I, p. 9).
2. It has been suggested that the power to stop and search for firearms should be extended to cover persons reasonably suspected of carrying any offensive weapon in a public place (see *Home Office Evidence to the Royal Commission on Criminal Procedure, Memorandum No. III*, pp. 28–30; (*Written Evidence of the Commissioner of Police of the Metropolis* Part I, pp. 8–9).

Misuse of Drugs Act 1971

23 (2) If a constable has reasonable grounds to suspect that any person is in possession of a controlled drug in contravention of this Act or of any regulations made thereunder, the constable may—
    (a) search that person, and detain him for the purpose of searching him;
    (b) search any vehicle or vessel in which the constable suspects that the drug may be found, and for that purpose require the person in control of the vehicle or vessel to stop it;
    (c) seize and detain, for the purposes of proceedings under this Act, anything found in the course of the search which appears to the constable to be evidence of an offence under this Act.
In this subsection 'vessel' includes a hovercraft within the meaning of the Hovercraft Act 1968; and nothing in this subsection shall prejudice any power of search or any power to seize or detain property which is exercisable by a constable apart from this subsection.

NOTES

1. The power of search without a warrant contained in the forerunner to this provision (Dangerous Drugs Act 1967, s. 6) was found by the Advisory Committee on Drug Dependence to be much more controversial than the power to search under a warrant considered above at pp. 70, 74. (*Powers of Arrest and Search in Relation to Drug Offences* (1970) pp. 34–49). A minority of the committee favoured the abolition of the power (ibid., p. 37–40), and the substitution of arrest, with search following either in the street or at the police station. They argued that this would simplify the law and clarify and restrict police power.

The number of persons stopped and searched each year for controlled drugs is given in the annual Report of Her Majesty's Chief Inspector of Constabulary. In 1978, 18, 107 were searched, of whom 22 % were found to be in illegal possession of drugs. Thirty five formal complaints were made. Between 1972 and 1977 the 'success rate' varied from 24 % to 31 %.
2. In *Terry v Ohio* 392 US 1 (1968) the Supreme Court held that a police officer has the power, consistent with the Fourth Amendment (above p. 53), to 'stop and frisk' a suspicious person. He may stop him, question him and, for his own protection if he reasonably believes him to be armed, pat his outer clothing for a weapon. 'Probable cause' which would justify an arrest is not necessary, this being an exception to the principle stated at p. 53 above. (See LaFave, 67 Mich LR 39) In *Pennsylvania v Mimms* 434 US 106 (1977), the Supreme Court held constitutional a police practice of ordering motorists out of their cars when lawfully stopped for traffic

violations, even where there was no reason to suspect foul play. The interest in the officer's safety outweighed what was at most a mere inconvenience to the driver.

In addition to this, searches which are warrantless are permitted where ancillary to arrest (above p. 88), where there is probable cause to suspect that a vehicle contains items which by law are subject to seizure (*Carroll v US* 267 US 132 (1925)), where a police officer is in hot pursuit of an offender (*Warden v Hayden* 387 US 294 (1967)), or, perhaps, where there is a need for immediate action (e.g. *People v Sirhan* 497 P 2d 1121 (1972) where the Supreme Court of California upheld a warrantless search of the home of Sirhan Sirhan following his assassination of Robert F. Kennedy. The crime was of enormous gravity, and the mere possibility that there might be evidence of a conspiracy to assassinate prominent political leaders fully warranted the officers' actions; cf. *Vale v Louisiana* 399 US 30 (1970)).

7 *Ghani v Jones* and its progeny

Ghani v Jones [1970] 1 QB 693, [1969] 3 All ER 1700, [1969] 3 WLR 1158, Court of Appeal

The police were investigating the disappearance of the daughter-in-law of Abdul Ghani and Razia Begum, two of the plaintiffs (the third plaintiff being their daughter). They believed that the daughter-in-law had been murdered. Two police officers went to G's house. G asked them in. He was questioned about the disappearance by one officer while the other searched the house. At the request of the police, G handed over the passports for himself and his wife, and some letters. Six days later, G gave the police his daughter's passport. The plaintiffs issued a writ against the police asking for a mandatory order that the passports and letters be returned. The police made affidavits to the effect that in the event of charges being preferred 'some of the documents will be of evidential value and others certainly of potential evidential value', and that if the plaintiffs were to leave the United Kingdom 'they may not return'. Talbot J ([1970] 1 QB 695) made the order sought. The police appealed to the Court of Appeal. The police now conceded that preventing the plaintiffs from leaving the country was no justification for retaining the passports. Instead they relied on the passports' 'potential evidential value'.

Lord Denning MR: . . . The first thing to notice is that the police officers had *no search warrant*. The reason is simple. No magistrate—no judge even—has any power to issue a search warrant for murder. He can issue a search warrant for stolen goods and for some statutory offences, such as coinage. But not for murder. Not to dig for the body. Nor to look for the axe, the gun or the poison dregs. The police have to get the consent of the householder to enter if they can: or, if not, do it by stealth or by force. Somehow they seem to manage. No decent person refuses them permission. If he does, he is probably implicated in some way or other. So the police risk an action for trespass. It is not much risk.

The second thing to notice is that the police officers kept the passports and letters *without the consent of the holders*. Mr. Leonard suggested that they took them with consent. This is a little far-fetched. Here were two police officers asking a Pakistani for the passports of himself and his wife. Of course he handed them to them. It would look bad for him if he did not. He bowed to their authority. Even if he consented to their looking at the passport, he did not consent to their *keeping* them. Even if he did consent to their *keeping* them, it was only for a while: and he could withdraw it at any time. As in fact he did. So it is all the same. They detain the passports *without his consent*.

The third thing to notice is that *no one has been arrested* for the murder or *charged* with it. The police officers believe that the woman has been murdered. They say so. In addition, although they do not say so, they must, I think, suspect that these three *may* in some way be implicated in it. Otherwise they would not hold on to the passports or papers as they do. But they have not arrested anyone or charged anyone. I can understand it. It would not be right for them to make an arrest or lay a charge unless the grounds were pretty strong.

So we have a case where the police officers, in investigating a murder, have seized property without a warrant and without making an arrest and have retained it without the consent of the party from whom they took it. Their justification is that they believe it to be of 'evidential value' on a prosecution for murder. Is this a sufficient justification in law?

I would start by considering the law where police officers enter a man's house by virtue of a warrant, or arrest a man lawfully, with or without a warrant, for a serious offence. I take it to be settled law, without citing cases, that the officers are entitled to take any goods which they find in his possession or in his house which they reasonably believe to be material evidence in relation to the crime for which he is arrested or for which they enter. If in the course of their search they come upon any other goods which show him to be implicated in some other crime, they may take them provided they act reasonably and detain them no longer than is necessary [our emphasis]. Such appears from the speech of Lord Chelmsford LC, in *Pringle v Bremner and Stirling* (1867) 5 Macph, (Ct of Sess) 55 at 60 and *Chic Fashions (West Wales) Ltd v Jones* [1968] 2 QB 299 [above, p. 80].

Accepting those cases, I turn to two cases where the police acted against a man without the authority of a warrant or of an arrest. The first is *Elias v Pasmore* [1934] 2 KB 164, [above, p.80]. It is reported in [1934] 2 KB 164, but the facts are given more fully in (1934) 50 TLR 196. Police officers there entered a house in Great Russell Street, of which Elias was the tenant. The police officers had only a warrant for the arrest of a man called Hannington. They had reasonable ground for believing that he had been guilty of sedition by attempting to cause disaffection among the police. They knew he was in the house. They entered and arrested him. They had no search warrant, authorising them to search the house. No search warrant is permissible to search for seditious papers. That is plain ever since since *Entick v Carrington* (1765) 19 State Tr 1029. Whilst there, however, they searched the place, seized a number of seditious papers and took them to Scotland Yard. These papers implicated, not only Hannington, but also Elias. They showed that Elias had been inciting Hannington to commit sedition. The police prosecuted first Hannington and second Elias. The papers were used at the trial of Elias. Both men were convicted. Elias afterwards said that the police had no right to take his papers and brought an action for their return and for damages for their detention. Horridge J rejected the claim. He said [1934] 2 KB 164 at 173: 'The interests of the state must excuse the seizure of documents, which seizure would otherwise be unlawful, if it appears in fact that such documents were evidence of a crime committed by anyone.'

I confess that I think those words 'by anyone' go too far. The decision itself can be justified on the ground that the papers showed that Elias was implicated in the crime of sedition committed by Hannington. If they had only implicated Elias in some other crime, such as blackmail or libel, I do not think the police officers would have been entitled to seize them. For that would be a flat contradiction of *Entick v Carrington* 19 State Tr 1029 [above, p. 74]. The common law does not permit police officers, or anyone else, to ransack anyone's house or to search for papers or articles therein, or to search his person, simply to see if he may have committed some crime or other. If police officers should so do, they would be guilty of a trespass. Even if they should find something incriminating against him, I should have thought that the court would not allow it to be used in evidence against him if the conduct of the police officers was so oppressive that it would not be right to allow the Crown to rely upon it: see *King v R* [1969] 1 AC 304.

[His Lordship then referred to *R v Waterfield*, above, p. 90]

The decision causes me some misgiving. I expect that the car bore traces of its impact with the brick wall. The police had reason to believe that Lynn and Waterfield were implicated in a crime of which the marks on the car might be most material evidence at the trial. If Lynn and Waterfield were allowed to drive the car away, they might very well remove or obliterate all incriminating evidence. My comment on that case is this: The law should not allow wrongdoers to destroy evidence against them when it can be prevented. Test it by an instance put in argument. The robbers of a bank 'borrow' a private car and use it in their raid, and escape. They abandon it by the roadside. The police find the car, i.e., the instrument of the crime, and want to examine if for finger prints. The owner of the 'borrowed' car comes up and demands the return of it. He says he will drive it away and not allow them to examine it. Cannot the police say to him: 'Nay, you cannot have it until we have examined it?' I should have thought they could. His conduct makes him look like an accessory after the fact, if not before it. At any rate it is quite unreasonable. Even though the raiders have not yet been caught, arrested or charged, nevertheless the police should be able to do whatever is necessary and reasonable to preserve the evidence of the crime. The Court of Criminal Appeal did not tell how *R v Waterfield* [1964] 1 QB 164, is to be distinguished from such a case. The court simply said, at 171, that the police constables were under no duty 'to prevent removal of the car in the circumstance.' They did not tell us what was the 'circumstance' which took it out of the general rule. It may have been sufficient. I do not know.

Other instances were put in argument to test the position when no one had been arrested or charged. Edmund Davies LJ drew from his unrivalled experience and told us that the great train robbers, when they were in hiding at Leatherslade Farm, used a saucer belonging to the farmer and gave the cat its milk. When seeking for the gang, before they were caught, the police officers took the saucer so as to examine it for finger prints. Could the farmer have said to them: 'No, it is mine. You shall not have it?' Clearly not. His conduct might well lead them to think that he was trying to shield the gang. At any rate it would have been quite unreasonable.

What is the principle underlying these instances? We have to consider, on the one hand, the freedom of the individual. His privacy and his possession are not to be invaded except for the most compelling reasons. On the other hand, we have to consider the interest of society at large in finding out wrongdoers and repressing crime. Honest citizens should help the police and not hinder them in their efforts to track down criminals. Balancing these interests, I should have thought that, in order to justify the taking of an article, when no man has been arrested or charged, these requisites must be satisfied:

First: The police officers must have reasonable grounds for believing that a serious offence has been committed—so serious that it is of the first importance that the offenders should be caught and brought to justice.

Second: The police officers must have reasonable grounds for believing that the article in question is either the fruit of the crime (as in the case of stolen goods) or is the instrument by which the crime was committed (as in the case of the axe used by the murderer) or is material evidence to prove the commission of the crime (as in the case of the car used by a bank raider or the saucer used by a train robber).

Third: The police officers must have reasonable grounds to believe that the person in possession of it has himself committed the crime, or is implicated in it, or is accessory to it, or at any rate his refusal must be quite unreasonable.

Fourth: The police must not keep the article, nor prevent its removal, for any longer than is reasonably necessary to complete their investigations or preserve it for evidence. If a copy will suffice, it should be made and the original returned. As soon as the case is over, or it is decided not to go on with it, the article should be returned.

Finally: The lawfulness of the conduct of the police must be judged at the time, and not by what happens afterwards.

Tested by these criteria, I do not think the police officers are entitled to hold on to these passports or letters. They may have reasonable grounds for believing that the woman has been murdered. But they have not shown reasonable grounds for believing that these passports and letters are material evidence to prove the commission of the murder. All they say is that they are of "evidential value," whatever that may mean. Nor have they shown reasonable grounds for believing that the plaintiffs are in any way implicated in a crime, or accessory to it. In any case, they have held them quite long enough. They have no doubt made photographs of them, and that should suffice.

It was suggested that a mandatory order should not be made for their return. The case, it was said, should go for trial, and the officers made liable in damages if they are wrong. But I think their affidavits fall so far short of any justification for retention that they should be ordered to return them forthwith. I cannot help feeling that the real reason why the passports have not been returned is because the officers wish to prevent the plaintiffs from leaving this country pending police inquiries. That is not a legitimate ground for holding them. Either they have grounds for arresting them, or they have not. If they have not, the plaintiffs should be allowed to leave—even if it means they are fleeing from the reach of justice. A man's liberty of movement is regarded so highly by the law of England that it is not to be hindered or prevented except on the surest grounds. It must not be taken away on a suspicion which is not grave enough to warrant his arrest.

I would, therefore, dismiss the appeal.

Edmund Davies LJ: Having already had the advantage of considering the judgment delivered by the Master of the Rolls, I have to say that I agree with it and cannot usefully add anything. I accordingly concur in holding that this appeal should be dismissed.

Sir Gordon Willmer: I also agree.

NOTES

1. In spite of the fact that much of Lord Denning's judgment is obiter, it has been treated as an authoritative statement of the law in subsequent cases in this country. Lord Denning deals with three situations:(1) seizure under a search warrant; (2) seizure ancillary to an arrest with or without a warrant; and (3) seizure 'when no man has been arrested or charged.' In the dictum italicized above at p. 95 his Lordship holds that the law is the same in (1) and (2). He subsequently holds that analogous principles apply in situation (3). These situations will be considered in turn. Note that the variable factors are:

a) From whom can property be seized: an arrested person; a person under suspicion but not arrested; a person under no suspicion?

b) Where can property be seized: from the person; from a person's immediate vicinity; from any part of premises where a person is found; from premises owned by a person but from which he is absent?

c) What kind of property can be seized: fruits of a crime; instruments by which a crime is committed; evidence?

d) In respect of what crimes can property be seized: the crime for which a person is arrested or for which a search warrant is executed; a similar crime; any serious crime; any crime?

e) Who must be suspected of the crime in connection with which the property is seized: the person arrested or whose person or premises are lawfully searched with or without a warrant; an associate of such a person; any person?

A further relevant point is: is the power to search narrower than the power to seize? Given so many variables, it is not surprising that there is a dearth of hard case law on a number of these factors. *Ghani v Jones* is a deliberate attempt by the Court of Appeal to widen the ambit of police powers.

(1) Seizure under a search warrant

2. Compare Lord Denning's dictum concerning search warrants in this case (the passage in italics at p. 95, above) with the passage in *Chic Fashions Ltd v Jones* [1968] 2 QB 299 at 313 (above, p. 83): 'when a constable enters a house by virtue of a search warrant for stolen goods, he may seize not only the goods which he reasonably believes to be covered by the warrant, but also any other goods which he believes on reasonable grounds to have been stolen and to be material evidence on a charge of stealing or receiving against the person in possession of them or anyone associated with him.' In what respects is his dictum in *Ghani v Jones* significantly wider?

3. Lord Denning's dictum in *Ghani v Jones* (the passage in italics at p. 95, above) has been applied in a number of cases in this country.

Garfinkel v Metropolitan Police Comr [1972] Crim LR 44. The plaintiffs were members of the 'Jake Prescott and Ian Purdie Defence Group'. Prescott and Purdie were awaiting trial on charges concerning an explosion at the house of Robert Carr. Police officers obtained a search warrant under the Explosive Substances Acts, which authorised them to enter the house of Ellesmore, one of the plaintiffs, and take samples of any explosive or ingredient of any explosive, or any substance reasonably believed to be an explosive or ingredient. When they searched the house, they found no such substances, but did find and seize a large number of leaflets, posters, broadsheets and stickers concerning the impending trial, and an organisation, Agitprop, which was associated with revolutionary movements. The plaintiffs sought an order for the return of the papers, which was refused by Ackner J. The Commissioner claimed (1) that all the documents had been seized as evidence of a crime such as conspiracy to pervert the course of justice or to commit contempt of court and had been sent to the Director of Public Prosecutions; and (2) that some of the documents were required for comparison with communiques purported to have been made by the Angry Brigade, which group had claimed responsibility for a series of explosions, including the one at Mr Carr's house. Ackner J held in relation to (1) that there was material which merited consideration by the Director of Public Prosecutions, and generally that the Commissioner was acting reasonably and was detaining the documents no longer than necessary. His Lordship rejected a claim that where multiple copies of documents had been seized, the copies should be returned for dissemination, in view of the possible charge of perverting the course of justice.

How far does this case go? Note that the second, narrower, ground of justification related to some only of the documents. See W. Birtles, (1974) 124 NLJ 425.

4. *Frank Truman Export Ltd v Metropolitan Police Comr* [1977] QB 952. The police arrested the second and third plaintiffs, respectively chief salesman and a director of the plaintiff company, on a charge of conspiracy to obtain money by deception. The charge related to a civil action which the company had brought against another company. Police officers obtained a warrant under section 16(1) of the Forgery Act 1913 authorising them to search the plaintiffs' solicitor's office for forged documents. The police, with the tacit consent of the solicitor, removed all the documents in his possession which related to the civil action, so that they could search them for forgeries. They subsequently retained 127: (1) forty-seven allegedly forged documents; (2) one invoice alleged to be material evidence that the alleged forgeries were such; and (3) seventy-nine documents alleged to be material evidence to prove the conspiracy charges (which were regarded as separate from the question of forgeries). The plaintiffs sought an interlocutory injunction to order the return of the documents and any copies, and to restrain the Commissioner from making use of any information derived from them. They claimed that the documents were protected by legal professional privilege. The plaintiffs had submitted the documents to their solicitor to obtain his advice upon them. Swanwick J refused to make the order sought. The documents in category (1) were expressly within the warrant, and this overrode any question of privilege. The seizure of the document in category (2) was justified ('whether privileged or not': p. 960) in view of the decision in *Chic Fashions Ltd v Jones* [1968] 2 QB 299 (above p. 80) and Lord Denning's dictum in *Ghani v Jones* [1970] 1 QB 693 at 706 (above p. 95).

The documents in category (3) were privileged, at least until they were handed over, but this had to be balanced against the interests of the state in seizing material evidence in the circumstances set out in Lord Denning's 'five principles' in *Ghani v Jones* (see note 10, below). As to this his Lordship stated at p. 965

'In the present case numbers 1, 2, 4 and 5 of these requirements are, in my judgment, clearly met. The only question arises over 3. Of course, Mr Wood was not implicated in any crime. However, Lord Denning MR was not drafting a statute or regulation, but giving guidelines, and I do not suppose that he was considering the application of the law of agency or bailment or envisaging every possible situation. Also, his reference to an unreasonable refusal shows that he was not considering a case where there was no refusal but a consent at the time of taking.'

His Lordship held that the police had acted reasonably:

'Search must involve sorting. The method of sorting was consented to and the documents handed over for that purpose. In the course of the sorting evidence came to light of a crime which the police were already investigating and for which they had already arrested one of the plaintiffs and interviewed the other, and, in my judgment, the police were acting reasonably . . .

'I should add that this does not mean that police entering a solictor's office under a search warrant should regard themselves as having an unlimited licence to search all his documents meticulously for evidence of any crime that his client may have committed. In the present case I have found that the police acted reasonably because Mr Wood consented to hand over all his files of papers dealing with these clients for the police to search and sort. What is reasonable when conducting a search in a solicitor's office must depend on the circumstances. What is reasonable in a man's house may well not be reasonable in the offices of his solicitor. Some sorting there must be in order to execute the warrant, but in conducting a search in the offices of a solicitor who is not suspected of complicity in any criminal activity, that sorting should, in my view, as far as possible, take place in the solicitor's office and be so conducted that documents which are clearly both privileged and inadmissible, such as those which have now been returned to Mr Wood, can be eliminated at once and without perusal of their text. Indeed, from a reputable solicitor police officers might well be prepared to accept his assurance as to which documents may be legitimate objects for the search and which clearly are not.'

Consider the following points. Which of the authorities apart from *Ghani v Jones* justify the seizure of items which are merely *evidence* as distinct from the *fruits* of a crime not specified in the warrant? How apt is the analogy with cases of stolen goods? Was it necessary for Swanwick J to rely on the 'five principles' as distinct from Lord Denning's dictum at p. 95 above? None of the cases to date involved questions of privilege. Do you think the judge gave sufficient seight to the point that some at least of the documents were privileged (see J. C. Smith [1977] Crim LR 477; N. P. Gravells, (1978) 41 MLR 72)

5. *Malone v Metropolitan Police Comr* [1980] QB 49, CA. Acting under a warrant to search for stolen goods police seized from a concealed wall cupboard certain items which turned out to have been stolen, and banknotes to the value of approximately £10,000. The plaintiff sought an order for the return of the money, but this was refused by the Court of Appeal on the ground that circumstances could arise under which it would form material evidence at the trial in respect of the stolen goods. However, it would not be lawful to retain the money for the purpose of making it available in the event of a conviction to satisfy a restitution order under section 28(1)(c) of the Theft Act 1968, or a compensation or forfeiture order under sections 35 or 43 of the Powers of Criminal Courts Act 1973. Had the money not been material to the charge, it would have had to be returned (see *R v Barnett* (1829) 3 C & P 600; *R v O'Donnell* (1835) 7 C & P 138; *R v Rooney* (1836) 7 C & P 515).

6. *McFarlane v Sharp* [1972] NZLR 838, the New Zealand Court of Appeal followed their own decision in *Barnett and Grant v Campbell* (1901–02) 4 GLR (NZ) 430 in preference to *Ghani v Jones*. It was held that the police acting under a search warrant relating to one offence were not entitled to seize property relating to a different offence except where that seizure was incidental to an arrest (see J. W. Bridge [1974] Crim LR 218). *Ghani* has, however, been applied in New South Wales (*G. H. Photography Ltd v McGarrigle* [1974] 2 NSWLR 635).

(2) Search and seizure ancillary to arrest

7. Does Lord Denning's dictum (the passage in italics above, p. 95) suggest that it is lawful to search the entire house of a person arrested? Cf. *Dillon v O'Brien and Davis*, above p. 85.

8. Does the dictum suggest that it is lawful for police to search the home of

a person arrested elsewhere?

In *Jeffrey v Black* [1978] QB 490, DC, B was arrested by police officers for the offence of stealing a sandwich from a public house. After he was charged at the police station, the officers told him that they intended to search his home. They went there with him. He let them in, although he did not consent to the search, and they had no search warrant. The Divisional Court rejected the argument of the police that they had a right to search. Lord Widgery CJ stated at 497:

'It may very well be that if the police officers in the instant case had had any sort of reason for thinking that the defendant's theft of the sandwich required an inspection of his premises, they might very well have made that inspection without further authority. But it is perfectly clear that when they sought to enter his premises, and did enter his premises they were not in the least bit concerned about the sandwich. Their concern was something quite different, namely, whether they would find drugs on the premises.'

Forbes J referred to the dictum by Lord Denning MR in *Ghani v Jones* and continued (at 499):

'I can find no unambiguous statement in that passage from the judgment of Lord Denning MR to the effect that police officers have a right when they have arrested a person in place A to search his dwelling house in place B with nothing more. The passage on that point, and on that narrow point only, seems to me to be equivocal and one could read it one way or another.'

'For myself, taking that view of that passage, I would not be prepared to hold that at any rate at present the police had wide authority which Mr. Farquharson seeks to justify.'

His Lordship also agreed with the reason given by Lord Widgery CJ. Croom-Johnson J agreed with both judgments.

It is apparently the practice of the police to search the homes of arrested persons whenever they have reason to believe that evidence may be found there (*Home Office Evidence No. III to the Royal Commission on Criminal Procedure*, p. 34). Although there are few complaints, there are doubts as to its legality (see the Report of the *Royal Commission on Police Powers and Procedure* Cmd. 3297 (1929) paras. 120, 121). The practice was criticised on this ground by Mr. Norman J. Skelhorn QC in his *Report of Inquiry into the Action of the Metropolitan Police in relation to the case of Mr. Herman Woolf* (Cmnd. 2319 (1964) paras. 106, 107).

9. What is Lord Denning's view as to the power to seize property relating to a crime committed by a third party? Note his Lordship's rationalization of *Elias v Pasmore* (above p. 88). One problem relating to that rationalization is that the charges against Hannington and Elias were not in law connected. Hannington was arrested and subsequently convicted on a charge of attempting to cause disaffection among the police contrary to the Police Act 1919 and not, as Lord Denning suggests, a charge of sedition, (*The Times*, 9 November 1932 p. 6). Elias was convicted for inciting persons (Llewellyn, and, coincidentally, Hannington) to commit sedition. In the words of counsel for the prosecution Elias had incited H and L 'to stir up "hunger marchers" to accompany their march by acts of grave disorder.' (*The Times*, 10 December 1932, p. 7). Thus, E was not 'implicated in the crime of sedition committed by Hannington.' H was not charged in respect of any disorder at hunger marches. It is true that E and H were 'associates', and that H was implicated in the crime of incitement for which E was convicted, although it was not established that H had acted in response to the incitement. Do you think that these facts are sufficient to justify the seizure of property on H's arrest in relation to E?

Must the evidence against the third party which is seized relate to the offence for which entry is made?

(3) Seizure where no man is arrested or charged

10. Consider Lord Denning's 'five principles', which apply to justify the taking of an article 'where no man is arrested or charged.'

The first principle
What do you think 'serious' means here? An offence triable on indictment? An arrestable offence? An offence 'serious' according to its particular circumstances?

The second principle
This principle gives the police for the first time power at common law to seize evidence without either an arrest or a warrant. Is it appropriate for the courts to extend police powers in this way, irrespective of the merits and demerits of the actual extension? Is it more properly a matter for Parliament?

The third principle
The words 'or at any rate his refusal must be quite unreasonable' did not appear in the report of *Ghani v Jones* in *The Times*, (1969) 30 October, and appear to have been added subsequently (see R. M. Jackson [1970] CLJ 1, 3; (1969) 119 NLJ 1011; (1970) 120 NLJ 423). See *Wershof v Metropolitan Police Comr* (below).

The fourth principle
This appears to be consonant with the position where property is seized on arrest or under a warrant: cf. *Elias v Pasmore* (above p. 88).

The fifth principle
This confirms the points made in *Chic Fashions Ltd v Jones* (above p. 80), disapproving *Elias v Pasmore*.

11. The 'five principles' were applied by the Court of Appeal (Criminal Division) in *R v Hinde* [1977] RTR 328. H helped to load the proceeds of a burglary on to his car. When the police approached he ran away, and they seized the car. The court held that the seizure was lawful, and that the car was accordingly not in H's 'possession or under his control' so as to enable him to be deprived of it under the Powers of Criminal Courts Act 1973, s. 43. The police had reasonable grounds for believing (i) that a serious offence had been committed, (ii) that the car was both the instrument by which the crime was committed and material evidence to prove its commission; and (iii) that H was the owner of the car and had himself committed the crime.

12. *Wershof v Metropolitan Police Comr* [1978] 3 All ER 540. A ring in the window of a jewellers' shop was identified by the owner as having been stolen from her. It was handed to a police officer, who, after it had been examined by the owner, put it in his pocket. W's brother was in charge of the shop, and sought the help of W, a solicitor. W was given the ring, but refused to hand it back unless the officer gave a receipt, which the officer declined to do. W was arrested for obstructing the police officer in the execution of his duty (see above, pp. 35–37). He was awarded £1000 damages for assault and false imprisonment. May J held (inter alia):
(1) that there was no general *power* to arrest for obstruction of the police, and this was not one of the exceptional situations where a power existed (above p. 58);

(2) that the officer was not acting in the execution of his duty, as he had no right to seize the ring.

On the latter point, May J stated at 552:

'. . . I follow the guidance given by Lord Denning MR in *Ghani v Jones* [1969] 3 All ER 1700 at 1705, [1970] 1QB 693 at 708–709 to which I have already referred. In that case he set out a list of requirements or criteria, which he suggested should be satisfied to justify the seizure of an article by a police officer without the backing of a warrant. These are not, however, to be construed as if they were the words of a statute. They are objective guidelines which a court should follow to assist it in balancing the freedom of the individual against the interests of society at large, which is the basic legal principle applicable to these cases, and is an objective not a subjective exercise. . . .

In the present case nos 1 and 2 of the requirements are clearly met. The fourth is irrelevant because, at the time, the article was not then in the hands of the police, which is different from the position in *Ghani v Jones*. Following the fifth requirement, I have sought to look at the situation at the time of the arrest and have in no way been affected by the plaintiff's subsequent acquittal.

As in the [*Frank Truman* case, above, p.98], it is the third criterion (namely that the person taking the article must have reasonable grounds to believe that the person in possession of it is involved in the crime, or at any rate, his refusal to hand it over must be quite unreasonable) which is the important one in the present case. No one has ever suggested that the plaintiff's family's jewellery business was in any way implicated in the theft of the ring, or that its subsequent purchase of it was otherwise than entirely honest and in the belief that the person selling it to them was fully entitled to do so. On the facts as I have found them to be, the plaintiff did not refuse to allow Sgt Brand to take the ring away outright. Had Sgt Brand or Mrs Talbot [the owner] been able to give him what he considered to be more cogent evidence that the ring had been stolen and did belong to Mrs Talbot, then I am satisfied he would have allowed Sgt Brand to take it away. Further, and perhaps more importantly, even without that additional or more cogent evidence, I am quite satisfied that the plaintiff would have permitted Sgt Brand to take the ring away had Sgt Brand been prepared to give him a receipt for it. It would have been very simple to do, would have taken but a minute or two, and would in no way have prejudiced the rights of the relevant parties amongst themselves. In my view, Sgt Brand's refusal to give the plaintiff a receipt was itself unreasonable and the plaintiff's refusal to hand it over without a receipt was I think entirely reasonable. For these reasons I am satisfied that Sgt Brand had no right in law to seize the ring at any material time on that Saturday afternoon with which the court is concerned, and that consequently there could be no wilful obstruction by the plaintiff of the execution by the former of any duty which lay on him. I think the plaintiff was fully entitled, unless and until Sgt Brand was prepared to give a receipt, to refuse to hand over the ring.'

13. The facts of *Ghani v Jones* raised the issue of whether the police could *retain* items arguably handed over by consent. The 'five principles' seem to cover the *seizure* of items where police are lawfully on premises (e.g. searching under a warrant, exercising a legal right of entry, or entering with the occupier's consent). Can these principles be stretched to authorise *entry* or *search*? If not, do they nevertheless operate as an undesirable inducement to the police 'to secure entry to premises, to obtain documents, and to obtain permission to search by recourse to moral blackmail' (Leigh, *Police Powers* (1975) p. 196)? In the US, where a prosecutor seeks to rely upon consent to justify the lawfulness of a search, he has the burden of proving that the consent was, in fact, freely and voluntarily given, although he need not demonstrate that the subject knew he had the right to refuse consent (*Schneckloth v Bustamonte*, 412 US 218 (1973)).

14. The Metropolitan Police Commissioner has suggested that the police should be given power to seize property found in a public place believed to be of evidential value (Evidence to the Royal Commission on Criminal Procedure, Part I, pp. 10–11)

He also recommended that a provision be enacted so that if it is made to appear by information on oath before a justice of the peace that there is reasonable cause to believe that an offence has been or is intended to be committed, and that the object or proceeds of that offence, or evidence, is to be found in premises named in that information, the justice may grant a warrant to a constable to search any such premises for any such object, proceeds or evidence, and to seize property whether it relates to that or any other offence provided that any property so seized may be retained for no longer than is necessary in the circumstances (ibid. p. 16).

8 Other powers to obtain physical evidence

(a) FINGERPRINTING

Magistrates' Courts Act 1952

40. Taking finger-prints
(1) Where any person not less than fourteen years old who has been taken into custody is charged with an offence before a magistrates' court, the court may, if it thinks fit, on the application of a police officer not below the rank of inspector, order the finger-prints of that person to be taken by a constable.
(2) Finger-prints taken in pursuance of an order under this section shall be taken either at the place where the court is sitting or, if the person to whom the order relates is remanded in custody, at any place to which he is committed; and a constable may use such reasonable force as may be necessary for that purpose.
(3) The provisions of this section shall be in addition to those of any other enactment under which finger-prints may be taken.
(4) Where the finger-prints of any person have been taken in pursuance of an order under this section, then, if he is acquitted, or the examining justices determine not to commit him for trial, or if the information against him is dismissed, the finger-prints and all copies and records of them shall be destroyed.

Criminal Justice Act 1967

33. Taking and use of finger-prints and palm-prints.
Section 40 of the Magistrates' Courts Act 1952 . . . shall apply to any person of not less than fourteen who appears before a magistrates' court in answer to a summons for any offence punishable with imprisonment, and . . . any reference to finger-prints shall be construed as including a reference to palm-prints.

NOTES

1. For the fingerprinting of persons under 14 see H. Bevan, *Law Relating to Children* (1973) pp. 63–64.
2. In *R v Jones* [1978] 3 All ER 1098, CA, the appellant was arrested for causing criminal damage during the course of parking her car. She was taken to a police station and was there granted bail. The police asked her to give her finger-prints but she refused to agree to this. The police obtained an order from the magistrates under the Magistrates' Courts Act 1952, s. 40 and proceeded to attempt to take the appellant's finger-prints. The appellant resisted these attempts, biting and kicking police officers in the process. Appealing against conviction, inter alia, for assaulting officers in the execution of their duties, she argued that since she had been bailed the finger-prints could not be taken against her wishes at the police station but only at the courthouse where the order had been made (s. 40(2)). The Court of Appeal quashed her conviction.
3. In evidence to the Royal Commission on Criminal Procedure the

Metropolitan Police Commissioner criticised the limited (applying only to persons charged or summonsed) and discretionary (court to grant order 'if it thinks fit') scope of s. 40. He recommended its replacement by a provision authorising the police to use such force as is reasonable in the circumstances to take finger, palm, toe and foot prints of persons under arrest at a police station, if they believe such evidence to be necessary to confirm or refute evidence of the arrested person's involvement in the crime for which he was arrested, to confirm or refute the arrested person's involvement in other offences in respect of which finger or other print evidence may identify the offender, or to enable the arrested person's identity to be confirmed from police records. (*Written Evidence of the Commissioner of Police of the Metropolis* (1978) Part I, paras. 7.1–7.5)

4. See further, L. Leigh, *Police Powers in England and Wales* (1975) pp. 198–204; (1977) The Magistrate 151; (1978) LAG Bulletin 185.

(b) MEDICAL EVIDENCE

In evidence to the Royal Commission on Criminal Procedure the Metropolitan Police Commissioner outlined advances made in identification of such medical evidence as blood, hair, semen, saliva and the product of nail scrapings and anal and penile swabs. Apart from certain provisions relating to blood and urine samples contained in the Road Traffic Act 1972 the police possess no compulsory powers to obtain such evidence. The Commissioner recommended the police be given powers to obtain an order from a magistrate whereupon a medical practitioner could examine a suspect and obtain such samples. In situations where delay through having to obtain a magistrate's order would reduce the value of the evidence subsequently obtained it should be permissible for a senior police officer to authorize the medical examination. (*Written Evidence of Commissioner of Police of the Metropolis* (1978) Part I, paras. 7.9–7.19.)

9 The Judges' Rules and the 'right to silence'

(a) THE JUDGES' RULES AND ADMINISTRATIVE DIRECTIONS

Judges' Rules and Administrative Directions to the Police. Home Office Circular No. 89/1978, Appendices A and B

Appendix A

JUDGES' RULES

These Rules do not affect the principles
  (*a*) That citizens have a duty to help a police officer to discover and apprehend offenders;
  (*b*) That police officers, otherwise than by arrest, cannot compel any person against his will to come to or remain in any police station;
  (*c*) That every person at any stage of an investigation should be able to communicate and to consult privately with a solicitor. This is so even if he is in custody provided that in such a case no unreasonable delay or hindrance is caused to the processes of investigation or the administration of justice by his doing so;
  (*d*) That when a police officer who is making enquiries of any person about an offence has enough evidence to prefer a charge against that person for the offence, he should without delay cause that person to be charged or informed that he may be prosecuted for the offence;
  (*e*) That it is a fundamental condition of the admissibility in evidence against any person, equally of any oral answer given by that person to a question put by a police officer and of any statement made by that person, that it shall have been voluntary, in the sense that it has

not been obtained from him by fear of prejudice or hope of advantage, exercised or held out by a person in authority, or by oppression.

The principle set out in paragraph (*e*) above is overriding and applicable in all cases. Within that principle the following Rules are put forward as a guide to police officers conducting investigations. Non-conformity with these Rules may render answers and statements liable to be excluded from evidence in subsequent criminal proceedings.

RULES

I. When a police officer is trying to discover whether, or by whom, an offence has been committed he is entitled to question any person, whether suspected or not, from whom he thinks that useful information may be obtained. This is so whether or not the person in question has been taken into custody so long as he has not been charged with the offence or informed that he may be prosecuted for it.

II. As soon as a police officer has evidence which would afford reasonable grounds for suspecting that a person has committed an offence, he shall caution that person or cause him to be cautioned before putting to him any questions, or further questions, relating to that offence.

The caution shall be in the following terms:—

'You are not obliged to say anything unless you wish to do so but what you say may be put into writing and given in evidence.'

When after being cautioned a person is being questioned, or elects to make a statement, a record shall be kept of the time and place at which any such questioning or statement began and ended and of the persons present.

III. (*a*) Where a person is charged with or informed that he may be prosecuted for an offence he shall be cautioned in the following terms:—

'Do you wish to say anything? You are not obliged to say anything unless you wish to do so but whatever you say will be taken down in writing and may be given in evidence.'

(*b*) It is only in exceptional cases that questions relating to the offence should be put to the accused person after he has been charged or informed that he may be prosecuted. Such questions may be put where they are necessary for the purpose of preventing or minimising harm or loss to some other person or to the public or for clearing up an ambiguity in a previous answer or statement.

Before any such questions are put the accused should be cautioned in these terms:—

'I wish to put some questions to you about the offence with which you have been charged (*or* about the offence for which you may be prosecuted). You are not obliged to answer any of these questions, but if you do the question and answers will be taken down in writing and may be given in evidence.'

Any questions put and answers given relating to the offence must be contemporaneously recorded in full and the record signed by that person or if he refuses by the interrogating officer.

(*c*) When such a person is being questioned, or elects to make a statement, a record shall be kept of the time and place at which any questioning or statement began and ended and of the persons present.

IV. All written statements made after caution shall be taken in the following manner:—

(*a*) If a person says that he wants to make a statement he shall be told that it is intended to make a written record of what he said. He shall always be asked whether he wishes to write down himself what he wants to say; if he says that he cannot write or that he would like someone to write it for him, a police officer may offer to write the statement for him. If he accepts the offer the police officer shall, before starting ask the person making the statement to sign, or make his mark to, the following:—

'I, . . . , wish to make a statement. I want someone to write down what I say. I have been told that I need not say anything unless I wish to do so and that whatever I say may be given in evidence.'

(*b*) Any person writing his own statement shall be allowed to do so without any prompting as distinct from indicating to him what matters are material.

(*c*) The person making the statement, if he is going to write it himself, shall be asked to write out and sign before writing what he wants to say, the following:—

'I make this statement of my own free will. I have been told that I need not say anything unless I wish to do so and that whatever I say may be given in evidence.'

(*d*) Whenever a police officer writes the statement, he shall take down the exact words spoken by the person making the statement, without putting any questions other than such as may be needed to make the statement coherent, intelligible and relevant to the material matters; he shall not prompt him.

(*e*) When the writing of a statement by a police officer is finished the person making it shall be asked to read it and to make any corrections, alterations or additions he wishes. When he has finished reading it he shall be asked to write and sign or make his mark on the following Certificate at the end of the statement:—

'I have read the above statement and I have been told that I can correct, alter or add anything I wish. This statement is true, I have made it of my own free will.'

(*f*) If the person who has made a statement refuses to read it or to write the above mentioned Certificate at the end of it or to sign it the senior police officer present shall record on the statement itself and in the presence of the person making it, what has happened. If the person making the statement cannot read, or refuses to read it, the officer who has taken it down shall read it over to him and ask him whether he would like to correct, alter or add anything and to put his signature or make his mark at the end. The police officer shall then certify on the statement itself what he has done.

V. If at any time after a person has been charged with, or has been informed that he may be prosecuted for an offence a police officer wishes to bring to the notice of that person any written statement made by another person who in respect of the same offence has also been charged or informed that he may be prosecuted, he shall hand to that person a true copy of such written statement, but nothing shall be said or done to invite any reply or comment. If that person says that he would like to make a statement in reply, or starts to say something, he shall at once be cautioned or further cautioned as prescribed by Rule III(*a*).

VI. Persons other than police officers charged with the duty of investigating offences or charging offenders shall, so far as may be practicable, comply with these Rules.

Appendix B

ADMINISTRATIVE DIRECTIONS ON INTERROGATION AND THE TAKING OF STATEMENTS

1. Procedure generally

(*a*) When possible statements of persons under caution should be written on the forms provided for the purpose. Police officers' notebooks should be used for taking statements only when no forms are available.

(*b*) When a person is being questioned or elects to make a statement, a record should be kept of the time or times at which during the questioning or making of a statement there were intervals or refreshment was taken. The nature of the refreshment should be noted. In no circumstances should alcoholic drink be given.

(*c*) In writing down a statement, the words used should not be translated into 'official' vocabulary; this may give a misleading impression of the genuineness of the statement.

(*d*) Care should be taken to avoid any suggestion that the person's answers can only be used in evidence against him, as this may prevent an innocent person making a statement which might help clear him of the charge.

2. Record of interrogation

Rule II and Rule III(*c*) demand that a record should be kept of the following matters:—

(*a*) when, after being cautioned in accordance with Rule II, the person is being questioned or elects to make a statement of the time and place at which any such questioning began and ended and of the persons present;

(*b*) when, after being cautioned in accordance with Rule III(*a*) or (*b*) a person is being questioned or elects to make a statement—of the time and place at which any questioning and statement began and ended and of the persons present.

In addition to the records required by these Rules full records of the following matters should additionally be kept:—

(*a*) of the time or times at which cautions were taken, and

(*b*) of the time when a charge was made and/or the person was arrested, and

(*c*) of the matters referred to in paragraph 1(*b*) above.

If two or more police officers are present when the questions are being put or the statement made, the records made should be countersigned by the other officers present.

3. Comfort and refreshment

Reasonable arrangements should be made for the comfort and refreshment of persons being questioned. Whenever practicable both the person being questioned or making a statement and the officers asking the questions or taking the statement should be seated.

4. Interrogation of children and young persons

As far as practicable children and young persons under, the age of 17 years (whether suspected of crime or not) should only be interviewed in the presence of a parent or guardian, or in their absence, some person who is not a police officer and is of the same sex as the child. A child or young person should not be arrested, nor even interviewed, at school if such action can possibly be avoided. Where it is found essential to conduct the interview at school, this should be done only with the consent, and in the presence, of the head teacher, or his nominee.

4A. Interrogation of mentally handicapped persons

(a) If it appears to a police officer that a person (whether a witness or a suspect) whom he intends to interview has a mental handicap which raises a doubt as to whether the person can understand the questions put to him, or which makes the person likely to be especially open to suggestion, the officer should take particular care in putting questions and accepting the reliability of answers. As far as practicable, and where recognised as such by the police, a mentally handicapped adult (whether suspected of crime or not) should be interviewed only in the presence of a parent or other person in whose care, custody or control he is, or of some person who is not a police officer (for example a social worker).
(b) So far as mentally handicapped children and young persons are concerned, the conditions of interview and arrest by the police are governed by Administrative Direction 4 above.
(c) Any document arising from an interview with a mentally handicapped person of any age should be signed not only by the person who made the statement, but also by the parent or other person who was present during the interview. Since the reliability of any admission by a mentally handicapped person may even then be challenged, care will still be necessary to verify the facts admitted and to obtain corroboration where possible.

5. Statements in languages other than English

In the case of a person making a statement in a language other than English:
(a) The interpreter should take down the statement in the language in which it is made.
(b) An official English translation should be made in due course and be proved as an exhibit with the original statement.
(c) The person making the statement should sign that at (a).
Apart from the question of apparent unfairness, to obtain the signature of a suspect to an English translation of what he said in another language can have little or no value as evidence if the suspect disputes the accuracy of this record of his statement.

6. Supply to accused persons of written statement of charges

(a) The following procedure should be adopted whenever a charge is preferred against a person arrested without warrant for any offence:—
As soon as a charge has been accepted by the appropriate police officer the accused person should be given a written notice containing a copy of the entry in the charge sheet or book giving particulars of the offence with which he is charged. So far as possible the particulars of the charge should be stated in simple language so that the accused person may understand it, but they should also show clearly the precise offence in law with which he is charged. Where the offence charged is a statutory one, it should be sufficient for the latter purpose to quote the section of the statute which created the offence.
The written notice should include some statement on the lines of the caution given orally to the accused person in accordance with the Judges' Rules after a charge has been preferred. It is suggested that the form of notice should begin with the following words:—
'You are charged with the offence(s) shown below. You are not obliged to say anything unless you wish to do so, but whatever you say will be taken down in writing and may be given in evidence.'
(b) Once the accused person has appeared before the court it is not necessary to serve him with a written notice of any further charges which may be preferred. If, however, the police decide, before he has appeared before a court, to modify the charge or to prefer further charges, it is desirable that the person concerned should be formally charged with the further offence and given a written copy of the charge as soon as it is possible to do so having regard to the particular circumstances of the case. If the accused person has then been released on bail it may not always be practicable or reasonable to prefer the new charge at once, and in cases where he is due to surrender to his bail within forty-eight hours or in other cases of difficulty it will be sufficient for him to be formally charged with the further offence and served with a written notice of the charge after he has surrendered to his bail and before he appears before the court.

7. Facilities for defence

(*a*) A person in custody should be supplied on request with writing materials. Provided that no hindrance is reasonably likely to be caused to the processes of investigation or the administration of justice:
   (i) he should be allowed to speak on the telephone to his solicitor or to his friends;
   (ii) his letters should be sent by post or otherwise with the least possible delay;
   (iii) telegrams should be sent at once, at his own expense.
(*b*) Persons in custody should not only be informed orally of the rights and facilities available to them, but in addition notices describing them should be displayed at convenient and conspicuous places at police stations and the attention of persons in custody should be drawn to these notices.

[*Appendix C omitted—'inquiries involving deaf persons'*]

NOTES

1. For the history and origin of the Judges' Rules see G. Abraham, *Police Questioning and the Judges' Rules* (1964) pp. 12–19. First formally issued in 1912, the Rules were added to in 1918 and fully revised and amended in 1964. The 1978 circular set out above incorporates such minor amendments as had been made to the 1964 Rules and Directions. For a concise summary and explanation of the Rules see Thornton (1978) LAG Bulletin 86.
For the admissibility in evidence of evidence obtained following breach of the Judges' Rules see below, p. 115.
2. In *R v Osbourne and Virtue* [1973] QB 678 CA the appellants argued that certain evidence should have been excluded from their trial since it had been obtained following a failure to caution them as required by Rule II. The Court of Appeal held that there had been no breach of Rule II. Neither at the commencement nor during the interrogation of the appellants did the police have any evidence that 'could be put before the court as the beginnings of a case'. It was only once some such evidence emerged that the duty to caution arose. The police may have had reasonable suspicion to justify the arrest of the appellants – this did not necessarily mean that they had 'evidence' affording reasonable suspicion as required by Rule II. On ' reasonable suspicion' see above, pp. 51–53.
3. Few deny that the strict terms of the Rules and Directions are frequently not complied with by the police. To some extent the rules may impose unrealistic obligations on the police – see e.g. criticism of the 'cautioning' requirements below, pp. 109–114. Judges have not regularly excluded evidence obtained following breach of the Rules and Directions. Sanction for breach of the rules lies in the possibility of disciplinary proceedings being brought rather than in the acquittal of defendants because of pre-trial irregularities. See further below, pp. 115–122.
   A good deal of attention has centred on the extent of compliance with the obligations imposed by 'principle (c)' and Administrative Direction 7. Studies by M. Zander [1972] Crim LR 342 and J. Baldwin and M. McConville [1979] Crim LR 145 indicate common breach of these rules. Note also that the Fisher report on the *Confait* case (1977–78 HC 90) described the safeguard in 'principle (c)' as 'hollow and ineffective' (para. 2.23) and Administrative Direction 7 as a 'dead letter' (para. 15.6) in the Metropolitan area. In *R v Stephen King* [1980] Crim LR 40, CA, it was

stated that the police need not inform a prisoner of his right to telephone a solicitor until after questioning. Contrast the obligations on the police in England with the 'Miranda' requirements in the US (see below, p. 117).

(b) THE CRIMINAL LAW ACT 1977, S.62

Criminal Law Act 1977

62. Right to have someone informed when arrested
Where any person has been arrested and is being held in custody in a police station or other premises, he shall be entitled to have intimation of his arrest and of the place where he is being held sent to one person reasonably named by him, without delay or, where some delay is necessary in the interest of the investigation or prevention of crime or the apprehension of offenders, with no more delay than is so necessary.

NOTES

1. For an account of the parliamentary history of this section, which was added to the Criminal Law Bill against government advice, see (1977) 127 NLJ 751. Its provisions are discussed by D. W. Williams at (1978) 128 NLJ 9. In April 1978 a circular was issued to Chief Constables explaining the obligations imposed by the section and arranging for the compilation of statistics as to its operation (Home Office Circular no. 74/1978, set out in abbreviated form in Archbold, *Criminal Pleading* (40th edn., 1979) para. 1390a). See (1978) 128 NLJ 631, [1978] Crim LR 585 and (1978) LAG Bulletin 137 for comment on the circular.

2. Between 19 June 1978 (when s. 62 came into force) and 31 December 1979, of a total of over two million arrests, it was found necessary to delay notification for a period of 4 hours or more in about 2,100 cases (0.1 %) and for a period of 24 hours or more in about 300 cases (.014%). See Home Office Statistical Bulletin No. 5/1980 and comment at [1980] Crim LR 261.

(c) THE 'RIGHT TO SILENCE'

Criminal Law Revision Committee. 11th Report. Evidence (General) (Cmnd. 4991, 1972)

21. The scales used to be loaded against the defence in ways which it is difficult now to remember.
   (i) Trials were often conducted with indecent haste. . . . Nowadays there are few complaints that trials before judges and juries are too short.
   (ii) Accused persons enjoyed far less legal representation in the past than now. . . .
   (iii) It was not until the Criminal Evidence Act 1898 (c. 36) that the accused and his spouse were able in all cases to give evidence on oath. . . .
   (iv) There are now far greater rights of appeal against conviction. . . .
   (v) The quality of juries and of lay magistrates has greatly improved. . . .
   (vi) Criminals are far more sophisticated than they used to be. Petty criminals may be only a little less ignorant and feckless about defending themselves . . . but there is now a large and increasing class of sophisticated professional criminals who are not only highly skilful in organizing their crimes and in the steps they take to avoid detection but are well aware of their legal rights and use every possible means to avoid conviction if caught. These include refusal to answer questions by the police. . . .
The chief significance of these comparisons for present purposes is that strict and formal rules of evidence, however illogically they may have worked in some cases, may have been necessary in order to give accused persons at least some protection, however inadequate, against injustice. But with changed conditions they may no longer serve a useful purpose but on the contrary have become a hindrance rather than a help to justice. There has also been a good

deal of feeling in the committee and elsewhere that the law of evidence should now be less tender to criminals generally. . . .

27. We need hardly say that we have no wish to lessen the fairness of criminal trials. But it must be clear what fairness means in this connection. It means, or ought to mean, that the law should be such as will secure as far as possible that the result of the trial is the right one. That is to say, the accused should be convicted if the evidence proves beyond reasonable doubt that he is guilty, but otherwise not. . . . We . . . have in mind fairness 'in the general circumstances of the administration of justice.' It is as much in the public interest that a guilty person should be convicted as it is that an innocent person should be acquitted. . . .

28. We propose to restrict greatly the so-called 'right of silence' enjoyed by suspects when interrogated by the police or by anyone charged with the duty of investigating offences or charging offenders. By the right of silence in this connection we mean the rule that, if the suspect, when being interrogated, omits to mention some fact which would exculpate him, but keeps this back till the trial, the court or jury may not infer that his evidence on this issue at the trial is untrue. Under our proposal it will be permissible to draw this inference if the circumstances justify it. The suspect will still have the 'right of silence' in the sense that it is no offence to refuse to answer questions or tell his story when interrogated; but if he chooses to exercise this right, he will risk having an adverse inference drawn against him at his trial.

29. Since one cannot tell for certain what effect it has on the jury when the accused tells a story in court which he did not mention to the police when questioned, the practical importance of the restriction on comment concerns what the judge may say in summing up. Briefly, he may invite the jury, in considering the weight which they should give to the accused's evidence, to take into account the fact that, by not mentioning his story to the police, he has deprived them of the opportunity of investigating it [*Littleboy* [1934] 2 KB 408]. The judge may also, apparently, say simply that the jury may take the accused's failure to give his explanation into account when they are considering the weight to give to his evidence in court, without having to add that the reason for this is that he has deprived the police of the opportunity to check his story [*Ryan* (1964) 50 Cr App Rep 144]. But in several cases, including *Hoare* [(1966) 50 Cr App Rep 166] and *Sullivan* [(1966) 51 Cr App Rep 102], it has been held that it is a misdirection to suggest that the jury may infer that the story told in court is false because, if it had been true, the accused would naturally have told it to the police when they questioned him. . . .

30. In our opinion it is wrong that it should not be permissible for the jury or magistrates' court to draw whatever inferences are reasonable from the failure of the accused, when interrogated, to mention a defence which he puts forward at his trial. To forbid it seems to us to be contrary to common sense and, without helping the innocent, to give an unnecessary advantage to the guilty. Hardened criminals often take advantage of the present rule to refuse to answer any questions at all, and this may greatly hamper the police and even bring their investigations to a halt. Therefore the abolition of the restriction would help justice. . . .

31. So far as we can see, there are only two possible arguments for preserving the present rule.

(i) Some lawyers seem to think that it is somehow wrong in principle that a criminal should be under any kind of pressure to reveal his case before his trial. The reason seems to be that it is thought to be repugnant—or, perhaps rather, 'unfair'—that a person should be obliged to choose between telling a lie and incriminating himself. Whatever the reason, this is a matter of opinion and we disagree. There seems to us nothing wrong in principle in allowing an adverse inference to be drawn against a person at his trial if he delays mentioning his defence till the trial and shows no good reason for the delay. . . .

(ii) It has been argued that the suggested change would endanger the innocent because it would enable the police, when giving evidence, to suppress the fact that the accused did mention to them the story which he told in court. But we reject this argument for two reasons. First, we do not regard this possible danger as a good enough reason for leaving the law as it now is. Second, it is already permissible to draw an adverse inference from the fact that the suspect told a lie to the police or tried to run away. . . . In neither of these cases is it considered a fatal objection that the police might say falsely that the accused told the lie or that he failed to tell his story.

32. We propose [in clause 1 of the draft bill appended to the Committee's report] that the law should be amended so that, if the accused has failed, when being interrogated by anyone charged with the duty of investigating offences or charging offenders, to mention a fact which he afterwards relies on at the committal proceedings or the trial, the court or jury may draw such inferences as appear proper in determining the question before them. The fact would have to be one which the accused could reasonably have been expected to mention at the time. . . . The facts might include an alibi, belief that stolen goods were not stolen (on a charge of handling stolen goods), . . . , consent (on a charge of rape) and (on a charge of indecency with a child) innocent association (for example, that the accused took the child into the bushes to show him a bird's nest). . . .

. . . What, if any, inferences are proper will depend on the circumstances. In a straightforward case of interrogation by the police where the accused has no reason for withholding his story (apart from the fact that he has not had time to invent it or that he hopes to spring it on the court at his trial) an adverse inference will clearly be proper and, we think, should be readily drawn. Obviously there may be reasons for silence consistent with innocence. For example, the accused may be shocked by the accusation and unable at first to remember some fact which would clear him. Again, to mention an exculpatory fact might reveal something embarrassing to the accused, such as that he was in the company of a prostitute. Or he may wish to protect a member of his family. It will be for the court or (with the help of the judge's direction) for the jury to decide whether in all the circumstances they are justified in drawing an adverse inference. . . .

43. If our proposal to allow adverse inferences to be drawn from the accused's silence is accepted, it follows that the requirements of the Judges' Rules to caution a suspect must be abolished or replaced by different kinds of warnings or intimations. Rule II requires that the 'first caution' should be given when the police officer 'has evidence which would afford reasonable grounds for suspecting that [the person in question] has committed an offence'; and Rule III(*a*) requires that the 'second caution' should be given when the suspect is 'charged with or informed that he may be prosecuted for an offence'. Both cautions include the statement 'You are not obliged to say anything unless you wish to do so' and the warning that anything said may be given in evidence. The warnings included in the first and second cautions are, on the face of them, a discouragement to the suspect to make a statement. . . . Whatever may have been desirable in the past, we think that there are serious objections to the requirements to administer these cautions.

 (i) It is of no help to an innocent person to caution him to the effect that he is not obliged to make a statement. Indeed, it might deter him from saying something which might serve to exculpate him. On the other hand the caution often assists the guilty by providing an excuse for keeping back a false story until it becomes difficult to expose its falsity. . . .

(ii) It is illogical that, when the police have a duty to question persons for the purpose of discovering whether and by whom an offence has been committed, they should be required to tell a person being questioned that he need not answer. In particular, the first caution (under Rule II), which was introduced when the rules were revised in 1964, has been objected to on the ground that it interrupts the natural course of interrogation and unduly hampers the police, as there may be a good deal more information which they wish to get, perhaps involving other offences and persons, after the stage when they have 'evidence which would afford reasonable grounds for suspecting that [the person being questioned] has committed an offence.' Indeed there may be a strong temptation for police officers not to interrupt an interrogation at a critical point by administering a caution which may render the investigation fruitless.

44. On the other hand, the fact that adverse inferences may be drawn from the failure of the accused to mention a fact on which he is going to rely at his trial raises the question whether suspects should be warned, when being interrogated, of this danger to them. This does seem to us necessary, because the new rule makes a great change from the present law. No doubt the change will be given plenty of publicity; but it may be some time before it becomes known to all persons whom it is likely to affect. . . . Any procedure introduced for warning suspects of the danger of remaining silent should avoid as far as possible the disadvantages of the present rules as to cautions. In particular one does not want to interrupt the natural course of interrogations or to have side issues as to whether the proper warning was given. Nor must the need to give a warning be made an excuse for using threats. We think that the best course would be that there should be an administrative requirement . . . that, when the accused is charged (or officially informed that he may be prosecuted), he should be given a written notice to the following effect:

'You have been charged with [informed that you may be prosecuted for]—. If there is any fact on which you intend to rely in your defence in court, you are advised to mention it now. If you hold it back till you go to court, your evidence may be less likely to be believed and this may have a bad effect on your case in general. If you wish to mention any fact now, and you would like it written down, this will be done.'

The reasons for suggesting that the notice should be given in writing are that this will provide a record that it was given and also that some suspects try to interrupt and otherwise obstruct police officers trying to give them oral notices. We do not wish to recommend that there should be any general requirement to warn suspects at an earlier stage of the interrogations, because this might have the disadvantages mentioned above which result from the present cautions and because in any case the circumstances are likely to differ so much that it is difficult to lay down any fixed procedure in this respect. The matter must depend on what is fair and proper in each particular case. . . .

48. We have considered whether to recommend that provision should be made as to the use of

tape recorders in criminal interrogation. This is partly because of their increasing use generally and their value when rightly used and partly because our proposal to allow adverse inferences to be drawn from a person's silence when interrogated makes it even more important to have a reliable account of the interrogation. The latter consideration applies strongly to evidence of confessions. . . . The advantage of a requirement to use tape recorders in interrogations would sometimes be great, because, if the recording was made in favourable conditions, the playing over of the tape in court would show clearly what was said and in what tone of voice. . . .
50. . . . the majority of the committee hesitate to recommend that tape recorders should be brought into general use in interrogations at present. In their view this should not be done until experience of their use on an experimental basis . . . has shown that the difficulties mentioned in this paragraph, in particular the technical difficulties, can be overcome and that the use of recorders makes a sufficiently valuable contribution to the ascertainment of the truth concerning happenings at police interrogations without seriously impairing their efficiency.
(i) The police fear that criminal investigations would be hampered if interrogations had to be tape-recorded, because many criminals would refuse to answer questions. This would be partly because of the more inquisitorial atmosphere and partly because criminals are often ready to talk so long as no record is being made. When a written record is being made, a criminal will sometimes say something incriminating but add: "Don't take that down". He feels that, so long as it is not taken down, he will be able to deny having said it or to pretend that the police misrepresented the effect of the conversation or put pressure on him.
(ii) A tape recording is not always a better way of showing what was said at an interrogation than a written record of the effect of the questions and answers. It may be fairer to the accused that he should write down his statement (as many prefer to do) or that the police should take it down for him, because then he can control what goes into the final version by asking for omissions, additions or alterations and by refusing to sign it until he is satisfied with it. In the course of interrogations all kinds of things may be said which would in any event have to be left out when the tape was played over. Examples are references to the accused's criminal record or to his associates and statements which are irrelevant or otherwise inadmissible in evidence. Arrangements can be made at the request of the defence for parts not to be played over, just as arrangements are made for parts of an oral or written statement not to be put in evidence, but it might be more noticeable to the jury that part of a tape was not being played over and they might be more likely to suspect that something significant was being kept from them.
(iii) If the use of tape recorders became standard, evidence of an interrogation not tape-recorded might be regarded as inferior and so suspect. Yet it might in fact be very important and there might have been a good reason why it was not tape-recorded. For example a conversation when the accused was on the way to the police station could not in any case be required to be tape-recorded.
(iv) The quality of tape recordings varies greatly. . . .
(v) We have been informed that it is astonishingly easy to tamper with a tape so as to add to, alter or cut out something said, and that this can be done in a very short time and without leaving a trace of the interference.

51. The majority of the committee think that . . . careful consideration should be given by the police, in conjunction with the Home Office, to the possibilities of a wider use of tape recorders than at present. In particular they would suggest that experiments should be made in order to see how far their use would be helpful.
52. A minority of three members would go further in this matter than the rest of the committee. So far as concerns interrogation outside a police station – for example, when the police are interviewing in his consulting room a doctor who is suspected of performing illegal abortions—the minority are content with the recommendation of the majority that careful consideration should be given to the possibility of using tape recorders on an experimental basis. But in respect of interrogations in police stations the minority would go further. As mentioned in sub-paragraph (vi) below, they consider that statutory provision should be made for the compulsory use of tape recorders at police stations in the larger centres of population and that the operation of clause 1 should be suspended until this has been done. Their reasons are given below.
(i) That the police should be able to question suspects in custody is now generally thought to be necessary for the due administration of the law; but the practice is fraught with dangers. In the first place, there is the danger of the use of bullying and even brutal methods by the police in order to obtain confessions. Examples are the Sheffield case in 1963 and the Challenor case in 1964. These incidents are attributable to a small number of "black sheep" in the police force. However rare their occurrence may be, every effort should be made to erect safeguards against them. Our arrangements should not depend upon the good faith of

everyone concerned in the administration of the law. Perhaps a provision for the electronic recording of interrogations would not always eliminate the use of 'third degree' methods by officers who are tempted to use them; but the knowledge that a recorder is running during an interview would surely exercise a deterrent effect. It is of great importance for the police themselves that any public suspicion of their practices should be allayed. In America, misconduct by the police has been partly responsible for the alienation of sympathy of the public from the police, which leads the public to refuse to help the police with information, and so greatly increases the difficulty of enforcing the law. Also, every proven instance of third degree by the police, or credible allegation of it, increases the suspicion with which juries regard the ordinary confession, which in fact is very likely to be true and properly obtained.

(ii) The minority argue that the use of tape recorders may help to reduce the occasions on which the police are tempted to fabricate confessions. As with the use of violence, it is impossible to assess the extent to which the police at present commit perjury, but there is a widespread impression, not only among criminals, that in tough areas a police officer who is certain that he has got the right man will invent some oral admission (colloquially known as a 'verbal') to clinch the case. The Royal Commission on the Police, 1962, said in its report:

'There was a body of evidence, too substantial to disregard, which in effect accused the police of stooping to the use of undesirable means of obtaining statements and of occasionally giving perjured evidence in a court of law'. (Cmnd. 1728 para. 369)

If the accused alleges that the evidence against him is perjured he is not likely to be believed and the mere making of the allegation by the accused in giving evidence enables the prosecution . . . to elicit damaging facts relating to his previous record.

(iii) Short of using violence and perjury, the police may get confessions by the use of various kinds of persuasion, which is all the more effective when the suspect is isolated from his friends. The present position is that the courts do not exclude evidence of confessions merely because they were obtained by questioning at night or in the small hours . . . [see below at pp. 115–117] It is demonstrated from time to time that even ordinary questioning can produce false confessions, but the risk is greatly increased if oppressive methods are used. Often there is a conflict of evidence between the accused and the police as to the time and duration of questioning. Electronic recording might reduce the conflict, especially if a 'speaking clock' were superimposed on the recording; and incidentally, this would make it much more difficult to tamper with the recording afterwards.

(iv) A more subtle danger lies in the way in which confessions are generally taken. Most written statements produced in evidence are not in the suspect's handwriting and absolutely in his own words. As a result of questioning, the police officer may write a narrative which is in part a blend of question and answer. The statement reads as though it was volunteered by the suspect; but in fact it may have consisted of a monosyllabic answer to a leading question asked by the officer with one or more subordinate clauses. Since the statement does not distinguish between question and answer, one cannot tell from the statement what facts were suggested to the suspect by the way in which the question was worded. And the written word does not reproduce the inflection of the voice upon which meaning may depend. One may not even be sure that the officer understood what the suspect said, or that the suspect understood the written statement when he read it through or had it read to him. His signature is not a guarantee that the written statement exactly reproduces what he said.

(v) The possibilities of error are multiplied if, as often happens, the statement is not reduced to writing at the time and signed by the suspect. The investigating officer may simply embody what he regards as the kernel of the suspect's statement in his notebook. This notebook will be entered up after the interview, and the note may represent only a very small part of a long interrogation. It may be months before the case is heard, and by that time the officer may have no memory of the interview beyond his written note. If there are two or more investigating officers, they are allowed to agree their evidence together before writing up their notes; this practice was approved by the Court of Criminal Appeal in 1953 [*Bass* [1953] 1 QB 680]. The officers may even prepare a joint note. If they are inclined to stretch the case a bit against the accused, perhaps because he has a 'record' and appears to them to be guilty, they know that they will be able to back each other up at the trial and will be virtually impregnable from attack. The agreed note destroys any small chance that the accused might otherwise have had to set one officer against the other.

(vi) The practical effect of clause 1 of the draft Bill [appended to the Committee's report] will be to put a measure of compulsion upon suspects to answer questions, even when they are in custody. It will therefore give some kind of statutory sanction to the practice of police questioning. In the view of the minority, this step ought not to be taken without all proper safeguards having first been introduced, and the principal safeguard required is the recording of the voices of all those concerned in an interrogation in a police station. Therefore, in the view of the minority, the operation of clause 1 of the draft Bill should be suspended until such time as provision has been made for the electronic recording of interrogations in police stations in the major centres of population. These police stations would in due course be specified in statutory instruments, and statements made by suspected persons when under interrogation in a listed police station would not be admissible in evidence unless they had been recorded. In the view of the minority, this provision would often be to the advantage of the prosecution because the recording would help to answer unfounded objections to the genuineness of the confession. There would not generally be a need to play the whole of the recording in court; in most cases a transcript of the essential part would be sufficient; but it would be open to counsel for the defence to ask for the recording to be played when it was relevant—or indeed, the prosecution might wish to do so, since the way in which the accused told his story may itself convey a strong impression of authenticity. The argument that the recording may be tampered with is, as the majority accept, not a decisive one. Even if it were true that the recording can be falsified and that no steps could be taken to counter this (which the minority do not believe), it is equally true that the police can, if so minded, falsify the entry in their notebooks upon which evidence of alleged admissions by the accused is now often founded. Moreover, recordings are at present admissible in evidence (for example, in blackmail cases) without its being suggested as a fatal objection that they can be falsified. As for the argument that the use of recorders would cause offenders to refuse to answer questions, there is reason to believe that in practice the existence of the recorder would soon be forgotten by the person who is under interrogation, particularly when it comes to be realised that the law as it is proposed to be established by clause 1 provides a powerful sanction for the answering of questions by the police. At present the Judges's Rules provide that all statements made by a person in custody must be written down at the time, and the use of electronic recording would hardly be more inhibiting for an offender than the sight of a police officer writing down what he is saying, though it is true that the Judges' Rules on this point are often neglected. Even if some suspects refuse to answer when they know they are being recorded, the loss of this evidence must be accepted as the price paid for an essential safeguard.

NOTES

1. These proposals, which have not been implemented, provoked much comment. See e. g. Mackenna [1972] Crim LR 605; editorial [1973] Crim LR 325; Cross [1975] Crim LR 329; Miller [1973] Crim LR 343; Zuckerman (1973) 36 MLR 509; Zander in Glazebrook (ed.), *Reshaping the Criminal Law* (1978) pp. 349–354; Zander [1979] Crim LR 203 at 211. Much evidence submitted to the Royal Commission on Criminal Procedure dealt with this matter. Note that in his evidence the Metropolitan Police Commissioner made recommendations broadly similar to those of the majority of the Criminal Law Revision Committee (*Written Evidence of Commissioner of Police of the Metropolis* (1978) Part I, paras. 4.1–4.27).
2. In 1978 a limited experiment into tape recording police interrogations was announced (*The Times*, 9 June 1978). This followed recommendations of the *Hyde Committee on The Feasibility of an Experiment in the Tape Recording of Police Interrogations* (1976) Cmnd. 6630 (on which see editorial at [1977] Crim LR 1) and of the Fisher Report on the *Confait case* (1977–78 HC 90 para. 2.24) that such an experiment to assess the practical difficulties be undertaken. It was hoped that the results of the experiment would be available in late 1979 in time for the consideration of the Royal Commission on Criminal Procedure. (954 HC Deb written answer col 433–4). See further on tape recording, G. Williams, [1979] Crim LR 6.

10 Admissibility of evidence improperly obtained

(a) CONFESSIONS AND ADMISSIONS

R v Prager [1972] 1 ALL ER 1114, [1972] 1 WLR 260, 56 Cr App Rep, 151, Court of Appeal

Edmund Davies LJ read the judgment of the court (**Edmund Davies** and **Stephenson LJJ** and **Thompson J**):

Detective Chief Superintendent Craig and Detective Superintendent Sills and other police officers arrived at [Prager's] home near Rotherham at 8 am on Sunday, 31 January 1971. At the outset he was shown a search warrant issued under the Official Secrets Act 1911. He was then told that the police wanted to question him regarding a serious matter and was asked whether he preferred to go to the police station for the purpose. He said he did, and in the 25 minute journey to Doncaster Police Headquarters remarked: 'This whole thing is a fantasy, but I will help you all I can.' They arrived there at 9.15 am and his wife followed soon after. It has not been suggested to this court that the defendant then or at any time before he was charged thought, or had any grounds for thinking, that he was not free to leave the police station had he wanted to.

On arrival, the defendant was given refreshment and Detective Chief Superintendent Craig forthwith began questioning him, and, conforming to a decision previously arrived at, they gave him no caution before doing so. . . .

In his submissions before us, Mr Comyn [counsel for the defendant] conveniently divided the events of the day into session I, lasting from 9.15 am to 12.30 pm, session II from 5.40 pm to about 7.40 pm, and session III from 7.40 to about 11.30 pm.

During session I the defendant made no admissions, and in particular denied taking illicit photographs or meeting Czechs whom he knew to be intelligence agents working for their country. Questioning broke off at 12.30 pm, when (accompanied by a detective officer) the defendant took a walk in the precincts of the police headquarters, had lunch and then rested and slept in a room made available to him. When he awoke, he was given tea and freshened himself up.

At 5.40 pm his interrogation was resumed, thus beginning what Mr Comyn described as session II. At about 7.40 pm something significant occurred, for on being asked whether he had been regarded as an agent by the Czech intelligence, he replied: 'It did not happen like that. Anything I have done was done unwittingly, but you must know my family are out of this.' At this point Mr Craig cautioned the defendant in accordance with rule II of the Judges' Rules 1964, and it is to be observed that when Lord Widgery CJ came to sum up, he told the jury:

It is not perhaps without importance to remember that that caution was, according to the prosecution—the police officers—and really not challenged by the defence, given to the defendant *before* he made any kind of admission in this matter at all.'

Session III began with the caution at 7.40 pm. Between then and 9 pm the defendant orally admitted buying a polaroid camera and a 'close-up' kit in Sheffield, and photographing 'stuff' in his kitchen. Asked what 'stuff' he was referring to, he replied: 'Just pictures of general calculations.' Asked to which device these calculations related, he said: 'Blue Diver.' He went on to say that he had handed these over to Malek at the Czech Embassy in London, and spoke of later passing notes on 'Blue Diver' to two Czech intelligence officers at Jevaney when on holiday in Czechoslovakia and of being paid by them £200 or £300, which he regarded as 'an advance against the sale of my house.'

At 9.35 pm he was asked whether he was prepared to furnish a signed statement and he assented, but asked whether he might take another walk before doing so. He then took a short walk, again accompanied by a detective officer. At 9.50 pm he was cautioned in the terms laid down by rule III of the Judges' Rules 1964 and between then and 11.30 pm he dictated a long statement. On its completion, he read and initialled each page and signed the completed statement.

It is not contested that the statement, if true, constituted a complete admission of the two offences upon which he was later convicted by the jury. . . .

On 1 March the same two officers saw the defendant and his solicitor at the prison. Reading from a script, the defendant then made a statement, the opening words being:

'I wish to make a statement in which I will tell you the truth. The previous statement which I was required to make on 31 January 1971, is not true in most of its contents because I was induced to make that statement and I was in a state of fear.'

It constituted a complete denial of any participation in espionage activities.

[At the trial Mr Comyn had objected to the admissibility of the defendant's confession on two grounds: (A) that Rule II of the Judges' Rules had been breached (failure to caution at the proper time) and (B) that the confession was not made voluntarily. Dealing with these matters his Lordship continued:]

Question (A) was, in effect, treated by Mr Comyn as conclusive of this appeal. But as the Rules of 1964 make clear, they were

'put forward as a guide to police officers conducting investigations. Non-conformity with these rules may render answers and statements liable to be excluded from evidence in subsequent criminal proceedings.'

Nevertheless, Mr Comyn insisted that the admissibility of an alleged confession must, in the first place (and, he seemed to be saying, in the last place also) depend upon whether the Rules have been complied with. He submitted that it was incumbent upon Lord Widgery CJ to decide whether, when the interrogation of the defendant began, the police already had 'evidence' which would afford reasonable grounds for suspecting that he had committed offences against the Official Secrets Act 1911.

Lord Widgery CJ declined to rule whether or not such 'evidence' had existed. . . . Lord Widgery CJ added that, in the light of his conclusion regarding the overriding issue of voluntariness, he found it unnecessary to decide it.

Mr Comyn has strongly criticised this approach. He submitted before us that it was imperative that Lord Widgery CJ decided first whether rule II had or had not been breached, for, if it had been, the confession should not have been admitted unless there emerged 'some compelling reason why the breach should have been overlooked.' He cited no authority for that proposition, which, he claimed, involved a point of law of very great importance. This 'complete lack of authority' (to use Mr Comyn's phrase) is not surprising, for in our judgment, the proposition advanced involves no point of law and is manifestly unsound. Its acceptance would exalt the Judges' Rules into rules of law. That they do not purport to be, and there is abundant authority for saying that they are nothing of the kind. Their non-observance may, and at times does, lead to the exclusion of an alleged confession; but ultimately all turns on the judge's decision whether, breach or no breach, it has been shown to have been made voluntarily. In the present case, Lord Widgery C. J. was, without deciding the point, prepared to assume in the accused's favour that there *had* been a breach of rule II, and then proceeded to consider whether its voluntary nature had nevertheless been established. In our judgment, no valid criticism of that approach can be made. On the contrary, it appears to us entirely sound, ...

We, therefore, turn to question (B), namely: was the voluntary nature of the alleged oral and written confessions established? In *R v Harz; R v Power* [1967] 1 AC 760 at 818, Lord Reid, in a speech with which all the other Law Lords agreed, treated the test laid down in note (*e*) in the introduction to the Judges' Rules as a correct statement of the law. [see above at p. 104]. As we have already indicated, the criticism directed in the present case against the police is that their interrogation constituted "oppression." This word appeared for the first time in the Judges' Rules 1964 and it closely followed the observation of Lord Parker CJ in *Callis v Gunn* [1961] 1 QB 495 at 501, condemning confessions 'obtained in an oppressive manner.'

The only reported judicial consideration of 'oppression' in the Judges' Rules of which we are aware is that of Sachs J in *R v Priestly* (1965) 51 Cr App Rep 1, where he said:

'. . . to my mind, this word, in the context of the principles under consideration imports something which tends to sap, and has sapped, that free will which must exist before a confession is voluntary. . . . Whether or not there is oppression in an individual case depends upon many elements. I am not going into all of them. They include such things as the length of time of any individual period of questioning, the length of time intervening between periods of questioning, whether the accused person had been given proper refreshment or not, and the characteristics of the person who makes the statement. What may be oppressive as regards a child, an invalid or an old man or somebody inexperienced in the ways of this world may turn out not to be oppressive when one finds that the accused person is of a tough character and an experienced man of the world.'

In an address to the Bentham Club in 1968, Lord MacDermott described 'oppressive questioning' as

'questioning which by its nature, duration, or other attendant circumstances (including the fact of custody) excites hopes (such as the hope of release) or fears, or so affects the mind of the subject that this will crumbles and he speaks when otherwise he would have stayed silent.'

We adopt these definitions or descriptions and apply them to the present case. . . .

In the judgment of this court, nothing has emerged during the hearing of this application to indicate any reason for holding that Lord Widgery CJ erred in exercising his undoubted discretion as he did in admitting the defendant's oral and written statements. After the jury had returned to the court, the detective officers were strongly cross-examined on this issue of voluntariness. . . . .

In the course of the summing up, repeated warnings were given to the jury of the necessity of their being sure that the confessions were both true and voluntary. Nevertheless, the criticism was advanced before us that the long, detailed questioning of the accused called for a stronger warning than those given. We find this criticism baseless.
Appeal dismissed.

NOTES

1. In *R v McGregor* [1975]Crim LR 514 (Crown Court) M was arrested on a Thursday night and detained in custody until brought before the magistrates on the following Saturday afternoon. M had not been cautioned at any time during this period in custody. The evidence against him consisted of oral admissions made on the Saturday morning. It was held that the Magistrates' Courts Act 1952, s. 38 required that M should have been brought before the magistrates as soon as practicable, ie in this case, on the Friday morning. In the circumstances, bearing in mind the absence of caution, the Court could not be sure that the admissions had been made voluntarily.

Note also the failure to prove voluntariness in *R v Hume* [1979]Crim LR 724 (Crown Court) and *R v Allerton* [1979] Crim LR 725 (Crown Court).
2. See further on the test to be applied in determining the voluntariness of confessions, *Director of Public Prosecutions v Ping Lin* [1976] AC 574, HL.
3. For recent cases demonstrating that breach of the Judges Rules or Administrative Directions does not of itself render a confession inadmissible see *Conway v Hotten* [1976] 2 All ER 213, DC: breach of Rule 3(b); *R v Elliott* [1977] Crim LR 551, Crown Court, *R v Lemsatef* [1977] 2 All ER 835, CA: failure to allow access to solicitor – though contrast, in this connection, *R v Allen* [1977] Crim LR 163, Crown Court.

Note, however, cases where breaches of the Directions have cast particular doubt on the reliability of admissions of young or mentally deficient persons and where the judges have excluded the evidence without, apparently, finding it necessary to hold the confession to be involuntary. See e.g. *R v Williams* [1979]Crim LR 47, Crown Court and *R v Glyde* [1979] Crim LR 385, Crown Court,: breaches of Directions 4 and 4A.

(b) PHYSICAL EVIDENCE

Physical evidence which is relevant to the matter to be proved is admissible notwithstanding any illegality in the manner in which it was obtained. This rule is, however, subject to an ill-defined discretion of trial judges to exclude evidence when to admit the evidence would be 'unfair' to the accused. On the limited extent of this discretion see *R v Sang* [1979] 3 WLR 263 (House of Lords); commentary at [1979] Crim LR 656; *Cross on Evidence* 5th edn. (1979) Addendum and Chapter 1 Section 6; *Heydon (1980) Crim LR 129.*

(c) THE AMERICAN POSITION

In the US the use of evidence obtained contrary to the Fourth Amendment (above p. 53) has been barred in federal prosecutions since 1914 (*Weeks v United States* 232 US 383 (1914)). The exclusionary rule was applied to state prosecutions in *Mapp v Ohio* 376 US 643 (1961). The reasons for the rule are the deterrence of constitutional violations and the desire of the courts to avoid being party to such violations. The rule extends to bar the use of evidence obtained through the use of information acquired during an unlawful search (the 'fruit of the poisoned tree': *Silverthorpe Lumber Co v United States* 251 US 385 (1920)). Many, including Chief Justice Burger, have criticised the rule and although *Mapp v Ohio* has not been overruled its scope has been restricted. Information based on illegal searches may be used in grand jury proceedings (*United States v Calandra* 414 US 238 (1974)), in civil proceedings (*United States v Janis* 428 US 433 (1976)) and to impeach statements by the accused in evidence (*Walder v United States* 347 US 62 (1954)).

More generally the reluctance of the English courts to use the rules as to admissibility of evidence and their discretion to exclude evidence to deter unlawful or improper police conduct may be contrasted with the decision of the US Supreme Court in *Miranda v Arizona* (384) US 436 (1966). The Supreme Court ruled that whenever a person is questioned by the police after being "taken into custody or otherwise deprived of his freedom by the authorities in any significant way" (this last phrase covering the situation when a person being questioned would be arrested if he tried to leave but not other situations involving non-custodial interrogation), two safeguards have to be observed to protect the right to silence. Firstly, the following information has to be given to him: 'He must be warned prior to any questioning that he has the right to remain silent, that anything he says can be used against him in a court of law, that he has the right to the presence of an attorney, and that if he cannot afford an attorney one will be appointed for him prior to any questioning if he so desires'. (p. 479).

Secondly, as the 'Miranda warnings', above, indicate, the person being questioned is entitled to the presence and participation of a lawyer during the interrogation. Evidence obtained without compliance with these safeguards is inadmissible.

The decision in *Miranda* was taken by a bare majority of 5 to 4, the dissenting judges arguing that it unduly handicapped the police. The case remains good law, though much of the sting has been taken out of it by a ruling by a differently composed Supreme Court in *Harris v New York* 401 US 222 (1971) that although evidence contrary to *Miranda* cannot be led, it can be introduced on cross-examination to impeach the defendant's testimony.

11 Complaints against the police

Report of the Police Complaints Board 1977 (1977–78 HC 359)

THE BOARD'S FUNCTIONS

3. The main purpose of the Police Act 1976 was to introduce an independent element into the arrangements for dealing with complaints by members of the public against members of police forces in England and Wales. . . . The new procedures apply only in respect of complaints against members of a police force up to and including the rank of chief superintendent and only to complaints relating to police officers' conduct on or after 1 June 1977.

4. Section 49 of the Police Act 1964 provides that where the chief officer for any police area receives a complaint from a member of the public against a member of the police force for that area he shall forthwith record the complaint and cause it to be investigated. Where it appears from the complaint that a disciplinary offence may have been committed, the chief officer is further required by the Police (Discipline) Regulations 1977 to appoint an investigating officer who, except in certain circumstances, must be of the rank of superintendent or above and from a different division of the force. In the Metropolitan Police District, the investigating officer may be from the same division, but not in the same chain of command, and he may be of the rank of chief inspector . . .

5. After the investigating officer has completed his investigation, he submits his report to the chief officer or, in practice, to his deputy. Unless the deputy chief constable, or his equivalent in the Metropolitan and City of London police forces, is satisfied that no criminal offence has been committed by the officer who is the subject of the complaint, he must refer the report to the Director of Public Prosecutions for his decision whether or not the officer should be prosecuted. It is only after the deputy chief constable has complied with all the requirements of section 49 . . . and after any necessary reference to the Director of Public Prosecutions, that the new procedures involving the Police Complaints Board come into play.

6. . . . The Board have no power to conduct investigations into complaints, although they may seek further information from the police about complaints cases submitted to them. The Board cannot take action on complaints sent to them direct except to send them straight on to the chief officer of police concerned . . .

7. . . . After a complaint has been investigated and after any necessary reference to the Director of Public Prosecutions, the deputy chief constable—unless the complaint has meanwhile been withdrawn—then considers whether or not disciplinary charges should be preferred against the officer complained of in respect of any breach of the discipline code which the investigation reveals.

8. Where the deputy chief constable decides to bring a disciplinary charge, and this is denied by the officer concerned, the papers in the case must be sent to the Board before the formal disciplinary hearing takes place. The Board's task is to consider whether there are exceptional circumstances making it desirable that the charges should be heard by a disciplinary tribunal rather than by the chief officer sitting alone as is the normal practice. The tribunal, if appointed, will consist of the chief officer and two members of the Board not previously concerned with the case and will decide, by a majority if necessary, whether or not the officer is guilty of the charges preferred. Any punishment to be awarded is decided by the chief officer after consultation with the other members.

9. If the officer admits the charge preferred by the deputy chief constable there is no reference to the Board at that stage and the charge is heard by the chief officer sitting alone. The outcome of such cases must be reported to the Board in due course . . .

12. If, as in the majority of cases, the deputy chief constable decides that disciplinary charges are not called for he must send the papers to the Board, including a copy of the original complaint, the investigating officer's report and an explanation of his reasons for not preferring disciplinary charges. At this stage, he will inform no one else of the decision he has reached. If the Board accept his decision they must inform him and the complainant accordingly. If, on the other hand, the Board consider that charges should be brought they may recommend to the deputy chief constable that this be done. Should he decline to follow that recommendation, the Board (in the absence of agreement following further discussions with the deputy chief constable) may direct that charges nevertheless be brought. Charges brought on a direction of the Board, unless admitted, must be heard by a disciplinary tribunal and in notifying the complainant and the police officer concerned, the deputy chief constable will inform them that the charges have been brought at the Board's direction . . .

14. Where the police investigation is still continuing four months after a complaint was first received the police must send to the Board a copy of the complaint together with a report on the stage reached in dealing with it . . .

Report of the Police Complaints Board 1978 (1979–80 HC 4)

27. Of the 13,079 complaints on which the Board completed action in 1978, 11,940, or about 91%, had been submitted under section 2(1) of the Act.

[i.e. cases where no criminal offence appears to have been committed, the officer complained about denies the charge and the complainant has not withdrawn the complaint.]

28. In 59 of these complaints the deputy chief constable had decided to prefer disciplinary charges against the officer concerned and the sole decision for the Board was whether to exercise our power . . . to direct that the charges should be heard by a disciplinary tribunal. In no case did we find that there were any exceptional circumstances which would justify such a direction.

29. In the remaining 11,881 complaints submitted under section 2(1), the deputy chief constable had decided not to prefer disciplinary charges and we had to decide whether or not to accept that view. We decided to recommend . . . that disciplinary charges should be brought with respect to 15 complaints. On all our recommendations we were able to reach agreement with the deputy chief constable concerned, either that charges should be preferred or that other action should be taken in pursuance of the complaint . . .

42. The range of considerations which may properly influence a deputy chief constable and the Board when contemplating possible disciplinary proceedings is very wide . . .

43. As far as evidential considerations are concerned, . . . we continue to be impressed by the standard and depth of police investigation . . .

44. Fears have been expressed that the police, in investigating complaints against their own members, might not be as diligent in their enquiries as a non-police investigator might be. We have found no evidence to support this as a general proposition and have indeed noted the great care which has been taken to unravel difficult and complicated complaints cases. The fact that during 1978 we found it necessary to ask the police for further information in less than 1 % of the matters of complaints submitted to us speaks for itself . . .

45. In some of the reports which have come to us we have seen signs of undue emphasis being given to points favourable to the police officer and unfavourable to the complainant. We have also detected in some cases a readiness to discount evidence in support of the complainant on the grounds that the witness could not be truly regarded as independent. Little is achieved by this since the Board are perfectly capable of drawing their own conclusions from the facts.

46. There can be no prescribed standard of evidence required before disciplinary proceedings are instituted. Our approach has been that where there is a prima facie case of a disciplinary offence and the evidence suggests that there is a reasonable prospect that a charge can be proved it may be right that the case should proceed to a hearing. This would enable the truthfulness of witnesses to be tested under cross examination and it is therefore appropriate in such cases to consider preferring charges. This does not mean that disciplinary charges should only be preferred where there is a virtual certainty of proving the case; an acquittal does not mean that the decision to bring charges was wrong. A reasonable prospect of a finding of guilt should, however, be a precondition to the bringing of charges. . . .

47. . . . Our examination of the cases which come to us (i.e. those which are not withdrawn) suggests that most of these "unsubstantiated" complaints fall broadly into two categories. The first comprises those many cases where the investigation will have shown the complaint to have been without substance or merit. There remains, however, a second category, consisting of a substantial number of cases where there are conflicting accounts of what took place and it is impossible to establish from the evidence where the truth lies. The conflict is unfortunate but inevitable given the nature of much police work, which involves encounters between the police and the public often in private, or at unusual times of the day or night, when there is little likelihood of other witnesses being present. This applies particularly where a complaint arises from detention or questioning within the police station. Such witnesses as are present may be colleagues or acquaintances of the police officer or the complainant whose detachment may be questionable. A judgement about whom to believe may not be easy to make and we have sometimes found ourselves taking a different view from the police about the weight to attach to the independence of witnesses. Neither the police nor the Board will discount the evidence of a police officer on the grounds that he is a colleague of the officer complained of but by the same token we believe that evidence in support of the complaint should not be discounted solely because it is given by a friend or acquaintance of the complainant.

48. Where there is a direct conflict of evidence which there is no way of resolving we must normally accept that an offence cannot be proved beyond reasonable doubt and consequently that disciplinary proceedings would not be justified. In taking this view we are not giving more weight to the police officer's version of the events than to the complainant's, nor are we casting doubt on the veracity or motives of the complainant or, for that matter, of the police officer. We well recognise that some of these complaints appear to have at least an element of justification but neither the deputy chief constable nor the Board can take action without adequate evidence. The inconclusive outcome in these cases is as unsatisfactory to the Board as it must be to the complainant and to the police service.

COMPLAINTS INVOLVING ALLEGATIONS OF CRIMINAL CONDUCT

49. Special considerations arise where the evidence reveals matters of a criminal nature. The deputy chief constable must send the papers resulting from the investigation to the Director of Public Prosecutions . . . The Board cannot question the Director's decision on whether criminal proceedings should be instituted. . . .

50. In considering whether disciplinary charges should follow where the evidence has first been referred to the Director of Public Prosecutions the Board are bound by two provisions of the 1976 Act. . . . Section 3(8) of the Act provides that in discharging their functions the Board shall have regard to guidance given to them . . . by the Secretary of State . . . This guidance . . . states that where the Director decides on evidential grounds not to prosecute a police officer, "there should normally be no disciplinary charges if the evidence required to substantiate a disciplinary charge is the same as that required to substantiate the criminal charge".

56. It is self-evident that the more serious the nature of the offence, the more likely the justification for disciplinary charges. A complaint of incivility, for example, is generally speaking less likely to give rise to formal charges than a complaint of neglect of duty. An equally important consideration may be whether or not the officer acted in good faith. Where an officer is forced to act without time for reflection and makes an error of judgment, it is difficult to see that formal disciplinary charges could be appropriate, even though the consequences of the error may have been quite serious and afford grounds for a civil action for damages. The officer is probably already aware that he made an error, and advice from a senior officer may be the appropriate way of dealing with the disciplinary aspect. On the other hand, where an officer acts with an improper motive, disciplinary charges may be appropriate even though the act itself, or its consequences, may have been comparatively minor.

57. . . . It can also happen that an officer's actions are considered by the Board to have been at fault, but to have resulted from a force policy or procedure for which the officer himself was not responsible. In such circumstances, disciplinary action would be inappropriate and the sensible course will normally be to seek a more general remedy with the deputy chief constable.

58. The circumstances surrounding the complaint may also need to be considered. Provocation may be a relevant factor, although more self-control is expected of police officers than of those with less demanding positions in society. . . .

60. Finally, there are broader considerations of the public interest and the effect of the Board's decision on the force or the police service in general. . . . The case for action against a police officer for breach of a provision of the discipline code may have to be balanced against considerations of force morale and the effect of the decision on the police in general. To bring formal charges against a police officer may have an inhibiting effect on his colleagues in carrying out their duties if they see the decision as oppressive or as showing insufficient regard for the particular difficulties faced by police officers. The deputy chief constable will obviously give particular weight to these latter considerations. From the Board's point of view it may be necessary to seek a balance between what can sometimes be conflicting public interests: on the one hand that police morale should be maintained and that the police should not seem to be hindered in the active discharge of their duties; and on the other that firm action should be taken in response to a justified complaint.

61. Even where evidence of an offence is available it is long established police practice, and in this the police are no different from many other organisations, that formal disciplinary action is normally reserved for more important matters, small matters being disposed of without recourse to a disciplinary hearing, i.e. by word of warning or advice from a senior officer.

62. We believe that advice or warning is not taken lightly by police officers. Not infrequently complainants state that they have no particular wish for formal proceedings or for severe punishments. What they generally seek in such cases is some sort of acknowledgment that the police erred and will try not to repeat the mistake . . .

65. There remain those comparatively few cases where there is evidence of a disciplinary offence which is sufficiently serious to justify instituting formal disciplinary action . . .

66. . . . In [some of] these cases, where we ha[d] initially been disposed to consider charges, we have found that consultation with the deputy chief constable has brought to light significant factors which did not emerge from the initial submission to us. The personal knowledge and experience of deputy chief constables inevitably plays a part in their decisions and a certain amount of subjective assessment is essential, both for them and for the Board. This serves to underline both the importance of the consultation process required by the Act and the need for deputy chief constables to set out as fully as possible the considerations which lie behind their decisions, particularly where disciplinary charges are seriously in issue.

NOTES

1. Members of the Police Complaints Board are appointed on a full-time or part-time basis by the Prime Minister. Membership is not open to any person who is or has been a constable in any part of the United Kingdom (Police Act 1976, s. 1). The present Chairman is Lord Plowden.

2. For a critical account of the police complaints system see D. Humphry, 'The Complaints System', in P. Hain (ed.), *Policing the Police*, Vol 1 (1979) pp. 43–103. See also Sir Robert Mark, *In the Office of Constable* (1978) pp. 209–228.

3. The *Police Discipline Code* and the rules that govern disciplinary

proceedings are set out at 1977 S.I. 580. For the arrangements for dealing with complaints against officers above the rank of Superintendent see 1977 S.I. 581.

4. For the handling of complaints against the police in Northern Ireland see the *Report of the Committee of Inquiry into Police Interrogation Procedures in Northern Ireland (Bennett Report)* Cmnd. 7497 (1979) Part V.

CHAPTER 3

Public order

1 Introduction

The liberty of the people to assemble in public in order to express their views on political matters is generally regarded as an essential element in a free and open society. The extent to which that liberty may be exercised in this country depends partly on the existing state of the law, and partly on the way in which the law is enforced by police, prosecutors and courts. As this chapter shows there are many ways in which public meetings or processions may fall foul of the law, both civil and criminal. Just as important is what is likely to happen in practice. On this latter point it is extremely difficult to generalise. Much depends on 'the policeman on the spot' (see *Williams*, Chap. 5). Moreover, the attitude of the authorities seems to vary according to current political circumstances. The more stable the political system, the greater is the toleration of political protest. As the effectiveness, or likely or even feared effectiveness of protest increases, so toleration is reduced: the law is enforced more rigorously, and may be strengthened. In addition to being concerned with the mechanics of protest (how many protesters? where are they? are they disorderly? are they violent?), the authorities may be more inclined to focus their attention on the content of the protest (is it seditious? does it incite to disaffection?)

At present, most of the law in the context of political protest relates to its 'public order' aspect. A major theme is the control of the advocacy or use of violence as a means of obtaining political change (in other words the prevention of breaches of the peace (see pp. 50–51)). Another theme is the protection of other legitimate interests of citizens (e.g. the right to use the highway; the right not to have an unwanted crowd gathering in one's own front garden). This concentration on the 'public order' aspect has three consequences. Firstly, the control of political assemblies is seen as part of the general police function of keeping the peace. The problems posed by disorderly political demonstrators are regarded as analogous to those posed by vandals, quarrelling neighbours, 'mods' and 'rockers', 'football hooligans' and drunks. The laws applicable are the same for all. It is open to argument whether the law should operate in the same way in relation to all the categories mentioned, although this is a point on which a very firm view was expressed in *R v Caird* (1970) 54 Cr App Rep 499 (below p. 160).

Secondly, by checking violent protest, it is possible that the law checks the very kind of protest which is most likely to obtain fundamental change. The justifications advanced are that any violence in society is unacceptable, and that violence in this context distorts the 'proper' democratic political process for obtaining reform.

Thirdly, laws which seek to maintain public order are easier to justify than those which impinge directly on freedom of expression. Indeed free expression is essential to the operation of those democratic processes which the maintenance of order is supposed to facilitate. However, laws preserving public order may have significant effects on freedom of expression (1) if they are enforced discriminatorily according to the nature of the political opinions held by particular defendants (as has frequently been alleged: see R. Kidd, *British Liberty in Danger* (1940) Chap. 5; B. Cox, *Civil Liberties in Britain* (1975) Chap. 1); (2) if they interfere with the *effective* communication of views (see, e.g. *Duncan v Jones* [1936] 1 KB 218, DC, below, p. 172); and (3) in so far as the use of words which incite or provoke violence are proscribed (see e.g. *Wise v Dunning* [1902] 1 KB 167, DC, below, p. 166, Public Order Act 1936, section 5, below, pp. 151–157 the law of sedition etc., pp. 291–298.) The law relating to public order is currently under review. See *Review of the Public Order Act 1936 and related legislation* (Green Paper, Cmnd. 7891 1980) and the minutes of evidence of the Home Affairs Committee of the House of Commons 1979–80 HC 384.

The main works cited in this chapter are: *Williams*: D. G. T. Williams, *Keeping the Peace* (1967); *Brownlie*: I. Brownlie, *The Law Relating to Public Order* (1968); *Smith and Hogan*: J. C. Smith and B. Hogan, *The Criminal Law* (4th edn, 1978), See also: R. Benewick and T. Smith (eds), *Direct Action and Democratic Politics* (1972); V. T. Bevan [1979] PL 163; T. A. Critchley, *The Conquest of Violence* (1970); A. D. Grunis (1978) 56 Can Bar Rev 393; E. R. H. Ivamy (1949) CLP 183; P. E. Kilbride and P. T. Burns (1966) 2 NZULR 1; O. Hood Phillips (1970) 86 LQR 1; D. G. T. Williams, [1970] CLJ 96; [1974] Crim L R 635–8; (1975) 1 UNSW Law Journal 94.

The constitutional status of public protest in Britain and the US is discussed by D. G. Barnum at [1977] PL 310. See also L. A. Stein [1971] PL 115; *Village of Skokie v National Socialist Party of America* 373 NE 2d 21 (1978); *Collin v Smith* 578 F 2d 1197 (1978).

The Red Lion Square Disorders of 15 June 1974 Report of Inquiry by the Rt. Hon. Lord Scarman OBE (Cmnd. 5919 1975)

FIRST PRINCIPLES

5. Amongst our fundamental human rights there are, without doubt, the rights of peaceful assembly and public protest and the right to public order and tranquillity. Civilised living collapses—it is obvious—if public protest becomes violent protest or public order degenerates into the quietism imposed by successful oppression. But the problem is more complex than a choice between two extremes—one, a right to protest whenever and wherever you will and the other, a right to continuous calm upon our streets unruffled by the noise and obstructive pressure of the protesting procession. A balance has to be struck, a compromise found that will accommodate the exercise of the right to protest within a framework of public order which enables ordinary citizens, who are not protesting, to go about their business and pleasure without obstruction or inconvenience. The fact that those who at any one time are concerned to secure the tranquillity of the streets are likely to be the majority must not lead us to deny the protesters their opportunity to march: the fact that the protesters are desperately sincere and are exercising a fundamental human right must not lead us to overlook the rights of the majority.
6. This Inquiry has been concerned to discover where the balance should be struck, and the role of the police in maintaining it. Indiscipline amongst demonstrators, heavy-handed police reaction to disorder are equally mischievous: for each can upset the balance. Violent demonstrators by creating public disorder infringe a fundamental human right which belongs

to the rest of us: excessively violent police reaction to public disorder infringes the rights of the protesters. The one and the other are an affront to civilised living.

THE ROLE OF THE POLICE

7. The police are not to be required in any circumstances to exercise political judgment. Their role is the maintenance of public order—no more, and no less. When the National Front marches, the police have no concern with their political message; they will intervene only if the circumstances are such that a breach of the peace is reasonably apprehended. Even if the message be 'racist', it is not for the police to 'ban the march' or compel it to disperse unless public order is threatened. If, of course, the message appears to infringe the race relations legislation, the police have a duty to report the facts so that consideration may be given to subsequent prosecution: moreover in such circumstances a senior police officer, accompanying the march, might think it wise to warn the organisers of the march that, if it proceeds with its slogans, he will report the fact. But it is vital, if the police are to be kept out of political controversy, that in a public order situation their sole immediate concern is, and is seen to be, with public order.

2 Demonstrations in London

The Metropolitan Police and political demonstrations by Sir Robert Mark QPM (Appendix 8 to the Report of the Commissioner of Police of the Metropolis for the year 1974)

2 . . . The total number of political demonstrations in London during 1972, 1973 and 1974 was 1,321. Only 54 of these demonstrations involved disorder, resulting in a total of 623 arrests. In these three years 297 police officers, 49 persons who were arrested and 27 other participants were reported to have been injured, none fatally until Red Lion Square. However, not every civilian participant will report minor injury and there cannot, therefore, be any true record of all casualties. The figures nevertheless suggest an avoidance of extreme violence and a tradition of containment of activities which, though usually lawful, are often controversial, sometimes provocative and occasionally open to exploitation and misrepresentation, and which are frequently the cause of inconvenience to the public. . . .
4. It is not possible to attribute to any one factor the general avoidance of extreme disorder and the comparative rarity of serious casualties in so long a history of political demonstrations. The underlying reason is perhaps our long-standing tradition of changing governments without bloodshed or tumult and a freedom of expression unsurpassed elsewhere. This has allowed a unique relationship between the people and the police, who traditionally depend on goodwill rather than force in carrying out their duties. Of the more immediate reasons for the avoidance of serious disorder and casualties, perhaps the most obvious is an adequate police presence and a lack of weaponry. The police have never had any special weapons or equipment for crowd control. We rely on manpower, supported by horses where necessary, as the most effective and least harmful means of control, and we have nothing more lethal than a wooden truncheon on which to rely in emergencies. Similarly, demonstrators in this country rarely have recourse to lethal weapons, possession of which is, in any case, in many circumstances an offence involving liability to arrest. There is usually no intentional separation of police and demonstrators. The one escorts the other when walking in procession and even when facing each other outside an embassy or police station they are usually within touching distance; their mutual vulnerability being more evident than if seen at a distance.
5. Although the support of the public at large for police aims and methods is a major factor in keeping down the temperature at demonstrations and minimizing casualties, the lack of fatal and serious casualties has allowed unjustified complacency in the public attitude to political demonstrations. These are occasionally both violent and frightening and there has emerged a small minority of extremist causes whose adherents leave no doubt of their belief in the use of force and lack of scruple to further political aims. That these groups are contained without more serious consequences is in the main due to the fortitude, the training and the tolerance of the police and the inhibitions natural to their role. The limitation of police powers in dealing with demonstrations and demonstrators, the accountability of the police and their constant exposure to the news media and to parliamentary questions, and not least the fact that police have learnt from experience that in the long run restraint is usually the most effective way to preserve order and maintain control; all these factors have the effect of creating an unwillingness to abandon persuasion except as a last resort. This unwillingness has perhaps been reinforced over the years by growing police awareness of the tolerance of the courts in dealing with those found guilty of an offence.

6. During 1972, in only 12 of 231 proved cases of threatening behaviour, assault on police, obstruction of police and of the highway, possessing offensive weapons and criminal damage did a court actually impose a prison sentence, none longer than three months. In 1973 not one of 84 proved cases resulted in a sentence of imprisonment that was not suspended; 17 of these cases were of assault on police and 10 of obstruction, which in practice is usually an attempt to liberate a prisoner. During 1974, notwithstanding an increase in violence and arrests, only 19 of 278 proved cases resulted in prison sentences, 13 of them suspended and none of the remaining six longer than three months.

7. The level of fines has generally been very low . . . From the administrative point of view it could be argued that in present circumstances prosecutions involve a waste of scarce and expensive police manpower for no worthwhile result and that in London they could, without disadvantage, be abandoned except in very serious cases intended for the higher courts, such as unlawful assembly or riot. . . .

13. Political demonstrations seem to give satisfaction in the main to those taking part. The public as a whole are usually not interested unless affected by inconvenience or aroused by disorder and violence. Nevertheless, the right to hold them is much valued and jealously preserved. In the event of violence there is usually much comment on the extent to which the police exercised or failed to exercise control. Speculation as to whether the police should have prohibited or regulated a political demonstration usually betrays a lack of knowledge of the law or of the difficulties of applying it. No useful purpose is achieved by prohibitions or regulations incapable of enforcement, or in respect of which judicial penalties are likely to be slight. Demonstrators who can rely on massive support, such as The Committee of 100 in the sixties, are unlikely to be deterred by such restrictions and political extremists are likely to welcome them. For both, disregard or defiance is sure to achieve maximum publicity at very little cost. . . .

16. When considering what action to take in respect of the declared intention to hold extremist demonstrations in support of any political persuasion, police observe scrupulously the principle declared to the House of Commons by a former Home Secretary:—

'If this is indeed a free country and we are free people, a man is just as much entitled to profess the Fascist philosophy as any other, and he is perfectly entitled to proclaim it and expound it so long as he does not exceed the reasonable bounds which are set by law.'

18. The Metropolitan Police have always been disinclined to seek the approval of the Secretary of State for an Order prohibiting political processions for a specified period on the grounds that this encourages extremist minority groups to threaten violence with the object of achieving the suppression of opposition opinion. We believe that attempts by coercion or force to suppress free speech are not only wrong but unlawful and that behaviour of that kind must be resisted no matter what the inconvenience or cost. To give way to such threats is not just to defer to mob-rule but to encourage it. . . .

NOTES

1. Annex B to the Commissioner's paper shows that of 623 persons arrested during demonstrations in the Metropolitan Police District in 1972, 1973 and 1974, the following charges were brought: threatening or insulting words or behaviour (234); assault on police (148); obstructing police (102); possession of offensive weapon (34); obstruction of the highway (148); criminal damage (15), and other offences (77). Annex G (a note by the Metropolitan Police Solicitor) states that prosecutions for affray, riot, unlawful assembly or conspiracy would only be used in 'exceptional cases, for example the Bloody Sunday Irish Demonstration or the Notting Hill Anti-Police March.' The paper is also printed in Mark, *Policing a Perplexed Society* (1977).

2. CS smoke was used in 1971 to dislodge a person suspected of three murders who had barricaded himself in an upstairs room. There has been a gradual extension of the kinds of equipment used by the police in Great Britain. 'CS smoke is available only for dealing with armed beseiged criminals in specific circumstances' (*Report of the Commissioner of Police of the Metropolis for 1971*, Cmnd: 4986, p. 43). Protective shields were first used in disturbances arising out of a National Front march in Lewisham in 1977, and were used again at the Notting Hill carnival in the same year. The

Commissioner stated in his Report for 1977 that it 'was with extreme reluctance that the Force had to resort to the use of defensive equipment and I must stress that it does not mean that we have forsaken traditional methods of policing demonstrations and the like' (Cmnd. 7238, p. 6). Riot equipment is used much more extensively in Northern Ireland.
3. On the Southall disturbances see *Southall 23 April 1979 The Report of the Unofficial Committee of Enquiry* (NCCL) (1980).

3 Freedom of association

There are few legal limits on the freedom of people to associate together for political purposes. The criminal law of conspiracy only applies to agreements to commit a crime, to defraud or to do an act which tends to corrupt public morals or outrage public decency (Criminal Law Act 1977, Part I; *Smith and Hogan*, pp. 216–246). Accordingly, the fact that people associate to perform certain acts will not render them criminally liable unless those acts would be illegal if performed by an individual, subject to the three limited exceptions stated. The tort of conspiracy is committed where two or more people agree to do an unlawful act, or to do a lawful act by unlawful means, or to perform acts other than for their own legitimate benefit, with the object of inflicting damage on a third party (*Clerk and Lindsell on Torts*, 14th edn. paras 810–815) *Hubbard v Pitt* [1976] QB 142, CA, below, p. 136). The tort of conspiracy is thus now appreciably wider in scope than the crime, although it is necessary in tort for the plaintiff to prove that he has suffered damage.

The following section illustrates some statutory limitations on freedom of association in the public order context.

Public Order Act 1936

An Act to prohibit the wearing of uniforms in connection with political objects and the maintenance by private persons of associations of military or similar character; and to make further provision for the preservation of public order on the occasion of public processions and meetings and in public places.
1. Prohibition of uniforms in connection with political objects
(1) Subject as hereinafter provided, any person who in any public place or at any public meeting wears uniform signifying his association with any political organisation or with the promotion of any political object shall be guilty of an offence:
    Provided that, if the chief officer of police is satisfied that the wearing of any such uniform as aforesaid on any ceremonial, anniversary, or other special occasion will not be likely to involve risk of public disorder, he may, with the consent of a Secretary of State, by order permit the wearing of such uniform on that occasion either absolutely or subject to such conditions as may be specified in the order.
(2) Where any person is charged before any court with an offence under this section, no further proceedings in respect thereof shall be taken against him without the consent of the Attorney-General [except such as are authorised by section 6 of the Prosecution of Offences Act 1979] so, however, that if that person is remanded in custody he shall, after the expiration of a period of eight days from the date on which he was so remanded, be entitled to be [released on bail] without sureties unless within that period the Attorney-General has consented to such further proceedings as aforesaid.

NOTES

1. The maximum penalty under s. 1 is currently three months' imprisonment, a fine of £500 or both (1936 Act s.7 as amended by the Criminal Law

Act 1977, s.31, Sch.6). The words in square brackets in s.1(2) were substituted respectively by (1) the Prosecution of Offences Act 1979 Sch. 1, and (2) the Bail Act 1976 Sch. 2 para. 10. 'Public place' and 'public meeting' are defined in s.9 (see below p. 151). Section 7(3) gives a power of arrest (ibid.).
2. The Public Order Act 1936 does not extend to Northern Ireland (s.10(2)). The equivalent legislation there is the Public Order Act (NI) 1951 as amended in 1970 and 1971 (see H. Calvert, *Constitutional Law in Northern Ireland* (1968) pp. 388–389; Public Order (Amendment) Acts (NI) 1970 and 1971). The provision relating to political uniforms is s.6 of the 1970 Act. See also the Prevention of Terrorism (Temporary Provisions) Act 1976, s.2 (below, p. 129) and the Northern Ireland (Emergency Provisions) Act 1978, s.25 (below, p. 185).
3. S. 1 was introduced in response to the increasing use of uniforms by political groups, notably the Fascists (see *Williams*, pp. 216–220). The first prosecutions were of Blackshirts: *R v Wood* (1937) 81 Sol Jo 108 (D sold fascist newspapers while wearing a black peak cap with two emblems, black shirt, tie and leather motoring coat, dark trousers and dark footwear: fined £2); *R v Charnley* (1937) 81 Sol Jo 108 (at public meetings D wore black trousers, dark navy blue pullover, and red brassard on his left arm: convicted and bound over) See also (1937) 81 Sol Jo 509; E. R. H. Ivamy [1949] CLP 184–187. Thus the wearing of a complete outfit is not necessary for a conviction. The section has also been used against members of the Ku Klux Klan (*The Times*, 8 October 1965) and supporters of the Irish republican movement (*O'Moran v Director of Public Prosecutions; Whelan v Director of Public Prosecutions* [1975] QB 864, DC).

In *O'Moran*, members of a funeral party accompanying the body of Michael Gaughan, a self-confessed IRA member who died on hunger strike while in Parkhurst prison, wore black or dark blue berets, dark glasses and dark clothing. They were not identically dressed. An oration beside the coffin referred to the Irish republican movement, and an Irish tricolour flag was placed on the coffin. In *Whelan,*the defendants assembled with others at Speakers' Corner in order to march as a protest on the first anniversary of internment in Northern Ireland. The march was organised by Provisional Sinn Fein and other groups. The leaders all wore black berets and some also wore dark clothing, dark glasses and carried Irish flags and banners. The Divisional Court upheld convictions under s.1(1).

Per Lord Widgery CJ at pp. 873–4: . . . '"Wearing" in my judgment implies some article of wearing apparel. I agree with the submission made in argument that one would not describe a badge pinned to the lapel as being a uniform worn for present purposes. In the present instance however the various items relied on, such as the beret, dark glasses, the pullovers and the other dark clothing, were clearly worn and therefore satisfy the first requirement of the section.
The next requirement is that that which was worn was a uniform, . . . policeman or the soldier is accepted as wearing uniform without more ado, but the isolated man wearing a black beret is not to be regarded as wearing a uniform unless it is proved that the beret in its association has been recognised and is known as the uniform of some particular organisation, proof which would have to be provided by evidence in the usual way.
In this case [O'Moran] the eight men in question were together. They were not seen in isolation. Where an article such as a beret is used in order to indicate that a group of men are together and in association, it seems to me that that article can be regarded as uniform without any proof that it has been previously used as such. The simple fact that a number of men deliberately adopt an identical article of attire justifies in my judgment the view that that article is uniform if it is adopted in such a way as to show that its adoption is for the purposes of showing association between the men in question. Subject always to the de minimis rule, I see no reason why the article or articles should cover the whole of the body or a major part of the body, as was argued at one point, or indeed should go beyond the existence of the beret by itself. In this case the articles did go beyond the beret. They extended to the pullover, the dark glasses and the dark clothing, and I have no doubt at all in my own mind that those men

wearing those clothes on that occasion were wearing uniform within the meaning of the Act.

Evidence has been called in this case from a police sergeant to the effect that the black beret was commonly used, or had been frequently used, by members of the IRA, and I recognise that it is possible to prove that an article constitutes uniform by that means as well.

The next point, and perhaps the most difficult problem of all, is the requirement of the section that the uniform so worn shall signify the wearer's association with any political organisation. This can be done in my judgment in two ways. The first I have already referred to. It is open to the prosecution, if they have the evidence and wish to call it, to show that the particular article relied upon as uniform has been used in the past as the uniform of a recognised association, and they can by that means, if the evidence is strong enough, and the court accepts it, prove that the black beret, or whatever it may be, is associated with a particular organisation. In my judgment it is not necessary for them to specify the particular organisation because in many instances the name of the organisation will be unknown or may have been recently changed. But if they can prove that the article in question has been associated with a political organisation capable of identification in some manner, then that would suffice for the purposes of the section.

Alternatively, in my judgment the significance of the uniform and its power to show the association of the wearer with a political organisation can be judged from the events to be seen on the occasion when the alleged uniform was worn. In other words, it can be judged and proved without necessarily referring to the past history at all, because if a group of persons assemble together and wear a piece of uniform such as a black beret to indicate their association one with the other, and furthermore by their conduct indicate that that beret associates them with other activity of a political character, that is enough for the purposes of the section.'

Public Order Act 1936

2. Prohibition of quasi-military organisations
(1) If the members or adherents of any association of persons, whether incorporated or not, are—
  (*a*) organised or trained or equipped for the purpose of enabling them to be employed in usurping the functions of the police or of the armed forces of the Crown; or
  (*b*) organised and trained or organised and equipped either for the purpose of enabling them to be employed for the use or display of physical force in promoting any political object, or in such manner as to arouse reasonable apprehension that they are organised and either trained or equipped for that purpose;
then any person who takes part in the control or management of the association, or in so organising or training as aforesaid any members or adherents thereof, shall be guilty of an offence under this section:

Provided that in any proceedings against a person charged with the offence of taking part in the control or management of such an association as aforesaid it shall be a defence to that charge to prove that he neither consented to nor connived at the organisation, training, or equipment of members or adherents of the association in contravention of the provisions of this section.

(2) No prosecution shall be instituted under this section without the consent of the Attorney-General.

(3) [This authorises the forfeiture of the property of an association which is unlawful under this section]

(5) [This gives a power to issue search warrants identical to the power in the Incitement to Disaffection Act 1934 s.2(2) and (3), below, p. 296, apart from the provisos to s.2(2)]

(6) Nothing in this section shall be construed as prohibiting the employment of a reasonable number of persons as stewards to assist in the preservation of order at any public meeting held upon private premises, or the making of arrangements for that purpose or the instruction of the person to be so employed in their lawful duties as such stewards, or their being furnished with badges or other distinguishing signs.

NOTES

1. The maximum penalties under this section are six months' imprisonment, a £1000 fine or both on summary conviction, and two years, a fine of any amount or both on conviction on indictment (Public Order Act 1936, s.7(1); Criminal Law Act 1977, ss. 28(2), 32(1)).

2. This section was passed to meet the growth of private armies, in

particular Fascist groups, between 1933 and 1936 (*Williams*, pp. 220–221:
R. Benewick, 'The Threshold of Violence' in Benewick and Smith (eds.)
Direct Action and Democratic Politics (1972)).
3. Note that there is no reference to the promotion of a political object in
s.2(1)(a). Vigilante groups might accordingly offend against this provision.
4. The first prosecution under s.2(1)(b) was *R v Jordan and Tyndall* [1963]
Crim LR 124, CCA, (*Williams* pp. 222–223). J and T took part in the
organisation of 'Spearhead', part first of the British National Party and
later of the National Socialist Movement. At various times in 1961 and
1962 uniformed members of Spearhead were seen practising foot drill,
carrying out attack and defence exercises at a tower building and
exchanging Nazi salutes. At a camp near Cheltenham, the Horst Wessel
song was sung and cries of 'Sieg Heil' were heard. The police searched the
Movement's headquarters under a warrant issued under s.2, and found
documents referring to the former German National Socialist Storm
Troopers and containing phrases such as 'Task Force', 'Front Line
Fighters' and 'Fighting Efficiency'. They also found tins of sodium chlorate
(weed killer) which could be used in making bombs. On one tin, the words
'Jew Killer' had been written. J and T were convicted of organising
Spearhead members in such a way as to arouse reasonable apprehension
that they were organised to be employed for the use or display of physical
force promoting a political object. The Court of Criminal Appeal approved
the trial judge's direction that: 'reasonable apprehension means an
apprehension or fear which is based not upon undue timidity or excessive
suspicion or still less prejudice but one which is founded on grounds which
to you appear to be reasonable. Moreover the apprehension or fear must be
reasonably held by a person who is aware of all the facts . . . You must try
to put yourselves in the position of a sensible man who knew the whole of
the facts'. J was sentenced to nine, and T to six months' imprisonment, the
Court of Criminal Appeal regarding it as an appropriate occasion for the
imposition of deterrent sentences (See further M. Walker, *The National
Front* (1977) pp. 39–42, 44–45). See also below p.294. The prosecution of
members of the 'Free Wales Army' under s.2 is described by D. G. T.
Williams at [1970] CLJ 103.
5. Unauthorised meetings of persons for the purpose of being trained to
the use of arms or of practising military exercises, are still prohibited by the
Unlawful Drilling Act 1819, s.1. Prosecutions under the Act were not
brought against those responsible for drilling the Ulster Volunteer Force in
resistance to Home Rule before the First World War, or in relation to the
military activities of the British Fascists in the 1930s, despite, in the latter
case, assurances from the Home Secretary that appropriate action would
be taken (28 HC Deb 31 January 1934 cols 360–1).
6. For a discussion of the use of conspiracy charges in the context of public
order see R. Hazell, *Conspiracy and Civil Liberties* (1974) Chap. 6. This
must now be read in the light of the Criminal Law Act 1977, Part I.

Prevention of Terrorism (Temporary Provisions) Act 1976

PART I

PROSCRIBED ORGANISATIONS

1. Proscribed organisations
(1) Subject to subsection (6) below, if any person—
  (*a*) belongs or professes to belong to a proscribed organisation:
  (*b*) solicits or invites financial or other support for a proscribed organisation, or knowingly

makes or receives any contribution in money or otherwise to the resources of a proscribed organisation; or

(*c*) arranges or assists in the arrangement or management of, or addresses, any meeting of three or more persons (whether or not it is a meeting to which the public are admitted) knowing that the meeting is to support or to further the activities of, a proscribed organisation, or is to be addressed by a person belonging or professing to belong to a proscribed organisation,

he shall be liable—

(i) on summary conviction to imprisonment for a term not exceeding six months or to a fine not exceeding [£1,000], or both, or

(ii) on conviction on indictment to imprisonment for a term not exceeding five years or to a fine, or both.

(2) Any organisation for the time being specified in Schedule I to this Act is a proscribed organisation for the purposes of this Act; and any organisation which passes under a name mentioned in that Schedule shall be treated as proscribed, whatever relationship (if any) it has to any other organisation of the same name.

(3) The Secretary of State may by order add to Schedule I to this Act any organisation that appears to him to be concerned in terrorism occurring in the United Kingdom and connected with Northern Irish affairs, or in promoting or encouraging it.

(4) The Secretary of State may also by order remove an organisation from Schedule I to this Act.

(5) In this section "organisation" includes an association or combination of persons.

(6) A person belonging to a proscribed organisation shall not be guilty of an offence under this section by reason of belonging to the organisation if he shows that he became a member when it was not a proscribed organisation and that he has not since he became a member taken part in any of its activities at any time while it was a proscribed organisation.

In this subsection the reference to a person becoming a member of an organisation shall be taken to be a reference to the only or last occasion on which he became a member.

(7) The court by or before which a person is convicted of an offence under this section may order the forfeiture of any money or other property which, at the time of the offence, he had in his possession or under his control for the use or benefit of the proscribed organisation.

2. Display of support in public for a proscribed organisation
(1) Any person who in a public place—

(*a*) wears any item of dress, or

(*b*) wears, carries or displays any article,

in such a way or in such circumstances as to arouse reasonable apprehension that he is a member or supporter of a proscribed organisation, shall be liable on summary conviction to imprisonment for a term not exceeding six months or to a fine not exceeding [£1000], or both.

(2) A constable may arrest without warrant a person whom he reasonably suspects to be a person guilty of an offence under this section.

(3) In this section 'public place' includes any highway and any other premises or place to which at the material time the public have, or are permitted to have, access whether on payment or otherwise.

PART II

EXCLUSION ORDERS (See below, pp. 133–135)

PART III

GENERAL AND MISCELLANEOUS

10. Contributions towards acts of terrorism
(1) If any person—

(*a*) solicits or invites any other person to give or lend, whether for consideration or not, any money or other property, or

(*b*) receives or accepts from any other person, whether for consideration or not, any money or other property,

intending that the money or other property shall be applied or used for or in connection with the commission, preparation or instigation of acts of terrorism to which this section applies, he shall be guilty of an offence.

(2) If any person gives, lends or otherwise makes available to any other person, whether for consideration or not, any money or other property, knowing or suspecting that the money or other property will or may be applied or used for or in connection with the commission, preparation or instigation of acts of terrorism to which this section applies, he shall be guilty of an offence.

(3) [The same penalties are prescribed as in s.1(1)]

(4) [authorises a court to make an order for the forfeiture of such money or property]
(5) This section and section II of this Act apply to acts of terrorism occurring in the United Kingdom and connected with Northern Irish affairs.

NOTES

1. The 1976 Act is a re-enactment, with some amendments, of the Prevention of Terrorism (Temporary Provisions) Act 1974 (see H. Street, [1975] Crim LR 192). The 1974 Act was passed in the aftermath of the Birmingham public house bombings of 21 November 1974 when 21 people were killed and over 180 injured. The Bill was introduced on 27 November and received the Royal Assent on 29 November. Part II of the Act, and related provisions, concerning 'exclusion orders', are discussed at pp. 133–135. The maximum fines were increased from £400 to £1000 by the Criminal Law Act 1977, ss.28(2), 32(1) and Sch.6. Proceedings under ss.1, 2, 9, 10 and 11 may not be instituted without the consent of the Attorney-General (in England and Wales) or the Attorney-General for Northern Ireland (in that province) (Sch. 3 para. 3). Statistics as to the operation of the Act are now given regularly in the Home Office Statistical Bulletin.
2. For the definition of 'terrorism', see above p. 38.
3. Part I does not extend to Northern Ireland. The power to proscribe terrorist organisations in Northern Ireland is contained in the Northern Ireland (Emergency Provisions) Act 1978, s.21, below, p. 184.
4. The 'Irish Republican Army' (which term covers both the 'Official' and 'Provisional' wings) was proscribed under the 1974 Act and is still proscribed (Sch. 1). The Irish National Liberation Army was proscribed in July 1979 (S.I. 1979 No. 745). The group had claimed responsibility for the killing of Mr Airey Neave, Opposition spokesman on Northern Ireland.
5. The operation of the 1976 Act has been monitored by the National Council for Civil Liberties (see C. Scorer (NCCL), *The Prevention of Terrorism Acts 1974 and 1976* (1976)). It has been reviewed by Lord Shackleton in a report for the Home Office (*Review of the Operation of the Prevention of Terrorism (Temporary Provisions) Acts 1974 and 1976* Cmnd. 7324 (1978)). There was one conviction under Part I during the currency of the 1974 Act (*Fegan*: NCCL Report pp. 6–7. F solicited support for the IRA by offering posters for sale. He was sentenced to 6 months' imprisonment). According to the NCCL the ban on the IRA has 'led to the curtailing of legitimate political activity by a number of groups who campaign peacefully for the unification of Ireland' (p. 7). This point is not mentioned by Lord Shackleton. Statistics of persons charged are given in Tables 4 and 9 of Appendix E to the Shackleton Report. To June 1978, 7 persons were charged in Great Britain under s. 1(1) (b), none under s.2 and 15 under s.10. The equivalent figures for Northern Ireland were none, none and 4. Lord Shackleton concluded:

'118. These powers [i.e. sections 1 and 2] were considered very important at the time the legislation was introduced. There was considerable public indignation at the fact that the IRA was a legal organisation in Great Britain. As a result of sections 1 and 2 the public displays, processions, funerals and collections on behalf of the IRA have effectively ceased. The temper of public feeling has moderated considerably as a result. There is, I believe, little doubt about this.
119. But these sections are rather different from others in the Act, since their effect is largely presentational. They have not led to any significant number of charges, but bearing in mind the limited significance of the statistics the effect has largely been one of deterrence; in this sense, sections 1 and 2 have been of some benefit. Without them, there could well have been serious provocation, with the possible result that feelings could have run high against the Irish community here, the vast majority of whom are horrified by the activities of the IRA. . . .

121. Proscription of the IRA has not, in the view of the police, made more than a marginal contribution to the curtailment of the activities of the IRA, and the justification for it does not derive principally from its "operational" value. The police do not regard these sections as of great importance in this respect. On the other side of the argument, the theoretical objections to proscription naturally remain. Nevertheless, it must be recognised that it would be a major affront to many people, bearing in mind the strength of feeling in the past, to legalise an organisation which has carried out acts of terrorism in Great Britain, which has declared its intention of resuming such attacks in Great Britain, and which is continuing to act with brutal savagery against the civil community and the security forces in Northern Ireland.'

Lord Shackleton considered the provisions of s.10 to be a 'useful supplement' to s.1, although they were not limited to support of proscribed organizations (*Shackleton Report*, p. 41).

6. Sections 11 (Information about acts of terrorism) and 12 (Powers of arrest and detention) are given above at pp. 38 and 43. Sch. 3 para. 4 gives a power to a justice of the peace to issue warrants to enable the police to search for evidence of the commission of an offence under ss.1, 9, 10 or 11, or evidence to justify an order under s.1 or an exclusion order. If a police officer of the rank of superintendent or above 'has reasonable grounds for believing that the case is one of great emergency and that in the interests of the State immediate action is necessary' he may give a police officer the authority which a warrant could have given. Para. 6(1) provides that in any circumstances in which a constable could arrest a person under s.12 (above, p. 43) 'he may also, for the purpose of ascertaining whether he has in his possession any document or other article which may constitute evidence that he is a person liable to arrest, stop that person and search him.' There is also an express power to search for evidence on a s.12 arrest (para. 6(2)).

Review of the Operation of the Prevention of Terrorism (Temporary Provisions) Acts 1974 and 1976 by the Rt. Hon. Lord Shackleton (Cmnd. 7324, 1978)

EXCLUSION ORDERS (PART II OF THE ACT)

33. Part II of the Act contains the provisions relating to the making of exclusion orders. These may be summarised briefly. Section 3 enables the Secretary of State to exercise his powers in relation to exclusion orders in such a way as appears to him expedient to prevent acts of terrorism (whether in the United Kingdom or elsewhere) designed to influence public opinion or Government policy with respect to affairs in Northern Ireland. An exclusion order may be made where the Secretary of State is satisfied that any person is or has been concerned in the commission, preparation or instigation of acts of terrorism, or is attempting or may attempt to enter the relevant territory (that is, Great Britain, Northern Ireland, or the United Kingdom) with a view to being so concerned. Orders made under section 4 of the Act exclude persons from Great Britain and orders under section 5 from Northern Ireland. Orders under section 6 exclude persons from the United Kingdom; they may not be made against citizens of the United Kingdom and Colonies. There are certain exemptions under sections 4 and 5 for a citizen of the United Kingdom and Colonies. Such a person is exempt from an order (if the order is to be made under section 4) if he is at the time ordinarily resident in Great Britain and has then been ordinarily resident in Great Britain throughout the previous 20 years, or if he was born in Great Britain and has, throughout his life, been ordinarily resident in Great Britain, or if he is at the time subject to an order excluding him from Northern Ireland; (that is, he cannot be excluded from Great Britain and Northern Ireland at the same time). If the order is to be made under section 5 (in the case of a person in Northern Ireland) comparable exemptions apply. . . .

35. The exclusion order power is one of the central provisions in this Act. There is no disguising that it may have drastic implications for the individual concerned. A person against whom an exclusion order is made who has, perhaps, been living in Great Britain for a number of years, may be removed either to Northern Ireland or outside the United Kingdom and may not legally return until the exclusion order is revoked. The penalty for failing to comply with an exclusion order can be up to five years' imprisonment and an unlimited fine. The removal of people whose homes are in Great Britain may cause a great deal of immediate and permanent disruption for the person concerned and for his family. . . .

45. The Act recognises the serious implications of a power of this kind by providing in section 7 that a person served with an exclusion order may make representations against the order. This section provides that where a person makes representations in writing within 96 hours of being served with the exclusion order, the Secretary of State is bound to consider these representations (unless he considers them frivolous) and to refer them for the advice of one or more persons nominated by him. If a person includes in his representations a request for a personal interview with the person or persons so nominated, he is entitled to that interview so long as he has not been removed with his consent from the territory from which he is being excluded. When representations are referred to one of the persons nominated, the Secretary of State must consider that person's report and the representations and reconsider the case as soon as possible, and when he has made his decision as to whether or not to revoke the exclusion order the subject of it must be notified of it if this is reasonably practicable.

46. . . . The persons nominated are known as the Advisers. . . . No cases have been rejected on the grounds that they are frivolous, which would seem to imply that this particular provision serves little purpose.

47. The Adviser system is not a judicial proceeding and is not intended as such. It is an independent review of the decision of the Secretary of State, consisting of a review of the material on which the Secretary of State bases his decision and an interview with the subject where he has requested this and has not already been removed with his consent. It is thus a means of taking account of any points the subject of the order might wish to make (at his own instigation) and of obtaining a second opinion on the case, based upon a personal interview. The Adviser sees in the course of his review of the case all the material which the Secretary of State has seen in considering the exclusion order application. Both the Advisers thought that the material they saw was adequate for thier purpose; both thought it sufficient as a basis on which the Secretary of State could make his judgment. . . .

50. . . . Part II of the Act has been criticised on a number of grounds. There are objections in principle to the idea of restricting the area within the United Kingdom in which a person can live. It is also suggested that the power is inherently arbitrary and oppressive, offensive to the Northern Irish community and unlikely to assist in the defeat of terrorism.

51. A more detailed objection is that exclusion orders lack any evidential basis. This is exemplified particularly in the criticism that the excluded person is not told the nature of the case against him, nor is he afforded the means of subjecting it to cross-examination or otherwise testing it. The counter-argument has always been that exclusion orders are not intended to be judicial decisions based upon evidence acceptable in court. Indeed, much of the material on which they are based could not be produced in court, nor would it be sufficient in evidential terms. But such material, together with other factors, may nevertheless strongly suggest that a person is engaged in terrorism. Clearly a decision to exclude a person on the basis of information such as this is in no sense a judicial decision and I believe that the arguments will be better understood if this is recognised clearly from the outset.

52. The justification for denying to the subject of the exclusion order the information on which the decision is based cannot however derive merely from the fact that the process is an executive one. An executive procedure carries no absolute right to deny information—far from it. In the case of exclusion orders, the justification is said to derive from the nature of the information itself. It is intelligence information, whose disclosure may involve unacceptable risks. Information which is specific about a person's participation in an act of terrorism may be known to only two or three people. It could, without difficulty, be traced back to its source if it became known to the subject of the exclusion order or to a wider circle of his associates and friends. From this might follow the death of the informant. The flow of information which can lead, and in many cases has led, to convictions in the courts would be endangered.

53. It has been suggested that when a person makes representations he should be told the information about him, since he is otherwise unable to refute the case against him. When he comes to be interviewed, his disadvantage may strike him even more forcibly. But the arguments against disclosure of information in the first place remain equally valid, and indeed the danger that intelligence information will be revealed may be greater since the subject may—understandably—try to find out what the information consists of. That is why the purpose of the interview is limited to enabling the Adviser to form a first-hand impression of the subject and to hear what he has to say. It is not an occasion on which intelligence information can be discussed. . . .

55. Being served with an exclusion order has the consequence that it is an offence to enter the territory to which the exclusion relates. This may have far-reaching effects on the person and his family. If he has been latterly resident, say, in Great Britain, and is removed to Northern Ireland, he may be separated immediately from his wife and family. They may not wish to join him in Northern Ireland . . . [H]e may have considerable difficulty in finding a job. If he is resident in Northern Ireland but is returned there after a visit here, he may be deprived of contact with friends and family here; if his job involves travelling here regularly (in the case of a lorry driver, for example) exclusion may have severe effects on him. The possibility that he

may be genuinely trying to get away from the violence in Northern Ireland has also to be considered; clearly it would be against the longer-term interests of both the individual and the community in Northern Ireland to deprive him, especially if he is a young man, of the chance to do this. These are factors which are borne in mind but the criteria on which exclusion orders are based relate strictly of course to the question of involvement in terrorism. . . .

57. Exclusion has been used against people who are members of organisations other than the Provisional and Official IRA, on both the Protestant and Republican sides of the sectarian divide, even though such organisations have not been proscribed in Great Britain. There is no restriction on this in the Act, and the exclusion order powers can therefore be used in respect of such people, provided that the criteria applied are the same as in all other cases. But these cases represent no more than a small proportion of the exclusion orders made, most of which relate to members of the Provisional IRA . . .

63. The police believe that exclusion has brought about the removal from Great Britain of many of those who were involved in the leadership and organisation of the IRA terrorist campaigns in Great Britain and that this has resulted in considerable disruption of the IRA here. They are in no doubt about this. The alternative to exclusion, in their view, would be to allow people strongly suspected of being terrorists but against whom there is insufficient evidence for a charge, or who escape detection, free rein to plan and commit terrorist activities here, carry messages and money, and organise local support and safe houses, all for the purpose of inflicting death, injury and damage on the community in Great Britain. . . .

127. . . . . If the Act is to continue it must be recognised that the longer it does so the greater the possibility that the circumstances of any particular case may have changed. **I recommend that consideration be given to a general review of all the exclusion order cases so as to establish whether there are any in which the order might with safety be revoked.**

129. I doubt that the strong objections in principle to the exclusion order power would be removed by any changes in the procedure which would be largely cosmetic. I am not attracted by schemes which attempt to disguise the reality of exclusion. That would probably be more dangerous in the long term. Nor do I see any alternative to a procedure of this kind being exercised by the Secretary of State who may be called upon to account for his actions in Parliament.

130. Exclusion can be justified only so long as it contributes significantly to the prevention of terrorism. On the one hand, it is held that exclusion is unacceptable in principle and makes no contribution in practice to the prevention of terrorism. On the other hand, the police have no doubt that exclusion has made a significant contribution in this respect. On the basis of the cases I have seen I have no reason to doubt their judgment.

NOTES

1. See also C. Scorer (NCCL), *The Prevention of Terrorism Acts 1974 and 1976* (1976); P. Hain (ed.), *Policing the Police*, Vol. 1, Section 2 'Police Powers and Terrorism Legislation', (1979).

2. This limited conformity with natural justice has close parallels with the procedures adopted to review orders for detention in wartime (*Liversidge v Anderson* [1942] AC 206, HL; C. K. Allen, *Law and Orders*, (3rd edn., 1965) Appendix 1; R. F. V. Heuston, (1970) 86 LQR 33, (1971) 87 LQR 161); the deportation of aliens for reasons of national security or foreign relations (*R v Secretary of State for Home Affairs, ex parte Hosenball* [1977] 1 WLR 776, CA); the internment procedures in Northern Ireland (below, p. 187) and the procedures for the security vetting of civil servants (see p. 280). The procedures in these other contexts do not seem to be satisfactory. Is it ever possible to reconcile satisfactorily the interests of persons affected by such decisions with the needs of national security?

3. 220 orders were made between 29 November 1974 and 29 November 1979. Orders may be reviewed after 3 years. (See 980 HC Debs 4 March 1980 col 405–412).

4 Public meetings and processions

In this country there are no unfettered legal rights to hold public meetings or processions. The law regulates (1) the location and (2) the conduct of public assemblies.

(a) THE LOCATION OF MEETINGS AND PROCESSIONS

All land is vested in some person or institution. People may be permitted to assemble at the landowner's discretion. Assembling without permission is a trespass, although proceedings may well not be taken. Meetings and processions must also conform to the common law of nuisance and to any specific statutory restrictions as to location. The residual freedom or 'liberty' to assemble must be exercised without infringement of the rights of others, and with due regard for their liberties. It is an important question whether English law gives sufficient weight to freedom of assembly. It is also open to argument whether judges have attached sufficient importance to this interest where the law only proscribes conduct that is 'unreasonable', and the conflicting interests of different people have accordingly to be balanced.

(i) The highway

1. Tort

The use of the highway for meetings and processions is restricted by both the law of tort and the criminal law. Aspects of the law of tort which are theoretically relevant include trespass, public nuisance and private nuisance. The position in *trespass* was set out by Lopes LJ in *Harrison v Duke of Rutland* [1893] 1 QB 142, 154:

'If a person uses the soil of the highway for any purpose other than that in respect of which the dedication was made and the easement acquired, he is a trespasser. The easement acquired by the public is a right to pass and repass at their pleasure for the purpose of legitimate travel, and the use of the soil for any other purpose, whether lawful or unlawful, is an infringement of the rights of the owner of the soil, . . .'

In addition, the use of a highway for purposes incidental to passage may well be a proper use:

'Thus a tired pedestrian may sit down and rest himself. A motorist may attempt to repair a minor breakdown. Because the highway is used also as a means of access to places abutting on the highway, it is permissible to queue for tickets at a theatre or other place of entertainment, or for a bus.'

(Forbes J in *Hubbard v Pitt* [1976] QB 142, cf *Hickman v Maisey* [1900] 1 QB 752). Such user must be reasonable in extent (ibid). Technically, therefore, a stationary meeting held on the highway, or even the picketing of premises other than in furtherance of a trade dispute (according to Forbes J in *Hubbard v Pitt*) may constitute trespass against the owner of the soil of the highway. Where a highway is maintainable at the public expense, as is usually the case with made up roads, it vests in the highway authority (Highways Act 1959 ss. 1, 226, 228–230). There is in fact no reported case of such an authority suing demonstrators or the participants in a meeting for trespass. In *Hubbard v Pitt* [1976] QB 142 the defendants picketed a firm of estate agents as part of a campaign against property developers. The estate agents brought an action alleging nuisance, libel and conspiracy, and were granted an interlocutory injunction by the Court of Appeal (affirming Forbes J, although not necessarily agreeing with all aspects of his judgment). Do you think that the highway authority *could* successfully have sued for trespass in this case? Why should orderly picketing not constitute 'a reasonable and usual mode of using a highway'? Is it significantly different from resting or sketching, which A. L. Smith LJ suggested in

Hickman v Maisey would not constitute trespass ([1900] 1 QB at 756) or queuing for theatre tickets (Forbes J in *Hubbard v Pitt*)? Note that the conduct of those held to be trespassers in *Harrison v Duke of Rutland* and *Hickman v Maisey* (below, p. 305) was detrimental to the interests of the owners of the soil of the highway in respect of their adjacent land. In what ways could picketing be detrimental to the highway authority's interests? Should a finding of some detrimental effect on the plaintiff's interests be a pre-requisite of a finding that the user of a highway is unreasonable?

To constitute *public nuisance*, the misuse of a highway must amount to 'unreasonable user' (*Lowdens v Keaveney* [1903] 2 IR 82; *R v Clark (No 2)* [1964] 2 QB 315). In *Hubbard v Pitt* Forbes J assumed that 'unreasonable-ness' was established if it could be shown that passage was obstructed. That assumption has been criticised (see P. Wallington [1976] CLJ 82, 101–106). Wallington argues:

'The test is . . . not whether a demonstration is something reasonably incidental to passage, but whether it is reasonable in the context of rights of highway users generally. If passers-by must make a detour, their inconvenience must be balanced against the interest in allowing the demonstration; it will be relevant to consider the degree of obstruction and whether the demonstration could conveniently have been held at a less obstructive venue or off the highway' (ibid. p. 104).

A civil action may be brought in respect of a public nuisance only by the Attorney-General, or by a person who suffers some particular or special loss over and above the inconvenience suffered by the public at large (*Winfield and Jolowicz on Tort*, 11th edn, pp. 353–5).

Private nuisance is described in *Winfield and Jolowicz on Tort* (11th edn, p. 355) as 'unlawful interference with a person's use or enjoyment of land, or some right over, or in connection with it'. This includes infringement of a servitude (ibid. p. 356). The person who creates the nuisance may be liable whether or not he is in occupation of the land on which it originates (ibid., pp. 373–4). The blocking of access to private premises is an example of private nuisance (ibid., pp. 390–1). Watching and besetting may constitute private nuisance (ibid., p. 526, based on *Lyons & Sons v Wilkins* [1899] 1 Ch 255) but Lord Denning MR took a different view in *Hubbard v Pitt*.

In his Report on the Red Lion Square disorders Lord Scarman discussed demonstrations and the public highway (Cmnd. 5919, paras. 122, 123):

'English law recognises as paramount the right of passage: a demonstration which obstructs passage along the highway is unlawful. The paramount right of passage is, however, subject to the reasonable use of the highway by others. A procession, therefore, which allows room for others to go on their way is lawful; but it is open to question whether a public meeting held on a highway could ever be lawful for it is not in any way incidental to the exercise of the right of passage . . . . I think the priority that the law gives to the right of passage is sound. Free movement between place and place and access to premises may seem workaday matters when compared with such rights as those of demonstration and protest; but society could grind to a halt if the law adopted any other priority. There is, therefore, a case, as was suggested by one party, for the specific provision of public meeting-places in our town and cities. Public meeting-places, whether they be a speaker's corner in the centre of a great city or a village green, are as essential to civilised life as is priority for the right of passage along our highways.'

2. Crime

As we have seen, obstruction of the highway may constitute public nuisance. A public nuisance may be the subject of criminal proceedings.

In *R v Clark (No 2)* [1964] 2 QB 315, C, the field secretary of the Campaign for Nuclear Disarmament, led a crowd through various streets in London in the course of a Committee of 100 demonstrations during the visit of the King and Queen of Greece. Several streets were partially or completely blocked. C was convicted on a charge of inciting persons to commit a public nuisance by obstructing the highway and sentenced to 18 months' imprisonment. His conviction was quashed as the deputy chairman at the London Sessions had failed to direct the jury on the question whether, granted obstruction, there was an unreasonable user of the highway. He had merely directed that if there was a physical obstruction, that constituted nuisance, and that C, if he incited it, was guilty.

Much more commonly, criminal proceedings for obstruction of the highway are brought under the following provision.

Highways Act 1959

121. Penalty for wilful obstruction
(1) If a person, without lawful authority or excuse, in any way wilfully obstructs the free passage along a highway he shall be guilty of an offence and shall be liable in respect thereof to a fine not exceeding [fifty pounds].
(2) A constable may arrest without warrant any person whom he sees committing an offence against this section.

NOTES

1. This section is much used in respect of demonstrations – particularly where people sit down in the street. It provides a power of arrest which is not available in relation to the crime of public nuisance.
2. It is not open to the local authority to authorise an obstruction of the highway so as to afford a defence to criminal proceedings: *Redbridge London Borough Council v Jacques* [1970] 1 WLR 1604; *Cambridgeshire and Isle of Ely County Council v Rust* [1972] 2 QB 426.
3. Cases under s. 121 and analogous statutory provisions have consistently taken the line that the obstruction of any part of the highway constitutes obstruction for these purposes, notwithstanding that there is room for persons to pass by, or that delay is minimal.

In *Homer v Cadman* (1886) 16 Cox CC 51, DC, H marched into the Bull Ring, Sedgley, an irregular triangle where six highways converge. He was accompanied by a band. He stood on a chair and addressed a crowd of between 150 and 200 people for an hour and a half. There was space between the crowd and the footpaths for vehicles or pedestrians to pass. H was convicted under the Highway Act 1835, s. 72. His appeal to the Divisional Court failed. Per Smith J at p. 54:

'The appellant was only entitled to use the highway in an authorised manner, that is, to pass over it to and fro. He certainly had used it in an unauthorised manner, and the magistrate has found that, as no person could have gone across that part of the highway where the appellant and his band were without considerable inconvenience and danger, there was an obstruction to the highway. The fact that only a part of the highway was so obstructed seems to me to make no difference.'

cf. *Aldred v Miller* 1924 JC 117 (High Court of Justiciary).
4. Reasonable user of the highway will constitute 'lawful excuse' under s. 121. In *Nagy v Weston* [1965] WLR 280, 1 All ER 78, Lajos Nagy parked his van in a lay-by where there was a bus stop, in order to sell hot-dogs from it. He was there for five minutes before he was arrested under s. 121. The justices found that although the road was wide, it was nevertheless busy at that time of night (10.15 p.m.), carrying heavy traffic including buses which would be pulling out of the lay-by. There was therefore unreasonable user

by parking a van even for five minutes. His conviction under S. 121 was affirmed by the Divisional Court. Per Lord Parker CJ at p. 284.

'There must be proof that the use in question was an unreasonable use. Whether or not the user amounting to an obstruction is or is not an unreasonable use of the highway is a question of fact. It depends upon all the circumstances, including the length of time the obstruction continues, the place where it occurs, the purpose for which it is done, and of course whether it does in fact cause an actual obstruction as opposed to a potential obstruction. . . [T]he justices, . . . have clearly found that in the circumstances of this case there was an unreasonable use of the highway. Indeed, on the facts stated, it is difficult to see how they could conceivably arrive at any other conclusion.'

Wallington (op. cit. pp. 108–9) argues that the term 'lawful' excuse could be interpreted more generously to cover all demonstrations reasonably conducted with due regard to the interests of others.

Arrowsmith v Jenkins [1963] 2 QB 561, [1963] 2 All ER 210, [1963] 2 WLR 856, 127 JP 289, 61 LGR 312, Queen's Bench Divisional Court

On 13 April 1962, a meeting was held in Nelson Street, Bootle, at which the main speaker was Pat Arrowsmith. This street linked two main roads. Meetings had been held there from time to time and police officers had on occasions attended to ensure the free passage of traffic. There was no evidence that these meetings had led to prosecutions for obstruction. At this meeting the carriageway and pavements were completely blocked from 12.35 p.m. to 12.40 p.m. A passageway for vehicles was then cleared by the police and a fire engine and other vehicles were guided through the crowd. Police officers requested the defendant to ask her audience to draw closer to her to help clear the carriageway and the defendant did so by means of a loud-hailer through which she was addressing the crowd. But the carriageway remained partly obstructed until after 12.55 p.m. when the defendant finished speaking. If it had not been for the fact that the defendant was speaking, the crowd would have dispersed and the highway would have been cleared.

A was convicted under the Highways Act 1959, section 121. She appealed unsuccessfully to quarter sessions and to the Divisional Court.

Lord Parker CJ: I think that the defendant feels that she is under a grievance because—and one may put it this way—she says: 'Why pick on me? There have been many meetings held in this street from time to time. The police, as on this occasion, have attended those meetings and assisted to make a free passage, and there is no evidence that anybody else has ever been prosecuted. Why pick on me?' That, of course, has nothing to do with this court. The sole question here is whether the defendant has contravened section 121 (1) of the Highways Act, 1959 . . .

I am quite satisfied that section 121 (1) of the Act of 1959, on its true construction, is providing that if a person, without lawful authority or excuse, intentionally as opposed to accidentally, that is, by an exercise of his or her free will, does something or omits to do something which will cause an obstruction or the continuance of an obstruction, he or she is guilty of an offence. Mr. Wigoder, for the defendant, has sought to argue that if a person—and I think that this is how he puts it—acts in the genuine belief that he or she has lawful authority to do what he or she is doing then, if an obstruction results, he or she cannot be said to have wilfully obstructed the free passage along a highway.

Quite frankly, I do not fully understand that submission. It is difficult, certainly, to apply in the present case. I imagine that it can be put in this way: that there must be some mens rea in the sense that a person will only be guilty if he knowingly does a wrongful act. I am quite satisfied that that consideration cannot possibly be imported into the words 'wilfully obstructs' in section 121 (1) of the Act of 1959. If anybody, by an exercise of free will, does something which causes an obstruction, then an offence is committed. There is no doubt that the defendant did that in the present case . . .

Ashworth and **Winn JJ** agreed.

Appeal dismissed

(ii) Open spaces

Open spaces, parks, recreation grounds and the like are usually vested in the Crown, or in a local authority. They may be subject to regulations or byelaws made under a variety of statutory powers (see *Brownlie*, pp. 32–35; Public Health Act 1875, section 164; Open Spaces Act 1906, section 15). The Local Government Act 1972, section 235 empowers district and London Borough councils to make byelaws for the 'good rule and government' of the whole or any part of their area, 'and for the prevention and suppression of nuisances therein'. These commonly cover such topics as the use in public of musical instruments, amplifiers or indecent language.

De Morgan v Metropolitan Board of Works (1880) 5 QBD 155, 49 LJ MC 51, 42 LT 238, 44 JP 296, Queen's Bench Divisional Court

By a scheme made under the Metropolitan Commons Act 1866, and confirmed by the Metropolitan Commons Supplemental Act 1877, it was provided that Clapham Common should be dedicated to the use and recreation of the public as an open and uninclosed space for ever, and the Metropolitan Board of Works were empowered to frame bye-laws and regulations for the prevention of nuisances and the preservation of order on the common. The Metropolitan Board of Works made a bye-law prohibiting the delivery of any public speech, lecture, sermon, or address of any kind, except with the written permission of the board first obtained, and upon such portions of the common and at such times as might be by such written permission directed and sanctioned by the board. De M delivered a sermon on the common without permission. He was convicted of an offence under the bye-law and appealed to the Divisional Court, contending that the bye-law was ultra vires and void.

Lush J [delivered the judgment of the court (Lush and Manisty JJ)]: . . . The appellant . . . impeached the validity of the bye-law on two grounds: First, he contended that the public had acquired a right to hold meetings on the common prior to the passing of the Act, and that it was therefore repugnant to the scheme to put any restriction upon the exercise of that right.
   The magistrate reports to us that some evidence was given of public meetings being held without remonstrance on the part of the commoners, or of the lords of the manor, though scarcely going back so long as twenty years; but finds that such user did not constitute a right or prove anything more than an excused or licensed trespass. In this opinion we entirely concur. The common was the soil of the lord of the manor, and the only rights over it were rights of pasture and other commonable rights of the commoners, and perhaps private rights of way. These are the rights which, not having been purchased by the board, are preserved. No such right as that claimed by the appellant on behalf of the public is known to the law. This ground of objection, therefore, entirely fails.
   Secondly, he contended that the common having been 'dedicated to and for the use and recreation of the public as an open and uninclosed space for ever,' the board could not prevent the public from assembling there whenever they pleased for the purpose of hearing sermons, or lectures, or addresses, on any subject, religious, political, or otherwise. If this argument were sound it would follow that any number of public meetings might be held at the same time in various parts of the common, even to the extent of monopolising the whole area, to the disturbance of the neighbourhood and the exclusion of that portion of the public who desired to use it for the purpose of recreation. We are satisfied that such was not the intention of the scheme which Parliament has sanctioned. Its object was to secure in perpetuity the common as a place which the public might use as of right for the purpose of recreation, and in order that all classes may at all times share in its enjoyment, the user of the common is necessarily placed under regulations. Bye-laws are a code of restrictions. Modes of user which, if enjoyed without limitation as to time or place, would unduly interfere with the comfort and enjoyment of

others, such as riding, boating, cricketing, bathing, and the like, are put under reasonable restrictions. It is equally necessary that the holding of public meetings on the common should be also put under regulation. And what can be a more reasonable mode of regulating such meetings, than to require information beforehand what the object and character of the meeting are, in order that the board may be able to judge whether it is such as ought to be allowed on the common, and if so to prescribe reasonable limits as to time and place? Mr De Morgan contends that order may be sufficiently preserved by the arrest and punishment of persons who by becoming riotous, or committing a breach of the peace violate the law. These, however, are retributive measures which operate only indirectly; whereas the Act contemplates and requires precautionary and preventive measures, tending directly to secure the comfortable enjoyment of the common by all classes.

We are therefore of opinion that the bye-law is valid, and consequently the conviction must be affirmed with costs.
Conviction affirmed

NOTES

1. This case, and *Brighton Corpn v Packham* (1908) 72 JP 318, Ch D, confirm that the general public may not acquire a legal right to hold meetings. In the *Brighton* case the corporation was granted a declaration that the defendants had no right to use the beach, which was vested in the corporation, for meetings. Warrington J. stated at 319:

'They say that from time immemorial the public have enjoyed the right of holding open air meetings upon the said seashore uninterruptedly. Is that defence a good defence in law? It is not founded on prescription, which is the right of an individual; it is not founded on custom, which could give a right to a limited section of the public, but it is an alleged right in the public as a whole. No authority has been cited in support of any such claim or right on the part of the public, but authority has been cited to the contrary. If there were such right in the public, it is a little difficult to imagine how such cases as those in which the right of recreation, for example, on a village green, has been held to be necessarily confined to a limited section of the public, have ever been decided, because it is notorious that many claims to that kind of right have been denied because the evidence has shown that it has been enjoyed by the public as a whole. But if a right in the public could have been shown to be a dedication for that purpose then the decision must have been the reverse of that which it in fact was.'

See further, *Brownlie*, pp. 136–7.
2. Challenges to byelaws which prohibit the holding of meetings at particular places or without prior consent have generally been unsuccessful: *Slee v Meadows* (1911) 75 JP 246 DC; *Aldred v Miller* 1925 JC 21; *Aldred v Langmuir* 1932 JC 22. See generally on bye-laws C. A. Cross, *Principles of Local Government Law* (5th edn.), Chap. 6 and *Kruse v Johnson* [1898] 2QB 91, DC.
3. In *Llandudno UDC v Woods* [1899] 2 Ch 705, the council obtained a declaration that W, a clergyman, was not entitled to hold meetings without their consent on the foreshore, of which they were lessees. Cozens Hardy J stated at 709:

'The public are not entitled to cross the shore even for purposes of bathing or amusement. The sands on the seashore are not to be regarded as . . . a highway'.

There was no evidence of any more extensive right gained by prescription or custom. Cozens Hardy J, however, refused in the exercise of his discretion to grant an injunction as there was no evidence of any breach of the peace or disorder:

'I consider this action wholly unnecessary and one that ought not to have been brought' (ibid.)

4. *Bailey v Williamson* (1873) LR 8 QB 118 concerned the validity of regulations under the Parks Regulation Act 1872 which (inter alia) prohibited public addresses in Hyde Park except at certain places. S. 1 of the Act provided that nothing in the Act authorized 'any interference with any right whatever to which any person or persons may be by law entitled'. The Court of Queen's Bench held that there was no 'right' to hold public meetings in the Park. Cockburn CJ said at 125: ' . . . whatever enjoyment the public have been allowed to have of these parks and royal possessions for any purpose has been an enjoyment which the public have had by the gracious concession of the Crown'. The use of Hyde Park is now regulated by the Royal and other Parks and Gardens Regulations, 1977, S. I. 1977 No. 217.

The Trafalgar Square Regulations 1952, S.I. 1952 No. 776

The Minister of Works in exercise of the powers conferred upon him by the Trafalgar Square Act 1844, and the Parks Regulation Acts 1872 and 1926, and of all other powers enabling him in that behalf, hereby makes the following Regulations: . . .
2. Prohibited Acts.—Within the Square the following acts are prohibited:
(1) wilfully interfering with the comfort or convenience of any person in the Square;
(2) dropping or leaving litter or refuse except in a receptacle provided for the purpose;
(3) polluting any water;
(4) walking on any shrubbery or flower bed;
(5) damaging, cutting or picking any tree or plant;
(6) damaging, defacing or climbing on any structure, seat or other Government property;
(7) bathing or paddling.
3. Acts for which Written Permission is required.—Within the Square the following acts are prohibited unless the written permission of the Minister has first been obtained:
(1) selling or distributing anything or offering anything for sale or hire;
(2) carrying on any trade or business;
(3) using artificial light or a tripod or stand for photography;
(4) organising, conducting or taking part in any assembly, parade or procession;
(5) making or giving a public speech or address;
(6) placing or exhibiting any display or representation;
(7) erecting or using any apparatus for the transmission, reception, reproduction or amplification of sound or speech by electrical or mechanical means unless the sound emitted is audible to the user only;
(8) causing any obstruction to free passage;
(9) singing or playing a musical instrument.

NOTES

1. The regulations were made on 8 April 1952, and came into operation on 8 June 1952. The powers are now exercised by the Secretary of State for the Environment. Under the present policy, the Square may be booked for meetings from 2 pm to sunset on Saturdays and from sunrise to sunset on Sundays, Bank Holidays and Good Fridays. No application is considered more than 3 months in advance of the date of a proposed meeting, and there must be at least 5 clear working days in which to consider an application (information supplied by the Department of the Environment).
2. The history of Trafalgar Square as a place of public meeting is discussed in R. Mace, *Trafalgar Square* (1976). Appendix 5 gives a list of applicants for the use of the Square for political meetings. A small minority of applications have been refused since 1952. In 1972 the Home Secretary placed a ban on all meetings concerning Ireland following the Aldershot bombing (See 833 HC Deb 22 March 1972 cols 1497–8).

3.   Two cases in 1888 confirmed that there was no right of public meeting in Trafalgar Square. In *R v Cunninghame Graham and Burns* (1888) 16 Cox CC 420 (below, p. 162) Charles J directed the jury that there was no right of public meeting 'either in Trafalgar-square' or any other public thoroughfare . . . '[T]he use of public thoroughfares is for people to pass and repass along them' (p. 429). In *Ex parte Lewis* (1888) 21 QBD 191, DC, L sought summonses against Henry Matthews, the Home Secretary, and Sir Charles Warren, the Metropolitan Police Commissioner, alleging, inter alia, conspiracy to prevent Her Majesty's subjects from exercising their constitutional and lawful rights, to endanger the public peace, and to inflict grievous bodily harm, and nuisance. The allegations were based upon the conduct of the authorities in relation to the Trafalgar Square riots of 13 November 1887 (below, p. 162). The Divisional Court declined to interfere with the magistrate's decision to refuse the summonses, and rejected the claim that there was a right of public meeting (see above, p. 141). Wills J pointed out at 198 that Trafalgar Square was vested by statute in the Crown with the powers of control and management exercised by the Commissioners of Works.

'Trafalgar Square . . . is completely regulated by Act of Parliament and whatever rights exist must be found in the statute if at all. The right of public meeting is not among them. The right of control appears to be unqualified except by what else is to be found in the Acts [53 Geo 3, cl21, 7 & 8 Vict c 60 and 14 & 15 Vict c 42] and must therefore cover the right of saying under what circumstances, and for what purposes, other than the public rights of passage given by the Acts, it shall be used . . . '

(iii) Near Parliament

In addition to the legislature provisions mentioned below, both Houses of Parliament at the commencement of each session direct the Metropolitan Police Commissioner to keep the streets leading to Parliament open and order that the access to Parliament of Lords and members is not to be obstructed. This power to give such sessional orders derives from parliamentary privilege (see Erskine May, *Parliamentary Practice*, 19th edn. p. 220). The Commissioner enforces these orders by giving directions under section 52 of the Metropolitan Police Act 1839 (below)

Seditious Meetings Act 1817

23. Restriction on meetings in Westminister, etc., during sitting of Parliament or of courts
. . . It shall not be lawful for any person or persons to convene or call together or to give any notice for convening or calling together any meeting of persons consisting of more than fifty persons, or for any number of persons exceeding fifty to meet, in any street, square, or open place in the city or liberties of Westminster, or county of Middlesex, within the distance of one mile from the gate of Westminster Hall, save and except such parts of the parish of Saint Paul's Covent Garden as are within the said distance, for the purpose or on the pretext of considering of or preparing any petition, complaint, remonstrance, declaration, or other address to the King, . . . or to both Houses or either House of Parliament, for alteration of matters in Church or State, on any day on which the two Houses or either House of Parliament shall meet and sit, or shall be summoned or adjourned or prorogued to meet or sit, . . . and . . . if any meeting or assembly, for the purposes or on the pretexts aforesaid, of any persons shall be assembled or holden on any such day, contrary to the intent and meaning of this enactment, such meeting or assembly shall be deemed and taken to be an unlawful assembly, by whomsoever or in consequence of what notice soever such meeting or assembly shall have been holden: . . .

NOTES

1.   In 1932, Tom Mann was required to enter a recognisance of £200, and find two sureties of £100, to keep the peace. He was a leading member of the National Unemployed Workers Movement, which was organising a hunger-march due to arrive in London to present a petition to Parliament. It was alleged that he was an 'inciter of persons to take part in mass demonstrations which are calculated to involve . . . contraventions of the provisions of the Seditious Meetings Act 1817' (see A Barrister, *Justice in England* (1938) pp. 243–246). Mann refused and was sent to prison for two months.
2.   It is an offence under the Tumultuous Petitioning Act 1661 for more than ten persons at any one time to 'repair' to the Queen or to Parliament to present any address.

Sessional Order of the House of Commons 3 November 1977

METROPOLITAN POLICE

Motion made, and Question proposed,
    That the Commissioner of the Police of the Metropolis do take care that during the Session of Parliament the passages through the streets leading to this House be kept free and open, and that no obstruction be permitted to hinder the passage of Members to and from this House, and that no disorder be allowed in Westminster Hall, or in the passages leading to this House, during the Sitting of Parliament, and that there be no annoyance therein or thereabouts; and that the Serjeant at Arms attending this House do communicate this Order to the Commissioner aforesaid.

Metropolitan Police Act 1839

52. Commissioners may make regulations for the route of carriages, and persons, and for preventing obstruction of the streets during public processions, etc., or in the neighbourhood of public buildings, etc.
. . . It shall be lawful for the commissioners of police from time to time, and as occasion shall require, to make regulations for the route to be observed by all carts, carriages, horses, and persons, and for preventing obstruction of the streets and thoroughfares within the metropolitan police district, in all times of public processions, public rejoicings, or illuminations, and also to give directions to the constables for keeping order and for preventing any obstruction of the thoroughfares in the immediate neighbourhood of her Majesty's palaces and the public offices, the High Court of Parliament, the courts of law and equity, the police courts, the theatres, and other places of public resort, and in any case when the streets or thoroughfares may be thronged or may be liable to be obstructed.

NOTES

1.   By s. 54(9) of this Act, 'every person' commits an offence 'who, after being made acquainted with the regulations or directions' made under s. 52, 'shall wilfully disregard or not conform himself thereunto'. The maximum penalty is a £50 fine (Criminal Law Act 1977 s. 31 and Sch. 6). There is a power under s. 54 for a constable to arrest without warrant any person who commits an offence under that section within his view.
2.   The following direction was made by the Commissioner on 21 April 1966:

    '*Processions prohibited during the sitting of Parliament.* By virtue of the powers conferred on me by section 52 of the Metropolitan Police Act 1839, I the undersigned Commissioner of

Police of the metropolis do hereby give directions to all constables that during the session of Parliament the following sessional order shall be enforced: [the order was recited] And I further direct all constables in pursuance of the said order and by virtue of my powers under the said Act: (1) That all assemblies or processions of persons shall be dispersed and shall not be in or proceed along any street, square or open place within the area specified hereunder on any day on which Parliament is sitting: South side of the river Thames between Waterloo and Vauxhall Bridges, Vauxhall Bridge Road, Victoria Street (between Vauxhall Bridge Road and Buckingham Palace Road), Grosvenor Gardens, Grosvenor Place, Piccadilly, Coventry Street, New Coventry Street, Leicester Square (north side), Cranbourn Street, Long Acre, Bow Street, Wellington Street, crossing Strand and Victoria Embankment west of Waterloo Bridge. Provided that processions may be routed along the thoroughfares named except Victoria Embankment west of Waterloo Bridge. (2) That they shall prevent or remove any cause of obstruction within the area named in paragraph (1) hereof, so that every facility shall be afforded for the free passage of members to and from the Houses of Parliament on any day on which Parliament is sitting.'

This direction was at issue in *Papworth v Coventry* [1967] 2 All ER 41 [1967] 1 WLR 663, DC. P and others took part in a 'vigil' in Whitehall on both sides of Downing Street to call attention to the situation in Vietnam. They were spaced out and stationary, and were not disorderly. They refused to move when requested and were prosecuted under s.54(9) for failure to comply with the direction. The court held (1) that the sessional order itself could have no effect outside the walls and precincts of the Houses of Parliament; and (2) that the direction was to be construed as if it referred only to such assemblies or processions of persons as are capable of causing consequential obstruction to the free passage of members to and from the Houses of Parliament or their departure therefrom, or disorder in the neighbourhood or annoyance thereabouts. Any wider sense would have been ultra vires the Commissioner. The case was remitted to the stipendiary magistrate to determine whether the conduct 'constituted an assembly which was capable of giving rise consequentially either to obstruction of streets and thoroughfares in the immediate neighbourhood of the Houses of Parliament, or to disorder, annoyance of the kind itself likely to lead to a breach of the peace.' Papworth was subsequently acquitted (*Brownlie*, p. 29).

3. The enforcement of sessional orders has also been secured by the prosecution of persons for wilfully obstructing the police in the execution of their duty. See *Pankhurst v Jarvis* (1909) 22 Cox CC 228, DC, and *Despard v Wilcox* (1910) 22 Cox CC 258, DC, cases concerning suffragettes.

4. Processions are stopped at the boundary of the 'Sessional Area' and marchers are allowed to proceed independently to Parliament to lobby MPs (Report of the *Commissioner of Police of the Metropolis for 1971*, Cmnd. 4986 pp. 17, 44–45).

5. Disorder within the precincts of Parliament is dealt with by police under the direction of the Serjeant at Arms, as in 1966, where some members of the Committee of 100 attempted to make speeches in the House of Commons, and others sat down in Old Palace Yard (*Report of the Commissioner of Police of the Metropolis for 1966*, Cmnd. 3315, p. 13).

(iv) Publicly owned premises

As the holding of street meetings is likely to be unlawful (see above, pp. 136–139), and therefore dependent in practice upon the goodwill of the police, it becomes even more crucial to those that wish to organize meetings that premises be available. Political meetings today seem to arouse such little public enthusiasm that finding premises is less of a problem than filling them. Extremist groups which are likely to arouse opposition naturally have most difficulty. One of the contributory factors in the decline of Mosley's British Union of Fascists after 1936 was the difficulty in hiring halls for their rallies (J. Stevenson and C. Cook, *The Slump* (1977) p. 210). Prior to the Olympia meeting in June 1934, the police prevented a B.U.F. rally at White City by persuading the chairman of the White City Board to demand so high a bond upon the safety of the hall that Mosley had to decline the booking.

The traditional importance of meetings during elections is recognised by section 82 of the Representation of the People Act 1949 (below). In addition the discretionary powers of management of public premises must be exercised within the constraints of the ultra vires doctrine. Accordingly, a fixed policy to refuse the use of premises to particular groups or for particular purposes may fall foul of the rule that requires individual exercises of discretion (de Smith, *Judicial Review of Administrative Action* 4th edn., pp. 311–317), and decisions based on improper considerations may also be challenged (ibid., pp. 322–343). There do not appear however, to have been any such legal proceedings in this context.

Representation of the People Act 1949

ELECTION MEETINGS

82. Right to use certain schools and halls for meetings at parliamentary elections
(1) Subject to the provisions of this section a candidate at a parliamentary election shall be entitled for the purpose of holding public meetings in furtherance of his candidature to the use at reasonable times between the receipt of the writ and the date of the poll of-
    (*a*) a suitable room in the premises of any school to which this section applies;
    (*b*) any meeting room to which this section applies.

(2) This section applies—
    (*a*) in England and Wales, to county schools and voluntary schools of which the premises are situated in the constituency or an adjoining constituency; . . .
but a candidate shall not be entitled under this section to the use of a room in school premises outside the constituency if there is a suitable room in other premises in the constituency which are reasonably accessible from the same parts of the constituency as those outside and are premises of a school to which this section applies.
(3) This section applies to meeting rooms situated in the constituency, the expense of maintaining which is payable wholly or mainly out of public funds or out of any rate, or by a body whose expenses are so payable.
(4) Where a room is used for a meeting in pursuance of the rights conferred by this section, the person by whom or on whose behalf the meeting is convened—
    (*a*) may be required to pay for the use of the room a charge not exceeding the amount of any actual and necessary expenses incurred in preparing, warming, lighting and cleaning the room and providing attendants for the meeting and restoring the room to its usual condition after the meeting; and
    (*b*) shall defray any damage done to the room or the premises in which it is situated, or to the furniture, fittings or apparatus in the room or premises.
(5) A candidate shall not be entitled to exercise the rights conferred by this section except on reasonable notice; and this section shall not authorise any interference with the hours during which a room in school premises is used for educational purposes, or any interference with the use of a meeting room either for the purposes of the person maintaining it or under a prior agreement for its letting for any purpose. . . .
(7) For the purposes of this section (except those of paragraph (*b*) of subsection (4) thereof), the premises of a school shall not be taken to include any private dwelling house, and in this section—
    (*a*) the expression 'meeting room' means any room which it is the practice to let for public meetings; and
    (*b*) the expression 'room' includes a hall, gallery or gymnasium.
(8) This section shall not apply to Northern Ireland.

NOTES

1. S. 83 makes similar provision in respect of local government elections. Any question arising under ss. 82 or 83 as to what is reasonable or suitable is to be determined by the Secretary of State (s.83(2); Sch. 7, para. 1(2)). Local authorities are to maintain lists of rooms which may be used (ibid. Sch. 7).

2. Local councils with a general policy of refusing to allow their premises to be used for National Front meetings have been compelled to accede to requests to hold election meetings where the Front have had candidates in parliamentary elections (e.g. Manchester City Council: *The Times*, 20 April 1978).

What is the position if the organisers of a National Front meeting, purportedly held under s.82, only allow Front members or ticket holders into the meeting? What if the decision is taken by police outside in order to preserve the peace? In July 1978, Manchester City Council refused the National Front permission to hold an election meeting in a local school claiming that it would not be a public meeting, and that council employees had said they would refuse to take the steps necessary to make the room available such as opening the school. The local county court judge held that he had no jurisdiction to entertain the Front's claim for damages for breach of statutory duty (*The Times* 8 and 11 July, 1978, J. F. Garner (1978) Local Government Chronicle, p. 778).

3. In October 1979, the Court of Appeal held that the Labour-controlled Great Yarmouth Council could not veto a booking for the annual conference of the National Front which had been accepted by the council when the Conservatives had been in power. The NF had paid over £6,000 for the booking fee and insurance to cover the risk of damage to council property. Lord Denning stated that the conference should go ahead in the interests of freedom of speech and assembly and of the importance of upholding a contract *Verrall v Great Yarmouth Borough Council* [1980] 1 All ER 839.

4. See the Green Paper on public order legislation (1980) Cmnd. 7891, pp. 24–26.

(v) Powers to ban or control processions

There are no general powers whereby public bodies or officials may prohibit in advance the holding of a meeting, although there are such powers in relation to land whose management or control is vested in the state (see, for example, pp. 140–143, 143–145). There are, however, general statutory powers to ban or control processions contained in section 3 of the Public Order Act 1936 (below). Moreover, any meeting or procession which constitutes an unlawful assembly may be dispersed (see pp. 159–166), and it may be lawful to disperse a lawful assembly where necessary to prevent a breach of the peace (see pp. 167–176).

Public Order Act 1936

3. Powers for the preservation of public order on the occasion of processions
(1) If the chief officer of police, having regard to the time or place at which and the circumstances in which any public procession is taking place or is intended to take place and to the route taken or proposed to be taken by the procession, has reasonable ground for apprehending that the procession may occasion serious public disorder, he may give directions imposing upon the persons organising or taking part in the procession such conditions as appear to him necessary for the preservation of public order, including conditions prescribing the route to be taken by the procession and conditions prohibiting the procession from entering any public place specified in the directions:

Provided that no conditions restricting the display of flags, banners, or emblems shall be imposed under this subsection except such as are reasonably necessary to prevent risk of a breach of the peace.

(2) If at any time the chief officer of police is of opinion that by reason of particular circumstances existing in any borough or urban district or in any part thereof the powers conferred on him by the last foregoing subsection will not be sufficient to enable him to prevent serious public disorder being occasioned by the holding of public processions in that borough, district or part, he shall apply to the council of the borough or district for an order prohibiting for such period not exceeding three months as may be specified in the application the holding of all public processions or of any class of public procession so specified either in the borough or urban district or in that part thereof, as the case may be, and upon receipt of the application the council may, with the consent of a Secretary of State, make an order either in terms of the application or with such modifications as may be approved by the Secretary of State.

This subsection shall not apply within the City of London as defined for the purposes of the Acts relating to the City police or within the Metropolitan police district.

(3) If at any time the Commissioner of the City of London police or·the Commissioner of police of the Metropolis is of opinion that by reason of particular circumstances existing in his police area or in any part thereof, the powers conferred on him by subsection (1) of this section will not be sufficient to enable him to prevent serious public disorder being occasioned by the holding of public processions in that area or part, he may, with the consent of the Secretary of State, make an order prohibiting for such period not exceeding three months as may be specified in the order the holding of all public processions or of any class of public procession so specified either in the police area or in that part thereof, as the case may be.

(4) Any person who knowingly fails to comply with any directions given or conditions imposed under this section, or organises or assists in organising any public procession held or intended to be held in contravention of an order made under this section or incites any person to take part in such a procession, shall be guilty of an offence.

NOTES

1. The term 'urban district' is to be construed as a reference to a new district council under the Local Government Act 1972 (1972 Act, s.79(3)). This means that the powers under s.3(2) may be exercised throughout England and Wales, including those areas which formerly had a rural district council. Boroughs existing before Local Government reorganisation were abolished by the 1972 Act, but it is possible for a new district to be conferred the status of borough under section 245 of that Act. The term 'public procession' is defined in s.9 (see p. 151). The maximum penalty under s.3(4) is now a fine of £500, 3 months' imprisonment, or both (Public Order Act 1936 s.7; Criminal Law Act 1977 s.31 and Sch. 6).

2. Under s.3(1) note the difference between the subjectively worded power to give directions as to route etc., and the objectively worded power in relation to flags, banners and emblems.

3. May a specified procession be banned under s.3(2)? If it is known that only one group are planning a march on a particular day, would it be lawful to ban 'all marches' on that day?

4. Directions and orders under this section are potentially reviewable in the courts under the ultra vires doctrine. A challenge might be made directly, on an application for judicial review under RSC Order 53, or collaterally, as a defence to a prosecution under s.3(4). There is, however, no challenge on the merits. Cf. *The Times*, 21 April 1980, p. 2.

5. In *Flockhart v Robinson* [1950] 2 KB 498, DC, F was prosecuted under section 3. The Metropolitan Police Commissioner on 3 October 1949 banned all public processions of a political character within the Metropolitan Police District. On 15 October, F organised a procession of members of a political group, the Union Movement, which procession lawfully dispersed on reaching Temple Bar. Later that day he met about 150 members at Hyde Park Corner who followed him in loose formation when he moved along Piccadilly, and then closed ranks. He gave signals to guide them through the traffic and direction signals. Members other than F sang the Horst Wessel song and shouted political slogans. F led them round Piccadilly Circus and into Coventry Street, where they were broken up by the police. F's conviction for 'organising' a procession contrary to s.3(4) was upheld by the Divisional Court (Lord Goddard CJ and Morris J, Finnemore J dissenting). Lord Goddard CJ stated at 502 'A procession is not a mere body of persons: it is a body of persons moving along a route. Therefore the person who organises the route is the person who organises the procession'.

6. In recent years, bans under s.3(2) and (3) have been uncommon. In November 1974 the Home Secretary approved orders made by Birmingham, Solihull and Coventry councils banning any funeral procession for James McDade, who was killed when planting a bomb in Coventry. According to the report of H. M. Chief Inspector of Constabulary, this was the first time s.3(2) had been used for many years (1974–75 HC 406, p. 61). When a proposed National Front march in Hyde was to be met by a large counter-demonstration, the Chief Constable of Greater Manchester obtained an order banning all political processions in Tameside for some 6 weeks.

'In the event, one of the leaders of the National Front announced that he would walk through Hyde on 8 October in protest against the ban. It also became clear that the National Front were determined to hold some other activity in Greater Manchester on that day—either a march or possibly some other form of demonstration which could not be prohibited under existing legislation. The Chief Constable of Greater Manchester decided that the best hope of avoiding serious disorder was not to publicise the venue for the National Front demonstration and to deploy some 6,000 officers drawn from Greater Manchester and other police forces, under mutual aid arrangements, to preserve the peace. These arrangements were operational decisions for the Chief Constable but you had made it clear following the disturbances at Lewisham and Ladywood that the Government was determined to support chief officers in the use of their powers to prevent violence and you publicly declared your support for the Chief Constable avoiding what could have been a major disturbance with injuries to public and the police and damage to property.'
(*Report of H M Chief Inspector of Constabulary for 1977* (1977–78 HC 545) (p. 63).

In 1978, the Metropolitan Police Commissioner reported:

'Candidates representing the National Front contested the parliamentary by-elections at Ilford and Brixton. After carefully weighing all the circumstances of the campaign at Ilford I sought your consent to a ban under the Public Order Act 1936. From the 24 February for a period of two months, public processions, other than those of a religious, festive or ceremonial character, were banned within the Metropolitan Police District. The purpose was to restrain those extremists who were deliberately seeking confrontation to further their political ends. The Brixton by-election also fell within the period of the ban. The ban, of course, did not affect public meetings and large numbers of police were deployed during each by-election to prevent serious disorder. Later in the year three National Front marches took place and, as the circumstances had changed, I decided not to seek prohibition; in the event there was little disorder.'
(*Report for 1978*, Cmnd. 7580, p. 7).

A ban on all but religious, educational, festive or ceremonial marches was imposed in Leeds in May 1978 as the local elections approached because of high feelings between extremists. The Leeds stipendiary magistrate ruled that the trade union movement's traditional May Day march did not have a 'ceremonial' character. The trades council secretary was fined £40 for assisting in the organisation of an illegal march (*Daily Telegraph*, 22 September 1978).

A list of bans under the 1936 Act is given in the NCCL newpaper *Rights* Vol. 2 No. 5 June/July 1978 p. 9.

7. It has been suggested that the Public Order Act 1936 be strengthened (1) by giving the authorities power to ban meetings as well as processions; and (2) by imposing a legal requirement that prior notice of processions be given to the authorities. The Public Order Act (N I) 1951 covers both these points in Northern Ireland.

There are, apparently, 115 precedents for notice requirements in local legislation since 1910, although many only apply to processions which involve live circus animals (968 HC Deb 21 June 1979 col 1585). Local authorities promoting 'general powers' bills to replace their local legislation, which is due to lapse under the Local Government Act 1972 s.262, have tended to include 'notice' provisions, (see e.g. the West Midlands County Council Act 1980, s. 14, which requires notice to be given at least 72 hours before a procession or as soon thereafter as is reasonably practicable: 977 HC Deb 21 January 1980 col 101–115.).

Lord Scarman, in his Report on the Red Lion Square disorders (above, p. 124) rejected suggestions for notice requirements for public processions (paras. 128, 129).

'I do not think the need for it has been established: and it does present really insuperable difficulty for the urgently called demonstration . . . It cannot be said too often that our law assumes that people will be tolerant, self-disciplined, and willing to co-operate with the police. The assumption is still sound: that is why the police go unarmed, and also why, with no legal requirement of notice, the police are in fact notified in at least 80 per cent of the cases. There are some who—law or no law—would never give notice: but they are on the very fringe of our society and should not, I suggest, force upon the law a largely unnecessary requirement, which can at times be an embarrassment to law-abiding citizens. In the few instances where no notification is given, the police have so far experienced no difficulty in finding out that a demonstration is planned. An effective demonstration needs a degree of advance publicity: the police, therefore, are seldom ignorant of what is planned.'

8. The Metropolitan Police Commissioner suggested to the Scarman Inquiry on the Red Lion Square disorders (see above p. 124) that s.3(1) should be amended so as to make it an offence to disobey the directions of a police constable when taking part in a public procession. Lord Scarman commented (para. 131):

'This, I think, goes too far but it is of critical importance that the law should be clarified. It should not be possible to challenge a route direction given by a senior police officer to a procession that is under way. I think it likely that a police officer already has the power to direct a procession en route if a breach of the peace is reasonably apprehended, or if it is required by the exigencies of traffic exercising its right of passage. I recommend that the statute be amended so as to confer upon the senior officer present a power to give a direction as to the route to be taken, if he thinks it necessary in the interests of public order.'

He did, however, reject a suggestion that a ban on processions under s.3 should be open to judicial review (e.g. by an appeal to a judge in chambers), as this would be 'undesirable (involving the courts in 'political' decisions), and impracticable' (para. 134). See also the Green Paper on public order legislation (Cmnd. 7891 1980) pp. 10–24.

(b) THE CONDUCT OF MEETINGS AND PROCESSIONS

(i) Introduction

There are many criminal offences which may be committed by those who take part in or disrupt meetings and processions. Some have already been mentioned, of which the most important in practice are the Police Act 1964 section 51 (above p. 36) and the Highways Act 1959, section 121 (above

p. 138). The Criminal Damage Act 1971 makes it an offence to destroy or damage property belonging to another without lawful excuse (section 1(1)). It is also an offence for a person to have with him in any public place any offensive weapon without lawful authority or reasonable excuse (Prevention of Crime Act 1953, section 1; cf. Public Order Act 1936, section 4). The common law offence of affray was brought back into use by prosecutors in the late 1950s. (See *R v Sharp* [1957] 1 QB 552, CCA). It covers unlawful fighting or violence or an unlawful display of force, in such a manner that a bystander of reasonably firm character might reasonably be expected to be terrified (*Smith and Hogan* pp. 757–760; *Button v Director of Public Prosecutions* [1966] AC 591, HL, *R v Summers* (1972) 56 Cr App Rep 604 CA; *Taylor v Director of Public Prosecutions* [1973] AC 964, HL. The Criminal Law Act 1977 made it an offence to use or threaten violence to secure entry to premises (section 6); to occupy premises as a trespasser and fail to leave on being required to do so by a displaced residential occupier or a protected intending occupier (section 7); to trespass with a weapon of offence (section 8); to trespass upon consular or diplomatic premises (section 9); and to obstruct court officers executing process for possession against unauthorised occupiers (section 10). We deal here with the following offences against public order: offensive conduct conducive to breaches of the peace; riot; unlawful assembly; disorder at public meetings.

(ii) Section 5 of the Public Order Act 1936

Public Order Act 1936

5. Prohibition of offensive conduct conducive to breaches of the peace
[Any person who in any public place or at any public meeting—
    (*a*) uses threatening, abusive or insulting words or behaviour, or
    (*b*) distributes or displays any writing, sign or visible representation which is threatening, abusive or insulting.
with intent to provoke a breach of the peace or whereby a breach of the peace is likely to be occasioned, shall be guilty of an offence.]

7. Enforcement
(3) A constable may arrest without warrant any person reasonably suspected by him to be committing an offence under ss. 1, 4 or 5 of this Act.

9. Interpretation, etc.
(1) In this Act the following expressions have the meanings hereby respectively assigned to them, that is to say:—
'Meeting' means a meeting held for the purpose of the discussion of matters of public interest or for the purpose of the expression of views on such matters;
'Private premises' means premises to which the public have access (whether on payment or otherwise) only by permission of the owner, occupier, or lessee of the premises;
'Public meeting' includes any meeting in a public place *and* any meeting which the public or any section thereof are permitted to attend, whether on payment or otherwise;
['Public place' includes any highway and any other premises or place to which at the material time the public have or are permitted to have access, whether on payment or otherwise']
'Public procession' means a procession in a public place; . . .

NOTES

1. The current s.5 was substituted for the original by the Race Relations Act 1965, s.7. The maximum penalty is now six months' imprisonment or a £1000 fine or both (Criminal Law Act 1977, s.15(1) and Sch. 17). Between 1963 and 1978 it was a hybrid offence (Public Order Act 1963, s.1(1)), but it is now triable only summarily (Criminal Law Act 1977 s.15 and Sch. 1(1); Report of the James committee on *The Distribution of Criminal Business* *between the Crown Court and the Magistrates' Courts* (1975) Cmnd. 6323 paras. 151–155.)

2. This is the key public order offence. It is used in preference to the more serious charges of riot, unlawful assembly and affray (see above p. 126). There are provisions analogous to s.5 in the Metropolitan Police Act 1839, s.54(13), the Theatres Act 1968, ss. 5 and 6, and the Public Order Act 1936, s.5A (see p. 393–397). The 1839 Act proscribes the use in any thoroughfare or public place within the Metropolitan Police District of any threatening, abusive or insulting words or behaviour with intent to provoke a breach of the peace, or whereby a breach of the peace may be occasioned. The maximum penalty is a £ 50 fine. It was on this and similar offences in local legislation that s.5 was modelled when introduced in 1936 on a nationwide basis.

3. The definition of 'public place' was substituted for the previous, narrower, definition by s.33 of the Criminal Justice Act 1972. The previous definition included highways, parks etc. and 'any open space to which . . . the public have access . . . ' In *Cooper v Shield* [1971] 2 QB 334, DC, threatening behaviour on a station platform was held not to be in a public place for the purpose of a prosecution under s.5, as the platform was not an 'open space'. In *Cawley v Frost* [1976] 3 All ER 743, [1976] 1 WLR 1207, DC, the speedway track between the pitch and the stands at the ground of Halifax Town A.F.C. was held to constitute a 'public place' within the revised definition, notwithstanding that the public were not permitted to have access to it. Where the public had access to the premises, those premises were to be considered in their entirety, and the fact that the public were denied access to certain areas did not exclude them from being part of a 'public place'. Cf. *Anderson v Miller* [1976] Crim LR 743, DC, where the area behind a counter in a shop was held to be part of a 'public place' for the purposes of s.19 of the Firearms Act 1968, which makes it an offence to have a loaded firearm in a public place without lawful authority or reasonable excuse. Public place is defined as in the Public Order Act 1936 (Firearms Act 1968, s.57(4)).

The front garden of a private house is not a 'public place' notwithstanding that there is normally implied permission for members of the public with legitimate business to approach the premises through the garden (*R v Edwards and Roberts* (1978) 67 Cr App Rep 228, [1978] Crim LR 564 CA). However, an offence under s.5 may be committed where the words or behaviour are used by or directed to a person in a public place (Ibid; *Wilson v Skeock* (1949) 113 JP 294 at 295 per Lord Goddard CJ; *Ward v Holman* [1964] 2 QB 580, DC) In *Ward v Holman* the Divisional Court rejected an argument (based on the long title of the Act, above, p. 127) that the Public Order Act 1936 was limited to conduct at political meetings and the like, and could not be extended to cover disputes between neighbours.

4. The operation of s.5 in practice has been considered by D. G. T. Williams [1967] Crim LR 385 and A. Dickey [1971] Crim LR 265.

It is clear that a conviction under s.5 is only justified where (1) the defendant's conduct has been more than merely 'offensive' or 'annoying' and (2) there has been some threat to the peace. Williams and Dickey show that it does not seem that magistrates are consistently rigorous in observing these restrictions. Consider for example the convictions of (1) the person who took off his clothes in one of the fountains in Trafalgar Square (*The Times*, 7 November 1967; Dickey, op. cit. p. 269); (2) the persons who shouted 'Remember Biafra' during the two minutes' silence at the 1969

Remembrance Day ceremony in Whitehall (*The Times*, 11 November 1969; Dickey, op. cit p. 269); and the person who painted the word 'Jews' in two-foot high letters on the garden wall of a house occupied by a Jewish family, the father of whom had been a prisoner at Dachau (Dickey, op. cit. p. 270–1). The section has been used in prosecutions of 'streakers'. See also *Brutus v Cozens*, below, p. 155.

The Court of Appeal (Criminal Division) have warned that it is important that s.5 'should not be misused' (*R v Ambrose*, (1973) 57 Crim App Rep 538 at 540).

The significance of s.5 prosecutions in relation to disorder at football matches is illustrated by the figures given by P. E. Marsh, (1977) 4 British Journal of Law and Society, p. 257. In 1974/75, 55 arrests out of a total of 78 at Oxford United's ground were under s.5. (See also R. Ingham and others, *Football Hooliganism*, (1978)).

5. S.3D of the New Zealand Police Offences Act 1927 provides that a person commits an offence 'who, in or within view of any public place . . . ., or within the hearing of any person therein, behaves in a riotous, offensive, threatening, insulting, or disorderly manner, or uses any threatening, abusive, or insulting words.' This is significantly wider than s.5 of the Public Order Act 1936, but the judges in New Zealand have been concerned to avoid the penalising of mildly anti-social conduct. Thus in *Melser v Police* [1967] NZLR 437, CA, Turner J stated at 444 that

'Disorderly conduct is conduct . . . which, while sufficiintly ill-mannered, or in bad taste, to meet with the disapproval of well-conducted and reasonable men and women, is also something more—it must, in my opinion, tend to annoy or insult such persons as are faced with it—and sufficiently deeply or seriously to warrant the interference of the criminal law . . . It cannot on the other hand be necessary to go so far as to prove a likely or imminent breach of the peace.'
McCarthy J stated at 446:
'an offence against good manners, a failure of good taste, a breach of morality, even though these may be contrary to the general order of public opinion, is not enough to establish this offence. There must be conduct which not only can fairly be characterised as distorderly, but also is likely to cause a disturbance or to annoy others considerably.'

The court upheld the convictions for disorderly conduct of persons who demonstrated against American involvement in the Vietnam war by chaining themselves to the pillars at the entrance to Parliament House at the time of the visit of the US Vice President. In *Kinney v Police* [1971] NZLR 924 the court allowed K's appeal against conviction for disorderly conduct. He had waded into an ornamental pond in a public park normally occupied only by goldfish and a few wild ducks: 'The ducks seemed unperturbed – they remained on the surface of the water with scarcely an increase in their rate of stroke. The attitude of the goldfish is unknown.' Woodhouse J regarded this as a 'mildly incongruous prank' (p. 296) '[T]he section should not be allowed to scoop up all sorts of minor troubles and it certainly is not designed to enable the police to discipline every irregular or inconvenient, or exhibitionist activity or to put a criminal sanction on over-exuberant behaviour, even when it might be possible to discern a few conventional hands raised in protest or surprise' (p. 926).

The defendant's loud reference to a police officer as an 'officious bastard' was held not to justify a disorderly conduct conviction given that he was unaware that the officer had followed him from the hotel where they had just had an altercation. The officer was 'the one and only person to whom [the remarks] could be both a serious insult and a source of annoyance' (*O'Connor v Police* [1972] NZLR 379). (See also *Derbyshire v Police* [1967] NZLR 391).

Jordan v Burgoyne [1963] 2 QB 744, [1963] 2 All ER 225, [1963] 2 WLR 1045, Queen's Bench Divisional Court

On 1 July 1962, at a public meeting in Trafalgar Square, there was a crowd of some 2,000 people at about 3 p.m. which increased to some 5,000 by about 5 p.m. The speakers' platform was divided from the crowd by a line of police. A group of young people positioned near the speakers' platform contained many Jews, supporters of the Campaign for Nuclear Disarmament and communists who intended to prevent the meeting. During the address of John Tyndall, the police stopped the meeting on four occasions to restore order. After that address, the defendant read a prepared speech to the crowd. During both speeches there was considerable opposition from the crowd, but the main disorder was concentrated in the group near the platform. At about 5.15 p.m. when the defendant used the following words: '. . . more and more people every day . . . are opening their eyes and coming to say with us Hitler was right. They are coming to say that our real enemies, the people we should have fought, were not Hitler and the National Socialists of Germany but world Jewry and its associates in this country,' there was complete disorder, an outcry and a general surge forward by the crowd towards the speakers' platform. At that point, the police stopped the meeting. The defendant was charged with using insulting words whereby a breach of the peace was likely to be occasioned, contrary to section 5 of the Public Order Act 1936. The justices convicted the defendant who appealed to quarter sessions. Quarter sessions were of the opinion that the words used by the defendant were highly insulting, but were not likely to lead ordinary, reasonable persons to commit breaches of the peace, and allowed the appeal.

Lord Parker CJ: . . . Speaking for myself, I had great difficulty in understanding what quarter sessions were intending to convey. It seems to me, however, that what they had in mind was a hypothetical audience of ordinary, reasonable citizens, whatever their creed, faith, race or political views might be. In other words, they were eliminating from the audience anybody who was intent, for instance, on breaking up the meeting, whatever words the speaker used.

It may be that that is what quarter sessions had in mind, but, even if that be so, I cannot myself, having read the speech, imagine any reasonable citizen, certainly one who was a Jew, not being provoked beyond endurance, and not only a Jew but a coloured man, and quite a number of people of this country who were told that they were merely tools of the Jews, and that they had fought in the war on the wrong side, and matters of that sort.

But, be that as may, in my judgment, there is no room here for any test as to whether any member of the audience is a reasonable man or an ordinary citizen, or whatever epithet one might like to apply . . .

This is, as I have said, a Public Order Act, and if in fact it is apparent that a body of persons are present—and let me assume in the defendant's favour that they are a body of hooligans— yet if words are used which threaten, abuse or insult—all very strong words—then that person must take his audience as he finds them, and if those words to that audience or that part of the audience are likely to provoke a breach of the peace, then the speaker is guilty of an offence. I will assume in the defendant's favour that this body of young persons was a body of hooligans, although I am not saying that they were, and I will assume that they came with the preconceived idea of preventing him from speaking, yet the police prevented them from obstructing the defendant and enabled him to speak and then, in his opening words, directed to those 200 or 300 people, he said: 'As for the red rabble here present with us in Trafalgar Square it is not a very good afternoon at all. Some of them are looking far from wholesome, more than usual I mean. We shall of course excuse them if they have to resort to smelling salts or first aid. Meanwhile, let them howl these multi-racial warriors of the Left. It is a sound that comes natural to them, it saves them from the strain of thinking for themselves.'

Those were words which were intended to be and were deliberately insulting to that body of persons being restrained by the police and on that, and on that alone, it seems to me that there was a clear contravention of section 5 of the Act of 1936.

The defendant, who has conducted his own case with great skill and industry, has been inclined to elevate this case into a cause célèbre in the sense that, if he is convicted, then there is some inroad into the doctrine of free speech. It is nothing of the sort. A man is entitled to express his own views as strongly as he likes, to criticise his opponents, to say disagreeable things about his opponents and about their policies, and to do anything of that sort. But what he must not do is—and these are the words of the section—he must not threaten, he must not be abusive and he must not insult them, 'insult' in the sense of 'hit by words.' It seems to me that this is a perfectly clear case and that the defendant was guilty of the offence charged.

Ashworth and **Winn JJ** agreed

Appeal allowed.

NOTES

1. See D. G. T. Williams (1963)26 MLR 425; A. Dickey [1971] Crim LR 265, 272–275.
2. How far does the proposition that 'if words are used which threaten, abuse or insult . . . then that person must take his audience as he finds them' extend? Consider these cases:

D uses words which on their face are not insulting, but which are in fact, unknown to D, insulting to members of the audience. (See Williams, op. cit. p. 429)

D uses words which on their face are insulting of persons known not to be present, but which cause a breach of the peace (e.g. 'X is a crook' where X is known to be elsewhere but there are friends of his in the audience). (See *Smith and Hogan*, pp. 761–762; *Brownlie*, pp. 7–8)

Brutus v Cozens [1973] AC 854, [1972] 2 All ER 1297, [1972] 2 WLR 521, 56 Cr App Rep 799, House of Lords

Members of the public were admitted to watch the annual open tennis tournament at Wimbledon from stands around the courts. They were not allowed access to the courts. During a tennis match involving Drysdale, a South African, B stepped on to No. 2 court blowing a whistle. He threw around leaflets, attempted to give one to a player and sat down on the court. Upon the blowing of the whistle other persons, some bearing banners or placards on which slogans were written, came on to the court and more leaflets were distributed. Play was stopped. The appellant was charged with using insulting behaviour whereby a breach of the peace was likely to be occasioned contrary to section 5 of the Public Order Act 1936. The justices held that his behaviour had not been insulting, and dismissed the information without calling on him to give evidence.

On appeal by the respondent prosecutor, the Divisional Court held that 'insulting . . . behaviour' in section 5 of the Act of 1936 was behaviour which affronted other people and evidenced a disrespect or contempt for their rights, and which reasonable persons would foresee as likely to cause resentment or protest; that on the findings of the justices, which were to be regarded as provisional, insulting behaviour by the appellant had been established and the case would be sent back to them to continue the hearing. B appealed to the House of Lords.

Lord Reid: . . . It appears that the object of this demonstration was to protest against the apartheid policy of the Government of South Africa. But it is not said that that government was insulted. The insult is said to have been offered to or directed at the spectators.

The spectators at No. 2 Court were upset: they made loud shouts, gesticulated and shook their fists and while the appellant was being removed some showed hostility and attempted to strike him. . . .

It is not clear to me what precisely is the point of law which we have to decide. The question in the case stated for the opinion of the court is 'Whether, on the above statement of facts, we came to a correct determination and decision in point of law.' This seems to assume that the meaning of the word 'insulting' in section 5 is a matter of law. And the Divisional Court appear to have proceeded on that footing.

In my judgment that is not right. The meaning of an ordinary word of the English language is not a question of law. The proper construction of a statute is a question of law. If the context shows that a word is used in an unusual sense the court will determine in other words what that unusual sense is. But here there is in my opinion no question of the word 'insulting' being used in any unusual sense. It appears to me, for reasons which I shall give later, to be intended to have its ordinary meaning. It is for the tribunal which decides the case to consider, not as law but as fact, whether in the whole circumstances the words of the statute do or do not as a matter of ordinary usage of the English language cover or apply to the facts which have been proved. If it is alleged that the tribunal has reached a wrong decision then there can be a question of law but only of a limited character. The question would normally be whether their decision was unreasonable in the sense that no tribunal acquainted with the ordinary use of language could reasonably reach that decision.

Were it otherwise we should reach an impossible position. When considering the meaning of a word one often goes to a dictionary. There one finds other words set out. And if one wants to pursue the matter and find the meaning of those other words the dictionary will give the meaning of those other words in still further words which often include the word for whose meaning one is searching.

No doubt the court could act as a dictionary. It could direct the tribunal to take some word or phrase other than the word in the statute and consider whether that word or phrase applied to or covered the facts proved. But we have been warned time and again not to substitute other words for the words of a statute. And there is very good reason for that. Few words have exact synonyms. The overtones are almost always different.

Or the court could frame a definition. But then again the tribunal would be left with words to consider. No doubt a statute may contain a definition—which incidentally often creates more problems than it solves—but the purpose of a definition is to limit or modify the ordinary meaning of a word and the court is not entitled to do that.

So the question of law in this case must be whether it was unreasonable to hold that the appellant's behaviour was not insulting. To that question there could in my view be only one answer—No.

But as the Divisional Court [1972] 1 WLR 484, have expressed their view as to the meaning of 'insulting' I must, I think, consider it. It was said at 487:

'The language of section 5, as amended, of the Public Order Act 1936, omitting words which do not matter for our present purpose, is: "Any person who in any public place . . . uses . . . insulting . . . behaviour, . . . with intent to provoke a breach of the peace or whereby a breach of the peace is likely to be occasioned, shall be guilty of an offence." It therefore becomes necessary to consider the meaning of the word "insulting" in its context in that section. In my view it is not necessary, and is probably undesirable, to try to frame an exhaustive definition which will cover every possible set of facts that may arise for consideration under this section. It is, as I think, quite sufficient for the purpose of this case to say that behaviour which affronts other people, and evidences a disrespect or contempt for their rights, behaviour which reasonable persons would foresee is likely to cause resentment or protest such as was aroused in this case, and I rely particularly on the reaction of the crowd as set out in the case stated, is insulting for the purpose of this section.'

I cannot agree with that. Parliament had to solve the difficult question of how far freedom of speech or behaviour must be limited in the general public interest. It would have been going much too far to prohibit all speech or conduct likely to occasion a breach of the peace because determined opponents may not shrink from organising or at least threatening a breach of the peace in order to silence a speaker whose views they detest. Therefore vigorous and it may be distasteful or unmannerly speech or behaviour is permitted so long as it does not go beyond any one of three limits. It must not be threatening. It must not be abusive. It must not be insulting. I see no reason why any of these should be construed as having a specially wide or a specially narrow meaning. They are all limits easily recognisable by the ordinary man. Free speech is not impaired by ruling them out. But before a man can be convicted it must be clearly shown that one or more of them has been disregarded.

We were referred to a number of dictionary meanings of 'insult' such as treating with insolence or contempt or indignity or derision or dishonour or offensive disrespect. Many things otherwise unobjectionable may be said or done in an insulting way. There can be no definition. But an ordinary sensible man knows an insult when he sees or hears it.

Taking the passage which I have quoted, 'affront' is much too vague a word to be helpful; there can often be disrespect without insult, and I do not think that contempt for a person's rights as distinct from contempt of the person himself would generally be held to be insulting. Moreover, there are many grounds other than insult for feeling resentment or protesting. I do not agree that there can be conduct which is not insulting in the ordinary sense of the word but which is 'insulting for the purpose of this section.' If the view of the Divisional Court was that in this section the word 'insulting' has some special or unusually wide meaning, then I do not agree. Parliament has given no indication that the word is to be given any unusual meaning. Insulting means insulting and nothing else.

If I had to decide, which I do not, whether the appellant's conduct insulted the spectators in this case, I would agree with the magistrates. The spectators may have been very angry and justly so. The appellant's conduct was deplorable. Probably it ought to be punishable. But I cannot see how it insulted the spectators.

I would allow the appeal with costs.

Lords Morris of Borth-y-Gest and **Kilbrandon** and **Viscount Dilhorne** delivered concurring speeches. **Lord Diplock** agreed

Appeal allowed.

NOTES

1. Viscount Dilhorne stated at pp. 865–6 that it was relevant to the issue whether the behaviour was insulting for the magistrates 'to consider whether the behaviour was such as to indicate an intention to insult anyone, and if so whom; and if the magistrates in this case did so, they may well have concluded that the appellant's behaviour did not evince any intention to insult either players or spectators, and so could not properly be regarded as insulting.'

2. The decision of magistrates on a question of fact will only be reversed on appeal to the High Court if it is one which no reasonable bench of magistrates could reach or if it is totally unsupported by evidence (*Bracegirdle v Oxley* [1947] 1 KB 349, DC). In most cases it is accepted that different magistrates may reasonably come to different conclusions, and the court will not interfere solely because the judges would personally have taken a different view.

An example of a case where a conviction was upset is *Hudson v Chief Constable, Avon and Somerset Constabulary* [1976] Crim LR 451. H was on the terraces at a football match. He became excited, jumping up and down and clapping his hands above his head. He fell forward and knocked the persons in front, causing a surge in the crowd. He was convicted of using threatening behaviour whereby a breach of the peace was likely to be occasioned, but the Divisional Court held that the facts found contained nothing which constituted a threat. Conversely, in *Simcock v Rhodes* (1977) 66 Cr App Rep 192, [1977] Crim LR 751, the Divisional Court upheld a conviction under s.5. A police sergeant instructed a disorderly group of about 15 young people who had emerged from a dance hall to be quiet and go home. The defendant shouted to him to 'fuck off'. The words were insulting and could have resulted in a breach of the peace.

3. S.5 has been used in prosecutions for fighting, although charges of affray or assault are more appropriate (*R v Oakwell* [1978] 1 All ER 1223, [1978] Crim LR 168, (1977) 66 Cr App Rep 175, CA). In a melee, each act of violence constitutes a separate breach of the peace (*R v Gedge* [1978] Crim LR 167 CA). Hence, threatening or inflammatory words used in the course of a disturbance may constitute an offence inasmuch as they may 'add fuel to the flames and lead to further breaches of the peace' (Ibid., p. 168).

4. In *Bryan v Robinson* [1960] 1 WLR 508, DC, a hostess at a non-alcoholic refreshment house in Dean Street London stood at the doorway, leaned out, smiled, beckoned and spoke to three men in the street. The men were annoyed and walked across the street. The Divisional Court allowed the hostess' appeal against conviction under the Metropolitan Police Act 1839, s.54(13) (above, p. 152). Per Lord Parker CJ at 509:

'I find it very difficult to see how a mere leaning out, smiling and beckoning without more could amount to such insulting behaviour of a character whereby a breach of the peace may be occasioned. It is true that three men were annoyed, but quite clearly somebody can be annoyed by behaviour which is not insulting behaviour. The mere fact that they were annoyed really carries the matter no further. Even if it can be said that a reasonable person would be likely to treat the gestures as insulting, they were certainly not, in my judgment, of such a character whereby a breach of the peace may be occasioned.'

(iii) Riot

Field v Metropolitan Police Receiver [1907] 2 KB 853, 76 L JKB 1015, 97 LT 639, 71 JP 494, 23 TLR 736, 5 LGR 1121, King's Bench Divisional Court

At nine o'clock on 30 October 1906 a number of youths of ages varying from fourteen to eighteen years were congregated together upon the pavement of Martindale Road, Canning Town, shouting and using rough language. The pavement adjoined a nine-inch wall of considerable length enclosing a yard and let into a house. Some of the youths were standing with their backs against the wall, and others were running against them, or against the wall, with their hands extended. After they had gone backwards and forwards in this way for about fifteen minutes, the wall, to the extent of about twelve feet, fell. As soon as it fell the caretaker of the premises came out into the street, and the youths then ran off in different directions.

The plaintiffs, owners of the wall, sought compensation under the Riot (Damages) Act 1886, section 2(1). This provides that:

'Where a house, shop or building in any police district has been injured or destroyed, or the property therein has been injured, stolen, or destroyed, by any persons riotously and tumultuously assembled together, such compensation as herein-after mentioned, shall be paid out of [the police fund] of such district to any person who has sustained loss by such injury, stealing, or destruction; but in fixing the amount of such compensation regard shall be had to the conduct of the said person, whether as respects the precautions taken by him or as respects his being a party or accessory to such riotous or tumultuous assembly, or as regards any provocation offered to the persons assembled or otherwise.'

The County Court judge held that these facts constituted a riot, and gave judgment for the plaintiffs for £3 10s. The Receiver appealed.

The judgment of the court (**Phillimore** and **Bray JJ**) was read by **Phillimore J**: . . . [His Lordship referred to the authorities, and continued:]

From these passages we deduce that there are five necessary elements of a riot—(1) number of persons, three at least; (2) common purpose; (3) execution or inception of the common purpose; (4) an intent to help one another by force if necessary against any person who may oppose them in the execution of their common purpose; (5) force or violence not merely used in demolishing, but displayed in such a manner as to alarm at least one person of reasonable firmness and courage. In this case element No. 1 was present. As to elements Nos. 2 and 3, there was evidence upon which the learned judge could have found their existence, though, as far as we can judge from the notes of the evidence and without seeing the witnesses, we think we should not have found the same way. But as to elements Nos. 4 and 5 there is no evidence. The youths ran away as soon as the single caretaker came forward; there is no reason to suppose that they would have resisted if he had come forward earlier and required them to desist. It is true that the caretaker's wife was frightened by the noise of the falling wall, but no one says that he was alarmed by the youths, though the witnesses may have been frightened by other youths on other occasions. Nor was the conduct of the youths such as would be calculated to alarm persons of reasonable firmness and courage. We cannot hold that there was a riot . . . .
Appeal allowed.

NOTES

1. It has been argued that either the common purpose must be unlawful or, if it is lawful, the force or violence must be displayed needlessly and without any reasonable occasion (*Smith and Hogan*, p. 755).
2. Alarm may be inferred from the circumstances without the necessity of calling a witness to say he was alarmed (*Devlin v Armstrong* [1971] NI 13; *O'Brien v Friel* [1974] NI 29).
3. Most of the recent reported cases on riot have concerned claims under the Riot (Damages) Act 1886 (see A. Samuels [1970] Crim LR 336). That Act was passed to remedy defects in the previous legislation (1827, 7 & 8 Geo IV c 31) under which compensation was paid by the hundred only in cases of the felonious destruction of certain specified kinds of property by persons riotously and tumultuously assembled. Pressure from people whose property was damaged in the Trafalgar Square riots of 8 February 1886, and who had no claim under the previous legislation, led to special provision being made for them by the Metropolitan Police (Compensation)

Act 1886. The general legislation followed shortly afterwards. Claims are met by the police authority, or, in the metropolitan police district, by the Receiver (1886 Act ss. 3, 9 and see S.R & O. 1921 No. 1536).

Other cases under this Act include *Gunter v Metropolitan Police District Receiver* (1889) 53 JP 249, Mathews J; *Rance v Hastings Corpn* (1913) 136 LT Jo 117, Hastings Cty Ct, (attack on a hotel where three ladies, wrongly thought by the mob to be militant suffragettes, had taken refuge: claim successful); *Ford v Metropolitan Police District Receiver* [1921] 2 KB 344, Bailhache J (a 'good humoured' crowd, some armed with crowbars and pickaxes, took woodwork and floorboards from an empty house as fuel for a 'peace night' bonfire; a neighbour gave evidence that he was afraid: claim successful); *Munday v Metropolitan Police District Receiver* [1949] 1 All ER 337, Pritchard J, (crowd unable to get into Chelsea F.C.'s ground to see a match again Moscow Dynamos broke into neighbouring premises in order to watch from there, the owner's daughter was held against a wall, and gave evidence that she was afraid: claim successful). In order to establish a claim, the conduct must be 'tumultuous' as well as 'riotous' (*J. W. Dwyer Ltd v Metropolitan Police District Receiver* [1967] 2 QB 970, Lyell J)

4. The relationship between the offences of riot and unlawful assembly is considered in *R v Caird* below, p. 160.

5. It is a statutory offence under the Ecclesiastical Courts Jurisdiction Act 1860, s. 2 for any person to be guilty of 'riotous, violent, or indecent behaviour' in any church or chapel of any denomination, or any churchyard or burial ground. The maximum penalty is two months' imprisonment or a fine of £20. In *Abrahams v Cavey* [1968] 1 QB 479, the defendants interrupted a televised service in a Brighton Methodist church connected with the Labour party's annual conference. The object was to protest against alleged support for United States policies in Vietnam. The Foreign Secretary, George Brown, had read a passage from Micah 4, and the Prime Minister was to read Matthew 7, 17–29. One defendant shouted 'Oh you hypocrites, how can you use the word of God to justify your policies', and other interventions were made. They were convicted under s. 2, the magistrates holding that this conduct offended against the recognised standards of propriety. Two were sentenced to two months' imprisonment and the rest fined £5 each. The Divisional Court held that 'indecent' in this context had no sexual connotation, and affirmed the convictions.

(iv) Unlawful assembly

The modern authorities on the scope of the common law misdemeanour of unlawful assembly place it firmly in the context of offences against public order. The constituents of the offence, according to Smith and Hogan (*Criminal Law*, (4th edn. 1978) p. 750), are

'1) An assembly of three or more persons;
2) A common purpose (a) to commit a crime of violence or (b) to achieve some other object, whether lawful or not, in such a way as to cause reasonable men to apprehend a breach of the peace.'

The same writers state that to establish the necessary mens rea

'it must be proved that D intended to use or abet the use of violence; or do or abet acts which he knows to be likely to cause a breach of the peace' (p. 753).

R v Caird (1970) 54 Cr App Rep 499, Court of Appeal (Criminal Division)

The eight applicants were convicted of a variety of offences arising out of a disturbance at the Garden House Hotel, Cambridge. The hotel planned a dinner and dance to coincide with a 'Greek week' in Cambridge. A crowd of about 300 or 400 people assembled. The following facts were stated in the judgment. From the outset there was shouting. Soon it became clear that a large number of them had developed a common purpose of wrecking the dinner. They tried to stop people entering the hotel. One person was injured and others were frightened. A proportion of those present were determined to break through the police cordon and into the hotel. Some pounded on the windows, others climbed onto the roof. The dining room windows were broken and various missiles thrown in, including rocks, clods of earth and lighted mole fuses. Inside, tables were overturned, glass and crockery smashed, chairs brandished and thrown and curtains torn down. A constable and a proctor received serious injuries; many others received minor injuries. Many of the guests were terrified. The disturbance lasted over two and a half hours.

Fifteen defendants were tried at Hertford Assizes before Melford Stevenson J on a variety of charges. Seven were acquitted on all charges. Caird was convicted of riot, assaulting a police constable in the execution of his duty, and possessing an offensive weapon; John of riot and malicious damage; Household of unlawful assembly; Lagden of riot and malicious damage; Emley of riot and assaulting a police constable in the execution of his duty; Williams of possessing an offensive weapon; Bodea and Newton of unlawful assembly. Caird was sentenced to a total of two years imprisonment; John and Emley to borstal training; Lagden to a total of fifteen months' imprisonment; and the others to nine months' imprisonment each. Williams and Bodea were recommended for deportation. They appealed to the Court of Appeal (Criminal Division).

Sachs LJ delivered the judgment of the court (**Sachs LJ, Lyell** and **Cusack JJ**): . . . That on 13 February at Cambridge there was an unlawful and riotous assembly of most serious proportions at the Garden House Hotel is something which is obvious. It has not been and could not have been disputed in this Court. . . .

There has been canvassed before this Court the distinction between unlawful and riotous assemblies. Unlawful assemblies and riotous assemblies take many forms. Without, of course, attempting a full definition, the difference can be stated in broad terms applicable to occasions of the particular type under consideration. The moment when persons in a crowd, however peaceful their original intention, commence to act for some shared common purpose supporting each other and in such a way that reasonable citizens fear a breach of the peace, the assembly becomes unlawful. In particular that applies when those concerned attempt to trespass, *or* to interrupt *or* disrupt an occasion where others are peacefully and lawfully enjoying themselves, *or* show preparedness to use force to achieve the common purpose. The assembly becomes riotous *at latest* when alarming force or violence begins to be used.

The borderline between the two is often not easily drawn with precision. In the nature of things some participation in an unlawful assembly when a mob is threatening violence may, according to its degree, constitute no less serious an offence than some participation in the riotous stage of actual violence. In each case the Court has, amongst other things, to take into account how grave the situation had become from the point of view of the public peace. When the point has been reached when violence is about to erupt, a situation can already be grave indeed.

It is the law—and, indeed, in common sense it should be the case—that any person who actively encourages or promotes an unlawful assembly or riot, whether by words, by signs or by actions, or who participates in it, is guilty of an offence which derives its great gravity from the simple fact that the persons concerned were acting in numbers and using those numbers to achieve their purpose. . . .

[The conviction of Williams was quashed]

Before now turning to individual sentences, it is appropriate first to mention certain general points which have been much canvassed. First, it should be observed that a plea in mitigation of 'provocation' made at one stage by Mr Myers was very properly withdrawn shortly after having been put forward. This Court could not entertain a political plea of that sort in the circumstances of this case as constituting mitigation, whatever other views it may have on it. Any suggestion that a section of the community strongly holding one set of views is justified in banding together to disrupt the lawful activities of a section that does not hold the same views so strongly or which holds different views cannot be tolerated and must unhesitatingly be rejected by the courts. When there is wanton and vicious violence of gross degree the Court is not concerned with whether it originates from gang rivalry or from political motives. It is the degree of mob violence that matters and the extent to which the public peace is being broken. It makes no difference whether the mob has attacked a first-class hotel in Cambridge or some dance hall frequented by the less well-circumstanced.

The next point to be mentioned is what might be called the 'Why pick on me?' argument. It has been suggested that there is something wrong in giving an appropriate sentence to one convicted of an offence because there are considerable numbers of others who were at the same time committing the same offence, some of whom indeed, if identified and arrested and established as having taken a more serious part, could have received heavier sentences. This is a plea which is almost invariably put forward where the offence is one of those classed as disturbances of the public peace—such as riots, unlawful assemblies and affrays. It indicates a failure to appreciate that on these confused and tumultuous occasions each individual who takes an active part by deed or encouragement is guilty of a really grave offence by being one of the number engaged in a crime against the peace. It is, moreover, impracticable for a small number of police when sought to be overwhelmed by a crowd to make a large number of arrests. It is indeed all the more difficult when, as in the present case, any attempt at arrest is followed by violent efforts of surrounding rioters to rescue the person being arrested. It is worse still when steps have been taken, as in the present case, to immerse the mob in darkness.

If this plea were acceded to, it would reinforce that feeling which may undoubtedly exist that if an offender is but one of a number he is unlikely to be picked on, and even if he is so picked upon, can escape proper punishment because others were not arrested at the same time. Those who choose to take part in such unlawful occasions must do so at their peril.

The present case was one of a long-lasting concerted attempt of grave proportions by aggressive force of numbers to overpower the police, to embark on wrecking, and to terrify citizens engaged in following peaceable and lawful pursuits. Any participation whatever, irrespective of its precise form, in an unlawful or riotous assembly of this type derives its gravity from becoming one of those who, by weight of numbers, pursued a common and unlawful purpose. The law of this country has always leant heavily against those who, to attain such a purpose, use the threat that lies in the power of numbers.

The general scale of the sentences adopted by the trial judge on this particular occasion was stern—but correctly so. The occasion was far more serious than that of most affrays and other disturbances of the public peace that have become all too common. In this connection it must also be emphasised that neither on the law applicable to ascertaining guilt, nor on the matter of sentencing, is an adult student in any better position than any other citizen. He most certainly cannot by virtue of his education claim preferential treatment—as, for instance, to receive lighter punishment than one less well educated. . . .

It is to be emphasised that in each and every case where the jury convicted one of the seven applicants either of riotous or unlawful assembly the person convicted had been in the very forefront of the mob and had been an active participator in attempts to get past and override the police in their protective tasks. It was indeed because he was thus in the forefront that he could be identified and in certain instances seized or arrested, often after a turbulent struggle in which those alongside attempted to rescue him. Moreover, each applicant was taking his part in the course of a protracted attack, and it was of no avail to plead sudden impulse. On that footing immediately custodial sentences were clearly required. . . .

In conclusion this Court feels it necessary to advert to the clear line that exists between the freedom of citizens to assemble peaceably in a permissible place to express their views in a lawful manner, a right which the courts always safeguard, and the unlawful act of doing something which threatens a breach of the peace. As has already been stated, a common purpose of thus disrupting by tumult the peaceful pursuits of other citizens whether at their work or in proper enjoyment of their leisure is unlawful in this country, even if unaccompanied by acts of frightening violence.

Moreover, it cannot be too plainly stated or too widely known that the moment when men join in an attempt to overpower the police who are performing their protective duties, that line has been considerably overstepped, and every person joining in the mob effort for that purpose is committing a grave crime even if he is not identified as having committed some specific assault or some specific piece of malicious damage. Those acting thus against the police, who, as in the present case, deserve the very highest commendation for their restraint in an intolerable position, must expect custodial sentences. That applies indeed to cases where there is not the hooligan trail of wreckage, injury and terrified women that was left here. Gross affronts to good order cannot be lightly treated and those of adult age cannot claim to be an exception because they are students.

[The sentences were confirmed except that Lagden was put on probation and the recommendation for deportation of Bodea was quashed].

NOTES

1. For a critical comment on *R v Caird* see S. Sedley. The Listener (1970) pp. 469–472, 783, 911; cf. A. W. Bradley, ibid. pp. 734–6; F. Bresler, ibid. pp. 736–7, 847.

2. An unlawful assembly, like a riot and an affray, may take place on private premises, although, as in affray, an essential element in such a case is 'the presence or likely presence of innocent third parties, members of the public not participating in the illegal activities in question' (per Lord Hailsham LC in *Kamara v Director of Public Prosecutions* [1974] AC 104, 116, HL: unlawful assembly on the premises of the High Commission of Sierra Leone).

3. Most of the authorities on unlawful assembly are directions to juries. In *R v Vincent* (1839) 9 C & P 91, a case arising out of Chartist disturbances in Newport, Alderson B emphasised that the jury had to consider

'the way in which the meetings were held, the hour of the day at which the parties met, and the language used by the persons assembled and by those who addressed them. . . . You will consider . . . whether firm and rational men . . . would have reasonable ground to fear a breach of the peace, for I quite agree . . . that the alarm must not be merely such as would frighten any foolish or timid person, but must be such as would alarm persons of reasonable firmness and courage.'

The other leading case is *R v Cunninghame Graham and Burns* (1888) 16 Cox CC 420, which followed the Trafalgar Square riots of 'Bloody Sunday' (13 November 1887). The Metropolitan Radical Federation resolved to hold a meeting in the Square to demand the release of 'Irish patriots'. The authorities anticipated disorder. The Metropolitan Police Commissioner (Sir Charles Warren)(1) issued a notice on 8 November with the sanction of the Secretary of State and the Commissioners of Works banning all public meetings in the Square until further intimation, and (2) made a regulation on 12 November under the Metropolitan Police Act 1839 s. 52 (above p. 144) that no organised procession was to be allowed to approach the Square on 13 November. Nevertheless a crowd of between 15,000 and 25,000 assembled in the vicinity of the Square and there were several attempts by demonstrators to break the police cordon in the Square itself. Cunninghame Graham (an MP) and John Burns (who subsequently became a cabinet minister) took part in one of these attacks. They were acquitted on charges of riot and assaulting the police but were convicted of unlawful assembly, and received sentences of six weeks' imprisonment. Among the points made to the jury by Charles J were (1) that the notice issued on 8 November did 'not create the meeting . . . an unlawful meeting unless for other reasons it was an unlawful meeting' (p. 431); (2) that a meeting initially lawful might become unlawful subsequently: 'although you may have gathered together with a most innocent intention, still, if while you are so gathered together you determine to do an act of violence, then you become a member of an unlawful assembly; if you do the act of violence then . . . you become a member of a riotous assembly' (p. 434). See also above, p. 143.

4. A count of unlawful assembly was preferred with counts of conspiracy to intimidate and affray in the 'Shrewsbury pickets' case (*R v Jones* (1974) 59 Crim App Rep 120, CA).

Beatty v Gillbanks [1882] 9 QBD 308, 51 LJMC 117, 47 LT 194, 46 JP 789, 15 Cox CC 138, Queen's Bench Divisional Court

Case stated by the Axbridge Justices.

The three appellants, Beatty, Mullins and Bowden, were charged on the complaint of Superintendent Gillbanks that they had unlawfully and tumultuously assembled with more than 100 others in public thoroughfares and other places in Weston-super-Mare to the disturbance of the public peace. The Justices found the allegations proved and bound the appellants over to keep the peace for twelve months. They stated a case for the opinion of the Divisional Court. The following facts were found to be proved. The Salvation Army had for some time organised processions in the streets of Weston-super-Mare. The Salvationists formed at the Army's Hall, were headed by a band and flags and banners, and collected a mob as they marched. There was much shouting and singing and noise. Beatty was a captain, and the other appellants leaders, of the Salvation Army, and they organized its meetings and processions. There was another organized body of persons called the Skeleton Army which also paraded the streets, and was antagonistic to the Salvationists. Other people collected in support of one or other faction. On several occasions 'a free fight, great uproar, blows, tumults, stone-throwing and disorder' ensued between the two groups. On 23 March 1882 the Salvation Army's procession was accompanied by a disorderly and riotous mob of over 2,000. The police were for a long time unable to cope with the fighting and disturbance in this mob. The Salvation Army forced their way through the streets to the Railway-parade where a general fight took place. B led the Salvationists on this occasion but neither he nor the other appellants were seen to commit any overt act of violence. In consequence, two justices issued a notice, copies of which were posted in the town and served on B, which stated that there were 'reasonable grounds for apprehending a repetition of such riotous and tumultuous assembly' and that 'we do hereby require, order, and direct all persons to abstain from assembling to the disturbance of the public peace' in the parish.

On Sunday 26 March, the Salvation Army, under the appellants' direction, formed a procession of 100 or more and marched off. They were surrounded by a tumultuous and shouting mob of some 100 persons, which rapidly increased as they passed on. They were met and stopped by the police. The sergeant in charge told B that he must obey the notice, and disperse at once, or he would be arrested. B refused to comply, marched on at the head of the procession some twenty yards, told the sergeant that he should still proceed, and was arrested. Mullins and Bowden were also arrested when they persisted in leading the procession on. None of the appellants were guilty of any overt act of violence, and all submitted quietly to their arrest. The final two paragraphs of the case stated that this assembling of the Salvation Army was a terror to the peaceable inhabitants of Weston-super-Mare,

'and was calculated to endanger and did endanger, and was calculated to cause a breach of the public peace; and there was good and sufficient cause for the inhabitants to suppose, and any rational person knowing the aforesaid circumstances would suppose that, unless the procession and mob were dispersed, there would be a repetition of the aforesaid violent and tumultuous acts, and that there would be a breach of the peace. The appellants intended to parade their procession through the principal streets and public places of the town, and to collect on their march a large mob of persons to accompany them; and they had good reason to expect that they would come into collision with the said Skeleton Army and other persons antagonistic to the procession, and they had good reason to expect that there would be the same fighting, stone-throwing, and disturbance, as there had been on previous occasions, and intended on meeting such opposition to force their way through the said streets and places as they had done on previous occasions.'

The questions of law stated for the opinion of the court were, whether these facts so found to be proved as aforesaid constituted the offence charged in the complaint, and whether the order made – that the defendants should find sureties to keep the peace – was valid.

Field J: I am of opinion that this order cannot be supported, and must therefore be discharged. The appellants, it appears, together with a large number of other people, belong to a body of persons called the Salvation Army, who are associated together for a purpose which cannot be said to be otherwise than lawful and laudable, or at all events cannot be called unlawful, their object and intention being to induce a class of persons who have little or no knowledge of religion and no taste or disposition for religious exercises or for going to places of worship, to join them in their processions, and so to get them together to attend and take part in their religious exercises, in the hope that they may be reclaimed and drawn away from vicious and irreligious habits and courses of life, and that a kind of revival in the matter of religion may be brought about amongst those who were previously dead to any such influences. That undoubtedly is the object of the Salvation Army, and of the appellants, and no other object or intention has been or can be imputed to them; and, as has been said by their learned counsel, and doubtless with perfect truth, so far are they from desiring to carry out that object by means of any force or violence, their principles are directly and entirely opposed to any conduct of that kind, or to the exercise or employment of anything like physical force; and, indeed, it appears that on the occasion in question they used no personal force or violence, but, on the contrary, when arrested by the police, they submitted quietly without the exhibition of any resistance either on their own parts or on that of any other member of their body. Such being their lawful object and intention, and having no desire or intention of using force or violence of any kind, it appeared that on this 26th day of March they assembled, as they had previously done on other occasions, in considerable numbers at their hall, and proceeded to march thence in procession through the streets of the town of Weston-super-Mare. Now that, in itself, was certainly not an unlawful thing to do, nor can such an assembly be said to be an unlawful one. Numerous instances might be mentioned of large bodies of persons assembling in much larger numbers, and marching, accompanied by banners and bands of music, through the public streets, and no one has ever doubted that such processions were perfectly lawful. Now the appellants complain that, for having so assembled as I have before stated, they have been adjudged guilty of the offence of holding an unlawful assembly, and have in consequence been ordered to find sureties to keep the peace, in the absence of any evidence of their having broken it. It was of course necessary that the justices should find that some unlawful act had been committed by the appellants in order to justify the magistrates in binding them over. The offence charged against them as "unlawfully, and tumultuously assembling with others to the disturbance of the public peace, and against the peace of the Queen," and of course before they can be convicted upon the charge clear proof must be adduced that the specific offence charged has been committed. Now was that charge sustained? There is no doubt that the appellants did assemble together with other persons in great numbers, but that alone is insufficient. The assembly must be a 'tumultuous assembly,' and 'against the peace.' in order to render it an unlawful one. But there was nothing so far as the appellants were concerned to show that their conduct was in the least degree 'tumultuous' or 'against the peace'. All that they did was to assemble together to walk through the town, and it is admitted by the learned counsel for the respondent, that as regards the appellants themselves, there was no disturbance of the peace, and that their conduct was quiet and peaceable. But then it is argued that, as in fact their line of conduct was the same as had on previous similar occasions led to tumultuous and riotous proceedings with stone-throwing and fighting, causing a disturbance of the public peace and terror to the inhabitants of the town, and as on the present occasion like results would in all probability be produced, therefore the appellants, being well aware of the likelihood of such results again occurring, were guilty of the offence charged against them. Now, without doubt, as a general rule it must be taken that every person intends what are the natural and necessary consequences of his own acts, and if in the present case it had been their intention, or if it had been the natural and necessary consequence of their acts, to produce the disturbance of the peace which occurred, then the appellants would have been responsible for it, and the magistrates would have been right in binding them over to keep the peace. But the evidence as set forth in the case shows that, so far from that being the case, the acts and conduct of the appellants caused nothing of the kind, but, on the contrary, that the disturbance that did take place was caused entirely by the unlawful and unjustifiable interference of the Skeleton Army, a body of persons opposed to the religious views of the appellants and the Salvation Army, and that but for the opposition and molestation offered to the Salvationists by these other persons, no disturbance of any kind would have taken place. The appellants were guilty of no offence in their passing through the streets, and why should other persons interfere with or molest them? What right had they to do so? If they were doing anything unlawful it was for the magistrates and police, the appointed guardians of law and order, to interpose. The law relating to unlawful assemblies, as laid down in the books and the cases, affords no support to the view of the matter for which the learned counsel for the respondent was obliged to contend, viz., that persons acting lawfully are to be held responsible and punished merely because other persons are thereby induced to act unlawfully and create a disturbance. In 1 Russell on Crimes (4th edn. p. 387), an unlawful assembly is defined as follows: "unlawful assembly, according to the common opinion, is a disturbance of the peace by persons barely assembling together with the intention to do a thing which, if it were executed, would make them rioters, but neither actually executing it nor making a motion towards the execution of it." It is clear that, according to this definition of the offence, the appellants were not guilty, for it is not pretended that they had, but, on the contrary, it is admitted that they had not, any intention to create a riot, or to commit any riotous or other unlawful act. Many examples of what are unlawful assemblies are given in Hawkins' Pleas of the Crown, book 1 cap. 28, sects. 9 and 10, in all of which the necessary circumstances of terror are present in the assembly itself, either as regards the object for which it is gathered together, or in the manner of its assembling and proceeding to carry out that object. The present case, however, differs from the cases there stated; for here the only terror that existed was caused by the unlawful resistance wilfully and designedly offered to the proceedings of the Salvation Army by an unlawful organisation outside and distinct from them, called the Skeleton Army. It was suggested by the respondent's counsel that, if these Salvation processions were allowed, similar opposition would be offered to them in future, and that similar disturbances would ensue. But I cannot believe that that will be so. I hope, and I cannot but think, that when the Skeleton Army, and all other persons who are opposed to the proceedings of the Salvation Army, come to learn, as they surely will learn, that they have no possible right to interfere with or in any way to obstruct the Salvation Army in their lawful and peaceable processions, they will abstain from opposing or disturbing them. It is usual happily in this country for people to respect and obey the law when once declared and understood, and I hope and have no doubt that it will be so in the present case. But, if it should not be so, there is no doubt that the magistrates and police, both at Weston-super-Mare and everywhere else, will understand their duty and not fail to do it efficiently, or hesitate, should the necessity arise, to deal with the Skeleton Army and other disturbers of the public peace as they did in the present instance with the appellants, for no one can doubt that the authorities are only anxious to do their duty and to prevent a disturbance of the public peace. The present decision of the justices, however, amounts to this, that a man may be punished for acting lawfully if he knows that his so doing may induce another man to act unlawfully—a proposition without any authority whatever to support it. Under these circumstances, the questions put to us by the justices must be negatively answered, and the order appealed against be discharged.

Cave J: I am entirely of the same opinion . . .

[His Lordship referred to Hawkins' Pleas of the Crown and Dalton's Country Justice]

Now, putting these several passages from these old authorities together, it seems to me to be impossible to hold that the appellants here have been brought within them as being guilty of unlawfully and tumultuously assembling. The meeting or assembly of the Salvation Army was for a purpose not unlawful. Was there an intention on their part to use violence? If, though their meeting was in itself lawful, they intended, if opposed, to meet force by force, that would render their meeting an unlawful assembly; but it does not appear that they entertained any such intention. On the contrary, when met and resisted by the Skeleton Army, they used no violence of any kind, and manifested no intention of meeting their opponents with like violence to that which the latter offered to them . . .

Appeal allowed.

NOTES

1. This was not a *prosecution* for unlawful assembly. The justices had no jurisdiction to try that offence. To what extent can it be regarded as an authority on the scope of unlawful assembly? See *Brownlie*, p. 42, where it is stated that the case 'had little to do with unlawful assembly'. Note, however, that the Divisional Court was asked by the justices whether the facts 'constituted the offence charged'. Moreover, the court took the view that a binding over order was only justified where an offence had been committed. (Subsequent cases have, however, made it clear that a binding over order may be made even where no offence has been committed (*Wilson v Skeock* (1949) 113 JP 294 DC), or following acquittal on the offence charged (*R v Sharp* [1957] 1 QB 552, CCA).)

2. How convincing is the argument that the disturbances were not *caused* by the Salvationists? Had the Salvationists not marched there would have been no disturbances. Moreover, the disturbances were both foreseeable and foreseen. To what extent would you regard the court's interpretation of the facts found as unduly favourable to the Salvationists? Note the criticisms expressed in *O'Kelly v Harvey* below, p. 170.

3. The question whether those who 'innocently' provoke a breach of the peace can be guilty of unlawful assembly is separate from the question whether direct action may be taken against them in order to preserve the peace (see below, pp. 167–176).

4. In *R v Londonderry JJ* (1891) 28 LR Ir 440, QBD, the court granted certiorari to quash orders binding over certain Salvationists to keep the peace. Their parades attracted a hostile crowd, but there was no act of hostility and no act of misconduct on the part of the Salvationists. The court held there was no evidence to support the orders.

5. *Beatty v Gillbanks* was distinguished in *Wise v Dunning* [1902] 1 KB 167 DC. 'Pastor' George Wise conducted a Protestant 'crusade' in Liverpool. He addressed a series of street meetings, using insulting and provocative language and gestures. At one meeting he put beads round his neck and waved a crucifix above his head. At another he referred to Roman Catholics as 'rednecks'. He did not himself commit any breach of the peace, nor did he incite his supporters to do so, but his conduct provoked his opponents to do so. He was bound over to keep the peace and be of good behaviour for twelve months. He appealed by case stated arguing that the magistrate had no jurisdiction (1) to bind him over to keep the peace because there was no evidence that he had committed a breach of the peace, or (2) to bind him over to be of good behaviour because it was not 'justly suspected' that he intended to break the peace. 'The appellant's conduct was lawful, and he cannot be bound over because the conduct of others was, or was likely to be, unlawful: *Beatty v Gillbanks*' (F. E. Smith, in argument). The Divisional Court upheld the order. Darling and Channell JJ held that breaches of the peace were the 'natural consequence' of W's provocative conduct. Channell J stated at 179 and 180 that while

'the law does not as a rule regard an illegal act as being the natural consequence of a temptation which may be held out to commit it . . . the cases with respect to apprehended breaches of the peace show that the law does regard the infirmity of human temper to the extent of considering that a breach of the peace, although an illegal act, may be the natural consequence of insulting or abusive language or conduct'.

Darling J pointed out (at p. 179) in relation to *Beatty v Gillbanks* and *R v Londonderry JJ* 'the whole question is one of fact and evidence'.

Lord Alverstone CJ referred to the Liverpool Improvement Act 1842 s. 149, which was identical in terms to the Metropolitan Police Act 1839 s. 54(13), (above p. 152), and said that it had a 'very important bearing on this case' (p. 176), (although no charge was actually brought under the Act).

'[W's] language and conduct went very far indeed towards inciting people to commit, or was, at any rate, language and behaviour likely to occasion, a breach of the peace' (p. 177).

Note that there was no allegation of unlawful assembly. Do you think that the facts would have justified a conviction for that offence?

(v) Disorder at lawful meetings

The statutory provisions given below afford a measure of protection to lawful meetings. Those who disrupt lawful meetings may commit other criminal offences not related in particular to meetings (see pp. 150–166) They may be ejected, and those who organize a meeting on private premises may employ stewards to preserve order (Public Order Act 1936, section 2(6), above, p. 129). It is arguable that the police should act first against persons who disrupt or threaten to disrupt a lawful meeting, and disperse the meeting itself only if necessary in the last resort (see pp. 167–176). As to police powers of entry to present disorder, see *Thomas v Sawkins*, above.

Public Meeting Act 1908

1. Penalty on endeavour to break up public meeting
(1) Any person who at a lawful public meeting acts in a disorderly manner for the purpose of preventing the transaction of the business for which the meeting was called together shall be guilty of an offence . . .
(2) Any person who incites others to commit an offence under this section shall be guilty of a like offence.
[(3) If any constable reasonably suspects any person of committing an offence under the foregoing provisions of this section, he may if requested so to do by the chairman of the meeting require that person to declare to him immediately his name and address and, if that person refuses or fails so to declare his name and address or gives a false name and address he shall be guilty of an offence under this subsection and liable on summary conviction thereof to a fine not exceeding forty shillings, and if he refuses or fails so to declare his name and address or if the constable reasonably suspects him of giving a false name and address, the constable may without warrant arrest him.]

NOTES

1. Sub-s. (3) was added by the Public Order Act 1936, s. 6. The maximum penalty is now six months' imprisonment, a £1000 fine or both. It was previously a hybrid offence, but is now triable only summarily (Criminal Law Act 1977 ss. 15, 30 and Schs. 1, 13, repealing the Public Order Act 1963, s. 1(1)). The Act does not apply to election meetings, but they are protected by analogous provisions in the Representation of the People Act 1949 s. 84. Breach of s. 84 is an 'illegal practice' under election law (see the 1949 Act ss. 139(2), 140, 147 and 150).
2. In *Burden v Rigler* [1911] 1 KB 337, DC, justices hearing a prosecution brought under the Act held that any meeting on the highway was ipso facto unlawful. The Divisional Court held that the justices had 'no right to assume that, simply because the meeting was held on a highway it could be interrupted notwithstanding the provisions of the Public Meeting Act 1908' (Lord Alverstone CJ at 340).The case was remitted for the justices to consider inter alia whether there was an obstruction.

(c) PREVENTIVE POWERS

(i) Powers of dispersal

The police are under a duty to disperse unlawful or riotous assemblies (see above, pp. 157–166). Magistrates are technically subject to the same duty although the preservation of public order is in practice today regarded as a police function. According to the cases in this section, police or magistrates may take direct action against persons not acting unlawfully where necessary to preserve the peace. This action may include committing what would otherwise be assaults (*Humphries v Connor*, below; *O'Kelly v Harvey*, below p. 170). *Duncan v Jones* (below p. 172) goes one step further: it supports the proposition that resistance to a police order to disperse may constitute the offence of obstruction of the police in the execution of their duty. These cases have been adversely criticised by commentators, although not in the courts.

Humphries v Connor (1864) 17 ICLR 1, Court of Queen's Bench in Ireland

Anne Humphries sued Daniel Connor for assault. C pleaded that he was a sub-inspector of Constabulary in Cavan; and at the time of the committing of the alleged assault, H was walking through Swanlinbar at about noon wearing a party emblem (an orange lily) the wearing of which 'was calculated and tended to provoke animosity between different classes of Her Majesty's subjects'. A number of people were provoked by the emblem, followed her, caused great noise and disturbance and threatened her with personal violence. She refused C's request to remove the emblem. C's pleadings continued:

> 'Whereupon the defendant, . . . in order to preserve the public peace, which was likely to be broken by and in consequence of the said conduct of the plaintiff, and to protect the plaintiff from the said threatened violence, and which violence the said several persons who were provoked by the conduct of the plaintiff, as aforesaid, in consequence of her said conduct, were likely to inflict on the plaintiff, and in order to restore order and tranquillity in said town, then gently and quietly, and *necessarily and unavoidably*, removed said emblem from the plaintiff, doing her no injury whatever; and in so doing, and for the purpose of so doing, *necessarily* committed the said alleged trespass . . . and thereby protected the plaintiff from said threatened personal violence, which would otherwise have been inflicted on her, and preserved the public peace, which was likely to be, and would otherwise have been broken.'

The plaintiff demurred to this defence on the grounds that the wearing of the lily was a perfectly legal act, and afforded no excuse for any turbulence on the part of others, and that it was the duty of the defendant to protect the plaintiff and not to assault or restrain her in the exercise of a legal right. The court held that, on the assumption that the facts alleged were true, the defence was good in law.

> **O'Brien J**: . . . With respect to the first ground, . . . that it was defendant's duty as a constable to preserve the public peace, and to prevent the breach of it by disturbance or otherwise; and it appears to me that some of the authorities cited in the argument show that, under the circumstances stated in the defence, he was justified in acting as therein mentioned. The observations of Baron Alderson in *Cook v Nethercote* ((1835) 6 C & P 744), and in *R v Brown* (1841) Can & M 314), and those of Baron Parke, in *Ingle v Bell* ((1836) IM & W 516). show the power which policemen have, even to arrest a party, in order to prevent a breach of the peace being committed or renewed. In another case—*R v Hogan* ((1837) 8 C & P 167)— where it appeared that a man playing the bagpipes at night had attracted a crowd of dissolute persons about him, Coltman, J., held that a constable who had directed the man to move on did not exceed his duty by merely laying his hand on the man's shoulder, with that view only.
>   According to the statements in the defence now before us, the act complained of . . . though an assault in point of law, was not a greater one than those complained of in some of the cases referred to; and it was done by defendant for the purpose of preventing a breach of the public peace, &c., and was necessary for that purpose. It has, however, been urged by plaintiff's Counsel that injurious consequences would result from our decision in defendant's favour—giving to constables a power so capable of being abused. I think it sufficient, in answer to this argument, to say that our decision would not be applicable to a state of facts where the power was abused; and that it would not protect a constable from any unnecessary, excessive, or improper exercise of such power in other cases.

Hayes J: . . . A constable, by his very appointment, is by law charged with the solemn duty of seeing that the peace is preserved. The law has not ventured to lay down what precise measures shall be adopted by him in every state of facts which calls for his interference. But it has done far better; it has announced to him, and to the public over whom he is placed, that he is not only at liberty, but is bound, to see that the peace be preserved, and that he is to do everything that is necessary for that purpose, neither more nor less. What he does, he does upon the peril of answering to a jury of his country, when his conduct shall be brought into question, and he shall be charged either with exceeding or falling short of his duty. In the present case it is said that it would be a lamentable thing if an individual were to be obstructed and assaulted when doing a perfectly legal act; and that there is no law against wearing an emblem or decoration of one kind or another. I agree with that in the abstract; but I think it is not straining much the legal maxim, *sic utere tuo ut alienum non lædas*—to hold that people shall not be permitted to use even legal rights for illegal purposes. When a constable is called upon to preserve the peace, I know no better mode of doing so than that of removing what he sees to be the provocation to the breach of the peace; and, when a person deliberately refuses to acquiesce in such removal, after warning so to do, I think the constable is authorised to do everything necessary and proper to enforce it. It would seem absurd to hold that a constable may arrest a person whom he finds committing a breach of the peace, but that he must not interfere with the individual who has wantonly provoked him to do so. But whether the act which he did was or was not, under all the circumstances, *necessary* to preserve the peace, is for the jury to decide. The defendant in his defence asserts that it was; and, for the purposes of this demurrer, we must take that assertion to be true. In my opinion the plea is good.

Fitzgerald J: . . . I entertain a doubt—and I may add a very serious doubt—as to the correctness of the judgment of the Court, though I defer to the greater experience and sounder opinions of my Brothers. . . . With respect to a constable, I agree that his primary duty is to preserve the peace; and he may for that purpose interfere, and, in the case of an affray, arrest the wrong-doers; or, if a breach of the peace is imminent, may, if necessary, arrest those who are about to commit it, if it cannot otherwise be prevented. But the doubt which I have is, whether a constable is entitled to interfere with one who is not about to commit a breach of the peace, or to do, or join in any illegal act, but who is likely to be made an object of insult or injury by other persons who are about to break the Queen's peace. . . .

I do not see where we are to draw the line. If a constable is at liberty to take a lily from one person, because the wearing of it is displeasing to others, who may make it an excuse for a breach of the peace, where are we to stop? It seems to me that we are making, not the law of the land but the law of the mob supreme, and recognising in constables a power of interference with the rights of the Queen's subjects, which, if carried into effect to the full extent of the principle, might be accompanied by constitutional danger. If it had been alleged that the lady wore the emblem with an intent to provoke a breach of the peace, it would render her a wrongdoer; and she might be chargeable as a person creating a breach of the peace.

NOTES

1. According to the pleadings the plaintiff's conduct was 'calculated and tended' to provoke animosity. The term 'calculated' normally means 'likely' rather than 'intended'. See G. Williams, *Textbook on Criminal Law* (1978) p. 94. Note the difference of view as to the relevance of the plaintiff's intentions. What would be the position where a person totally unwittingly provokes a breach of the peace, as where a person wears an emblem unaware of any political connotations? Should the availability of this defence depend upon the state of mind of the person against whom the action is taken? If so, what should the relevant state of mind be?

2. In *Hughes v Casares* (1967) 111 Sol Jo 637, the defendant, a police officer, was struggling with a person under arrest in the course of transferring him to a police car. The plaintiff stood in front of the door and did not move when requested. The defendent pushed the plaintiff aside and the latter fell injuring his ankle. His claim for damages failed. Blain J held that there was no evidence of deliberate or unnecessary violence, and that the defendant's reaction was reasonable and 'no more than the occasion demanded'.

O'Kelly v Harvey (1883) 15 Cox CC 435, 10 LR Ir 285, 14 LR Ir 105, Exchequer Division and Court of Appeal in Ireland

The plaintiff claimed damages for assault and battery. H, a magistrate, had laid his hand on him in the course of dispersing a meeting held on 7 December 1880 to encourage tenant farmers not to pay their rents. The 13th paragraph of the defence stated that the meeting had been advertised in advance as a 'Great Land Demonstration' which would probably be addressed by C. S. Parnell and other MPs. In response the following notice was circulated:

> Orangemen of Fermanagh, will you allow your county to be disgraced by letting a Land League meeting be held (as advertised) at Brookeborough, on 7th Dec. inst., where addresses are to be delivered not only dishonest but treasonable, and opposed to your principles?
> When the Government won't protect Protestant life and property, it is time we should do so ourselves, and put a stop to all treasonable proceedings in our loyal county Fermanagh.
> Remember the treatment of your brethren at Lough Mask!!! Assemble in your thousands at Brookeborough on Tuesday, and give Parnell and his associates a warm reception.
> God save the Queen.
> Brookeborough, Dec. 4th, 1880.

The defendant claimed that he believed, and had reasonable and probable grounds for believing that if the meeting were held many Orangemen would meet in pursuance of the second notice and the public peace would be broken. Para. 13 continued:

> 'The defendant . . . believed, *and had reasonable and probable grounds for believing*, that a breach of the peace would occur if said meeting were allowed to be held and continued; and that the public peace and tranquillity could not otherwise be preserved than by separating and dispersing the plaintiff and said other persons so assembled as aforesaid; and defendant, being present at said meeting, requested the plaintiff and said other persons so assembled to disperse, which they neglected to do; and thereupon the defendant laid his hand on the plaintiff, in order to separate and disperse the plaintiff and said other persons so assembled as aforesaid, using no more violence than was necessary for the purpose aforesaid, which is the assault and battery complained of.'

The plaintiff demurred on the ground that this did not disclose a defence. The Exchequer Division (Palles CB, Fitzgerald and Dowse BB) and the Court of Appeal (Law LC, Morris CJ, Deasy and Fitzgibbon LJJ) held that the defence was good.

The judgment of the Court of Appeal was delivered by Law LC: . . . The question then seems to be reduced to this: assuming the plaintiff and others assembled with him to be doing nothing unlawful, but yet that there were reasonable grounds for the defendant believing as he did that there would be a breach of the peace if they continued so assembled, and that there was no other way in which the breach of the peace could be avoided but by stopping and dispersing the plaintiff's meeting—was the defendant justified in taking the necessary steps to stop and disperse it? In my opinion he was so justified under the peculiar circumstances stated in the defence, and which for the present must be taken as admitted to be there truly stated. Under such circumstances the defendant was not to defer action until a breach of the peace had actually been committed. His paramount duty was to preserve the peace unbroken, and that by whatever means were available for the purpose. Furthermore, the duty of a justice of the peace being to preserve the peace unbroken, he is, of course, entitled, and in fact bound to intervene the moment he has reasonable apprehensions of a breach of the peace being imminent; and, therefore, he must in such cases necessarily act on his own reasonable and *bonâ fide* belief as to what is likely to occur. Accordingly, in the present case, even assuming that the danger to the public peace arose altogether from the threatened attack of another body on the plaintiff and his friends, still; if the defendant believed and had just grounds for believing that the peace could only be preserved by withdrawing the plaintiff and his friends from the attack with which they were threatened, it was I think the duty of the defendant to take that course. This indeed was, as it appears to me, substantially decided here some years ago by the Court of Queen's Bench in the case of *Humphries v Connor* (17 Ir CLR 1). . . .

So also here the vital averment that the defendant had reasonable grounds for his belief that

the peace could not be preserved by any other means than those which he adopted must, I think, be regarded as a sufficient statement of a matter of fact on which the plaintiff could safely take issue, as no doubt he has done, and which, if not proved at the trial to the satisfaction of the jury, the defence must necessarily fail. If it be suggested that the defence should have been more communicative and distinct as to the defendant's grounds of belief, the answer is that any embarrassment so caused—if, indeed, there was any, which I do not myself believe there was—should have been dealt with by motion. On the record, however, as it stands, no such point as this is open for consideration. During the argument the recent case of *Beatty v Gillbanks* ((1882)9 QBD 308) was much relied on by the plaintiff's counsel. I frankly own that I cannot understand that decision, having regard to the facts stated in the special case there submitted to the court, and which, with all deference to the learned judges who decided it, appear to me to have presented all the elements necessary to constitute the offence known as 'unlawful assembly.' Field J quotes a passage from Serjeant Hawkins to the effect that any meeting of great numbers of people, with such circumstances of terror as cannot but endanger the public peace and raise fears and jealousies among the King's subjects, is an unlawful assembly, and suggests that, for this purpose, the 'circumstances of terror' must exist in the assembly itself. Well, even supposing this to be so, what is to be said as to the paragraph of the case which stated (sect. m) that the particular assemblage in question was a terror to the peaceable inhabitants of the town, and especially to those then going to their respective places of worship, and was calculated to endanger, and did endanger, the public peace, I should have thought that an assemblage of that character had in itself sufficient 'circumstances of terror' to make it unlawful. But, again, we find it stated that Beatty and his friends constituting this Salvation Army procession knew they were likely to be attacked on this occasion, as before, by the body which had been organised in antagonism to them, and that there would be fighting, stone-throwing, and disturbance as there had been on previous occasions; and further, that they intended, on meeting such opposition, to fight and force their way through the streets and public places as they had done before. I confess I should have thought that this, too, was no bad description of an unlawful assembly. Indeed, I have always understood the law to be that any needless assemblage of persons in such numbers and manner and under such circumstances as are likely to provoke a breach of the peace, was itself unlawful; and this, I may add, appears to be the view taken by the very learned persons who revised the Criminal Code Bill in 1878. But, after all, that decision of Field and Cave JJ is no authority against the view I take of the case now before us. I assume here that the plaintiff's meeting was not unlawful. But the question still remains, Was not the defendant justified in separating and dispersing it if he had reasonable ground for his belief that by no other possible means could he perform his duty of preserving the peace? For the reasons already given I think he was so justified, and therefore that the defence in question is good; . . .
Appeal dismissed.

NOTES

1. The reference to Lough Mask relates to the social ostracism of Captain Charles Boycott, land agent for Lord Erne, who lived at Lough Mask House, Co. Mayo (see J. Marlow, *Captain Boycott and the Irish* (1973)). The Land League was founded in 1879 under the presidency of C. S. Parnell, and proceeded to hold meetings, particularly in Connaught. Its aims were the reduction of rent and evictions, and the ultimate achievement of tenant ownership. The first meeting organised in Ulster was at Belleek on 9 November 1880:

'Some disturbance was anticipated and an opposition meeting was talked of, but it did not take place, and the proceedings passed off quietly. A large force of police and military was sent down from Eniskellen and kept under arms during the day, but there was no need for their services' (*The Times*, 10 November 1880).

For the meeting on 7 December 1880, over 100 extra police were brought into Brookeborough, and over 100 men of the 2nd Dragoons were billeted nearby. J. J. O'Kelly MP and others arrived by train from Dublin. They drove to the field

'and found it occupied by a crowd of people and a strong force of police under the direction of Mr Harvey RM. When Mr O'Kelly entered the field, Mr Harvey, advancing to him, asked what he had come for, and on his replying that he had come to attend the meeting, Mr Harvey took him by the shoulders and gave him into the custody of a constable. He demanded by what authority the magistrate did so, and Mr Harvey directed the constables to remove him from the field . . . Mr O'Kelly and his friends . . .drove away to the distance of about half a mile, in the direction of the railway, where a crowd collected and a meeting was hastily formed. Apprehending the interference of the police, the promoters of it cut short the proceedings . . . ' (*The Times*, 8 December 1880).

Interestingly, the authorities took a different approach in respect of a meeting at Scotstown, Co. Monaghan on 9 December, which O'Kelly and John Dillon MP attended. A counter demonstration by Orangemen had been announced. The 2nd Dragoons were moved in from Brookeborough and there was a strong force of police. This time, the land league meeting was not prohibited. Instead, Major Blair RM and others persuaded Lord Rossmore, County Grand Master of the Orange Order, to adjourn the Orange meeting. (*The Times*, 10 December 1880).

O'Kelly had formerly been a soldier in the French Foreign Legion, a captain in the French army and a war correspondent in Cuba and the USA. In this last capacity he had been with US troops in the war against the Sioux chief, Sitting Bull (H. Boyland, *A Dictionary of Irish Biography* (1978) p. 272).

2. Compare the principle of *Humphries v Connor* and *O'Kelly v Harvey* with (1) the law on arrest for breach of the peace, above, p. 51 and (2) s. 3 of the Criminal Law Act 1967, above p. 59. If the circumstances are such as to justify detention, then the use of force short of arrest is similarly justified. Cf. the Northern Ireland (Emergency Provisions) Act 1978, s. 24, below, p. 184.

3. It is clear that ample legal powers are available to deal with the persons who are threatening disorder in situations such as these. The principle of these cases is designed to assist the policeman on the spot who may be faced with practical problems. Nevertheless, the principle is dangerous, if acceptable at all. It should be confined to cases of genuine last resort. If not it might become too easy to suppress the expression of unpopular views by threatening violence against those who express them. Where the police have advance warning of a problem of the *O'Kelly v Harvey* kind, should they be allowed to rely on the principle endorsed by that case, or should they be required to mobilise sufficient support to deal with the 'hostile' group?

4. Does the lawful assembly in these circumstances become unlawful if those present refuse to disperse when ordered to do so? See *Smith and Hogan*, p. 752, cf. *Duncan v Jones*, below.

5. These Irish cases are generally accepted as good law in England, although the acceptance has been described as 'uncritical' (W. Birtles (1973) 36 MLR 587)

Duncan v Jones [1936] 1 KB 218, 105 LJKB 71, 154 LT 110, 99 JP 399, 52 TLR 26, 79 Sol Jo 903, 33 LGR 491, 30 Cox CC 279, King's Bench Divisional Court
Case stated by County of London Quarter Sessions.

At 1 p.m. on 30 July 1934, about thirty people, including the appellant, Mrs Katherine Duncan, collected with a view to holding a meeting in Nynehead Street, New Cross, Deptford, a cul-de-sac, near to the entrance to an unemployed training centre. The meeting was to protest against the Incitement to Disaffection Bill. At the entrance to Nynehead Street a notice was written across the roadway as follows:—

'SEDITION'

Meeting at the Test Centre to-day (now) 1 p m
Speakers: R. Kidd (Council for Civil Liberties),
A. Bing (Barrister-at-Law),
E. Hanley (Amalgamated Engineers' Union),
K. Duncan (National Unemployed Workers' Movement),
Defend the right of free speech and public meeting.

A box was placed in the roadway opposite the entrance to the training centre, on which the appellant was about to mount, when the chief constable of the district, with whom was Inspector Jones, told her that a meeting could not be held in Nynehead Street, but that it could be held in Desmond Street, some 175 yards distant. The appellant then said: 'I'm going to hold it,' stepped on to the box, and started to address the people who were present, when the respondent immediately took her into custody, to which she submitted without resistance.

D. was convicted by a magistrate of obstructing J. in the execution of his duty contrary to the Prevention of Crimes Act 1871, s. 12, as amended by the Prevention of Crimes Amendment Act 1885, s. 2. She was fined 40s, and appealed to London Quarter Sessions.

At the hearing of the appeal it was not alleged . . . that there was any obstruction of the highway or of the access to the training centre, save in the sense of the obstruction necessarily caused by the box which was placed in the roadway and by the presence of the people surrounding it. Neither was it alleged that the appellant nor any of the persons present at the meeting had either committed, incited or provoked any breach of the peace.

It was proved or admitted that on 25 May 1933, a meeting had been held opposite the entrance to the training centre, and the appellant had addressed that meeting. Following that meeting and on the same day a disturbance took place inside the training centre. The superintendent of the training centre, who attributed the disturbance to the meeting, sent for the police to prevent a breach of the peace. Subsequently, and in spite of the disturbance and of warnings by the police, the appellant, for some reason unexplained by her, made one or more attempts to hold a meeting at the same spot, which were frustrated by the police. Before 30 July 1934, the superintendent of the training centre, who feared a repetition of the previous disturbance, communicated with the police, and by reason of such communication and of reports by the police in the course of their duty, the chief constable of the district and the respondent apprehended that a breach of the peace would result if the meeting now in question were held.

The deputy-chairman of quarter sessions was of opinion: (1.) that in fact (if it be material) the appellant must have known of the probable consequences of her holding the meeting—namely, a disturbance and possibly a breach of the peace—and was not unwilling that such consequences should ensue; (2.) that in fact the respondent reasonably apprehended a breach of the peace; (3.) that in law it thereupon became his duty to prevent the holding of the meeting; and (4.) that in fact, by attempting to hold the meeting, the appellant obstructed the respondent when in the execution of his duty. The appeal was, therefore, dismissed.

On the application of the appellant, quarter sessions stated this case for the opinion of the Court whether there was evidence on which the deputy-chairman could so decide in point of law.

Lord Hewart CJ: There have been moments during the argument in this case when it appeared to be suggested that the Court had to do with a grave case involving what is called the right of public meeting. I say 'called,' because English law does not recognize any special right of public meeting for political or other purposes. The right of assembly, as Professor Dicey puts it (Dicey's Law of the Constitution, 8th edn., p. 499), is nothing more than a view taken by the Court of the individual liberty of the subject. If I thought that the present case raised a question which has been held in suspense by more than one writer on constitutional law—namely, whether an assembly can properly be held to be unlawful merely because the holding of it is expected to give rise to a breach of the peace on the part of persons opposed to those who are holding the meeting—I should wish to hear much more argument before I expressed an opinion. This case, however, does not even touch that important question.

Our attention has been directed to the somewhat unsatisfactory case of *Beatty v Gillbanks*. ((1882) 9 QBD 308) The circumstances of that case and the charge must be remembered, as also must the important passage in the judgment of Field J, in which Cave J concurred. Field J said (Ibid. 314): 'I entirely concede that everyone must be taken to intend the natural consequences of his own acts, and it is clear to me that if this disturbance of the peace was the natural consequence of acts of the appellants they would be liable, and the justices would have been right in binding them over. But the evidence set forth in the case does not support this contention; on the contrary, it shows that the disturbances were caused by other people antagonistic to the appellants, and that no acts of violence were committed by them.' Our attention has also been directed to other authorities where the judgments in *Beatty v Gillbanks* have been referred to, but they do not carry the matter any further, although they more than once express a doubt about the exact meaning of the decision. In my view, *Beatty v Gillbanks* is apart from the present case. No such question as that which arose there is even mooted here.

The present case reminds one rather of the observations of Bramwell B in *R v Prebble* ((1858) I F&F 325 at 326), where, in holding that a constable, in clearing certain licensed premises of the persons thereon, was not acting in the execution of his duty, he said: 'It would have been otherwise had there been a nuisance or disturbance of the public peace, or any danger of a breach of the peace.'

The case stated which we have before us indicates clearly a causal connection between the meeting of May 1933, and the disturbance which occurred after it—that the disturbance was not only *post* the meeting but was also *propter* the meeting. In my view, the deputy-chairman was entitled to come to the conclusion to which he came on the facts which he found and to hold that the conviction of the appellant for wilfully obstructing the respondent when in the execution of his duty was right. This appeal should, therefore, be dismissed.

Humphreys J I agree. I regard this as a plain case. It has nothing to do with the law of unlawful assembly. No charge of that sort was even suggested against the appellant. The sole question raised by the case is whether the respondent, who was admittedly obstructed, was so obstructed when in the execution of his duty.

It does not require authority to emphasize the statement that it is the duty of a police officer to prevent apprehended breaches of the peace. Here it is found as a fact that the respondent reasonably apprehended a breach of the peace. It then, as is rightly expressed in the case, became his duty to prevent anything which in his view would cause that breach of the peace. While he was taking steps so to do he was wilfully obstructed by the appellant. I can conceive no clearer case within the statutes than that.

Singleton J: On the facts stated in the case I am satisfied that the respondent at the material time was doing that which it was his duty to do, and that, therefore, the obstruction of him by the appellent constituted obstruction of him when in the execution of his duty. Authorities in other branches of the law do not carry the matter any further. I agree that the appeal should be dismissed.

Appeal dismissed.

NOTES

1. This case has received widespread condemnation from academic commentators. See E.C.S. Wade, (1937) 6 CLJ 175; *Williams*, pp. 119–123; *Brownlie*, pp. 18–22; T. C. Daintith [1966] PL 248. It has been followed in New Zealand: *Burton v Power* [1940] NZLR 305.

2. An alternative version of events is given in A Barrister, *Justice in England* (1938) pp. 247–260. The author was D. N. Pritt, who defended Mrs Duncan in the court, sponsored by the NCCL. See also *Williams*, pp. 127–128 on the ban on meetings.

3. 'The police are set up by this judgment as the arbiters of what political parties or religious sects shall and shall not be accorded the rights of freedom of speech and freedom of assembly' (R. Kidd, *British Liberty in Danger* (1940) p. 24). Do you agree?

4. How convincing is the finding of fact that a breach of the peace was reasonably apprehended? Consider the width of the discretion which may be exercised by the police. Is there any suggestion that the police action was *necessary* in the *last resort*? Should this be a precondition to dispersal of a lawful meeting? (cf. *Humphries v Connor*, *O'Kelly v Harvey*, above). Note that the meeting in *Duncan v Jones* was not alleged to be unlawful. On the facts given, however, what offences might have been committed?

5. Is it possible to reconcile *Duncan v Jones* with *Beatty v Gillbanks* (above, p. 163) (1) in law; (2) in spirit? (See T. C. Daintith, [1966] PL 248; S. A. de Smith, *Constitutional and Administrative Law*, (3rd edn., 1977) pp. 493–496). Does it matter, given that both are merely decisions of the Divisional Court? An important point made by Daintith is that obstructing the police in the execution of their duty was a summary offence under a variety of statutory provisions at the time of *Beatty v Gillbanks* and could have been used by the prosecutor in that case (op. cit. p. 251). He suggests that the reason why it was not used was that 'not until 1936 was it revealed that facts insufficient to establish the offence of unlawful assembly might yet amount to obstruction of the police in the execution of their duty . . . unless an assembly was unlawful, the police had no duty to disperse it . . . ' (op. cit. pp. 251–2).

6. Compare the reasoning in *Duncan v Jones* with that of *Thomas v Sawkins* (above p. 64), and that of *R v Waterfield and Lynn* (above, p. 90). Note that other cases have taken a more restrictive view of what conduct, and in particular, disobedience to what commands, may amount to obstruction of the police in the execution of their duty (above pp. 35–37, 39–43).

7. D. N. Pritt told the House of Commons: 'You can always lend an air of plausibility to the enterprise of stopping the meeting by offering . . . an alternative site 175 yards away . . . . [I]f you cannot get an audience 175 yards away you might as well be 175 miles away' (314 HC Deb 10 July 1936 col 1551).

8. The basic issue is one of policy. Where X 'innocently' provokes Y to commit breaches of the peace, and the police wish to take direct action against X, the alternatives are (1) the police pay compensation (damages) to X (who is after all 'innocent'), with the money coming out of public (police) funds; or (2) the police needn't pay damages (*Humphries v Connor*) or (3) the police needn't pay damages, and any resistance is an offence (*Duncan v Jones*).

9. The police in practice rely on *Duncan v Jones* to control the numbers of pickets outside places of work, and the judges do not show much inclination to challenge assertions by police officers that they had reasonable grounds to apprehend breaches of the peace. See *Piddington v Bates* (below).

Piddington v Bates [1961] 1 WLR 162, [1960] 3 All ER 660, Queen's Bench Divisional Court

Eighteen men arrived to picket printer's works where about eight of the normal complement of twenty-four were working. Chief Inspector Bates told the appellant that two pickets at each of the two entrances were sufficient. He replied 'I'm going there and you can't stop me,' 'I know my rights', and 'I can stand by the gate if I want to' and finally, 'I'm going to join them. If you don't want me to, you'd better arrest me'. He then pushed gently past the prosecutor and was gently arrested. He was convicted of obstructing the prosecutor in the execution of this duty, and appealed.

Lord Parker CJ: . . . First, the mere statement by a constable that he did anticipate that there might be a breach of the peace is clearly not enough. There must exist proved facts from which a constable could reasonably anticipate such a breach. Secondly, it is not enough that his contemplation is that there is a remote possibility; there must be a real possibility of a breach of the peace. Accordingly, in every case, it becomes a question of whether, on the particular facts, it can be said that there were reasonable grounds on which a constable charged with this duty reasonably anticipated that a breach of the peace might occur . . . The magistrate found, so far as it is material: 'Having regard to the whole of the evidence the [prosecutor] was in my opinion justified in anticipating the possibility of a breach of the peace unless steps were taken to prevent it, and in my opinion it was his duty to decide what those steps should be.' That is challenged by the defendant on two grounds. The first and lesser ground is a criticism of the word 'possibility' of a breach of the peace. It is said that there must be something more than a mere possibility. I agree with that, but I do not read the finding of the magistrate as saying that it was just a mere remote possibility. I think he was referring to it as a real possibility.

The other point goes to an analysis of the evidence, from which it is said that no reasonable man could possibly anticipate a breach of the peace. It is pointed out that there was no obstruction in the street; that there was no actual intimidation; and that there were no threats or intimations of violence. It is said that there was really nothing save the fact that picketing was going on to suggest that a breach of the peace was a real possibility.

As I have said, every case must depend upon its exact facts, and the matter which influences me in this case is the matter of numbers. It is, I think, perfectly clear from the wording of the case, although it is not expressly so found, that the police knew that in these small works there were only eight people working. They found two vehicles arriving, with 18 people milling about the street, trying to form pickets at the doors. On that ground alone, coupled with the telephone call which, I should have thought, intimated some sense of urgency and apprehension, the police were fully entitled to think as reasonable men that there was a real danger of something more than mere picketing to collect or impart information or peaceably to persuade. I think that in those circumstances the prosecutor had reasonable grounds for anticipating that a breach of the peace was a real possibility. It may be, and I think this is the real criticism, that it can be said: Well, to say that only two pickets should be allowed is purely arbitrary; why two? Why not three? Where do you draw the line? I think that a police officer charged with the duty of preserving the Queen's peace must be left to take such steps as on the evidence before him he thinks are proper. I am far from saying that there should be any rule that only two pickets should be allowed at any particular door. There, one gets into an arbitrary area, but so far as this case is concerned I cannot see that there was anything wrong in the action of the prosecutor.

Finally, I would like to say that all these matters are so much matters of degree that I would hesitate, except on the clearest evidence, to interfere with the findings of magistrates who have had the advantage of hearing the whole case and observing the witnesses. . . .

Ashworth and **Elwes JJ** agreed.

Appeal dismissed

NOTES

1. See also *Tynan v Balmer* [1967] 1 QB 91, DC, and *Kavanagh v Hiscock* [1974] QB 600, DC. Wallington ([1972] 1 ILJ 219, 222) observes that 'any form of mass picketing almost inevitably involves the commission of offences, unless the pickets remain quiet and orderly, do not obstruct the street or the footway, and do as they are told by the police.'

2. The current statutory protection for peaceful picketing is section 15 of the Trade Union and Labour Relations Act 1974:

'It shall be lawful for one or more persons in contemplation or furtherance of a trade dispute to attend at or near—

   (a) a place where another person works or carries on business; or
   (b) any other place where another person happens to be, not being a place where he resides,

for the purpose only of peacefully obtaining or communicating information, or peacefully persuading any person to work or abstain from working.'

This protects pickets from actions in trespass, but not in respect of unreasonable obstruction of access to premises or unreasonable obstruction of the highway (B. Hepple and P. O'Higgins, *Encyclopedia of Labour Relations Law*, para. 1A-084). No one can be obliged to stop and listen (*Broome v Director of Public Prosecutions* [1974] AC 587, HL, *Kavanagh v Hiscock* [1974] QB 600). See further on picketing: R. Rideout *Principles of Labour Law*, (3rd edn., 1979), pp. 326–332; R. Kidner, [1975] Crim LR 256; J. E. Trice [1975] Crim LR 271; P. Wallington, [1972] 1 ILJ 219 and [1974] 3 ILJ 109; R. Kidner, *Trade Union Law* (1979) Chap. 13. The 1980 Employment Bill seeks to alter s. 15.

(ii) Binding over

The common law power of justices, (and any court of record having a criminal jurisdiction: Justices of the Peace Act 1968, section 1(7); Administration of Justice Act 1973, Schedule 5) to bind persons over to keep the peace, and their wider power under the Justices of the Peace Act 1361 (34 Edw III c 1) to bind persons over to be of good behaviour, have frequently been employed in the context of public order.

The power to require a person to enter into a recognisance to keep the peace, either generally, or towards a particular person, may be exercised where there is reasonable apprehension of a future breach of the peace (see above pp. 50–1). The recognisance may be forfeited by any unlawful action that tends to a breach of the peace.

The statutory power 'to take all of them that be [not] of good fame, where they shall be found, sufficient surety and mainprise of their good behaviour towards the King and his people, . . .', according to Blackstone (Book IV, Chap. XVIII), may be exercised:

'for causes of scandal, *contra bonos mores*, as well as *contra pacem*: as, for haunting bawdy-houses with women of bad fame; or for keeping such women in his own house; or for words tending to scandalize the government, or in abuse of the officers of justice, especially in the execution of their office. Thus also a justice may bind over all night-walkers; eaves-droppers; such as keep suspicious company, or are reported to be pilferers or robbers; such as sleep in the day, and wake in the night; common drunkards; whoremasters; the putative fathers of bastards; cheats; idle vagabonds; and other persons whose misbehaviour may reasonably bring them within the general words of the statute, as persons not of good fame . . .'

NOTES

1. On binding-over generally see G. Williams, 'Preventive Justice and the Rule of Law' (1953) 16 MLR 417; *Williams*, Chap. 4; *Brownlie*, pp. 119–120; (1961) 25 Journal of Criminal Law 220; A. D. Grunis, [1976] PL 16; D. G. T. Williams, [1970] CLJ 96, 104–106.
2. An appeal lies against a binding over order to the Crown Court (The Magistrates' Courts (Appeals from Binding Over Orders) Act 1956), or, by case stated on a point of law, to the Divisional Court (e.g. *Beatty v Gillbanks*, above p. 163, *Wise v Dunning*, above p. 166). An order may be challenged by an application for certiorari under RSC Order 53 (see *R v Londonderry JJ* (1891) 28 LR Ir 440).
3. Binding over orders have been made in many cases following conviction for a criminal offence against public order (see *Williams*, pp. 94–95). In addition, they have been made against persons who incite disorder. The most celebrated instance is *Lansbury v Riley* [1914] 3 KB 229, DC, where George Lansbury spoke in support of militant suffragettes at a time when there were many attacks on property. He said that women 'ought to break the law on every possible occasion, short of taking human life.' (*Williams*, p. 97). He was bound over in the sum of £1,000 with two sureties of £500. In the 1930s, several officers of the National Unemployed Workers' Movement were imprisoned for refusing to be bound over (Wal Hannington in 1922 and 1931; Sid Elias in 1931; Tom Mann and Emrhys Llewellyn in 1932; *Williams*, pp. 99–100; J. Stevenson and C. Cook, *The Slump* (1977) p. 227–8). See also *Wise v Dunning*, above p. 166, and *Beatty v Gillbanks*, above p. 163.

5 Emergency powers

(a) INTRODUCTION

The most extreme form of emergency which the country may face is war. In earlier times, the Crown relied on prerogative powers to take steps necessary for the conduct of war (see Wade and Phillips, *Constitutional and Administrative Law*, 9th edn., pp. 237–8). Each of the two world wars saw the creation of a complex edifice of statutory powers, mostly contained in delegated legislation made under the Defence of the Realm Acts 1914–15 and the Emergency Powers (Defence) Acts 1939–40. Every aspect of national life was closely regulated. Commentators were able to poke fun at the inevitable fatuity of some of the controls (see, e.g., C. K. Allen, *Law and Disorders* 1954). The interest of civil liberties was equally inevitably and equally swiftly relegated to a lesser rank in the order of national priorities. These measures have attracted both support, inasmuch as Britain has 'created the means of preserving itself from disaster without sacrificing the essential processes of democracy' (C. P. Cotter, (1953) 5 Stanford LR 382, 416), and stringent criticism (see C. K. Allen, *Law and Orders*, 1st edn. (1945); R. Kidd, *British Liberty in Danger* (1940), Part Two). Economic difficulties caused certain aspects of wartime regulation to be prolonged after the cessation of hostilities. In addition, the Emergency Powers Act 1920 enables the state to obtain wide ranging powers by regulation to meet peacetime emergencies. Section 1(1) of the Act (as amended by the Emergency Powers Act 1964) provides that

> 'If at any time it appears to His Majesty that [there have occurred, or are about to occur, events of such a nature] as to be calculated, by interfering with the supply and distribution of food, water, fuel, or light, or with the means of locomotion, to deprive the community, or any substantial portion of the community, of the essentials of life, His Majesty may, by proclamation (hereinafter referred to as a proclamation of emergency), declare that a state of emergency exists...'

A proclamation may not be in force longer than a month, without prejudice to the issue of further proclamations (ibid.). During the currency of a proclamation, regulations may be made by Order in Council 'for securing the essentials of life to the community'. The Act has been used solely in relation to major strikes. The most recent proclamation was in the winter of 1973/1974. The regulations were contained in S. I. 1974 No. 350. See generally, G. Morris [1979] PL 317.

(b) NORTHERN IRELAND

The situation in Ireland has long generated a requirement for additional legal powers to aid the preservation of peace.

'Emergency Powers' or 'special powers' have existed in Ireland without a break from the nineteenth century. The current provisions for Northern Ireland are contained in the Northern Ireland (Emergency Provisions) Act 1978 (below p. 181 ff.) In recent times particular issues have arisen concerning the ill-treatment of persons under interrogation (*Ireland v United Kingdom*, below p. 191) and the employment of troops to aid the civil power (below, p. 198).

The materials which follow concentrate upon Northern Ireland's security problems. This is not the whole picture. Between the inception of the state of Northern Ireland in 1921 and 1972 its government was in the hands of the Protestant Ulster Unionist Party. The decision that Northern Ireland should comprise six of the nine counties in the Province of Ulster was indeed based on the desire to ensure a Unionist majority in the Parliament of Northern Ireland. The voting strength of Unionists and Nationalists in Ulster as a whole was roughly equal (see N. Mansergh, *The Irish Question 1840–1921*, 3rd edn. (1975) Chap. VI). The Catholic minority during this period was the object of serious discrimination in a number of important areas. Official recognition of this came in 1969 with the report of the Cameron Commission on *Disturbances in Northern Ireland*, whose conclusions in this regard are summarised below. Both before and after the imposition of direct rule a number of legislative measures sought to end the regime of discrimination. Fourteen reforms are listed in the Report of the Standing Advisory Commission on Human Rights on *The protection of human rights by law in Northern Ireland* (1977) Cmnd. 7009, p. 11–14, covering such matters as universal adult suffrage in local elections, and the establishment of a Parliamentary Commissioner for Administration (government departments), a Commissioner for Complaints (local councils and public bodies), a Police Complaints Board, a central housing authority, an independent police authority, a Director of Public Prosecutions and a Fair Employment Agency. All legislative and executive actions of central and local government and statutory bodies which are discriminatory on religious or political grounds are unlawful under Part III of the Northern Ireland Constitution Act 1973. Nevertheless, as the Commission point out (at p. 14):

'What might have succeeded at another time or in different circumstances has not been sufficient to change a situation where violence has become a way of life for some and a perpetual terror for others. . . . The continuing state of emergency has not only seriously impaired the effectiveness of the substantial legislative and administrative reforms which have been made since 1969 for the better protection of human rights but has also inevitably resulted in the restrictions of certain basic rights and freedoms in Northern Ireland.'

One matter of concern for those who believe that legal processes may be of value in the protection of civil liberties has been why the minority did not seek legal redress for such of their grievances as lay against public authorities. The discriminatory abuse of statutory powers is potentially reviewable under the ultra vires doctrine. Judicial review of administrative action may in theory at least be used as a vehicle for civil rights litigation. The Government of Ireland Act 1920 contained specific guarantees against discriminatory legislation. However, commentators have pointed to the absence of 'the necessary confidence in the judicial system as a means of securing justice' (K. Boyle, T. Hadden and P. Hillyard, *Law and State* (1975) p. 11). See generally, Boyle, Hadden and Hillyard, Chap. 2; W. D. Carroll, (1973) 6 NY Univ Journal of International Law and Politics p. 28, 47–53; T. Hadden and P. Hillyard, *Justice in Northern Ireland* (1973) Chap. II; Northern Ireland Constitution Act 1973 Part III; *Purvis v Magherafelt District Council* [1978] NI 26.

The problems of the control of emergency powers are considered by M. P. O'Boyle, (1977) 28 NILQ 160.

Disturbances in Northern Ireland: Report of a Commission appointed by the Governor of Northern Ireland, Chairman: Lord Cameron [Cmd. 532, 1969]

SUMMARY OF CONCLUSIONS ON CAUSES OF DISORDERS

(*a*) *General*

(1) A rising sense of continuing injustice and grievance among large sections of the Catholic

population in Northern Ireland, in particular in Londonderry and Dungannon, in respect of (i) inadequacy of housing provision by certain local authorities (ii) unfair methods of allocation of houses built and let by such authorities, in particular, refusals and omissions to adopt a 'points' system in determining priorities and making allocations (iii) misuse in certain cases of discretionary powers of allocation of houses in order to perpetuate Unionist control of the local authority.

(2) Complaints, now well documented in fact, of discrimination in the making of local government appointments, at all levels but especially in senior posts, to the prejudice of non-Unionists and especially Catholic members of the community, in some Unionist controlled authorities.

(3) Complaints, again well documented, in some cases of deliberate manipulation of local government electoral boundaries and in others a refusal to apply for their necessary extension, in order to achieve and maintain Unionist control of local authorities and so to deny to Catholics influence in local government proportionate to their numbers.

(4) A growing and powerful sense of resentment and frustration among the Catholic population at failure to achieve either acceptance on the part of the Government of any need to investigate these complaints or to provide and enforce a remedy for them.

(5) Resentment, particularly among Catholics, as to the existence of the Ulster Special Constabulary (the 'B' Specials) as a partisan and para-military force recruited exclusively from Protestants.

(6) Widespread resentment among Catholics in particular at the continuance in force of regulations made under the Special Powers Act, and of the continued presence in the statute book of the Act itself.

(7) Fears and apprehensions among Protestants of a threat to Unionist domination and control of Government by increase of Catholic population and powers, inflamed in particular by the activities of the Ulster Constitution Defence Committee and the Ulster Protestant Volunteers, provoked strong hostile reaction to civil rights claims as asserted by the Civil Rights Association and later by the People's Democracy which was readily translated into physical violence against Civil Rights demonstrators. . . .

Report of a Committee to consider, in the context of civil liberties and human rights, measures to deal with terrorism in Northern Ireland, Chairman: Lord Gardiner (Cmnd. 5847, 1975)

CIVIL LIBERTIES AND HUMAN RIGHTS

15. Our terms of reference require us to consider the problem of terrorism and subversion . . . with due consideration for the preservation of civil liberties and human rights. We have been set the difficult task of maintaining a double perspective; for, while there are policies which contribute to the maintenance of order at the expense of individual freedom, the maintenance without restriction of that freedom may involve a heavy toll in death and destruction. Some of those who have given evidence to us have argued that such features of the present emergency provisions as the use of the Army in aid of the civil power, detention without trial, arrest on suspicion and trial without jury are so inherently objectionable that they must be abolished on the grounds that they constitute a basic violation of human rights. We are unable to accept this argument. While the liberty of the subject is a human right to be preserved under all possible conditions, it is not, and cannot be, an absolute right, because one man may use his liberty to take away the liberty of another and must be restrained from doing so. Where freedoms conflict, the state has a duty to protect those in need of protection . . .

17. The suspension of normal legal safeguards for the liberty of the subject may sometimes be essential, in a society faced by terrorism, to counter greater evils. But if continued for any period of time it exacts a social cost from the community; and the price may have to be paid over several generations. It is one of the aims of terrorists to evoke from the authorities an over-reaction to the violence, for which the terrorists are responsible, with the consequence that the authorities lose the support of those who would otherwise be on the side of government.

18. In the present situation there are neighbourhoods in Northern Ireland where natural social motivation is being deployed against lawful authority rather than in support of it. Any good society is compounded of a network of natural affection and loyalties; yet we have seen and heard of situations in which normal human responses such as family affection, love of home, neighbourliness, loyalty to friends and patriotism are daily invoked to strengthen terrorist activity.

19. The imposition of order may be successful in the short term; but in the long term, peace and stability can only come from that consensus which is the basis of law. The tragedy of

Northern Ireland is that crime has become confused with politically motivated acts. The common criminal can flourish in a situation where there is a convenient political motive to cover anti-social acts; and the development of a 'prisoner-of-war' mentality among prisoners with social approval and the hope of an amnesty, lends tacit support to violence and dishonesty.

20. We acknowledge the need for firm and decisive action on the part of the security forces; but violence has in the past provoked a violent response. The adoption of methods of interrogation 'in depth', which involved forms of ill-treatment that are described in the Compton Report (Cmnd. 4823), did not last for long. Following the Report of the Parker Committee in 1972 (Cmnd. 4901) these methods were declared unlawful and were stopped by the British Government; but the resentment caused was intense, widespread and persistent.

21. **The continued existence of emergency powers should be limited both in scope and duration.** Though there are times when they are necessary for the preservation of human life, they can, if prolonged, damage the fabric of the community, and they do not provide lasting solutions. **A solution to the problems of Northern Ireland should be worked out in political terms, and must include further measures to promote social justice between classes and communities. Much has been done to improve social conditions in recent years, but much remains to be done.**

Northern Ireland (Emergency Provisions) Act 1978

PART I

Scheduled offences

[Part I contains various provisions as to proceedings for 'scheduled offences' i.e. those listed in Schedule 4. These are the crimes commonly committed by terrorists, including, for example, murder, manslaughter, riot, kidnapping, assault occasioning actual bodily harm, robbery involving weapons, and various firearms and explosives offences. In relation to some of these the Attorney-General for Northern Ireland may certify that a particular case is not to be treated as a scheduled offence. All trials on indictment of scheduled offences are held at the Belfast City Commission (section 6) and are conducted by a judge sitting without a jury (section 7). Reasons for conviction must be given (section 7(5)). A person convicted may appeal to the Court of Criminal Appeal on any ground without leave.]

8. Admissions by persons charged with scheduled offences
(1) In any criminal proceedings for a scheduled offence, or two or more offences which are or include scheduled offences, a statement made by the accused may be given in evidence by the prosecution in so far as—
    (*a*) it is relevant to any matter in issue in the proceedings; and
    (*b*) it is not excluded by the court in pursuance of subsection (2) below.

(2) If, in any such proceedings where the prosecution proposes to give in evidence a statement made by the accused, prima facie evidence is adduced that the accused was subjected to torture or to inhuman or degrading treatment in order to induce him to make the statement, the court shall, unless the prosecution satisfies it that the statement was not so obtained—
    (*a*) exclude the statement, or
    (*b*) if the statement has been received in evidence, either—
      (i) continue the trial disregarding the statement;
    or
      (ii) direct that the trial shall be restarted before a differently constituted court (before which the statement in question shall be inadmissible).

(3) This section does not apply to a summary trial.

9. [This section reverses the onus of proof in relation to certain offences of possessing firearms, explosives etc.]

PART II

Powers of arrest, detention, search and seizure, etc.

11. Arrest of terrorists
(1) Any constable may arrest without warrant any person whom he suspects of being a terrorist.
(2) For the purpose of arresting a person under this section a constable may enter and search any premises or other place where that person is or where the constable suspects him of being.
(3) A person arrested under this section shall not be detained in right of the arrest for more than seventy-two hours after his arrest . . .
(4) Where a person is arrested under this section, an officer of the Royal Ulster Constabulary not below the rank of chief inspector may order him to be photographed and to have his finger prints and palm prints taken by a constable, and a constable may use such reasonable force as may be necessary for that purpose.

12. Dentention of terrorists, etc
Schedule 1 to this Act shall have effect with respect to the detention of terrorists and persons suspected of being terrorists.

13. Constables' general power of arrest and seizure
(1) Any constable may arrest without warrant any person whom he suspects of committing, having committed or being about to commit a scheduled offence or an offence under this Act which is not a scheduled offence.
(2) For the purposes of arresting a person under this section a constable may enter and search any premises or other place where that person is or where the constable suspects him of being.
(3) A constable may seize anything which he suspects is being, has been or is intended to be used in the commission of a scheduled offence or an offence under this Act which is not a scheduled offence.

14. Powers of arrest of members of Her Majesty's forces
(1) A member of Her Majesty's forces on duty may arrest without warrant, and detain for not more than four hours, a person whom he suspects of committing, having committed or being about to commit any offence.
(2) A person effecting an arrest under this section complies with any rule of law requiring him to state the ground of arrest if he states that he is effecting the arrest as a member of Her Majesty's forces.
(3) For the purpose of arresting a person under this section a member of Her Majesty's forces may enter and search any premises or other place—
 (*a*) where that person is, or
 (*b*) if that person is suspected of being a terrorist or of having committed an offence involving the use or possession of an explosive, explosive substance or firearm, where that person is suspected of being.

15. Power to search for munitions and radio transmitters
(1) Any member of Her Majesty's forces on duty or any constable may enter any premises or other place other than a dwelling-house for the purpose of ascertaining—
 (*a*) whether there are any munitions unlawfully at that place; or
 (*b*) whether there is a transmitter at that place;
and may search the place for any munitions or transmitter with a view to exercising the powers conferred by subsection (4) below.

(2) Any member of Her Majesty's forces on duty authorised by a commissioned officer of those forces or any constable authorised by an officer of the Royal Ulster Constabulary not below the rank of chief inspector may enter any dwelling-house in which it is suspected that there are unlawfully any munitions or that there is a transmitter and may search it for any munitions or transmitter with a view to exercising the said powers.

(3) Any member of Her Majesty's forces on duty or any constable may—
 (*a*) stop any person in any public place and, with a view to exercising the said powers, search him for the purpose of ascertaining whether he has any munitions unlawfully with him or any transmitter with him; and
 (*b*) with a view to exercising the said powers, search any person not in a public place whom he suspects of having any munitions unlawfully with him or any transmitter with him.

(4) A member of Her Majesty's forces or a constable—
 (*a*) authorised to search any premises or other place or any person under this Act, may seize any munitions found in the course of the search unless it appears to the person so authorised that the munitions are being, have been and will be used only for a lawful purpose and may retain and, if necessary, destroy them;

(*b*) authorised to search any premises or other place or any person, may seize any transmitter found in the course of the search unless it appears to the person so authorised that the transmitter has been, is being and is likely to be used only lawfully and may retain it.

(5) In this section—
'munitions' means—
    (*a*) explosives, explosive substances, firearms and ammunition; and
    (*b*) anything used or capable of being used in the manufacture of any explosive, explosive substance, firearm or ammunition; . . .

17. Entry to search for persons unlawfully detained
(1) Where any person is believed to be unlawfully detained in such circumstances that his life is in danger, any member of Her Majesty's forces on duty or any constable may, subject to subsection (2) below, enter any premises or other place for the purpose of ascertaining whether that person is so detained there.
(2) A dwelling-house may be entered in pursuance of sub-section (1) above—
    (*a*) by a member of Her Majesty's forces, only when authorised to do so by a commissioned officer of those forces; and
    (*b*) by a constable, only when authorised to do so by an officer of the Royal Ulster Constabulary not below the rank of chief inspector.

18. Power to stop and question
(1) Any member of Her Majesty's forces on duty or any constable may stop and question any person for the purpose of ascertaining—
    (*a*) that person's identity and movements;
    (*b*) what he knows concerning any recent explosion or any other incident endangering life or concerning any person killed or injured in any such explosion or incident; or
    (*c*) any one or more of the matters referred to in paragraphs (*a*) and (*b*) above.

(2) Any person who—
    (*a*) fails to stop when required to do so under this section, or
    (*b*) refuses to answer, or fails to answer to the best of his knowledge and ability, any question addressed to him under this section,
shall be liable on summary conviction to imprisonment for a term not exceeding six months or to a fine nor exceeding £400, or both.

19. General powers of entry and interference with rights of property and with highways
(1) Any member of Her Majesty's forces on duty or any constable may enter any premises or other place—
    (*a*) if he considers it necessary to do so in the course of operations for the preservation of the peace or the maintenance of order; or
    (*b*) if authorised to do so by or on behalf of the Secretary of State.

20. Supplementary provisions
(1) Any power conferred by this Part of this Act—
    (*a*) to enter any premises or other place includes power to enter any vessel, aircraft or vehicle;
    (*b*) to search any premises or other place includes power to stop and search any vehicle or vessel or any aircraft which is not airborne and search any container;
and in this Part of this Act references to any premises or place shall be construed accordingly.
(2) In this Part of this Act references to a dwelling-house include references to a vessel or vehicle which is habitually stationary and used as a dwelling.
(3) Any power conferred by this Part of this Act to enter any place, vessel, aircraft or vehicle shall be exercisable, if need be, by force.
(4) Any power conferred by virtue of this section to search a vehicle or vessel shall, in the case of a vehicle or vessel which cannot be conveniently or thoroughly searched at the place where it is, include power to take it or cause it to be taken to any place for the purpose of carrying out the search.
(5) Any power conferred by virtue of this section to search any vessel, aircraft, vehicle or container includes power to examine it.
(6) Any power conferred by this Part of this Act to stop any person includes power to stop a vessel or vehicle or an aircraft which is not airborne.
(7) Any person who, when required by virtue of this section to stop a vessel or vehicle or any aircraft which is not airborne, fails to do so shall be liable [to the same penalty as in s. 18(2)]
(8) A member of Her Majesty's forces exercising any power conferred by this Part of this Act when he is not in uniform shall, if so requested by any person at or about the time of exercising that power, produce to that person documentary evidence that he is such a member.

PART III

Offences against public security and public order

21. Proscribed organisations
[Section 21 contains provisions similar to those of the Prevention of Terrorism (Temporary Provisions) Act 1976, section 1, above p. 130. The main differences are: – section 1(1)(c) is replaced here by:

'(c) solicits or invites any person to become a member of a proscribed organisation or to carry out on behalf of a proscribed organisation orders or directions given, or requests made, by a member of that organisation (s. 21(1)(c))';

– the maximum penalty on conviction on indictment is ten years imprisonment not five and the maximum fine on summary conviction is £400 not £1,000 (section 21(1)).
– an organisation may be proscribed where it appears to the Secretary of State 'to be concerned in acts of terrorism or in promoting or encouraging it' (section 21(4)).
– the following provision has no counterpart in section 1:

21(6) The possession by a person of a document
(a) addressed to him as a member of a proscribed organisation; or
(b) relating or purporting to relate to the affairs of a proscribed organisation; or
(c) emanating or purporting to emanate from a proscribed organisation or officer of a proscribed organisation,
shall be evidence of that person belonging to the organisation at the time when he had the document in his possession.]

22. Unlawful collection, etc. of information
(1) No person shall, without lawful authority or reasonable excuse (the proof of which lies on him)—
(a) collect, record, publish, communicate or attempt to elicit any information with respect to any person to whom this paragraph applies which is of such a nature as is likely to be useful to terrorists;
(b) collect or record any information which is of such a nature as is likely to be useful to terrorists in planning or carrying out any act of violence; or
(c) have in his possession any record of or document containing any such information as is mentioned in paragraph (a) or (b) above.

(2) Subsection (1)(a) above applies to any of the following persons, that is to say—
(a) any constable or member of Her Majesty's forces;
(b) any person holding judicial office;
(c) any officer of any court; and
(d) any person employed for the whole of his time in the prison service in Northern Ireland.

(3) In subsection (1) above any reference to recording information includes a reference to recording it by means of photography or by any other means. . . .
(4) [The same penalties are prescribed as in s. 21(1)]

23. Training in making or use of firearms, explosives or explosive substances
(1) Subject to subsection (2) below, any person who instructs or trains another or receives instruction or training in the making or use of firearms, explosives or explosive substances shall be liable [to the same penalties as in s. 21(1)]
(2) In any prosecution for an offence under this section it shall be a defence for the person charged to prove that the instruction or training was given or received with lawful authority or for industrial, agricultural or sporting purposes only or otherwise with good reason. . . .

24. Failure to disperse when required to do so
(1) Where any commissioned officer of Her Majesty's forces or any officer of the Royal Ulster Constabulary not below the rank of chief inspector is of opinion that any assembly of three or more persons—
(a) may lead to a breach of the peace or public disorder; or
(b) may make undue demands of the police or Her Majesty's forces,
he, or any member of those forces on duty or any constable, may order the persons constituting the assembly to disperse forthwith.

(2) Where an order is given under this section with respect to an assembly, any person who thereafter joins or remains in the assembly or otherwise fails to comply with the order shall be liable [to the same penalty as in s. 18(2)].

25. Dressing or behaving in a public place like a member of a proscribed organisation
Any person who in a public place dresses or behaves in such a way as to arouse reasonable apprehension that he is a member of a proscribed organisation shall be liable [to the same penalty as in s. 18(2)].

26. Wearing of hoods, etc. in public places
Any person who, without lawful authority or reasonable excuse (the proof of which lies on him), wears in a public place or in the curtilage of a dwelling-house (other than one in which he is residing) any hood, mask or other article whatsoever made, adapted or used for concealing the identity or features shall be liable [to the same penalty as in s. 18(2)].

PART IV

Miscellaneous and general

27. Supplementary regulations for preserving the peace, etc.
(1) The Secretary of State may by regulations make provision additional to the foregoing provisions of this Act for promoting the preservation of the peace and the maintenance of order. . . .

28. Compensation
(1) Where under this Act any real or personal property is taken, occupied, destroyed or damaged, or any other act is done interfering with private rights of property, compensation shall, subject to the provisions of this section, be payable by the Secretary of State. . . .

29. Restriction of prosecutions
(1) A prosecution shall not be instituted in respect of any offence under this Act except by or with the consent of the Director of Public Prosecutions for Northern Ireland. . . .

31. Interpretation
(1) In this Act, except so far as the context otherwise requires— . . .
'terrorism' means the use of violence for political ends and includes any use of violence for the purpose of putting the public or any section of the public in fear;
'terrorist' means a person who is or has been concerned in the commission or attempted commission of any act of terrorism or in directing, organising or training persons for the purpose of terrorism; . . .

Schedule 3

THE NORTHERN IRELAND (EMERGENCY PROVISIONS) REGULATIONS 1978

Road traffic

2. The Secretary of State may by order prohibit, restrict or regulate in any area the use of vehicles or any class of vehicles on highways or the use by vehicles or any class of vehicles of roads or classes of roads specified in the order, either generally or in such circumstances as may be so specified.

Railways

3. The Secretary of State, or any officer of the Royal Ulster Constabulary not below the rank of assistant chief constable, may direct any person having the management of a railway to secure that any train specified in the direction or trains of any class so specified shall stop, or shall not stop, at a station or other place so specified.

Funerals

4. Where it appears to an officer of the Royal Ulster Constabulary not below the rank of chief inspector that a funeral may—
    (*a*) occasion a breach of the peace or serious public disorder, or
    (*b*) cause undue demands to be made on Her Majesty's forces or the police,

he may give directions imposing on the persons organising or taking part in the funeral such conditions as appear to him to be necessary for the preservation of public order including (without prejudice to the generality of the foregoing) conditions—
    (i) prescribing the route to be taken by the funeral;
    (ii) prohibiting the funeral from entering any place specified in the directions;
    (iii) requiring persons taking part in the funeral to travel in vehicles. . . .

NOTES

1. There have been many occasions in Irish history when the government of the day has secured the enactment of wider statutory powers to deal with the problem of security than those normally available in Great Britain. In the nineteenth century, for example, the Protection of Person and Property Act (Ireland) 1881, 44 Vict c4, the Peace Preservation (Ireland) Act 1881, 44 Vict c5, the Prevention of Crime (Ireland) Act 1882, 45 & 46 Vict c25, and the Criminal Law and Procedure Act 1887, 50 & 51 Vict c20, included many provisions similar to those contained in the 1978 Act, including powers of detention, arrest and search, and trial without a jury for certain kinds of offence. In addition there were at various times powers to prohibit meetings, provisions as to special juries and the change of venue of trials, and provisions making intimidation an offence.

In the twentieth century, the main piece of 'emergency' legislation in Northern Ireland was the Civil Authorities (Special Powers) Act (NI) 1922 and the regulations made thereunder. This was originally intended as a temporary measure, but was renewed annually until 1928 and then for five years to 1933. It was then provided that the Act 'shall continue in force until Parliament otherwise determines' by the Civil Authorities (Special Powers) Act (NI) 1933, s. 2. The content of the regulations was altered from time to time, and certain features were strongly criticised (see the *Report of a Commission of Inquiry appointed to examine the purpose and effect of the Civil Authorities (Special Powers) Acts (NI) 1922 and 1933*, NCCL (1936); *A Review of the 1936 NCCL Commission of Inquiry in the light of subsequent events*, NCCL (1972); J.Ll. J. Edwards, [1956] Crim LR 7; H. Calvert, *Constitutional Law in Northern Ireland* (1968) pp. 380–386; *Emergency Powers: A Fresh Start*, Fabian Tract 416 (1972). One of the most objectionable provisions was section 2(4) of the 1922 Act which provided that:

'If any person does any act of such a nature as to be calculated to be prejudicial to the preservation of the peace or maintenance of order in Northern Ireland and not specifically provided for in the regulations, he shall be deemed to be guilty of an offence against the regulations.'

This has no counterpart in the 1973 and 1978 Acts.

The legal procedures to deal with terrorist activities were reviewed by the Diplock Commission (Report, December 1972, Cmnd. 5185; see W.L. Twining [1973] Crim LR 407). The Northern Ireland (Emergency Provisions) Act 1973 (which repealed the Special Powers Acts) was based upon their recommendations. *The Report of a Committee to consider, in the context of civil liberties and human rights, measures to deal with terrorism in Northern Ireland* (Chairman: Lord Gardiner, January 1975, Cmnd. 5847) was followed by legislation amending the 1973 Act Northern Ireland (Emergency Provisions) (Amendment) Act 1975, and most of these provisions are now consolidated in the 1978 Act. The Act is very fully annotated by K. Boyle in '*Current Law*' *Statutes Annotated*. A number of aspects of the 1978 Act were considered in the *Report of the Committee of Inquiry into Police Interrogation Procedures in Northern Ireland* (1979) Cmnd. 7497 (the Bennett Report):

2. *Trial by judge alone*

This was introduced following recommendations of the Diplock Commission (Cmnd. 5185, pp. 17–19). The Commission took the view that there was a serious threat of intimidation to jurors, and a danger of perverse acquittals of 'loyalist extremists' by the predominantly Protestant juries. The Gardiner Committee concluded (Cmnd. 5847 p. 11) that the new system 'has worked fairly and well', that 'the right to a fair trial has been respected and maintained and that the administration of justice has not suffered.' Accordingly they supported the continuation of these provisions. Boyle (op. cit., note to s.7) gives figures which show a pattern of declining acquittal rates for trials by judge alone over the period 1973–1977, and notes that 'concern has been voiced over the spectre of judges becoming case-hardened . . .'

3. *Admissions*

It has been held that while section 8 (formerly s.6 of the 1973 Act) has replaced the common law test of voluntariness, the judges retain their discretion to disallow relevant evidence where its prejudicial effect outweighs its probative value, or where to admit it 'would not be in the interests of justice' (*R v Corey* (1973) December (unreported: NIJB, cited in *R v McCormick* [1977] NI 105 at 112); *R v Hetherington* [1975] NI 164 at 169–170). In *R v McCormick* [1977] NI 105, 114 McGonigal LJ stated that this discretion should not be used so as to negative the effect of s.6 of the 1973 Act 'and under the guise of the discretionary power have the effect of reinstating the old common law test in so far as it depended on the proof of physical or mental maltreatment.' It should only be exercised where maltreatment has rendered a statement 'in itself' suspect by reason of the method as a result of which it was obtained. See also *R v Milne* [1978] NI 110 (Belfast City Commission) and *R v O'Halloran* (1979) 2 NIJB (CCA). In the latter case, Lowry LCJ observed:

'This Court finds it difficult in practice to envisage any form of physical violence which is relevant to the interrogation of a suspect in custody and which, if it had occurred, could at the same time leave a court satisfied beyond reasonable doubt in relation to the issue for decision under section 6.'

Once a prima facie case has been raised that the defendant has been subjected to improper treatment under the section, the onus shifts to the Crown to establish *beyond reasonable doubt* that admissions were not so obtained (*R v Hetherington* [1975] NI 164 at 166). McGonigal LJ recognized in *R v McCormick* that s. 6 'leaves it open to an interviewer to use a moderate degree of physical maltreatment for the purpose of inducing a person to make a statement' ([1977] NI 105, 111).

The Bennett Committee concluded that the reports of cases decided by the judges as to the discretion to exclude evidence 'necessarily leave areas of uncertainty from the point of view of police practice' (Bennett Report, p. 136). This led the Committee 'to consider whether the control exercised by the court over the means by which statements are induced and obtained should be supplemented by more direct regulation operating immediately on the interviewing officers' (ibid. p. 31).

4. *Internment*

The detention of persons without trial has been employed by the authorities in both Northern Ireland and the Republic of Ireland (see J. McGuffin, *Internment*, (1973)).

The changes in legislation authorising the 'extrajudicial deprivation of liberty' are traced in the Judgment of the European Court of Human Rights in *Ireland v The United Kingdom* (1978) pp. 31–39. These were in turn (1) Regulation 12(1) of the Special Powers Regulations; (2) the Detention of Terrorists (Northern Ireland) Order 1972 (made under the Northern Ireland (Temporary Provisions) Act 1972 and in operation between 7 November 1972 and 8 August 1973); (3) the Northern Ireland (Emergency Provisions) Act 1973 s. 10(5) and Sch. 1 (7 August 1973–21 August 1975) and (4) the Northern Ireland (Emergency Provisions) (Amendment) Act 1975 s. 9 and Sch. 1 (21 August 1975–: now consolidated in s. 12 and Sch. 1 of the 1978 Act).

The internment powers were invoked on 9 August 1971 (see The Sunday Times Insight Team, *Ulster* (1972) Ch. 15; *Ireland v UK*, pp. 16–18).

The power to order internment under the Special Powers Regulation 12 was vested in the Minister of Home Affairs for Northern Ireland acting on the recommendation of a senior police officer or advisory committee, and could be exercised where he was satisfied that it was expedient for securing the preservation of peace and the maintenance of order. Following direct rule, the Detention of Terrorists Order (Northern Ireland) 1972 provided for an independent review of decisions. An interim custody order could be made by the Secretary of State for Northern Ireland where it appeared that an individual was suspected of having been concerned in the commission or attempted commission of any act of terrorism or the organization of persons for the purpose of terrorism. The person could only be held for 28 days unless the case was referred to a commissioner appointed under the Order. The commissioner was to order release unless satisfied that the person had been concerned in acts of the kind described above and that his detention was necessary for the protection of the public. There was a right of appeal to an appeal tribunal. Proceedings were to take a quasi-judicial form subject to the requirements of security. The Gardiner Committee concluded:

> 148. After long and anxious consideration, we are of the opinion that detention cannot remain as a long-term policy. In the short term, it may be an effective means of containing violence, but the prolonged effects of the use of detention are ultimately inimical to community life, fan a widespread sense of grievance and injustice, and obstruct those elements in Northern Ireland society which could lead to reconciliation. Detention can only be tolerated in a democratic society in the most extreme circumstances; it must be used with the utmost restraint and retained only as long as it is strictly necessary. We would like to be able to recommend that the time has come to abolish detention; but the present level of violence, the risks of increased violence, and the difficulty of predicting events even a few months ahead make it impossible for us to put forward a precise recommendation on the timing.'

Should such measures still be regarded as necessary, the Committee recommended a return to the system where the sole and ultimate responsibility for detention should be that of the Secretary of State, advised by a Detention Advisory Board, but with no attempt to emulate, even approximately, quasi-judicial procedures (Cmnd. 5847, pp. 45–49). Revised arrangements were incorporated in the 1975 and 1978 statutes but have not been used. The last detainees were released on 5 December 1975, and the policy of 'internment' abandoned. See R. J. Spjut (1975) 10 Irish Jurist (n s) 272; K. Boyle, T. Hadden and P. Hillyard, *Law and State* (1975) Chap. 5.

The compatibility of internment with the European Convention on Human Rights was considered in *Ireland v UK* (below).

5. *Arrest*
(i) The powers of arrest are wider in various respects than the powers normally granted (see above pp. 46–63). Only s. 14(2), however, dispenses with the *Christie v Leachinsky* requirements (as to which see above pp. 55–59). This was justified by the Diplock Commission (Cmnd. 5185) on the ground that it was not practicable for the initial arrest of a suspected terrorist in 'extremist strongholds' to be effected by a police officer:

> '45. It is, we think, preposterous to expect a young soldier making an arrest under these conditions to be able to identify a person whom he has arrested as being a man whom he knows to be wanted for a particular offence so as to be able to inform him accurately on the grounds on which he is arresting him. It is impossible to question arrested persons on the spot to establish their identity. In practice this cannot usually be ascertained until they have been taken to the safety of battalion headquarters. Even here it may be a lengthy process, as suspects often give false names or addresses or, giving their true names, which are often very common ones, assert that some relation or other person of the same name is the real person who is 'wanted' for a particular offence. It is only when his identity has been satisfactorily established that it is possible to be reasonably certain of the particular ground on which he was liable to arrest and to inform him of it.'

(ii) Many regulations made under the Civil Authorities (Special Powers) Act 1922 purported to give powers to members of the armed forces on duty. It was held in *R(Hume) v Londonderry JJ* [1972] NI 91 that such regulations were *ultra vires* in view of the Government of Ireland Act 1920 s. 4 (1), which provided that the Northern Ireland Parliament was not to have power to make laws in respect of 'the navy, the army, the air force, . . . or the defence of the realm, or any other naval, military, or air force matter . . .'

Parliament immediately passed legislation to regularise the position retrospectively in the Northern Ireland Act 1972 s. 1:

> **'1. Effects of Government of Ireland Act 1920 s. 4(1) para. 3**
> The limitations imposed by paragraph (3) of section 4(1) of the Government of Ireland Act 1920 on the powers of the Parliament of Northern Ireland to make laws shall not have effect, and shall be deemed never to have had effect, to preclude the inclusion in laws made by that Parliament for the peace, order or good government of Northern Ireland of all provisions relating to members of Her Majesty's forces as such or to things done by them when on duty, and in particular shall not preclude, and shall be deemed never to have precluded, the conferment on them by, under or in pursuance of any such law of powers, authorities, privileges or immunities in relation to the preservation of the peace or maintenance of order in Northern Ireland.'

The Attorney-General gave an undertaking that 'any prosecution now pending, which would fail if today's Judgment stood, will be abandoned or stopped and no new prosecution of that kind will be initiated in relation to the past' (831 HC Deb 23 February 1972 col 1370). He also stated that 'the Bill will not act retrospectively affecting civil claims based on any matter other than the technical defect in the powers of the troops, affected by the Bill.' (831 HC Deb 23 February 1972 col 1445). See P. O'Higgins, (1972) 35 MLR 295.

In *R v Gorman* [1974] NI 152, Lowry LCJ held that G could be charged with the offence of escaping from lawful custody where the original arrest had been unlawful, but had been retrospectively validated by the 1972 Act. The Act had been passed after G had escaped.
(iii) In *Re McElduff* [1972] NI 1, McGonigal J held that the usual requirements as to arrests (above pp. 53–59) were applicable to arrests under the Civil Authorities (Special Powers) Act Regulations. Accordingly, a person could not be validly arrested unless (1) the arrestor

took reasonable steps to bring the fact of the arrest to the notice of the person arrested; (2) the person arrested was informed at the time of the arrest or at the earliest opportunity thereafter, (i) under what powers he had been arrested, and (ii) of the general nature of the suspicion leading to the arrest. McElduff was arrested on 9 August 1971 under Regulation 10 (power to arrest and detain for up to 48 hours for the purposes of interrogation) as part of 'Operation Demetrius' (see *Ireland v UK*, below, p. 191). Later the same day, he was purportedly rearrested under Regulation 11(1) (power to arrest persons suspected of acting in a manner prejudicial to peace or order). The arresting officer did not sufficiently distinguish this from the earlier arrest, merely stating that McElduff was 'being arrested' under the Special Powers Act. As a valid and subsisting arrest under Regulation 11(1) was a necessary prerequisite for a valid detention order under Regulation 11(2), habeas corpus was granted. McGonigal J stated obiter that the power to arrest a person whom the arrestor 'suspects' of acting in the prescribed manner did not import a standard of reasonableness:

> 'The test is therefore whether the arrestor suspected. That does not appear to me to be open to an objective test. It may be based on purely arbitrary grounds, on grounds which the courts, if this were an objective test of reasonableness might consider unreasonable. . . . What is required by the regulation is a suspicion existing in the mind of the constable. That is a subjective test. If that is correct, the courts in enquiring into the exercise of the power, can only enquire as to the bona fides of the existence of the suspicion. Did the constable in his own mind suspect? And in my view the only other question for the courts is, "Was this an honest suspicion?" ' (p. 19)

[An earlier attempt by McElduff to obtain habeas corpus from the High Court in London failed on jurisdictional grounds: In *re Keenan* [1972] 1 QB 533. See K. Boyle, (1972) 23 NILQ 334 and *Kelly v Faulkener* [1973] NI 31.]

(iv) The Army have found it necessary to obtain information about the population in Republican areas. Indeed, a population census has been described as 'the fundamental tool for defeating terrorism and insurrection' (R. Evelegh, *Peace-Keeping in a Democratic Society* (1978) p. 119). One aspect of this has been the use of the arrest powers under the Emergency Provisions Acts to detain people in Republican areas for questioning (see K. Boyle, T. Hadden and P. Hillyard, *Law and State* (1975), pp. 41–48; Evelegh, op. cit. pp. 63–67, 119–122). The use of powers of arrest for purposes other than of commencing criminal proceedings is of dubious legality. Moreover, according to Evelegh (who commanded an army battalion in Belfast in 1972 and 1973) 'the vast majority of those arrested by the Army in Northern Ireland were arrested without being suspected of anything except in the most general sense' (op. cit. p. 120).

Is the proper response to criticise the illegality, or to argue the case for the extension of powers to detain for questioning, or both?

Evelegh argues for the introduction of (1) powers to compel all citizens to attend security surveillance census interviews, (2) identity cards and (3) a computerized intelligence system (op. cit. Chap. 6) Boyle, Hadden and Hillyard (op. cit. p. 53) state that it was doubtful 'whether the adverse effects of the screening policy, when combined with the obvious risk that large numbers of innocent persons would be ill-treated or abused . . . . . . was not counter productive in the sense that it increased the alienation of the civilian population in troubled areas. . . .'.

(v) The power of arrest in s. 11 was originally designed to be used as the start of a procedure leading to detention without trial under s. 12 and Sch.

1. The detention powers have not been used but s. 11 is still widely used as the start of a procedure leading to questioning and, possibly, proceedings for a specific criminal offence. Note that the power of arrest contained in the Prevention of Terrorism (Temporary Provisions) Act 1976, s. 12 (above, p. 43) is applicable within Northern Ireland except in relation to suspected offences under s. 1 of that Act. It is R.U.C. policy to arrest every terrorist suspect, even if caught in the act of committing a specific offence, under their powers either under s. 11 of the 1978 Act or s. 12 of the 1976 Act. This gives them more time to carry out their investigations.

6. *Proscription*

The following organizations have been proscribed:

The IRA (Official and Provisional wings) (8 August 1973–)
Cumann na mBan (Women's Branch of the IRA) (8 August 1973–)
Fianna na hEireann (Youth Branch of the IRA) (8 August 1973–)
Saor Eire (IRA splinter group) (8 August 1973–)
Ulster Freedom Fighters ('loyalist' terrorist group) (12 November 1973–)
Red Hand Commando ('loyalist' terrorist group) (12 November 1973–
Sinn Fein (8 August 1973–23 May 1974)
Ulster Volunteer Force (8 August 1973–23 May 1974; 4 October 1975–)
Irish National Liberation Army (3 July 1979–)

Some of these groups were proscribed under previous legislation (see also *McEldowney v. Forde* [1971] AC 632; D. N. MacCormick (1970) 86 LQR 171; (1969) 20 NILQ 1; (1970) 21 NILQ 191: proscription of ' "Republican Clubs" or any like organization howsoever described').

In *R v Adams* (1978) 5 NIJB (Belfast City Commission), Lowry LCJ declined to infer IRA membership from the defendant's conduct in parading in a compound of the Maze Prison run by the inmates on quasi-military lines.

Ireland v United Kingdom Eur. Court HR, Series A, Judgment of 18 January 1978

Ireland lodged two applications against the United Kingdom arising out of events in Northern Ireland. The first application in 1971 was declared admissible in respect of claims under Articles 1, 3, 5, and 6 and under the last two of these Articles read in conjunction with Article 14. (see above, pp. 18, 19 and 20) As to the second application, see below, p. 198.

The claims in the first application that were admitted for consideration on the merits concerned the introduction and operation of the policy of internment and detention that applied in Northern Ireland between 1971 and 1975. Following an increase in IRA activities, it was decided in 1971 to intern without trial persons suspected of serious terrorist activities but against whom there was not sufficient evidence to bring court proceedings. Powers to detain persons for questioning over a forty-eight hour period or longer were also brought into operation. Implementation of this policy, which was originally based upon regulations made under the Civil Authorities (Special Powers) Act (NI) 1922, began with 'Operation Demetrius' on 9 August 1971. Some 350 persons were arrested, of whom 104 were released within forty-eight hours. Of those detained further, twelve were sent to unidentified centres for 'interrogation in depth.' This involved use of the 'five techniques' described in the Court's judgment. Many more suspects were interned or detained for questioning in the following months. Of these, two more (making a total of fourteen) were subjected to the 'five techniques.' The claims admitted for consideration on their merits were mainly to the effect that the policy of internment and detention infringed Articles 5 and 6 and that persons interned or detained had been subjected to ill-treatment that constituted an 'administrative practice' in violation of Article 3. The ill-treatment, it was alleged, had occurred at the unidentified interrogation centres where the 'five techniques' were used and at other named interrogation centres including Palace Barracks, where, it was alleged, more familiar forms of assault occurred. In support of its allegations, the Irish Government presented evidence relating to the treatment of 228 persons. The procedure agreed upon by the Commission and parties to handle this mass of evidence was for the Commission to concentrate on sixteen 'illustrative cases' selected by Ireland. The Commission heard oral as well as written evidence in these cases and received medical reports. The Commission had regard to another 'forty-one cases' in respect of which it heard written (but not oral) evidence and received medical reports. It also took account of the remaining cases, but did not examine them in detail.

Judgment

As to the facts . . .

III ALLEGATIONS OF ILL-TREATMENT . . .

B. The unidentified interrogation centre or centres

96. Twelve persons arrested on 9 August 1971 and two persons arrested in October 1971 were singled out and taken to one or more unidentified centres. There, between 11 to 17 August and 11 to 18 October respectively, they were submitted to a form of 'interrogation in depth' which involved the combined application of five particular techniques.

These methods, sometimes termed 'disorientation' or 'sensory deprivation' techniques, were not used in any cases other than the fourteen so indicated above. It emerges from the Commission's establishment of the facts that the techniques consisted of:

(a) *wall-standing*: forcing the detainees to remain for periods of some hours in a 'stress position', described by those who underwent it as being 'spreadeagled against the wall, with their fingers put high above the head against the wall, the legs spread apart and the feet back, causing them to stand on their toes with the weight of the body mainly on the fingers';

(b) *hooding*: putting a black or navy coloured bag over the detainees' heads and, at least initially, keeping it there all the time except during interrogation;

(c) *subjection to noise*: pending their interrogations, holding the detainees in a room where there was a continuous loud and hissing noise;

(d) *deprivation of sleep*: pending their interrogations, depriving the detainees of sleep;

(e) *deprivation of food and drink*: subjecting the detainees to a reduced diet during their stay at the centre and pending interrogations. . . .

97. From the start, it has been conceded by the respondent Government that the use of the five techniques was authorised at 'high level'. Although never committed to writing or authorised in any official document, the techniques had been orally taught to members of the RUC by the English Intelligence Centre at a seminar held in April 1971.

98. The two operations of interrogation in depth by means of the five techniques led to the obtaining of a considerable quantity of intelligence information, including the identification of 700 members of both IRA factions and the discovery of individual responsibility for about 85 previously unexplained criminal incidents.

99. Reports alleging physical brutality and ill-treatment by the security forces were made public within a few days of Operation Demetrius. . . . A committee of enquiry under the chairmanship of Sir Edmund Compton was appointed by the United Kingdom Government on 31 August 1971 to investigate such allegations. Among the 40 cases this Committee examined were 11 cases of persons subjected to the five techniques in August 1971; its findings were that interrogation in depth by means of the techniques constituted physical ill-treatment but not physical brutality as it understood that term. The Committee's report [Cmnd. 4823], adopted on 3 November 1971, was made public, as was a supplemental report of 14 November by Sir Edmund Compton in relation to 3 further cases occurring in September and October, one of which involved the techniques.

100. The Compton reports came under considerable criticism in the United Kingdom. On 16 November 1971, the British Home Secretary announced that a further Committee had been set up under the chairmanship of Lord Parker of Waddington to consider 'whether, and if so in what respects, the procedures currently authorised for interrogation of persons suspected of terrorism and for their custody while subject to interrogation require amendment'.

The Parker report, which was adopted on 31 January 1972, contained a majority and a minority opinion. The majority report concluded that the application of the techniques, subject to recommended safeguards against excessive use, need not be ruled out on moral grounds. On the other hand, the minority report by Lord Gardiner disagreed that such interrogation procedures were morally justifiable, even in emergency terrorist conditions. Both the majority and the minority considered the methods to be illegal under domestic law, although the majority confined their view to English law and to 'some if not all the techniques'.

101. The Parker report [Cmnd. 4901] was published on 2 March 1972. On the same day, the United Kingdom Prime Minister stated in Parliament:

'[The] Government, having reviewed the whole matter with great care and with reference to any future operations, have decided that the techniques . . . will not be used in future as an aid to interrogation.'
He further declared:
'The statement that I have made covers all future circumstances. If a Government did decide . . . that additional techniques were required for interrogation, then I think that . . . they would probably have to come to the House and ask for the powers to do it.'

As foreshadowed in the Prime Minister's statement, directives expressly prohibiting the use of the techniques, whether singly or in combination, were then issued to the security forces by the Government . . .

102. At the hearing before the Court on 8 February 1977, the United Kingdom Attorney-General made the following declaration:
'The Government of the United Kingdom have considered the question of the use of the "five techniques" with very great care and with particular regard to Article 3 of the Convention. They now give this unqualified undertaking, that the "five techniques" will not in any circumstances be reintroduced as an aid to interrogation.'

103. The Irish Government referred to the Commission 8 cases of persons submitted to the five techniques during interrogation at the unidentified centre or centres between 11 and 17 August 1971. The Commission examined as illustrative the cases of T 6 and T 13, which were among the 11 cases investigated by the Compton Committee.

104. T 6 and T 13 were arrested on 9 August 1971 during Operation Demetrius. Two days later they were transferred from Magilligan Regional Holding Centre to an unidentified interrogation centre where they were medically examined on arrival. Thereafter, with intermittent periods of respite, they were subjected to the five techniques during four or possibly five days; neither the Compton or Parker Committees nor the Commission were able to establish the exact length of the periods of respite.

The Commission was satisfied that T 6 and T 13 were kept at the wall for different periods totalling between twenty to thirty hours, but it did not consider it proved that the enforced stress position had lasted all the time they were at the wall. It stated in addition that 'the required posture caused physical pain and exhaustion. The Commission noted that, later on during his stay at the interrogation centre, T 13 was allowed to take his hood off when he was alone in the room, provided that he turned his face to the wall. It was not found possible by the Commission to establish for what periods T 6 and T 13 had been without sleep, or to what extent they were deprived of nourishment and whether or not they were offered food but refused to take it.

The Commission found no physical injury to have resulted from the application of the five techniques as such, but loss of weight by the two case-witnesses and acute psychiatric symptoms developed by them during interrogation were recorded in the medical and other evidence. The Commission, on the material before it, was unable to establish the exact degree of any psychiatric after-effects produced on T 6 and T 13, but on the general level it was satisfied that some psychiatric after-effects in certain of the fourteen persons subjected to the techniques could not be excluded. . . .

T 6 . . . alleged that he was also assaulted in various ways at, or during transport to and from, the centre. On 17 August 1971 he was medically examined on leaving the centre and also on his subsequent arrival at Crumlin Road Prison where he was then detained until 3 May 1972. The medical reports of these examinations and photographs taken on the same day revealed on T 6's body bruising and contusions that had not been present on 11 August. While not accepting all T 6's allegations, the Commission was 'satisfied beyond a reasonable doubt that certain of these injuries . . . [were] the result of assaults committed on him by the security forces at the centre'. As a general inference from the facts established in T 6's case, the Commission also found it 'probable that physical violence was sometimes used in the forcible application of the five techniques'.

107. T 13 and T 6 instituted civil proceedings in 1971 to recover damages for wrongful imprisonment and assault; their claims were settled in 1973 and 1975 respectively for £15,000 and £14,000. The twelve other individuals against whom the five techniques were used have all received in settlement of their civil claims compensation ranging from £10,000 to £25,000.

C. *Palace Barracks*

110 . . . Despite the absolute denials given in evidence by witnesses from the security forces at Palace Barracks, the Commission held the following facts, amongst others, to be established beyond reasonable doubt:
'The four men [T 2, T 8, T 12 and T 15] . . . were severely beaten by members of the security forces . . . The beating was not occassional but it was applied in a sort of scheme in order to make them speak . . .'

Each man instituted civil proceedings for damages and rejected the offer of £750 made in settlement of his claim. . . .
111 . . . The medical evidence disclosed injuries described as 'substantial' in T 9's case and 'massive' in T 14's case. The Commission concluded that 'the proved injuries must have been caused while the two men were at Palace Barracks'. Fourteen members of the security forces at the centre gave evidence completely denying any knowledge of the injuries or their causes, but these denials were not believed by the Commission. While viewing certain of the two men's assertions as exaggerated, invented or improbable, the Commission made the following finding:
'T 9 and T 14 . . . were subjected to physical violence, especially kicking and beating, during or between a series of "interviews" conducted by the Special Branch.'
Civil proceedings seeking damages were instituted by T 14 and T 9; their claims were settled for £2,250 and £1,975 respectively. They also, it seems, complained to the police, but no evidence was produced to the Commission of a police enquiry into their complaints. . . .
118. The Commission considered on a number of grounds that the police officers in command at Palace Barracks at the relevant time could not have been ignorant of the acts of ill-treatment found to have been committed. Yet, on their own evidence, these officers took no action to prevent the occurrence or repetition of such ill-treatment.
Knowledge on the part of the higher authorities of allegations regarding this centre was inferred by the Commission from various facts. Nevertheless, no evidence of police investigations into these allegations was produced to the Commission and, apart from Sir Edmund Compton's 'supplemental' report into three Palace Barracks cases . . ., no general enquiry took place. Furthermore, no disciplinary or criminal proceedings seem to have been instituted against any of the police officers who either committed or failed to react against the acts established. No special instructions relating to the proper treatment of persons in custody were issued to the RUC until April 1972 . . . . Through their inaction, the authorities in Northern Ireland were held by the Commission to have shown indifference towards the treatment of prisoners at Palace Barracks in the autumn of 1971.

[The court then considered evidence of ill-treatment at Gridwood Park and Ballykinler Regional Holding Centres, and at various army posts, police stations, a prison, at home or during transport.]

G.   Measures concerning the treatment of persons arrested or held by the security forces

4.   Compensation
142. Procedures to obtain compensation were available before the domestic courts to all persons who considered themselves to have been ill-treated by the security forces. There is no suggestion that domestic courts were or are anything other than independent, fair and impartial. . . . Like any plaintiff in a civil action, a plaintiff alleging ill-treatment by the security forces was entitled to obtain disclosure of relevant documents, for example medical reports, in the possession of the defendant authorities.
143. Between 9 August 1971 and 31 January 1975, compensation totalling £302,043 had been paid in settlment of 473 civil claims for wrongful arrest, false imprisonment, assault and battery, leaving 1,193 actions still outstanding. At the time of the Commission's report, compensation ranging from about £200 to £25,000, had been paid in settlement of 45 of the 228 cases submitted by the applicant Government. In the only case of alleged physical ill-treatment which seems to have been fought, namely the case of *Moore v Shillington* (18 February (1972), Armagh County Court), the judge disbelieved the evidence of the security forces.

As to the law . . .

I. ON ARTICLE 3 . . .

1.   The unidentified interrogation centre or centres

(A)   *The 'five techniques'*
165. The facts concerning the five techniques are summarised at paragraphs 96–104 and 106–107 above. In the Commission's estimation, those facts constituted a practice not only of inhuman and degrading treatment but also of torture. The applicant Government ask for confirmation of this opinion which is not contested before the Court by the respondent Government.
166. The police used the five techniques on fourteen persons in 1971, . . . Although never authorised in writing in any official document, the five techniques were taught orally by the

English Intelligence Centre to members of the RUC at a seminar held in April 1971. There was accordingly a practice.

167. The five techniques were applied in combination, with premeditation and for hours at a stretch; they caused, if not actual bodily injury, at least intense physical and mental suffering to the persons subjected thereto and also led to acute psychiatric disturbances during interrogation. They accordingly fell into the category of inhuman treatment within the meaning of Article 3. The techniques were also degrading since they were such as to arouse in their victims feelings of fear, anguish and inferiority capable of humiliating and debasing them and possibly breaking their physical or moral resistance.

On these two points, the Court is of the same view as the Commission.

In order to determine whether the five techniques should also be qualified as torture, the Court must have regard to the distinction, embodied in Article 3, between this notion and that of inhuman or degrading treatment.

In the Court's view, this distinction derives principally from a difference in the intensity of the suffering inflicted.

The Court considers in fact that, whilst there exists on the one hand violence which is to be condemned both on moral grounds and also in most cases under domestic law of the Contracting States but which does not fall within Article 3 of the Convention, it appears on the other hand that it was the intention that the Convention, with its distinction between 'torture' and 'inhuman or degrading treatment', should by the first of these terms attach a special stigma to deliberate inhuman treatment causing very serious and cruel suffering.

Moreover, this seems to be the thinking lying behind Article 1 *in fine* of Resolution 3452 (xxx) adopted by the General Assembly of the United Nations on 9 December 1975, which declares: 'Torture constitutes an *aggravated* and deliberate form of cruel, inhuman or degrading treatment or punishment'.

Although the five techniques, as applied in combination, undoubtedly amounted to inhuman and degrading treatment, although their object was the extraction of confessions, the naming of others and/or information and although they were used systematically, they did not occasion suffering of the particular intensity and cruelty implied by the word torture as so understood.

168. The Court concludes that recourse to the five techniques amounted to a practice of inhuman and degrading treatment, which practice was in breach of Article 3.

[The holdings as to torture was by thirteen votes to four. The holding as to inhuman treatment was by sixteen votes to one]

(B) *Ill-treatment alleged to have accompanied the use of the five techniques*
170. As far as T 6 is concerned, the Court shares the Commission's opinion that the security forces subjected T 6 to assaults severe enough to constitute inhuman treatment. This opinion, which is not contested by the respondent Government, is borne out by the evidence before the Court. . . .

[As this was the only case where, ill-treatment in addition to the use of the five techniques was established, the Court was unable to hold that there was a 'practice' of ill treatment. On the other allegations of breaches of Article 3, the Court:]

6. *holds* unanimously that there existed at Palace Barracks in the autumn of 1971 a practice of inhuman treatment, which practice was in breach of Article 3;

7. *holds* by fourteen votes to three that the last-mentioned practice was not one of torture within the meaning of Article 3;

8. *hold* unanimously that it is not established that the practice in question continued beyond the autumn of 1971;

9. *holds* by fifteen votes to two that no practice in breach of Article 3 is established as regards other places;

10. *holds* unanimously that it cannot direct the respondent State to institute criminal or disciplinary proceedings against those members of the security forces who have comitted the breaches of Article 3 found by the Court and against those who condoned or tolerated such breaches; . . .

II ON ARTICLE 5

[The Irish Government alleged that the powers relating to extrajudicial deprivation of liberty:

i) did not comply with Article 5;
ii) were not in conformity with the conditions for derogation under Article 15;
iii) were exercised with discrimination and consequently also violated article 14 taken together with Article 5.

The Court agreed with proposition i). As to derogation:]

1. On the 'public emergency threatening the life of the nation'
205. . . . The existence of such an emergency is perfectly clear from the facts . . . and was not questioned by anyone before either the Commission or the Court. The crisis experienced at the time by the six counties therefore comes within the ambit of Article 15. [This holding was unanimous]
2. On the 'extent strictly required'
206. The Contracting States may make use of their right of derogation only 'to the extent strictly required by the exigencies of the situation'. . . .
(A) *The role of the court*
207. . . . It falls in the first place to each Contracting State, with its responsibility for 'the life of [its] nation', to determine whether that life is threatened by a 'public emergency' and, if so, how far it is necessary to go in attempting to overcome the emergency. By reason of their direct and continuous contact with the pressing needs of the moment, the national authorities are in principle in a better position than the international judge to decide both on the presence of such an emergency and on the nature and scope of derogations necessary to avert it. In this matter Article 15 §I leaves those authorities a wide margin of appreciation.
    Nevertheless, the States do not enjoy an unlimited power in this respect. The Court, which, with the Commission, is responsible for ensuring the observance of the States' engagements (Article 19), is empowered to rule on whether the States have gone beyond the 'extent strictly required by the exigencies' of the crisis (*Lawless* judgment of 1 July 1961, Series A no. 3, p. 55, §22, and pp. 57–59, §§36–38). The domestic margin of appreciation is thus accompanied by a European supervision. . . .
(C) *Questions concerning the merits*
211. The Court has to decide whether the United Kingdom went beyond the "extent strictly required". For this purpose the Court must, . . . enquire into the necessity for, on the one hand, deprivation of liberty contrary to paragraph 1 of Article 5 and, on the other hand, the failure of guarantees to attain the level fixed by paragraphs 2 to 4.
(i) On the necessity for derogation from paragraph 1 of Article 5 by extrajudicial deprivation of liberty
212. Unquestionably, the exercise of the special powers was mainly, and before 5 February 1973 even exclusively, directed against the IRA as an underground military force. The intention was to combat an organisation which had played a considerable subversive rôle throughout the recent history of Ireland and which was creating, in August 1971 and thereafter, a particularly far-reaching and acute danger for the territorial integrity of the United Kingdom, the institutions of the six counties and the lives of the province's inhabitants . . . Being confronted with a massive wave of violence and intimidation, the Northern Ireland Government and then, after the introduction of direct rule (30 March 1972), the British Government were reasonably entitled to consider that normal legislation offered insufficient resources for the campaign against terrorism and that recourse to measures outside the scope of the ordinary law, in the shape of extrajudicial deprivation of liberty, was called for. When the Irish Republic was faced with a serious crisis in 1957, it adopted the same approach and the court did not conclude that the 'extent strictly required' had been exceeded (*Lawless* judgment of 1 July 1961, Series A no. 3, pp. 35–36, §14, and pp. 57–58, § 36).
    However, under one of the provisions complained of, namely Regulation 10, a person who was in no way suspected of a crime or offence or of activities prejudicial to peace and order could be arrested for the sole purpose of obtaining from him information about others – and this sometimes occurred . . . This sort of arrest can be justifiable only in a very exceptional situation, but the circumstances prevailing in Northern Ireland did fall into such a category. Many witnesses could not give evidence freely without running the greatest risks . . . .; the competent authorities were entitled to take the view, without exceeding their margin of appreciation, that it was indispensible to arrest such witnesses so that they could be questioned in conditions of relative security and not be exposed to reprisals. Moreover and above all, Regulation 10 authorised deprivation of liberty only for a maximum of forty-eight hours.
213. From 9 August 1971 to 5 February 1973, the measures involving deprivation of liberty taken by the respondent State were used only against Republican terrorism even though as early as this period outrages, at first sporadic but later constantly more numerous, were attributable to Loyalist terrorism; even after 5 February 1973, the measures were applied

against Republican terrorism to a much greater extent than against Loyalist terrorism despite the latter's organisation and extensive development shortly after 30 March 1972.

The Court will examine below (paragraphs 228–232) whether the difference of treatment between the two types of terrorism was such as to violate Article 14 of the Convention.

This issue apart, it appears to the Court that the extrajudicial measures brought into operation could, in the situation described above, reasonably have been considered strictly required for the protection of public security and that, in the context of Article 15, their intrinsic necessity, once recognised, could not be affected by the restriction of their field of application.

214. The Irish Government submit that experience shows extrajudicial deprivation of liberty to have been ineffectual. They contend that the policy introduced on 9 August 1971 not only failed to put a brake on terrorism but also had the result of increasing it. Consequently, the British Government, after attenuating the policy in varying degrees following the introduction of direct rule abandoned it on 5 December 1975: since then, it appears that no one has been detained in the six counties under the emergency legislation, despite the persistence of an intense campaign of violence and even though the Emergency Provisions Amendment Act has remained in force . . . . This, claim the applicant Government, confirms that extrajudicial deprivation of liberty was not an absolute necessity.

The Court cannot accept this argument.

It is certainly not the Court's function to substitute for the British Government's assessment any other assessment of what might be the most prudent or most expedient policy to combat terrorism. The Court must do no more than review the lawfulness, under the Convention, of the measures adopted by that Government from 9 August 1971 onwards. For this purpose the Court must arrive at its decision in the light, not of a purely retrospective examination of the efficacy of those measures, but of the conditions and circumstances reigning when they were originally taken and subsequently applied.

Adopting, as it must, this approach, the Court accepts that the limits of the margin of appreciation left to the Contracting States by Article 15 § 1 were not overstepped by the United Kingdom when it formed the opinion that extrajudicial deprivation of liberty was necessary from August 1971 to March 1975.

(ii) On the necessity for derogation from the guarantees under paragraphs 2 to 4 of Article 5

220 . . . [T]he crisis experienced at the time by the six counties was serious and, hence, of a kind that justified far-reaching derogations from paragraphs 2 to 4 of Article 5. In view of the contracting states' margin of appreciation, the Court does not find it established that the United Kingdom exceeded in this respect the 'extent strictly required' referred to in Article 15 § 1. . . .

[The holdings as to the necessity for derogation were by sixteen votes to one].

[The Court held that no discrimination contrary to Articles 14 and 5 taken together was established. The much wider use of extrajudicial deprivation of liberty against Republicans than Loyalists was to be explained by the fact that the vast majority of outrages before March 1972 were attributable to Republicans; that the IRA, with its far more structured organisation, constituted a far more serious menace than Loyalist terrorists; and that it was easier to institute criminal proceedings against Loyalist terrorists, such prosecutions having actually taken place]

NOTES

1. In relation to the proceedings before the Commission in this and other Northern Irish cases see H. Hannum and K. Boyle (1972) 7 *Irish Jurist* (n.s.) 329; K. Boyle, T. Hadden and P. Hillyard, *Law and State* (1975) Chap. 8; 13 Yearbook of the European Convention on Human Rights 340. For discussion of the Court's judgment see D. Bonner, (1978) 27 ICLQ 897; D. J. Harris, (1978) 49 BYIL 301.

2. The 'psychiatric side-effects' of the 'five techniques' are considered in J. McGuffin, *The Guineapigs* (1974) and R. M. Fields, *Society under Siege* (1977).

In his dissent to the report of the Parker Committee (Cmnd. 4901 (1972)), Lord Gardiner referred to medical evidence that:

'Sensory isolation is one method of inducing an artificial psychosis or episode of insanity. We know that people who have been through such an experience do not forget it quickly and may experience symptoms of mental distress for months or years. We know that some artificially induced psychoses, for instance those produced by drugs like LSD or mescaline, have in fact proved permanent; and there is no reason to suppose that this may not be a danger with psychoses produced by sensory deprivation. Even if such psychotic symptoms as delusions and hallucinations do not persist, a proportion of persons who have been subjected to these procedures are likely to continue to exhibit anxiety attacks, tremors, insomnia, nightmares, and other symptoms of neurosis. . . .' (p. 17).

3. Allegations of ill-treatment in the period following that considered by the European Court have been substantiated. See the *Report of an Amnesty International Mission to Northern Ireland* (1978) and the Bennett Report, Cmnd. 7497 (1979). The Bennett Committee's examination of medical evidence revealed 'cases in which injuries, whatever their precise cause, were not self-inflicted and were sustained in police custody' (Bennett Report, p. 136). The Committee made a number of suggestions for improving the supervision of interrogations and the police complaints procedures. In addition, prisoners should be given an unconditional right of access to a solicitor after 48 hours and every 48 hours thereafter, although the solicitors should not be permitted to be present at interviews.
4. An application in which the Republic of Ireland argued that the Northern Ireland Act 1972 (above, p. 189) conflicted with Article 7 of the Convention (above, p. 19) was withdrawn when the UK Attorney-General gave an undertaking in proceedings before the Commission that no one had or would be held guilty as a result of the 1972 Act for an act or omission which did not constitute a criminal offence at the time it was committed (A 5451/72, 41 CDE Comm HR, pp. 82–83 (1972)).

Attorney-General for Northern Ireland's Reference (No. 1 of 1975) [1977] AC 105, [1976] 2 All ER 937, [1976] 3 WLR 235, House of Lords [NI]

A British soldier on patrol in Northern Ireland in the exercise of his power to prevent crime under section 3(1) of the Criminal Law Act (NI) 1967 (which is in the same terms as the Criminal Law Act 1967 s.3(1), above p. 59) shot and killed an unarmed man, who had run away when challenged. The soldier had the honest and reasonable, though mistaken, belief that he was a terrorist. A judge sitting without a jury acquitted him of murder holding that he had no conscious intention to kill or seriously injure and that the killing was justifiable. The Attorney-General referred two matters to the Court of Criminal Appeal in Northern Ireland, and an appeal was taken to the House of Lords. The House held that the first matter raised no point of law, since it was in essence whether or not the soldier had used reasonable force, and that was a question of fact for the judge. The second matter accordingly did not arise. Lord Diplock made some observations as to the legal position.

Lord Diplock: . . . There is little authority in English law concerning the rights and duties of a member of the armed forces of the Crown when acting in aid of the civil power; and what little authority there is relates almost entirely to the duties of soldiers when troops are called upon to assist in controlling a riotous assembly. Where used for such temporary purposes it may not be inaccurate to describe the legal rights and duties of a soldier as being no more than those of an ordinary citizen in uniform. But such a description is in my view misleading in the circumstances in which the army is currently employed in aid of the civil power in Northern Ireland . . . In theory it may be the duty of every citizen when an arrestable offence is about to be committed in his presence to take whatever reasonable measures are available to him to prevent the commission of the crime; but the duty is one of imperfect obligation and does not place him under any obligation to do anything by which he would expose himself to risk of personal injury, nor is he under any duty to search for criminals or seek out crime. In contrast to this a soldier who is employed in aid of the civil power in Northern Ireland is under a duty, enforceable under military law, to search for criminals if so ordered by his superior officer and to risk his own life should this be necessary in preventing terrorist acts. For the performance of this duty he is armed with a firearm, a self-loading rifle, from which a bullet, if it hits the human body, is almost certain to cause serious injury if not death. . . .

What amount of force is 'reasonable in the circumstances' for the purpose of preventing crime is, in my view, always a question for the jury in a jury trial, never a 'point of law' for the judge.

The form in which the jury would have to ask themselves the question in a trial for an offence against the person in which this defence was raised by the accused, would be: Are we satisfied that no reasonable man (a) with knowledge of such facts as were known to the accused or reasonably believed by him to exist (b) in the circumstances and time available to him for reflection (c) could be of opinion that the prevention of the risk of harm to which others might be exposed if the suspect were allowed to escape justified exposing the suspect to the risk of harm to him that might result from the kind of force that the accused contemplated using?

The jury would have also to consider how the circumstances in which the accused had to make his decision whether or not to use force and the shortness of the time available to him for reflection, might affect the judgment of a reasonable man. In the facts that are to be assumed for the purposes of the reference there is material upon which a jury might take the view that the accused had reasonable grounds for apprehension of imminent danger to himself and other members of the patrol if the deceased were allowed to get away and join armed fellow-members of the Provisional IRA who might be lurking in the neighbourhood, and that the time available to the accused to make up his mind what to do was so short that even a reasonable man could only act intuitively. This being so, the jury in approaching the final part of the question should remind themselves that the postulated balancing of risk against risk, harm against harm, by the reasonable man is not undertaken in the calm analytical atmosphere of the court-room after counsel with the benefit of hindsight have expounded at length the reasons for and against the kind and degree of force that was used by the accused; but in the brief second or two which the accused had to decide whether to shoot or not and under all the stresses to which he was exposed.

In many cases where force is used in the prevention of crime or in effecting an arrest there is a choice as to the degree of force to use. On the facts that are to be assumed for the purposes of the reference the only options open to the accused were either to let the deceased escape or to shoot at him with a service rifle. A reasonable man would know that a bullet from a self-loading rifle if it hit a human being, at any rate at the range at which the accused fired, would be likely to kill him or to injure him seriously. So in one scale of the balance the harm to which the deceased would be exposed if the accused aimed to hit him was predictable and grave and the risk of its occurrence high. In the other scale of the balance it would be open to the jury to take the view that it would not be unreasonable to assess the kind of harm to be averted by preventing the accused's escape as even graver—the killing or wounding of members of the patrol by terrorists in ambush, and the effect of this success by members of the Provisional IRA in encouraging the continuance of the armed insurrection and all the misery and destruction of life and property that terrorist activity in Northern Ireland has entailed. The jury would have to consider too what was the highest degree at which a reasonable man could have assessed the likelihood that such consequences might follow the escape of the deceased if the facts had been as the accused knew or believed them reasonably to be.

Lords Simon of Glaisdale, Edmund-Davies and **Russell of Killower** expressed their agreement with **Lord Diplock's** opinion.

NOTES

1. In *R v MacNaughton* [1975] NI 203, a sergeant was tried by Lowry LCJ (sitting without a jury) on charges of attempted murder and causing grievous bodily harm. He was in command of a foot patrol in South Armagh. They met a man, W, coming from the direction of an explosion and, suspecting him of being implicated in it, arrested him. The defendant claimed that W then tried to escape over a fence, and that he had shot at W after calling on him to stop. Lowry LCJ held that there had been a lawful arrest, that the defendant's evidence raised a triable issue that the force used was reasonable, and that the prosecution had been unable to prove beyond

reasonable doubt that the degree of force was not reasonable on this occasion.

His Lordship took into account the factors that the patrol was working in active service conditions in a hostile area; that judging by the explosion, it was operating in the possible presence of an ambush; that there was a danger of booby-traps; that there was the possibility of masking a line of fire; the gravity of the suspected offence; and the likelihood that if W escaped he would undertake terrorist acts.

See also *McLaughlin v Ministry of Defence* (1978) 7 NIJB, CA; *Report of the Tribunal appointed to inquire into the events on Sunday, 30 January 1972, which led to loss of life in connection with the procession in Londonderry on that day by The Rt Hon Lord Widgery (1972)* HC 220; S. Dash, *Justice Denied* (NCCL) (1972); *Ireland v UK*, A 5310/71 41 CDE Comm HR p. 3 (1972) (application under Article 2 ECHR in respect of the deaths of certain persons in Northern Ireland declared inadmissible); *R v Bohan* (1979) 5 NIJB, Belfast Crown Court.

2. The absence of clear guidelines has been criticised by R. Evelegh (*Peace Keeping in a Democratic Society* (1978) pp. 76–78). He suggests that in consequence the actions of the security forces have been unpredictable to the disorderly and that the forces have tended to permit disorder in order to avoid legal liability (op. cit. p. 78). One of his proposals is for the reintroduction of something resembling the 'reading of the Riot Act': 'To have been able to say . . . "Disperse in one hour or be shot dead" would have quickly put an end to all rioting in Northern Ireland' (op. cit. p. 159).

The gap between theory and practice as regards military aid to the civil power is discussed by Evelegh (op. cit.). See also *the Manual of Military Law*, Part II, Section V, (1968); *Queen's Regulations for the Army*, Reg. J 11.002; *Report of the Committee appointed to inquire into the Circumstances connected with the Disturbances at Featherstone on 7th of September, 1893* (C 7234); R. Neville, '*The Yorkshire Miners and the 1893 Lockout: The Featherstone 'Massacre'* (1976) XXI International Review of Social History, 337; *Report of the Departmental Committee on Riot* (1895, C 7650); *Report of the Commissioner of Police of the Metropolis for 1975*, Cmnd. 6496, Appendix 9; *Report of the Tribunal of Inquiry into violence and Civil Disturbances in Northern Ireland* (Chairman, Scarman J) (1972) Cmnd. 566, especially Part VI, and pp. 193–195, 201–206, 220–221.

CHAPTER 4

Freedom of expression: censorship and obscenity

1 Theatre censorship

Theatres Act 1968

1. Abolition of censorship of the theatre

(1) The Theatres Act 1843 is hereby repealed; and none of the powers which were exercisable thereunder by the Lord Chamberlain of Her Majesty's Household shall be exercisable by or on behalf of Her Majesty by virtue of Her royal prerogative.

(2) In granting, renewing or transferring any licence under this Act for the use of any premises for the public performance of plays or in varying any of the terms, conditions or restrictions on or subject to which any such licence is held, the licensing authority shall not have power to impose any term, condition or restriction as to the nature of the plays which may be performed under the licence or as to the manner of performing plays thereunder:

Provided that nothing in this subsection shall prevent a licensing authority from imposing any term, condition or restriction which they consider necessary in the interests of physical safety or health or any condition regulating or prohibiting the giving of an exhibition, demonstration or performance of hypnotism within the meaning of the Hypnotism Act 1952.

NOTES

1. For accounts of the Lord Chamberlain's exercise of his powers of censorship prior to the Theatres Act 1968 see R. Findlater, *Banned! A Review of Theatrical Censorship in Britain* (1967); P. O'Higgins, *Censorship* (1972) pp. 95–99; G. Robertson, *Obscenity* (1979) pp. 246–250.

2. The Theatres Act 1968 ended 'official' censorship of plays. Theatre managers as distinct from authors and directors had for long favoured the Lord Chamberlain's activities since it was unlikely that any prosecution (e.g. for obscenity) would be brought in respect of the performance of a play which had met with his approval. This official guidance they preferred to the prospect of themselves having to assess the likelihood of such prosecution and possible conviction. Some opponents of the Lord Chamberlain's censorship powers feared lest undue caution on the part of theatre managements might impose on authors and directors a greater 'institutional' censorship than that formerly exercised by the Lord Chamberlain.

3. For provisions of the Theatre Act 1968 affecting criminal liability in respect of the performance of plays see below. pp. 232–234.

2 Film censorship

Cinematograph Act 1909

1. Provision against cinematograph exhibition except in licensed premises
[No cinematograph exhibition (as defined in the Cinematograph Act 1952) shall][1] be given unless the regulations made by the Secretary of State [under this Act][1] are complied with, or, save as otherwise expressly provided by this Act, elsewhere than in premises licensed for the purpose in accordance with the provisions of this Act.

2. Provisions as to licences
(1) A [district][2] council may grant licences to such persons as they think fit to use the premises specified in the licence [for the purpose of cinematographic exhibitions (as defined in the Cinematograph Act 1952)][1] on such terms and conditions and under such restrictions as, subject to regulations of the Secretary of State, the council may by the respective licences determine.

3. Penalties
If the owner of [any][1] apparatus uses the apparatus, or allows it to be used, or if the occupier of any premises allows those premises to be used, in contravention of the provisions of this Act or the regulations made thereunder, or of the conditions or restrictions upon or subject to which any licence relating to the premises has been granted under this Act, he shall be liable, on summary conviction, to a fine not exceeding [£200][3], and the licence (if any)[1] shall be liable to be revoked by the [district][2] council.

4. Power of entry
A constable or any officer appointed for the purpose by a [district][4] council may at all reasonable times enter any premises, whether licensed or not, in which he has reason to believe that such an exhibition as aforesaid is being or is about to be given, with a view to seeing whether the provisions of this Act, or any regulations made thereunder, and the conditions of any licence granted under this Act [and any restrictions subject to which any licence has been so granted][5] have been complied with, and if any person prevents or obstructs the entry of a constable or any officer appointed as aforesaid, he shall be liable, on summary conviction, to a penalty not exceeding [fifty][6] pounds.

7. Application of Act to special premises
(4) This Act shall not apply to an exhibition given in a private dwelling-house to which the public are not admitted, whether on payment or otherwise.

Cinematograph Act 1952

1. Extension of 9 Edw 7 c 30 to cinematograph exhibitions using non-inflammable films or television, etc.
Subject to the provisions of section seven of the Act of 1909 and to the exemptions hereinafter provided, the said Act and (except so far as they otherwise provide) any regulations made

---

1. Words in brackets substituted by the Cinematograph Act 1952, s.8 and Schedule.
2. 'District'substituted for 'county' by the Local Government Act 1972, s.204 (5). The GLC remains the licensing authority within Greater London.
3. Maximum fine raised to £200 by the Criminal Justice Act 1967, s.92(1) and Sch.3, Part I.
4. 'District' substituted for 'county' by the Local Government Act 1972, s.204(5). The GLC remains the licensing authority within Greater London.
5. Words in brackets substituted by the Cinematograph Act 1952, s.8 and Schedule.
6. Maximum fine raised to £50 by the Criminal Law Act, 1977 s.31(5)(6).

thereunder shall apply as respects all cinematograph exhibitions, whether given by means involving the use of inflammable films or non-inflammable films, or by means not involving the use of films.

3. Provisions as to conditions in licences

(1) It shall be the duty of the licensing authority, in granting a licence under the Act of 1909 as respects any premises,—

(*a*) to impose conditions or restrictions prohibiting the admission of children to cinematograph exhibitions involving the showing of works designated, by the licensing authority or such other body as may be specified in the licence, as works unsuitable for children; and

(*b*) to consider what (if any) conditions or restrictions should be imposed as to the admission of children to other cinematograph exhibitions involving the showing of works designated by the authority or such other body as aforesaid as of such other description as may be specified in the licence.

(2) Neither the last foregoing section nor subsection (1) of this section shall be construed as derogating from the generality of the power of the licensing authority, as respects any premises, to impose conditions or restrictions.

5. Exemptions for non-commercial exhibitions

(1) The following exemptions shall have effect in the case of cinematograph exhibitions (hereinafter referred to as 'exempted exhibitions') to which the public are not admitted or to which the public are admitted without payment, that is to say:—

(*a*) a licence under the Act of 1909 shall not be required by reason only of the giving of an exempted exhibition . . .

(*b*) . . . .

(*c*) regulations made by the Secretary of State under the Act of 1909 . . . shall not apply in relation to an exempted exhibition[7].

(*d*) in connection with the giving of an exempted exhibition in premises in respect of which a licence under the Act of 1909 is in force no condition or restriction on or subject to which the licence was granted shall apply[8].

(2) For the purposes of this section an exhibition shall not be treated as an exempted exhibition if organised wholly or mainly as an exhibition for children who are members of a club, society or association the principal object of which is attendance at cinematograph exhibitions, so however that this subsection shall not apply to any exhibition given as part of the activities of an educational or religious institution.

9. Interpretation

(1) In this Act the following expressions have the meanings hereby assigned to them respectively, that is to say: . . .

'child' means a person under the age of sixteen;

'cinematograph exhibition' means an exhibition of moving pictures produced on a screen by means which include the projection of light;

NOTES

1. In *R v Greater London Council, ex parte Blackburn* [1976] 1 WLR 550, CA, Lord Denning MR said, at p. 553:

' . . . [The Cinematograph Act 1909] was passed in the early days and was concerned with safety in cinemas, not with censorship . . . . Although the Act was concerned with safety, nevertheless the courts two years later held that a county council could impose conditions which related to other matters so long as they were not unreasonable. So, in 1911, the courts held that a condition saying that premises should not be opened on Sundays was valid: see *LCC v Bermondsey Bioscope Co Ltd* [1911] 1 KB 445. Soon afterwards the county councils began to insert a condition that no film shown should be of a licentious or indecent character. Such a condition was accepted as valid, but it did not permit any censorship beforehand. Next the county councils tried to insert a power of censorship by delegating it to three justices. This was held to be invalid: see *R v Burnley JJ, ex parte Longmore* [1916–17] All ER Rep 346. Once again they tried. They sought to hand over all power of censorship to the British Board of Film

---

7. Remainder of paragraph repealed by Fire Precautions Act 1971, s.12(11), (12).

8. Remainder of paragraph and proviso repealed by Fire Precautions Act 1971, s.12(11), (12).

Censors, but this was held invalid because the county councils were not allowed to delegate their powers: see *Ellis v Dubowski* [1921] 3 KB 621. But in 1924 there was a breakthrough. The courts gave a decision which allowed censorship by the British Board of Film Censors provided that that body did not have the final say, but was subject to review by the county council itself: see *Mills v LCC* [1925] 1 KB 213. That decision has held the field since that time and must, I think, be accepted as good law. It was recognised as such by Parliament itself in 1952 when it made it compulsory for conditions to be imposed for the protection of children: see s. 3 of the Cinematograph Act 1952. Under that section the county council are under a duty to impose conditions so as to ensure that, if a film is designated as unsuitable for children, then children are not to be admitted to see it. Such designation is to be done 'by the licensing authority or such other body as may be specified in the licence'. In speaking of such other body Parliament no doubt had in mind the British Board of Film Censors. To that extent, therefore, the Board has Parliamentary approval. . . . The British Board of Film Censors . . . goes back for 60 years. There is a president, at present Lord Harlech, who is responsible for broad policy. There is a secretary, Mr James Ferman, who makes executive decisions. There are four film examiners, who work full-time. These work in pairs, viewing films on three days each week. They put films into four categories, according to their suitability for various age groups: U, A, AA, and X. 'U' for everyone, 'X' for those over 18. They sometimes require cuts before giving a certificate. The examiners are recruited from outside the film industry. They are paid salaries. The money is provided by the manufacturers of films through the Incorporated Association of Kinematograph Manufacturers. The extent of their work is shown by what they did in 1975. They saw 417 Feature Films. They passed 400 and refused 17. But of those 17, they passed five after cuts had been made. They passed 73 documentary films.

Although the board is not a body known to the law, it is, I think, a 'body' within s.3(1) of the 1952 Act. I do not think the county councils can delegate the whole of their responsibilities to the board . . . but they can treat the board as an advisory body whose views they can accept or reject, provided that the final decision – aye or nay – rests with the county council. If the exhibitor – or any member of the public – brings the film up before the county council, they ought themselves to review the decision of the British Board of Film Censors and exercise their own judgment on it. That is, I think, the right way to interpret *Mills v LCC*. When the Board issues a certificate permitting the exhibition of a film – and the county council take no objection – that is equivalent to a permission by the county council themselves. When the board refuses a certificate, the exhibitor can appeal to the county council . . .

The upshot of it all is this. The county council are in law the body which has the power to censor films for exhibitions in cinemas, but in practice it is the board which carries out the censorship, subject to review by the county council.'

Note that the statutory duty in s.3(1) of the 1952 Act refers to persons under 16 whereas the classifications of the British Board of Film Censors relate to suitability for persons under 18.

See further on the history of film censorship, N. March Hunnings, *Film Censors and the Law* (1967) pp. 29–125.

2. For the work of the British Board of Film Censors see N. March Hunnings, op. cit., pp. 126–148; J. Trevelyan (a former secretary of the BBFC), *What the Censor Saw* (1973) and 'Film Censorship and the Law' in R. Dhavan and C. Davies (eds.), *Censorship and Obscenity* (1978) pp. 98–108; G. Phelps, *Film Censorship* (1975).

3. For the practice of local authorities, and variations between authorities, in relation to film censorship see E. Wistrich (a former chairman of the GLC Film Viewing Board), *I Don't Mind the Sex it's the Violence – Film Censorship Explored* (1978); H. Street, *Freedom, the Individual and the Law* (4th edn., 1977) pp. 70–77; P. O'Higgins, *Censorship* (1972) pp. 85–89; C. R. Munro (1965) Public Law 279; *R v Greater London Council, ex parte Blackburn* [1976] 3 All ER 184, [1976] 1 WLR 550, CA. – though this case must now be read in the light of the Criminal Law Act 1977, s.53(1) and the Obscene Publications Act 1959, s.2(4A) below, p. 219.

For the opinion that local authorities are generally too busy with other matters to enforce their own licensing conditions see D. Holbrook (1973) 123 NLJ 701 and correspondence at pp. 754, 775, 794, 833 and 915. For the influence of often uninformed press reports about particular films on the decisions of the BBFC and local councils see G. Phelps, Sight and Sound

Vol 42, No. 3 p. 138 (account of press reports of, and decisions taken in relation to, *Last Tango in Paris*). Local council decisions may be better informed since the BBFC began in 1975 publishing monthly bulletins explaining decisions taken in relation to particular films (see McDonald, Index on Censorship (1977) Vol. 6, No. 4, p. 51)

4. The Williams Committee on Obscenity and Film Censorship (1979) Cmnd. 7772 recommended that the censorship functions of local authorities and the BBFC should be transferred to a new statutory Film Examining Board consisting of about a dozen persons representative of a range of interests (including local government and the film industry). The Board would appoint film examiners, guide their decisions and hear appeals from their decisions. Films would be classified as (*U*) – suitable for all ages, (*11A*) – those under 11 to be accompanied by an adult,-(*16*) – no persons under 16 to be admitted, (*18*) – no person under 18 to be admitted, (*18R*) – restricted exhibition and no person under 18 to be admitted. In addition a certificate might be refused. A film would be classified for restricted exhibition only if its visual content and the manner in which it deals with violence, cruelty, or horror, or sexual, faecal or urinary functions or genital organs is such that in the judgment of the examiners it is appropriate that the film be shown only under restricted conditions. A film so classified could be shown only at a cinema licensed by a local authority to show such films and the authority's decision would be final. An auditorium in a multi-screen cinema complex would be eligible for designation for showing restricted films. The Williams Committee intended that the (18R) classification would be used for films that are currently denied a certificate. Current 'X' certificate films would be classified as (18). Commercial cinema clubs would be brought within this censorship system. The Film Review Board should refuse a certificate altogether if the film is considered unfit for public exhibition either because it contains material prohibited by law (see, e.g. below, p. 240) or where, even having had regard to the importance of allowing the development of artistic expression and of not suppressing truth or reality, the film is unacceptable because of the manner in which it depicts violence or sexual activity or crime.

Prosecutions should be restricted to the police or by or with the consent of the DPP.

3 Broadcasting

Report of the Committee on the Future of Broadcasting, Chairman: Lord Annan (Cmnd. 6783 1977)

POWERS OF THE GOVERNMENT AND RESPONSIBILITIES OF PARLIAMENT IN RELATION TO BROADCASTING

5.1. The Government and Parliament must have the power to decide the number and nature of the broadcasting services—who should provide them, how they should be financed and what priority should be given to them. But these powers should give them the minimum opportunity to intervene in the day-to-day business of providing broadcasting services. Do their present powers need to be changed?

5.2. The Government's powers over broadcasting and the present relationship between the Home Secretary and the BBC and the IBA are defined by the provisions of several Acts of Parliament. [Principally the Wireless Telegraphy Act 1949, the Post Office Act 1969 and the Independent Broadcasting Authority Acts 1973 and 1974 and by the terms of the BBC's Royal Charter, and the BBC's Licence and Agreement.] Since broadcasting services can operate only under a licence from the Home Secretary, he is able to control the number of services and the manner in which they are provided . . . .

The Government's powers on financial questions

5.3. The Home Secretary also has some powers over the Broadcasting Authorities on financial questions. At present, the Home Secretary's powers enable the Government to decide in broad terms the amount of money which should be devoted to broadcasting. The Wireless Telegraphy Act 1949 empowers the Home Secretary to prescribe the level of the broadcast receiving licence fee and thus the amount of the BBC's main source of income. Under the terms of the Independent Broadcasting Authority Act 1974, the Home Secretary may, after consultation with the Authority, increase or reduce the rate of the additional payments or 'levy' paid by the Independent Television contractors, ie the companies. Similarly, the Independent Broadcasting Authority Act 1973 empowers the Home Secretary to impose payments on the Independent Radio contractors to prevent them making what are currently considered excessive profits.

5.7 . . . Does the Government use the licence fee and the levy as a lever to exercise control over programme policies? Discussions with the Government on the levy are normally conducted by the IBA, but the Independent Television Companies Association volunteered the information that such discussions as they had had were solely concerned with estimating what was necessary to run an efficient television service and what would be a reasonable return for the companies' shareholders. We discussed with Home Office and Treasury officials and with the BBC's Director-General and Director of Finance what happened when the BBC had applied for an increase in the licence fee. They too assured us that this power has not been used to attempt to influence programme policies, and that the Home Office and Treasury were conscious of the need for particular care in this matter. We accept their assurance. There is a sufficient safeguard. If there were to be improper pressure, there would be an uproar within and outside Parliament. . . .

The Government's powers over programmes

5.8. The Home Secretary also has some direct powers over programming. The terms of the BBC's Licence and Agreement and the IBA Act 1973 empower the Minister responsible for broadcasting to prescribe in writing the hours during which broadcasting may take place . . . . In January 1972, the Minister of Posts and Telecommunication announced the end of the restriction on the hours of television and radio broadcasting. But the power to regulate the hours of broadcasting remains, and was used in the winter of 1973–74 to close down broadcasting by 10.30 pm in the interests of fuel economy. Clearly the Government needs such emergency powers, and we recommend that this power should remain and should be applied to all the Broadcasting Authorities in future.

5.9. Any Minister of the Crown may require the Broadcasting Authorities to broadcast on their stations announcements in connection with his functions. (Clause 13(3) of the BBC's Licence and Agreement and section 22(1) of the IBA Act 1973). They are also required to broadcast any other matter at the request of a Minister in whose opinion an emergency has arisen or continues. The BBC and IBA may announce or not, as they please, that the Minister has required them to do so. In practice, the making of announcements (such as police messages, appeals for blood donors, reports of outbreaks of animal disease and the like) is a matter of day-to-day arrangements rather than of formal requirement. We note that the term 'announcements' has always been interpreted very strictly and has not been regarded as covering explanations of Government policies. We recommend that there should be no change in these powers . . . .

5.10. The Home Secretary's other main power over programmes is the power to veto, by a notice in writing, the broadcasting of any matter or classes of matter. (Clause 13(4) of the BBC's Licence and Agreement and section 22(3) of the IBA Act 1973). The Broadcasting Authorities can announce that such a direction has been given. This power has always been regarded as a reserve power and only five directions of a general kind have ever been given. Two of these are still in force. In 1927, when the original Licence was granted to the BBC, the Corporation was directed not to broadcast its own opinion on current affairs or on matters of public policy. This direction still stands. A similar prescription for the IBA and its programme contractors, is embodied in the IBA Act so that no direction is necessary. . . . The BBC was also directed in 1927 not to broadcast matters of political, industrial or religious controversy, but this prohibition was speedily withdrawn in 1928. In July 1955, the BBC and the IBA were directed to refrain from anticipating parliamentary discussions by broadcasting statements or discussions on matters during the fortnight before they were due to be debated in Parliament (the '14 day Rule'). This too was subsequently suspended; initially for a six-months' experimental period and then indefinitely, on assurance from both bodies that they would so act as not to derogate from the primacy of Parliament as the forum for debating the affairs of the nation. In July 1955, the BBC was directed to refrain at all times from broadcasting controversial party political broadcasts other than those arranged in agreement with the leading political parties for broadcasting throughout the United Kingdom. Ten years later this direction too was withdrawn . . . . In 1964 the BBC and the IBA were required to refrain at all times from broadcasting matter which uses subliminal techniques.

5.11. Although no direction has ever been made by the Postmaster General or his successors on a particular broadcast this power is, in our view, the one which poses the greatest threat to the independence of the Broadcasting Authorities. We understood that at least on one occasion in recent years the possibility of it being exercised in relation to an individual programme had arisen. This was over the BBC programme *The Question of Ulster*, which was broadcast in January 1972. We discussed this matter at some length with the BBC Chairman and Director-General. They told us that after the Home Secretary, who was then responsible for Northern Ireland but did not have Departmental responsibility for broadcasting, had made representations to the BBC early in December 1971, the Director-General and the then Chairman of the BBC had had a meeting with the Home Secretary. The Chairman had suggested that if the Government wished to stop the programme they should direct the BBC not to transmit it and the BBC would announce that this had been done. In the event, the Government did not exercise their powers of direction and despite further representations from the Home Secretary, the programme was shown. The BBC told us that, while they could not say the Home Secretary was wrong in making the representations he did, they thought they were right to continue with their plans for this programme. . . .

5.14. It is inevitable that Ministers will be tempted to intervene. In the last resort, the Government, not the broadcasters, must make decisions about national security. Moreover, it would be undesirable and impracticable to try to prevent Ministers and Government Departments making representations to the broadcasting organisations about programmes dealing with matters for which they are responsible. Even so, distinctions can, and should, be made. There are on the one hand representations about specific programme matters made through political channels, or by Departments with responsibilities for the subject matter of the programme; these the broadcasting organisations should consider on their merits as they would representations from other individuals and organisations. On the other hand, there are attempts to influence programmes or programme content generally, by Ministers brandishing the threat of using the Home Secretary's powers of direction or, to the BBC, the threat of withholding an increase in the licence fee. Representations of the first kind are inevitable but few allegations of instances of the second have come to us from any source. We consider that if politicians attempt to influence programmes before transmission, they do so at their peril, and broadcasters have every right to make such intervention known. . . .

NOTE

See further on the relationship between the broadcasting authorities and the politicians, C. R. Munro, *Television Censorship and the Law* (1979); J. Dearlove, Index on Censorship (1974) Vol. 3 No. 1 p. 23.

White Paper on Broadcasting (Cmnd. 7294 1978)

100. . . .The provision and content of programmes are the responsibility of the broadcasting authorities, and their independence in matters of programme content is central to the constitutional arrangements for broadcasting in the United Kingdom. This independence carries with it certain obligations as to programmes and programme standards and for the IBA these are set out in sections 2(2), 4 and 5 of the IBA Act 1973. The obligations of the BBC, most of which correspond with those of the IBA, are set out in its Royal Charter, in Ministerial prescriptions under Clause 13(4) of the Corporation's Licence and Agreement and in a letter of 19 June 1964 from the then Chairman of the BBC, Lord Normanbrook, to the Postmaster General. The contents of this letter are noted in the prescribing memorandum under Clause 13(4) of the Licence and Agreement). . . .

101. The main obligations which are broadly common to the existing broadcasting authorities in relation to the services and programmes they provide are set out in the table below.

BBC	IBA

(1) Each Authority has a duty to provide its respective radio and television services as public services for the dissemination of information, education and entertainment, and to

ensure that its programmes maintain a high general standard, in particular as respects their quality and content, and a proper balance and wide range of subject matter, having regard to the programmes as a whole and the days on which, and the times at which, programmes are broadcast.

(BBC's Royal Charter, Article 3(a);   *(IBA Act 1973, section 2(2)*
Lord Normanbrook's letter)

---

(2) Each Authority must ensure that, so far as possible, nothing is included in its programmes which offends against good taste or decency or is likely to encourage or incite to crime or lead to disorder or to be offensive to public feeling.

(Lord Normanbrook's letter)   *(section 4(1)(a))*

(3a) The BBC must ensure that, so far as possible, due impartiality is preserved in news programmes and programmes dealing with matters of public policy, and also in the treatment of controversial subjects generally.

(Lord Normanbrook's letter)

(3b) The IBA must ensure that, so far as possible, a sufficient amount of [time is given to news and news] features and that all news is presented with due accuracy and impartiality. It must also ensure that, so far as possible, due impartiality is preserved on the part of persons providing the programmes as respects matters of political or industrial controversy or relating to current public policy.

(section 4(1)(b) and (f))

(4a) The BBC must ensure that programmes do not include any expression of the Corporation's opinions on current affairs or on matters of public policy.

(Ministerial prescription under clause 13(4) of the Licence and Agreement)

(4b) The IBA must ensure that programmes do not include any expression of the opinions of the Authority (or its Members or officers, or programme contractors, their directors or officers, or persons having control over programme contractors) on matters of political or industrial controversy or relating to current public policy.

(section 4(2))

---

(5) Each Authority must ensure that programmes do not include any technical device to convey messages to, or influence, members of an audience without their being aware of what is being done.

(Ministerial prescription under clause 13(4) of the Licence and Agreement)   *(section 4 (3))*

---

(6) Each Authority must ensure that proper proportions of programmes are of British origin and British performance.

(Lord Normanbrook's letter)   *(section 4(1)(c))*

(7a) The BBC is obliged to exclude from the earlier part of the evening's programmes those which might be unsuitable for children.

(Lord Normanbrook's letter)

(7b) The IBA is required to draw up, from time to time review, and secure compliance with, a code of guidance on the rules to be observed in regard to the portrayal of violence and 'such other matters concerning programme standards and practice as it considers suitable for inclusion in the code.' In drawing up the code the IBA must have particular regard to programmes broadcast when large numbers of children and young persons may be expected to be watching or listening.

(section 5(1))

The portrayal of violence and related questions

103. The programme issue which has caused most concern to the public is the portrayal of violence on television and its effects. . . . The effects of television programmes on viewers are of their nature difficult to determine. However, the Government is in no doubt that the only safe course is for the broadcasting authorities to assume undesirable effects unless convincing evidence to the contrary emerges. This means that the authorities must be cautious in

broadcasting programmes, particularly programmes in which violence is portrayed, if these might have effects on susceptible people, especially young people and children. The BBC and the IBA are alert to the dangers, but the Government believes that they should both review their codes and guidance on the portrayal of violence in the light of the comments made in this White Paper, and should then publish these, if possible with their next annual reports. The codes and guidance should be subject to regular review thereafter. . . .

105. There is evidence that many children spend a great deal of time watching television and that their choice of programme is not always supervised by their parents. It is known, moreover, that there is no time of the evening when there are not some children viewing, perhaps even in quite substantial numbers, though there is a progressive decline throughout the evening in the proportion of children present in the audience. It would not be reasonable to require the broadcasters to ensure that no material that might be considered unsuitable for children was broadcast at any time. However, while the Government endorses the Annan Committee's recommendation that the BBC and the IBA should continue to operate a policy of not showing before 9 pm television programmes which may be unsuitable for children, it does not consider that the broadcasting authorities are entitled to assume that the entire responsibility for protecting children after 9 pm can be safely left to the parents. Although parents should take the primary responsibility thereafter—and more particularly the later in the evening it gets—the Government considers that the broadcasting authorities should always have regard (as the IBA is now required to have regard) in planning their programmes to the likely nature of the audience at a particular time.

106. The Government sympathises with the intention behind the Annan Committee's recommendations that the original classification given by the British Board of Film Censors to a film should be shown when it is broadcast and that a warning symbol should be given in programmes likely to disturb a number of viewers. Both the recommendations were designed to enable viewers to protect themselves from receiving broadcasts which they, or those in their family, might find highly objectionable. However, there is some evidence that to give a warning in this way would sometimes positively attract viewers, which would be contrary to the object of the exercise. The IBA has been conducting research into these matters and in the light of this the Government will discuss with the BBC and the IBA . . . how practical effect might be given to the spirit of the recommendations.

Due impartiality

107. The Annan Committee recommended that the broadcasting authorities should continue to ensure that, so far as possible, controversial subjects are treated with due impartiality, which they distinguished from a mathematical balance of different views, neutrality or indifference. They considered due impartiality to be composed of three elements—the expression of the widest possible range of views and opinions, the taking into the account of the weight of opinion which holds those views and the fact that both the range of views and weight of opinion are constantly changing. The requirement of due impartiality is fundamental to our concept of public service broadcasting. . . .

NOTES

1. In *A-G ex rel McWhirter v Independent Broadcasting Authority* [1973] 1 QB 629, CA the late Ross McWhirter sought an injunction to restrain the IBA from broadcasting a programme entitled 'Warhol: Artist and Film-maker'. The programme had been heralded by the News of the World as a 'Programme which goes further than anything . . . seen on TV . . . Millions of viewers will find its frankness offensive'. The IBA had not itself viewed the film and McWhirter alleged that the IBA had failed to comply with its statutory duty to satisfy itself, so far as possible, that programmes broadcast include nothing which offends good taste or decency or is offensive to public feeling. The Court of Appeal, by a majority, granted an interim injunction preventing the imminent scheduled broadcast of the programme. At this point the IBA and its General Advisory Council saw the film and decided that it was suitable for showing on television at the late night time scheduled. At the subsequent court hearing the Court of Appeal discharged the interim injunction. In the course of his judgment Lord Denning MR said, at 358:

. . . The Independent Broadcasting Authority are the people who matter. They are the censors. The courts have no right whatever – and I might add no desire whatever – to interfere with their decisions so long as they reach them in accordance with law . . . Counsel for Mr McWhirter submitted, however, that the Independent Broadcasting Authority had misdirected themselves. He said that they had regarded the film as a whole, and not piece by piece as the statute required. Alternatively, he said that their decision was one to which they could not reasonably have come.

To test these submissions we ourselves saw the film. I hesitate to express my own views on it, . . . I can understand that some people would think it entertaining, but I must speak as I find. Viewing it as a whole, the film struck me as dreary and dull. It shows the sort of people—the perverts and homosexuals–who surround Mr Warhol and whom he portrays in his work. But, taken as a whole it is not offensive. Viewing it piece by piece, there are some incidents which seemed to me to be inserted in an attempt to liven up the dullness—an attempt which did not succeed, at least so far as I was concerned. These are the incidents which struck the newspaper reporters and were described by them, . . . They only form about one-tenth of the whole. Speaking for myself, I would take the same view as the newspaper reporters . . . I should have thought that those individual incidents could be regarded as indecent and likely to be offensive to many. But my views do not matter, unless they go to show that the Independent Broadcasting Authority misdirected themselves or came to a conclusion to which they could not reasonably come. I am certainly not prepared to say that. Quite the contrary. On seeing the film, they came to a decision to which they might reasonably come, and this court has no right whatever to interfere with it.

I would therefore lift the injunction. The programme can be shown as soon as can be arranged. No doubt many will wish to see it to form their own view. Some will write to the Independent Broadcasting Authority and tell them. It should give the Independent Broadcasting Authority a good guide to public feeling, and so help them in the difficult decisions which they have to make in the future. But they should always remember that there is a silent majority of good people who say little but view a lot. Their feelings are to be respected as well as those of the vociferous minority who, in the name of freedom, shout for ugliness in all its forms.'

Note that the *locus standi* aspects of this case must now be read in the light of the decision of the House of Lords in *Gouriet v Union of Post Office Workers* [1978] AC 435, [1977] 3 All ER 70.

2. Note the following comment of the BBC on the problem of programme standards:

'Violence, bad language, sexual explicitness are all aspects of the very difficult problems that confront us. . . . [T]he theatre, the cinema and the written word have become, in recent years, far more permissive, and as a result we are under continual pressure to change our standards to theirs. In fact we assert a far stricter control than any of the other media. . . . We are all clear that writers, directors and producers must observe the difference between television's artistic conventions as a medium that comes straight into the home and those that impinge elsewhere. And if that distinction is properly observed the problem diminishes. . . . . . .[W]e believe that we shall, by degrees, achieve a balance between what is broadly acceptable to viewers and the demands of worthwhile creative work which may sometimes pull in the opposite direction.' (Quoted in *BBC Handbook* 1979 p. 3).

The BBC has published successively revised Codes on the portrayal of violence on television in 1960, 1972 and 1979. ITV issued a Code on Violence in 1964 and the Code is kept under review.

3. For accounts of decisions taken by the broadcasting authorities in relation to programme content see H. Street, *Freedom, the Individual and the Law* (4th edn., 1977) pp. 79–83, 92–3; C. R. Munro, *Television Censorship and the Law* (1979). Note, for example, the decisions of the BBC in 1978 against the broadcasting of two television plays. One – 'Scum' by Roy Minton and Alan Clarke – portrayed violence between inmates of a Borstal Institution. The BBC explained that the compressed presentation of events in the play produced a 'gross distortion of normal conditions'. Such 'distortion by compression' was made the subject of particular warning to producers in the 1979 guidelines on the portrayal of violence issued by the BBC. Subsequently the play was made into a feature film released with an 'X' certificate in 1979. The other play – 'Solid Geometry' by Ian McEwan – was banned at rehearsal stage. Particular exception was taken to certain lines about menstruation and the appearance on screen of a preserved penis in a specimen jar (See Index on Censorship (1978) Vol. 8 No. 4 p. 65).

4. Some criticism has been expressed of decisions taken by the broadcasting authorities in respect of the reporting of Northern Irish affairs. See e.g. Anthony Smith, Index on Censorship (1972) Vol. 1 No. 2, p. 15; P. Taylor, Index on Censorship (1978) Vol. 7 No. 6, p. 3; *The British Media and Ireland* (Campaign for Free Speech in Ireland) (1979).

5. In 1971 both the BBC and the IBA set up bodies to consider complaints from members of the public about broadcast programmes. The BBC's Programme Complaints Committee has a rather narrower jurisdiction than that of the IBA's Complaints Review Board. Whereas the latter can consider general complaints from the public about programmes, the former is limited to considering complaints by individuals or organisations about their allegedly unjust or unfair treatment in connection with a programme or programmes. On the other hand the membership of the BBC's Commission is more obviously 'independent' than that of the IBA's Board. For further information about these bodies see the annual *BBC Handbook* and *IBA Yearbook*.

The Annan Committee considered there to be a lack of public confidence about the way in which these bodies dealt with complaints. In their place the Committee recommended a single Broadcasting Complaints Commission whose members would be appointed by the Home Office and which would be seen, the Committee thought, as more independent than the present bodies. Its jurisdiction should, however, more closely resemble that of the present BBC Commission than that of the IBA. It would be authorised to make adjudications (and award 'costs' to successful complainants) in respect of allegations of misrepresentation, unjust or unfair treatment in broadcast programmes and complaints of invasion of privacy in the making of programmes. The Committee felt, however, that more general complaints relating to 'taste' or the standard of programmes were, however, less suited to such a quasi-judicial procedure and should be left to the consideration of the broadcasting authorities themselves. The Committee made certain recommendations which it hoped would make the authorities more open to such complaints than in the past (e.g. proposals for more public hearings for discussion of the services provided by the authorities). These recommendations were broadly accepted by the *White Paper on Broadcasting*, (1978) Cmnd. 7294, and form the basis of the complaints provisions in the Broadcasting Bill 1980.

4 The Press

(a) FREEDOM OF THE PRESS

In its Final Report the Royal Commission on the Press commented:

'Freedom of the press carries different meanings for different people. Some emphasise the freedom of proprietors to market their publications, others the freedom of individuals, whether professional journalists or not, to address the public through the press; still others stress the freedom of editors to decide what shall be published. These are all elements in the right to freedom of expression. But proprietors, contributors and editors must accept the limits to free expression set by the need to reconcile claims which may often conflict. The public, too, asserts a right to accurate information and fair comment which, in turn, has to be balanced against the claims both of national security and of individuals to safeguards for their reputation and privacy except when these are overridden by the public interest. But the public interest does not reside in whatever the public may happen to find interesting, and the press must be careful not to perpetrate abuses and call them freedom. Freedom of the press cannot be absolute. There must be boundaries to it and realistic discussion concerns where those boundaries ought to be set.

We define freedom of the press as that degree of freedom from restraint which is essential to enable proprietors, editors and journalists to advance the public interest by publishing the facts and opinions without which a democratic electorate cannot make responsible judgments . . . ' (Cmnd. 6810, 1977, paras. 2.2 and 2.3).

Materials elsewhere in this book illustrate a number of areas where the law restricts absolute press freedom – see e.g. the sections on obscenity, contempt of court, official secrecy, 'D' Notices, sedition, incitement to disaffection, racial discrimination and privacy.

During the mid-1970s much discussion of freedom of the press centred on the alleged dangers of 'closed shop' agreements entered into between newspapers and the NUJ. In particular it was feared lest such agreements should restrict editorial freedom to commission work from non-NUJ members. See further, *Royal Commission on the Press – Final Report* 1977 Cmnd. 6810, Chapter 17; *Annual Report of the Press Council* 1977 p. 118; debates in Parliament on the Trade Union and Labour Relations (Amendment) Act 1976, conveniently summarised at *Keesings Archives* 1976, 28006–28008; England and Rees (1977) 127 NLJ 256 and (1976) 39 MLR 699 – 700; G. Scott and others, Index on Censorship (1977) Vol. 6 No. 1, pp. 8–16.

Note also the examples of action taken by print unions interfering with newspaper production because of the content of items in newspapers cited in the *Annual Report of the Press Council,* 1977, Chapter 4. The disputes involved an article in *The Times*, an advertisement placed in *The Observer* by the National Association for Freedom, and a leader in *The Sun*. On each occasion the Press Council issued a statement condemning these 'grave attacks' on freedom of the Press. The article in *The Times* was a report of an article by David Astor (former editor of the *Observer*), which had appeared in Index on Censorship (1977) Vol. 6 No. 1, pp. 5–8 in which Astor had been highly critical of unions in the newspaper industry. The NGA refused to allow the report to be published despite an offer by the editor of *The Times* of a right of reply in a subsequent issue. The report was ultimately printed the following day. (See Index on Censorship (1977) Vol. 6 No. 3, pp. 47–60).

The materials that follow relate not to *restrictions* on press freedom but rather illustrate the role of the Press Council in protecting individuals and organisations from *abuses* of press freedom.

(b) THE PRESS COUNCIL

This body was set up in 1953 by the Press following recommendations of the first *Royal Commission on the Press*, Cmnd. 7700 1947–1949. Its objects include the preservation of the established freedom of the British press, the maintenance of the character of the British press in accordance with the highest professional and commercial standards and the consideration of complaints about the conduct of the press. The Council's membership consisted initially entirely of press representatives. Following recommendations of the second *Royal Commission on the Press* (1962) Cmnd. 1811, the *Report of the Committee on Privacy* (1972) Cmnd. 5012 and the

Royal Commission on the Press (1977) Cmnd. 6810 the Council now consists of an independent chairman and thirty-six members, consisting of an equal number of press and lay members. The important complaints committee consists of six lay members, six press members and the independent chairman of Press Council.

For information about the work of the Press Council see H. Phillip Levy, *The Press Council* (1967) and the *Annual Reports of the Press Council.* The range of matters about which complaints are received is large. The list includes mis-reporting, sensationalism and distortion, the publication of corrections and apologies, matters of taste and unethical methods of obtaining information. For the attitude of the Press Council to invasions of privacy see below, pp. 324–325.

Royal Commission on the Press – Final Report (Cmnd. 6810 1977)

NEED FOR A PRESS COUNCIL

20.1 The Press Council plays a key role in maintaining public confidence in the press, and a basic condition for such confidence is that it must be wholly independent of government. We reject as potentially authoritarian suggestions for a standing commission for broadcasting and the press, representative of all major sections of the community and responsible to a Minister for monitoring the performance of the press. The Press Council must also show a determination to be independent of the press. The public will not believe that a Council dominated by journalists and others from the press can keep an effective watch on the standards of the press or can deal satisfactorily with complaints by citizens. In discussing privacy . . . we insisted that willingness on the part of the press to accept and conform to the rulings of the Council is the only alternative to the introduction of a legal right of privacy, and, perhaps, of a statutory Press Council. Finally, an effective Press Council must be expert and influential enough for its judgement to carry weight within the press, with proprietors, editors and journalists. . . .

20.3 . . . Though we make many criticisms in this chapter, we emphasise at the outset that [its] virtues are great and we record our recognition of the service which the Press Council has given to the community for nearly a quarter of a century. . . .

20.12 Witnesses held strong views about the Press Council, varying from wholehearted approval to outright opposition. Some suggested that it should be abolished or replaced. The press was broadly satisfied; lay critics were unhappy to a greater or lesser extent; the most extreme charged the Council with bias in favour of the press, unwillingness to censure it and even with reluctance to consider complaints against it. It is unhappily certain that the Council has so far failed to persuade the knowledgeable public that it deals satisfactorily with complaints against newspapers, notwithstanding that this has come to be seen as its main purpose. . . .

COMPLAINTS PROCEDURE

20.25 Most of the work of the Press Council has come to concern complaints and most of the comment made to us was about its procedure for dealing with them. A number of critics . . . complained to us that the Press Council's procedures were too slow. Where a story has damaged the reputation of an individual, or has been misleading, it is important for an adjudication to be made quickly; the sooner it is made, the better the chance of removing the false impression which has been given. . . .

20.26 . . . we acquit the staff of the Press Council of the charge that they delay cases.

20.27 . . . a considerable number of letters is often needed before a case can be considered by the Complaints Committee. These letters may be requests for copies of correspondence, for articles complained of, or for elucidation of the precise form and basis of complaints. . . . However, if the Complaints Committee is to carry out its work properly we do not see how such requests can be avoided.

20.28 Nevertheless, speed is highly important when dealing with certain types of complaint and it is also necessary for complainants to have some help in advancing their grievances and achieving remedies. The Press Council agrees. Its Commentary on Representations to the Royal Commission says: 'the Council believes that conciliation of some kind might serve the interests of both the public and the press by offering more rapid resolution of compalints with less documentary work'. . . .

20.29 We are very encouraged by this move of the Press Council. . . .

20.34 . . . we **recommend** that the task of conciliation should be carried out by a named conciliator. The figure we have in mind would not be separate from the Press Council but on its staff, exercising powers delegated to him by the Council. His role in conciliation would include proposing a remedy if he thought that right; and if his remedy were rejected by the complainant or the newspaper, we would expect the rejection to be taken into account by the Complaints Committee when the complaint reached them. Only when he had failed to conciliate would a dossier be prepared in order to enable a case to be brought formally before the Complaints Committee. This task would require an officer of the Council with great ability and invested with considerable authority.

CASE FOR WRITTEN CODE

20.51 We heard a wide range of opinions about the adjudications of the Press Council on complaints. From inside the industry, both in formal evidence and in informal discussion, we were often told that the adjudications issued by the Press Council had built up a body of case law which was most useful in guiding journalists as to the standards they should employ. This is the attitude of the Press Council itself, and it was thus expressed by Lord Devlin:

> It has given many rulings, some of general application, and others doing hardly more than decide a particular case. . . . Inevitably a collection of rulings of this sort indicates, if it does not settle, professional standards. Even where a principle is not expressed, it can often be induced from a group of similar decisions. The Press Council has not, unlike many other professional bodies, drafted a code. It has, whether it realised it or not, adopted the methods of generations of judges who produced the common law of England. They let it grow out of the decisions they gave. (H. Phillip Levy, *The Press Council* (1967), p. xi).

20.52 On the other hand, there was criticism from some who thought that the decisions of the Council did not give sufficient basis to guide the conduct of the press. For example, Mr Alexander Irvine suggested to us in a long and detailed paper that adjudications do not always make adequately clear the basis on which they are made. Since there are quite often two or more possible reasons for a particular decision, each with different implications for conduct by other journalists, Mr Irvine argues that, if adjudications are to be useful guides to future conduct, the reasons for them should always be given. His submission was based on decisions made some years ago, but his points are still relevant.

20.53 As an example of vagueness, Mr Irvine quoted cases, dating from 1962 and 1963, in which the same issue had been raised—that of publicity about the private lives of well-known people who were living together while married to other people. In one case a complaint was upheld. In the other it was not. The adjudications did not make clear why the different results were arrived at. The cases are old, but the point is general. The Press Council meets it by saying that since its decisions are those of a jury, and different members of the Council may have acted for somewhat different reasons, it is not possible to give full reasons.

20.54 Carried to its logical conclusion, this argument would leave the Press Council free to come to completely inconsistent decisions. It would prevent the building up by case law of consistent principles and cause great problems for journalists and the public in knowing what was permitted and what was not. The Council does not generally act as inconsistently as that, but the form in which its adjudications have been expressed in the past make it difficult to determine what standards it applies.

20.55 A concise statement of criticism of the standards applied by the Press Council was submitted to us by Mr John M Dickie. After commenting on a series of adjudications he summarised their implications as he saw them as follows:

> . . . we have sanctions of a free hand for misreporting and for the exercise of editorial bias, permission of headline misleadingness, no censure of doubtfully proper methods of obtaining information, an escape from editorial blame by the mere passage of time, establishment of unhampered editorial right to close a correspondence at any moment, sanction of autocratic and unfair editorial behaviour in dealing with correspondence, support for arbitrary editorial refusal to entertain correction of alleged factual error merely out of concern for the preserving of editorial authority and *amour propre*, approval of editorial escape by means of word juggling from a charge of misrepresentation; acceptance of the right of denial of news coverage to minority news, establishment of the freedom of editorial discretion in the acceptance of advertising regardless of the rightness or wrongness of that decision.

20.56 We conclude from our examination of the adjudications of the Press Council that the standards they apply and the terms in which they are expressed fall short of what is desirable. In particular, we consider that adjudications do not contain sufficient argument, and that they sometimes make too many allowances for editorial discretion and errors of fact. The adjudication of the Council upon a complaint that *The Sunday Times* had caused a fall in the value of sterling by irresponsible reporting is a case in point and illustrates the ambiguity and inadequacy of some of its rulings. The Council first states that 'the most that can be insisted upon is that the Editor should honestly believe the truth of what he publishes and that his belief should be based on reasonable grounds'. That clearly implies that two conditions have to be fulfilled: one subjective—honest belief on the part of the Editor; and the other objective—reasonable grounds for that belief. But this adjudication then goes on to hold that the second condition was fulfilled because 'whether the story was true or not, there existed in the minds of the Editor and Mr Crawford reasonable grounds for holding it to be true'. In other words, both tests are subjective. The test becomes 'the Editor should honestly believe the truth of what he publishes and honestly believe that he has reasonable grounds for so doing'. This is a very different and far less stringent test. The Press Council abdicates its responsibility for determining whether there are reasonable grounds and leaves it to the Editor.

20.57 It has been suggested that the Press Council should draw up a code of conduct to make clearer the basis of its decisions and to improve standards in other ways. The Council has already produced two 'Declarations of Principle'. The first dealt with cheque book journalism in the aftermath of the Moors Murder trial; the second with privacy, following extensive adverse comment on gossip columns in 1975 and early 1976. These provide obvious precedents for a code.

20.58 The Press Council itself has opposed the preparation of a code. It claims that any code would be too rigid in its operations and lead to evasions of the spirit of the rules by those who adhered to its letter. It argues that in a world of rapidly changing standards, such a code itself would need frequent amendment, pointing out that its Declaration of Principle on cheque-book journalism needed amendment soon after it had been adopted. We do not accept that a written code would of necessity impose rigidity on the Press Council. Nor do we believe that such a code would need to be amended more often than would be practicable. The experience of the Advertising Standards Authority in operating a code which deals with questions similar to those which would come within the scope of a code of journalistic behaviour supports our view. We believe that the Panel on Takeovers and Mergers operates another code in accordance with its spirit and not just its letter. Accordingly, we **recommend** that the Press Council should draw up a code of behaviour on which to base its adjudications. We believe that such a code would be a natural way of demonstrating that the Press Council is carrying out its stated objects, and we consider that it should set out in some detail the spirit which should govern the conduct of editors and journalists. The Council should be free to censure conduct in breach of the spirit as well as of the letter of the code, and to decline to censure conduct technically breaching the code, if there are sufficient extenuating circumstances. The existence of a code would also enable the public to judge the performance of the press by known and accepted standards.

20.59 So far as possible we think that the code should be based on past adjudications. After more than twenty years of complaints such codification would certainly be useful. We know that work has been going on to bring up to date the classifications in Mr Levy's book, following the recommendation of the Committee on Privacy, but what we have in mind goes further than that, and would involve drawing up a set of rules and standards based on those adjudications rather than simply marshalling them under headings. It would be a codification both bringing together previous adjudications and filling gaps in them. It would also be designed to provide a comprehensive set of guidelines for the conduct of those gathering and presenting news and information. We were strengthened in our view when the Guild of British Newspaper Editors told us in evidence that they believe there is now a case for such a code. We attach particular importance to the early implementation of this recommendation, and we invite the Council to consider employing someone specifically to undertake this task.

EFFECTIVENESS OF COUNCIL SANCTIONS

20.60 The Press Council itself believes that there has been a great improvement in the behaviour of newspapers in the last twenty years, and naturally takes some of the credit for this. Some witnesses have agreed. Others have suggested that there has been a decline.

20.61 The Press Council and those who generally support it hold that publicity and condemnation are the most effective sanctions which can be used against journalists. Those in the profession have suggested to us that they really do feel the Press Council breathing down their necks as they practise, and plead that any stronger sanctions would be impracticable and undesirable. Fines on journalists would involve turning the occupation into a 'closed' licensed profession; only in this way could a sanction beyond a fine and suspension of the right to have work published be provided. Suspension from publication of a paper would be tantamount to censorship and the suppression of opinion.

20.62 On the other hand, the critics of the Press Council think that the sanction of publicised criticism is inadequate. They argue that only fines or suspension would make a real difference to the conduct of journalists. But no witness gave us a clear idea of how he envisaged that stronger sanctions might work.

20.64   In our opinion, there are still flagrant breaches of acceptable standards. . . .

20.68   . . . One reason why such instances continue is no doubt that newspapers will often run the risk that those involved in a story will not want to prolong the unpleasantness involved by complaining to the Press Council or even co-operating with the Council in an investigation. This must be an important consideration, which will often frustrate the efforts of the Press Council. But we consider that there is a strong case to be made for increasing the risk which newspapers run when they gamble on the likelihood that the parties involved in a story will take this attitude. Not only might an increase in sanctions make newspapers think twice before breaking Press Council standards; it might also persuade some people that it would be worth their while to accept the unpleasantness involved in co-operating with a Press Council enquiry. However true it is that the individual journalist feels profoundly ashamed of being criticised in an adjudication, this is by no means clear to potential complainants. We are not suggesting that the Press Council should satisfy an appetite for revenge, but that it would be desirable if adjudication could become a more worthwhile remedy than it now is.

20.69   Because we feel strongly that the Press Council should have more power over the press it is with reluctance that we have accepted, as did the Committee on Privacy, the arguments against Press Council fines or suspensions. One reason is that they would represent a potentially dangerous weapon of control over the press if they were given statutory backing. Nor are we convinced that the law should be available to enforce penalties for what are in many cases breaches of taste. . . .

20.70   A voluntary or a statutory scheme would present severe practical problems. For example, the level of fines would be difficult to set. Would it depend on the ability of the newspaper or periodical to pay, or of the individual journalist, and how would such ability be assessed? Or on the gravity of the offence alone? On whom should fines be levied in particular cases: journalist, editor, sub-editor or publisher? How far would it be proper to expect those in the industry to bind themselves to pay such fines, and how would they signify that they were bound? Similarly, in exactly what circumstances would it be right for a journalist to be suspended, and should someone under threat of suspension not have the right to appeal, and, if so, to whom? And how could suspensions be enforced against a journalist who was a freelance or part-time employee? These questions seem to us to amount to grave objections to any scheme of formal penalties involving fines or suspensions. We prefer to rely on the sanction of censure by an independent and forceful Press Council.

IMPROVEMENTS REQUIRED

20.71   There is therefore a pressing call to enhance the standing of the Press Council in the eyes of the public and potential complainants. In the first place we consider that increased publicity for the Press Council, together with a greater number of complaints and adjudications, would bring it more into public notice. To this end we **recommend** that the Press Council should be provided with enough funds to enable it to advertise its services in the same way as the Advertising Standards Authority. . . .

20.73   The Council needs a more obvious sanction than it now possesses. There should be wider publicity for adjudications, if need be by publishing them in the advertising columns of the press. . . .

20.74   We have referred to the sense of humiliation said to be felt by a journalist who is criticised by the Press Council. We believe that this would carry more public weight if the humiliation was generally more obvious than it sometimes is. We also **recommend** that the Press Council should be prepared to undertake a wider review than it normally does at present of the record of the publication or journalist concerned. We have in mind here a point made in evidence to us by Times Newspapers:

> Newspapers can shrug off the finding that they made a mistake in a particular case. To be told in public, with evidence, that their achievement in a recurrent part of their work has been persistently shoddy is in itself a punishment of a different order, and a real stimulus to reform.

20.75   To some extent this would be met by the Press Council itself taking the initiative more frequently than in the past in investigating the conduct of the press without waiting for formal complaints. We have been glad to note that Council proposes to do this more often and we **recommend** that they make this a regular practice. A code of conduct such as we have recommended would also help. But at the same time we consider that more fully argued adjudications are called for. We do not comment in detail on individual adjudications, because we do not wish to seem to condemn individual journalists, but we take the view that adjudications are often too terse.

20.76 Finally, we **recommend** that the Press Council should change its position on two important questions, accuracy and bias. In our consideration of editorial standards we have given great weight, following commentators from the time of the first Royal Commission, to fairness and accuracy. In its initial evidence to us, the Press Council offered as its list of the foundations of editorial standards 'judgement, courage, honesty, fairness, and tenacity'. The Council does not regard inaccuracy alone as adequate grounds for a complaint against a newspaper or periodical. Someone who complains of inaccuracy must show that it arises from an impropriety such as malice or recklessness. The argument for this is that it would be unreasonable, in the hurried conditions in which newspapers are produced, to expect every fact to be checked, and to hold an editor accountable if he failed to do so. The burden of proof to be discharged before malice and recklessness can be shown is heavy indeed. There can be very few cases where this could be demonstrated beyond doubt.

20.77 At the same time the Press Council has resolutely and rightly defended the right of newspapers to be partisan in their commentary in the news. The potential complainant can thus find that if he complains about inaccuracy or recklessness, and if he prays in aid the nature of the commentary on that event in order to demonstrate bias or malice, he will be told that a newspaper has the right to be partisan. In other words, the Council leaves newspapers free to present contentious opinions on the basis of inaccurate reports.

20.78 In oral evidence to us, the Press Council explained that when considering a complaint on the grounds of inaccuracy they consider failure to correct as a reason for upholding a complaint if the inaccuracy has concerned an important matter. We were glad to hear this, but we are not satisfied that Council practice is strict enough in protecting the public against the dangers of partisan opinion exacerbated by factual inaccuracy.

20.79 Not only does a combination of inaccuracy and partisanship, whenever it occurs, seem to us to amount to serious misconduct on the part of the press, it is also the abuse which the first Royal Commission had in mind when they recommended the setting up of the Press Council. They said:

> Political partisanship alone . . . deprives the citizen of the evidence on which conclusions should be based: political partisanship in conjunction with a high degree of distortion for news value may lead him to forget that conclusions are, or should be, grounded on evidence.

20.80 We believe that inaccuracy, even if subsequently corrected, should be prima facie evidence for upholding a complaint, and we **recommend** that contentious opinions based on inaccurate information should be grounds for censure.

NOTES

1. For an assessment of the achievements of Press Council during its first twenty-five years see, 'Past Performance, Future Tasks – a personal view' by Rt Hon Lord Shawcross (then Chairman of Press Council) in *Annual Report of Press Council*, 1977, Chap. 1. Lord Shawcross notes what he regards as a marked improvement in the press in matters of accuracy and bias and believes Press Council decisions to have been influential. He is less sure of the Council's achievements in relation to sensationalism, violence, sex, and above all, trivia. For the future he accepts and stresses the importance of the Press Council itself initiating inquiries rather than acting only on complaints received, and the need for decisions of the Council to be more fully reasoned. Lord Shawcross does not, however, favour the drawing up of a 'code' covering press behaviour.

2. A controversial issue in relation not only to the Press Council but also the BBC Programme Complaints Commission and IBA Complaints Review Board is whether a complainant should be required to waive his right to take legal action before these bodies consider the complaint. Should these bodies be regarded as providing alternative or additional remedies to those available at law? The arguments in favour of retention of the legal waiver centre around fears that only if subsequent legal proceedings are excluded will the press and broadcasting authorities co-operate fully with the voluntary adjudicating bodies. See further on this issue the *Report of the Committee on Privacy* (1972) Cmnd. 5012 paras. 153–155 ('unavoidable feature of voluntary complaints system'); the *Annan*

Committee on the Future of Broadcasting (1973) Cmnd. 6753 para 6.18 (majority opposed to waiver); *Royal Commission on the Press* (1977) Cmnd. 6810 paras. 20.43–20.49 (Commission divided; Press Council should reconsider waiver); *White Paper on Broadcasting* (1978) Cmnd. 7294 paras. 79–80 (arguments finely balanced; comments sought).

3. The Press Council put into effect the recommendations of the *Royal Commission on the Press* concerning conciliation in 1978. See *Annual Report of the Press Council,* 1977, pp. 99 and 114.

5 Obscenity and indecency

(a) OBSCENE PUBLICATIONS ACTS 1959 AND 1964

(i) The offences

Obscene Publications Act 1959

An Act to amend the law relating to the publication of obscene matter; to provide for the protection of literature; and to strengthen the law concerning pornography.

2. Prohibition of Publication of Obscene Matter

(1) Subject as hereinafter provided, any person who, whether for gain or not, publishes an obscene article [or who has an obscene article for publication for gain (whether gain to himself or gain to another)][9] shall be liable—

    (a) on summary conviction to a fine not exceeding [£1000] or to imprisonment for a term not exceeding six months[10];

    (b) on conviction on indictment to a fine or to imprisonment for a term not exceeding three years or both.

(2)[11] Notwithstanding anything in section one hundred and four of the Magistrates' Courts Act 1952, summary proceedings for an offence against this section may be brought at any time within twelve months from the commission of the offence; . . . .

(3) A prosecution [on indictment][11] for an offence against this section shall not be commenced more than two years after the commission of the offence.

(3A)[12] Proceedings for an offence under this section shall not be instituted except by or with the consent of the Director of Public Prosecutions in any case where the article in question is a moving picture film of a width of not less than sixteen millimetres and the relevant publication or the only publication which followed or could reasonably have been expected to follow from the relevant publication took place or (as the case may be) was to take place in the course of a cinematograph exhibition; and in this subsection 'the relevant publication' means–

    (a) in the case of any proceedings under this secton for publishing an obscene article, the publication in respect of which the defendant would be charged if the proceedings were brought; and

    (b) in the case of any proceedings under this section for having an obscene article for publication for gain, the publication which, if the proceedings were brought, the defendant would be alleged to have had in contemplation.

(4) A person publishing an obscene article shall not be proceeded against for an offence at common law consisting of the publication of any matter contained or embodied in the article where it is of the essence of the offence that the matter is obscene.

---

9. Words in square brackets added by the Obscene Publications Act 1964, s.1(1).

10. Penalty on summary conviction raised to present level by the Criminal Law Act 1977, ss.16(4), 28(2), 28(7).

11. S.2(2) and words in square brackets in s.2(3) repealed by the Criminal Law Act 1977, s.65, Sch.13 and S.I. 1978 No.712.

12. S.2(3A) added by the Criminal Law Act 1977, s.53.

$(4A)^{13}$ Without prejudice to subsection (4) above, a person shall not be proceeded against for an offence at common law–

(a) in respect of a cinematograph exhibition or anything said or done in the course of a cinematograph exhibition, where it is of the essence of the common law offence that the exhibition or, as the case may be, what was said or done was obscene, indecent, offensive, disgusting or injurious to morality; or

(b) in respect of an agreement to give a cinematograph exhibition or to cause anything to be said or done in the course of such an exhibition where the common law offence consists of conspiring to corrupt public morals or to do any act contrary to public morals or decency.

(5) [See below, p. 231]

(6) [See below, p. 222]

(7) In this section 'cinematograph exhibition' means an exhibition of moving pictures produced on a screen by means which include the projection of light.

NOTES

1. The Obscene Publications Act 1964, s. 1 (2) provides that for the purpose of any proceedings for an offence under s.2 of the 1959 Act 'a person shall be deemed to have an article for publication for gain if with a view to such publication he has the article in his ownership, possession or control.'

2. The Obscene Publications Act 1964, s.1 (5) provides that the term 'publication for gain' shall mean 'any publication with a view to gain, whether the gain is to accrue by way of consideration for the publication or in any other way.'

3. The Obscene Publications Acts 1959 and 1964 have superseded, though without actually abolishing, the common law offence of obscene libel. The 1959 Act followed recommendations of a committee set up by the Society of Authors (Chairman, Sir Alan Herbert) in response to a 'spate' of prosecutions of 'serious literature' during 1954, and the deliberations of a Parliamentary Select Committee (1956–57 HC 245; 1957–58 HC 122 and 123). For the 1954 prosecutions and the unsatisfactory features of the common law offence they revealed see C. H. Rolph, *Books in the Dock* (1969) pp. 93–109; N. St. John-Stevas [1954] Crim LR 817 and *Obscenity and the Law* (1956); series of unattributed articles in (1954) 118 JPN at 664, 680, 694, 709, 725, 812; G. Robertson, *Obscenity* (1979), Chap. 2. Note however the much praised summing-up of Stable J in *R v Martin Secker and Warburg* [1954] 2 All ER 683, [1954] 1 WLR 1178. The 1964 Act was passed to remedy certain flaws that had become apparent in the provisions of the 1959 Act (see e.g. *R v Clayton and Halsey* [1963] 1 QB 163, CCA and *Mella v Monahan* [1961] Crim LR 175, DC). Substantial further amendment to the 1959 and 1964 Acts was made by Criminal Law Act 1977, s. 53.

The 1959 Act was intended to provide greater safeguards for those who create or deal in works of 'art' or 'literature' whilst, at the same time, making better provision for the prosecution of those who create or deal in 'pornography' and for the seizure and forfeiture of such material. Neither aim appears to have been achieved. The protection afforded to literature depends more on levels of tolerance of jurors and magistrates than on the law itself, and pornography is such profitable business that the possibility of conviction, or forfeiture of material, provides no real deterrent. Moreover, the publicity which such proceedings bring may well provide a more than compensatory boost to future sales. The difficulties of enforcing the obscenity laws prompted Sir Robert Mark, then Metropolitan Police

---

13. S.2(4A) added by the Criminal Law Act 1977, s.53.

Commissioner, to describe the task as 'a self-defeating attempt to eradicate the ineradicable' (Sir R. Mark, *Policing a Perplexed Society* (1977) p. 60). See also *R v Metropolitan Police Comr, ex parte Blackburn (No. 3)* [1973] 1 QB 141, CA; Hay and Hoddinott, 47 Police Journal 28. A further difficulty for the police has been the vigilance necessary to ensure that their own officers do not succumb to offers of bribes held out by the pornographers. For accounts of such corruption and its 'rooting out' see B. Cox, J. Shirley and M. Short, *The Fall of Scotland Yard* (1977); Sir R. Mark, *In the Office of Constable* (1978) pp. 173–4, 263–269.

Inevitably there have been many proposals for reform of the law. Some have sought to provide a more workable legal formula for distinguishing what is permissible from what is not. See e.g. *Pornography: The Longford Report* (1972); *The Pollution of the Mind: New Proposals to Control Public Indecency and Obscenity* – Society of Conservative Lawyers (1972). Others have favoured relaxation of the obscenity laws, though usually recognising the need to afford children some protection. A distinction has commonly been drawn between those who foist offensive displays on others and those who simply supply material to those who actively seek it. See e.g. *The Obscenity Laws: Report of Arts Council Working Party* (1969); proposals of the *Defence of Literature and the Arts Society* (DLAS), reported at (1978) 128 NLJ 423. For appraisals of a variety of possible reforms see C. H. Rolph, *Books in the Dock* (1969), Chap. 6; G. Robertson, *Obscenity* (1979), Chap. 11. A Committee was appointed in July 1977 by the then Home Secretary to 'review the laws concerning obscenity, indecency and violence in publications, displays and entertainments in England and Wales, except in the field of broadcasting, and to review the arrangements for film censorship in England and Wales; and to make recommendations'. See the closely reasoned, though nonetheless controversial, recommendations of that Committee (1979) Cmnd. 7772, set out below at pp. 239–241.

4. The provisions in s.2(4) of the 1959 Act were intended to prevent defendants being denied the various safeguards contained in the 1959 Act by being charged at common law with obscene libel. It has, however, been held that the subsection does not prevent charges of conspiracy to corrupt public morals or conspiracy to outrage public decency since in such cases the essence of the offence is not the publication of obscene matter but the agreement to act in a corrupting or outrageous manner. See *Shaw v Director of Public Prosecutions* [1962] AC 220, HL, at 268, 290, 291; and *Knuller v Director of Public Prosecutions* [1973] AC 435, HL, at 456 per Lord Reid: 'Technically the distinction . . . is correct but it appears to me to offend against the policy of the Act . . .' Fears lest the bringing of such charges might circumvent the Obscene Publications Acts led to assurances to Parliament from the Law Officers that such charges would not be brought where to do so would deprive defendants of those Acts' safeguards. See 695 HC Deb 3 June 1964 col 1212; 698 HC Deb 7 July 1964 cols 315–6.

For full discussion of these conspiracy offences see Smith and Hogan, *Criminal Law* (4th edn., 1978) pp. 234–236; *Law Commission Report No. 76 Conspiracy and Criminal Law Reform* (1976) pp. 74–80; G. Robertson, *Obscenity* (1979) pp. 210–236.

Note the more comprehensive words in the 1959 Act s.2(4A) (the parallel provisions relating to prosecutions in respect of films added by Criminal Law Act 1977, s.53) and also in the Theatres Act 1968, s.2(4) (below, p. 232) in respect of obscene plays.

5. Prior to 1978 the police were obliged, in the interest of achieving some degree of national consistency, to send full information to the DPP in respect, inter alia, of offences involving obscene exhibitions or publications. By S. I. 1978 No. 1846 this obligation was altered to one of having to provide such information as the DPP might require. During 1979 the DPP, after consultation with the Attorney-General, wrote to all Chief Constables stating that in respect of forfeiture proceedings involving articles of no conceivable literary merit no reporting of the case to the DPP was necessary. This would save much administrative work in meritless cases. Cases that should still be reported are:

'Cases involving obscene exhibitions or publications in respect of which (a) a criminal charge including conspiracy (whether under s.2 of the Obscene Publications Act 1959, any other statute or at common law), as opposed to forfeiture proceedings under s.3 of the 1959 Act, is contemplated; or

(b) the issue of obscenity or the defence of public good may be raised in forfeiture proceedings by a reputable seller, keeper or publisher; or

(c) where an application for forfeiture under s.3 of the 1959 Act has been made against a seller or keeper but the publisher wishes to intervene and seek a jury trial.'

(Change of practice noted in (1979) 143 JPN 513).

6. The time limit on prosecutions contained in the 1959 Act, s.2(3) protects those who 'publish' or 'have for publication' rather than secondary parties who aid and abet such 'publication', e.g. authors, cameramen, actors. Time runs from the 'publication' or 'having for publication' rather than from the, perhaps much earlier, date of the secondary party's contribution to that eventual 'having' or 'publication'. See G. Robertson, *Obscenity* (1979) at pp. 74–6 quoting from transcript of Court of Appeal judgment in *R v Barton* [1976] Crim LR 514. The Court of Appeal suggested that a person will not be regarded as having aided or abetted publication if he 'disassociated' himself from such publication but did not give guidance as to what conduct would amount to such a 'disassociation'.

7. In *R v Anderson* [1972] 1 QB 304, CA, Lord Widgery CJ made the following comments about penalties for breach of the 1959 Act: ' . . . Mr Mortimer [counsel for the appellants] has drawn our attention to the fact, which is undoubtedly true, that prison sentences for offences of obscenity have been very rare in the past. What the reason for this is is something on which we do not wish to speculate, but it is true that to send a man to prison for offences in this classification has been a relatively unusual thing in the past. However, those of us who sit regularly in this court are only too familiar with the fact that, when a particular offence becomes prevalent and a wave of it appears, the only course which can be taken is to increase the sentences in order to adjust for the increase in the incidence of the offence. That is one of our responsibilities which we must exercise to the best of our ability. We would therefore like to make it quite clear in general terms that any idea that an offence of obscenity does not merit a prison sentence should be eradicated . . . '

The appellants, the editors and publishers of '*Oz No. 28 School Kids Issue*' had been convicted of offences under s.2 of the 1959 Act and s.11 of the Post Office Act 1953 (see below, p. 234). The jury had acquitted them of charges of conspiracy to corrupt public morals by conspiring to produce a magazine with intent to debauch and corrupt the morals of young persons and children. Prison sentences had been imposed on the editors by the trial judge. On appeal the convictions under the 1959 Act were quashed because of misdirection on the meaning of obscenity. The convictions under the Post Office Act 1953 and the sentences of six months imprisonment, suspended for two years, were upheld.

8. In the *Handyside* case, Eur Court HR, Series A, Vol 24, Judgment of 7 December 1976, the applicant was the publisher of *The Little Red Schoolbook*. The book, which was aimed at children, had chapters on education, learning, teachers, pupils and 'the system'. The chapter on pupils had subsections on masturbation, intercourse, homosexuality and abortion. The applicant was convicted under the Obscene Publications Acts of having in his possession obscene articles for gain. The European Court of Human Rights held, by 13 votes to 1, that the conviction was not a breach of the freedom of speech guarantee in Article 10, ECHR. It could be justified as being for 'the protection of morals' (Article 10(2)).

(ii) The definition of 'obscene'

Obscene Publications Act 1959

1. Test of Obscenity
(1) For the purposes of this Act an article shall be deemed to be obscene if its effect or (where the article comprises two or more distinct items) the effect of any one of its items is, if taken as a whole, such as to tend to deprave and corrupt persons who are likely, having regard to all relevant circumstances, to read, see or hear the matter contained or embodied in it.
(2) In this Act 'article' means any description of article containing or embodying matter to be read or looked at or both, any sound record, and any film or other record of a picture or pictures.

2. Prohibition of publication of obscene matter
(6) In any proceedings against a person under this section the question whether an article is obscene shall be determined without regard to any publication by another person unless it could reasonably have been expected that the publication by the other person would follow from publication by the person charged.

Obscene Publications Act 1964

1. Obscene articles intended for publication for gain
(3) In proceedings brought against a person under the said section 2[14] for having an obscene article for publication for gain the following provisions shall apply in place of subsections (5) and (6) of that section, that is to say,—
   (a) [See below, p. 231]
   (b) the question whether the article is obscene shall be determined by reference to such publication for gain of the article as in the circumstances it may reasonably be inferred he had in contemplation and to any further publication that could reasonably be expected to follow from it, but not to any other publication.

NOTES

1. The Obscene Publications Act 1964, s.2(1) extends the meaning of 'article' as defined in s.1(2) of the 1959 Act. It provides:

'The Obscene Publications Act 1959 (as amended by this Act), shall apply in relation to anything which is intended to be used, either alone or as one of a set, for the reproduction or manufacture therefrom of articles containing or embodying matter to be read, looked at or listened to, as if it were an article containing or embodying that matter so far as that matter is to be derived from it or from the set.'

---

14. I.e. Obscene Publications Act 1959, s.2.

Whether or not such an article is obscene is to be determined in accordance with the Obscene Publications Act 1964, s.2(2) which provides:

'For the purposes of the Obscene Publications Act 1959 (as so amended), an article shall be deemed to be had or kept for publication if it is had or kept for the reproduction or manufacture therefrom of articles for publication; and the question whether an article so had or kept is obscene shall—

(a) for the purposes of section 2 of the Act be determined in accordance with section 1(3)(b) above as if any reference to publication of them were a reference to publication of articles reproduced or manufactured from it; and

(b) for purposes of section 3 of the Act be determined on the assumption that articles reproduced or manufactured from it would be published in any manner likely having regard to the circumstances in which it was found, but in no other manner.'

(For the Obscene Publications Act 1959, s.3, see below, p. 227).

2. In *Director of Public Prosecutions v Whyte* [1972] AC 849 HL at 860, Lord Wilberforce, commenting on the statutory test of obscenity, said:

'. . . the Act has adopted a relative conception of obscenity. An article cannot be considered obscene in itself: it can only be so in relation to its likely readers. . . . in every case, the magistrates, or the jury are called upon to ascertain who are likely readers and then to consider whether the article is likely to deprave and corrupt them.'

An example of the application of the test was given by Lord Pearson at 864:

'The question whether an article is obscene depends not only on its inherent character but also on what is being or is to be done with it. Suppose that there is a serious book on *Psychopathia Sexualis* designed to be read only by medical men or scientists concerned with such matters, and that it is kept in the library of a hospital or university and so far as possible reserved for use by such medical men or scientists. Such a book should not be regarded as obscene for the purpose of the Act, because it is not likely to come (though possibly it might come) into the hands of anyone who might be corrupted by it.'

Lord Simon commented at 867

'The intention of the Act was . . . to enable serious literary, artistic, scientific or scholarly work to draw on the amplitude of human experience without fear of allegation that it could conceivably have a harmful effect on persons other than those to whom it was in truth directed . . .'

The defence raised in *Whyte*, which the Magistrates had accepted, was that by virtue of a policy of excluding young persons from the defendant's bookshop, the likely purchasers of the pornographic books were males of middle age and upwards described by the magistrates as 'inadequate, pathetic, dirty-minded men . . . addicts to this type of material, whose morals were already in a state of depravity and corruption'. Since this likely audience was no longer open to immoral influence (being already corrupt and depraved) the articles could not be considered obscene within the meaning of the 1959 Act. The prosecutor appealed to the House of Lords. The majority held that the facts as found by the Magistrates were sufficient to constitute the offence charged. The minority (Lords Simon and Salmon) held that the Magistrates' conclusions on the facts could not be interfered with, as it had not been shown that they lacked any evidential basis. Their Lordships were generally agreed that the Act covered more than cases of once and for all corruption. Lord Wilberforce explained at 863:

'. . . the Act's purpose is to prevent the depraving and corrupting of men's minds by certain types of writing: it could never have been intended to except from the legislative protection a large body of citizens merely because, in different degrees, they had previously been exposed, or exposed themselves, to the "obscene" material. The Act is not merely concerned with the once for all corruption of the wholly innocent; it equally protects the less innocent from, further corruption, the addict from feeding or increasing his addiction.'

Lord Simon said at 867:

'. . . a defence is available not merely that the likely expose is too aesthetic, too scientific or too scholarly to be likely of corruption by the particular matter in question, but also that he is too corrupt to be further corrupted by it. I would, however, express my concurrence with the view . . . that the language of the statute is apt to extend to the maintenance of a state of corruption which might otherwise be escaped, and . . . that a person can be re-corrupted . . .'

Lord Salmon at 876 commented . . . there was no finding that these dirty minded old men were other than depraved and corrupted long before they became customers of the respondents, nor that what they found there made them any worse than they already were or kept them in a state of depravity or corruption from which they might otherwise have escaped.'

3. The courts have deprecated judicial attempts to explain to juries the meaning of the terms 'corrupt and deprave'. See, for example, Salmon LJ in *R v Calder and Boyars Ltd* [1969] 1 QB 151 at 168 referring to 'attempts to improve upon or re-define' the statutory formula. In general the matter should be left at large for the jury. However judges have stressed the seriousness of the terms. For example, in *Knuller v Director of Public Prosecutions* [1973] AC 435 HL at 456 Lord Reid commented that one may 'lead persons morally astray without depraving and corrupting them.' On the other hand, in *Director of Public Prosecutions v Whyte* [1972] AC 849 the House of Lords stressed that the formula covered moral or spiritual corruption and depravity not manifesting itself in corrupt and depraved conduct. If an article produces in the mind of its audience thoughts which a magistrate or jury, as the case may be, regards as having corrupted and depraved the audience's minds, the article is obscene.

4. A consequence of defining obscenity in terms of tendency to deprave and corrupt is that the concept is not confined to sexual matters. In *John Calder (Publications) Ltd v Powell* [1965] 1 QB 509, DC, Lord Parker CJ said at 515:

'In my judgment it is perfectly plain that depravity, and, indeed, obscenity (because obscenity is treated as a tendency to deprave) is quite apt to cover what was suggested by the prosecution in this case. This book – the less said about it the better – concerned the life, or imaginary life, of a junkie in New York, and the suggestion of the prosecution was that the book high-lighted the favourable effects of drug-taking and, so far from condemning it, advocated it, and that there was a real danger that those into whose hands the book came might be tempted at any rate to experiment with drugs and get the favourable sensations high-lighted by the book.

In my judgment there is no reason whatever to confine obscenity and depravity to sex, and there was ample evidence upon which the justices could hold that this book was obscene.'

What other matter might be regarded as having a tendency to deprave and corrupt? Violence? See *Director of Public Prosecutions v A and BC Chewing Gum Ltd* [1968] 1 QB 159, DC.

5. Some guidance has been given by the courts as to what proportion of an article's audience a magistrate or jury need regard as being susceptible to an article's corrupting and depraving effect for the article to be obscene. In *R v Calder and Boyars Ltd* [1969] 1 QB 151 Salmon LJ said at 168: 'the jury should have been directed to consider whether the effect of the book was to tend to deprave and corrupt a significant proportion of those persons likely to read it. What is a significant proportion is a matter entirely for the jury to decide.' Earlier he had said that the term 'persons' in s.1 of the 1959 Act 'clearly . . . cannot mean all persons, nor can it mean any one person, for there are individuals who may be corrupted by almost anything. On the other hand, it is difficult to construe "persons" as meaning the majority of persons or the average reader . . .' Salmon LJ's formulae were approved by the House of Lords in *Director of Public Prosecutions v Whyte* [1972] AC 849, Lord Cross explaining that 'a significant proportion of a class means a part which is not numerically negligible but which may be much less than half' and Lord Pearson stating that 'if a seller of pornographic books has a large number of customers who are not likely to be corrupted by such books, he does not thereby acquire a licence to expose for sale or sell such books to a small number of customers who are likely to be corrupted by them.'

6. A defence sometimes raised is that an article does not deprave and corrupt its audience if it so revolts them that it averts them from the sort of conduct it depicts. In *R v Calder and Boyars Ltd* [1969] 1 QB 151, CA, Salmon LJ said at 168:

> The defence . . . was that the book . . . gave a graphic description of the depths of depravity and degradation in which life was lived in Brooklyn. This description was compassionate and condemnatory. The only effect that it would produce in any but a minute lunatic fringe of readers would be horror, revulsion and pity; it was admittedly and intentionally disgusting, shocking and outrageous; it made the reader share in the horror it described and thereby so disgusted, shocked and outraged him that, being aware of the truth, he would do what he could to eradicate those evils and the conditions of modern society which so callously allowed them to exist. In short, according to the defence, instead of tending to encourage anyone to homosexuality, drug-taking or senseless, brutal violence, it would have precisely the reverse effect. Unfortunately, whilst the judge told the jury in general terms that it was not enough for the Crown to prove merely that the book tended to horrify, shock, disgust or nauseate, he never put a word of the specific defence to the jury when he summed up on the issue of obscenity.
>
> This is a serious defect in the summing-up . . . With a book such as this, in which words appear on almost every page and many incidents are described in graphic detail which, in the ordinary, colloquial sense of the word, anyone would rightly describe as obscene, it is perhaps of particular importance to explain to the jury what the defendants allege to be the true effect of those words and descriptions within their context in the book.'

In *R v Anderson* [1972] 1 QB 304, CA, Lord Widgery CJ said at 314:

> '. . . the defence . . . said this material in the magazine was not likely to deprave or corrupt; that it may shock is accepted, but it is not likely to cause people to act in a depraved or corrupted fashion. One of the arguments advanced in support of that line of defence was that many of the illustrations in the magazine were so grossly lewd and unpleasant that they would shock in the first instance and then would tend to repel. In other words, it was said that they had an aversive effect and that far from tempting those who had not experienced the acts to take part in them, they would put off those who might be tempted so to conduct themselves. The argument which Mr Mortimer [counsel for the defendant] put forward on this point is that the trial judge never really got over to the jury this argument of aversion, . . . Strangely enough the same situation arose in the earlier decision in this court . . . *R v Calder and Boyars Ltd* . . . was in fact a then well-publicised criminal trial dealing with the book *Last Exit to Brooklyn* and Mr Mortimer appeared for the defence, and in this court Mr Mortimer argued, and this court held rightly argued, that the failure of the judge to put what one might call the aversion argument was fatal to the retention of the conviction.'

7. Section 1(1) of the 1959 Act requires that an article be considered as a whole in estimating its effect on its likely audience. This contrasts with the position prior to 1959 in trials for obscene libel when prosecutors might read 'purple passages' in isolation from their context to juries. Note the effect, however, of s.1(1) of the 1959 Act on articles comprising more than one item. In *R v Anderson* [1972] 1 QB 304, CA, Lord Widgery CJ said at 312:

> '. . . At the trial the prosecution accepted the proposition that in deciding whether the offences under the Act of 1959 had been made out, it was right for the jury to consider the magazine as a whole and not to look at individual items in isolation. That was a proposition accepted by the prosecution . . . largely in fairness to the defence, and, being accepted by both parties, it was a proposition which was accepted by the judge as well. It certainly did the defence no harm; it was much to their interests; but in the judgment of this court it was entirely wrong. It is in our view quite clear from section 1 that where you have an article such as this comprising a number of distinct items, the proper view of obscenity under section 1 is to apply the test to the individual items in question. It is equally clear that if, when so

applied, the test shows one item to be obscene that is enough to make the whole article obscene.

Now that may seem unfair at first reading, but it is the law in our judgment without any question. A novelist who writes a complete novel and who cannot cut out particular passages without destroying the theme of the novel is entitled to have his work judged as a whole, but a magazine publisher who has a far wider discretion as to what he will, and will not, insert by way of items is to be judged under the Act on what we call the "item by item" basis. This was not done in this case. Our main concern in mentioning the point now is to ensure that it will be done in future . . .'

8. The courts have refused to permit expert evidence as to the effect that an article may have on its likely audience. The matter is one for the jury to assess without expert guidance (cf. the use of expert testimony under s.4 of the 1959 Act, see below, p. 229). In *R v Anderson* [1972] 1 QB 304, CA, Lord Widgery CJ said at 313:

'. . . a majority of the expert evidence called by the defence in this case . . . was . . . directed to showing that the article was not obscene. In other words, it was directed to showing that in the opinion of the witness it would not tend to deprave or corrupt. Now whether the article is obscene or not is a question exclusively in the hands of the jury, and it was decided in this court in *R v Calder and Boyars Ltd* [1969] 1 QB 151 that expert evidence should not be admitted on the issue of obscene or no. It is perfectly true that there was an earlier Divisional Court case in which a somewhat different view had been taken. It was *Director of Public Prosecutions v A and BC Chewing Gum Ltd* [1968] 1 QB 159. That case in our judgment should be regarded as highly exceptional and confined to its own circumstances, namely, a case where the alleged obscene matter was directed at very young children, and was of itself of a somewhat unusual kind. In the ordinary run of the mill cases in the future the issue "obscene or no" must be tried by the jury without the assistance of expert evidence on that issue, and we draw attention to the failure to observe that rule in this case in order that that failure may not occur again.

We are not oblivious of the fact that some people, perhaps many people, will think a jury, unassisted by experts, a very unsatisfactory tribunal to decide such a matter. Those who feel like that must campaign elsewhere for a change of the law. We can only deal with the law as it stands, and that is how it stands on this point.'

In *Director of Public Prosecutions v Jordan* [1977] AC 699, HL, Viscount Dilhorne expressed some doubt about the correctness of the *Chewing Gum* case and felt the exception certainly should not be extended. Lord Wilberforce stated the alleged exception to the general rule and commented, at 718: 'we are not obliged to validate, or otherwise this exception or to define its scope, because the evidence was not directed to showing that the class of likely readers consisted of, or as to a significant number included, sexual abnormals or deviants. The case was one of normal readers, and was to be judged by the jury in relation to them, and, since normal readers were in question here, [expert] evidence . . . was inadmissible at the stage when section 1 was being considered.'

9. For summaries of research into the effect of the portrayal of sex and violence in the various media see S. Brody, *Screen Violence and Film Censorship* – Home Office Research Study No. 40 (1977); E. Wistrich, *I Don't Mind the Sex it's the Violence – Film Censorship Explored* (1978) pp. 45–47, 83–89, 96–101; R. Dhavan and C. Davies (eds.) *Censorship and Obscenity* (1978), pp. 111–182; Belson, *Television Violence and the Adolescent Boy* (1978). Report of the Williams *Committee on Obscenity and Film Censorship* (1979) Cmnd. 7772 Chapter 6 and para. 10.8 (burden of proving harm caused by pornography fairly clearly not discharged).

(iii) The definition of 'publication'

Obscene Publications Act 1959

1 (3) For the purposes of this Act a person publishes an article who –
(a) distributes, circulates, sells, lets on hire, gives, or lends it, or who offers it for sale or for letting on hire; or
(b) in the case of an article containing or embodying matter to be looked at or a record, shows, plays or projects it:
Provided that paragraph (b) of this subsection shall not apply to anything done in the course of [. . . . .][15] television or sound broadcasting.

NOTE

As originally enacted the 1959 Act excluded from the definition of 'publication' within s.1(3)(b) 'anything done in the course of a cinematograph exhibition . . . other than one excluded from the Cinematograph Act 1909' by s.7(4) of that Act (above, p. 202). In other words, the 1959 Act only applied to exhibitions taking place in a private dwelling-house to which the public were not admitted. A separation had been intended between exhibitions subject to local authority licensing control and exhibitions not subject to licensing control in respect of which the 1959 Act would apply. However, excluded from either control were the 'exempted exhibitions' within the Cinematograph Act 1952, s.5(1) (above, p. 203). These included exhibitions to which the public were not admitted, including those of commercial film clubs. See further Zellick [1971] Crim LR 126.

Since the 1959 Act did not apply to licensed or exempted exhibitions the bars it would have imposed on the charging of common law offences did not prevent prosecutions of cinema proprietors for indecent exhibition or keeping disorderly houses. In 1975, for example, a licensed cinema proprietor was convicted of these offences for showing a film ('More about the Language of Love') notwithstanding that the film had been granted a GLC licence (*R v Jacey (London) Ltd* (unreported)).

The Law Commission (*Report No. 76 Conspiracy and Criminal Law Reform*) recommended that the 1959 Act apply to all cinematograph exhibitions and the Criminal Law Act 1977, s.53(1) achieves this result by repealing in part the proviso to the 1959 Act, s.1(3)(b). Note also the new s.2(4A) added by the 1977 Act, s.53(3) (above, p. 219).

(iv) Forfeiture of obscene articles

Obscene Publications Act 1959

3. Powers of search and seizure
(1) If a justice of the peace is satisfied by information on oath that there is reasonable ground for suspecting that, in any premises in the petty sessions area for which he acts, or on any stall or vehicle in that area, being premises or a stall or vehicle specified in the information, obscene articles are, or are from time to time, kept for publication for gain, the justice may issue a warrant under his hand empowering any constable to enter (if need be by force) and search the premises, or to search the stall or vehicle, within fourteen days from the date of the warrant, and to seize and remove any articles found therein or thereon which the constable has reason to believe to be obscene articles and to be kept for publication for gain.
(2) A warrant issued under the foregoing subsection shall, if any obscene articles are seized under the warrant, also empower the seizure and removal of any documents found in the

---

15. Repealed by the Criminal Law Act 1977 s.53.

premises or, as the case may be, on the stall or vehicle which relate to a trade or business carried on at the premises or from the stall or vehicle.

(3) [Subject to subsection (3A) of this section][16] any articles seized under subsection (1) of this section shall be brought before a justice of the peace acting for the same petty sessions area as the justice who issued the warrant, and the justice before whom the articles are brought may thereupon issue a summons to the occupier of the premises or, as the case may be, the user of the stall or vehicle to appear on a day specified in the summons before a magistrates' court for that petty sessions area to show cause why the articles or any of them should not be forfeited; and if the court is satisfied, as respects any of the articles, that at the time when they were seized they were obscene articles kept for publication for gain, the court shall order those articles to be forfeited:

Provided that if the person summoned does not appear, the court shall not make an order unless service of the summons is proved.

Provided also that this subsection does not apply in relation to any article seized under subsection (1) of this section which is returned to the occupier of the premises or, as the case may be, the user of the stall or vehicle in or on which it was found[17].

Obscene Publications Act 1964

1. Obscene articles intended for publication for gain

(4) Where articles are seized under section 3 of the Obscene Publications Act 1959 . . . and a person is convicted under section 2 of that Act of having them for publication for gain, the court on his conviction shall order the forfeiture of those articles: . . . .

Obscene Publications Act 1959

3. Powers of search and seizure

(3A)[18] Without prejudice to the duty of a court to make an order for the forfeiture of an article where section 1 (4) of the Obscene Publications Act 1964 applies (orders made on conviction), in a case where by virtue of subsection (3A) of section 2 of this Act proceedings under the said section 2 for having an article for publication for gain could not be instituted except by or with the consent of the Director of Public Prosecutions, no order for the forfeiture of the article shall be made under this section unless the warrant under which the article was seized was issued on an information laid by or on behalf of the Director of Public Prosecutions.

(4) In addition to the person summoned, any other person being the owner, author or maker of any of the articles brought before the court, or any other person through whose hands they had passed before being seized, shall be entitled to appear before the court on the day specified in the summons to show cause why they should not be forfeited.

(5) Where an order is made under this section for the forfeiture of any articles, any person who appeared, or was entitled to appear, to show the cause against the making of the order may appeal to [the Crown Court][19]; . . . .

(6) If as respects any articles brought before it the court does not order forfeiture, the court may if it thinks fit order the person on whose information the warrant for the seizure of the articles was issued to pay such costs as the court thinks reasonable to any person who has appeared before the court to show cause why those articles should not be forfeited; and costs ordered to be paid under this subsection shall be enforceable as a civil debt.

(7) For the purposes of this section the question whether an article is obscene shall be determined on the assumption that copies of it would be published in any manner likely having regard to the circumstances in which it was found, but in no other manner.

(8) The Obscene Publications Act 1857, is hereby repealed, ...

NOTES

1. The Criminal Justice Act 1967, s. 25 provides that a warrant under s. 3 may not be issued except on an information laid by or on behalf of the DPP

---

16. Words in square brackets added by the Criminal Law Act 1977, s.53.
17. Second proviso to s.3(3) added by the Criminal Law Act 1977, s.65 and Sch.12.
18. S.3(3A) added by the Criminal Law Act 1977, s.53.
19. Words in brackets substituted by the Courts Act, 1971 s.56, Sch.9.

or by a constable. This restriction followed the successful private forfeiture proceedings, in 1966, against *Last Exit to Brooklyn*. These proceedings forced the hand of the DPP to reverse his original decision not to prosecute the publishers under s. 2. See further *R v Calder and Boyars Ltd* [1969] 1 QB 151, CA.

2. For criticism of the way in which magistrates operate the burden of proof under s. 3 see G. Robertson, *Obscenity* (1979) pp. 93–100.

3. The provision in s. 3(4) of the 1959 Act granting rights to appear to interested parties other than the occupier of the premises searched was regarded as an important new provision in the 1959 Act. The opportunity it provides to authors etc. to defend their work is somewhat diminished by the absence of any procedure for making such interested persons aware of the existence of the forfeiture proceedings. Much depends on press publicity of the seizure or the actions of the person from whom the articles were seized in contacting such other interested parties.

4. Prior to the 1959 Act a practice had developed whereby the police, having discovered articles which they and the DPP considered obscene, would persuade the occupier of the premises to sign a form disclaiming any interest in the articles. The police would then destroy the articles and no court proceedings would take place. This practice was disapproved by the 1957 *Parliamentary Select Committee on Obscene Publications* (1957–58 HC 123–1). S. 3(3) of the 1959 Act (as amended) requires articles seized to be returned to the occupier or brought before the magistrates. See also the adverse comments of the court of Appeal concerning the 'disclaimer' practice in *R v MetropolitanPolice Comr, ex parte Blackburn, No. 3* [1973] QB 241 at 252–254.

5. It sometimes appears that there are differences between the attitudes of magistrates and juries in their application of the test of obscenity. For example, comment was aroused when magistrates at Watford ordered forfeiture of an edition of the magazine *Men Only* at about the time that an Old Bailey jury acquitted the editors of *Nasty Tales* of the offence under s. 2 (see (1973) 137 JPN 82). Note also the jury acquittal of the publishers of *Inside Linda Lovelace* in 1976 and comment at (1976) 126 NLJ 126.

(v) Defence of 'public good'

Obscene Publications Act 1959

4. Defence of Public Good

(1) [Subject to subsection (1A) of this section][20] a person shall not be convicted of an offence against section two of this Act, and an order for forfeiture shall not be made under the foregoing section, if it is proved that publication of the article in question is justified as being for the public good on the ground that it is in the interests of science, literature, art or learning, or of other objects of general concern.

(1A)[1] Subsection (1) of this section shall not apply where the article in question is a moving picture film or soundtrack, but –
    (a) a person shall not be convicted of an offence against section 2 of this Act in relation to any such film or soundtrack, and
    (b) an order for forfeiture of any such film or soundtrack shall not be made under section 3 of this Act,
if it is proved that publication of the film or soundtrack is justified as being for the public good on the ground that it is in the interests of drama, opera, ballet or any other art, or of literature or learning.

---

20. Words in square brackets added by the Criminal Law Act 1977, s.53.

1. S.4(1A) added by the Criminal Law Act 1977, s.53.

(2) It is hereby declared that the opinion of experts as to the literary, artistic, scientific or other merits of an article may be admitted in any proceedings under this Act either to establish or to negative the said ground.

(3)[2] In this section 'moving picture soundtrack' means any sound record designed for playing with a moving picture film, whether incorporated with the film or not.

NOTES

1. S. 4 provides that the publication of an article which, taken as a whole, is regarded by a magistrate or a jury as having a tendency to corrupt and deprave its likely audience may nevertheless be found to be justified as being for the public good as furthering certain objects or ends. Expert evidence may be presented as to the merit (or lack of merit) of the articles though the ultimate question whether such merit justifies the adverse effect of the articles is one for the court or jury and not a matter for expert opinion. In *R v Calder and Boyars Ltd* [1969] 1 QB 151, CA, Salmon LJ explained at 171:

> . . . In the view of this court, the proper direction on a defence under section 4 in a case such as the present is that the jury must consider on the one hand the number of readers they believe would tend to be depraved and corrupted by the book, the strength of the tendency to deprave and corrupt, and the nature of the depravity or corruption; on the other hand, they should assess the strength of the literary, sociological or ethical merit which they consider the book to possess. They should then weigh up all these factors and decide whether on balance the publication is proved to be justified as being for the public good. A book may be worthless; a book may have slight but real merit; it may be a work of genius. Between those extremes the gradations are almost infinite. A book may tend to deprave and corrupt a significant but comparatively small number of its readers or a large number or indeed the majority of its readers. The tendency to deprave and corrupt may be strong or slight. The depravity and corruption may also take various forms. It may be to induce erotic desires of a heterosexual kind or to promote homosexuality or other sexual perversions or drug-taking or brutal violence. All these are matters for the jury to consider and weigh up; it is for them to decide in the light of the importance they attach to these factors whether or not the publication is for the public good. The jury must set the standards of what is acceptable, of what is for the public good in the age in which we live . . .

2. In *Director of Public Prosecutions v Jordan* [1977] AC 699, HL, the defence sought to argue that the publication of the articles in question, which they admitted to be 'hard pornography', was justified in that the articles had 'some psychotherapeutic value for various categories of persons of heterosexual taste unable to achieve satisfactory heterosexual relationships, for persons of deviant sexuality, and for homosexuals and other perverts . . . providing . . . approprite material to relieve their sexual tensions by way of sexual fantasy and masturbation'. Also 'that such release was beneficial to such persons and would act as a safety valve to save them from psychological disorders and . . . divert them from anti-social and possibly criminal activities directed at others'. The House of Lords rejected this argument. Lord Wilberforce said at 718:

> '. . . Whatever the exact meaning of the expressions used in section 4 may be, one thing is apparent. The section is dealing with a different range, or dimension, of considerations from that with which section 1 is concerned. . . . It assumes that, apart from what section 4 itself may do, that issue would be resolved in favour of "deprave and corrupt" and having assumed that, it allows a contention to be made and evidence to be given that publication of the material is, on specified grounds, for the public good.
>
> Each of its subsections provides guidance as to the conception of public good which is in mind. Subsection (1) provides a list which one may suspect (from the long title) started with "literature" and was expanded to include science, art and learning and still further to include

---

2. S.4(3) added by the Criminal Law Act 1977, s.53.

"other objects of general concern." The latter phrase is no doubt a mobile phrase; it may, and should, change in content as society changes. But . . . even if this is not strictly a case for applying a rule of eiusdem generis (the genus being one of intellectual or aesthetic values), the structure of the section makes it clear that the other objects, or, which is the same argument, the nature of the general concern, fall within the same area, and cannot fall in the totally different area of effect on sexual behaviour and attitudes, which is covered in section 1. In other words it introduces a new type of equation—possibly between incommensurables—between immediate and direct effect on people's conduct or character (section 1) and inherent impersonal values of a less transient character assumed, optimistically perhaps, to be of general concern (section 4). . . . The judgment to be reached under section 4(1), and the evidence to be given under section 4(2), must be in order to show that publication should be permitted in spite of obscenity—not to negative obscenity. Section 4 has been diverted from its proper purpose, and indeed abused, when it has been used to enable evidence to be given that pornographic material may be for the public good as being therapeutic to some of the public. I respectfully agree with the observations to this effect of Lord Denning MR and of Phillimore and Roskill LJJ in *R v Metropolitian Police Comr Ex parte Blackburn (No 3)* [1973] QB 241 and I consider that such cases as *R v Gold* (unreported), 3 November, 1972, Central Criminal Court (see [1973] QB 241 at 250) took a wrong turning. Indeed, I have the impression that if those cases are right the more "obscene" an article, the more likely it would be that the appellant's defence would apply to it. To produce such a result would in my opinion involve a total alteration in the Act. . . . '

3. In *A–G's Reference (No. 3 of 1977)* [1978] 3 All ER 1166, CA, the respondents had been allowed to produce at their trial expert witnesses as to the merit of the magazines, which they had sold, in providing information to their readers about sexual matters. They had contended, successfully before the trial judge, that his sex-education role of the magazines brought them within the term 'learning' in s. 4(1). On appeal, Lord Widgery CJ, giving the judgement of the court, said, at 1169: '. . . it seems to us that the fundamental question is whether "learning" in this context is a noun, in which case . . . it must mean the product of scholarship. The only possible meaning of "learning" as a noun . . . would have been something whose inherent excellence is gained by the work of the scholar. I would reject at once the idea that "learning" in this context is a verb.' Accordingly, since 'learning' could not be equated with 'teaching' or 'education' the trial judge had been wrong in allowing the expert testimony.

(vi) Ignorance as to nature of article

Obscene Publications Act 1959

2. Prohibition of obscene matter
(5) A person shall not be convicted of an offence against this section if he proves that he had not examined the article in respect of which he is charged and had no reasonable cause to suspect that it was such that his publication of it would make him liable to be convicted of an offence against this section

Obscene Publications Act 1964

1. Obscene articles intended for publication for gain
(3) In proceedings brought against a person under the said section 2[3] for having an obscene article for publication for gain the following provisions shall apply in place of subsections (5) and (6) of that section, that is to say –
  (a) he shall not be convicted of that offence if he proves that he had not examined the article and had no reasonable cause to suspect that it was such that his having it would make him liable to be convicted of an offence against that section; and
  (b) [above, p. 222]

---

3. Obscene Publications Act 1959, s.2.

(b) THEATRES ACT 1968

Theatres Act 1968

2. Prohibition of presentation of obscene performances of plays
(1) For the purpose of this section a performance of a play shall be deemed to be obscene if, taken as a whole, its effect was such as to tend to deprave and corrupt persons who were likely, having regard to all the circumstances, to attend it.
(2) Subject to sections 3 and 7 of this Act, if an obscene performance of a play is given, whether in public or private, any person who (whether for gain or not) presented or directed that performance shall be liable –
    (a) on summary conviction, to a fine not exceeding [£1000] or to imprisonment for a term not exceeding six months;
    (b) on conviction on indictment, to a fine or to imprisonment for a term not exceeding three years, or both.
(3) A prosecution on indictment for an offence under this section shall not be commenced more than two years after the commission of the offence.
(4) No person shall be proceeded against in respect of a performance of a play or anything said or done in the course of such a performance –
    (a) for an offence at common law where it is of the essence of the offence that the performance or, as the case may be, what was said or done was obscene, indecent, offensive, disgusting or injurious to morality; or
    (b) for an offence under section 4 of the Vagrancy Act 1824 consisting of wilfully exposing to public view an indecent exhibition, ...
    (c) [*Omitted*]
and no person shall be proceeded against for an offence at common law of conspiring to corrupt public morals, or to do any act contrary to public morals or decency, in respect of an agreement to present or give a performance of a play, or to cause anything to be said or done in the course of such a performance.

3. Defence of public good
(1) A person shall not be convicted of an offence under section 2 of this Act if it is proved that the giving of the performance in question was justified as being for the public good on the ground that it was in the interests of drama, opera, ballet or any other art, or of literature or learning.
(2) It is hereby declared that the opinion of experts as to the artistic, literary or other merits of a performance of a play may be admitted in any proceedings for an offence under section 2 of this Act either to establish or negative the said ground.

5. Incitement to racial hatred by means of public performance of a play
(1) Subject to section 7 of this Act, if there is given a public performance of a play involving the use of threatening, abusive or insulting words, any person who (whether for gain or not) presented or directed that performance shall be guilty of an offence under this section if—
    (*a*) he did so with intent to stir up hatred against any section of the public in Great Britain distinguished by colour, race or ethnic or national origins; and
    (*b*) that performance, taken as a whole, is likely to stir up hatred against that section on grounds of colour, race or ethnic or national origins.
(2) A person guilty of an offence under this section shall be liable—
    (*a*) on summary conviction, to a fine not exceeding [£ 1000] or to imprisonment for a term not exceeding six months, or both;
    (*b*) on conviction on indictment, to a fine or to imprisonment for a term not exceeding two years, or both.

6. Provocation of breach of peace by means of public performance of a play
(1) Subject to section 7 of this Act, if there is given a public performance of a play involving the use of threatening, abusive or insulting words or behaviour, any person who (whether for gain or not) presented or directed that performance shall be guilty of an offence under this section if—
    (*a*) he did so with intent to provoke a breach of the peace; or
    (*b*) the performance, taken as a whole, was likely to occasion a breach of the peace.
(2) A person guilty of an offence under this section shall be liable—
[on summary conviction to a fine not exceeding £1000 or to imprisonment for a term not exceeding 6 months or to both].

7. Exceptions for performances given in certain circumstances
(1) Nothing in sections 2 to 4 of this Act shall apply in relation to a performance of a play given on a domestic occasion in a private dwelling.
(2) Nothing in sections 2 to 6 of this Act shall apply in relation to a performance of a play given solely or primarily for one or more of the following purposes, that is to say—
    (*a*) rehearsal; or
    (*b*) to enable—
        (i) a record or cinematograph film to be made from or by means of the performance; or
        (ii) the performance to be broadcast; or
        (iii) the performance to be transmitted to subscribers to a diffusion service;
but in any proceedings for an offence under section 2, 5 or 6 of this Act alleged to have been committed in respect of a performance of a play or an offence at common law alleged to have been committed in England and Wales by the publication of defamatory matter in the course of a performance of a play, if it is proved that the performance was attended by persons other than persons directly connected with the giving of the performance or the doing in relation thereto of any of the things mentioned in paragraph (*b*) above, the performance shall be taken not to have been given solely or primarily for one or more of the said purposes unless the contrary is shown.
(3) In this section—
    'broadcast' means broadcast by wireless telegraphy (within the meaning of the Wireless Telegraphy Act 1949), whether by way of sound broadcasting or television;
    'cinematograph film' means any print, negative, tape or other article on which a performance of a play or any part of such a performance is recorded for the purposes of visual reproduction;
    'record' means any record or similar contrivance for reproducing sound, including the sound-track of a cinematograph film;

8. Restriction on institution of proceedings
Proceedings for an offence under section 2, 5 or 6 of this Act or an offence at common law committed by the publication of defamatory matter in the course of a performance of a play shall not be instituted in England and Wales except by or with the consent of the Attorney-General.

18. Interpretation
(1) In this Act . . .
'play' means—
    (*a*) any dramatic piece, whether involving improvisation or not, which is given wholly or in part by one or more persons actually present and performing and in which the whole or a major proportion of what is done by the person or persons performing, whether by way of speech, singing or acting, involves the playing of a role; and
    (*b*) any ballet given wholly or in part by one or more persons actually present and performing, whether or not it falls within paragraph (*a*) of this definition;
'premises' includes any place;
'public performance' includes any performance in a public place within the meaning of the Public Order Act 1936 and any performance which the public or any section thereof are permitted to attend, whether on payment or otherwise;
(2) For the purposes of this Act—
    (*a*) a person shall not be treated as presenting a performance of a play by reason only of his taking part therein as a performer;
    (*b*) a person taking part as a performer in a performance of a play directed by another person shall be treated as a person who directed the performance if without reasonable excuse he performs otherwise than in accordance with that person's direction; and
    (*c*) a person shall be taken to have directed a performance of a play given under his direction notwithstanding that he was not present during the performance;
and a person shall be not be treated as aiding or abetting the commission of an offence under section 2, 5 or 6 of this Act in respect of a performance of a play by reason only of his taking part in that performance as a performer.

NOTES

1. The maximum fines were raised to the levels shown by the Criminal Law Act 1977, ss. 15, 16(4), 28(2)(7), 30, 32 and Sch. 1.

2. For the prosecution of indecent performances not coming within the terms of the 1968 Act see Stone (1977) 127 NLJ 452

(c) OFFENCES INVOLVING INDECENCY

Post Office Act 1953

11. Prohibition on sending by post of certain articles
(1) A person shall not send or attempt to send or procure to be sent a postal packet which–
(a) . . . . or
(b) encloses any indecent or obscene print, painting, photograph, lithograph, engraving, cinematograph film, book, card or written communication, or any indecent or obscene article whether similar to the above or not; or
(c) has on the packet, or on the cover thereof, any words, marks or designs which are grossly offensive or of an indecent or obscene character.
(2) If any person acts in contravention of the foregoing subsection, he shall be liable on summary conviction to a fine not exceeding [£1000] or on conviction on indictment to imprisonment for a term not exceeding twelve months.

NOTES

1. The maximum fine on summary conviction was raised to £1000 by the Criminal Law Act 1977, ss. 16(4), 28(2)(7). A fine may be imposed on conviction on indictment (Powers of Criminal Courts Act 1973, s.30).
2. The meaning of the words 'indecent or obscene' was considered in *R v Stanley* [1965] 2 QB 327, CCA. Lord Parker CJ explained, at 333:

' . . . The words "indecent or obscene" convey one idea, namely, offending against the recognised standards of propriety, indecent being at the lower end of the scale and obscene at the upper end of the scale . . . As it seems to this court, an indecent article is not necessarily obscene, whereas an obscene article almost certainly must be indecent . . .'

Lord Parker also quoted with approval the following passage from Lord Sands' judgment in *McGowan v Langmuir* 1931 JC 10:

'I do not think that the two words "indecent" and "obscene" are synonymous. The one may shade into the other, but there is a difference of meaning. It is easier to illustrate than define, and I illustrate thus. For a male bather to enter the water nude in the presence of ladies would be indecent, but it would not necessarily be obscene. But if he directed the attention of a lady to a certain member of his body his conduct would certainly be obscene . . .'

In *R v Anderson* [1972] 1 QB 304, CA, it was held to have been no misdirection on the charge under the Post Office Act 1953 for the trial judge to have directed the jury to consider whether the material was 'repulsive', 'filthy', 'loathsome' or 'lewd'.
In assessing 'indecency' under this section the courts have refused to look beyond the intrinsic qualities of the material itself to consider the circumstances of its distribution – e.g. to consider its effect on its recipient. See *Kosmos Publications v Director of Public Prosecutions* [1975] Crim LR 345, DC. Such effect would be crucial to a charge under the Obscene Publications Act 1959, s. 2.

Customs Consolidation Act 1876

42. Prohibitions and restrictions
The goods enumerated and described in the following table of prohibitions and restrictions inwards are hereby prohibited to be imported or brought into the United Kingdom, save as thereby excepted . . .

Goods prohibited to be imported

Indecent or obscene prints, paintings, photographs, books, cards, lithographic or other engravings, or any other indecent or obscene articles.

Customs and Excise Management Act 1979

49. Forfeiture of goods improperly imported
(1) Where–
    (a) . . . .
    (b) any goods are imported, landed or unloaded contrary to any prohibition or restriction for the time being in force with respect thereto under or by virtue of any enactment; or
    (c) . . . .
those goods shall, ... be liable to forfeiture.

SCHEDULE 3

Provisions Relating to Forfeiture

Notice of seizure
1.—(1) The Commissioners shall, except as provided in sub-paragraph (2) below, give notice of the seizure of any thing as liable to forfeiture and of the grounds therefor to any person who to their knowledge was at the time of the seizure the owner or one of the owners thereof.
    (2) Notice need not be given under this paragraph if the seizure was made in the presence of—
    (*a*) the person whose offence or suspected offence occasioned the seizure; or
    (*b*) the owner or any of the owners of the thing seized or any servant or agent of his; or
    (*c*) in the case of any thing seized in any ship or aircraft, the master or commander.

Notice of claim
3. Any person claiming that any thing seized as liable to forfeiture is not so liable shall, within one month of the date of the notice of seizure or, where no such notice has been served on him, within one month of the date of the seizure, give notice of his claim in writing to the Commissioners at any office of customs and excise.

Condemnation
5. If on the expiration of the relevant period under paragraph 3 above for the giving of notice of claim in respect of any thing no such notice has been given to the Commissioners . . . the thing in question shall be deemed to have been duly condemned as forfeited.
6. Where notice of claim in respect of any thing is duly given in accordance with paragraphs 3 and 4 above, the Commissioners shall take proceedings for the condemnation of that thing by the court, and if the court finds that the thing was at the time of seizure liable to forfeiture the court shall condemn it as forfeited.

NOTES

1. In *Henn and Darby v Director of Public Prosecutions* [1980] 2 WLR 597, ECJ and HL, the ECJ held that although s.42 constitutes a quantitive restriction on imports contrary to Art. 30, EEC Treaty such a measure may be justified under Art. 36 (permitting prohibitions or restrictions on grounds, inter alia, of public morality or public policy but not as a means of arbitrary discrimination or a disguised restriction on trade between member states). The ECJ stated:

'. . . it is permissible to conclude, on a comprehensive view, that there is no lawful trade in [indecent although not obscene] goods in the United Kingdom. A prohibition on imports which may in certain respects be more strict than some of the laws applied within the United Kingdom cannot therefore be regarded as amounting to a measure designed to give some indirect protection to some national product . . . '.

2. Note that a directive issued by the Customs Department in 1978 instructs officers to ignore the importation by individuals of small quantities of

single copies of prohibited material if imported purely for personal use. See
G. Robertson, *Obscenity* (1979) p. 194.
3. For offences relating to breach of s. 42 see the Customs and Excise
Management Act 1979, ss. 50 and 170. Note also the provisions of the 1979
Act, s. 154(2) as to the burden of proof in proceedings relating to customs
and excise.

Vagrancy Act 1824

Persons committing certain offences shall be deemed rogues and vagabonds . . ..
4. . . . . every person wilfully exposing to view, in any street, road, highway, or public place,
any obscene print, picture, or other indecent exhibition; . . . . shall be deemed a rogue and
vagabond, within the true intent and meaning of this Act; . . ..

NOTES

1. For penalties for being found 'a rogue and vagabond' see above, p. 50.
2. By s. 2 of the Vagrancy Act 1838, ' . . . Every person who shall wilfully
expose or cause to be exposed to public view in the window or other part of
any shop or other building situate in any street, road, highway, or public
place, any obscene print, picture, or other indecent exhibition, shall be
deemed to have wilfully exposed' the obscene matter to public view within
the intent and meaning of the Vagrancy Act 1824. The Home Office
Working Paper on Vagrancy and Street Offences (1974) pointed to some
uncertainty as to the scope of the 1838 Act provisions:

' . . . The 1824 Act appears to be confined to streets and open spaces. The 1838 Act
extended the offence to material in, or visible from, shops or buildings in public places if it
was exposed to public view. Does this extend to material exposed inside a building and not
visible from the street? Does it make any difference whether the public have paid or
admission or not? There has been a conviction under these provisions in respect of material
in an art gallery although the "place" point was not argued. An attempt to institute
proceedings in respect of the public showing of a film in a commercial cinema however, has
been rejected. There has been no authoritative pronouncement on the scope of these
provisions by a higher court' (para. 134).

The *Working Paper* favoured repeal and replacement with provisions
which would limit offences of this sort to:

'displays which force themselves on the attention of the public, but not those which persons
have in some sense "volunteered" to see, e.g. by entering premises on payment which is for
the display. This principle brings in the interior of certain buildings; for example we think it
should be possible to deal with the mischief of children in a sweet shop being faced with a row
of "adult" magazines' (para. 135).

This was endorsed in the Working Party's Report (1976).

Town Police Clauses Act 1847

28. Every person who in any street, to the obstruction, annoyance, or danger of the residents
or passengers, commits any of the following offences, shall be liable to a penalty not exceeding
twenty pounds for each offence, or, in the discretion of the justice before whom he is convicted,
may be committed to prison, there to remain for a period not exceeding fourteen days;
and . . . . any constable shall take into custody, without warrant, and forthwith convey
before a justice, any person who within his view commits any such offence; . . .
Every person who publicly offers for sale or distribution, or exhibits to public view any
profane, indecent, or obscene book, paper, print, drawing, painting, or represention, or sings
any profane or obscene song or ballad, or uses any profane or obscene language.

NOTE

The maximum penalty on summary conviction was raised to the level shown by the Criminal Justice Act 1967, s.92 (1) and Sch. 3 Part I.

Metropolitan Police Act 1839

54. Penalty on persons committing in thoroughfares the offences herein mentioned
. . . . Every person shall be liable to a penalty not more than twenty pounds who, within the limits of the metropolitan police district, shall in any thoroughfare or public place, commit any of the following offences; (that is to say,) . . . .
12. Every person who shall sell or distribute or offer for sale or distribution, or exhibit to public view, any profane, indecent, or obscene book, paper, print, drawing, painting or representation, or sing any profane, indecent, or obscene song or ballad, or write or draw any indecent or obscene word, figure, or representation, or use any profane indecent or obscene language to the annoyance of the inhabitants or passengers: . . . .
And it shall be lawful for any constable belonging to the metropolitan police force to take into custody, without warrant, any person who shall commit any such offence within view of any such constable.

NOTE

The maximum penalty was raised to the level shown by the Criminal Justice Act 1967, s. 92 (1) and Sch. 3 Part I.

Indecent Advertisements Act 1889

3. Summary proceedings against persons affixing, etc., indecent or obscene pictures or printed or written matter
Whoever affixes to or inscribes on any house, building, wall, hoarding, gate, fence, pillar, post, board, tree, or any other thing whatsoever so as to be visible to a person being in or passing along any street, public highway, or footpath, and whoever affixes to or inscribes on any public urinal, or delivers or attempts to deliver, or exhibits, to any inhabitant or to any person being in or passing along any street, public highway, or footpath, or throws down the area of any house, or exhibits to public view in the window of any house or shop, any picture or printed or written matter which is of an indecent or obscene nature, shall, on summary conviction . . ., be liable to a penalty not exceeding twenty pounds; or, in the discretion of the Court, to imprisonment for any term not exceeding one month . . .

4. Summary proceedings against persons sending others to do the acts punishable under s. 3
Whoever gives or delivers to any other person any such pictures, or printed or written matter mentioned in section three of this Act, with the intent that the same, or some one or more thereof, should be affixed, inscribed, delivered, or exhibited as therein mentioned, shall, on conviction in manner provided by the Summary Jurisdiction Acts, be liable to a penalty not exceeding fifty pounds, or, in the discretion of the Court, to imprisonment for any term not exceeding three months . . .

5. Certain advertisements declared indecent
Any advertisement relating to syphillis, gonorrhoea, nervous debility, or other complaint or infirmity arising from or relating to sexual intercourse, shall be deemed to be printed or written matter of an indecent nature within the meaning of section three of this Act, if such advertisement is affixed to or inscribed on any house, building, wall, hoarding, gate, fence, pillar, post, board, tree, or other thing whatsoever, so as to be visible to a person being in or passing along any street, public highway, or footpath, or is affixed to or inscribed on any public urinal, or is delivered or attempted to be delivered to any person being in or passing along any street, public highway, or footpath.
Provided that this section shall not apply to advertisements affixed or inscribed as aforesaid by reason of their relating to any venereal disease, if they are so affixed or inscribed for a local or public authority or for a person publishing them with the sanction of the Secretary of State.

NOTES

1. The maximum fine under s. 3 was raised to £20, and that under s. 4 to £50 by the Criminal Justice Act 1967, s.92 (1)(a), Sch. 3 Part I. The proviso to s. 5 was added by Indecent Advertisements (Amendment) Act 1970, s.1. **2.** Note also the Venereal Disease Act 1917, s. 2 prohibiting advertisements or offers to treat or offer advice in connection with treatment of VD. Here also a proviso excludes advertisements etc. by public authorities or made with the sanction of the Secretary of State. See further G. Robertson, *Obscenity* (1979) pp. 202–3.

3. At various times in recent years private members' bills designed to impose further curbs on indecent displays (e.g. in newsagents' shops, cinema entrances, outside striptease clubs) have been introduced into Parliament. A bill introduced in 1973 received all-party support but during committee stage the defects of its drafting became apparent. In particular there was uncertainty as to the scope of the term 'indecent' used in the bill. The bill lapsed with the 1974 election and was not re-introduced in the following session. A bill, in almost identical terms, was introduced by a Conservative MP, Mr Hugh Rossi in 1978, and was given an unopposed second reading. This bill also lapsed with the election of May 1979. See further G. Robertson, *Obscenity* (1979) pp. 203–4.

Protection of Children Act 1978

1. Indecent photographs of children
(1) It is an offence for a person—
  (*a*) to take, or permit to be taken, any indecent photograph of a child (meaning in this Act a person under the age of 16); or
  (*b*) to distribute or show such indecent photographs; or
  (*c*) to have in his possession such indecent photographs, with a view to their being distributed or shown by himself or others; or
  (*d*) to publish or cause to be published any advertisement likely to be understood as conveying that the advertiser distributes or shows such indecent photographs, or intends to do so.
(2) For purposes of this Act, a person is to be regarded as distributing an indecent photograph if he parts with possession of it to, or exposes or offers it for acquisition by, another person.
(3) Proceedings for an offence under this Act shall not instituted except by or with the consent of the Director of Public Prosecutions.
(4) Where a person is charged with an offence under subsection (1) (*b*) or (*c*), it shall be a defence for him to prove—
  (*a*) that he had a legitimate reason for distributing or showing the photographs or (as the case may be) having them in his possession; or
  (*b*) that he had not himself seen the photographs and did not know, nor had any cause to suspect, them to be indecent. . . .

2. Evidence . . .
(3) In proceedings under this Act a person is to be taken as having been a child at any material time if it appears from the evidence as a whole that he was then under the age of 16.

6. Punishments
(1) Offences under this Act shall be punishable either on conviction on indictment or on summary conviction.
(2) A person convicted on indictment of any offence under this Act shall be liable to imprisonment for a term of not more than three years, or to a fine or to both.
(3) A person convicted summarily of any offence under this Act shall be liable—
  (*a*) to imprisonment for a term not exceeding six months; or
  (*b*) to a fine not exceeding the prescribed sum for the purposes of section 28 of the Criminal Law Act 1977 (punishment on summary conviction of offences triable either way: £1,000 or other sum substituted by order under that Act), or to both.

7. Interpretation
(1) The following subsections apply for the interpretation of this Act.
(2) References to an indecent photograph include an indecent film, a copy of an indecent photograph or film, and an indecent photograph comprised in a film.
(3) Photographs (including those comprised in a film) shall, if they show children and are indecent, be treated for all purposes of this Act as indecent photographs of children.
(4) References to a photograph include the negative as well as the positive version.
(5) 'Film' includes any form of video-recording.

NOTES

1. Sections 4 and 5 of this Act provide powers of entry, search, seizure and forfeiture in terms substantially similar to the provisions of the Obscene Publications Act 1959, s. 3, above, p. 227.
2. See further the annotation of this Act by M. D. A. Freeman in *Current Law Statutes Annotated.*

(d) REFORM

Report of the Committee on Obscenity and Film Censorship, Chairman: Bernard Williams, (Cmnd. 7772 1979)

13.4 We propose that:

GENERAL

1. The existing variety of laws in this field should scrapped and a comprehensive new statute should start afresh.
2. Terms such as 'obscene', 'indecent' and 'deprave and corrupt' should be abandoned as having outlived their usefulness.
3. The law should rest partly on the basis of harms caused by or involved in the existence of the material: these alone can justify prohibitions; and partly on the basis of the public's legitimate interest in not being offended by the display and availability of the material: this can justify no more than the imposition of restrictions designed to protect the ordinary citizen from unreasonable offence.
4. The principal object of the law should be to prevent certain kinds of material causing offence to reasonable people or being made available to young people.
5. Only a small class of material should be forbidden to those who want it, because an objective assessment of likely harm does not support a wider prohibition.
6. The printed word should be neither restricted nor prohibited since its nature makes it neither immediately offensive nor capable of involving the harms we identify, and because of its importance in conveying ideas.

RESTRICTION

7. Restrictions should apply to matter (other than the printed word) and to a performance whose unrestricted availability is offensive to reasonable people by reason of the manner in which it portrays, deals with or relates to violence, cruelty or horror, or sexual, faecal or urinary functions or genital organs.
8. Restriction is to consist in a ban
 (i) on the display, sale, hire etc. of restricted material other than by way of postal or other delivery and
 (ii) on the presentation of any restricted performance
other than in premises (or a part of premises having a separate access from the street)
  (a) to which persons under the age of eighteen are not admitted, and
  (b) to which access is possible only by passing a prominent warning notice in specified terms, and
  (c) which make no display visible to persons not passing beyond the warning notice, other than the name of the business and an indication of its nature.
9. No material or performance should be exempt from these restrictions on the ground of any intrinsic merit it might possess.

10. It should be an offence to display, sell, hire etc. any restricted matter or to present a restricted performance in contravention of the restrictions laid down.

11. This offence should not apply to the showing of films, for which we propose separate controls. [See above, p. 205.]

12. It should be an offence to send or deliver restricted material, or advertisements for such material, to

(a) a person whom the sender knew or ought reasonably to have known was under the age of eighteen, or

(b) a person whom the sender knew or ought reasonably to have known had not solicited the material.

13. It should not be an offence for a person under the age of eighteen to seek to gain entry to premises in which restricted material is being displayed, sold or hired or in which a restricted performance is being presented, or to order restricted material to be sent to him or her.

14. It should not be freely open to any individual to institute proceedings for the criminal offences proposed above; prosecutions should be brought by the police or by or with the consent of the Director of Public Prosecutions.

15. Restriction offences should be triable only by magistrates and punishable by fines of up to £1,000 and imprisonment of up to six months.

16. The police should have power to obtain a magistrate's warrant to enter and search premises for material which they believe is being displayed, sold or hired in contravention of the restrictions, and to seize such material as may be needed for the purposes of evidence.

17. A magistrates' court convicting an offender for a restriction offence should have power to order, if it thinks fit, that seized material should be forfeited.

18. There should be no separate procedure aimed at the forfeiture of restricted material divorced from criminal proceedings against an alleged offender.

PROHIBITION

19. Prohibited material should consist of photographs and films whose production appears to the court to have involved the exploitation for sexual purposes of any person where either

(a) that person appears from the evidence as a whole to have been at the relevant time under the age of sixteen, or

(b) the material gives reason to believe that actual physical harm was inflicted on that person.

20. It should be an offence to take any prohibited photograph or film, to distribute or show it, to have it with a view to its being distributed or shown, or to advertise it as being available for distribution or showing.

21. No proceedings in respect of this offence should lie in relation to any film exhibited under the authority of a film censorship certificate.

22. Prohibited material should be included in the list of goods prohibited from importation, and imports contravening the prohibition should be dealt with according to the normal customs procedures for prohibited imports, save for certain exceptions relating to films.

23. Prohibited material should be included among articles prohibited from transmission through the post but there should be an additional prohibition as regards overseas mail on articles of which the importation and circulation is prohibited in the country of destination.

24. A live performance should be prohibited if

(a) it involves actual sexual activity of a kind which, in the circumstances in which it was given, would be offensive to reasonable people (sexual activity including the act of masturbation and forms of genital, anal or oral connection between humans and animals as well as between humans), or

(b) it involves the sexual exploitation of any person under the age of sixteen.

25. It should be an offence to present, organise or take part in a performance which contravenes the prohibition.

26. The law should not be so framed as to apply to what is performed in a private house so long as no person under eighteen is present and no charge is made.

27. The law on live performances should not apply to what is performed solely for the purposes of being filmed or photographed where the resulting material would not be liable to prohibition.

28. No material or performance should be exempt from the prohibition on the grounds of any intrinsic merit it might possess.

29. No proceedings should be instituted in respect of a prohibition offence other than by or with the consent of the Director of Public Prosecutions.

30. Prohibition offences should be triable either in the Crown Court or in a magistrates' court, with a maximum term of three years' imprisonment and an unlimited fine on conviction in the Crown Court.

31. The police should have power to obtain a magistrate's warrant to enter and search premises and seize what they believe to be prohibited material kept in circumstances in which they believe an offence is being committed.

32. The court convicting a person of an offence involving prohibited material shall order that any material seized which is in their view prohibited material shall be forfeited.

33. There should be no separate procedure aimed at the forfeiture of prohibited material divorced from criminal proceedings against an alleged offender.

CHAPTER 5

Freedom of expression: contempt of court

1 Introduction

It is obvious that the administration of justice must be preserved free from improper interference and obstruction, and more or less inevitable that the courts will play a significant part in securing that end. There are a number of substantive criminal offences relating to the administration of justice, for example, perjury, subornation, (i.e. inducing a witness to commit perjury), embracery (i.e. attempting to corrupt or improperly to influence a jury), perversion or obstruction of the course of public justice, and impeding the prosecution of a person who has committed an arrestable offence, contrary to section 4(1) of the Criminal Law Act 1967. These offences have recently been under consideration by the Law Commission, who have proposed the creation or retention of over 20 specific offences in order to bring more certainty into this area of the law (see *Law Commission Report No. 96 on Offences relating to Interference with the Course of Justice* (1979).

Superimposed upon these criminal offences is the power of the superior courts to punish contempts. The contempt power is of wide and uncertain scope, and in the United Kingdom is exercised according to a summary procedure unknown to any other branch of the law. Trial on indictment is a theoretical possibility, but proceedings are today invariably conducted summarily. The summary procedure is of doubtful historical origin (see *R v Almon* (1765) Wilm. 243; Sir John Fox *Contempt of Court* (1927); Frankfurter and Landis, 37 Harv LR 1010, 1046 ff.). However, it is now too late to argue that the courts may not punish contempts summarily, given that many judges of high authority have acted on the then unchallenged assumption that they could (see *James v Robinson* (1963) 109 CLR 593; Frankfurter J in *Green v United States* 356 US 165 at 189 (1958)).

Classification of contempt is not easy. A basic distinction is drawn in England (although not in Scotland) between 'civil' and 'criminal' contempts. The former are cases of disobedience to an order of a court made in civil proceedings such as an injunction, the object of such contempt proceedings being essentially coercive. The latter are cases of interference with the administration of justice, and the aims of the proceedings are punitive and deterrent. There are some minor differences between the two forms, the most significant being that in civil contempt, committals can be *sine die*, until the contempt is purged. In criminal contempts, committals can only be for fixed terms.

Criminal contempts may be grouped under five headings (see *Borrie and Lowe*): (1) Publications prejudicial to a fair criminal trial; (2) publications prejudicial to fair civil proceedings; (3) scandalising the court; (4) contempt in the face of the court; and (5) acts which interfere with the course of justice. The materials given here concentrate on the first three aspects, as these tend to impinge most on freedom of expression, and the fourth, as this generates problems of natural justice. The general principles underlying the law of contempt are discussed in *A-G v Times Newspapers Ltd* [1974] AC 273, the first contempt case to reach the House of Lords (see below, p. 256, in the section on publications prejudicial to civil proceedings).

The contempt power gives rise to concern on a number of points. Firstly, there is uncertainty as to its scope, which is undesirable given the heavy punishments that may be imposed. Secondly, it may inhibit unduly freedom of expression. Thirdly, the summary process may lack the qualities of procedural fairness thought essential for orthodox criminal proceedings. These considerations have led the Phillimore Committee on Contempt of Court (1974: Cmnd. 5794) to recommend that conduct *intended* to pervert the course of justice should be dealt with as a criminal offence unless there are compelling reasons requiring it to be dealt with as a matter of urgency by means of summary contempt procedures. Where there is no such intention, then the law of contempt should apply, but on a much narrower basis than at present. Accordingly, strict liability should only attach to publications (and no other kinds of conduct) which create a risk of serious prejudice to the course of justice and which are addressed to the public at large during the currency of proceedings. The relevant time limits should be more narrowly drawn than the present sub judice period. 'Scandalising the court' should no longer be punished as contempt, but as a criminal offence. Contempt in the face of the court should where appropriate be dealt with as a criminal offence, and where dealt with summarily there should be additional procedural safeguards for the defendant. The distinctions between 'civil' and 'criminal' contempt should be abolished. These proposals have not yet been implemented. In a Green Paper issued in 1978 the Government indicated that on a number of points the Phillimore proposals for reducing the scope of contempt might be regarded as too radical (Cmnd. 7145) A Bill is to be placed before Parliament in 1980/1.

In the United States of America, the contempt power has been much more narrowly defined by comparison with the British position. The Supreme Court has applied the Constitution's First Amendment guarantees of freedom of speech and of the press strictly against exercises of the contempt power. In *Bridges v California; Times-Mirror v California* 314 US 252 (1941), the Court held by 5–4 that utterances can only be punished as contempt where there is a clear and present danger to the orderly and fair administration of justice in relation to pending litigation: 'The substantive evil must be extremely serious and the degree of imminence extremely high before utterances can be punished' (per Black J at p. 263). A 'reasonable tendency' is not sufficient. Subsequent cases have shown that the law of contempt is virtually a dead letter in protecting the trial process from prejudicial comment (see below, p. 251). In addition, the constitutional right to jury trial in serious criminal cases (Fifth, Sixth and Fourteenth Amendments) has been held applicable to contempt cases (*Bloom v Illinois* 391 US 194 (1968); *Miller* pp. 45–47). In federal courts, the summary contempt power is limited by statute (18 US Code, Section 401, as derived originally from an Act of 1831) to: '(1) Misbehaviour of any person in its presence or so near thereto as to obstruct the administration of justice;

(2) Misbehaviour of any of its officers in their official transactions; (3) Disobedience or resistance to its lawful writ, process, order, rule, decree, or command.' The words 'so near thereto' have been held by the Supreme Court to bear a geographical rather than a causative meaning (*Nye v United States* 313 US 33 (1941)). Some states have similar legislation narrowing the scope of the contempt power.

The main works cited in this chapter are: *Abraham*: H. J. Abraham, *Freedom and the Court*, (3rd edn. 1977); *Borrie and Lowe*: G. Borrie and N. Lowe, *The Law of Contempt*, (1973); *Dobbs*: D. B. Dobbs, 'Contempt of Court: A Survey', (1971) 56 Cornell LR 183; *Goldfarb*: R. L. Goldfarb, *The Contempt Power* (1963); *Miller*: C. J. Miller, *Contempt of Court* (1976); *Phillimore*: *Report of the Committee on Contempt of Court* (1974) Cmnd. 5794; *Smith and Hogan*: J. C. Smith and B. Hogan, *Criminal Law* (4th edn. 1978). In addition, see: Zelman Cowen, *Individual Liberty and the Law*, Chapters 6 and 7 (1977); Zelman Cowen, *Sir John Latham and other papers*, Chapter 2 (1965); *Contempt of Court: A Discussion Paper* (1978) Cmnd. 7145; A.L. Goodhart, (1935) 48 Harv LR 885; B. Harris, *The Courts, the Press and the Public* (1976); A. E. Hughes, (1900) 16 LQR 292; M. Jones, *Justice and Journalism* (1974) Justice Report on Contempt of Court (1959); Justice Report on Law and the Press (1965) pp. 5–17; H. J. Laski, (1928) 41 Harv LR 1031; Law Reform Commission of Canada Working Paper No. 21: Contempt of Court (1977); M. Lippman and T. Weber, [1978] 2 Crim LJ 198; Oswald, *Contempt of Court* (3rd edn., 1910); H. Street, *Freedom, the Individual and the Law*, (4th edn., 1977) pp. 166–187.

2 Publications prejudicial to a fair criminal trial

The main area where uncertainties in the law of contempt cast a shadow over free expression is that of publications which tend to prejudice the fair trial of either criminal or civil proceedings, or otherwise interfere with the course of justice. The important criticisms made to the Phillimore Committee were (1) 'the lack of clear definition of the kind of statement, criticism or comment which will be held to amount to contempt' (para. 83) and (2) 'the uncertainty as to the time when the law of contempt applies' (para. 84). The balance between freedom of expression and the right to a fair trial is different in the UK and the United States, and there are important sectors of opinion in each country which express dissatisfaction with their country's own position.

(a) WHAT CONSTITUTES CONTEMPT?

R v Evening Standard Co Ltd [1954] 1 QB 578, [1954] 1 All ER 1026, [1954] 2 WLR 861, Queen's Bench Divisional Court

On 23 February 1954, a prisoner was indicted at Chelmsford Assizes for the murder of his wife, who had been dead for a considerable time before his arrest and whose body was discovered in a trunk which the prisoner had caused to be moved with his effects. Part of the case for the Crown was that the prisoner had told many lies with regard to the disappearance of his wife. A Miss Briggs gave evidence that the prisoner had told her that he was unmarried, and a Mrs Darmody said that he had told her that he had been married but that his wife had died. That evening, the *Evening Standard* carried a report of the trial under the headline 'Trunk Trial Story of Marriage Offer – Husband is Accused', which stated that Mrs Darmody 'said at the assizes here that a man accused of murdering his wife asked her to marry him.'

In fact, Mrs Darmody had not given that evidence. Miss Briggs had given evidence before the examining justices that the prisoner had, after the death of his wife, asked her to marry him; but at the trial, when Miss Briggs had just begun to give evidence the judge ruled, after a discussion in the absence of the jury, that that part of her evidence should not be given as it was highly prejudicial to the prisoner; and no such evidence was given at the trial.

The reporter at the trial was responsible for the error – he had attended the committal proceedings, and had left the trial during the discussion as to the admissibility of part of Miss Briggs' evidence, returning just after she had completed her evidence. In fact the jury found the prisoner not guilty.

The Attorney-General applied for leave to issue a writ of attachment against the Evening Standard Co Ltd, the editor of the *Evening Standard* and the reporter.

According to an affidavit filed by the editor the reporter had for 10 years been a trusted reporter on the staff of the newspaper and had previously reported many trials without any complaint as to the accuracy of his reports, and had proved himself a thoroughly competent and reliable reporter. He had thought the report perfectly accurate and genuine and he and the proprietors had published it in good faith.

Lord Goddard CJ delivered the judgement of the court (**Lord Goddard CJ**, **Hilbery** and **Hallett JJ**): . . .

This is surely a proper matter to bring before this court. It is just as well that the nature of the jurisdiction which this court exercises on these occasions with regard to reports of trials in newspapers should be understood. It is called contempt of court, and that is a convenient expression because it is akin to a contempt. But the essence of the jurisdiction is that reports, if they contain comments on cases before they are tried, or alleged histories of the prisoner who is on trial—such as in the case of the *Daily Mirror* (*R v Bolam, ex parte Haigh* (1949) 93 Sol Jo 220), in which this court had to intervene about five years ago—and all misreports are matters which tend to interfere with the due course of justice. The foundation of the jurisdiction is that such reports are an interference with the due course of justice, and one of the earliest cases, if not the earliest, in which this jurisdiction was invoked was in 1742, in a case known as *The St. James's Evening Post* ((1742) 2 Atk 469) before that great judge, Lord Hardwicke LC. In that case there was a motion to commit an editor for publishing a libel upon a litigant and it was objected that it was not a matter for the summary jurisdiction of the court because there was a remedy at law for libel. Lord Hardwicke pointed out that he was dealing with the matter of the publication of a libel upon a litigant in a case which had not then come to a conclusion or been heard. He started his judgment by saying (ibid.): 'Nothing is more incumbent upon courts of justice, than to preserve their proceedings from being misrepresented;'—that is, of course, what has happened here—'nor is there any thing of more pernicious consequence, than to prejudice the minds of the public against persons concerned as parties in causes, before the cause is finally heard.' After rejecting the argument that he could not deal summarily with the case because there was a remedy at law, he considered the different sorts of contempt. The last one was (ibid. p. 471): 'There may be also a contempt of this court, in prejudicing mankind against persons before the cause is heard. There cannot be any thing of greater consequence, than to keep the streams of justice clear and pure, that parties may proceed with safety both to themselves and their characters.' . . .

We have said, perhaps more frequently in recent years, that the summary jurisdiction of this court should only be invoked and will only be exercised in cases of real and serious moment; and have deprecated in certain cases a motion to attach where there has not really been a serious interference with justice. This case might have been a disastrous interference with justice; but, as Lord Hewart CJ said in *R v Editor of the New Statesman, ex parte Director of Public Prosecutions* (1928) 44 TLR 301 at 303 the gravity of the penalty or sanction which the court will impose must depend upon the circumstances of each particular case. If a comment is gratiuitiously published either in a newspaper or in any other form of public dissemination, this court would not hesitate to impose a severe penalty, and even, as in the recent case of the *Daily Mirror* (*R v Bolam ex parte Haigh* (1949) 93 Sol Jo 220) to inflict the penalty of imprisonment. In this case, however, I am glad to be able to come to the conclusion that there was here no intentional interference with the course of justice. I cannot believe that the reporter for a moment deliberately or intentionally sent out false information. He, as a responsible journalist, would know that doing so would land him in the gravest possible difficulty. Nor can one attach moral blame, if I may use that expression, to the editor, who had no reason to suppose that a reporter of the 'Standard' had sent him information in an inaccurate form. There are, therefore, mitigating circumstances, and one can only be thankful that the matter did not react unfavourably on the prisoner, though, as I have said whether it reacts favourably or unfavourably upon the prisoner is not the test.

Sir Hartley Shawcross said that, while his clients desired to abide by the well understood rule of journalism that the editor and proprietors of papers must in a case such as this take responsibility, he would suggest to the court that vicarious liability, as it is called, ought not in law to be visited upon them and that they ought not to be made vicariously liable for the mistake or misconduct of the reporter. I do not think that we can possibly agree with that submission, which seems contrary to what Lord Russell and Wright J said in *R v Payne* [1896] 1 QB 577 where they pointed out that the court would interfere where the publication was intended or calculated or likely to interfere with the course of justice. Wright J (ibid. p. 582) used the word 'likely,' Lord Russell (ibid. 580) used the word 'calculated'.

[The court held that all the defendants were guilty of contempt, but that no penalty should be imposed on the editor and reporter. The publishers were fined £1,000.]

R v Savundranayagan and Walker [1968] 1 WLR 1761, [1968] 3 All ER 439, 52 Cr App Rep 637, Court of Appeal (Criminal Division)

The appellants, S and W, were directors of an insurance company [the Fire, Auto and Marine Insurance Co Ltd]. In July 1966, considerable press coverage was given to the company's affairs, the disappearance of S and his unsavoury record. In February 1967, S was interviewed on television [by David Frost] when he was questioned about his own record and the company's affairs. In January 1968, the appellants were tried and subsequently convicted of, inter alia, conspiring to defraud policy holders of the company by fraudulently applying for their own benefit the proceeds of premiums paid. S appealed against conviction on the ground, inter alia, that he did not have a fair trail because the jury's minds might have been affected by attacks made upon him in the press, on television and in books which purported to prejudge issues which were subsequently before the jury . . .

The judgment of the court (**Salmon LJ, Geoffrey Lane** and **Fisher JJ**) was delivered by **Salmon LJ**: . . . [I]n July of 1966 a press campaign of considerable magnitude was mounted in relation to the parlous state of FAMIC's affairs, the disappearance of Savundra and his past unsavoury record. At that stage there was nothing to suggest that criminal proceedings were even in contemplation. There is accordingly no question of contempt of court. When an insurance company fails and its policy holders are left stranded, this is undoubtedly a matter of public interest and indeed public concern. When, in such circumstances, the moving figure in the company is a man with an unsavoury record who appears to have used large sums of the company's money for his own purposes and disappeared abroad, the matter becomes a public scandal. There is no doubt that a free press has the right, and indeed the duty, to comment on such topics so as to bring them to the attention of the public. It is in the public interest that this should be done. Indeed it is sometimes largely because of facts discovered and brought to light by the press that criminals are brought to justice. The private individual is adequately protected by the law of libel should defamatory statements published about him be untrue or if any defamatory comment made about him is unfair. This court does not consider that any real complaint can be made about the press campaign in July 1966, 18 months before the trial.

The court, however, takes a very different view of the television programme of February 1967, in which Savundra was interviewed shortly after his return to England. At this time it must surely have been obvious to everyone that he was about to be arrested and tried on charges of gross fraud. It must not be supposed that proceedings to commit for contempt of court can be instituted only in respect of matters published after proceedings have actually begun. No one should imagine that he is safe from committal for contempt of court if, knowing or having good reason to believe that criminal proceedings are imminent, he chooses to publish matters calculated to prejudice a fair trial. On any view the television interview with Savundra was deplorable. With no experience of television he was faced with a skilled interviewer whose clear object was to establish his guilt before an audience of millions of people. None of the ordinary safeguards for fairness that exist in a court of law were observed, no doubt because they were not understood. They may seem prosaic to those engaged in the entertainment business but they are the rocks upon which freedom from oppression and tyranny have been established in this country for centuries—as one well-known journalist subsequently pointed out in an evening paper. On the other hand, surprisingly and regrettably, virtually the whole interview was reproduced verbatim in one of the Sunday newspapers. This court hopes that no interview of this kind will ever again be televised. The court has no doubt that the television authorities and all those producing and appearing in televised programmes are conscious of their public responsibility and now also of the peril in which they all stand if any such interview were ever to be televised in the future. Trial by television is not to be tolerated in a civilised society.

On the facts of this case, however, it seems to the court, regrettable though this interview undoubtedly was, it affords no ground for quashing Savundra's conviction. In the first place Savundra voluntarily went to the television interview when he must have strongly suspected that he was about to be arrested and eventually tried. He should have had a fair idea of what was in store for him at the interview, but in his self-confidence or conceit he thought that he could get the better of the interviewer. It hardly lies in his mouth to complain. Secondly, in the event, the trial did not take place until 11 months after the interview. The evidence lasted for close on 40 days and the judge gave a strong warning, both at the beginning of the trial and in his summing up, that the jury must pay attention only to the evidence and not take any notice of anything they may have heard or read or seen out of court. This court is quite satisfied that, in the particular circumstances of this case, there was no real risk that the jury was influenced by the pre-trial publicity. Also, perhaps, most importantly, the case for the Crown was so overwhelming that no jury could conceivably have returned any different verdicts against Savundra. . . .
Appeal dismissed.

NOTES

1. Note that the Divisional Court is not concerned with the actual effect upon proceedings, but the potential effect, particularly on a jury. The following are some examples of contempt:

(i) Prejudging the merits of a case

R v Bolam, ex parte Haigh (1949) 93 Sol Jo 220. B, the editor of the *Daily Mirror*, was imprisoned for three months, and the proprietors were fined £10,000 for describing Haigh as a 'vampire' and, after saying that he was charged with one murder, stating that he had committed others, giving the names of the victims (cf. *R v Odham's Press, ex parte A-G* [1957] 1 QB 73).

In the 1920s, various newspapers conducted systematic 'criminal investigations' whose results were then published. This led to fines of £1,000 imposed on the *Evening Standard*, and of £300 on two other newspapers, with a warning that repetition of the offence would lead to imprisonment (*R v Evening Standard, ex parte Director of Public Prosecutions* (1924) 40 TLR 833).

In the *Sunday Times* case, below p. 256, the House of Lords held that prejudgement of the merits amounted to a contempt of court. The facts concerned civil proceedings, but a distinction between civil and criminal proceedings was not drawn for this purpose. However, in recent cases the Divisional Court has held that prejudgment will only amount to contempt where it creates a real risk that the fair and proper trial of pending proceedings might be prejudiced. So, in *Blackburn v British Broadcasting Corpn* (1976) *Times* 15 December James Ferman, secretary designate of the British Board of Film Censors, referred in a television interview to pending criminal proceedings instituted by B in relation to the showing of the film 'The Language of Love', and said 'The context of the film was seriously educational and could do nothing but good in the board's opinion and my opinion.' The court held that there was no risk of prejudice given that the words were spoken in the middle of a general discussion about film censorship and were immediately followed by an expression of F's opinion that the courts should be the final arbiter. Moreover, the programme was only shown in the south-west, and it was unlikely that a prospective Old Bailey juror would see or recollect the words. The same test was applied in *R v Bulgin, ex parte British Broadcasting Corpn* (1977) *Times* 14 July.

(ii) Comments on a defendant's character

R v Thomson Newspapers Ltd, ex parte A-G [1968] 1 All ER 268. The *Sunday Times* published an article about Michael Abdul Malik who was awaiting trial on a charge under the Race Relations Act 1965. Beneath a photograph of M was the comment that he 'took to politics after an unedifying career as brothel keeper, procurer and property racketeer.' The proprietors were fined £5,000 for contempt. However, M's appeal against conviction on the ground (inter alia) that there was a danger that he had not had a fair trial was dismissed. The Court of Appeal (Criminal Division) felt that in the light of all the evidence at the trial, M had not been prejudiced (*R v Malik* [1968] 1 All ER 582). In *R v Border Television Ltd, ex parte A-G; R v Newcastle Chronicle and Journal Ltd, ex parte A-G* (1978) 68 Cr App R 375, DC, the defendants had stated that a person being tried by jury on six charges of obtaining by deception and six charges of theft had pleaded guilty to four deception charges. That information had been kept from the jury, which had to be discharged. The publication was held to be a contempt. Lord Widgery CJ pointed out at 380 that 'every fledgling reporter' should be aware of two simple forms of contempt: 'publishing material relating to other offences or publishing material which has been deliberately kept from the jury's ears'.

(iii) The publication of photographs

R v Evening Standard Co Ltd, ex parte A-G (1976) *Times* 3 November DC. The Company was fined £1,000 for publishing a photograph of Peter Hain, together with an article, on the front page of the *Evening Standard*, on the day that he was due to take part in an identification parade after he had been charged with the theft of £490 from a bank in Putney. H was ultimately acquitted. In assessing the penalty, the court took into account the nature of the contempt, how the contempt happened, the degree of distribution of the newspaper, and the effect on the administration of justice. The court seemed to think that it had had no effect on the identification parade, but Peter Hain has stated that several bank officials who attended the parade as witnesses had seen a copy of the paper that morning at the bank (P. Hain, *Mistaken Identity* (1976), pp. 21–2, 39–40, 42, 85). Another factor the court took into account was that 'it would be a great pity if the courts allowed newspapers to think that the cost of their legal department was unjustified.'

2. Inferior courts generally only have power to punish contempts in the face of the court (see below, p. 270). However, the Divisional Court fulfils a protective role, as a corollary to its supervisory jurisdiction, over the proceedings of inferior courts and tribunals. Accordingly, it has been held that that court can punish publications likely to prejudice proceedings before quarter sessions (see *R v Davies* [1906] 1 KB 32), consistory courts

(*R v Daily Herald, ex parte Bishop of Norwich* [1932] 2 KB 402) and local valuation courts (*A-G v British Broadcasting Corpn* [1979] 3 All ER 45, CA).

3. The disclosure of jury secrets may amount to contempt: *A-G v New Statesman and Nation Publishing Ltd* [1980] 1 All ER 644, DC (defendants not liable on the facts).

4. Recent cases have established the proposition that a judge has jurisdiction to order that the name of a witness should not be disclosed in the proceedings if there is a danger that a lack of anonymity would deter such witnesses from coming forward. Disclosure may then amount to contempt. In *R v Socialist Worker Printers and Publishers Ltd, ex parte A-G* [1975] 1 All ER 142, DC, prosecution witnesses at the trial of Janie Jones on charges (inter alia) of blackmail were referred to in court as 'Y' and 'Z' by direction of the judge. Their names were published in the *Socialist Worker*. There was no specific direction to the press not to publish the names. Nevertheless, the publishers and editor (Paul Foot) were each fined £250 for contempt. This was both 'an affront to the authority of the court' and 'an act calculated to interfere with the due course of justice' (per Lord Widgery CJ at 151).

The New Zealand Court of Appeal has similarly held that it is contempt to disobey directions not to reveal the identities of members of the NZ Security Intelligence Service who were prosecution witnesses in a well publicised trial (*A-G v Taylor* [1975] 2 NZLR 675; *A-G v Hancox* [1976] 1 NZLR 171; W. C. Hodge, (1976) 7 NZ Universities LR 171).

In *A-G v Leveller Magazine Ltd* [1979] 1 All ER 745, HL, three newspapers (*Leveller, Peace News* and *Journalists*) published the name of a witness in the committal proceedings which led to the 'ABC trial' (below p. 278). He had been allowed to give evidence as 'Colonel B' for security reasons. They were convicted of contempt and fined, on the ground that 'a flouting (or deliberate disregard) outside the court will be a contempt if it frustrates the court's ruling' (per Lord Widgery CJ, [1978] 3 All ER 731 at 736). The House of Lords allowed the defendants' appeals on a variety of grounds.

(1) (Lord Diplock, Viscount Dilhorne and Lord Russell). In evidence at the committal proceedings 'Colonel B' gave the name and number of his unit and referred to the fact that his posting was recorded in a particular issue of 'Wire', the Royal Signals magazine, which was available to the general public. His identity could thus be deduced from evidence given in open court without objection from the prosecution. Accordingly, the disclosure could not interfere with the due administration of justice and could not amount to contempt. In the words of Lord Russell, 'the gaff was already blown' (p. 764). Viscount Dilhorne (at 754) and Lord Russell (at 764) gave this as the only reason for their decision.

(2) (Lord Edmund-Davies) The Attorney-General had sought the orders of committal on the basis that the defendants had ignored an explicit *direction* of the magistrates. It subsequently appeared from the affidavit of the court clerk that no such direction had been given. Lord Edmund-Davies held at 759 that

> 'it was not open to the Divisional Court (and particularly after refusing to allow him to amend his grounds of application) to entertain an entirely different case on which to commit the appellants for criminal contempt . . . Persons charged with criminal misconduct are entitled to know with reasonable precision the basis of the charge'.

The speeches of their Lordships do not, however, give clear guidance as to when a publication of information will amount to contempt. Would it be sufficient for the court simply to rule that a witness' name should not be revealed in the court? That publication of the name, following the ruling, might well amount to contempt in the opinions of Viscount Dilhorne at 755, 756 and Lord Russell of Killowen at 764.

Viscount Dilhorne:

'... Were it not for the evidence given by Colonel B in open court from which his identity could be ascertained without difficulty, I would have been in favour of dismissing these appeals. It must have been clear to all in court and to all who learnt what had happened in court that the object sought to be achieved by the justices allowing Colonel B to write down his name was the preservation of his anonymity ... [A] person who seeks to frustrate what the court has done may well be guilty of contempt.'

Lord Russell:

'... (1) The decision of the examining magistrates should have been recognised by the appellants as one designed to preserve the anonymity of Colonel B. (2) That decision should be taken as made in the interests of the due administration of justice, both in that case and in the due administration of justice as a continuing process ... (5) But for the substantially self-identifying content of Colonel B's legitimately reportable deposition I would have been for dismissal of these appeals'.

The speeches of the other members of the House seemed to require further conditions to be fulfilled before a conviction for contempt. Lord Edmund-Davies' view was nearest to that of Viscount Dilhorne and Lord Russell, although he did express doubts as to the ratio decidendi of *R v Socialist Worker*. Viscount Dilhorne at 756 (as did Lord Scarman) expressly approved the decision in that case and Lord Russell can be taken as having done so by implication.

Lord Diplock: ...

[I]n adopting this particular device which on the face of it related only to how proceedings within the courtroom were to be conducted it behoved the magistrates to make it clear what restrictions, if any, were intended by them to be imposed on publishing outside the courtroom information relating to those proceedings and whether such restrictions were to be precatory only or enforceable by the sanction of proceedings for contempt of court. ... [W]here (1) the reason for a ruling which involves departing in some measure from the general principle of open justice within the courtroom is that the departure is necessary in the interests of the due administration of justice and (2) it would be apparent to anyone who was aware of the ruling that the result which the ruling is designed to achieve would be frustrated by a particular kind of act done outside the courtroom, the doing of such an act with knowledge of the ruling and of its purpose may constitute a contempt of court, not because it is a breach of the ruling but because it interferes with the due administration of justice.

What was incumbent on [the magistrates] was to make it clear to anyone present at, or reading an accurate report of, the proceedings, what in the interests of the due administration of justice, was the result that was intended by them to be achieved by the limited derogation from the principle of open justice within the courtroom which they had authorised, and what kind of information derived from what happened in the courtroom would if it were published frustrate that result.

There may be many cases in which the result intended to be achieved by a ruling by the court as to what is to be done in court is so obvious as to speak for itself; it calls for no explicit statement.Sending the jury out of court during a trial within a trial is an example of this; so may be the common ruling in prosecutions for blackmail that a victim called as a witness be referred to in court by a pseudonym.

Lord Edmund-Davies: ...

For [contempt] to arise something more than disobedience of the court's direction needs to be established. That something more is that the publication must be of such a nature as to threaten the administration of justice either in the particular case in relation to which the prohibition was pronounced or in relation to cases which may be brought in the future. ...

[T]he Press and others could, as I believe, be helped were a court when sitting in public to draw express attention to any procedural decisions it had come to and implemented during the hearing, to explain that they were aimed at ensuring the due and fair administration of justice, and to indicate that any who by publishing material or otherwise acting in a manner calculated to prejudice that aim would run the risk of contempt proceedings being instituted against them. ...

[N]othing I have said should be regarded as implying that there can be no committal for contempt unless there has been some sort of warning against publication. While, for the reasons I have indicated, it would be wise to warn, the court is under no obligation to do so. And there will remain cases where a court could not reasonably have considered a warning even desirable, such as where the later conduct complained of should not have been contemplated as likely to occur. *R v Newcastle Chronicle and Journal Ltd* [above, p. 248] is an example of such a case.

Lord Scarman: . . .

'If a court is satisfied that for the protection of the administration of justice from interference it is necessary to order that evidence either be heard in private or be written down and not given in open court, it may so order. Such an order or ruling may be the foundation of contempt proceedings against any person who, with knowledge of the order, frustrates its purpose by publishing the evidence kept private or information leading to its exposure. The order or ruling must be clear and can be made only if it appears to the court reasonably necessary. There must be material (not necessarily evidence) made known to the court on which it could reasonably reach its conclusion, and those who are alleged to be in contempt must be shown to have known, or to have had a proper opportunity of knowing of the existence of the order. . . . '

Note that there are three distinct statements by justices which are possible.
(a) A 'ruling' that a witness should be allowed to remain anonymous in court;
(b) a 'direction' that the witness' identity should not be published in or out of court;
(c) a 'warning' that publication may amount to or be dealt with as contempt.
Which of these statements do you think each of their Lordships has in mind as a precondition of liability in contempt? There seemed to be general agreement that disobedience to statements of any of these kinds would not *automatically* constitute contempt. See Viscount Dilhorne at 734, Lord Edmund Davies at 761 and Lord Scarman at 768. Lord Diplock at 751 left the point open.

5. The strong line taken by the Supreme Court of the United States against inhibitions on freedom of expression and freedom of the press (see above, p. 243) has meant that broadcasting and press publication of prejudicial material has been a considerable problem. There has been an extensive debate on whether the balance between the right of free expression and the right to a fair trial is correctly drawn (see e.g. *Abraham*, pp. 178–186; Donnelly and Goldfarb, (1961) 24 MLR 239). The Supreme Court has had to quash convictions in some extreme *causes célèbres: Irvin v Dowd* 366 US 717 (1961); *Estes v Texas* 381 US 532 (1965) (where the courtroom, according to the *New York Times* 'was turned into a snake-pit by the multiplicity of cameras, wires, microphones and technicians milling about the chamber' (*Abraham*, p. 183); and *Sheppard v Maxwell* 384 US 333 (1966). In the last case, Sheppard's conviction was quashed after he had been in prison for ten years convicted of murder after a sensationalised 'circus-like' trial. He was acquitted following a re-trial. The disquiet engendered by such cases has led to the employment of a number of safety devices: use of the voir dire examination of jurors to determine whether they are capable of ignoring pre-trial publicity; sequestration of the jury during the trial; transferring a case to another county; and the exercise of control by judges and public authorities over police officers, lawyers and court officials to prevent the release of prejudicial information. In addition, there is the encouragement of self-regulation by the press – the voluntary observation of proper standards of press coverage. These devices are constitutional, but doubts are expressed as to their efficacy. Following *Sheppard v Maxwell*, with its emphasis on the defendant's right to a fair trial under the Sixth and Fourteenth Amendments, trial courts have imposed specific reporting restrictions ('gag orders') on the press in individual cases where prejudicial publicity is apprehended. In *Nebraska Press Association v Stuart* 427 US 539 (1976), the Supreme Court held that a 'gag order' will normally be an unconstitutional restriction on press freedom (see A. M. Schatz, (1975) 10 Harvard Civil Rights–Civil Liberties Law Review 608; Note (1977) 87 Yale LJ 342). The debate in the United States continues.

(b) WHEN DOES THE SUB JUDICE RULE APPLY?

(i) Commencement

There are uncertainties both as to the commencement and the conclusion of the period within which matters are sub judice so as to render comments or acts that are prejudicial, contempts. If proceedings are 'pending' they are clearly sub judice. Proceedings have been held to be 'pending' where a defendant has been arrested by virtue of a warrant (*R v Clarke, ex parte Crippen* (1910) 103 LT 636, DC), and it was suggested obiter in the same case that they are 'pending' from the time the warrant is issued. The authorities conflict on the question whether matters are sub judice when proceedings are merely 'imminent'. In *James v Robinson* (1963) 109 CLR 593, the High Court of Australia held that as a matter of law, contempt of court could not be committed before the proceedings in question began. It is possible that *James v Robinson* would not be followed in this country (see *Borrie and Lowe*, p. 142; *Miller*, p. 80). The view that the law of contempt applies when proceedings are merely imminent was expressed in *R v Savundranayagan* (above p. 246), but those were not contempt proceedings. In *R v Beaverbrook Newspapers Ltd* [1962] NI 15, QBD, Sheil and McVeigh JJ. held that the word 'imminent' in section 11 of the Administration of Justice Act 1960 'cannot be ignored if effect is to be given to the section as a whole. Whatever may be said to be the distinction between 'proceedings pending' and 'proceedings imminent', it is clear from the use of the words 'as the case may be' that a distinction was intended' (Shiel J at 21). The *Daily Express* published photographs and other details (including the past criminal record) of a man who was arrested and charged with murder within two days of the publication. At the time of the publication, the reporter who supplied the material knew that the man was under close police surveillance, and indeed the *Daily Express* referred to him as the 'No. 1 Suspect'. Fines were imposed on the editors and proprietors of the *Daily Express*. Section 11 is given below, p. 254.

Report of the Committee on Contempt of Court, Chairman: Phillimore LJ (Cmnd. 5794, 1974)

[*James v Robinson* was endorsed by the Committee (paras. 70–72; 84; 115–123)]

ARGUMENTS AGAINST RESTRICTING THE PERIOD OF APPLICATION OF THE LAW

116. It has many times been pointed out that statements made before proceedings begin can be just as prejudicial as those made at a later stage . . . A fixed starting point, whether at the moment proceedings begin or at any other time, would be arbitrary. Secondly, it is hardly more difficult for a publisher to have to take care not to issue a prejudicial publication if he knows that proceedings are 'imminent' and will be instituted as soon as the court office is open than it is to take care not to publish immediately afterwards. In this connection, it is relevant

that many of the formal steps which initiate proceedings are not taken in public, so that, unless they are informed by those who have set the law in motion, the press would not necessarily know whether proceedings have begun or not until the matter comes before the court. Finally, in England and Wales, the press have some protection by virtue of section 11 of the Administration of Justice Act 1960 [below, p. 254] . . .

ARGUMENTS IN FAVOUR OF RESTRICTING THE PERIOD OF APPLICATION OF THE LAW.

117. Impressive as these arguments are, the application of the concept of 'imminence' presents too many problems. The difficulties surrounding the day-to-day application of the law of contempt are already unavoidably great without adding to them by uncertainties of this kind. For example, there is no way of knowing what period the word 'imminent' is intended to cover. An ex post facto test would be liable to be unjust, because the publisher cannot foresee what may happen. The evidence submitted to us suggests that this uncertainty has an inhibiting effect upon the freedom of the press which is out of proportion to any value there may be in preserving it. Our analysis of the need to protect the administration of justice points clearly to the conclusion that, although there may be some risks before proceedings begin, the dangers increase as the trial approaches. Certainly this is true with regard to jurors and witnesses, who by the time the trial takes place are likely to have forgotten all but relatively recent publications. It is also true of the danger of undermining public confidence in the administration of justice. The risks of creating prejudice and of damaging public confidence before proceedings begin undoubtedly exist, but they should not be exaggerated and can largely be eliminated if a sufficiently early starting point for the operation of the law is selected. Finally, and perhaps most important, a restriction of time accords with the principles . . . that the law of contempt, combining strict liability and a summary procedure, should be invoked only where there is a serious and immediate threat to the administration of justice. This in practice is only likely to arise when the trial is due to take place in the near future. These arguments confirm our view . . . that the law of contempt should not apply before proceedings begin.

[The Committee recommended that the right starting point in England and Wales is the moment when the suspected man is charged or a summons served; and in Scotland when the person is firstly publicly charged on petition or otherwise, or at the first calling in court of a summary complaint, as the case may be.]

(ii) Conclusion

Technically, the proceedings will not be over until the trial has been completed and either the time for appealing has expired, or any appeals have finally been determined (see *Delbert-Evans v Davies and Watson* [1945] 2 All ER 167, DC; *R v Duffy, ex parte Nash* [1960] 2 QB 188, DC). However, it is very unlikely that any comment would be regarded as giving rise to any risk of prejudice to the fair conduct of proceedings. 'A judge is in a very different position to a juryman. Though in no sense superhuman, he has by his training no difficulty in putting out of his mind matters which are not evidence in the case.' (Per Lord Parker CJ in *R v Duffy, ex parte Nash* [1960] 2 QB 188 at 198). The Phillimore Committee recommended that the law of contempt should cease to apply at the conclusion of the trial or hearing at first instance unless (1) sentence is postponed, in which case restrictions should continue until sentence is passed; or (2) no verdict is reached, in which case restrictions should continue unless and until it is clear that there will be no further trial; or (3) a new trial is ordered on appeal, in which case restrictions should again apply; or(4) there is an appeal from a magistrate's court to the Crown Court, in which case restrictions should apply from the moment the appeal is set down (para. 132).

(c) THE SCOPE OF LIABILITY

A defendant will be liable for contempt if he publishes matter in circumstances where such publication, objectively judged, creates a real risk that the fair trial of proceedings may be prejudiced. An intention to prejudice proceedings will not apparently be enough if there is in fact no risk of prejudice: *R v Ingrams, ex parte Goldsmith* (1976) 120 Sol Jo 835 [1977] Crim LR 40. However authorities to the contrary collected in *Borrie and Lowe* at pp. 57–59 were not mentioned by the members of the Divisional Court in *R v Ingrams*, and Eveleigh J is reported as saying that he did not think the article in question 'would – or had been intended to – prejudice the fair trial of the litigation' against *Private Eye*.

There appears to be no requirement of mens rea beyond an intention to publish the matter in question (*R v Odhams Press Ltd* [1957] 1 QB 73, DC, *R v Griffiths ex parte A-G* [1957] 2 QB 192, DC), although section 11 of the Administration of Justice Act 1960 does now provide defences in two situations where publication can be said to be 'innocent' (below). The person who supplies information to a newspaper should not be held liable unless he has mens rea (see *Smith and Hogan*, pp. 744–745, criticising *R v Evening Standard Co Ltd* [1954] 1 QB 578; but cf. *Borrie and Lowe*, pp. 198–201).

The Phillimore Committee recommended that the unintentional creation of a risk of prejudice should continue to be regarded as contempt:

> 'The risk of damage resulting from potentially prejudicial publications is such that we are sure that, broadly speaking, no change of principle is required. A liability which rested only on proof of intent or actual foresight would favour the reckless at the expense of the careful. Most publishing is a commercial enterprise undertaken for profit, and the power of the printed or broadcast word is such that the administration of justice would not be adequately protected without a rule which requires great care to be taken to ensure that offending material is not published.' (para. 74).

Administration of Justice Act 1960

11. Innocent publication and distribution
(1) A person shall not be guilty of contempt of court on the ground that he has published any matter calculated to interfere with the course of justice in connection with any proceedings pending or imminent at the time of publication if at that time (having taken all reasonable care) he did not know and had no reason to suspect that the proceedings were pending, or that such proceedings were imminent, as the case may be.
(2) A person shall not be guilty of contempt of court on the ground that he has distributed a publication containing such matter as is mentioned in subsection (1) of this section if at the time of distribution (having taken all reasonable care) he did not know that it contained any such matter as aforesaid and had no reason to suspect that it was likely to do so.
(3) The proof of any fact tending to establish a defence afforded by this section to any person in proceedings for contempt of court shall lie upon that person.

NOTES

1. Sub-s. 2 of s. 11 was introduced to meet the situation highlighted by *R v Griffiths, ex parte A-G* [1957] 2 QB 192. Here, the distributors of the American magazine *Newsweek* were held guilty of contempt, on the ground that an issue of the magazine contained an article prejudicial to the pending trial on a charge of murder of Dr. John Bodkin Adams. The Divisional Court held that there was no defence of 'innocent dissemination' in the law of contempt, although there was such a defence in the law of defamation.

Accordingly, the distributors, W. H. Smith and Son, could not escape liability by arguing that they did not in fact know and had no reason to suspect that the issue contained the offending matter. Distributors subsequently took protective measures when dealing with imported magazines (see [1957] Crim LR 467.)

2. See generally on the 1960 Act: D. G. T. Williams [1961] Crim LR 87. The Act also created rights of appeal against any order or decision of a court in the exercise of jurisdiction to punish for contempt of court (s.13) and clarified the law relating to the publication of information relating to proceedings in private (s. 12).

3. Note that s. 11 has no application to publications which 'scandalise' the court (see below pp. 262–267).

4. The Phillimore Committee recommended that further defences should be created by statute:

(1) that the publication was a fair and accurate report of legal proceedings in open court published contemporaneously and in good faith (paras. 134–141);

(2) that the publication forms part of a legitimate discussion of matters of general public interest and that it only incidentally and unintentionally created a risk of serious prejudice to particular proceedings (para. 142)

However, they rejected proposals for a defence of public benefit (paras. 143–145).

5. Do you think that strict liability is appropriate in this context? Do the s. 11 defences go far enough to protect the innocent publisher of a contempt?

6. How should the law of contempt apply in the following cases (based on the 'Justice' Report on Contempt of Court, p. 11)?

(a) Mrs K is found strangled, her husband has disappeared, and (it is stated) the police are looking for him as he may be able to assist them in their inquiries. A newspaper states

(i) that Mr K has been acquitted of murdering a previous wife of his; and

(ii) that the police are not looking for anyone else (cf. press coverage of the Lucan affair: see R. Callender Smith, *Press Law* (1978) pp. 104–106)

(b) A notorious and dangerous ex-convict is on the run, suspected of a series of violent crimes. A newspaper publishes his name and photograph, and the crimes which he is suspected to have committed, with a view to securing his arrest and protecting the public meanwhile.

7. The law commission have proposed, inter alia, that it should be an offence 'if a person, intending thereby to achieve a miscarriage of justice in any current or future judicial proceedings, publishes or distributes a statement whose publication or distribution creates a risk of a miscarriage' (Report No. 96, pp. 71–2).

3 Publications prejudicial to civil proceedings

As the jury is today rarely used in civil proceedings, so the risk of prejudice to the fairness of trials from the publication of information and comments concerning pending litigation is acordingly reduced. However, where there is trial by jury the law of contempt will obviously apply in the same way as in criminal proceedings, see above, pp. 244 ff., and the recent *Sunday Times* case (below) illustrates that the law will protect litigants and witnesses from improper pressure, and indeed protect the administration of justice from being devalued by the development of 'trial by newspaper'.

Attorney-General v Times Newspapers Ltd [1974] AC 273, [1973] 3 All ER 54, [1973] 3 WLR 298, House of Lords

In 1958 Distillers, a drug company, began to make and sell in the United Kingdom a sedative which contained the drug thalidomide. The product was . . . prescribed for many pregnant women for whom it was said to be quite safe. Many of the mothers who had taken the drug gave birth to babies suffering from grave deformities. It was subsequently established that the deformities were caused by the action of thalidomide on the unborn child at certain stages of the pregnancy. As soon as that was realised Distillers withdrew the product in 1961. Between 1962 and 1968 some 70 actions for negligence were brought against Distillers on behalf of the deformed children. Early in 1968 a settlement was reached in those proceedings. Subsequently further writs were issued; by February 1969, 248 writs had been issued in proceedings which were not covered by the 1968 settlement. Negotiations took place with a view to a settlement and no further steps were taken in the proceedings in which writs had been issued to bring the actions to trial. Distillers made it a condition of any settlement that all claimants should accept it. The parties were, however, unable to come to agreement. In June 1972 Distillers made new proposals but they were not accepted; there were then some 389 claims outstanding. The editor of the *Sunday Times* took a keen interest in the matter. On 24 September 1972 the newspaper published a long and powerful article which criticised the law relating to the liability of drug companies and the methods of assessing damages. The sting of the article was however contained in a paragraph which stated that 'the thalidomide children shame Distillers' and urged Distillers to offer much more than they had done so far. The paragraph continued: ' . . . the law is not always the same as justice. There are times when to insist on the letter of the law is as exposed to criticism as infringement of another's legal rights. The figure in the proposed settlement is £3.25m., spread over 10 years. This does not shine as a beacon against pre-tax profits last year of £64.8 million and company assets worth £421 million. Without in any way surrendering on negligence, Distillers could and should think again.' Distillers brought the article to the attention of the Attorney-General maintaining that it was a contempt of court. The Attorney-General decided to take no action and Distillers let the matter drop. The editor of the *Sunday Times* was, however, minded to publish a further article of a different character. That article consisted in the main of detailed evidence and argument intended to show that Distillers had not exercised due care to see that thalidomide was safe for pregnant mothers before they put it on the market. The editor sent the article to the Attorney-General who commenced proceedings for an injunction against the respondents, the proprietors of the *Sunday Times*, restraining them from publishing that article. The Divisional Court ([1972] 3 All ER 1136) granted an injunction but the Court of Appeal([1973] 1 All ER 815) allowed the respondents' appeal and discharged the injunction on the grounds, inter alia, that the article contained comments which the authors honestly believed to be true on matters of outstanding public interest and did not prejudice pending litigation since the litigation had been dormant for several years and no active steps had been taken or were likely to be taken to bring it before the courts. The Attorney-General appealed.

The House held unanimously (1) that the Attorney-General was a proper person to commence contempt proceedings, and (2) that an injunction should be granted to restrain publication of the second article. Lords Reid and Cross of Chelsea stated obiter that the first article did not amount to contempt. Lords Diplock and Simon of Glaisdale disagreed. They held that the first article improperly held Distillers up to public obloquy. Lord Simon would in addition have held that 'private pressure' to forego legal rights was in general impermissible, and could only be justified within narrow limits as where there existed such a common interest that fair, reasonable and moderate personal representations could be appropriate. Lord Diplock took the view that 'private pressure' could not constitute contempt.

Lord Reid: . . . The law on this subject is and must be founded entirely on public policy. It is not there to protect the private rights of parties to a litigation or prosecution. It is there to prevent interference with the administration of justice and it should, in my judgment, be limited to what is reasonably necessary for that purpose. Public policy generally requires a balancing of interests which may conflict. Freedom of speech should not be limited to any greater extent than is necessary but it cannot be allowed where there would be real prejudice to the administration of justice. . . .

We are particularly concerned here with 'abusing parties' and 'prejudicing mankind' against them. Of course parties must be protected from scurrilous abuse: otherwise many litigants would fear to bring their cases to court. But the argument of the Attorney-General goes far beyond that. His argument was based on a passage in the judgment of Buckley J in *Vine Products Ltd* v *Green* [1966] Ch 484 at 495–496:

'It is a contempt of this court for any newspaper to comment on pending legal proceedings in any way which is likely to prejudice the fair trial of the action. That may arise in various ways. It may be that the comment is one which is likely in some way or other to bring pressure to bear upon one or other of the parties to the action, so as to prevent that party from prosecuting or from defending the action, or encourage that party to submit to terms of compromise which he otherwise might not have been prepared to entertain, or influence him in some other way in his conduct in the action, which he ought to be free to prosecute or to defend, as he is advised, without being subject to such pressure.'

I think that this is much too widely stated. It is true that there is some authority for it but . . . it does not seem to me to be in accord with sound public policy. Why would it be contrary to public policy to seek by fair comment to dissuade Shylock from proceeding with his action? Surely it could not be wrong for the officious bystander to draw his attention to the risk that, if he goes on, decent people will cease to trade with him. Or suppose that his best customer ceased to trade with him when he heard of his lawsuit. That could not be contempt of court. Would it become contempt if, when asked by Shylock why he was sending no more business his way, he told him the reason? Nothing would be more likely to influence Shylock to discontinue his action. It might become widely known that such pressure was being brought to bear. Would that make any difference? And though widely known must the local press keep silent about it? There must be some limitation of this general statement of the law.

And then suppose that there is in the press and elsewhere active discussion of some question of wide public interest, such as the propriety of local authorities or other landlords ejecting squatters from empty premises due for demolition. Then legal proceedings are begun against some squatters, it may be by some authority which had already been criticised in the press. The controversy could hardly be continued without likelihood that it might influence the authority in its conduct of the action. Must there then be silence until that case is decided? And there may be a series of actions by the same or different landlords. Surely public policy does not require that a system of stop and go shall apply to public discussion.

I think that there is a difference between direct interference with the fair trial of an action and words or conduct which may affect the mind of a litigant. Comment likely to affect the minds of witnesses and of the tribunal must be stopped for otherwise the trial may well be unfair. But the fact that a party refrains from seeking to enforce his full legal rights in no way prejudices a fair trial, whether the decision is or is not influenced by some third party. There are other weighty reasons for preventing improper influence being brought to bear on litigants, but they have little to do with interference with the fairness of a trial. There must be absolute prohibition of interference with a fair trial but beyond that there must be a balancing of relevant considerations. . . .

So I would hold that as a general rule where the only matter to be considered is pressure put on a litigant, fair and temperate criticism is legitimate, but anything which goes beyond that may well involve contempt of court. But in a case involving witnesses, jury or magistrates, other considerations are involved: there even fair and temperate criticism might be likely to affect the minds of some of them so as to involve contempt. But it can be assumed that it would not affect the mind of a professional judge. . . .

The crucial question on this point of the case is whether it can ever be permissible to urge a party to a litigation to forgo his legal rights in whole or in part. The Attorney-General argues that it cannot and I think that the Divisional Court has accepted that view. In my view it is permissible so long as it is done in a fair and temperate way and without any oblique motive. The *Sunday Times* article of 24 September 1972, affords a good illustration of the difference between the two views. It is plainly intended to bring pressure to bear on Distillers. It was likely to attract support from others and it did so. It was outspoken. It said: 'There are times when to insist on the letter of the law is as exposed to criticism as infringement of another's legal rights' and clearly implied that that was such a time. If the view maintained by the Attorney-General were right I could hardly imagine a clearer case of contempt of court. It could be no excuse that the passage which I quoted earlier was combined with a great deal of other totally unobjectionable material. And it could not be said that it created no serious risk of causing Distillers to do what they did not want to do. On the facts submitted to your

Lordships in argument it seems to me to have played a large part in causing Distillers to offer far more money than they had in mind at that time. But I am quite unable to subscribe to the view that it ought never to have been published because it was in contempt of court. I see no offence against public policy and no pollution of the stream of justice by its publication.

Now I must turn to the material to which the injunction applied . . . [I]t consists in the main of detailed evidence and argument intended to show that Distillers did not exercise due care to see that thalidomide was safe before they put it on the market.

If we regard this material solely from the point of view of its likely effect on Distillers I do not think that its publication in 1972 would have added much to the pressure on them created, or at least begun, by the earlier article of September 24. . . .

But, to my mind, there is another consideration even more important than the effect of publication on the mind of the litigant. The controversy about the tragedy of the thalidomide children has ranged widely but as yet there seems to have been little, if any, detailed discussions of the issues which the court may have to determine if the outstanding claims are not settled. The question whether Distillers were negligent has been frequently referred to but, so far as I am aware, there has been no attempt to assess the evidence. If this material were released now, it appears to me to be almost inevitable that detailed answers would be published and there would be expressed various public prejudgments of this issue. That I would regard as very much against the public interest.

There has long been and there still is in this country a strong and generally held feeling that trial by newspaper is wrong and should be prevented. I find, for example, in the report in 1969 of Lord Salmon's committee dealing with the Law of Contempt in relation to Tribunals of Inquiry (Cmnd. 4078) a reference to the 'horror' in such a thing (p. 12, para. 29). What I think is regarded as most objectionable is that a newspaper or television programme should seek to persuade the public by discussing the issues and evidence in a case before the court, whether civil or criminal, that one side is right and the other wrong. If we were to ask the ordinary man or even a lawyer in his leisure moments why he has that feeling, I suspect that the first reply would be—'well, look at what happens in some other countries where that is permitted.' As in so many other matters, strong feelings are based on one's general experience rather than on specific reasons, and it often requires an effort to marshal one's reasons. But public policy is generally the result of strong feelings, commonly held, rather than of cold argument. . . .

There is ample authority for the proposition that issues must not be prejudged in a manner likely to affect the mind of those who may later be witnesses or jurors. But very little has been said about the wider proposition that trial by newspaper is intrinsically objectionable. That may be because if one can find more limited and familiar grounds adequate for the decision of a case it is rash to venture on uncharted seas.

I think that anything in the nature of prejudgment of a case or of specific issues in it is objectionable, not only because of its possible effect on that particular case but also because of its side effects which may be far reaching. Responsible 'mass media' will do their best to be fair, but there will also be ill-informed, slapdash or prejudiced attempts to influence the public. If people are led to think that it is easy to find the truth, disrespect for the processes of the law could follow, and, if mass media are allowed to judge, unpopular people and unpopular causes will fare very badly. Most cases of prejudging of issues fall within the existing authorities on contempt. I do not think that the freedom of the press would suffer, and I think that the law would be clearer and easier to apply in practice if it is made a general rule that it is not permissible to prejudge issues in pending cases. . . .

There is no magic in the issue of a writ or in a charge being made against an accused person. Comment on a case which is imminent may be as objectionable as comment after it has begun. And a 'gagging' writ ought to have no effect.

But I must add to prevent misunderstanding that comment where a case is under appeal is a very different matter. For one thing it is scarcely possible to imagine a case where comment could influence judges in the Court of Appeal or noble and learned Lords in this House. And it would be wrong and contrary to existing practice to limit proper criticism of judgments already given but under appeal.

Now I must deal with the reasons which induced the Court of Appeal to discharge the injunction. It was said that the actions had been dormant or asleep for several years. Nothing appears to have been done in court, but active negotiations for a settlement were going on all the time. No one denies that it would be contempt of court to use improper pressure to induce a litigant to settle a case on terms to which he did not wish to agree. So if there is no undue procrastination in the negotiations for a settlement I do not see how in this context an action can be said to be dormant.

Then it was said that there is here a public interest which counter-balances the private interests of the litigants. But contempt of court has nothing to do with the private interests of the litigants. I have already indicated the way in which I think that a balance must be struck between the public interest in freedom of speech and the public interest in protecting the administration of justice from interference. I do not see why there should be any difference in principle between a case which is thought to have news value and one which is not. Protection of the administration of justice is equally important whether or not the case involves important general issues. . . .

Lord Diplock: My Lords, in any civilised society it is a function of government to maintain courts of law to which its citizens can have access for the impartial decision of disputes as to their legal rights and obligations towards one another individually and towards the state as representing society as a whole. The provision of such a system for the administration of justice by courts of law and the maintenance of public confidence in it, are essential if citizens are to live together in peaceful association with one another. 'Contempt of court' is a generic term descriptive of conduct in relation to particular proceedings in a court of law which tends to undermine that system or to inhibit citizens from availing themselves of it for the settlement of their disputes. Contempt of court may thus take many forms. . . .

The due administration of justice requires *first* that all citizens should have unhindered access to the constitutionally established courts of criminal or civil jurisdiction for the determination of disputes as to their legal rights and liabilities; *secondly*, that they should be able to rely upon obtaining in the courts the arbitrament of a tribunal which is free from bias against any party and whose decision will be based upon those facts only that have been proved in evidence adduced before it in accordance with the procedure adopted in courts of law; and *thirdly* that, once the dispute has been submitted to a court of law, they should be able to rely upon there being no usurpation by any other person of the function of that court to decide it according to law. Conduct which is calculated to prejudice any of these three requirements or to undermine the public confidence that they will be observed is contempt of court.

The commonest kind of conduct to come before the courts on applications for committal for contempt of court has been conduct which has been calculated to prejudice the second requirement. This is because trial by jury has been, as it still is, the mode of trial of all serious criminal offences, and until comparatively recently has also been the mode of trial of most civil cases at common law which are likely to attract the attention of the public. Laymen, whether acting as jurymen or witnesses (or, for that matter, as magistrates), were regarded by the judges as being vulnerable to influence or pressure which might impair their impartiality or cause them to form preconceived views as to the facts of the dispute, or, in the case of witnesses, to be unwilling to give evidence with candour at the trial. The conduct most commonly complained of was the publication, generally in a newspaper, of statements or comments about parties to pending litigation or about facts at issue in the litigation; so the discussion in the judgments tends to be directed to consideration of the question whether the publication complained of involved a risk of causing someone who might be called upon to serve as a juror to be prejudiced against a party or to form a preconceived view of the facts before the evidence was adduced in court, or a risk of influencing someone who might be called as a witness to alter his evidence or to decline to testify.

Contempt of court, except the rare offence of scandalising the court after judgment, is committed before the trial is concluded. Whether in the result the publication will have had any influence upon jurors or witnesses is not known when the proceedings for committal for contempt of court are heard. The mischief against which the summary remedy for contempt of court is directed is not merely that justice will not be done but that it will not be manifestly seen to be done. Contempt of court is punishable because it undermines the confidence not only of the parties to the particular litigation but also of the public as potential suitors, in the due administration of justice by the established courts of law.

My Lords, to hold a party up to public obloquy for exercising his constitutional right to have recourse to a court of law for the ascertainment and enforcement of his legal rights and obligations is calculated to prejudice the *first* requirement for the due administration of justice: the unhindered access of all citizens to the established courts of law. Similarly, 'trial by newspaper,' i.e., public discussion or comment on the merits of a dispute which has been submitted to a court of law or on the alleged facts of the dispute before they have been found by the court upon the evidence adduced before it, is calculated to prejudice the *third* requirement: that parties to litigation should be able to rely upon there being no usurpation by any other person of the function of that court to decide their dispute according to law. If to have recourse to civil litigation were to expose a litigant to the risk of public obloquy or to public and prejudicial discussion of the facts or merits of the case before they have been determined by the court, potential suitors would be inhibited from availing themselves of courts of law for the purpose for which they are established.

It is only where a case is to be heard by a tribunal which may be regarded as incapable of being influenced by public criticism of the parties or discussion of the merits or the facts and any witnesses likely to be called are similarly immune, that conduct of this kind does not also offend against the *second* requirement for the due administration of justice;

[His Lordship went on to hold that the second article was in contempt as it 'discussed prejudicially the facts and merits of Distillers' defence to the charge of negligence brought against them in the actions before these have been determined by the court or the actions disposed of by settlement'. The first article was also in contempt as a passage in it 'does hold Distillers up to public obloquy for . . . . relying upon the defence, available to them under the law as it stands, that they were not guilty of any negligence. .' That did not mean that action should have been taken as it was a 'short passage in a long and trenchant article which was otherwise unobjectionable']

Lord Cross of Chelsea: . . . I agree with my noble and learned friend [Lord Reid] that we should maintain the rule that any 'prejudging' of issues, whether of fact or of law, in pending proceedings—whether civil or criminal—is in principle an interference with the administration of justice although in any particular case the offence may be so trifling that to bring it to the notice of the court would be unjustifiable. . .
Appeal allowed

NOTES

1. See casenotes by C. J. Miller (1974) 37 MLR 96; M O'Boyle [1974] NILQ 57; D.G.T. Williams [1973] CLJ 177; and see C. J. Miller [1975] Crim LR 132. The injunction was discharged in 1976 (*The Times* 24 June) and the article subsequently appeared in the *Sunday Times*.
2. The Phillimore Committee did not like the 'prejudgment' test propounded by the House of Lords, while recognising the force of the policy arguments against 'trial by newspaper' or 'trial by television':

'111. The test of prejudgment might well make for greater certainty in one direction – provided a satisfactory definition of prejudgment could be found – but it is by no means clear that it is satisfactory in others, for instance, in the case of the "gagging" writs . . . It can be arbitrary in its application. For example, an opinion expressed on a legal issue in a learned journal would fall within the description of prejudgment given by Lord Cross of Chelsea. Again, there has been much discussion and expression of opinion in scientific journals as to the manner in which thalidomide operates to produce deformities. These, too, would fall within the test of prejudgment and would therefore be contempts. Furthermore, the scope and precise meaning of the words "prejudge" or "prejudgment" as used in the House of Lords are no easier to determine in practice than the phrase "risk of prejudice". At what point does legitimate discussion or expression of opinion cease to be legitimate and qualify as prejudgment? This may depend as much upon the quality and the authority of the party expressing the opinion as upon the nature of the opinion and the form of its expression . . . Further, the expression of opinion and even its repetition can be so framed as to disclaim clearly any intention to offer a concluded judgment and yet be of highly persuasive and influential character. The simple test of prejudgment therefore seems to go too far in some respects and not far enough in others. We conclude that no satisfactory definition can be found which does not have direct reference to the mischief which the law of contempt is and always has been designed to suppress. That mischief is the risk of prejudice to the due administration of justice.'

The Committee recommended in relation to publications which are alleged to affect particular proceedings (civil or criminal) a statutory definition 'on the following lines:'

'The test of contempt is whether the publication complained of creates a risk that the course of justice will be seriously impeded or prejudiced' (para. 113).

This is based on the formula adopted by the Divisional Court in the *Sunday Times* case, namely that 'the test of contempt is whether the words complained of create a serious risk that the course of justice may be interfered with (per Lord Widgery CJ [1972] 3 All ER 1136 at 1145).
3. The 'prejudgment' test was presumably intended to be applicable to criminal proceedings as well as civil – it has not been so applied: see above, p. 247.

4. In view of the length of civil proceedings as compared with criminal, the decrease in jury trials and the unlikelihood that judges will be improperly influenced, the Phillimore Committee took the view that strict liability need not be imposed from the commencement of proceedings in civil cases. The starting points they recommend are (1) the date of setting down for trial in the High Court in England and Wales; (2) the date of allowance of proof or jury trial in the Court of Session and Sheriff Courts in Scotland; and (3) six weeks before the date fixed for a hearing in county courts and magistrates' courts. The sub judice period should expire on the same basis as for criminal proceedings (above p. 253).

5. It has been thought that once a writ for libel is issued, subsequent repetition of the libel will amount to contempt of court. So, persons with little or no intention of pursuing proceedings have issued so-called 'gagging' writs in order to stifle further comment. The best view is that the issue of a writ does not *automatically* render repetition of the alleged libel contempt, but that repetition may be contempt if there is a risk of prejudice to the pending proceedings. If a court is not convinced that the plaintiff genuinely intends to proceed, or if the repetition is well before the trial, then there is likely to be no risk of prejudice and so no contempt. Salmon LJ seemed to go further when he offered the following encouragement to the press (obiter) in *Thomson v Times Newspapers Ltd* [1969] 3 All ER 648, CA, at 651:

'It is a widely held fallacy that the issue of a writ automatically stifles further comment. There is no authority that I know of to support the view that further comment would amount to contempt of court. Once a newspaper has justified, and there is some prima facie support for the justification, the plaintiff cannot obtain an interlocutory injunction to restrain the defendants from repeating the matters complained of. In these circumstances it is obviously wrong to suppose that they could be committing a contempt by doing so. It seems to me to be equally obvious that no other newspaper that repeats the same sort of criticism is committing a contempt of court. They may be publishing a libel, and if they do so, and they have no defence to it, they will have to pay whatever may be the appropriate damages; but the writ does not, in my view, preclude the publication of any further criticism: it merely puts the person who makes the further criticism on risk of being sued for libel; and he takes the same risk whether or not there has been any previous publication. I appreciate that very often newspapers are chary about repeating criticism when a writ for libel has been issued because they feel they are running some risk of being proceeded against for contempt. Without expressing any final view, because the point is not before this court for decision, I think that in this they are mistaken. No doubt the law relating to contempt could and should be clarified in this respect.'

This was approved by Lord Denning MR in *Wallersteiner v Moir* [1974] 3 All ER 217, CA at 230 and supported in the *Sunday Times* case by Lord Reid (above p. 258). The Phillimore Committee's recommendation that the sub-judice period should not start with the commencement of proceedings would solve the problem – only serious cases would get as far as setting down for trial. See further on 'gagging writs': *Borrie and Lowe*, pp. 90–96; *Miller*, pp. 145–149.

6. Do you think that the test for contempt suggested by the Phillimore Committee will make the determination of what is and is not a contempt any easier in individual cases? Is it possible to construct a definition that would make it easier? Do you think that the 'prejudgment' test should be applicable in addition to the Phillimore test to make it clear that 'trial by newspaper' is unacceptable? Or will the Phillimore test be itself sufficient to that end? Do you think that commencement of proceedings in respect of contempt consisting of the creation of a risk of serious prejudice by a publication should be in the sole hands of the Attorney-General?

7. In the *Sunday Times* case, Eur Court HR, Series A, Vol 30, Judgment of 26 April 1979, the European Court of Human Rights held, by 11 votes to 9, that the restriction imposed upon the applicants' freedom of speech by the injunction granted by the House of Lords was contrary to Article 10, ECHR, above, p. 20. The British judge, Sir Gerald Fitzmaurice, dissented. The Court's judgment reads in part:

'Whilst they [the courts] are the forum for the settlement of disputes, this does not mean that there can be no prior discussion of disputes elsewhere, be it in specialised journals, in the general press or amongst the public at large. . . . Not only do the media have the task of imparting such information and ideas: the public also has a right to receive them. . . . The Court observes . . . that, following a balancing of the conflicting interests involved, an absolute rule was formulated by certain of the Law Lords to the effect that it was not permissible to prejudge issues in pending cases . . . Whilst emphasising that it is not its function to pronounce itself on an interpretation of English law adopted in the House of Lords . . . the Court points out that it has to take a different approach. The Court is faced not with a choice between two conflicting principles but with a principle of freedom of expression [in Article 10] that is subject to a number of exceptions which must be narrowly interpreted . . . the Court has to be satisfied that the interference was necessary having regard to the facts and circumstances prevailing in the specific case before it. . . . the families of numerous victims of the tragedy, who were unaware of the legal difficulties involved, had a vital interest in knowing all the underlying facts and the various possible solutions. They could be deprived of this information, which was crucially important for them, only if it appeared absolutely certain that its diffusion would have presented a threat to the "authority of the judiciary".

' . . . the facts of the case did not cease to be a matter of public interest merely because they formed the background to pending litigation. By bringing to light certain facts, the article might have served as a brake on speculative and unenlightened discussion.

Having regard to all the circumstances of the case . . . the Court concludes that the interference complained of did not correspond to a social need sufficiently pressing to outweigh the public interest in freedom of expression within the meaning of the Convention. The Court therefore finds the reasons for the restraint imposed on the applicants not to be sufficient under Article 10 § 2. That restraint proves not to be proportionate to the legitimate aim pursued; it was not necessary in a democratic society for maintaining the authority of the judiciary.'

The legislation the Government is preparing on contempt of court will take account of the *Sunday Times* case.

8. On threats against parties to civil litigation see the Phillimore Report pp. 25–30 and the Law Commission Report No. 96 pp. 59–62.

4 Scandalising the court

R v Gray [1900] 2 QB 36, 69 LJQB 502, 82 LT 534, 64 JP 484 Queen's Bench Divisional Court

On 15 March 1900, one Wells was tried before Darling J at Birmingham Assizes for publishing certain obscene and filthy words, and for publishing an obscene libel. Before the trial commenced Darling J made some observations in Court, pointing out that, whatever might be the rights of the case, it was inexpedient that the press should give anything like a full or detailed account of what passed at the trial, and that, although a newspaper had the right to publish accounts of proceedings in a law court, and for many purposes was protected for doing so, there was absolutely no protection to a newspaper for the publication of objectionable, obscene, and indecent matter, and any newspaper which did so might as easily be prosecuted as anybody else. He further said that, although he hoped and believed that his advice would be taken, if it was disregarded he should make it his business to see that the law was in that respect enforced.

The following day, after the Wells trial was over, Gray wrote and published in the Birmingham Daily Argus an article which included the following passage (printed in 82 LT 534):

'No newspaper can exist except upon its merits, a condition from which the Bench, happily for Mr Justice Darling, is exempt. There is not a journalist in Birmingham who has anything to learn from the impudent little man in horsehair, a microcosm of conceit and empty-headedness, who admonished the Press yesterday. It is not the credit of journalism, but of the English Bench, that is imperilled in a speech like Mr Justice Darling's. One is almost sorry that the Lord Chancellor had not another relative to provide for on that day that he selected a new judge from among the larrikins of the law. One of Mr Justice Darling's biographers states that "an eccentric relative left him much money". That misguided testator spoiled a successful bus conductor. Mr Justice Darling would do well to master the duties of his own profession before undertaking the regulation of another.'

The Attorney-General brought the matter to the attention of the Queen's Bench Divisional Court on 27 March.

Lord Russell of Killowen CJ delivered the judgment of the court (**Lord Russell CJ, Gramtham** and **Phillinore JJ**): . . .

Any act done or writing published calculated to bring a Court or a judge of the Court into contempt, or to lower his authority, is a contempt of Court. That is one class of contempt. Further, any act done or writing published calculated to obstruct or interfere with the due course of justice or the lawful process of the Courts is a contempt of Court. The former class belongs to the category which Lord Hardwicke LC characterised as 'scandalising a Court or a judge.' (*Re Read and Huggonson* (1742) 2 Atk 291, 469) That description of that class of contempt is to be taken subject to one and an important qualification. Judges and Courts are alike open to criticism, and if reasonable argument or expostulation is offered against any judicial act as contrary to law or the public good, no Court could or would treat that as contempt of Court. The law ought not to be astute in such cases to criticise adversely what under such circumstances and with such an object is published; but it is to be remembered that in this matter the liberty of the press is no greater and no less than the liberty of every subject of the Queen. Now, as I have said, no one has suggested that this is not a contempt of Court, and nobody has suggested, or could suggest, that it falls within the right of public criticism in the sense I have described. It is not criticism: I repeat that it is personal scurrilous abuse of a judge as a judge. We have, therefore, to deal with it as a case of contempt, and we have to deal with it brevi manu. This is not a new-fangled jurisdiction; it is a jurisdiction as old as the common law itself, of which it forms part. . . It is a jurisdiction, however, to be exercised with scrupulous care, to be exercised only when the case is clear and beyond reasonable doubt; because, if it is not a case beyond reasonable doubt, the Courts will and ought to leave the Attorney-General to proceed by criminal information.

[The court fined Gray £100, with £25 costs]

R v Metropolitan Police Commissioner, ex parte Blackburn (No. 2) [1968] 2 QB 150, [1968] 2 All ER 319, [1968] 2 WLR 1204, Court of Appeal

In January 1968 the Court of Appeal delivered judgments in an application by a private citizen, [Raymond Blackburn], for an order of mandamus against the Metropolitan Police Commissioner in connection with the non-enforcement of the Gaming Acts. In their judgments the court expressed opinions on the conduct of the police and on earlier decisions on the Acts in the Queen's Bench Divisional Court [See [1968] 2 QB 118]. After reports of the judgments had appeared in the Press, [Quintin Hogg], a Privy Councillor who was also a Member of Parliament and Queen's Counsel, wrote an article in the weekly newspaper *Punch* in a section entitled 'Political Parley' in which he vigorously criticised the Court of Appeal and its dicta, wrongly attributing to that court decisions of the Divisional Court.

The applicant applied to the same Court of Appeal for an order that the writer had been guilty of contempt of court in (a) that the article falsely stated that the Act was 'rendered virtually unworkable by the unrealistic, contradictory and, in the leading case, erroneous decisions of the courts, including the Court of Appeal' and ridiculed that court by suggesting that it should apologise for the expense and trouble to which it had put the police; (b) that without proper knowledge of the facts the writer sought to ridicule the court for its alleged 'blindness'; and (c) that the writer had stated that 'a prudent policeman may well turn a somewhat blind eye towards a law which does not make sense and which Parliament may be about to repeal,' thereby encouraging police officers to flout the court's decision and commit breaches of their duty to enforce the law. For the writer it was stated that no disrespect of the court was intended but that he was exercising his right to criticise on a matter which he believed to be of public importance.

Lord Denning MR: . . .

That article is certainly critical of this court. In so far as it referred to the Court of Appeal, it is admittedly erroneous. This court did not in the gaming cases give any decision which was erroneous, nor one which was overruled by the House of Lords. But is the article a contempt of court?

This is the first case, so far as I know, where this court has been called on to consider an allegation of contempt against itself. It is a jurisdiction which undoubtedly belongs to us but which we will most sparingly exercise: more particularly as we ourselves have an interest in the matter.

Let me say at once that we will never use this jurisdiction as a means to uphold our own dignity. That must rest on surer foundations. Nor will we use it to suppress those who speak against us. We do not fear criticism, nor do we resent it. For there is something far more important at stake. It is no less than freedom of speech itself.

It is the right of every man, in Parliament or out of it, in the Press or over the broadcast, to make fair comment, even outspoken comment, on matters of public interest. Those who comment can deal faithfully with all that is done in a court of justice. They can say that we are mistaken, and our decisions erroneous, whether they are subject to appeal or not. All we would ask is that those who criticise us will remember that, from the nature of our office, we' cannot reply to their criticisms. We cannot enter into public controversy. Still less into political controversy. We must rely on our conduct itself to be its own vindication.

Exposed as we are to the winds of criticism, nothing which is said by this person or that, nothing which is written by this pen or that, will deter us from doing what we believe is right; nor, I would add, from saying what the occasion requires, provided that it is pertinent to the matter in hand. Silence is not an option when things are ill done.

So it comes to this: Mr Quintin Hogg has criticised the court, but in so doing he is exercising his undoubted right. The article contains an error, no doubt, but errors do not make it a contempt of court. We must uphold his right to the uttermost.

I hold this not to be a contempt of court, and would dismiss the application.

Salmon LJ The authority and reputation of our courts are not so frail that their judgments need to be shielded from criticism, even from the criticism of Mr Quintin Hogg. Their judgments, which can, I think, safely be left to take care of themselves, are often of considerable public importance. It is the inalienable right of everyone to comment fairly upon any matter of public importance. This right is one of the pillars of individual liberty—freedom of speech, which our courts have always unfailingly upheld.

It follows that no criticism of a judgment, however vigorous, can amount to contempt of court, providing it keeps within the limits of reasonable courtesy and good faith. The criticism here complained of, however rumbustious, however wide of the mark, whether expressed in good taste or in bad taste, seems to me to be well within those limits. . . .

No one could doubt Mr Hogg's good faith. I, of course, entirely accept that he had no intention of holding this court up to contempt; nor did he do so. Mr Blackburn complains that Mr Hogg has not apologised. There was no reason why he should apologise, for he owes no apology, save, perhaps, to the readers of *Punch* for some of the inaccuracies and inconsistencies which his article contains. I agree that this application should be dismissed.

Edmund Davies LJ delivered a concurring judgment.

Application dismissed.

NOTES

1. In *McLeod v St. Aubyn* [1899] AC 549, PC, attacks upon the competence and partiality of St. Aubyn, the Acting Chief Justice of St. Vincent, appeared in the 'Federalist' newspaper. McLeod gave a copy of the newspaper to a librarian. It was not alleged that he was the author of either the article or the letter in question, although he was the paper's agent and correspondent in St. Vincent. Neither was he aware of the contents of the offending issue. The Privy Council held that McLeod was not guilty of contempt. 'A printer and publisher intends to publish, and so intending cannot plead as a justification that he did not know the contents. The appellant in this case never intended to publish' (per Lord Morris at 562). Lord Morris also stated (at 561):

'The power summarily to commit for contempt of Court is considered necessary for the proper administration of justice. It is not to be used for the vindication of the judge as a person. He must resort to action for libel or criminal information. Committal for contempt of Court is a weapon to be used sparingly, and always with reference to the interests of the administration of justice. Hence, when a trial has taken place and the case is over, the judge or the jury are given over to criticism.

It is a summary process, and should be used only from a sense of duty and under the pressure of public necessity, for there can be no landmarks pointing out the boundaries in all cases. Committals for contempt of Court by scandalising the Court itself have become obsolete in this country. Courts are satisfied to leave to public opinion attacks or comments derogatory or scandalous to them. But it must be considered that in small colonies, consisting principally of coloured populations, the enforcement in proper cases of committal for contempt of Court for attacks on the Court may be absolutely necessary to preserve in such a community the dignity of and respect for the Court.'

The case of *R v Gray*, decided the following year, showed that this aspect of contempt was not obsolete. A. E. Hughes ((1900) 16 LQR 292) argued strongly that Lord Morris's view was to be preferred. According to Abel-Smith and Stevens (*Lawyers and the Courts* (1967) pp. 126–7): 'within a decade [of *R v Gray*] the criticism of judicial behaviour which had been so outspoken was replaced in the press by almost unbroken sycophantic praise for the judges.'

2. In *Ambard v A-G for Trinidad and Tobago* [1936] AC 322, PC, a reasoned criticism of the sentences passed in two cases in a Port of Spain court was held by the Privy Council not to constitute contempt. There was no evidence to support the finding of the Supreme Court of Trinidad that the article was written 'with the direct object of bringing the administration of the criminal law in this Colony by the judges into disrepute and disregard.' Lord Atkin stated at 335: 'But whether the authority and position of an individual judge, or the due administration of justice, is concerned, no wrong is committed by any member of the public who exercises the ordinary right of criticising, in good faith, in private or public, the public act done in the seat of justice. The path of criticism is a public way: the wrong headed are permitted to err therein: provided that members of the public abstain from imputing improper motives to those taking part in the administration of justice, and are genuinely exercising a right of criticism, and not acting in malice or attempting to impair the administration of justice, they are immune. Justice is not a cloistered virtue: she must be allowed to suffer the scrutiny and respectful, even though outspoken, comments of ordinary men.'

3. In *R v New Statesman Editor, ex parte Director of Public Prosecutions* (1928) 44 TLR 301, DC, the defendant wrote that the verdict in a libel action against Marie Stopes was a miscarriage of justice – prejudice against her work 'ought not to be allowed to influence a court of justice in the manner in which they appeared to influence Mr Justice Avory in his summing-up . . . [A]n individual owning to such views as those of Dr Stopes cannot apparently hope for a fair hearing in a Court presided over by Mr Justice Avory – and there are so many Avorys.' The Divisional Court held this to be a contempt, although they imposed no penalty in view of the editor's unqualified expressions of regret, and the absence of any intention to interfere with the performance of Avory J's judicial duties.

4. The last successful contempt proceedings of this nature in England were in the 1930s (*R v Wilkinson* (1930) *Times* 16 July; *R v Colsey* (1931) *Times* 9 May). It is noteworthy that contempt proceedings were not instituted in respect of attacks on the National Industrial Relations Court which were at times virulent (see *Phillimore*, para. 160 and Chap. 11). There have, however, been more recent examples in the Commonwealth. In See *R v Glanzer* (1962) 38 DLR (2d) 402, *Re Wiseman* [1969] NZLR 55, *Re Borowski* (1971) 19 DLR (3d) 537, and *Re Ouellet* (1976) 67 DLR (3d) 73.

5. *Mens Rea.* It is not clear whether mens rea is required for liability for this form of contempt (see *Miller*, pp. 191–2). *R v New Statesman Editor, ex parte Director of Public Prosecutions* (1928) 44 TLR 301, above p. 265, seems to indicate that it does not. This was followed in New Zealand in *Solicitor General v Radio Avon Ltd* [1977] 1 NZLR 301. Authorities to the contrary are *S v Van Niekerk* [1970] 3 SA 655 (T) and *Re Ouellet* (1976) 67 DLR (3d) 73, 91–92 (Qu Sup Ct).

In *S v Van Niekerk* [1970] 3 S A 655(T), the defendant, a senior lecturer in law, wrote in an article in the South African Law Journal ((1969) 86 SALJ 457 and (1970) 87 SALJ 60) that a significant proportion of judges and advocates who responded to a questionnaire believed that justice as regards capital punishment was meted out to the different races on a deliberately differential basis. Claassen J held at 657 that 'before a conviction can result the act complained of must not only be wilful and calculated to bring into contempt but must also be made with the intention of bringing the judges in their judicial capacity into contempt or of casting suspicion on the administration of justice'. As Van N did not have that intention he was not convicted. See H. R. Hahlo (1971) 21 U of Toronto LJ 378 and J. R. L. Milton (1970) 87 SALJ 424.

6. This variety of the law of contempt is virtually a dead letter in the United States. In *Bridges v California; Times-Mirror Co v California* 314 US 252 (1941), in applying the 'clear and present danger' test (see above, p. 243), Black J discounted 'disrespect for the judiciary' as a 'substantive evil' which could properly be averted by restricting freedom of expression: 'The assumption that respect for the judiciary can be won by shielding judges from published criticism wrongly appraises the character of American public opinion. For it is a prized American privilege to speak one's mind, although not always with perfect good taste, on all public institutions. And an enforced silence, however limited solely in the name of preserving the dignity of the bench, would probably engender resentment, suspicion, and contempt much more than it would enhance respect' (pp. 270–271).

Press allegations of judicial bias, directed to pending proceedings, have been held not to constitute a clear and present danger to the administration of justice (*Pennekamp v Florida* 328 US 331 (1946), *Re Turner* 174 NW (2d) 895 (1969)).

7. *Reform.* The Phillimore Committee recommended that attacks on courts or judges should not be dealt with under the law of contempt, unless there is a risk of serious prejudice to particular proceedings in progress. However, there should be a substantive criminal offence consisting of the publication of matter imputing improper or corrupt judicial conduct with the intention of impairing confidence in the administration of justice. It should be triable only on indictment, and only with the leave of the Attorney-General or the Lord Advocate. Cf. Law Commission Report No. 96, pp. 67–8.

8. (i) Is the law of defamation sufficient to protect the judges from scurrilous abuse, or do you agree with the Phillimore Committee's proposal for a criminal offence to replace contempt proceedings in this context? Should mens rea be a requirement? Should justification and fair comment be defences?

(ii) Does the present law of contempt give sufficiently clear guidance to those who wish to criticise the judiciary?

(iii) Do you agree with Harold Laski's view that 'To argue that the expression, even the strong expression, of . . . doubts [as to judicial impartiality] is an "interference with the course of justice" because the result is to undermine public confidence in the judiciary is to forget that public confidence is undermined not so much by the comment, as by the

habit which led to the comment . . . ' ((1928) 41 Harv LR 1031 at 1036)?
(iv) Should reports of research into the administration of justice ever be
regarded as contempt? (cf. *S v Van Niekerk*)

5 Contempt in the face of the court

It is obvious that the public interest in the due administration of justice
requires that legal proceedings be free from disruption or direct interference. Some kinds of disruption are ordinary criminal offences, for
example violent attacks on judges or jurors. All kinds of disruption will also
amount to contempt in the face of the court, and may be dealt with
summarily. The law of contempt in this context does to an extent inhibit
freedom of expression; such as the expression of the views of a disappointed
litigant as to the defects of the English legal system in general, and the
defects of the judge who has just tried his case in particular. Moreover, the
disruption of legal proceedings in order to gain publicity for a particular
cause has been roundly condemned in the Court of Appeal (*Morris v Crown
Office* [1970] 2 QB 114, below p. 270). However, the law here cannot
convincingly be criticised on the basis of interference with free speech.
Most of the criticism has centred on the summary nature of the procedure.
The two main criticisms made to the Phillimore Committee were, 'first, that
the judge appears to assume the role of prosecutor and judge in his own
cause, especially where the missile or insult is directed against him
personally; and secondly, that the contemnor usually has little or no
opportunity to defend himself or make a plea in mitigation.' (*Phillimore,*
para. 29).

**Balogh v St. Albans Crown Court [1975] QB 73, [1974] 3 All ER 283, [1974] 3 WLR 314,
Court of Appeal**

Balogh, a temporary clerk in a solicitor's office, while attending a criminal
trial at a Crown Court, devised a plan to enliven the proceedings by
releasing nitrous oxide ('laughing gas') down a ventilation duct on the roof
into the trial court. He stole a cylinder of the gas from a hospital lorry and
climbed up on to the roof at night to locate the particular inlet duct. The
next morning he left the cylinder in his brief case in the public gallery of the
court next door (Court 1) from which there was access to the roof,
intending to carry out his plan later in the day. Police, who had seen him on
the roof, found his brief case, opened it, and later cautioned Balogh who
at once admitted what he had done and planned to do. He was charged
with theft of the cylinder. The police reported the matter to Melford
Stevenson J, the senior judge, who was presiding in Court 1. Balogh was
brought before the judge who said that his admitted conduct was a serious
contempt of court and that he would consider the penalty overnight.
Balogh was to be kept in custody.
   The next morning Balogh told the judge that he did not feel competent to
conduct his own case on contempt and that he understood that the only
charge against him was theft. The judge said that he would not deal with
that charge, but committed him to six months' imprisonment for contempt
of court. Balogh then said: 'You are a humourless automaton. Why don't
you self-destruct.' Subsequently, he wrote from prison to the Official

Solicitor asking to be allowed to apologise in the hope that his contempt would be purged. Accordingly, he appealed to the Court of Appeal.

Lord Denning MR: . . .

The jurisdiction of the Crown Court

The Crown Court is a superior court of record: section 4 (1) of the Courts Act 1971. In regard to any contempt of court, it has the like powers and authority as the High Court: section 4 (8). . . .
[RSC Order 52 r. 5] . . . preserves the power of the High Court 'to make an order of committal of its own motion against a person guilty of contempt of court' . . . .
In what circumstances can the High Court make an order 'of its own motion?' In the ordinary way the High Court does not act of its own motion. An application to commit for contempt is usually made by motion either by the Attorney-General or by the party aggrieved: . . . and such a motion can, in an urgent case, be made ex parte: see *Warwick Corpn v Russell* [1964] 2 All ER 337, [1964] 1 WLR 613. . . . All I find in the books is that the court can act upon its own motion when the contempt is committed 'in the face of the court.' Wilmot CJ in his celebrated opinion in *R v Almon* (1765) Wilm 243 at 254 said: 'It is a necessary incident to every court of justice to fine and imprison for a contempt to the court, acted in the face of it.' *Blackstone* in his *Commentaries*, 16th edn. (1825), Book IV, p. 286, said: 'If the contempt be committed in the face of the court, the offender may be instantly apprehended and imprisoned, at the discretion of the judges.' In *Oswald on Contempt*, 3rd edn. (1910), p. 23 it is said: 'Upon contempt in the face of the court an order for committal was made instanter' and not on motion. But I find nothing to tell us what is meant by 'committed in the face of the court.' It has never been defined. Its meaning is, I think, to be ascertained from the practice of the judges over the centuries. It was never confined to conduct which a judge saw with his own eyes. It covered all contempts for which a judge of his own motion could punish a man on the spot. So 'contempt in the face of the court' is the same thing as 'contempt which the court can punish of its own motion.' It really means 'contempt in the cognisance of the court.'
Gathering together the experience of the past, then, whatever expression is used, a judge of one of the superior courts or a judge of Assize could always punish summarily of his own motion for contempt of court whenever there was a gross interference with the course of justice in a case that was being tried, or about to be tried, or just over—no matter whether the judge saw it with his own eyes or it was reported to him by the officers of the court, or by others—whenever it was urgent and imperative to act at once. This power has been inherited by the judges of the High Court and in turn by the judges of the Crown Court. To show the extent of it, I will give some instances:
(i) *In the sight of the court.* There are many cases where a man has been committed to prison at once for throwing a missile at the judge, be it a brickbat, an egg, or a tomato. Recently, too, when a group of students broke up the trial of a libel action Lawton J very properly sent them at once to prison: see *Morris v Crown Office* [1970] 2 QB 114. There is an older case, too, of great authority, where a witness refused to answer a proper question. The judge of Assize at York Castle at once sentenced him to prison for six months and imposed a fine of £500: see *Ex parte Fernandez* (1861) 10 CBNS 3.
(ii) *Within the court room but not seen by the judge.* At the Old Bailey a man distributed leaflets in the public gallery inciting people to picket the place. A member of the public reported it to a police officer, who reported it to the judge. The offender denied it. Melford Stevenson J immediately heard the evidence on both sides. He convicted the offender and sentenced him to seven days' imprisonment. The man appealed to this court. His appeal was dismissed: *Lecointe v Court's Administrator of the Central Criminal Court* (1973) 8 February Bar Library Transcript No. 57A of 1973.
(iii) *At some distance from the court.* At Bristol 22 men were being tried for an affray. The first witness for the prosecution was a school girl. After she had given her evidence, she went to a café for a meal. A man clenched his fist at her and threatened her. She told the police, who told the judge. Park J had the man arrested. He asked counsel to represent him. He broke off the trial. He heard evidence of the threat. He committed the man. He sentenced him to three months' imprisonment. The man appealed to this court. His appeal was dismissed: *Moore v Clerk of Assize, Bristol* [1972] 1 All ER 58. Another case was where a man was summoned to serve on a jury. His employer threatened to dismiss him if he obeyed the summons. Melford Stevenson J said it was a contempt of court which made him liable to immediate imprisonment: see 'The Rule of Law and Jury Service' (1966) 130 JP 622.
Those are modern instances. I have no doubt that there were many like instances in the past which were never reported, because there was until recently no right of appeal. They bear out the power which I have already stated—a power which has been inherited by the judges of the Crown Court.

This power of summary punishment is a great power, but it is a necessary power. It is given so as to maintain the dignity and authority of the court and to ensure a fair trial. It is to be exercised by the judge of his own motion only when it is urgent and imperative to act immediately—so as to maintain the authority of the court—to prevent disorder—to enable witnesses to be free from fear--and jurors from being improperly influenced—and the like. It is, of course, to be exercised with scrupulous care, and only when the case is clear and beyond reasonable doubt: see *R v Gray* [1900] 2 QB 36 at 41 by Lord Russell of Killowen CJ. But properly exercised it is a power of the utmost value and importance which should not be curtailed.

Over 100 years ago Erle CJ said that ' . . . these powers, . . . as far as my experience goes, have always been exercised for the advancement of justice and the good of the public': see *Ex parte Fernandez* (1861) 10 CBNS 3 at 38. I would say the same today. From time to time anxieties have been expressed lest these powers might be abused. But these have been set at rest by section 13 of the Administration of Justice Act 1960, which gives a right to appeal to a higher court.

As I have said, a judge should act of his own motion only when it is urgent and imperative to act immediately. In all other cases he should not take it upon himself to move. He should leave it to the Attorney-General or to the party aggrieved to make a motion in accordance with the rules in RSC Ord 52. The reason is so that he should not appear to be both prosecutor and judge: for that is a role which does not become him well.

Returning to the present case, it seems to me that up to a point the judge was absolutely right to act of his own motion. The intention of Mr. Balogh was to disrupt the proceedings in a trial then taking place. His conduct was reported to the senior judge then in the court building. It was very proper for him to take immediate action, and to have Mr Balogh brought before him. But once he was there, it was not a case for summary punishment. There was not sufficient urgency to warrant it. Nor was it imperative. He was already in custody on a charge of stealing. The judge would have done well to have remanded him in custody and invited counsel to represent him. If he had done so counsel would, I expect, have taken the point to which I now turn.

The conduct of Mr Balogh

Contempt of court is a criminal offence which is governed by the principles applicable to criminal offences generally. In particular, by the difference between an attempt to commit an offence and an act preparatory to it.
[His Lordship held that B's conduct amounted at most to 'acts preparatory'] . . .
So here Mr Balogh had the criminal intent to disrupt the court, but that is not enough. He was guilty of stealing the cylinder, but no more.

On this short ground we think the judge was in error. We have already allowed the appeal on this ground. But, even if there had not been this ground, I should have thought that the sentence of six months was excessive. Balogh spent 14 days in prison: and he has now apologised. That is enough to purge his contempt, if contempt it was.

Conclusion

There is a lesson to be learned from the recent cases on this subject. It is particularly appropriate at the present time. The new Crown Courts are in being. The judges of them have not yet acquired the prestige of the Red Judge when he went on Assize. His robes and bearing made everyone alike stand in awe of him. Rarely did he need to exercise his great power of summary punishment. Yet there is just as much need for the Crown Court to maintain its dignity and authority. The judges of it should not hesitate to exercise the authority they inherit from the past. Insults are best treated with disdain—save when they are gross and scandalous. Refusal to answer with admonishment—save where it is vital to know the answer. But disruption of the court or threats to witnesses or to jurors should be visited with immediate arrest. Then a remand in custody and, if it can be arranged, representation by counsel. If it comes to a sentence, let it be such as the offence deserves—with the comforting reflection that, if it is in error, there is an appeal to this court. We always hear these appeals within a day or two. The present case is a good instance. The judge acted with a firmness which became him. As it happened, he went too far. That is no reproach to him. It only shows the wisdom of having an appeal.
Stephenson and **Lawton LJJ** delivered concurring judgments.
Appeal allowed.

NOTES

1. In *Morris v Crown Office* [1970] 2 QB 114, CA, a group of young Welsh students interrupted the proceedings in a libel action (*Broome v Cassell & Co*) being heard by Lawton J. They shouted slogans, scattered pamphlets and sang songs. The judge adjourned the hearing. When order was restored, the judge returned to court and sentenced three students to three months' imprisonment each for contempt. At the rising of the court, he dealt with nineteen others. Eight apologised, and were fined £50 each and bound over to keep the peace. Eleven did not apologise, saying that they acted as a matter of principle on behalf of the Welsh language. They each received 3 month sentences. The eleven students appealed to the Court of Appeal, arguing (inter alia) (1) that s. 39(1) and (3) of the Criminal Justice Act 1967 required the sentences to be suspended, and (2) that the sentences were too severe. The Court of Appeal held that the 1967 Act was not applicable as there was no machinery for following up a suspended sentence passed in such circumstances, and that the sentences when passed were appropriate. However, as the students had spent a week in prison, and shown respect to the court, the prison sentences were remitted and the defendants bound over to be of good behaviour, to keep the peace, and to come up to judgment if called on to do so.

2. In England, inferior courts have statutory power to punish certain kinds of conduct amounting to contempt in the face. See the County Courts Act 1959, ss. 30(1) (assault on officer of the court), 84(1) (refusals to produce documents, to be sworn or to give evidence), 157(1) (insults towards judge, juror, witness or officer of the court, and misbehaviour in court); and the Magistrates' Courts Act 1952, s. 77(4) (refusals to produce documents, to be sworn or to give evidence). Binding-over powers may be used, and offenders can be removed from the court. The Phillimore Committee recommend that magistrates courts be given statutory power to punish contempt in the face of the court, the maximum penalty being the same as that prescribed by s. 77(4) of the 1952 Act, namely 7 days' imprisonment or a £20 fine.

3. An example of contempt in the face of the court of significance for press freedom is the refusal of a witness to answer a question. In *A-G v Mulholland; A-G v Foster* [1963] 2 QB 477, the Court of Appeal held that a journalist has no legal privilege entitling him to refuse to divulge his sources of information. He must answer any question put to him which is relevant to the inquiry and one which, in the opinion of the judge, it is proper for him to be asked. See also *A-G v Clough* [1963] 1 QB 773. These cases arose out of refusals by journalists to answer questions put by the Tribunal of Inquiry into the Vassall case (Report, Cmnd. 2009). The chairman of the Tribunal, Viscount Radcliffe, referred the matter to the High Court pursuant to s. 1(2) of the Tribunals of Inquiry (Evidence) Act 1921. The United States Supreme Court has also held that journalists enjoy no privilege against disclosing their sources (see *Miller*, pp. 60–61 and the cases cited therein). See also *Senior v Holdsworth* [1975] 2 All ER 1009 where the Court of Appeal set aside a county court summons to ITN to produce all the film they had taken at the Windsor Great Park pop festival in August 1974, issued at the instigation of a plaintiff in an assault action against the police. ITN were held not to be entitled to any privilege against production of untransmitted film, but the particular order was regarded as excessively wide and oppressive given that much of the film was taken on days other than the one on which the alleged assault took place.

4. The fact that many examples of contempt in the face of the court have their humorous side should not conceal the very real difficulties faced by judges in 'political' trials. These seem to be more endemic in the United States than in Britain. See, for example, the Transcript of the Contempt Citations, Sentences, and Responses of the Chicago Conspiracy 10 (1970). For entertainment, see Megarry, *A Second Miscellany-at-Law* (1973) pp. 70–83.

5. An excellent illustration of the dangers inherent in use of the summary procedures in this context is *McKeown v R* (1971) 16 DLR (3d) 390, where the Supreme Court of Canada managed to uphold a contempt conviction based on slender evidence, over strong dissents by Spence and Laskin JJ. See also *Maharaj v A-G for Trinidad and Tobago* [1977] 1 All ER 411, where the Privy Council held that the failure of a judge to make plain the specific nature of the contempt with which M was being charged vitiated the judge's order committing M to the 'Royal Goal' [sic] for contempt in the face of the court. Subsequently the Privy Council held that M was entitled to claim damages for the imprisonment, under the Constitution of Trinidad and Tobago, on the ground that he had been deprived of his liberty otherwise than by due process of law (*Maharaj v A-G for Trinidad and Tobago (No 2)* [1978] 2 All ER 670, PC). For a discussion of the problems arising out of alleged misconduct by lawyers in the face of the court, see P. Butt [1978] Crim LR 463.

6. The Phillimore Committee recommended (in Chap. 3) that the practice whereby the judge deals with contempts in the face of the court himself should continue, and that:

'(a) the judge should always ensure that the contemnor is in no doubt about the nature of the conduct complained of, and give him an opportunity of explaining or denying his conduct, and of calling witnesses;
(b) before any substantial penalty is imposed there should be a short adjournment, with power to remand the contemnor in custody. The judge should have power to obtain a background report on the contemnor, and the contemnor should be entitled to speak in mitigation of sentence;
(c) for the purposes of defending himself and of making a plea in mitigation the contemnor should be entitled to legal representation, and the court should have power to grant legal aid immediately for this purpose where appropriate;
(d) if the contempt also amounts to a criminal offence, the judge should consider referring it to the prosecuting authorities to be dealt with under the ordinary criminal law, and should so refer it in serious cases unless reasons of urgency or convenience require that it be dealt with summarily.' (p. 95).

7. Is it contempt of court for a member of the public to raise two fingers in the direction of a limousine carrying two High Court Judges on their way to court? Should it make any difference that the member of the public believes the car to be that of the local mayor, whom he regards as responsible for the latest increase in rates? Cf. the case of Mr Bangs (*Miller*, p. 53, *The Times*, 24 May, 1973, *The Daily Telegraph*, May 23, 1973). Mr Bangs spent two hours in a cell before being admonished by Lawson J.

CHAPTER 6

Freedom of expression: national security

1 Government secrecy and national security

(a) INTRODUCTION

The materials in this chapter illustrate a variety of legal and extra-legal inhibitions on freedom of expression and access to information which protect the interest of the state in keeping certain matters secret. At the heart of the legal restrictions are the Official Secrets Acts (below pp. 273–276) which cover matters ranging from serious breaches of national security to the unauthorised disclosure of any official information. These have reinforced the tendency towards excessive secrecy which has been one of the hallmarks of the public service. Currently there are moves towards more open government (below, pp. 290–291). Government departments are prepared to release more information than formerly. There are proposals which have attracted widespread support for restricting the scope of criminal sanctions. There are rather more tentative suggestions for the creation of legal rights of access to information. The courts have restricted the circumstances in which a public authority may decline to divulge information in the course of legal proceedings on the ground that it would be contrary to the public interest (below, p. 289). At the same time, the Lord Widgery CJ has held that the state may take advantage of the developing law relating to the restraint by injunction of breaches of confidence (below, pp. 286–289).

Extra-legal factors are equally significant in the maintenance of secrecy and security. The press have acceded to a system of self-censorship in defence and security matters ('D' Notices: below pp. 284–285). There are extensive measures for maintaining the physical security of classified information. There are procedures for vetting applicants for positions in the Civil Service aimed in particular at excluding persons with Communist associations or character defects from sensitive positions. Civil Servants responsible for unauthorised disclosures may be disciplined or dismissed. See generally, D. G. T. Williams, *Not in the Public Interest* (1965), and (1968) 3 Federal LR 20; H. Street, *Freedom, the Individual and the Law*, 4th edn. (1977) Chap. 8.

(b) THE OFFICIAL SECRETS ACTS

Official Secrets Act 1911

1. Penalties for spying
(1) If any person for any purpose prejudicial to the safety or interests of the State—
    (*a*) approaches [inspects, passes over] or is in the neighbourhood of, or enters any prohibited place within the meaning of this Act; or
    (*b*) makes any sketch, plan, model, or note which is calculated to be or might be or is intended to be directly or indirectly useful to an enemy; or
    (*c*) obtains, [collects, records, or publishes,] or communicates to any other person [any secret official code word, or pass word, or] any sketch, plan, model, article, or note, or other document or information which is calculated to be or might be or is intended to be directly or indirectly useful to an enemy;
he shall be guilty of felony . . .
(2) On a prosecution under this section, it shall not be necessary to show that the accused person was guilty of any particular act tending to show a purpose prejudicial to the safety or interests of the State, and, notwithstanding that no such act is proved against him, he may be convicted if, from the circumstances of the case, or his conduct, or his known character as proved, it appears that his purpose was a purpose prejudicial to the safety or interests of the State; and if any sketch, plan, model, article, note, document, or information relating to or used in any prohibited place within the meaning of this Act, or anything in such a place [or any secret official code word or pass word], is made, obtained, [collected, recorded, published], or communicated by any person other than a person acting under lawful authority, it shall be deemed to have been made, obtained, [collected, recorded, published] or communicated for a purpose prejudicial to the safety or interests of the State unless the contrary is proved.

2. Wrongful communication, etc., of information
(1) If any person having in his possession or control [any secret official code word, or pass word, or] any sketch, plan, model, article, note, document, or information which relates to or is used in a prohibited place or anything in such a place, or which has been made or obtained in contravention of this Act, or which has been entrusted in confidence to him by any person holding office under His Majesty or which he has obtained [or to which he has had access] owing to his position as a person who holds or has held office under His Majesty, or as a person who holds or has held a contract made on behalf of His Majesty, or as a person who is or has been employed under a person who holds or has held such an office or contract,—
    (*a*) communicates the [code word, pass word,] sketch, plan, model, article, note, document, or information to any person, other than a person to whom he is authorised to communicate it, or a person to whom it is in the interest of the State his duty to communicate it, or,
    [(*aa*) uses the information in his possession for the benefit of any foreign power or in any other manner prejudicial to the safety or interests of the State;]
    (*b*) retains the sketch, plan, model, article, note, or document in his possession or control when he has no right to retain it [or when it is contrary to his duty to retain it or fails to comply with all directions issued by lawful authority with regard to the return or disposal thereof] [or
    (*c*) fails to take reasonable care of, or so conducts himself as to endanger the safety of the sketch, plan, model, article, note, document, secret official code or pass word or information]:
that person shall be guilty of a misdemeanour.
    [(1A) If any person having in his possession or control any sketch, plan, model, article, note, document, or information which relates to munitions of war, communicates it directly or indirectly to any foreign power, or in an other manner prejudicial to the safety or interests of the State, that person shall be guilty of a misdemeanour;]
    (2) If any person receives any [secret official code word, or pass word, or] sketch, plan, model, article, note, document, or information, knowing, or having reasonable ground to believe, at the time when he receives it, that the [code word, pass word,] sketch, plan, model, article, note, document, or information is communicated to him in contravention of this Act, he shall be guilty of a misdemeanour, unless he proves that the communication to him of the [code word, pass word,] sketch, plan, model, article, note, document, or information was contrary to his desire.

3. Definition of prohibited place
For the purposes of this Act, the expression 'prohibited place' means—
    [(*a*) Any work of defence, arsenal, naval or air force establishment or station, factory, dockyard, mine, minefield, camp, ship, or aircraft belonging to or occupied by or on behalf

of His Majesty, or any telegraph, telephone, wireless or signal station, or office so belonging or occupied, and any place belonging to or occupied by or on behalf of His Majesty and used for the purpose of building, repairing, making, or storing any munitions of war, or any sketches, plans, models, or documents relating thereto, or for the purpose of getting any metals, oil, or minerals of use in time of war]; and

(*b*)   any place not belonging to His Majesty where any [munitions of war], or any [sketches, models, plans] or documents relating thereto, are being made, repaired, [gotten] or stored under contract with, or with any person on behalf of, His Majesty, or otherwise on behalf of His Majesty; and

(*c*)   any place belonging to [or used for the purposes of] His Majesty which is for the time being declared [by order of a Secretary of State] to be a prohibited place for the purposes of this section on the ground that information with respect thereto, or damage thereto, would be useful to an enemy; and

(*d*)   any railway, road, way, or channel, or other means of communication by land or water (including any works or structures being part thereof or connected therewith), or any place used for gas, water, or electricity works or other works for purposes of a public character, or any place where any [munitions of war], or any [sketches, models, plans] or documents relating thereto, are being made, repaired, or stored otherwise than on behalf of His Majesty, which is for the time being declared by order of a Secretary of State] to be a prohibited place for the purposes of this section, on the ground that information with respect thereto, or the destruction or obstruction thereof, or interference therewith, would be useful to an enemy.

6. Power to arrest
Any person who is found committing an offence under this Act . . . or who is reasonably suspected of having committed, or having attempted to commit, or being about to commit, such an offence, may be apprehended and detained . . .

7. Penalty for harbouring spies
If any person knowingly harbours any person whom he knows, or has reasonable grounds for supposing, to be a person who is about to commit or who has committed an offence under this Act, or knowingly permits to meet or assemble in any premises in his occupation or under his control any such persons, or if any person having harboured any such person, or permitted to meet or assemble in any premises in his occupation or under his control any such persons, [wilfully omits or refuses] to disclose to a superintendent of police any information which it is in his power to give in relation to any such person he shall be guilty of a misdemeanour . . .

8. Restriction on prosecution
A prosecution for an offence under this Act shall not be instituted except by or with the consent of the Attorney-General.

9. Search warrants
(1)   If a justice of the peace is satisfied by information on oath that there is reasonable ground for suspecting that an offence under this Act has been or is about to be committed, he may grant a search warrant authorising any constable named therein to enter at any time any premises or place named in the warrant, if necessary, by force, and to search the premises or place and every person found therein, and to seize any sketch, plan, model, article, note, or document, or anything of a like nature or anything which is evidence of an offence under this Act having been or being about to be committed, which he may find on the premises or place or on any such person, and with regard to or in connexion with which he has reasonable ground for suspecting that an offence under this Act has been or is about to be committed.
(2)   Where it appears to a superintendent of police that the case is one of great emergency and that in the interests of the State immediate action is necessary, he may by a written order under his hand give to any constable the like authority as may be given by the warrant of a justice under this section.

12. Interpretation
In this Act, unless the context otherwise requires,—
Any reference to a place belonging to His Majesty includes a place belonging to any department of the Government of the United Kingdom or of any British possessions, whether the place is or is not actually vested in His Majesty; . . .
Expressions referring to communicating or receiving include any communicating or receiving, whether in whole or in part, and whether the sketch, plan, model, article, note, document, or information itself or the substance, effect, or description thereof only be communicated or received; expressions referring to obtaining or retaining any sketch, plan, model, article, note, or document, include the copying or causing to be copied the whole or

any part of any sketch, plan, model, article, note, or document; and expressions referring to the communication of any sketch, plan, model, article, note or document include the transfer or transmission of the sketch, plan, model, article, note or document;

The expression 'document' includes part of a document;

The expression 'model' includes design, pattern, and specimen;

The expression 'sketch' includes any photograph or other mode of representing any place or thing;

[The expression 'munitions of war' includes the whole or any part of any ship, submarine, aircraft, tank or similar engine, arms and ammunition, torpedo, or mine, intended or adapted for use in war, and any other article, material, or device, whether actual or proposed, intended for such use;]

The expression 'superintendent of police' includes any police officer of a like or superior rank [and any person upon whom the powers of a superintendent of police are for the purpose of this Act conferred by a Secretary of State];

The expression 'office under His Majesty' includes any office or employment in or under any department of the Government of the United Kingdom, or of any British possession;

The expression 'offence under this Act' includes any act, omission, or other thing which is punishable under this Act.

Official Secrets Act 1920

1. (2) If any person—

(*a*) retains for any purpose prejudicial to the safety or interests of the State any official document, whether or not completed or issued for use, when he has no right to retain it, or when it is contrary to his duty to retain it, or fails to comply with any directions issued by any Government Department or any person authorised by such department with regard to the return or disposal thereof; or

(*b*) allows any other person to have possession of any official document issued for his use alone, or communicates any secret official code word or pass word so issued, or, without lawful authority or excuse, has in his possession any official document or secret official code word or pass word issued for the use of some person other than himself, or on obtaining possession of any official document by finding or otherwise, neglects or fails to restore it to the person or authority by whom or for whose use it was issued, or to a police constable; or

(*c*) without lawful authority or excuse, manufactures or sells, or has in his possession for sale any such die, seal or stamp as aforesaid;

he shall be guilty of a misdemeanour.

(3) In the case of any prosecution under this section involving the proof of a purpose prejudicial to the safety or interests of the State, subsection (2) of section one of the principal Act shall apply in like manner as it applies to prosecutions under that section.

6. [(1) Where a chief officer of police is satisfied that there is reasonable ground for suspecting that an offence under section one of the principal Act has been committed and for believing that any person is able to furnish information as to the offence or suspected offence, he may apply to a Secretary of State for permission to exercise the powers conferred by this subsection and, if such permission is granted, he may authorise a superintendent of police, or any police officer not below the rank of inspector, to require the person believed to be able to furnish information to give any information in his power relating to the offence or suspected offence, and, if so required and on tender of his reasonable expenses, to attend at such reasonable time and place as may be specified by the superintendent or other officer; and if a person required in pursuance of such an authorisation to give information, or to attend as aforesaid, fails to comply with any such requirement or knowingly gives false information, he shall be guilty of a misdemeanour.

(2) Where a chief officer of police has reasonable grounds to believe that the case is one of great emergency and that in the interest of the State immediate action is necessary, he may exercise the powers conferred by the last foregoing subsection without applying for or being granted the permission of a Secretary of State, but if he does so shall forthwith report the circumstances to the Secretary of State.

(3) References in this section to a chief officer of police shall be construed as including references to any other officer of police expressly authorised by a chief officer of police to act on his behalf for the purposes of this section when by reason of illness, absence, or other cause he is unable to do so.]

7. Attempts, incitements, etc.

Any person who attempts to commit any offence under the principal Act or this Act, or solicits or incites or endeavours to persuade another person to commit an offence, or aids or abets and does any act preparatory to the commission of an offence under the principal Act or this Act, shall be guilty of a felony or a misdemeanour or a summary offence according as the offence in question is a felony, a misdemeanour or a summary offence, and on conviction shall be liable to the same punishment, and to be proceeded against in the same manner, as if he had committed the offence.

NOTES

1. The words in square brackets in the 1911 Act were added by the Official Secrets Act 1920. S. 6 of the 1920 Act was substituted by the Official Secrets Act 1939, s. 1. The maximum penalty under s. 1 of the 1911 Act is 14 years' imprisonment, and for the other offences under the two Acts (other than sections 4 and 5 of the 1920 Act) is two years' imprisonment.

There are special provisions concerning atomic energy. Section 12 of the Atomic Energy Act 1946 makes it an offence to communicate to an unauthorised person information relating to atomic energy plant (see S.R. & O. 1947 No. 100). Membership of, or any office or employment under, the UK Atomic Energy Authority is deemed to be an office under Her Majesty for the purposes of the Official Secrets Act 1911, s. 2 (Atomic Energy Authority Act 1954, Sch. 3). Any place belonging to or used for the purposes of the Authority may be declared to be a prohibited place under the Official Secrets Act 1911, s. 3(c) (Atomic Energy Authority Act 1954, s. 6(3)). Similar provisions apply to the Civil Aviation Authority (Civil Aviation Act 1971, s. 61) and the holders of a nuclear site licence (Nuclear Installations Act 1965, Sch. 1). It is also an offence for a member of any Euratom institution or committee, an officer or servant of Euratom or a person who has dealings with Euratom to disclose classified information acquired from that source (European Communities Act 1972, s. 11(2)). The current orders under s. 3(c) are The Official Secrets (Prohibited Places) Orders 1955 and 1975, S.I.s 1955 No. 1497 and 1975 No. 182. They cover the Capenhurst and Windscale works of British Nuclear Fuels Ltd., and various establishments of the Atomic Energy Authority, including Dounreay and Harwell.

2. It is an offence under section 1(1) of the 1920 Act to use specified false pretences for the purpose of gaining admission to a prohibited place or for any other purpose prejudicial to the safety or interests of the State. These include the use without lawful authority of official uniform (e.g. military or police) or any uniform so nearly resembling it as to be calculated to deceive; making false statements; forging or altering a pass (or similar document); using or possessing such a document; personating a person holding office under the Crown or a person entitled to use an official pass (or similar document), code word, or pass word; unauthorised use or possession of any die seal or stamp of a government department or any diplomatic, naval, military or air force authority under the Crown, or die seal or stamp so closely resembling one as to be calculated to deceive.

It is also an offence to obstruct, knowingly mislead or otherwise interfere with or impede any police officer, or any member of the forces on guard, patrol or similar duty, 'in the vicinity of a prohibited place' (1920 Act, s. 3).

3. The fact that a person has been in communication with a foreign agent constitutes evidence in proceedings against him under s. 1 of the 1911 Act that he has for a purpose prejudicial to the safety or interests of the State, obtained or attempted to obtain information which may be useful to an enemy (1920 Act, s. 2). There is also a power whereby a Secretary of State may require the production of telegrams (1920 Act, s. 4). Persons who carry on the business of receiving postal packets for delivery or forwarding must be registered with the police (1920 Act, s. 5).

4. If, in the course of any court proceedings under the Acts:

'. . . application is made by the prosecution, on the ground that the publication of any evidence to be given or of any statement to be made in the course of the proceedings would be prejudicial to the national safety, that all or any portion of the public shall be excluded during any part of the hearing, the court may make an order to that effect, but the passing of sentence shall in any case take place in public.' (1920 Act, s. 8(4)).

5. The term 'enemy' includes a potential enemy, and so all the provisions of section 1 are applicable in peace time (*R v Parrott* (1913) 8 Cr App Rep 186, CCA).

6. The origins of the Official Secrets Acts are discussed in D. G. T. Williams, *Not in the Public Interest* (1965) Chap. 1; Report of the Franks Committee on Section 2 of the Official Secrets Act 1911, Cmnd. 5104, Ch. 4 and Appendix III; D. French, 'Spy Fever in Britain, 1900–1915', The Historical Journal, 21, 2 (1978) p. 355. The 1911 Bill was presented by the Government as a measure which was aimed at spying and was essential on grounds of national security (Franks Report, p. 24). S. 2 was not mentioned. It passed all its Commons stages in less than an hour. The files show that the legislation had been desired for some time by governments, the Official Secrets Act 1889 having proved inadequate to prevent the leakage of official information by civil servants, and that it had been carefully prepared over a period of years (Franks Report, p. 25).

7. The leading case on section 1, *Chandler v Director of Public Prosecutions*, is given below at p. 280. S. 3 of the 1920 Act was used in a prosecution of four members of the Committee of 100, including Pat Arrowsmith, in 1964. They were fined £25 for inciting people to obstruct police officers at the USAF base at Ruislip in connection with a demonstration there (D. G. T. Williams, *Not in the Public Interest* (1965) p. 109). Williams points out (at p. 111) that it was not necessary for the Official Secrets Acts to be invoked against the nuclear disarmers in the 1960s, in preference to prosecutions for the general public order offences.

In *Adler v George* [1964] 2 QB 7, A obstructed a member of the armed forces engaged in security duty while within the boundaries of Marham RAF station. His conviction under s. 3 of the 1920 Act was upheld by the Divisional Court, which held that the words 'in the vicinity of' had to be read as meaning 'in or in the vicinity of'.

Another alteration in the statutory language to the detriment of a defendant was made by the Court of Criminal Appeal in *R v Oakes* [1959] 2 QB 350. The court treated section 7 of the 1911 Act as if it read 'aids or abets *or* does any act preparatory' so as to render liable a person who had done an 'act preparatory' without 'aiding or abetting'.

'It seems to the court that it is quite clear in the present case what the intention was, and that there has been merely a faultiness of expression'
(per Lord Parker CJ at p. 357).

O had also been convicted under s. 2 of the 1911 Act. In *R v Bingham* [1973] QB 870 the Court of Appeal (Criminal Division) held that an 'act preparatory' was 'an act done by the accused with the commission of an offence under the principal Act in mind', and that it was sufficient to show that the transmission of prejudicial information was 'possible' and not 'probable' (per Lord Widgery CJ at p. 875). Is it necessary for something to be an offence which is even more remote from the substantive offence than an attempt to commit it?

8. Proceedings which revealed the extent to which the authorities were still prepared to prefer charges under the Official Secrets Acts were instituted in 1978 (the *ABC* case: Nichol [1979] Crim LR 284). The defendants were John Berry, a former corporal in the Intelligence Corps, Duncan Campbell, a journalist with the *New Statesman*, and Crispin Aubrey, a journalist with *Time Out*. B communicated information to the journalists concerning Britain's signals intelligence (Sigint) organization. They were convicted under s. 2, but charges under s. 1 were dropped (see below p. 284). The journalists were given conditional discharges, and B a six month suspended prison sentence.

Mars-Jones J made some rulings of significance as to the scope of s. 2 (Nichol, op. cit. pp. 288–290). He held that the word 'information' in s. 2(2) was not qualified by the words 'secret official' which appear earlier in the subsection. Accordingly, the information did not have to be secret. He confirmed that *R v Crisp and Homewood* (1919) 83 JP 121 was still good law. There, C, a War Officer clerk handed to H, a director of a firm of tailors, details of procurement contracts for Army officers' clothing. Avory J held that the enacting words of s. 2 could not be altered or limited merely by the short title referring to 'Official Secrets', but that even if this could be done, there was evidence that these documents were official secrets.

As to *mens rea*, Mars–Jones J rejected B's argument that he was entitled to be acquitted if he honestly believed that in the interests of the State it was his duty to communicate the information to C. What was in the interests of the State was a wholly inappropriate question for a jury. He followed *R v Fell* [1963] Crim LR 207 where the Court of Criminal Appeal stated that the offence under s. 2(1) 'is absolute and is committed whatever the document contains, whatever the nature of the disclosure and whether or not the disclosure is prejudicial to the state.'

A different view as to *mens rea* had been taken in *R v Aitken* (1971). Four defendants were charged under s. 2 in connection with the communication and receipt of a confidential assessment of the situation in Nigeria during the Biafran conflict, written by the Defence Adviser at the British High Commission in Lagos. A copy was published in the *Sunday Telegraph*. The defendants were the newspaper, the editor, and two of those along the chain of communication. They were all acquitted. Caulfield J left to the jury A's defence that he believed it was his duty in the interests of the State to show that Ministers may have been deceiving the public (see J. Aitken, *Officially Secret* (1971)).

9. The repeal of s. 2 and its replacement by narrower and more specific provisions in an Official Information Act was recommended by a Departmental Committee under the chairmanship of Lord Franks, which reported in 1972 (Cmnd. 5104). The main proposals were as follows. Criminal sanctions should apply to the disclosure by a Crown Servant contrary to his official duty of certain limited classes of material ('official information'): information classified SECRET concerning defence, internal security, foreign relations, the currency and the reserves; information classified CONFIDENTIAL concerning military weapons and equipment; information likely to be helpful in the commission of offences, in facilitating an escape from legal custody or other acts prejudicial to prison security, or whose disclosure would be likely to impede the prevention or detection of offences or the apprehension or prosecution of offenders; cabinet documents; and information given in confidence to the government by private individuals or concerns. Other offences should include the use of 'official information' for private gain and failure to take reasonable care of 'official information' or to comply with directions for its return or disposal. Similar provisions should be applicable to government contractors. The unauthorised communication by any person of 'official information' which he knows or has reasonable grounds to believe has been communicated in contravention of the Official Information Act would be an offence, although the mere receipt of such information would not be. In relation to a prosecution where 'classification' of the information was a necessary element, the responsible minister should be required to determine whether at the time of the relevant disclosure the information was properly so classified. There would be various defences that the person charged did not know and had no reasonable, ground to know that, for example, information was classified, or that disclosure would be contrary to a Crown Servant's official duty.

The basic principles of the repeal of s. 2 and its replacement along the lines suggested by the Franks Committee were accepted by the Home Secretaries in both Conservative and Labour governments (Robert Carr, 858 HC Deb 29 June 1973 col 1885; Merlyn Rees, 919 HC Deb 22 November 1976 cols 1878–1881). There were, however, differences on point of detail.

The Labour proposals were in some respects narrower than the Franks categories. They did not regard criminal sanctions as necessary for economic information, and for cabinet documents (unless they fell by their content and security classification into one of the protected categories). However, there was a need to protect 'confidential' information in certain areas of defence policy and international relations and they agreed with the Conservatives that all confidences of the citizen, however acquired, should be protected (see also the White Paper published in July 1978, Cmnd. 7285). A private members bill presented by Clement Freud to repeal section 2, to create a public right of access to official information, and to make new provision in respect of the wrongful communication and handling of official information, had cross-party support, and some prospect for success, but lapsed with the fall of the Labour government in 1979 (Official Information Bill, 1978–79 Bill 96).

The Conservative Government introduced a Protection of Official Information Bill in October 1979 (1979–80 Bill 73 HL). This was still largely modelled on the Franks report though wider in some respects and narrower in others. This bill was withdrawn in November 1979. It was thought that the bill would have prevented the disclosures which led to the naming of Anthony Blunt as a Russian spy.

10. The Franks Committee proposals were shaped by their view that s. 2 was properly described as 'a long stop or a safety net . . . S. 2 is not the main protection: its function is to provide an extra margin of protection, in case other measures should fail' (Franks Committee, p. 30). The 'other measures' are discussed in Chapter 5 of the Committee's report. They point out that a civil servant who is regarded as unreliable, or who tends to overstep the mark and to talk too freely, may fail to obtain promotion or may be given less important and attractive jobs. Breach of the formal discipline code may lead to penalties ranging from reprimand to dismissal. (Action taken for the purpose of safeguarding national security may not form the basis of a complaint for unfair dimissal under the Employment Protection (Consolidation) Act 1978: ibid., Sch. 9, para. 2(1), and a certificate purporting to be signed by or on behalf of a Minister is conclusive evidence that the action was taken for that purpose: ibid., Sch. 9, para. 2(2).) The government's recruitment procedures are designed to ensure fitness for appointment. There are vetting procedures to check the suitability of those with access to particularly sensitive information (see 448 HC Deb 15 March 1948 cols 1703 ff; *Statement of the Findings of the Conference of Privy Counsellors on Security* (1956) Cmd. 9715; 563 HC Deb 29 January 1957 cols 152–156 written answer, *Report of the Committee on Security Procedures in the Public Service* (1961) Cmnd. 1681; D. C. Jackson (1957) 20 MLR 364; M. R. Joelson, [1963] PL 51). Security vetting has been applied to the personal assistants of Ministers from outside the Civil Service (873 HC Deb 7 May 1974 cols. 121–2 written answer), but does not apply to Ministers themselves (*Report of the Security Commission* (1973) Cmnd. 5367). Precautions are also taken to ensure the physical security of documents according to their classification.

Chandler v Director of Public Prosecutions [1964] AC 763, [1962] 3 All ER 142, [1962] 3 WLR 702, House of Lords

The appellants, five men and a w,oman, were members of the Committee of 100 who sought to further the aims of the Campaign for Nuclear Disarmament by non-violent demonstrations of civil disobedience. They took part in organising a demonstration held on 9 December 1961, at Wethersfield Airfield which was a 'prohibited place' within section 3 of the Official Secrets Act 1911, and which was occupied at the material time by United States Air Force squadrons assigned to the Supreme Commander Allied Forces, Europe. The plan was that on 9 December 1961, some demonstrators would take up a position outside the entrances to the airfield and would remain there sitting for five hours, while others would enter the airfield and, by sitting in front of aircraft, would prevent them from taking off. On that date, many demonstrators did travel to Wethersfield, but were prevented from entering the airfield. The admitted objects were to ground all aircraft, to immobilise the airfield and to reclaim the base for civilian purposes. The appellants were charged with conspiring together to incite divers persons to commit, and with conspiring together and with others to commit, 'a breach of section 1 of the Official Secrets Act 1911, namely, for a purpose prejudicial to the safety or interests of the State to enter a Royal Air Force Station . . . at Wethersfield.' A prosecution witness, Air Commodore Magill, gave evidence that interference with the ability of aircraft to take off was prejudicial to the safety or interests of the State. The judge refused to allow counsel for the defence to cross-examine or call evidence as to the appellants' beliefs that their acts would benefit the State or to show that the appellants' purpose was not in fact prejudicial to the safety or interests of the State. The appellants were convicted and sentenced to terms of imprisonment (eighteen months each for the men and twelve for the woman).

They appealed on the grounds that the facts did not disclose a conspiracy to commit a breach of section 1 of the Act of 1911, and that the judge was wrong in excluding cross-examination and evidence as to the facts on which the appellants' beliefs were based, and as to whether the appellants' purpose was in fact prejudicial to the State. Their appeals were dismissed by the Court of Criminal Appeal [1964] AC 771 and the House of Lords.

Lord Reid: . . . In cross-examination [of Air Commodore Magill] objection was taken to his being asked as to the armament of these squadrons. Counsel for the accused said that they sought to adduce evidence that their purpose was not prejudicial to the interests of the State, and that the basis of the defence was that these aircraft used nuclear bombs and that it was not in fact in the interests of the State to have aircraft so armed at that time there. So, he said, it would be beneficial to the State to immobilise these aircraft. Then counsel further submitted that he was entitled to adduce evidence to show that the accused believed, and reasonably believed, that it was not prejudicial but beneficial to the interests of the State to immobilise these aircraft: the jury were entitled to hold that no offence had been committed because the accused did not have a purpose prejudicial to the State, and it was for the jury to determine their purpose. . . . [C]ounsel said that his evidence would deal with the effect of exploding a nuclear bomb and . . . reference was made to the possibility of accident or mistake, and other reasons against having nuclear bombs. He said that he wished to cross-examine as to the basic wrongness of the conception of a deterrent force and the likelihood of it attracting hostile attack. In reply the Attorney-General submitted that an objective test must determine whether the purpose of grounding aircraft was a prejudicial purpose, that the accused's beliefs were irrelevant and so was the reasonableness of their beliefs. Havers J then ruled that the defence were not entitled to call evidence to establish that it would be beneficial for this country to give up nuclear armament or that the accused honestly believed that it would be. . . . [Section 1 of the Official Secrets Act 1911] has a side note 'Penalties for spying,' and it was argued that this limits its scope. In my view side notes cannot be used as an aid to construction. They are mere catchwords and I have never heard of it being supposed in recent times that an amendment to alter a side note could be proposed in either House of Parliament. Side notes in the original Bill are inserted by the draftsman. During the passage of the Bill through its various stages amendments to it or other reasons may make it desirable to alter a side note. In that event I have reason to believe that alteration is made by the appropriate officer of the House—no doubt in consultation with the draftsman. So side notes cannot be said to be enacted in the same sense as the long title or any part of the body of the Act. Moreover, it is impossible to suppose that the section does not apply to sabotage and what was intended to be done in this case was a kind of temporary sabotage.

The first word in the section that requires consideration is 'purpose'. . . . The accused both intended and desired that the base should be immobilised for a time, and I cannot construe purpose in any sense that does not include that state of mind. A person can have two different purposes in doing a particular thing and even if their reason or motive for doing what they did is called the purpose of influencing public opinion that cannot alter the fact that they had a purpose to immobilise the base. And the statute says 'for any purpose.' There is no question here of the interference with the aircraft being an unintended or undesired consequence of carrying out a legitimate purpose.

Next comes the question of what is meant by the safety or interests of the State. 'State' is not an easy word. It does not mean the Government or the Executive. And I do not think that it means, as counsel argued, the individuals who inhabit these islands. The statute cannot be referring to the interests of all those individuals because they may differ and the interests of the majority are not necessarily the same as the interests of the State . . . Perhaps the country or the realm are as good synonyms as one can find and I would be prepared to accept the organised community as coming as near to a definition as one can get.

Who, then, is to determine what is and what is not prejudicial to the safety and interests of the State? The question more frequently arises as to what is or is not in the public interest. I do not subscribe to the view that the Government or a Minister must always or even as a general rule have the last word about that.

But here we are dealing with a very special matter—interfering with a prohibited place which Wethersfield was. The definition in section 3 shows that it must either be closely connected with the armed forces or be a place such that information regarding it or damage to it or interference with it would be useful to an enemy. It is in my opinion clear that the disposition and armament of the armed forces are and for centuries have been within the exclusive discretion of the Crown and that no one can seek a legal remedy on the ground that such discretion has been wrongly exercised. I need only refer to the numerous authorities gathered together in *China Navigation Co Ltd v A-G* [1932] 2 KB 197. Anyone is entitled, in or out of Parliament, to urge that policy regarding the armed forces should be changed; but until it is changed, on a change of Government or otherwise, no one is entitled to challenge it in court.

Even in recent times there have been occasions when quite large numbers of people have been bitterly opposed to the use made of the armed forces in peace or in war. The 1911 Act was passed at a time of grave misgiving about the German menace, and it would be surprising and hardly credible that the Parliament of that date intended that a person who deliberately interfered with vital dispositions of the armed forces should be entitled to submit to a jury that Government policy was wrong and that what he did was really in the best interests of the country, and then perhaps to escape conviction because a unanimous verdict on that question could not be obtained. Of course we are bound by the words which Parliament has used in the Act. If those words necessarily lead to that conclusion then it is no answer that it is inconceivable that Parliament can have so intended. The remedy is to amend the Act. But we must be clear that the words of the Act are not reasonably capable of any other interpretation.

I am prepared to start from the position that, when an Act requires certain things to be established against an accused person to constitute an offence, all of those things must be proved by evidence which the jury accepts, unless Parliament has otherwise provided. But normally such things are facts and where questions of opinion arise they are on limited technical matters on which expert evidence can be called. Here the question whether it is beneficial to use the armed forces in a particular way or prejudicial to interfere with that use would be a political question—a question of opinion on which anyone actively interested in politics, including jurymen, might consider his own opinion as good as that of anyone else. Our criminal system is not devised to deal with issues of that kind. The question therefore is whether this Act can reasonably be read in such a way as to avoid the raising of such issues.

The Act must be read as a whole and paragraphs (*c*) and (*d*) of section 3 appear to me to require such a construction. Places to which they refer become prohibited places if a Secretary of State declares that damage, obstruction or interference there 'would be useful to an enemy.' Plainly it is not open to an accused who has interfered with or damaged such a place to a material extent to dispute the declaration of the Secretary of State and it would be absurd if he were entitled to say or lead evidence to show that, although he had deliberately done something which would be useful to an enemy, yet his purpose was not prejudicial to the safety or interests of the State. So here at least the trial judge must be entitled to prevent the leading of evidence and to direct the jury that if they find that his purpose was to interfere to a material extent they must hold that his purpose was prejudicial. If that be so, then, in view of the matters which I have already dealt with, it appears to me that the same must necessarily apply to the present case.

I am therefore of opinion that the ruling of Havers J excluding evidence was right and that his direction to the jury was substantially correct . . . .. I think it was proper to give to the jury a direction to the effect that if they were satisfied that the intention and desire of the accused was to procure the immobilisation of these aircraft in a way which they knew would or might substantially impair their operational effectiveness then the offence was proved and they should convict.

Viscount Radcliffe: . . . When a man has avowed that his purpose in approaching an airfield forming part of the country's defence system was to obstruct its operational activity, what, if any, evidence is admissible on the issue as to the prejudicial nature of his purpose? In my opinion the correct answer is, virtually none. This answer is not surprising if certain considerations that lie behind the protection of official secrets are borne in mind. The defence of the State from external enemies is a matter of real concern, in time of peace as in days of war. The disposition, armament and direction of the defence forces of the State are matters decided upon by the Crown and are within its jurisdiction as the executive power of the State. So are treaties and alliances with other States for mutual defence. An airfield maintained for the service of the Royal Air Force or of the air force of one of Her Majesty's allies is an instrument of defence, as are the airplanes operating from the airfield and their armament.

It follows, I think, that if a man is shown to the satisfaction of the jury to have approached an airfield with the direct purpose of obstructing its operational use, a verdict of guilty must result, provided that they are also satisfied that the airfield belongs to Her Majesty and was at the relevant date part of the defence system maintained by the Crown for the protection of the realm . . .

[E]ven if all these matters [on which the accused wished to adduce evidence] were to be investigated in court, they would still constitute only various points of consideration on the ultimate general issue, is it prejudicial to the interests of the State to include nuclear armament in its apparatus of defence? I do not think that a court of law can try that issue or, accordingly, can admit evidence upon it. It is not debarred from doing so merely because the issue is what is ordinarily known as 'political.' Such issues may present themselves in courts of law if they take a triable form. Nor, certainly, is it because Ministers of the State have any inherent general authority to prescribe to the courts what is or is not prejudicial to the interests of the State. But here we are dealing with a matter of the defence of the realm and with an Act designed to protect State secrets and the instruments of the State's defence. If the methods of arming the defence forces and the disposition of those forces are at the decision of Her Majesty's Ministers for the time being, as we know that they are, it is not within the competence of a court of law to try the issue whether it would be better for the country that that armament or those dispositions should be different.

Lords Hodson, Devlin and **Pearce** delivered concurring speeches.

Appeal dismissed.

NOTES

1. Lord Devlin's reasoning differed in some respects from the other members of the House, although he concurred in the result. The question whether an act was for a prejudicial purpose was for the jury to consider, and they should take account of all the consequences of the act which were reasonably to be apprehended. There was no justification for restricting the relevant consequences, as the Crown had argued, to those which occurred in the prohibited place or which could otherwise be regarded as 'immediate'. Whether the general immobilisation of nuclear weapons would be a good thing for the country would have had to be considered by the jury had it not been for the words 'to the safety and interests of the state'. In this context, the term 'state' denoted 'the organs of government' (p. 807), which in relation to the armed forces meant the Crown:

'So long as the Crown maintains armed forces for the defence of the realm, it cannot be in its interest that any part of them should be immobilised' (p. 807).

It was for the Crown to indicate, and not for the jury to determine, what its 'interests' were:

'Suppose that the statute made it an offence to be in a factory for a purpose prejudicial to the interests of the owner, I should not allow the accused to cross-examine the owner to suggest that the factory was unprofitable and that the sooner it closed down the better for the owner, nor to call expert evidence to show that his views were economically sound. A man is entitled to decide for himself how he should govern his life, his business and his other activities, and when the decision is taken, it dictates what his interests are. It is not to he point to say that if the decision had been a better one, his interests would have been different.' (p. 807) . . .
'In a case like the present, it may be presumed that it is contrary to the interests of the Crown to have one of its airfields immobilised just as it may be presumed that it is contrary to the interests of an industrialist to have his factory immobilised . . . But the presumption is not irrebuttable. Men can exaggerate the extent of their interests and so can the Crown. It is the duty of the Courts to be as alert now as they have always been to prevent abuse of the prerogative. But in the present case there is nothing at all to suggest that the Crown's interest in the proper operation of its airfields is not what it may naturally be presumed to be or that it was exaggerating the perils of interference with their effectiveness' (p. 809).

2. The decision in this case has been severely criticised by D. Thompson ([1963] PL 201). He points out that Parliament had been assured by two Attorneys-General (Sir Gordon Hewart and Sir Hartley Shawcross) and Lord Maugham LC that s.1 applied only to espionage, and that the expression 'for a purpose prejudicial to the safety or interests of the state' would be for the courts to construe and determine. Indeed the current form of section 6 of the 1920 was adopted in order to limit its operation to cases of espionage, and linking it with s.1 of the 1911 Act was thought to have that effect. While reference to proceedings in Parliament was not permissible as an aid to construction, 'it was indefensible on the part of the Attorney-General to press arguments upon the courts to give the section a wider meaning' (pp. 210–211). Thompson also challenges the legal reasoning (cf. *Smith and Hogan* pp. 809–811).

3. Apart from *Chandler v Director of Public Prosecutions*, prosecutions under s.1 have generally been confined to cases of espionage. It is certainly open to the Attorney-General to have regard to assurances given to Parliament in exercising the discretion whether to authorise a prosecution. However, the then Attorney-General, Sir Reginald Manningham-Buller said.

'In considering whether or not to prosecute, I must direct my mind to the language and spirit of the Acts and not to what my predecessors said about them many years ago in an entirely different context.'
(657 HC Deb 5 April 1962 col 611)

Persons convicted for contravening or conspiring to contravene section 1 since the war include Dr Fuchs, the members of the Portland 'spy ring', George Blake (sentenced to fourteen years' imprisonment on each of five separate counts the first three to run consecutively: (1961) 45 Cr App R 292), and W. J. C. Vassall (see the Report of the Radcliffe Tribunal of Inquiry, (1963) Cmnd. 2009). In 1978 proceedings were instituted under s. 1 and 2 against John Berry, a former corporal in the Intelligence Corps, and two journalists, Duncan Campbell and Crispin Aubrey. B communicated information to the journalists concerning Britain's Signals Intelligence Organization. Mars-Jones J hinted that the use of charges under s.1 was oppressive in a non-spying case. None of the defendants intended to use the information to assist an enemy. Counsel for the prosecution offered to prove that the defendants conduct was prejudicial, notwithstanding that the burden of proof as to this matter technically lay on the defendants under s.1(2). Mars-Jones J was unable to accept this arrangement in view of the clear words of the s.1(2). The Attorney-General decided to drop the s.1 charges (*The Times*, 31 October 1978). See A. Nichol, [1979] Crim LR 284.

Other matters of significance were (1) the proceedings for contempt of court brought in relation to the disclosure of the identity of one of the witnesses (see above pp. 249–251); and (2) the revelation that the potential jurors had been vetted for their potential loyalty or disloyalty. (see H. Harman and J. Griffith, *Justice Deserted* (NCCL 1979)).

(c) 'D' NOTICES

General introduction to 'D' notices nos. 1–12

The 'D' Notice system is entirely voluntary and has no legal authority. As the Committee on Security Procedures in the Public Service said in their report of April 1962 (Cmnd. 1681), 'Its success depends on goodwill, and in effect, upon very little else'.

A 'D' Notice may be issued only on the authority of the Defence, Press and Broadcasting Committee which is composed of officials from Government Departments concerned with defence and national security and representatives of all the Press and Broadcasting organisations. Notices are addressed to editors of newspapers, news editors in television and sound radio, editors of some periodicals which are particularly concerned with defence matters, and selected publishers who publish books on defence related subjects. Their purpose is to advise editors that the Government regards certain categories of information as being secret for reasons of national security, and to ask editors to refrain from publishing such information. An editor who is in doubt can contact the Secretary to the Defence, Press and Broadcasting Committee for advice.

'D' NOTICES AND THE OFFICIAL SECRETS ACTS 1911–1939

It is stressed that there is no direct relationship between the 'D' Notice system and the Official Secrets Acts, although information which is the subject of a 'D' Notice may also be covered by the Official Secrets Acts. In this context the practical effect of 'D' Notices is to remind editors that to publish such information could contravene the Official Secrets Acts. However, nothing in the 'D' Notice system relieves an editor of his responsibilities under the Acts.

THE WORKING OF THE 'D' NOTICE SYSTEM

Nothing in this introduction changes the existing position and the general description of the working of the 'D' Notice system which was contained in the 'Report of the Committee of Privy Counsellors appointed to inquire into 'D' Notice matters' (Cmnd. 3309) still holds good:
'The Secretary's office is therefore the central point of the system. He is the servant of the Committee as a whole, and his duties are whole-time. The greater part of his daily work consists in offering advice and assistance to different members of the Press as to the interpretation and application of the 'D' Notices. Sometimes a 'D' Notice can only be

expressed as a general guide to editors on the treatment of 'sensitive' subjects, and we have no doubt that from time to time questions of real difficulty arise as to the application of a particular Notice to some unpredictable combinations of circumstances. It is on such questions in particular that the Secretary is invited to advise. It must not be thought that he is invested with any authority to give 'rulings' or judicial interpretations. The system is not institutionalised and it operates throughout as one of free co-operation. But the evidence that we received satisfied us that, although individual editors vary from each other to some extent in their attitude on this matter, the Secretary's interpretations of the meaning and effect of the Notices are regarded with very great respect and would not be departed from by a particular newspaper until at any rate the matter had been fully discussed with him and a considered decision taken in the editorial chair'.

In an emergency the Government may request the Committee to issue a special 'D' Notice. Such a Notice cannot be issued without the prior approval of at least three members of the Press and Broadcasting side of the Committee. If an emergency Notice is issued it must be reviewed by the full Committee as soon as possible.

Finally editors are again reminded that the system is voluntary and that 'D' Notices do not have the force of law. The system offers editors guidance and advice but it does not give them decisions. In the end it is for an editor to decide whether to publish an item of information. 'D' Notices are intended only to help him to take account of national security in coming to his decision.

NOTES

1. This was printed as an annex to the submission of the Committee to the Franks Committee on s.2 of the Official Secrets Act 1911 (Minutes of Evidence, Vol 2 pp. 244–245).

2. The pre-1965 position as to 'D' Notices is discussed in D. G. T. Williams, *Not in the Public Interest* (1965) pp. 80–87. The Report of the (Radcliffe) Committee of Privy Counsellors (Cmnd. 3309) concerned the revelation by Chapman Pincher in the Daily Express that private cables and telegrams were vetted by the security authorities. The government claimed, and persisted in claiming notwithstanding the contrary view expressed by the Radcliffe Committee, that this contravened two 'D' Notices (see the White Paper, Cmnd. 3312 (1967), P. Hedley and C. Aynsley, *The D Notice Affair* (1967) and Chapman Pincher, *Inside Story* (1978).

Chapman Pincher suggests that the minority of Government repre-senatives on the Committee almost always got their way and that prior to 1967, journalists tended to rely heavily on the view of the Secretary as to whether a story was covered by a 'D' Notice, confident that clearance by the Secretary would cover them in practice as regards possible prosecution under the Official Secrets Act (although it could not affect the legal position). According to Pincher, the affair 'effectively destroyed the D-notice system', which he thereafter 'virtually ignored' (op. cit. p. 244). This seems to stem from his loss of confidence in the changed role of the Secretary and the emphasis in the revised arrangements that clearance by the Secretary would not affect the position under the Official Secrets Act. In the Oral Evidence to the Franks Committee the Chairman of the Defence, Press and Broadcasting Committee, Sir James Dunnett, stated that it would be an 'extreme case' in which the DPP would want to prosecute an editor where clearance had been given, and that the Attorney-General in deciding to give his fiat under the Act would wish to know whether the editor had been in touch with the Secretary to the Committee (p. 57).

(d) BREACH OF CONFIDENCE

**Attorney-General v Jonathan Cape Ltd Attorney-General v Times Newspapers Ltd [1976]
QB 752, [1975] 3 All ER 484, [1975] 3 WLR 606 Lord Widgery CJ**

Between 1964 and 1970 [Richard Crossman] a Cabinet Minister, with the knowledge of his Cabinet colleagues, kept a diary recording Cabinet discussions and political events with a view to their publication as a book. Following his death in April 1974, volume one of the book, *Diaries of a Cabinet Minister*, which covered the years 1964–66, was sent to the Secretary of the Cabinet for his approval but was rejected on the ground that publication was against the public interest in that the doctrine of collective responsibility would be harmed by the disclosure of details of Cabinet discussions, the revelation of differences between members of the Cabinet and the disclosure of advice given by, and discussions regarding the appointment of, civil servants. In July 1974 the literary executors gave an undertaking not to publish the book without giving prior notice to the Treasury Solicitor but, in January 1975, the first extracts from the book were published in the *Sunday Times* without the consent of the Secretary of the Cabinet. Subsequently extracts were submitted to the Secretary for his prior approval and in some instances deletions were made in accordance with his views.

The Attorney-General applied for injunctions against the publishers and literary executors of Mr Crossman to restrain publication of the book in the public interest, and against the publishers of the *Sunday Times* to restrain publication of the book or of extracts from it.

Lord Widgery CJ: . . . It is quite clear that no court will compel the production of Cabinet papers in the course of discovery in an action, and the Attorney-General contends that not only will the court refuse to compel the production of such matters, but it will go further and positively forbid the disclosure of such papers and proceedings if publication will be contrary to the public interest.

The basis of this contention is the confidential character of these papers and proceedings, derived from the convention of joint Cabinet responsibility whereby any policy decision reached by the Cabinet has to be supported thereafter by all members of the Cabinet whether they approve of it or not, unless they feel compelled to resign . . .

There is no doubt that Mr Crossman's manuscripts contain frequent references to individual opinions of Cabinet Ministers, and this is not surprising because it was his avowed object to obtain a relaxation of the convention regarding memoirs of ex-Ministers . . . The Attorney-General does not attempt a final definition but his contention is that [cabinet] proceedings are confidential and their publication is capable of control by the courts at least as far as they include (a) disclosure of Cabinet documents or proceedings in such a way as to reveal the individual views or attitudes of Ministers; (b) disclosure of confidential advice from civil servants, whether contained in Cabinet papers or not; (c) disclosure of confidential discussions affecting the appointment or transfer of such senior civil servants.

The Attorney-General contends that all Cabinet papers and discussions are prima facie confidential, and that the court should restrain any disclosure thereof if the public interest in concealment outweighs the public interest in a right to free publication. The Attorney-General further contends that, if it is shown that the public interest is involved, he has the right and duty to bring the matter before the court.

I do not understand . . . the Attorney-General to be contending, that it is only necessary for him to evoke the public interest to obtain an order of the court. On the contrary, it must be for the court in every case to be satisfied that the public interest is involved, and that, after balancing all the factors which tell for or against publication, to decide whether suppression is necessary.

The defendants' main contention is that whatever the limits of the convention of joint Cabinet responsibility may be, there is no obligation enforceable at law to prevent the publication of Cabinet papers and proceedings, except in extreme cases where national security is involved. In other words, the defendants submit that the confidential character of Cabinet papers and discussions is based on a true convention as defined in the evidence of Professor Henry Wade, namely an obligation founded in conscience only. Accordingly, the defendants contend that publication of these Diaries is not capable of control by any order of this court.

If the Attorney-General were restricted in his argument to the general proposition that Cabinet papers and discussion are all under the seal of secrecy at all times, he would be in difficulty . . . .

[I]t seems to me that the degree of protection afforded to Cabinet papers and discussion cannot be determined by a single rule of thumb. Some secrets require a high standard of protection for a short time. Others require protection until a new political generation has taken over. In the present action against the literary executors, the Attorney-General asks for a perpetual injunction to restrain further publication of the Diaries in whole or in part. I am far from convinced that he has made out a case that the public interest requires such a Draconian remedy when due regard is had to other public interests, such as the freedom of speech: . . . .

Some attempt has been made to say that the publication of these Diaries by Mr. Crossman would have been a breach of his oath as a Privy Councillor, . . . This is, however, not seriously relied upon . . . and the Attorney-General concedes that the present defendants are not in breach of the Official Secrets Acts . . .

In 1964, 1966 and 1969 the Prime Minister (who was in each case Mr Harold Wilson) issued a confidential document to Cabinet Ministers containing guidance on certain questions of procedure. Paragraph 72 of the 1969 edition provides:

'The principle of collective responsibility and the obligation not to disclose information acquired whilst holding Ministerial office apply to former Ministers who are contemplating the publication of material based upon their recollections of the conduct of Cabinet and Cabinet committee business in which they took part.'

The general understanding of Ministers while in office was that information obtained from Cabinet sources was secret and not to be disclosed to outsiders.

There is not much evidence of the understanding of Ministers as to the protection of such information after the Minister retires. It seems probable to me that those not desirous of publishing memoirs assumed that the protection went on until the incident was 30 years old, whereas those interested in memoirs would discover on inquiry at the Cabinet Office that draft memoirs were normally submitted to the Secretary of the Cabinet for his advice on their contents before publication. Manuscripts were almost always submitted to the Secretary of the Cabinet in accordance with the last-mentioned procedure. Sir Winston Churchill submitted the whole of his manuscripts concerned with the war years, and accepted the advice given by the Secretary of the Cabinet as to publication . . . .

In recent years, successive Secretaries of the Cabinet, when giving advice on the publication of a Minister's memoirs, were much concerned about (a) disclosure of individual views of Members of the Cabinet in defiance of the principle of joint responsibility; (b) disclosure of advice given by civil servants still in office; (c) disclosure of discussions relating to the promotion or transfer of senior civil servants.

Mr Crossman . . . disapproved of the submission of manuscripts to the Secretary of the Cabinet. He made no attempt to admit the three categories of information just referred to, and expressed the intention to obtain publication whilst memories were green.

Mr Crossman made no secret of the fact that he kept a diary which he intended to use for the writing of his memoirs. It was contended on behalf of the literary executors that any bond of confidence or secrecy normally attending upon Cabinet material had been lifted in Mr Crossman's case by consent of his colleagues. Even if, as a matter of law, a Minister can release himself from a bond of secrecy in this way, I do not find that Mr Crossman effectively did so. It is not enough to show that his colleagues accepted the keeping of the diary. It was vital to show that they accepted Mr Crossman's intention to use the diary whether it passed the scrutiny of the Secretary of the Cabinet or not.

I have already indicated some of the difficulties which face the Attorney-General when he relied simply on the public interest as a ground for his actions. That such ground is enough in extreme cases is shown by the universal agreement that publication affecting national security can be restrained in this way. It may be that in the short run (for example, over a period of weeks or months) the public interest is equally compelling to maintain joint Cabinet responsibility and the protection of advice given by civil servants, but I would not accept without close investigation that such matters must, as a matter of course, retain protection after a period of years.

However, the Attorney-General has a powerful reinforcement for his argument in the developing equitable doctrine that a man shall not profit from the wrongful publication of information received by him in confidence.

[His Lordship referred to *Prince Albert v Strange* (1849) 1 H & TW 1; *Saltman Engineering Co Ltd v Campbell Engineering Co Ltd* (1948) 65 RPC 203, *Coco v A. N. Clark (Engineers) Ltd* [1969] RPC 41, *Duchess of Argyll v Duke of Argyll* [1967] Ch 302 and *Fraser v Evans* [1969] 1 QB 349, below pp. 317–322].

Even so, these defendants argue that an extension of the principle of the *Argyll* case to the present dispute involves another large and unjustified leap forward, because in the present case the Attorney-General is seeking to apply the principle to public secrets made confidential in the interests of good government. I cannot see why the courts should be powerless to restrain the publication of public secrets, while enjoying the *Argyll* powers in regard to domestic secrets. Indeed, as already pointed out, the court must have power to deal with publication which threatens national security, and the difference between such a case and the present case is one of degree rather than kind. I conclude, therefore, that when a Cabinet Minister receives information in confidence the improper publication of such information can be restrained by the court, and his obligation is not merely to observe a gentleman's agreement to refrain from publication.

Mr Comyn's third submission [was] . . . that the evidence does not prove the existence of a convention as to collective responsibility, or adequately define a sphere of secrecy. I find overwhelming evidence that the doctrine of joint responsibility is generally understood and practised and equally strong evidence that it is on occasion ignored. The general effect of the evidence is that the doctrine is an established feature of the English form of government, and it follows that some matters leading up to a Cabinet decision may be regarded as confidential. Furthermore, I am persuaded that the nature of the confidence is that spoken for by the Attorney-General, namely, that since the confidence is imposed to enable the efficient conduct of the Queen's business, the confidence is owed to the Queen and cannot be released by the members of Cabinet themselves . . . . I cannot accept the suggestion that a Minister owes no duty of confidence in respect of his own views expressed in Cabinet. It would only need one or two Ministers to describe their own views to enable experienced observers to identify the views of the others . . . .

The Cabinet is at the very centre of national affairs, and must be in possession at all times of information which is secret or confidential. Secrets relating to national security may require to be preserved indefinitely. Secrets relating to new taxation proposals may be of the highest importance until Budget day, but public knowledge thereafter. To leak a Cabinet decision a day or so before it is officially announced is an accepted exercise in public relations, but to identify the Ministers who voted one way or another is objectionable because it undermines the doctrine of joint responsibility.

It is evident that there cannot be a single rule governing the publication of such a variety of matters. In these actions we are concerned with the publication of diaries at a time when 11 years have expired since the first recorded events. The Attorney-General must show (a) that such publication would be a breach of confidence; (b) that the public interest requires that the publication be restrained, and (c) that there are no other facets of the public interest contradictory of and more compelling than that relied upon. Moreover, the court, when asked to restrain such a publication, must closely examine the extent to which relief is necessary to ensure that restrictions are not imposed beyond the strict requirement of public need.

Applying those principles to the present case, what do we find? In my judgment, the Attorney-General has made out his claim that the expression of individual opinions by Cabinet Ministers in the course of Cabinet discussion are matters of confidence, the publication of which can be restrained by the court when this is clearly necessary in the public interest.

The maintenance of the doctrine of joint responsibility within the Cabinet is in the public interest, and the application of that doctrine might be prejudiced by premature disclosure of the views of individual Ministers.

There must, however, be a limit in time after which the confidential character of the information, and the duty of the court to restrain publication, will lapse . . . . I have . . . read the whole of volume one of the Diaries, and my considered view is that I cannot believe that the publication at this interval of anything in volume one would inhibit free discussion in the Cabinet of today, even though the individuals involved are the same, and the national problems have a distressing similarity with those of a decade ago. It is unnecessary to elaborate the evils which might flow if at the close of a Cabinet meeting a Minister proceeded to give the press an analysis of the voting, but we are dealing in this case with a disclosure of information nearly 10 years later.

It may, of course, be intensely difficult in a particular case, to say at what point the material loses its confidential character, on the ground that publication will no longer undermine the doctrine of joint Cabinet responsibility. It is this difficulty which prompts some to argue that Cabinet discussions should retain their confidential character for a longer and arbitrary period such as 30 years, or even for all time, but this seems to me to be excessively restrictive. The court should intervene only in the clearest of cases where the continuing confidentiality of the material can be demonstrated. In less clear cases—and this, in my view, is certainly one— reliance must be placed on the good sense and good taste of the Minister or ex-Minister concerned . . . .

It remains to deal with the Attorney-General's two further arguments, namely, (a) that the Diaries disclose advice given by senior civil servants who cannot be expected to advise frankly if their advice is not treated as confidential; (b) the Diaries disclose observations made by Ministers on the capacity of individual senior civil servants and their suitability for specific appointments. I can see no ground in law which entitle the court to restrain publication of these matters. A Minister is, no doubt, responsible for his department and accountable for its errors even though the individual fault is to be found in his subordinates. In these circumstances, to disclose the fault of the subordinate may amount to cowardice or bad taste,

but I can find no ground for saying that either the Crown or the individual civil servant has an enforceable right to have the advice which he gives treated as confidential for all time ..
Injunction refused.

NOTES

1. See further on cabinet secrecy, D. G. T. Williams, *Not in the Public Interest* (1965) Chap. 2; Hugo Young, *The Crossman Affair* (1976); R. K. Middlemass, (1976) 47 Political Quarterly 39.

2. In June 1976 extracts from Cabinet minutes were used in an article in *New Society* by Frank Field (17 June 1976) criticising the Government for deciding to postpone the introduction of a child benefit scheme (see 914 HC Deb 28 June 1976 cols 39–106). An investigation did not reveal the identity of the person responsible for the leak. A Committee of Privy Counsellors on Cabinet Document Security, chaired by Lord Houghton, subsequently made various recommendations for tightening the physical security of documents, applying the 'need to know' principle to the circulation of documents and improving the relevant administrative machinery (Cmnd. 6677). In general, they found that 'our public servants . . . maintain a very high standard for the protection of the written word' (p. 10).

3. Cabinet documents may also be protected from disclosure in litigation by a claim that disclosure would be contrary to the public interest (see generally de Smith, *Judicial Review of Administrative Action* 4th edn. pp. 35–46; J. Jacob, [1976] PL 134; *Conway v Rimmer* [1968] AC 910 952 (Lord Reid); *Burmah Oil Co Ltd v Bank of England* [1979] 2 All ER 461, CA; *Sankey v Whitlam* (1978) 53 ALJR 11, High Court of Australia; *Elston v State Services Commission* [1979] 1 NZLR 193, Supreme Court of New Zealand).

4. The conventions as to the publication of ministerial memoirs were considered by the *Committee of Privy Counsellors on Ministerial Memooirs* (Chairman, Lord Radcliffe, Cmnd. 6386, (1976)). The committee endorsed the view taken by the Cabinet in 1946 that it was necessary

'to keep secret information of two kinds, disclosure of which would be detrimental to the public interest:
(*a*) In the international sphere, information whose disclosure would be injurious to us in our relations with other nations, including information which would be of value to a potential enemy.
(*b*) In the domestic sphere, information the publication of which would be destructive of the confidential relationships on which our system of government is based and which may subsist between Minister and Minister, Ministers and their advisers, and between either and outside bodies or private persons.' (p. 7)

The committee suggested further 'working rules' as to the reticence due from an ex-Minister:

'(*a*) In dealing with the experience that he has acquired by virtue of his official position, he should not reveal the opinions or attitudes of colleagues as to the Government business with which they have been concerned. That belongs to their stewardship, not to his. He may, on the other hand, describe and account for his own.
(*b*) He should not reveal the advice given to him by individuals whose duty it has been to tender him their advice or opinions in confidence. If he wishes to mention the burden or weight of such advice, it must be done without attributing individual attitudes to identifiable persons. Again, he will need to exercise a continuing discretion in any references that he makes to communications received by him in confidence from outside members of the public.
(*c*) He should not make public assessments or criticisms, favourable or unfavourable, of those who have served under him or those whose competence or suitability for particular posts he has had to measure as part of his official duties.' (pp. 20–21).

As to enforcement, the committee did not regard the legal principles expounded by Lord Widgery CJ in the *Crossman Diaries* case as providing 'a system which can protect and enforce those rules of reticence that we regard as called for when ex-Ministers compose their memoirs. . . .' According to his Lordship, each case would have to be decided on its own facts – there were 'no fixed principles of legal enforceability' (p. 24) The Committee did not regard a Judge as 'so equipped as to make him the best arbitrator of the issues involved. The relevant considerations are political and administrative. . . .' Moreover, the legal principles did not protect confidences of or about Civil Servants. Neither did legislation offer the right solution. The 'burden of compliance' should be 'left to rest on the free acceptance of an obligation of honour' (p. 26).

(e) ACCESS TO INFORMATION

1. There is no general public right of access to official information. Public records in the Public Records Office are not available for public inspection

'[until the expiration of the period of thirty years beginning with the first day of January in the year next after that in which they were created, or such other period] . . . as the Lord Chancellor may, with the approval or at the request, of the Minister or other person, if any, who appears to him to be primarily concerned, for the time being prescribe as respects any particular class of public records.' (Public Records Act 1958 s. 5(1) as amended by the Public Records Act, 1967).

Longer periods have been prescribed for the following categories:

'Firstly, those containing information about individuals whose disclosure would cause distress or embarrassment to living persons or their immediate descendants, such as criminal or prison records, records of courts-martial, records of suspected persons and certain police records; secondly, those containing information obtained with a pledge of confidence, for example, the census returns; thirdly, certain papers relating to Irish affairs; fourthly, certain exceptionally sensitive papers, which affected the security of the State. . . .'

(The Attorney-General, Sir Elwyn Jones, 749 HC Deb 26 June 1967 col 25).

Documents mentioning the existence of the Secret Intelligence Service (MI6) have been withheld from production beyond the 30 years period, apparently because its existence is not officially acknowledged (*The Times*, 25 October 1978). This restriction is under review (see 398 HL Deb 13 February 1979 col 1092).

2. There are many specific statutory provisions preventing the disclosure without lawful authority of information acquired from citizens. See the list in Appendix V to the Franks Report.

3. In recent years, the government has taken a number of steps to encourage the publication of a wider range of information. The principles were outlined by Mr. Callaghan in 1977:

The Prime Minister: Departments have been advised that in future as much as possible of the factual and analytical material used as background to major policy studies should be published. The working assumption will be that, once Ministers have reached their conclusions on a particular study, the associated background material will be published unless Ministers have good reasons for deciding otherwise. This material will mainly consist of deliberate presentations in the later stages of the discussion and development of new policy. Most of it will be released on the initiative of the Department, probably through Her Majesty's Stationery Office. Material of lesser importance, or of interest to a limited audience, may well be put out through other means, such as being made available to newspapers, or through publication in magazines and journals in the usual way. Departments will also be ready to respond positively and sympathetically to specific requests in the same way as a good deal of otherwise unpublished material is already made available to bona fide researchers. The overall effect should be an increase in the already considerable amount of material put out by Departments but at a minimum cost, directly or indirectly, to public funds.'

(936 HC Deb written answer 26 October 1977 col 699–700). These were amplified in a letter sent by Lord Croham (then Sir Douglas Allen, Head of the Civil Service) to Heads of Department on 6 July 1977. Mrs. Thatcher has exhorted ministers to 'give close personal attention to and take the initiative in publishing information, especially on major issues of parliamentary interest, to the greatest possible extent' (The Times, 27 November 1979, p. 5). See also 968 HC Deb 20 June 1979 col 1316.

4. *Justice* have proposed the establishment of a Code of Practice on access to official information to which ministers would be committed. The monitoring authority would be the Parliamentary Commissioner (*Freedom of Information* (1978)). This approach was favoured by the Labour Government, (Green Paper on *Open Government* Cmnd 7520 (1979) p. 18), but has been criticised as an inadequate substitute for a legal right of access (J. Michael, *The Politics of Secrecy, The Case for a Freedom of Information Law*, NCCL (1979)). See also R. Wraith, *Open Government, The British Interpretation*, RIPA (1977) and *Disclosure of Official Information: A Report on Overseas Practice* (HMSO 1979).

2 Sedition and incitement to disaffection

(a) INTRODUCTION

This section illustrates a number of offences, most of them statutory, which impinge in particular upon freedom of expression in the political context. The common law of sedition sets the bounds for general political discourse, and as expounded in the modern cases, those bounds are set widely. A series of statutory offences proscribe the incitement of disaffection among the armed forces and the police, whose loyalty to the state is regarded by the state as being of particular importance for its own well being. Prosecutions in the 1970s show that these offences are by no means obsolete.

(b) SEDITION

R v Burns (1886) 16 Cox CC 355, 2 TLR 510, Central Criminal Court, Cave J

John Burns, William Champion, Henry Hyndman and John Williams were indicted for unlawfully and maliciously uttering seditious words of and concerning the Government with intent to incite to riot, and (in other counts) with intent to stir up ill-will between Her Majesty's subjects, and for conspiracy. The prosecution arose out of the serious riots in the West End of London which followed meetings in Trafalgar Square and Hyde Park on 8 February 1886 at which the allegedly seditious words were spoken. It was not suggested that the defendants incited the particular acts of disorder which followed these meetings, but only that the defendants must have been aware of, and were answerable for, the natural result of the language they used. The facts and arguments are given fully in 2 TLR 510.

Cave J directed the jury as follows:

. . . There are two offences, one is the offence of speaking seditious words, and the other offence is the publication of a seditious libel. It is obviously important to know what is meant by the word sedition, and Stephen J proceeds in a subsequent article to give a definition of it. [*Digest of the Criminal law* p. 56, art. 93; 8th edn, art. 114] He says:'A seditious intention is an intention to bring into hatred or contempt, or to excite disaffection against the person of Her Majesty, her heirs, or successors, or the government and constitution of the United Kingdom, as by law established, or either House of Parliament, or the Administration of justice, or to excite Her Majesty's subjects to attempt otherwise than by lawful means the alteration of any matter in Church or State by law established, or to raise discontent or disaffection amongst Her Majesty's subjects, or to promote feelings of ill-will and hostility between different classes of such subjects.' Stephen, J . . . goes on to point out what sort of intention is not seditious . . . 'An intention to show that Her Majesty has been misled or mistaken in her measures, or to point out errors or defects in the government or constitution as by law established, with a view to their reformation, or to excite Her Majesty's subjects to attempt by lawful means the alteration of any matter in Church or State by law established, or to point out, in order to their removal, matters which are producing, or have a tendency to produce, feelings of hatred and ill-will between classes of Her Majesty's subjects, is not a seditious intention.' . . . Now, the seditious intentions which it is alleged existed in the minds of the prisoners in this case are: first, an intention to excite Her Majesty's subjects to attempt otherwise than by lawful means the alteration of some matter in Church or State by law established; and, secondly, to promote feelings of hostility between different classes of Her Majesty's subjects. This is necessarily somewhat vague and general, particularly the second portion, . . . Any intention to excite ill-will and hostility between different classes of Her Majesty's subjects may be a seditious intention; whether in a particular case this is a seditious intention or not, you must judge and decide in your own minds, taking into consideration the whole of the circumstances of the case.

[I]f you think that these defendants . . .had a seditious intention to incite the people to violence, to create public disturbances and disorder, then undoubtedly you ought to find them guilty. If from any sinister motive, as, for instance, notoriety, or for the purpose of personal gain, they desired to bring the people into conflict with the authorities, or to incite them tumultuously and disorderly to damage the property of any unoffending citizens, you ought undoubtedly to find them guilty. On the other hand, if you come to the conclusion that they were actuated by an honest desire to alleviate the misery of the unemployed—if they had a real *bonâ fide* desire to bring that misery before the public by constitutional and legal means, you should not be too swift to mark any hasty or ill-considered expression which they might utter in the excitement of the moment.

I am unable to agree entirely with the Attorney-General when he says that the real charge is that, though these men did not incite or contemplate disorder, yet, as it was the natural consequence of the words they used, they are responsible for it. In order to make out the offence of speaking seditious words there must be a criminal intent upon the part of the accused, they must be words spoken with a seditious intent; and, although it is a good working rule, to say that a man must be taken to intend the natural consequences of his acts, and it is very proper to ask a jury to infer, if there is nothing to show the contrary, that he did intend the natural consequences of his acts, yet, if it is shown from other circumstances, that he did not actually intend them, I do not see how you can ask a jury to act upon what has then become a legal fiction. [His Lordship referred to Stephen's *History of the Criminal Law* vol. 2 p. 359] . . . It is one thing to speak with the distinct intention to produce disturbances, and another thing to speak recklessly and violently of what is likely to produce disturbances. I must, however, notwithstanding what I have said upon that subject, go on to tell you that . . . [I]t is not at all necessary to the offence of uttering seditious words that an actual riot should follow, that there should be an actual disturbance of the public peace, it is the uttering with the intent which is the offence, not the consequences which follow, and which have really nothing to do with the offence. A man cannot escape from the consequences of uttering words with intent to excite people to violence solely because the persons to whom they are addressed may be too wise or too temperate to be seduced into that violence.

 . . . [W]hen people go to a meeting there are circumstances under which a man may be responsible not only for what he says, but also for what someone else says. Now what are those circumstances? Stephen, J. says: 'If at a meeting lawfully convened seditious words are spoken, of such a nature as are likely to produce a breach of the peace, that meeting may become unlawful, and all those who speak the words undoubtedly are guilty of uttering seditious words, and those who do anything to help those who speak to produce upon the hearers the natural effect of the words spoken.' You must do something more than stand by and say nothing; if you express approval of the statements of speakers who utter seditious language that equally will do; if you make a speech calculated to help that part of the speech made by someone else, and which excited to disorder; if you do anything to help that part of the effect upon the hearers, then undoubtedly you will be guilty of uttering seditious words just as if you spoke them yourself. . . . Those even who make a speech themselves are not guilty of uttering seditious words unless you can gather from the language they use that they are endeavouring to assist the other man in carrying out that portion of his speech, and by that course endeavouring to assist him in causing his words which excite to disorder to produce their natural effect upon the people. . . .

[The defendants were acquitted on all counts]

NOTES

1. See *Smith and Hogan* pp. 802–806; *Brownlie*, pp. 85–90; *Williams*, p. 197–204; Law Commission Working Paper No. 72 on Treason, Sedition and Allied Offences; L. H. Leigh [1977] PL 128, 145–148; M. Head, [1979]3 Crim LJ 89. The emphasis on the intention to cause or likelihood of *disorder* as a necessary element in sedition given in this case, in *R v Aldred* (1909) 22 Cox CC 1 and in *R v Caunt* (1947) (reported in *An Editor on Trial* (Morecambe Press Ltd); (1948) 64 LQR 203) illustrates a narrowing in the scope of sedition as compared with 19th century cases (see *Brownlie*, op. cit.). In view of the modern limitation of the offence to cases of incitement to disorder, which could be dealt with by prosecutions for incitement to commit offences such as criminal damage, riot, unlawful assembly or assault, the Law Commission (op. cit. p. 48) have taken the provisional view that there would be no need for an offence of sedition in a criminal code.

2. The Supreme Court of Canada held by 5–4 in *Boucher v R* [1951] 2 DLR 369 that not only must there be proof of an incitement to violence, but also it must be violence or defiance for the purpose of 'disturbing constituted authority', i.e. the disorder must be aimed at the institutions of Government. Accordingly, the conviction of a Jehovah's Witness for publishing a pamphlet attacking the Roman Catholic church was set aside. This limitation does not appear in the English cases, although the Law Commission suggest that it would probably be accepted as good law in England.

3. The view that the defendant must actually *intend* to cause disorder was also expressed by Birkett J in *R v Caunt* (1947). A different view was taken by Coleridge J in *R v Aldred* (1909) 22 Cox CC 1, 3:

'The test is not either the truth of the language or the innocence of the motive with which he published it, but the test is this: was the language used calculated, or was it not, to promote public disorder or physical force or violence in a matter of State?'

Aldred was convicted of publishing seditious libels in the form of articles in the *Indian Sociologist*, including one written by himself, advocating political assassination with a view to securing Indian independence. He was sentenced to 12 months' imprisonment.

4. Other occasions in which charges relating to sedition have been brought this century include the prosecutions of Harry Pollitt, William Gallacher, Wal Hannington and nine other Communist leaders in 1925 (see W. Hannington, *Never on our Knees* (1967) pp. 188–193); Sidney Elias in 1932; and Tom Mann and Harry Pollitt later in 1932 (see *Williams*, pp. 185–186, 199–200; above p. 100). Incitement to racial hatred, which formed the subject matter of unsuccessful prosecutions for sedition in *R v Leese* (1936) *Times* 19 September and 22 and *R v Caunt* (1947) are now dealt with under the Public Order Act 1936 s. 5A (below, p. 393). In *Caunt*, the editor of a local paper, *The Morecambe and Heysham Visitor* wrote an article attacking British Jewry in the aftermath of the murder of two British sergeants in Palestine. He suggested that 'violence may be the only way to bring them to the sense of their responsibility to the country in which they live'. C claimed that this was intended only as a warning and that he did not intend to advocate any particular form of violence. The jury acquitted.

In 1972 three members of an organisation who were in England openly recruiting volunteers to go to Northern Ireland to take up arms in support of the Catholics in the event of civil war or widespread sectarian violence were charged with treason felony, seditious conspiracy, uttering seditious words and taking part in the management of an association contrary to the Public Order Act 1936 s.2 (above, p. 129). The first two counts were not proceeded with, and they were given suspended sentences on the other two counts (Law Commission Working Paper No. 72 pp. 30–31).

(c) INCITEMENT TO DISAFFECTION

Incitement to Mutiny Act 1797

[1.] Any person who shall attempt to seduce any sailor or soldier from his duty or incite him to mutiny, etc., to suffer death
From and after the passing of this Act, any person who shall maliciously and advisedly endeavour to seduce any person or persons serving in his Majesty's forces by sea or land from his or their duty and allegiance to his Majesty, or to incite or stir up any such person or persons to commit any act of mutiny, or to make or endeavour to make any mutinous assembly, or to commit any traiterous or mutinous practice whatsoever, shall, on being legally convicted of such offence, be adjudged guilty of felony . . .

NOTES

1. See *Williams*, pp. 179–187; T. Young, *Incitement to Disaffection* (1976); Law Commission Working Paper No. 72 on Treason, Sedition and Allied Offences, pp. 49–50, 57, 58,
2. The Act was extended to the Air Force in 1918 (SR & 0 1918 No. 548). The maximum penalty is now life imprisonment.
3. The word 'advisedly' means 'knowingly'. It is necessary to show that the defendant knew he was addressing a member of the armed forces (*R v Fuller* (1797) 2 Leach 790: the first prosecution under the Act).
4. The Act was introduced in the aftermath of the naval mutinies at Spithead and the Nore. It was originally a temporary measure, and lapsed in 1807, but it was revived and made permanent in 1817. There was a prosecution in 1804 (*R v Tierney* (1804) Russ & Ry 74), but apparently no more officially instigated prosecutions until 1912. In that year, 'An Open Letter to British Soldiers' published in *The Syndicalist* led to the prosecution of five people under the Act in three separate trials (see Young, op. cit. pp. 14–20). The letter exhorted soldiers not to fire upon strikers if ordered to do so. Fred Crowsley, a railwayman, was convicted under the Act for distributing copies of the letter, reprinted as a leaflet, to soldiers. The editor and printers of *The Syndicalist* were also convicted (*R v Bowman* (1912) 76 JP 271). Tom Mann made a point of reading the letter at various meetings and stating that he believed in every sentence, and admitted nominal responsibility for *The Syndicalist* in his capacity as Chairman of the Industrial Syndicalist League (see Tom Mann, *Memoirs* (1923) pp. 230–262). Terms of imprisonment were imposed, although the defendants were released early following a public outcry. Horridge J held in *R v Bowman* that the indictment need not specify the persons alleged to have been approached. The prosecutions were criticised on a number of grounds, including the fact that an old statute had been revived, that proceedings had been taken against the press, and that no proceedings had been taken against leading right-wing politicians who had incited the armed forces not to take action against armed resistance in Ulster to Home Rule (see A Barrister, *Justice in England* (1938) pp. 221–228).

In 1924, proceedings under the 1797 Act were instituted and then dropped against J. R. Campbell in respect of an 'Open Letter to the Fighting Forces' in *Workers' Weekly*. Suspicions that the Attorney-General, Sir Patrick Hastings, had bowed to Cabinet pressure, and that the Cabinet had been influenced by the Communist party, led to the fall of the Labour Government. It seems that the Cabinet had in fact decided that the prosecution should be withdrawn, but for the rather different reason that they did not wish to give free publicity to the communists (see F. H. Newark, (1969) 20 NILQ 19; N. D. Siederer, (1974) 9 Journal of Contemporary History p. 143).

Prosecutions under the 1797 Act were brought against twelve Communist leaders in 1925 (Young, op. cit. p. 45–47) in relation to exhortations similar to those at issue in 1912. Charges of incitement to contravene the 1797 Act have been employed in the 1970's in connection with the British Withdrawal from Northern Ireland Campaign leafletting (Young op. cit. p. 93).

5. W. I. Jennings (*The Sedition Bill Explained* (1934) p. 14) argued that 'an act of mutiny'

'involves more than a mere refusal to obey a lawful order. It implies a collective act. It is not mutiny for a soldier to overstay his leave, or to refuse to clear out a latrine. . . . or to strike a sergeant-major, or to use an army lorry for a joy ride. These are mere breaches of duty . . . A "mutiny" implies a general and co-ordinated refusal by a body of men to obey not merely a specific order but a class of orders.'

Encouragement of such less serious acts would not fall within the 1797 Act, although it would be proscribed by the Incitement to Disaffection Act 1934, s.l, below.

6. The Law Commission (op. cit. p. 58) have expressed the 'provisional view' that the Act should be repealed as it 'has not been invoked for very many years, and there are other offences which cover the conduct.' The other offences include the following (with maximum penalties as stated):

– Obstruction of or interference with a member of the Army or Air Force in the exercise of his duty (Army Act 1955, s.193; Air Force Act 1955 s.193: three months imprisonment, a £50 fine or both).

– Procuring or persuading a member of the forces to desert or to absent himself without leave (Army Act 1955, s.97: two years imprisonment, a fine or both if tried on indictment; three months' imprisonment, £1,000 or both on summary conviction.)

– Naval Discipline Act 1957 s. 94:

'Every person not subject to this Act who, being on board any of Her Majesty's ships or vessels, or being within any of Her Majesty's naval establishments outside Her Majesty's dominions, endeavours to seduce any person subject to this Act from his duty or allegiance to Her Majesty shall be liable on conviction by court-martial to imprisonment for any term.'

Mutiny or desertion by persons subject to military law are of course serious offences (Army Act 1955 ss. 31(1), (2), 37(1); Air Force Act 1955, ss. 31(1)(2), 37(1); Naval Discipline Act 1957, ss.9, 16.)

Aliens Restriction (Amendment) Act 1919

3. Incitement to sedition, etc.

(1) If any alien attempts or does any act calculated or likely to cause sedition or disaffection amongst any of His Majesty's Forces or the forces of His Majesty's allies, or amongst the civilian population, he shall be liable on conviction on indictment to penal servitude for a term

not exceeding ten years, or on summary conviction to imprisonment for a term not exceeding three months.

(2) If any alien promotes or attempts to promote industrial unrest in any industry in which he has not been bona fide engaged for at least two years immediately preceding in the United Kingdom, he shall be liable on summary conviction to imprisonment for a term not exceeding three months.

NOTE

Is it justifiable to make it an offence for an alien to do something which is not an offence if done by a non-alien?

Incitement to Disaffection Act 1934

1. Penalty on persons endeavouring to seduce members of His Majesty's forces from their duty or allegiance
If any person maliciously and advisedly endeavours to seduce any member of His Majesty's forces from his duty or allegiance to His Majesty, he shall be guilty of an offence under this Act.

2. Provisions for the prevention and detection of offences under this Act
(1) If any person, with intent to commit or to aid, abet, counsel, or procure the commission of an offence under section one of this Act, has in his possession or under his control any document of such a nature that the dissemination of copies thereof among members of His Majesty's forces would constitute such an offence, he shall be guilty of an offence under this Act.

(2) If a judge of the High Court is satisfied by information on oath that there is reasonable ground for suspecting that an offence under this Act has been committed, and that evidence of the commission thereof is to be found at any premises or place specified in the information, he may, on an application made by an officer of police of a rank not lower than that of inspector, grant a search warrant authorising any such officer as aforesaid named in the warrant together with any other persons named in the warrant and any other officers of police to enter the premises or place at any time within one month from the date of the warrant, if necessary by force, and to search the premises or place and every person found therein, and to seize anything found on the premises or place or on any such person which the officer has reasonable ground for suspecting to be evidence of the commission of such an offence as aforesaid:

Provided that—
(a) a search warrant shall only be issued in respect of an offence suspected to have been committed within the three months prior to the laying of the information thereof; and
(b) if a search warrant under this Act has been executed on any premises, it shall be the duty of the officer of police who has conducted or directed the search to notify the occupier that the search has taken place, and to supply him with a list of any documents or other objects which have been removed from the premises, and where any documents have been removed from any other person to supply that person with a list of such documents.

(3) No woman shall, in pursuance of a warrant issued under the last foregoing subsection, be searched except by a woman . . .

NOTES

1. See *Williams*, pp. 187–191; W. I. Jennings, *The Sedition Bill Explained* (1934); J. E. MacColl and W. T. Wells, (1934) Political Quarterly 352; T. Young, *Incitement to Disaffection* (1976); Larry Grant, Index on Censorship (1974) Vol. 3 No. 3.

2. The maximum penalty is two years' imprisonment, a fine, or both, on conviction on indictment (1934 Act, s. 3(1); Criminal Law Act 1977, s. 32) and four months' imprisonment a £1,000 fine or both on summary conviction (1934 Act, s. 3(1); Criminal Law Act 1977, s. 28(2)). One of the

reasons for the form of the 1934 legislation was the absence of possible summary trial under the 1797 Act. Prosecutions require the consent of the DPP (s. 3(2)). The Act extends to Northern Ireland (s. 4(3)).

3. The Bill was the subject of widespread criticism from persons such as Professors W. Holdsworth and J. L. Brierly. W. I. Jennings (op. cit. p. 8) described it as 'a danger to the essential liberties without which democratic government cannot exist.' It attempted to prevent members of the armed forces 'from learning that sometimes a refusal to obey orders may be right' (p. 15) and was a direct attack on pacifist doctrines (p. 28). In consequence of the criticism, the Bill was modified in a number of respects. Originally, mere possession of the documents 'without lawful excuse' was an offence. The reference to the intent of the possessor was substituted. The words 'maliciously and advisedly' were added after the second reading in the Commons. The very wide power to issue search warrants was originally to be exercised by magistrates, but was limited to a High Court Judge.

4. Note the difference in wording between the phrase 'duty and allegiance' in the 1797 Act (above) and 'duty or allegiance' in s. 1 of the 1934 Act. The government refused to agree to the substitution of 'and' for 'or' in the 1934 Act. The Law Commission (op. cit. p. 57) have taken the view that

'the offences under the Services legislation are . . . sufficient to cover persuading a member of the armed forces to be absent without leave, or, in the case of the Army and the Air Force, interfering with his military duty. The Incitement to Disaffection Act should . . . if it is to be retained, be amended to make it clear that it aims to penalise those who endeavour to seduce members of the Services from their allegiance to the Sovereign, which implies a breach of a fundamental duty of loyalty.'

5. The first prosecution, in 1937, was of an 18 year old, H. Phillips. He had met an R.A.F. corporal in a railway station cafe, and they discussed stealing a plane and flying to Spain to help the Republicans. He also wrote a letter suggesting that the corporal could either fly to Madrid, or stay and convert the whole squadron. He was convicted and sentenced to 12 months' imprisonment although he was released early following intervention by the Home Secretary in response to public pressure (T. Bunyan, *The Political Police in Britain* (1977) pp. 33–34; Young op. cit. p. 77). The next prosecution was in 1972. M. Tobin was sentenced to two years' imprisonment for possessing pamphlets which contained explicit appeals to soldiers to desert and offered a soldier £50 to go over to the I.R.A., £25 for delivering up an officer, and £80 for delivering up arms (Young, op. cit. p. 81). The Act has since been used in respect of pamphlets distributed in connection with the British Withdrawal from Northern Ireland Campaign.

In *R v Arrowsmith* [1975] QB 678, CA, Pat Arrowsmith distributed literature to soldiers in Colchester suggesting that they should leave the Army or desert rather than serve in Northern Ireland. She was arrested for insulting behaviour under the Public Order Act 1936, s. 5, and told the matter would be reported to the DPP for his consent to a prosecution under the 1934 Act. The DPP decided not to give that consent, and A was acquitted by the justices of insulting behaviour. She then distributed leaflets to soldiers in Warminster and was again arrested. She was convicted of offences under s. 1 and 2(1) of the 1934 Act and sentenced to 18 months' imprisonment concurrent on each count. On appeal, the Court of Appeal (Criminal Division) held (1) that 'maliciously' did not bear the meaning of spite or ill-will, but something which was wilful or intentional; (2) that a belief that she would not be prosecuted was no defence in law; (3) that her conduct was clearly unlawful; but (4) that she might 'have drawn the inference from the Director of Public Prosecutions' inaction and decision that nothing would happen to her if she went on distributing these leaflets' and have 'some grounds for thinking that she has not been treated fairly.' Accordingly, her sentence was reduced to allow for her immediate release 'in the interests, not of justice, but of the appearance of justice' (Lawton LJ at p. 691)

An application by Pat Arrowsmith claiming that her conviction under the Incitement of Disaffection Act 1934 violated Articles 9, 10 and 14, ECHR was admitted for consideration (*A. 7050/75*, 20 YBECHR 316 (1977)) but rejected on the merits (CM Res DH (79) 4).

Police Act 1964

53. Causing disaffection
(1) Any person who causes, or attempts to cause, or does any act calculated to cause, disaffection amongst the members of any police force, or induces or attempts to induce, or does any act calculated to induce, any member of a police force to withhold his services or to commit breaches of discipline, shall be guilty of an offence and liable—
    (*a*) on summary conviction, to imprisonment for a term not exceeding six months or to a fine not exceeding [£1,000], or to both;
    (*b*) on conviction on indictment, to imprisonment for a term not exceeding two years or to a fine or to both.
(2) This section applies to special constables appointed for a police area as it applies to members of a police force.

NOTES

1. The maximum fine on summary conviction was increased from £100 by the Criminal Law Act 1977, s. 28 (2).
2. This section is the re-enactment of the Police Act 1919, s. 3. That provision was introduced following strikes of the London police force in 1918, and agitation for a general police strike the following year (G. W. Reynolds and A. Judge, *The Night the Police went on strike* (1968); *Williams* pp. 192–193; *Young*, op. cit. pp. 23–27). Two people were prosecuted in 1921 for exhorting the police not to oppose the unemployed (*Williams*, p. 193). In 1932, Wal Hannington was convicted of attempting to cause disaffection among members of the Metropolitan Police and sentenced to 3 months imprisonment. He had urged the 'working class in uniform' to stand together with the unemployed, in a speech in Trafalgar Square (see *The Times*, 9 November 1932; *Williams*, pp. 194–5; W. Hannington, *Unemployed Struggles* (1936) pp. 259–266; W. Hannington, *Never on our Knees* (1967) pp. 268–277). The magistrate, Sir Chartres Biron, met Hannington's argument that there was already disaffection among the police as a result of pay cuts, by holding that there was a
    'distinction between dissatisfaction and disaffection. The effect of your speech would be to make use of the dissatisfaction and to make disaffection general.'
3. Consider the effect of the absence of the words 'maliciously and advisedly' from s. 53 (and the Aliens Restriction (Amendment) Act 1919 s. 3) in contrast with the 1797 and 1934 Acts.

CHAPTER 7

The right to privacy

1 Introduction

The right to privacy was described by Cooley as 'the right to be let alone' (*Torts* (2nd edn. 1888) p. 29). Both the Justice Report (*Privacy and the Law* (1970) p. 5) and the Younger Committee Report (*Report of the Committee on Privacy*, 1972, Cmnd, 5012, p. 17) pointed out the difficulty of finding 'a precise or logical formula which could either circumscribe the meaning of the word 'privacy' or define it exhaustively' (Justice Report, p. 5). Each, however, suggested a working definition. The Justice Report (ibid) understood privacy as meaning

'that area of a man's life which in any given circumstances, a reasonable man with an understanding of the legitimate needs of the community would think it wrong to invade'.

The Younger Committee (Report, p. 10) 'conceived of the right of privacy as having two main aspects':

'The first of these is freedom from intrusion upon oneself, one's home, family and relationships. The second is privacy of information, that is the right to determine for oneself how and to what extent information about oneself is communicated to others'.

Cf. the definition adopted by A. F. Westin, *Privacy and Freedom* (1970) p. 7:

'Privacy is the claim of individuals, groups, or institutions to determine for themselves when, how, and to what extent information about them is communicated to others. Viewed in terms of the relation of the individual to social participation, privacy is the voluntary and temporary withdrawal of a person from the general society through physical or psychological means, either in a state of solitude or small-group intimacy or, when among larger groups, in a condition of anonymity or reserve.'

Mr Walden's 1970 private member's bill (reprinted in the Younger Committee Report, pp. 276ff) proposed a right of action for invasion of privacy in the following terms:

1. Any substantial and unreasonable infringement of a right of privacy taking place after the coming into force of this Act shall be actionable at the suit of any person whose right of privacy has been so infringed . . ..

9.—(1) 'Right of privacy' means the right of any person to be protected from intrusion upon himself, his home, his family, his relationships and communications with others, his property and his business affairs, including intrusion by—

(a) spying, prying, watching or besetting;
(b) the unauthorised overhearing or recording of spoken words;
(c) the unauthorised making of visual images;
(d) the unauthorised reading or copying of documents;

(e) the unauthorised use or disclosure of confidential information, or of facts (including his name, identity or likeness) calculated to cause him distress, annoyance or embarrassment, or to place him in a false light;

(f) the unauthorised appropriation of his name, identity or likeness for another's gain.

The Bill provided for a number of defences: lack of knowledge that conduct invades privacy; consent; public interest; defence of the person, property, or business interests; absolute or qualified privilege; and lawful authority. See also the definitions in the US *Restatement*, below, p. 303, and in the conclusions of the 1967 Nordic Conference on the Right of Privacy (Justice Committee Report, Appendix B, and S. Stromholm, *Right of Privacy and Rights of the Personality* (1967) p. 237).

The 'principal areas of complaint with regard to intrusions into privacy' in the private sector were identified by the Younger Committee (Report, p. 7) as follows: (i) unwanted publicity (by the press and broadcasting); (ii) misuse of personal information (by credit rating agencies, banks, employers, educational institutions (student records) and the medical profession (particularly in industry)); (iii) intrusions on home life (by prying neighbours, landlords, the press, doorstep and postal and telephone sales and promotional methods and private detectives; and (iv) intrusion in business life (industrial espionage). To these may be added in the public sector (i) intrusion in the course of the administration of the criminal law, for example, by personal and property searches (the law as to which is considered in Chapter 2), telephone tapping, finger-printing, and the use of breathalysers and (ii) the misuse of personal information held by public authorities such as income tax, census, social security, council housing and family welfare authorities and the police. On the problem of the 1971 census, see *Security of the Census of Population* (Cmnd. 5365). On prying in the enforcement of the cohabitation rule by the Supplementary Benefits Commission, see the extracts in M. Jones (ed.), *Privacy* (1974) p. 107.

The protection afforded to privacy by English law is piecemeal, incomplete and indirect. There is no general right to privacy. Concern about the adequacy of the protection given has long been voiced (see, eg., Winfield, (1931) 47 LQR 23 and has in recent years reached the point where it has been the subject of two reports and several private members' bills. The reasons for this activity were identified by the Younger Committee Report, p. 6, as follows:

'18   To some extent the new public concern on this subject is the direct result of new technological developments. Numerous sophisticated electronic devices have been invented and marketed, which greatly increase the possibilities of surreptitious supervision of people's private activities and of spying upon business rivals. Computers have been designed which facilitate the centralisation of information about people's private affairs and its dissemination for purposes other than those for which it was supplied. And, accompanying these technical developments, there has been a spectacular growth in the collection and distribution of information as a commercial activity, which has given rise to anxiety in connection with the granting of credit, mail-order business and other forms of promotion.

19   Furthermore, but by no means least important, there has been a fairly steady flow of complaints about intrusions into privacy by the mass information media. This is a subject as old as the popular press, but its importance has been enhanced in the context of radio and television and by the growing tendency of all media to engage increasingly in "investigative journalism". Press and broadcasting organisations see themselves as the watchdogs of the public in investigating and exposing conduct of many kinds which, though not necessarily involving breaches of the law, may arguably be considered of concern to society and therefore fair game for revelation and public comment in the press or on the air. This may involve the reporting of intimate details of the lives of individuals which would not normally be thought of as being in the public domain.

20   From a wider point of view concern for the protection of privacy has been stimulated by the growing pressures exerted by modern industrial society upon the home and daily life, including such factors as the density of urban housing, the consequent difficulty of escaping

from the observation of neighbours, the annoyance of commercial advertising and the increasing inquisitiveness of social surveys, polls and market research about the lives of private citizens.'

On the right to privacy, see J. D. Baxter (1977) 8 Cambrian LR 7; L. Brittan, (1963) 37 Tul LR 235; P. Burns, (1976) 54 Can BR 1; Z. Cowen, *Individual Liberty and the Law* (1977) Chap 4 & 5; G. Dworkin, (1967) 2 U Tas LR 418; J. Fleming, *Law of Torts* (5th edn.) Ch 25; P. Goode, (1973–6) 5 Adelaide LR 13; P. Hewitt, *Privacy: The Information Gatherers* (1977); M. Jones (ed.) *Privacy* (1974); D. Madgwick, *Privacy under Attack* (1968); D. Madgwick and T. Smythe, *The Invasion of Privacy* (1974); G. Marshall, (1975) 21 McGill LJ 242; A. R. Miller, *The Assault on Privacy* (1971); B. Neill, (1962) 25 MLR 393; W. F. Pratt, [1975] PL 161; J. B. Rule, *Private Lives and Public Surveillance* (1973); J. Swanton, (1974) 48 Aust LJ 91; S. Stromholm, *Right of Privacy and Rights of the Personality* (1967); G. D. S. Taylor, (1971) 34 MLR 288; Wacks, 96 LQR 73 (1980); S. Warren and L. Brandeis, (1890) 4 Harv LR 193; A. F. Westin, *Privacy and Freedom* (1970); P. Winfield, 47 LQR 23 (1931); T. L. Yang, (1966) 15 ICLQ 175. And see the Justice Report (*Privacy and the Law* (1970)); the Younger Committee Report (*Report of the Committee on Privacy* (1972) Cmnd. 5012); and the Report of the Privacy Committee of the Society of Conservative Lawyers (*Price of Privacy* (1971)).

2 A general right of privacy?

Report of the Committee on Privacy, Chairman: Kenneth Younger MP (Cmnd. 5012 1972)

655   We have . . . examined . . . each of the specific areas in which substantial concern about intrusions into privacy has been brought to our attention. In some cases we have recommended that there should be legislation to create either a new offence in order to deal with new threats to privacy, for instance new technical surveillance devices; or a right of access by an individual to information held about him by a credit rating agency. In other cases we have thought it more effective to recommend that administrative controls should be established over a particular kind of activity, such as credit rating agencies and private detectives. In yet other cases where legal action has seemed too heavy an instrument and administrative control undesirable or unnecessary, we have preferred to rely on a measure of self-discipline being exercised by bodies whose activities involve a possible threat to privacy. Examples are the mass media, the universities, the medical profession and industrial employers . . .
657   Looking at the field as a whole, we have expressed the view that the existing law provides more effective relief from some kinds of intrusion into privacy than is generally appreciated . . . .
659   . . . We recognise that this piecemeal approach leaves some gaps. In the private sector (with which alone we are concerned) it is not difficult to think of some kinds of intrusion, most obviously by journalistic investigators or by prying neighbours, for which our recommendations provide no new legal remedy. In the second place, some of our proposals frankly rely, to an extent which some may find over-optimistic, upon the readiness of potentially intrusive agencies, such as the press, to respond not to legal sanctions but to the pressures of public and professional criticism and to the climate of society. Yet other proposals rely upon codes of conduct or on negotiated conditions of employment as means of maintaining ethical standards . . . .
664   This raises the question whether the method which we have adopted is . . . inadequate . . . . We have concluded that, so far as the principal areas of complaint are concerned, and especially those which arise from new technological developments, our specific recommendations are likely to be much more effective than any general declaration. Having covered these areas, we do not think that what remains uncovered is extensive; and our evidence does not suggest that the position in the uncovered area is deteriorating. We think moreover that to cover it by a blanket declaration of a right of privacy would introduce uncertainties into the law, the repercussions of which upon free circulation of information are difficult to foresee in detail but could be substantial . . . .

665   We have found privacy to be a concept which means widely different things to different people and changes significantly over relatively short periods.[1] In considering how the courts could handle so ill-defined and unstable a concept, we conclude that privacy is ill-suited to be the subject of a long process of definition through the building up of precedents over the years, since the judgments of the past would be an unreliable guide to any current evaluation of privacy . . . .

667   . . . Privacy, however defined, embodies values which are essential to a free society. It requires the support of society as a whole. But the law is only one of the factors determining the climate of a democratic society and it is often only a minor factor. Education, professional standards and the free interplay of ideas and discussion through the mass media and the organs of political democracy can do at least as much as the law to establish and maintain standards of behaviour. We have explained in this report that we see risks in placing excessive reliance on the law in order to protect privacy. We believe that in our recommendations we have given to the law its due place in the protection of privacy and we see no need to extend it further.

MINORITY REPORT OF MR LYON

Criticism of a general right

6   They [the Committee] begin by doubting whether privacy can be defined for the purpose of the law. I noticed in our discussions that there was rarely any doubt whether a specific complaint, e.g. noise, was a privacy situation or not. As a philosophic concept the limits may be imprecise . . . . For the purpose of the law, however, privacy is what the law says it is. If the statute said that only conversations in bed between husbands and wives were to be protected, that would be the limit of legal privacy . . . .

9   My colleagues . . . claim that a general law would be an unjustifiable suppression of truth. The law already puts curbs on dissemination of true facts in the area of breach of confidence, criminal libel, copyright and patent. To these we [i.e. the Committee] now propose to add curtailment of the use of electronic and photographic devices and the use of information obtained by unlawful methods . . . .

11   In other words truth is not inviolate, any more than any other value in our society . . . .

12   . . . The new tort, they say, would lead to a spate of blackmailing actions . . . . The press cite defamation as an area where unmeritorious cases succeed, but this is frequently because accident is no defence to defamation whereas all the suggested drafts of a tort of privacy have required a deliberate intention to intrude . . . .

13   Nevertheless, the critics continue, the threat of legal action may cause those whose duty is to reveal the truth for the public good to limit their activities . . . . All justifiable intrusions could be protected by the defences which would be written into any legislation.

14   If there are some disadvantages to the general right and the number of people assisted will be small is it necessary to legislate? The same argument might have been used in relation to the legal remedies of trespass, nuisance and even negligence . . . .They raise similar issues of a balance of conflicting interests and some imprecision of definition. Because the individual would feel a sense of outrage if he was injured in these ways without legal redress, society has thought it right to give legal protection. In a number of western countries similar general protection has been given for privacy without any of the consequences alleged by the critics . . . .

Advantages of the general tort

17   *First*, . . . Parliamentary time is restricted and every new advance demands a long and sometimes exhausting campaign. It is much better to set out the principles on which the courts can act and leave them to develop the law·as need required . . . .

19   *Second*, it gives a remedy to all those seriously prejudiced by intrusions into privacy . . . .

20   *Third*, it gives teeth to many of our other recommendations. If a computer operator knew that his activities might lead to a suit for damages, he would be more likely to respond to the code of principles we enunciate.

21   *Fourth*, it allows juries to set the standards in a constantly changing area of human values. If private enquiry agents are to lose their certificates of registration for unreasonable intrusion

1.   Ed. E.g. contrast the reaction now and 20 years ago to the information that an unmarried couple are living together. Note also that the revelation of a person's income was placed only below the revelation of facts about his sex life as an invasion of privacy in the public opinion survey done for the Younger Committee (Report, p. 239). In contrast, in Sweden one's income is a matter of public record in the sense that it is possible to buy a book which lists the income tax that everyone pays.

into privacy, who is to decide what is reasonable? The Home Office? The police? I would prefer a jury as more representative of public opinion.

22   *Fifth*, it would provide an effective remedy for any unreasonable behaviour. Not only would damages reimburse financial loss or mollify injured feelings, but an injunction would be a useful deterrent to prevent anticipated intrusions into privacy . . . .

23   *Sixth*, no general remedy is likely to gain Parliamentary approval if it did not include government activities. The result of my colleagues' recommendations is that the government has succeeded in keeping its activities to itself although many would agree that government intrusion is potentially more dangerous and annoying. A general tort would easily have been amended to cover all those government activities which were not authorised by law . . . .

24   *Seventh*, we would have fulfilled our obligations under the United Nations Declaration of Human Rights and the European Convention. One of the ironies of the majority report is that the European Court may choose in time to give a remedy for English litigants which my colleagues would deny to them. [See the *Klass* case, below, p.332] . . .

26   Early in my researches on this subject I came across the case of a Mrs X whose policeman husband took a mistress. The wife prevailed upon him to give up the mistress and they were reconciled. The jealous lover told a national newspaper. When their reporter was rebuffed by Mrs X, they printed the story under the headlines 'The love life of a detective'. The family had to move; the husband had to give up his job; the child was teased at school. What do I now tell Mrs X? 'Truth must prevail'. 'We cannot protect privacy except where there has been a breach of confidence or the intruder used offensive new methods like bugging devices.' 'A reformed Press Council will censure the newspaper!'

Mr Ross QC also appended a Minority Report dissenting from the Committee on the same issue.

NOTES

1. As Sir Robert Megarry VC stated in *Malone v MPC*, below, p. 328, 'no general right of privacy has been recognised by English law'. Cf. Lord Denning MR in *Re X (A Minor)*, below, p. 314, and Latham CJ in *Victoria Park Racing and Recreation Co Ltd v Taylor*, below, p. 310. Several torts (mainly trespass, nuisance and defamation) provide indirect remedies in some cases, as does the law of copyright and breach of confidence. Criminal law occasionally helps. The Press Council and other complaints or standard-setting bodies play a role, as would the proposed Data Protection Authority.

2. The position contrasts sharply with that in the United States where the courts in most jurisdictions have, sometimes with the aid of legislation, developed a tort of invasion of privacy. The inspiration to do so came from an article by Warren and Brandeis ((1890) 4 Harv LR 193) prompted by the press coverage of the wedding of the daughter of one of the authors. Somewhat ironically, the article argued for the existence of a right of privacy in tort largely on the basis of English precedents such as *Prince Albert v Strange*, below, p. 317. The tort—or more accurately the four interrelated torts—that has developed in the US is defined in the *Restatement, 2d, Torts*, 1977, para 652A, as follows:

'(1) One who invades the right of privacy of another is subject to liability for the resulting harm to the interests of the other.
(2) The right of privacy is invaded by
    (a) unreasonable intrusion upon the seclusion of another . . .; or
    (b) appropriation of the other's name or likeness . . .; or
    (c) unreasonable publicity given to the other's private life . . .; or
    (d) publicity that unreasonably places the other in a false light before the public.'

The *Restatement* represents the preponderance of opinion in American jurisdictions.

The classification is that first adopted by Prosser ((1960) 48 Cal LR 383).

To the tort must now be added the constitutional right to privacy which originated in *Griswold v Connecticut* (1965), above, p. 13.

3. In 1961 and 1967, Lord Mancroft and Mr Lyon respectively introduced unsuccessfully private member's bills (for texts, see Younger Committee Report, pp. 273ff) that would have created a right of action for invasion of privacy. A third such bill to the same effect was introduced in 1969 by Mr Walden (for text, see ibid, pp. 276ff; extracts above, p. 299) based upon a draft bill prepared by the Justice Committee (*Report on Privacy and the Law* (1970) Appendix J) which had reported in favour of a general statutory right of action. The 1969 bill was withdrawn when the Government undertook to establish the Younger Committee, whose terms of reference were as follows:

> 'To consider whether legislation is needed to give further protection to the individual citizen and to commercial and industrial interests against intrusions into privacy by private persons and organisations, or by companies, and to make recommendations.'

The Committee was not authorised to examine invasions of privacy in the public sector (by government and the police).

4. As the above extract indicates, the Younger Committee came out against a general right of privacy and in favour of strengthening and adding to existing legal and non-legal rules and remedies. Its main recommendations for changes in the law were for:

> i. a criminal offence of surreptitious unlawful surveillance by means of a technical device (below, p. 334);
> ii. a tort of unlawful surveillance by such means (below, p. 334);
> iii. a tort of disclosure or other use of information unlawfully acquired (below, p. 321).
> iv. a legally enforceable right of access to information held by a credit agency about one (implemented by the Consumer Credit Act 1974, s. 158).

The Committee also recommended changes in the working of the Press Council, see above, p. 212, and the BBC Complaints Commission; the taking of steps by the institutions and persons concerned to improve the confidentiality of personal information held by banks, universities and employers; the licensing of private detectives; and the adoption of a voluntary code by computer users (see now the recommendations of the Lindop Committee, below, pp. 334–339).

5. Whose arguments on the need for a general right of privacy do you prefer? The Committee's? Or Mr Lyon's? Would a bill such as Mr Walden's, above, p. 299, work? Lord Denning MR stated in Parliament (229 HL Deb March 13 1961 col 639):

> 'This is the law [on invasion of privacy] as evolved in the United States from our Common Law. Why cannot we have something similar? I am not in despair. The Judges may well do it. There is nothing in any decision of this House, judicially, which prevents it, in that whenever any grievous cases come up we find that the lawyers produce a remedy.'

But see the same judge's judgment in *Re X (A Minor)*, below, p. 314. For an argument against leaving the matter to the judges (as opposed to introducing a statutory right of action), see the Justice Committee Report, p. 30.

3 Existing remedies in law

(a) TRESPASS

Hickman v Maisey [1900] 1 QB 752, 69 LJQB 511, 82 LT 321, Court of Appeal

The plaintiff owned and occupied land on which for a fee he allowed a racehorse trainer to train horses. The defendant, a racing tout, observed the horses from a highway that crossed the plaintiff's land. The plaintiff brought an action in trespass for damages and an injunction. The jury found for the plaintiff, awarding damages of one shilling, and the judge granted an injunction. The defendant appealed to the Court of Appeal.

A. L. Smith LJ: . . . Many authorities shew that primâ facie the right of the public is merely to pass and repass along the highway; but I quite agree with what Lord Esher MR said in *Harrison v Duke of Rutland* [1893] 1 QB 142. . . . namely, that, though highways are dedicated primâ facie for the purpose of passage, 'things are done upon them by everybody which are recôgnised as being rightly done and as constituting a reasonable and usual mode of using a highway as such'; and, 'if a person on a highway does not transgress such reasonable and usual mode of using it,' he will not be a trespasser; but, if he does 'acts other than the reasonable and ordinary user of a highway as such' he will be a trespasser. . . . But I cannot agree with the contention of the defendant's counsel that the acts which this defendant did, not really for the purpose of using the highway as such, but for the purpose of carrying on his business as a racing tout to the detriment of the plaintiff by watching the trials of race-horses on the plaintiff's land, were within such an ordinary and reasonable user of the highway as I have mentioned. . . . In the case of *Harrison v Duke of Rutland* [1893] 1 QB 142 the point which arises in this case was substantially determined, though the user of the highway by the plaintiff in that case was not precisely similar to that in the present case. In that case the plaintiff went upon a highway, the soil of which was vested in the defendant, while a grouse drive was taking place on adjoining land of the defendant, for the purpose of interfering with the drive, which the defendant's keepers prevented him from doing by force. The plaintiff thereupon brought an action for assault against the defendant, and the defendant counter-claimed in trespass. . . . It was clear upon the facts that he was not using the highway for the purpose of passing or repassing along it, but solely for the purpose of interfering with the defendant's enjoyment of his right of shooting over his land, and it was held therefore that the plaintiff's user of the highway was a trespass. I cannot see any real distinction between that case and the present. . . . I do not agree with the argument of the defendant's counsel to the effect that the intention and object of the defendant in going upon the highway cannot be taken into account in determining whether he was using it in a lawful manner. I think that his intention and object were all-important in determining that question.
Collins and **Romer LJJ** delivered concurring judgments.
Appeal dismissed.

NOTES

1. The case concerned a highway the soil of which was the property of the plaintiff. In most cases (a private road would be an exception), the soil will be vested in a highway authority: usually a local authority or the Environment Secretary. Although the same rule (ordinary and reasonable user) applies, it will be unlikely in such cases that a person who wishes to rely upon it will be as fortunate as the racehorse trainer in *Hickman v Maisey* was in persuading the owner of the soil to bring proceedings.
2. The trainer could not have brought an action in trespass to land because he was not in possession of the land: see Salmond, *Torts*, (17th edn., 1977) p. 45. Similarly, in the cases which have reached the Press Council in which the press have entered hospitals surreptitiously to interview or photograph a patient (see, e.g., the Aneurin Bevan case, 8th Report 1961, p. 39), the hospital authorities could have brought proceedings in trespass, but not the patient or his family. So also, 'the ordinary overnight visitor at an hotel

may sleep in but does not "occupy" the bedroom allotted to him and hence has no remedy against an intruder who plants a microphone in the room; the hotel proprietor will have an action in trespass but he may be unwilling to bring it; indeed he may have put the microphone in the room himself or be in collusion with someone who did so' (Younger Report, p. 290). But 'where there is a contract between a hotel guest and the hotel proprietor it might be argued that it is an implied term of such a contract that the former's room should be free from devices intruding on his privacy' (ibid). This, of course, would only give a claim against the hotel.

3. The plaintiff would not have had a remedy in trespass to land if the defendant had watched the horses from land that was not the plaintiff's. Cf. Lord Camden's dictum quoted in *Malone v Metropolitan Police Commissioner*, above, p. 328. There has to be a physical presence on the plaintiff's land, as in *Sheen v Clegg, Daily Telegraph* (1961), 22 June cited in the Younger Committee Report, p. 289 (Microphone placed by trespass over plaintiff's marital bed) and *Greig v Greig* [1966] VR 376 S Ct Vict (microphone placed in plaintiff's flat by trespass). The Younger Committee (p. 289) suggested that a 'method of spying which involved the projection into airspace above the plaintiff's land of beams (as for radar) could presumably be treated as trespass to land or perhaps nuisance'. The Committee added:

'An entry is unauthorised . . . if permission to enter is obtained by fraud, as when an enquiry agent posing as a post office engineer obtains entry to a building and puts a bugging device in a telephone receiver; and an entry lawfully made may become trespassing when the entrant takes advantage of the occasion to do things (e.g. to carry out a search of the premises) not covered by his permission to enter.'

See the Press Council cases (e.g. 18th Report 1971, p. 49) in which reporters have been invited into a house and then taken a photograph without consent.

4. In addition to the limitations upon trespass to land as a remedy for invasion of privacy noted above, there is also the question of the measure of damages. As the Younger Committee Report states:

'In any case where invasion of privacy is the real issue, there is not likely to be any substantial claim for damage to the land, at least by comparison with what the plaintiff is likely to feel he ought to receive for the invasion of privacy. Damages for the latter can only be covered by a claim for aggravated or for punitive (or exemplary) damages i.e. for a sum which will offer the plaintiff some recompense for the attack made on his feelings and dignity or which will punish the defendant for the outrageous form which the trespass has taken . . . . It would seem that . . . a journalist, for example, who forced his way into a house to get a story for his newspaper might find himself liable to pay substantial damages, even though he had done little or no damage to the house. However, the cases in which punitive damages may be awarded appear to have been severely limited by the House of Lords in *Rookes v Barnard* [1964] AC 1129 and *Cassell & Co v Broome* [1972] AC 1027.'

In *Rookes v Barnard*, Lord Devlin stated that punitive damages were available only in (i) cases of 'oppressive, arbitrary or unconstitutional action by the servants of the government' (the government includes local government and the police: *Cassell v Broome*); (ii) cases 'in which the defendant's conduct has been calculated by him to make a profit for himself which may well exceed the compensation payable to the plaintiff'; and (iii) where 'exemplary damages are expressly authorised by statute'. Some privacy cases involving, for example, police or press action will come within the first or second of these categories. For a privacy case of breach of copyright in which punitive damages were awarded, see *Williams v Settle*, below. p. 316.

5. In 1965 the *Sunday Express* and *The People* published pictures of the

Queen and Princess Margaret showing them water-skiing at the Great Pond, Sunninghill Park. The Park is Crown land but has a public footpath running through it some distance from the lake and from which part of the lake can be seen. The pictures had been bought from a professional photographer who claimed to have taken them from the footpath with a telephoto lens. The case was investigated by the Press Council (12th Report 1965, p. 3) which found 'that the photographs . . . were taken surreptitiously by Mr R. Bellisario when the Queen and the Princess obviously were unaware that the pictures were being taken and that Mr Bellisario was trespassing on the private ground of Her Majesty [i.e. off the footpath] at the time.' After concluding that the newspapers had acted in good faith, having been deceived by the photographer, the Council 'unreservedly' condemned the photographer. It also censured a *Daily Express* photographer who was one of two photographers discovered 'hidden in the undergrowth lying on the ground, with their cameras trained on the hut where Her Royal Highness was changing her clothes'. Clearly actions in trespass could have been brought to protect privacy on these facts. Could one have been brought against Mr Bellisario if his claim to have taken the pictures from the footpath had been correct?

6. Another Press Council case (4th Report 1957, p. 22) in which there would have been a remedy in trespass was that in which the *Daily Sketch* published a reporter's story of how she had gatecrashed the Duke of Kent's 21st birthday party in the boot of a car. The editor was found 'guilty of a flagrant violation of good manners'. In a recent case, the Council (23rd Report 1976, p. 113) condoned trespass by deception when a *News of the World* reporter claimed to be homeless to gain admission to the Centrepoint hostel in London to check a story that homeless youngsters were sleeping in a mixed sex dormitory. The Press Council ruled that 'the use of subterfuge can be justified in cases involving public interest or the exposure of crime'. See further the Press Council Declaration of Principle on Privacy, below, p. 324.

7. In *Lord Bernstein of Leigh v Skyviews and General Ltd* [1978] QB 479, the plaintiff's land was flown over and an aerial photograph of his house taken without his knowledge or consent. He refused the offer to sell him the photograph and sued the defendant in trespass and invasion of privacy instead. Rejecting the claim, Griffiths J stated:

'I can find no support in authority for the view that a landowner's rights in the air space above his property extend to an unlimited height. In *Wandsworth Board of Works v United Telephone Co Ltd*, (1884) 13 QBD 904 Bowen LJ described the maxim, usque ad coelum, as a fanciful phrase, to which I would add that if applied literally it is a fanciful notion leading to the absurdity of a trespass at common law being committed by a satellite every time it passes over a suburban garden. . . . The problem is to balance the rights of an owner to enjoy the use of his land against the rights of the general public to take advantage of all that science now offers in the use of air space. This balance is in my judgment best struck in our present society by restricting the rights of an owner in the air space above his land to such height as is necessary for the ordinary use and enjoyment of his land and the structures upon it, and declaring that above that height he has no greater rights in the air space than any other member of the public.

Applying this test to the facts of this case, I find that the defendants' aircraft did not infringe any rights in the plaintiff's air space, and thus no trespass was committed. It was on any view of the evidence flying many hundreds of feet above the ground and it is not suggested that by its mere presence in the air space it caused any interference with any use to which the plaintiff put or might wish to put his land. The plaintiff's complaint is not that the aircraft interfered with the use of his land but that a photograph was taken from it. There is, however, no law against taking a photograph, and the mere taking of a photograph cannot turn an act which is not a trespass into the plaintiff's air space into one that is a trespass.

The present action is not founded in nuisance for no court would regard the taking of a single photograph as an actionable nuisance. But if the circumstances were such that a plaintiff was subjected to the harrassment of constant surveillance of his house from the air, accompanied by the photographing of his every activity, I am far from saying that the court would not regard such a monstrous invasion of his privacy as an actionable nuisance for which they would give relief.'

See R. Wacks (1977) 93 LQR 491.

8. There is no right in law to prevent a person taking one's picture. In *Sports and General Press Agency v 'Our Dogs' Publishing Co Ltd* [1916] 2 KB 880, the Ladies Kennel Association purported to sell the 'sole photographic rights' to their dog show (held at a place of which they were in exclusive occupation for the day). An injunction was sought to prevent a magazine publishing photographs taken at the show by another photographer whose ticket of admission said nothing about taking photographs. In the absence of any trespass, Horridge J held for the defendant:

'In my judgment no one possesses a right of preventing another person photographing him any more than he has a right of preventing another person giving a description of him, provided the description is not libellous or otherwise wrongful.'

The Younger Committee reported (Report, p. 35) that it was suggested to it that if a person is photographed by the press without permission 'the negative and all the prints should be considered his property'. Would you agree?

9. A lot of Press Council cases raising questions of privacy have concerned the publication of photographs. In one such case (12th Report 1965, p. 91), the *Sheffield Telegraph* was censured for publishing photographs taken by telephoto lens of three professional footballers who had been convicted on betting charges and who were photographed playing football in prison. In the context of the Manchester Utd Munich Air Crash, the Council stated that 'as a general principle a photograph of a seriously injured person likely to cause needless distress and pain to relatives should not be printed' (5th Report 1958, p. 35). The criterion in cases of personal tragedies generally (including pictures of accidents, funerals, victims of crimes) is whether the publication 'causes unnecessary suffering and distress to relatives and friends and does not serve the public interest' (13th Report 1966, p. 86). See further the Press Council Declaration of Principle on Privacy, below, p. 324.

10. The public opinion survey done for the Younger Committee (Report, Appendix E) showed that 'callers at the door' were regarded as invading privacy, with Jehovah's Witnesses being mentioned in particular. In *Robson v Hallett* [1967] 2 QB 939, DC, Diplock LJ stated that at 953–4

'when a householder lives in a dwelling house to which there is a garden in front and does not lock the gate of the garden, it gives an implied licence to any member of the public who has lawful reason for doing so to proceed from the gate to the front door or back door, and to inquire whether he may be admitted and to conduct his lawful business.'

Diplock LJ stated that such an implied licence may be rebutted, as by a notice on the gate (eg. 'No hawkers').

11. The above materials concern trespass to land. Trespass to goods may occasionally provide a remedy for invasion of privacy also, as where a document is taken.

(b) NUISANCE

Report of the Committee on Privacy, Chairman: Kenneth Younger MP (Cmnd. 5012, 1972)

Private nuisance, giving rise to a civil action at the suit of an aggrieved individual, has on occasions been very widely defined to cover virtually any unreasonable interference with that individual's enjoyment of land which he occupies. But an action for private nuisance is normally brought for *some physical invasion of the plaintiff's land by some deleterious subject-matter*—such as noise, smell, water or electricity—in circumstances which would not amount to trespass to land. It is much more doubtful if it would cover an activity which had no physical effects on the plaintiff's land, although it detracts from the plaintiff's enjoyment of that land. Thus spying on one's neighbour is probably not in itself a private nuisance[2] although watching and besetting a man's house with a view to compelling him to pursue (or not to pursue) a particular course of conduct has been said to be a nuisance at common law.[3] With regard to the latter type of conduct, however, it must be admitted that it is concerned with a situation very different from the typical case in which complaint is made of an invasion of privacy. The eavesdropper or spy does not seek to change the behaviour of his victim; on the contrary he hopes that it will continue unchanged, so that he may have the opportunity of noting it unobserved. . . .

As a remedy for invasions of privacy private nuisance has the same basic disadvantages as the action for trespass to land, namely that it can only be brought by the person who is from a legal point of view the "occupier" of the land, enjoyment of which is affected by the nuisance.

NOTES

1. Persistent telephoning may be a nuisance. In *Stokes v Brydges* [1958] QWN 5, S Ct Qu, the defendant, annoyed by the noise made by milkmen, retaliated by making telephone calls to the homes of directors of the milk company to disturb their sleep. The directors were granted an injunction to prevent further calls. A single telephone call, even in the middle of the night (see 11th Press Council Report 1964, pp. 32, 35), is not a nuisance. A person commits an offence contrary to the Post Office Act 1953, s. 66 if he

'(a) sends any message by telephone which is grossly offensive or of an indecent, obscene or menacing character;
(b) sends any message by telephone, or any telegram, which he knows to be false, for the purpose of causing annoyance, inconvenience or needless anxiety to any other person; or
(c) persistently makes telephone calls without reasonable cause and for any such purpose as aforesaid.'

In *Robbins v Canadian Broadcasting Corpn* (1958) 12 DLR (2d) 35, Quebec Sup Ct, the plaintiff wrote to the producer of a television programme criticizing it. The letter was read on the programme and viewers were invited to telephone (the number was given) or write to the plaintiff to cheer him up. For three days afterwards, the plaintiff's telephone rang nonstop until he was obliged to change his number. He also received 102 letters and had pranks played upon him. He was awarded damages by the Quebec Superior Court under the Quebec Civil Code for damage caused by the fault of another. Cf. a Press Council case (12th Report 1965, p. 97) in which the *Daily Sketch* was censured for publishing the telephone number of

2. (See the case, cited by Kenny (*Cases on Tort*, 4th ed. 1926, p. 367) but otherwise unreported, in which a dentist in Balham failed to obtain any remedy against his neighbours, who by means of large mirrors were able to observe what passed in his study and surgery. The fact that a person has not previously been in a position to watch his neighbour, when his house has had no windows on the side facing that neighbour, is not a ground for preventing him from later opening a window for that purpose: see *Tapling v Jones* (1865), 11 HL Cases 290). Ed. But planning permission might be refused: Neill, (1962) 25 MLR 393, 395.

3. Ed. *J Lyons & Sons v Wilkins* [1899] 1 Ch 255 CA, an industrial disputes case.

Christine Keeler at the height of Profumo Affair causing 'a constant stream of abusive calls'.

2. In *Victoria Park Racing and Recreation Grounds Co Ltd v Taylor* (1938) 58 CLR 479, H Ct Aust, the first defendant owned land adjacent to the plaintiff's racecourse. The second defendant erected a platform on the land and broadcast descriptions of the races from it. The plaintiff was refused an injunction to prevent the broadcasts. Latham CJ stated at 494–6:

> 'Any person is entitled to look over the plaintiff's fences and to see what goes on in the plaintiff's land. . . . The court has not been referred to any principle of law which prevents any man from describing anything which he sees anywhere if he does not make defamatory statements, infringe the law as to offensive language, &c, break a contract, or wrongfully reveal confidential information. . . .
>
> The claim under the head of nuisance has also been supported by an argument that the law recognizes a right of privacy which has been infringed by the defendant. However desirable some limitation upon invasions of privacy might be, no authority was cited which shows that any general right of privacy exists'.

The *Balham* case to which the Younger Committee refers (which was unreported and is 'worthless as an authority': Winfield, (1931) 47 LQR 23, 27) suggests that 'peeping toms', however persistent, do not commit a nuisance. But they may be bound over to be of good behaviour, see below, p. 323. The Younger Committee's recommendation on unlawful surveillance by technical devices (below, p. 334) would not apply. 'Peeping toms' would be liable for invasion of privacy in the form of 'intrusion upon seclusion' in the sense of the *Restatement, 2d, Torts*, above, p. 303.

3. Would newspaper reporters who gather at the door of a person's house and will not go away unless they are given an interview or a picture be 'watching or besetting'? See the Christian Keeler case, below, p. 314.

(c) DEFAMATION

Corelli v Wall [1906] 22 TLR 532, Chancery Division, Swinfen Eady J

The plaintiff, a well known authoress and a resident of Stratford on Avon, sought an injunction to restrain the defendants, publishers in the same town, from publishing a series of postcards depicting imaginary scenes in the private life of the plaintiff. The injunction was sought pending the hearing of a libel action based upon the cards. The scenes included the plaintiff feeding ponies, on the river Avon in a gondola, and in an imaginary garden. The plaintiff's annoyance reached its height when the defendant's hired sandwichmen to parade through Stratford, particularly near the plaintiff's home, to advertise the postcards.

Swinfen Eady J:
The real ground of the plaintiff's motion is that the cards constitute a libel upon her and that their sale ought to be restrained that ground. Although it is well settled that a person may be defamed as well by a picture or effigy as by written or spoken words, I am not satisfied that the cards are libellous; and in any event the case is not so clear as to justify the Court in intervening before the fact of libel has been established. The case of *Bonnard v Perryman* [1891] 2 Ch 269 shows how careful the Court should be in granting interlocutory injunctions in cases of alleged libel. It was also urged that the plaintiff as a private person was entitled to restrain the publication of a portrait of herself which had been made without her authority and which, although professing to be her portrait, was totally unlike her. No authority in support of this proposition was cited. The plaintiff has not established, for the purpose of this motion, that she has any such right. Under these circumstances I do not see my way to grant any interlocutory injunction. When it is known that the sale of the postcards is in direct opposition to the plaintiff's wishes, and is the subject of grave annoyance to her, most respectable persons will probably do as Messrs. W. H. Smith and Son have done, and refuse to have anything to do with them.
Motion dismissed

NOTES

1. The case illustrates that even if an action in defamation is available, the remedy may be limited to damages. Although an injunction will often be much the more effective remedy from a privacy point of view, one will only be granted under the rule in *Bonnard v Perryman* [1891] 2 Ch 269 at 284, CA 'in the clearest cases, where any jury would say that the matter complained of was libellous . . .'

2. Did *Corelli v Wall* decide that there was no remedy in English law for invasion of privacy in the form of the 'appropriation' of a person's 'name or likeness' (*Restatement, 2d, Torts*, above, p. 303)? Or only that an injunction could not be granted on the facts of the case?

3. In *Monson v Tussauds* [1894] 1 QB 671, CA, the plaintiff had been tried and acquitted of murder. He sued the defendants for libel for including in their exhibition a wax model of him with the gun that was thought to be the murder weapon close-by. Under the rule in *Bonnard v Perryman*, the Court of Appeal refused an injunction pending trial of the libel action. In the Divisional Court, Collins J expressly left open 'the question whether a private person can restrain the publication of a portrait or effigy of himself which has been obtained without his authority' (p. 679). In the Court of Appeal, Lord Halsbury touched upon the question of invasion of privacy in more general terms (p. 687):

'If I understand the argument correctly, it comes to this—that the exhibition in question is dedicated to the gratification of public curiosity in regard to every person or event which may for the moment be interesting. I confess I regard such a claim with something like dismay. Is it possible to say that everything which has once been known may be reproduced with impunity in print or picture; every incident of a criminal or other trial be produced, and its publication justified; not only trials, but every incident which has actually happened in private life, furnish material for the adventurous exhibitor, dramatized peradventure, and justified because, in truth, such an incident did really happen? That it is done for gain does not in itself make it unlawful if it be in other respects legitimate; but it is not altogether immaterial as excluding such a publication from the category of those which are made in the fulfilment of some moral or legal duty.'

4. In *Tolley v J. S. Fry & Sons Ltd* [1931] AC 333, HL, the defendants published an advertisement for their chocolate showing, without his knowledge or consent, a caricature of the plaintiff, a well known amateur golfer, playing golf with a packet of their chocolate in his pocket. The plaintiff recovered damages in defamation on the basis that the advertisement carried an innuendo that he had prostituted his amateur status by advertising the defendant's goods for reward. On the question whether a remedy would have existed if the advertisement had not been defamatory, Greer LJ stated in the Court of Appeal ([1930] 1 KB at 477–8):

'Some men and women voluntarily enter professions which by their nature invite publicity, and public approval or disapproval. It is not unreasonable in their case that they should submit without complaint to their names and occupations and reputations being treated as matters of public interest, and almost as public property. On the other hand a great many people outside the professions I have referred to resent any attempt to utilize their names or their doings as public property. And I can very well imagine that an amateur sportsman, though success necessarily brings about a certain amount of publicity, strongly objecting to the use of his name in connection with an advertising campaign aimed at increasing the sales of a commodity which he may either dislike, or at any rate in which he is not the least interested. I have no hesitation in saying that in my judgment the defendants in publishing the advertisement in question, without first obtaining Mr. Tolley's consent, acted in a manner inconsistent with the decencies of life, and in doing so they were guilty of an act for which there ought to be a legal remedy. But unless a man's photograph, caricature, or name be published in such a context that the publication can be said to be defamatory within the law of libel, it cannot be made the subject-matter of complaint by action at law: *Dockrell v Dougall* and *Corelli v Wall* [above].'

In *Dockrell v Dougall* (1899) 80 LT 556 at 557, CA, the defendant had used the plaintiff's name without his knowledge or consent in an advertisement for a quack medicine ('Dr Dockrell says "Nothing had done his gout so much good"'). After a jury had held that the advertisement was not libellous, the plaintiff unsuccessfully sought an injunction. Smith LJ stated:

> If it could be made out that a man has a property in his own name *per se* and there has been an unauthorised use of his name, then the plaintiff might be entitled to an injunction. In order, however, to be entitled to an injunction, it seems to me that the plaintiff must show injury to him in his property, business, or profession. Upon that ground I think that the appeal fails.

See also *Blennerhassett v Novelty Sales Services Ltd* (1933) 175 LT Jo 393. **5.** The Press Council (17th Report 1970, p. 80) upheld a complaint against the *Armagh Guardian* for publishing an advertisement for a hotel which contained a picture of the complainant's wedding reception at the hotel without his knowledge or consent. The publication was said to have caused 'embarrassment and humiliation'.

The Goolagong Case (20th Press Council Report 1973, p. 44)

Publication by the *Sun* of drawings purporting to show Miss Evonne Goolagong, the Australian tennis player, in the nude, was an infringement of privacy said the Council after the All England Lawn Tennis and Croquet Club had complained that the *Sun* published the drawings without Miss Goolagong's knowledge and consent and that the drawings caused her great distress. . . . The drawings . . . were published under the heading 'On Wimbledon's opening day Goolagong in the Altogether'.

Miss Goolagong wrote to the Secretary of the All England Club (Major A. D. Mills) saying (inter alia) that when she went on court on the first Tuesday she felt all eyes were turned on her and that she was being undressed publicly. . . . Major Mills protested to the Editor [Mr Lamb] about the drawings and the Editor's Personal Assistant . . . replied that they were published because they believed they had artistic merit and were in no way offensive. They had had no complaint from Miss Goolagong. They would be distressed to think they had upset her. They newspaper was the first to note her charm, professional potential and appeal in 1971 . . .

Mr Lamb replied that his information was that Miss Goolagong was distressed not so much by the drawings as the behaviour of a fellow competitor who publicly accused her of having posed for them. He was unable to accept that the drawings, which were wholly sympathetic, were below 'acceptable standards' or that they constituted an infringement of privacy . . .

The adjudication was: In the view of the Press Council the publication of drawings purporting to portray Miss Goolagong in the nude without her knowledge and consent was an infringement of her privacy. The complaints against the *Sun* are upheld.

NOTE

Would there have been a remedy at law on these facts?

Melvin v Reid 112 Cal App 285 (1931), 297 Pac 91, District Court of Appeal, 4th District, California

The plaintiff, a prostitute, was acquitted of murder in 1918. Thereafter, she abandoned her former way of life and became a respectable married house-wife. She made many friends who did not know of her past. In 1925, the defendants made a film without the plaintiff's knowledge or consent based upon her earlier life and trial and identifying the plaintiff by using her maiden name. The plaintiff sued in the California state courts inter alia for invasion of privacy. The plaintiff appealed against the judgment of the trial court rejecting her claim.

Marks J:
. . . the use of the incidents from the life of appellant in the moving picture is in itself not actionable. These incidents appeared in the records of her trial for murder, which is a public record, open to the perusal of all. . . . Had respondents, in the story of 'The Red Kimono,' stopped with the use of those incidents from the life of appellant which were spread upon the record of her trial, no right of action would have accrued. They went further, and in the formation of the plot used the true maiden name of appellant. If any right of action exists, it arises from the use of this true name in connection with the true incidents from her life together with their advertisements in which they stated that the story of the picture was taken from true incidents in the life of Gabrielle Darley, who was Gabrielle Darley Melvin.

In the absence of any provision of law, we would be loath to conclude that the right of privacy as the foundation for an action in tort, in the form known and recognized in other jurisdictions, exists in California. We find, however, that the . . . right to pursue and obtain happiness is guaranteed to all by the fundamental law of our state [Article 1(1) Calif. Const.]. This right by its very nature includes the right to live free from the unwarranted attack of others upon one's liberty, property and reputation. . . .

. . . [E]ight years before the production of 'The Red Kimono' appellant had abandoned her life of shame, had rehabilitated herself, and had taken her place as a respected and honored member of society. This change having occurred in her life, she should have been permitted to continue its course without having her reputation and social standing destroyed by the publication of the story of her former depravity with no other excuse than the expectation of private gain by the publishers. . . .

We believe that the publication by respondents of the unsavory incidents in the past life of appellant after she had reformed, coupled with her true name, was not justified by any standard of morals or ethics known to us, and was a direct invasion of her inalienable right guaranteed to her by our Constitution, to pursue and obtain happiness. Whether we call this a right of privacy or give it any other name is immaterial, because it is a right guaranteed by our Constitution that must not be ruthlessly and needlessly invaded by others. . . .
Barnard PJ and **Jennings J** concurred
Judgment reversed.

NOTES

1. This would have been a case of invasion of privacy in the form of 'unreasonable publicity' for a person's 'private life' according to the classification of invasion of privacy in the *Restatement, 2d, Torts*, above, p. 303. The *Restatement* states that publicity is not actionable if it is on a 'matter of legitimate public concern'. It also states that the private lives of both voluntary (e.g. politicians, actors, criminals) *and* involuntary (e.g. relatives of criminals, victims of crime, witnesses of catastrophes) public figures are such matters 'to some reasonable extent'. Some American courts are less protective of privacy than others. Contrast *Melvin v Reid* with *Sidis v F-R Pub Corpn* 113 F 2d 806 (2d Cir 1940) (a cruel 'where are they now' article on a failed childhood prodigy; no liability). There can be no liability for invasion of privacy for publishing a matter of public record: *Cox Broadcasting Corpn v Cohn* 420 US 469 (1975) (name of a rape victim discovered in court records and broadcast on TV).
2. There would have been no liability in defamation in English law in *Melvin v Reid* because justification, or truth, is always a defence (but see the Rehabilitation of Offenders Act 1974, below). 'Newspapers are free in this country to rake up a man's forgotten past, and ruin him deliberately in the process, without incurring tortious liability' (Street, *Torts* (6th edn., 1976) p. 308). In most Australian jurisdictions truth is only a defence to defamation if the publication is for the 'public benefit': see Fleming, *The Law of Torts* (5th edn. 1977) p. 546. Dworkin (2 U Tas LR 418 at 425 (1967)) suggests that if such a limitation were introduced into English law,

cases of invasion of privacy of the 'unjustified publicity' kind which were not controlled by law would be 'reduced to negligible proportions'.

3. Under the Rehabilitation of Offenders Act 1974, a conviction leading to a sentence of no more than 30 months imprisonment becomes 'spent' after a period of time ranging from 5 to 10 years. The effect of a conviction becoming 'spent' is, inter alia, that the convicted person (i) need not reveal it in judicial proceedings or for employment or insurance purposes and (ii) may recover against a person who reveals the conviction provided that he proves that the publication is made 'with malice' (s. 8). There are some exceptions. How effective is the remedy in defamation?

4. In *Re X (A Minor)* [1975] Fam 47, CA, X's parents were divorced shortly after her birth in 1960. Her father died in 1967. A friend of X's father wrote a book which described X's father's private life, showing him to have been a man who was 'utterly depraved in his sexual activities, who indulged in sordid and degrading conduct, and who was obscene and drank to excess'. X, who was highly strung, had been brought up to respect her father. Before the book was published, X was made a ward of court and an injunction sought to prevent the publication of the offending passages. The Court of Appeal refused the injunction as an impermissible extension of wardship jurisdiction. In the course of his judgment, Lord Denning MR stated at p. 58:

' . . . [I]s there any remedy in the law of defamation? Suppose the mother of the child were to bring an action for defamation on the ground that the passages were untrue and a gross libel on her dead husband. Many might think she should be able to prevent the publication, especially as it would bring such grief and distress to his relatives, and, in addition, emotiona damage to his child. But the law of defamation does not permit any such proceeding. It says simply that no action lies for a libel on a dead man: on the ground that on balance it is in the public interest that no such action should lie: see *R v Topham* (1791) 4 *Term Rep 126; R v Ensor* (1887) 3 TLR 366. . . . Suppose the dead man were still alive. . . . He could not sue for libel, or, if he did, he would fail because the words are true. But could he sue for infringement of privacy? Many might think that he should be able to do so; he should be able to prevent his public exposure. But again, as I understand it, it would be difficult to give him any remedy. We have as yet no general remedy for infringement of privacy, the reason given being that on balance it is not in the public interest that there should be: see the *Report of the Committee on Privacy* in 1972 (Cmnd. No. 5012), paras. 651–653.

The reason why in these cases the law gives no remedy is because of the importance it attaches to the freedom of the press . . .

5. Christine Keeler had been a prominent figure in the Profumo Affair in the early 1960s. In spite of a request by her, several newspapers published her new name and address when she married several years later. The Press Council (13th Report 1966, p. 95) considered that her request had been 'a reasonable one' and regretted 'that this was either overlooked or disregarded by a number of newspaper editors'. The complainant 'told the Council that from the Saturday afternoon on which her whereabouts were discovered by the Press, until the following Monday afternoon, reporters and photographers were almost continually outside her house. Repeated requests that she and her husband should pose for photographs were refused'. Eventually the photographers went away after Miss Keeler and her husband agreed to walk from the house to their car while photographs were taken. The Council did not comment specifically upon this but noted that it 'was inevitable that Miss Keeler's marriage should be reported as a matter of public interest'. Would these facts give a remedy in English law? Should they?

6. The Press Council has ruled upon a lot of complaints about the revelation of current information about a person's life. In one case (6th Report 1959, p. 30) the *Sunday Mercury* was censured for revealing, contrary to a coroner's request, the name of a married mother who had had an affair with a man who had committed suicide. The woman then committed suicide herself, apparently because of the revelation. In another, the *Sunday Pictorial* had, much to the embarrassment of the family, stopped a wedding in church because the bride was under age. The Council found that the family could have been given the opportunity to tell the clergyman beforehand but the press, quite improperly, were looking for a sensational story (4th Report 1957, p. 24). In two other cases, the Council censured the *Daily Mail* for revealing 'the name, age and school of a six year old girl from whom her parents had kept the opinion of doctors that she would die from a rare blood disease before she reached teen-age' (9th Report 1962, p. 36) and a story about a girl who had plagiarized a poem in a poetry competition and who, following the report (which gave her name and address) had received 'threats of violence, filthy letters and other kinds of abuse' (11th Report 1964, p. 53). In the early days of heart transplants, the Press Council (16th Report 1969, p. 70 and 17th Report 1970, p. 47) rejected complaints that newspapers had ignored hospital and, in one case, family requests that the name of the recipient should not be published. The Council considered that the matter was one for one editorial discretion. On the Press Council's adjudication on the Lord Lambton 'Call Girl' Affair (which partly concerned privacy), see the Council Booklet No. 5, *Press Conduct in the Lambton Affair*, 1974, and 20th Report 1973, p. 57.

In 1977, the Council (24th Report 1977, p. 72) rejected a complaint that the *Daily Mail* had invaded the privacy of Ms Maureen Colquhoun (then an MP, later defeated in the 1979 election) by revealing in its Dairy that Ms Colquhoun had left her matrimonial home to share a house with a close woman friend. Applying its Declaration of Principle on Privacy, below, p. 324, the Council considered that whereas her status as an MP would not by itself have justified the story, the fact that Ms Colquhoun was an MP 'who has taken a very strong stand on feminist issues and has not been loath to publicise her views upon them' did. It brought the story into 'the area of those matters which the public is entitled to know as being capable of affecting the performance of her public duties or affecting public confidence in her views as a Member of Parliament'.

7. For the most recent of a series of unsuccessful attempts in Parliament to restrict by law the publication in the media of the details of wills, see the suggestion by Sir Anthony Meyer in 1975: 895 HC Deb 14 July 1975 col 1059. In the public opinion survey conducted for the Younger Committee (Report, p. 238), publication of the details of a large legacy left to a person was regarded by most people as an invasion of privacy that ought to be prohibited by law. For a Press Council case on unwanted publicity for football pool winners, see 13th Report 1966, p. 80.

8. In a case of false attribution, the Press Council (23rd Report 1976, p. 111) upheld a complaint against the *Daily Express* in respect of the publication of 'an article on abortion purporting to have been written by Labour MP Mrs Helen Hayman, when in fact she was not the author and was not consulted about the presentation of her views in that way'. The *Express* had telephoned Mrs Hayman and asked for comment on the then current controversy in Parliament on abortion. Mrs Hayman's comments were used as the basis for an article under her name without her knowledge or consent that they would be used in this way. Had Mrs Hayman written the article, she would have presented her views in a very different way. 'The Council strongly criticised the practice of presenting interviews as if they· were the personal contribution of the interviewee'. Would there have been a

remedy for defamation in this case? Or for the tort of passing off?, see below, p. 323. In the US this would have been a case of invasion of privacy by placing a person in a 'false light' in the sense of the *Restatement, 2d, Torts*, above, p. 303. For a 'false light' case in which defamation provided a remedy in English law, see *Fry v Daily Sketch* (1968) *Times*, 29 June. See also the Press Council ruling in the same case: 15th Report 1968, p. 100.

(d) BREACH OF COPYRIGHT

Williams v Settle [1960] 1 WLR 1072, [1960] 2 All ER 806, Court of Appeal

The defendant, a professional photographer, took the photographs at the plaintiff's wedding. Two years later, when the plaintiff's wife was pregnant, her father was murdered. The case attracted publicity and, when the national press came looking for photographs, the defendant sold them copies of the wedding photographs. He did so without the knowledge or consent of the plaintiff, who held the copyright. One of the photographs—a family group with the father in it—was published 5 days after the wife gave birth with captions identifying the persons in it. One newspaper gave a particular description of the plaintiff's wife. The plaintiff successfully sued the defendant for breach of copyright in the county court. He was awarded £1000 damages. The defendant's appeal to the Court of Appeal on the ground that the County Court had lacked jurisdiction to award such a high amount of damages was rejected. The following extract concerns the appeal on the amount of damages.

Sellers LJ: In the present action the judge was clearly justified, in the circumstances in which the defendant, in breach of the plaintiff's copyright, handed these photographs to the press knowing the use to which they were going to be put, in awarding substantial and heavy damages of a punitive nature. The power so to do, quite apart from the ordinary law of the land, is expressly given by statute. By section 17 (3) of the Copyright Act 1956, it is provided: 'Where in an action under this section an infringement of copyright is proved or admitted, and the court, having regard (in addition to all other material considerations) to—(a) the flagrancy of the infringement, and (b) any benefit shown to have accrued to the defendant by reason of the infringement, is satisfied that effective relief would not otherwise be available to the plaintiff, the court, in assessing damages for the infringement, shall have power to award such additional damages by virtue of this subsection as the court may consider appropriate in the circumstances.' It seems that this is not a case where there is any effective relief which could be given. The benefit which can be shown to have accrued to the defendant is meagre . . . It is the flagrancy of the infringement which calls for heavy damages, because this was a scandalous matter in the circumstances, which I do not propose to elaborate and about which I do not propose to express a view. It is sufficient to say that it was a flagrant infringement of the right of the plaintiff, and it was scandalous conduct and in total disregard not only of the legal rights of the plaintiff regarding copyright but of his feelings and his sense of family dignity and pride. It was an intrusion into his life, deeper and graver than an intrusion into a man's property. **Willmer** and **Harman LJJ** delivered concurring judgments.
Appeal dismissed.

NOTES

1. See (1961) 77 LQR 12 and (1961) 24 MLR 185
2. The plaintiff also obtained £52 10s damages and costs from the *Daily Express*, an apology and undertakings from the *Daily Mail* and a ruling in his favour from the Press Council: [1960] 1 WLR 1074–5. Whether or not the award of punitive damages at common law in a case of this sort has survived *Rookes v Barnard*, see above, p. 306, the statutory provision on damages in s. 17(3) remains intact.

3. The Justice Committee (Report, p. 12) notes that the plaintiff would not have been able to have recovered 'had he signed the now prevalent contract form which vests the copyright in the photographer'. The copyright in a letter is in the author, not the recipient, Copyright Act 1956, s. 4.

4. In 1979, the *Daily Mail* was sued for breach of copyright by Princess Margaret's lady in waiting for publishing photographs taken by her at a party which 'showed Princess Margaret dressed as Mae West and a Valkyrie and Mr Llewellyn as a wizard and later removing his costume' (*The Guardian*, 9 March 1979) The photographs had been taken from the plaintiff's home and sold to the *Daily Mail* without her knowledge or consent. A court order was made against the defendant about the use and return of the photographs. Damages were agreed out of court.

(e) BREACH OF CONFIDENCE

Prince Albert v Strange (1849) 1 Mac and G 25, 1H & TW1, Court of Chancery

Queen Victoria and the plaintiff had for their private amusement made etchings of their children and other subjects of personal interest. The defendant obtained copies and planned to exhibit them and to publish a catalogue listing and describing the etchings for profit. The etchings had been kept privately by the Royal Family, although a few copies had been given to friends. The plates for the etchings had been entrusted to a printer in Windsor for him to make further impressions. It appeared that, without the printer's knowledge or consent, one of his employees had made unauthorised copies of the etchings and the defendant had purchased these. The plaintiff obtained an injunction preventing the exhibition and the publication of the catalogue. In these proceedings, the defendant, who accepted that the exhibition should not proceed, applied to have the injunction amended to allow him to publish the catalogue. He appealed to the Lord Chancellor against the refusal of his application by Knight Bruce VC ((1848) 2 De G and Sm 652), who had referred in his judgment to 'sordid spying into the privacy of domestic life' (p. 698).

Lord Cottenham LC: . . . the Defendant insists that he is entitled to publish a catalogue of the etchings, that is to say, to publish a description or list of works or compositions of another, made and kept for the private use of that other, the publication of which was never authorised, and the possession of copies of which could only have been obtained by surreptitious and improper means. It was said by one of the learned counsel for the Defendant, that the injunction must rest upon the ground of property or breach of trust; both appear to me to exist. The property of an author or composer of any work, whether of literature, art, or science, in such work unpublished and kept for his private use or pleasure, cannot be disputed . . . the Plaintiff is entitled to the injunction of this Court to protect him against the invasion of such right and interest by the Defendant, which the publication of any catalogue would undoubtedly be; but this case by no means depends solely upon the question of property, for a breach of trust, confidence, or contract, would of itself entitle the Plaintiff to an injunction . . . and upon the evidence on behalf of the Plaintiff, and in the absence of any explanation on the part of the Defendant, I am bound to assume that the possession of the etchings by the Defendant . . . has its foundation in a breach of trust, confidence, or contract . . . upon this ground also I think the Plaintiff's title to the injunction sought to be discharged, fully established. The observations of Vice-Chancellor Wigram in *Tipping* v *Clarke* (2 Hare, 393) are applicable to this part of the case. He says: 'Every clerk employed in a merchant's counting-house is under an implied contract that he will not make public that which he learns in the execution of his duty as clerk. If the Defendant has obtained copies of books, it would very probably be by means of some clerk or agent of the Plaintiff; and if he availed himself surreptitiously of the information which he could not have had except from a person guilty of a breach of contract in communicating it, I think he could not be permitted to avail himself of that breach of contract . . . . This was the opinion of Lord Eldon, expressed in the case of *Wyatt* v *Wilson* in 1820, respecting an engraving of George the Third during his

illness, in which, according to a note with which I have been favoured by Mr Cooper, he said, 'If one of the late king's physicians had kept a diary of what he heard and saw, this court would not, in the king's lifetime, have permitted him to print and publish it.'
Motion refused

NOTES

1. See on breach of confidence, G. Dworkin *Confidence in the Law* (1971); G. Forrai, (1971) 6 Sydney LR 382; J. Jacob and R. Jacob, (1969) 119 NLJ 133; G. Jones, (1970) 86 LQR 463; Meagher, Gummow and Lehane *Equitable Doctrines and Principles* (1975) pp. 713–22; P. M. North, (1972) 12 JSPTL 149; S. Ricketson, (1977) 11 Mel ULR 223, 289; R. Wacks (1977) 127 NLJ 328. And see Law Commission Working Paper No 58: on Breach of Confidence, 1974.

2.   The Younger Committee (Report, p. 26) considered that the 'law on breach of confidence offers the most effective protection of privacy in the whole of our existing law, civil or criminal'. In its opinion 'the extent of its potential effectiveness is not widely recognised and that it should be'. On its recommendation, breach of confidence was referred to the Law Commission with a view to its being clarified and placed on a statutory footing. The Law Commission produced an excellent working paper (see previous note), but no legislation has yet resulted. As the Younger Committee states, breach of confidence 'affords a measure of protection for all specific and reasonably implied confidences'.

3. *Prince Albert v Strange* is the seminal case in the development of the equitable doctrine of breach of confidence. Insofar as judgment was given for the plaintiff on a basis other than that of his property right in the etchings, was it given purely because of breach of confidence or because of an implied term in the rogue employee's contract of employment? As the cases Lord Cottenham refers to at the end of the above extract indicate, the common law has, in the absence of an express term, implied a term in a contract of employment by which an employee may not divulge confidential information obtained during employment to any third party without consent while he is still employed and thereafter. In practice this has mainly been relevant (as has the law of breach of confidence) in the context of trade secrets, but it can apply to more personal matters, as the unreported case of *Wyatt v Wilson*, above, indicates. The conditions of service of members of the Royal Household contain a confidentiality clause. The text is printed in the Press Council's 2nd Report 1955, p. 35, in connection with a case in which the *Sunday Pictorial* had published the memoirs of the Duke of Edinburgh's valet.

4. For the Press Council case concerning the publication in the *Daily Express* of photographs of the Queen in bed shortly after the birth of Prince Edward, see the Press Council's 16th Report 1969, p. 78. It is not clear from the Report how the *Daily Express* came to have the photographs.

Duke of Argyll v Duchess of Argyll [1967] Ch 302, [1965] 1 All ER 611, [1965] 2 WLR 790, Ungoed-Thomas J

The first defendant, the Duke of Argyll and former husband of the plaintiff, Margaret, Duchess of Argyll, had had published in *The People* the first two of a series of articles in which he wrote of their married life. The plaintiff sought injunctions against the first defendant and against the editor and publisher of *The People* to prevent the publication in the remaining articles of 'secrets of the plaintiff relating to her private life, personal affairs or private conduct, communicated to the first defendant in confidence during the subsistence of his marriage to the plaintiff and not hitherto made public property'.

Ungoed-Thomas J: . . . It is clear that the court may restrain breach of confidence arising out of contract or any right to property. The question whether the court's protection is limited to such cases was considered in two authorities to which I shall refer.

[His lordship discussed *Prince Albert v Strange*, above, and *Pollard v Photographic Co* (1889) 40 Ch D 345, Ch D. Referring to the latter, he said:]

. . . In that case a photographer, who had taken a negative likeness of a lady to supply her with copies for money, was restrained from selling or exhibiting copies, both on the ground that there was an implied contract not to use the negative for such purposes, and also on the ground that such sale or exhibition was a breach of confidence. . . .

These cases, in my view, indicate (1) that a contract or obligation of confidence need not be expressed but can be implied (2) that a breach of confidence or trust or faith can arise independently of any right of property or contract other, of course, than any contract which the imparting of the confidence in the relevant circumstances may itself create; (3) that the court in the exercise of its equitable jurisdiction will restrain a breach of confidence independently of any right at law.

. . . Marriage is, of course, far more than mere legal contract and legal relationship, and even legal status; but it includes legal contract and relationship. If, for the court's protection of confidence and, contrary to my view, the confidence must arise out of a' contractual or property relationship, marriage does not lack its contract. It is basically a contract to be and, according to our Christian conception of marriage, to live as man and wife. It has been said that the legal consideration of marriage—that is the promise to become and to remain man and wife—is the highest legal consideration which there is. And there could hardly be anything more intimate or confidential than is involved in that relationship, or than in the mutual trust and confidences which are shared between husband and wife. The confidential nature of the relationship is of its very essence and so obviously and necessarily implicit in it that there is no need for it to be expressed. To express it is superfluous; it is clear to the least intelligent. So it seems to me that confidences between husband and wife during marriage are not excluded from the court's protection by the criteria appearing in the cases to which I have referred. . . .

[His Lordship then considered and distinguished *Rumping v Director of Public Prosecution* [1964] AC 814, HL, in which the House of Lords ruled that an intercepted communication between a husband and wife was admissible in evidence in criminal proceedings against the husband.]

It thus seems to me that the policy of the law, so far from indicating that communication between husband and wife should be excluded from protection against breaches of confidence given by the court in accordance with *Prince Albert v Strange* strongly favours its inclusion, and in view of that policy it can hardly be an objection that such communications are not limited to business matters. . . . if there are communications which should be protected and which the policy of the law recognises should be protected, even to the extent of being a foundation of the old rule making husband and wife incompetent as witnesses against each other, then the courts is not to be deterred merely because it is not already provided with fully developed principles, guides, tests, definitions and the full armament for judicial decision. It is sufficient that the court recognises that the communications are confidential, and their publication within the mischief which the law as its policy seeks to avoid, without further defining the scope and limits of the jurisdiction: and I have no hesitation in this case in concluding that publication of some of the passages complained of is in breach of marital confidence. . . .

Should the plaintiff be denied the injunction which she would otherwise get because she has herself to an extent broken confidence and because she, after the confidences of whose breach she complains, adopted an immoral attitude towards her marriage? A person coming to Equity for relief—and this is equitable relief which the plaintiff seeks—must come with clean hands: but the cleanliness required is to be judged in relation to the relief that is sought.

First, I do not consider that the plaintiff's own articles [written in another Sunday newspaper before the defendant's articles and revealing information about him] justify the objectionable passages in the Duke's articles or, of themselves, should disentitle the plaintiff to the court's protection.

Secondly, with regard to the plaintiff's immorality. . . .
[it] is not in my view just that adultery should have retrospective operation on a marriage
and not only break the marriage for the future but nullify it for the past. The plaintiff's
adultery, repugnant though it be, should not in my view license the husband to broadcast
unchecked the most intimate confidences of earlier and happier days.

It is in my view established by *Lord Ashburton v Pape* [1913] 2 Ch 469, in accordance with
the references already made to *Prince Albert v Strange*, that an injunction may be granted to
restrain the publication of confidential information not only by the person who was a party to
the confidence but by other persons into whose possession that information has improperly
come.

Injunction granted.

NOTES

1. Ungoed-Thomas J's ruling that breach of confidence may be a basis for
a claim in equity in the absence of any express or implied term in a contract
is consistent with the earlier and often approved statement by Greene MR
in *Saltman Engineering Co v Campbell Engineering Co* (1948) (a trade secret
case), reported in [1963] 3 All ER 413 at 414, CA:

' . . . the obligation to respect confidence is not limited to cases where the parties are in
contractual relationship. . . . If a defendent is proved to have used confidential information, directly or indirectly obtained from a plaintiff, without the consent, express or
implied of the plaintiff, he will be guilty of an infringement of the plaintiff's rights.'

2. *Argyll v Argyll* is faithful to *Prince Albert v Strange* in confirming that
breach of confidence can provide protection for personal information of
the sort that one associates with the notion of privacy. (For its later
extension to public law, see *A-G v Jonathan Cape*, above, p. 286). What
kinds of personal information the law will recognise as deserving of
protection, in addition to secrets, disclosed during matrimony is an open
question. There are many candidates, including (1) information given to or
obtained by income tax, social security, housing, educational, census, or
other national or local public authorities and (2) information in the private
sector such as that given by a patient to a doctor or by a client to a bank
manager or solicitor. Information in some of these categories will be
covered by express or implied terms in employment, business or other
contracts. In *Coco v A. N. Clark (Engineers) Ltd* [1969] RPC 41 at 48 (a
trade secret case), Megarry J doubted, obiter, 'whether equity would
intervene unless the circumstances are of sufficient gravity; equity ought
not to be invoked merely to protect trivial tittle-tattle, however confidential'. Might some information revealed during matrimony be excluded
from protection on this basis?

3. In *Malone v Metropolitan Police Comr*, below, p. 328, Sir Robert
Megarry VC listed 'three elements' that are required for a claim in breach of
confidence to succeed: confidential information; an obligation of confidence; unauthorised use. Of the second, he had earlier suggested in *Coco v
A. N. Clark (Engineers) Ltd*, above, a 'reasonable man' test:

'It seems to me that if the circumstances are such that any reasonable man standing in the
shoes of the recipient of the information would have realised that upon reasonable grounds
the information was being given to him in confidence, then this should suffice to impose
upon him the equitable obligation of confidence.'

In *Malone v MPC*, a claim challenging telephone tapping under a Home
Office warrant for the police failed to meet the second and third
requirements. Street, *Torts* (6th edn., 1976) p. 376, suggests that 'it will also
be actionable to induce a breach of confidence'.

4. Could a person who, without the knowledge or consent of the person or
persons concerned, accidentally or intentionally overhears a conversation
or sees a letter or conduct be liable in *breach of confidence* (as opposed to
trespass, etc.) for revealing the information he has obtained? Suppose a

husband were to publish information obtained from his wife's private diary which she kept locked in a drawer the key to which he had stolen? Would the law of breach of confidence provide a remedy? See in this connection the Younger Committee's proposal (Report, p. 194) for a new tort of disclosing or using information unlawfully obtained:

> 632. There is another type of situation which, although it may be partially covered by the law relating to breach of confidence, raises problems which cannot be entirely solved by an application of that branch of the law, at least as it is generally understood. We think that the damaging disclosure or other damaging use of information acquired by means of any unlawful act, with knowledge of how it was acquired, is an objectionable practice against which the law should afford protection. We recommend therefore that it should be a civil wrong, actionable at the suit of any person who has suffered damage thereby, to disclose or otherwise use information which the discloser knows, or in all the circumstances ought to have known, was obtained by illegal means. It would be necessary to provide defences to cover situations where the disclosure of the information was in the public interest or was made in privileged circumstances. We envisage that the kinds of remedy available for this civil wrong would be similar to those appropriate to an action for breach of confidence.

Fraser v Evans [1969] 1 QB 349, [1969] 1 All ER 8, [1968] 3 WLR 1172, Court of Appeal

The plaintiff, a public relations consultant, was employed by the Greek Government to make a report for them. The contract imposed an obligation of confidence upon the plaintiff, but not the Government. A copy of the report was obtained surreptitiously from the Greek Government and came into the hands of a *Sunday Times* reporter. The reporter interviewed the plaintiff and planned an article quoting the report and the interview. The plaintiff sought an injunction to prevent its publication on grounds of libel, breach of copyright and breach of confidence. The *Sunday Times* admitted that the article was defamatory but said that they proposed to plead justification and fair comment. Crichton J issued an injunction restraining only the publication of extracts or information obtained from the report. The *Sunday Times* appealed against the injunction. The following extract concerns only the breach of confidence claim. The arguments based on libel and breach of copyright were also rejected.

Lord Denning MR: . . . Mr Fraser says that the report was a confidential document and that the publication of it should be restrained on the principles enunciated in the cases from *Prince Albert v Strange* to *Duchess of Argyll v Duke of Argyll*. Those cases show that the court will in a proper case restrain the publication of confidential information. The jurisdiction is based not so much on property or on contract as on the duty to be of good faith. No person is permitted to divulge to the world information which he has received in confidence, unless he has just cause or excuse for doing so. Even if he comes by it innocently, nevertheless once he gets to know that it was originally given in confidence, he can be restrained from breaking that confidence. But the party complaining must be the person who is entitled to the confidence and to have it respected. He must be a person to whom the duty of good faith is owed. It is at this point that I think Mr Fraser's claim breaks down. There is no doubt that Mr Fraser himself was under an obligation of confidence to the Greek Government. The contract says so in terms. But there is nothing in the contract which expressly puts the Greek Government under any obligation of confidence. Nor, so far as I can see, is there any implied obligation . . . . The Greek Government alone have any standing to complain if anyone obtains the information surreptitiously or proposes to publish it. . . .

Even if Mr Fraser had any standing to complain, *The Sunday Times* say that in any event they have just cause or excuse for publishing. They rely on the line of authority from *Gartside v Outram* ((1856) 26 LJ Ch 113) to the latest case, *Initial Services Ltd v Putterill*. ([1968] 1 QB 396) They quote the words of Woods V-C that "there is no confidence as to the disclosure of iniquity." I do not look upon the word "iniquity" as expressing a principle. It is merely an instance of just cause or excuse for breaking confidence. There are some things which may be required to be disclosed in the public interest, in which event no confidence can be prayed in aid to keep them secret. I feel it might be difficult for *The Sunday Times* to make out that case here. . . .

Davies and **Widgery LJJ** delivered concurring judgments.
Appeal allowed. Injunctions discharged.

NOTES

1. Does Lord Denning's 'good faith' basis for the doctrine suggest (the point appears undecided) that the breach of confidence need not be for profit for liability to arise? The 'public interest' justification for breach of confidence was persuasive in *Malone v Metropolitan Police Comr* below p. 328. In *Hubbard v Vosper* [1972] 2 QB 84, CA, a person had written a book in which he revealed damaging facts about the scientology movement based upon his former membership. The disclosures were held to be justified in the public interest as arguably revealing 'medical quackery of a dangerous kind'.

In *Woodward v Hutchins* [1977] 1 WLR 760, CA, the plaintiff 'pop' singers (Tom Jones, Englebert Humperdinck and Gilbert O'Sullivan) were refused an injunction to prevent the publication by their former public relations officer in the *Daily Mirror* of embarrassing details of their personal lives on the ground of public interest. Lord Denning MR stated that the plaintiffs had sought publicity about their private lives to further their careers and could not complain if the truth were told. 'If the image which they fostered was not a true image, it is in the public interest that it should be corrected.' In *Kashogi v Smith* (1980) 130 NLJ, CA, an application by Mrs K. for an injunction to prevent the publication by her former housekeeper of details of her private life in the *Daily Mirror* on the ground of breach of confidence was refused, partly because the applicant had courted publicity.

2. In all three of the cases from which extracts have been included in the text above the remedy sought was an injunction. On damages for breach of confidence (which will be the only satisfactory remedy if the newspaper article, for example, has already been published), Sir Robert Megarry VC in *Malone v Metropolitan Police Comr* said:

This is an equitable right which is still in course of development, and is usually protected by the grant of an injunction to prevent disclosure of the confidence. Under Lord Cairns' Act 1858 damages may be granted in substitution for an injunction; yet if there is no case for the grant of an injunction, as when the disclosure has already been made, the unsatisfactory result seems to be that no damages can be awarded under this head: see *Proctor v Bayley* (1889) 42 Ch D 390. In such a case, where there is no breach of contract or other orthodox foundation for damages at common law, it seems doubtful whether there is any right to damages, as distinct from an account of profits. It may be, however, that a new tort is emerging (see *Goff and Jones, The Law of Restitution* (2nd edn. 1978), pp. 518, 519, and Gareth Jones (1970) 86 LQR 463 at 491), though this has been doubted: see *Street, The Law of Torts* (6th edn. 1976), p. 377.

Damages were awarded in *Seager v Copydex* (a trade secrets case), [1967] 2 All ER 415, CA. They were to be 'assessed on the basis of reasonable compensation for the use of the confidential information' (Lord Denning MR). In *Seager v Copydex* (No 2) [1969] 2 All ER 718, CA, Winn LJ stated that the damages were to be recovered 'on a tortious basis' and Lord Denning MR drew an analogy with conversion. Relying upon this case, North 12 JoSPTL 149 (1972) argues that breach of confidence, which developed as an equitable principle, is now a tort.

3. Suppose that a newspaper buys a story reasonably believing that it has been obtained without a breach of confidence on the part of the writer? Can the newspaper (i) be restrained from publication or (ii) have damages awarded against it for publication? On the position of innocent third parties, see Jones (1970) 86 LQR 463, 477–81 and Meagher, Gummow and Lehane, *Equitable Doctrines and Principles* (1975) pp. 720–1. Was the defendant in *Prince Albert v Strange*, above, an innocent third party?

4. Would a doctor who revealed to the parents of a 16 year old patient that she was on the pill be in breach of confidence in law? For a complaint that confidential information about foreigners using the NHS is given by the Department of Health and Social Security to the Home Office, see *The Times*, 6 December 1979.

(f) OTHER REMEDIES IN LAW

It has been suggested (see Dworkin, (1967) 2 U Tas LR 418, 444) and Neill ((1962) 25 MLR 393, 402) that the tort of *intentional infliction of physical harm* (other than by trespass) established in *Wilkinson v Downton* [1897] 2 QB 57, QBD, could be developed to provide a remedy. In that case, as a practical joke the defendant told the plaintiff that the plaintiff's husband had broken his legs in an accident. The plaintiff suffered nervous shock causing 'serious and permanent physical consequences'. Wright J awarded her damages on the following basis

> The defendant has wilfully done an act calculated to cause physical harm to the plaintiff—that is to say, to infringe her legal right to personal safety, and has in fact thereby caused physical harm to her. That proposition without more appears to me to state a good cause of action, there being no justification alleged for the act. This wilful injuria is in law malicious, although no malicious purpose to cause the harm which was caused nor any motive of spite is imputed to the defendant.'

The decision was approved and relied on by the Court of Appeal in *Janvier v Sweeney* [1919] 2 KB 316. In that case, the defendants, private detectives, sought to persuade the plaintiff to hand over letters to which she had access by telling her falsely that she was wanted by Scotland Yard for corresponding with a German spy. The plaintiff recovered for physical illness resulting from shock. Cf. the Press Council case (11th Report 1964, p. 36) in which the press contacted a young girl and correctly informed her in the absence of her mother that her estranged father whom she had not seen since she was a baby had been granted a right of access to her by a court order. The girl 'suffered a serious emotional upset which required medical attention'.

Might there be liability in tort for *negligent misstatement* if a reporter failed to check his facts and published an inaccurate statement about someone's personal life (e.g. that he takes heroin or has a mistress) that causes him to lose his job? Is there a duty of care? In a Press Council case (14th Report 1967, p. 53), the *Sunday Times* mistakenly reported that a person had committed suicide when the coroner's verdict was otherwise. What if his widow suffered physical injury resulting from shock?

Breach of contract may provide a remedy in some cases. See, e.g., *Pollard v Photographic Co*, above, p. 319. On express or implied terms in contracts of employment, see above, p. 318.

The tort of *passing off* would appear to apply only to unfair trading competition Street, *Torts* (6th edn., 1976) pp. 365–372. In *Sim v Heinz* [1959] 1 WLR 313, CA, the question whether an action for passing off lies for the unauthorised use by impersonation of an actor's voice for commercial gain (as in an advertisement) was left open.

In *criminal law*, the harassment of tenants (Protection from Eviction Act 1977, s. 1) or of debtors (Administration of Justice Act 1970, s. 40) is a crime. But 'Parliament has not yet found itself able to make harassment by journalists an offence' (Glanville Williams, *Textbook of Criminal Law*, 1978, p. 147). The Unsolicited Goods and Services Act 1971, s. 4, makes it a criminal offence to send a person unsolicited material which 'describes or illustrates human sexual techniques'. Eavesdroppers and 'peeping toms' may be bound over to be of good behaviour (see above p. 177). See *R v*

London County Quarter Sessions Appeals Committee, ex parte Metropolitan Police Comr, [1948] 1 KB 670 DC (eavesdropping at Public Trustee's Office) and *R v Wyres* (1956) *2 Russell on Crime* (12th edn.,) 1397 (spying on woman undressing). Eavesdropping is not a criminal offence: Criminal Law Act 1967, s.13(1)(a). The Official Secrets Acts 1911–20, above, p. 273, protect confidential information above private individuals in official hands. See also the Post Office Act 1953, s.66, above, p. 309, and the Wireless Telegraphy Act 1949, ss.1, 5, below, p. 332. For other statutory provisions, see the Younger Committee Report, Appendix I. In *Director of Public Prosecutions v Withers* [1975] AC 842, HL, the defendants were private detectives. They were convicted on two counts of conspiracy to effect a public mischief by (on the first count) obtaining confidential information from banks and building societies about private accounts by making telephone calls pretending to be officials from other banks, etc., and (on the second count) by obtaining confidential information from the Criminal Records Office, vehicle registration authorities and the Ministry of Defence. The information in relation to the second count was obtained either by deceit or by persuading a public official to act contrary to his duty. The convictions were quashed by the House of Lords on the ground that conspiracy to effect a public mischief was not a crime. The decision is confirmed by the provisions on conspiracy (ss. 1, 5) in the Criminal Law Act 1977: A majority of the House of Lords in *Director of Public Prosecutions v Withers* thought the defendants might have been guilty on the second count of a conspiracy to defraud. Two members—Lord Reid and Viscount Dilhorne—would appear to have taken the same view in respect of the first count. Lord Kilbrandon, however, was of the opinion that there could be no conspiracy to defraud bank and building society officials, because they are not public officers. The Criminal Law Act 1977 retains conspiracy to defraud as an offence, but does not resolve the question whether private detectives (and others) may commit it only if they deceive public officials or define public officials for this purpose. One situation which criminal law does not cover is that in which a person 'steals' information (by, for example, photocopying a document). In *Oxford v Moss* (1978) 68 Cr App Rep 183, DC, a university student dishonestly obtained a copy of the proof of an examination paper and read and returned it. It was held that he could not be guilty of theft because information was not 'property' that could be stolen. See A. Tettenborn, RN (1979) 129 NLJ 967. On the Younger Committee's recommendation for a new tort of disclosure or other use of information unlawfully acquired, see above, p.321.

4 The Press Council

Press Council Declaration of Principle on Privacy (23rd Press Council Report 1976 p. 150)

The following statement represents the policy which the Press Council has and will continue to support and which accords with the practice of responsible journalists:

(i) The publication of information about the private lives or concerns of individuals without their consent is only acceptable if there is a legitimate public interest overriding the right of privacy.

(ii) It is the responsibility of editors to ensure that enquiries into matters affecting the private life or concerns of individuals are only undertaken where in the Editor's opinion at the time a legitimate public interest in such matters may arise. The right to privacy is however not involved if the individuals concerned have freely and clearly consented to the pursuit of enquiries and publication.

(iii) The public interest relied on as the justification for publication or inquiries which conflict with a claim to privacy must be a legitimate and proper public interest and not only a prurient or morbid curiosity. 'Of interest to the public' is not synonymous with 'in the public interest.' It should be recognised that entry into public life does not disqualify an individual from his right to privacy about his private affairs, save when the circumstances relating to the private life of an individual occupying a public position may be likely to affect the performance of his duties or public confidence in him or his office.

(iv) Invasion of privacy by deception, eavesdropping or technological methods which are not in themselves unlawful can however only be justified when it is in pursuit of information which ought to be published in the public interest and there is no other reasonably practicable method of obtaining or confirming it.

(v) The Council expects the obtaining of news or pictures to be carried out with sympathy and discretion. Reporters and photographers should do nothing to cause pain or humiliation to bereaved or distressed people unless it is clear that the publication of the news or pictures will serve a legitimate public interest and there is no other reasonably practicable means of obtaining the material.

(vi) Editors are responsible for the actions of those employed by their newspapers and have a duty to ensure that all concerned are aware of the importance of respecting all legitimate claims to personal privacy.

NOTES

1. On the Press Council, see above, p. 212. The Council adjudicates, inter alia, upon complaints of press invasion of privacy. 'In the whole period from the Council's inception in 1953 up to 30 June 1970 a total of 65 privacy cases were adjudicated upon, of which 37 were upheld and 28 rejected' (Younger Committee Report, p. 44). Although, as the Younger Committee states (ibid.), the percentage of complaints which the Council receives that are on privacy is 'a tiny proportion of the whole', the complaints are sufficient in number and diversity to indicate the hazards that press coverage present for the protection of privacy—as the examples in this Chapter taken from the Council's annual reports show.

2. In his foreword to the Council's 22nd Report 1975, Lord Shawcross was critical of gossip columns in the press and referred approvingly to Sir Harold Wilson's suggestion 'that the test of what is permissible might be that the Press would accord to public men and women the degree of privacy they would give to their own proprietors or to their own or other editors'. Cf. the following comment by Street, *Freedom, the Individual and the Law* (4th edn., 1977) p. 263:

'What is more sinister is that the privacy of certain persons only is invaded: we are told nothing of the private lives of newspaper proprietors; a Minister may have, to the general knowledge of Fleet Street, a mistress, but on this there will be silence. But let Mrs Gilliatt expose the methods of the leading gossip columnists in an article in *Queen*, and she will be hounded by squads of reporters from the *Daily Telegraph* and other national dailies who will report her minute-by-minute movements in the company of playwright John Osborne.'

In his Foreword in the following year, Lord Shawcross quoted the Royal Commission on the Press's opinion 'that the way in which a few national newspapers treat some private lives is one of the worst aspects of the performance of the press': *Final Report of the Commission*, 1977, p. 100.

3. On the BBC Complaints Commission and the IBA Complaints Review Board, which are competent to hear privacy complaints, see above, p. 211. Few privacy complaints have been made.

5 Surveillance by technical devices

Report of the Committee of Privy Councillors appointed to inquire into the Interception of Communications (Cmnd 283 1957)

The Committee (chaired by Birkett LJ) was established as a result of the Marrinan case. In that case, the Home Secretary authorised the tapping of the telephone line of a suspected criminal at the request of the police. He then authorised the police to show the Bar Council the transcript of conversations on the intercepted line to which a barrister who was being investigated by the Council for unprofessional conduct was a party. In the following extract from its Report, the Committee considers the procedure followed in the authorisation of telephone tapping, the kinds of cases in which it is permitted and makes recommendations for improvement in the system.

54. The exercise by the Secretary of State of the executive power to intercept communications is by warrant under his own hand . . .

56. The warrant . . . sets out the name and address or telephone number of the persons whose communications are to be intercepted. On occasion, a single warrant has been issued in the past to cover a number of names. We think this practice is undesirable. In our opinion each warrant should in future specify the name and address or telephone number of the person who is the subject of the warrant . . .

62. Since the Secretary of State's discretion is absolute he may issue a warrant for the interception of communications to any person, authority, agency or Department of State; but in fact such warrants have been granted to a limited number of authorities. . . .

63. The great majority of warrants for interception for the purpose of the detection of crime have been, and are now, granted to the Metropolitan Police and Board of Customs and Excise. . . .

64. The principles on which the Home Office acts in deciding whether to grant an application for a warrant to intercept communications for the detection of crime [are] . . .

(*a*) The offence must be really serious.

(*b*) Normal methods of investigation must have been tried and failed, or must, from the nature of things, be unlikely to succeed if tried.

(*c*) There must be good reason to think that an interception would result in a conviction.

65. It was indicated in the letter to the Police that what the Home Office regarded as 'serious crime' were offences for which a man with no previous record could reasonably be expected to be sentenced to three years' imprisonment, or offences of lesser gravity in which a large number of people were involved.

66. . . . The definition of 'serious crime' upon which the Home Office acts when considering the issue of warrants to the Customs is that 'the case involves a substantial and continuing fraud which would seriously damage the revenue or the economy of the country if it went unchecked.'

The principles governing the issue of warrants to the Security Service can be stated in these terms:—

(*a*) There must be a major subversive or espionage activity that is likely to injure the national interest.

(*b*) The material likely to be obtained by interception must be of direct use in compiling the information that is necessary to the security Service in carrying out the tasks laid upon it by the State . . .

74. We feel that the outstanding warrants should be reviewed more frequently. We therefore *recommend* that there should be a regular review not less than once a month both by the Home Office and by every authority that is granted a warrant to intercept. This review should be not only of the numbers of warrants outstanding, but of each particular warrant.

75. We *recommend* that warrants should no longer be valid until they are cancelled, but that their validity should be for a defined period that appears on their face. Normally this should be for a period no longer than a month and in no case should it be for a period longer than two months. If an extension of the validity of the warrant is desired, the reasons for this should be sent to the Home Office for their consideration before any extension is approved . . .

85. It has been urged in some quarters that the authority for the issue of warrants for interception should not be left exclusively in the hands of the Secretary of State. The chief suggested alternatives that have come to our attention are that the Home Secretary should be assisted by an Advisory Committee or that warrants should be issued only on a sworn information before magistrates or High Court Judge.

86. In our opinion, neither of these proposals would improve matters. If a number of magistrates or judges had the power to issue such warrants, the control of the use to which methods of interception can be put would be weaker than under the present system. It might very well prove easier in practice to obtain warrants. Moreover, it would be harder to keep and collate records. If an Advisory Committee were set up this would, at the best, leave things as at present because the ultimate discretion would still lie with the Secretary of State: at the worst it would tend to weaken the sense of responsibility of the Secretary of State, and might lead to a loosening of the principles, the strict maintenance of which is the chief means of ensuring that

interception of communications is limited to the uses for which it is intended . . .

NOTES

1. The Committee recommended (Report, p. 36) that, contrary to what happened in the *Marrinan* case, 'in no circumstances should material obtained by interception be made available to any body or person whatever outside the public service'. In 1959, the General Medical Council struck a doctor off the Medical Register because of his relationship with a female patient. The evidence came from a tape recording handed to the Council by the police of a telephone conversation overheard by the police who 'listened on a private extension of a telephone with the consent of the subscriber [the female patient] in the course of criminal investigations'. The police had suggested that the call be made. No request for a Home Office warrant was made or—because of the consent—needed. See the Home Secretary (Mr Butler), 614 HC Deb 3 December 1979 col 1379.
2. In addition to those named in the above extract, other authorities to whom warrants were issued between 1937 and 1956 included the Investigation Branch of the Post Office, the Port of London Authority Police, various Chief Constables, the Ministry of Food (during the war) and the Home Office itself (dangerous drugs, lotteries and obscene publications): Privy Councillors' Report, Appendix II. In 1956, 159 new Home Office warrants authorising telephone interceptions by the police, the customs authorities, the Post Office and the Security Service were issued. The Privy Councillors' Committee recommended that it 'would be against the public interest for the Secretary of State to give figures of the extent of the interception of communications' because to do so 'would greatly aid the operation of agencies hostile to the state' (Report, pp. 27, 37). Until 1980 the Government refused to give details of the numbers of warrants issued because of this recommendation. In 1973, it was confirmed (849 HC Deb 1 February 1973 col 1778–9), that the 'principles and procedures set out in the [Privy Councillors'] report have been scrupulously observed'. Cf. 399 HL Deb 19 March 1979 col 859. Although the Privy Councillors' Committee (Report, p. 27) took the view that 'a Member of Parliament is not to be distinguished from an ordinary member of the public, so far as the interception of communications is concerned', in 1966 the Prime Minister (Mr Wilson) announced that he had given instructions after taking office that MPs' telephones were to be immune (736 HC Deb 17 November 1966 col 639). Mr Heath, his successor, confirmed this (803 HC Deb 16 July 1970 col 1723). The number of Home Office warrants issued for the years 1958–79 was revealed in 1980 (Cmnd. 7873). 421 were *issued* in 1978. Altogether, 214 warrants *remained in force* at the end of that year. 411 warrants were issued in 1979. The number of interceptions is not indicated. The Post Office has the capacity to make 1000 interceptions at any one time: *New Statesman*, 1 February 1980, and see D. Campbell in P. Hain (ed.), *Policing the Police*, Vol 2, pp. 65–152. The Home Secretary (982 HC Deb 1 April 1980 col 205–220) has indicated that legislation will not be introduced to control telephone tapping; instead, a high court judge will be designated to monitor the operation of the present system. The Home Office warrant procedure does not control the use of 'bugs'.
3. The procedures described in the Report apply to the interception of letters as well as to telephone tapping. In 1956, 183 warrants were issued authorising the opening of letters. 52 warrants were issued in 1979.

4. The procedures described in the Report apply to the interception of letters as well as telephone tapping. In 1956, 183 warrants were issued authorising the opening of letters. The use of bugging devices by the police and the security services is not subject to the Home Office warrant or any other procedure.

Malone v Metropolitan Police Commissioner (No 2) [1979] 2 WLR 700, [1979] Ch 344, [1979] 2 All ER 620, Sir Robert Megarry VC

The plaintiff was prosecuted for various offences relating to the handling of stolen property. He was acquitted on certain counts; the jury disagreed on the others. The Crown acknowledged during the trial that the plaintiff's telephone had been tapped. In these proceedings the plaintiff sought declarations to the effect that the tapping had been illegal.

Sir Robert Megarry VC: . . . [The plaintiff's] first main contention was that by reason of the right of privacy and the right of confidentiality it was unlawful to tap a telephone, even under the authority of a warrant of the Home Secretary. . . .

First, I do not think that any assistance is obtained from the general warrant cases, or other authorities dealing with warrants. At common law, the only power to search premises under a search warrant issued by a justice of the peace is to search for stolen goods: see *Entick v Carrington* 19 State Tr 1029 at 1067. However, many statutes authorise searches under search warrants for many different purposes; and there is admittedly no statute which in terms authorises the tapping of telephones, with or without a warrant. Nevertheless, any conclusion that the tapping of telephones is therefore illegal would plainly be superficial in the extreme. The reason why a search of premises which is not authorised by law is illegal is that it involves the tort of trespass to those premises: and any trespass, whether to land or goods or the person, that is made without legal authority is prima facie illegal. Telephone tapping by the Post Office, on the other hand, involves no act of trespass. The subscriber speaks into his telephone, and the process of tapping appears to be carried out by Post Office officials making recordings, with Post Office apparatus on Post Office premises, of the electrical impulses on Post Office wires provided by Post Office electricity. . . . As Lord Camden CJ said in *Entick v Carrington*, 19 State Tr 1029 at 1066, 'the eye cannot by the laws of England be guilty of a trespass'; and, I would add, nor can the ear.

Second, I turn to the warrant of the Home Secretary. This contrasts with search warrants in that it is issued by one of the great officers of state as such, and not by a justice of the peace acting as such. Furthermore, it does not purport to be issued under the authority of any statute or of the common law. From the Birkett Report . . . it appears that the power to tap telephones has been exercised 'from time to time since the introduction of the telephone,' but that not until 1937 were any warrants issued. Until then, the Post Office took the view that any operator of telephones had a power to tap conversations without infringing any rule of law. The police authorities accordingly made arrangements directly with the Director-General of the Post Office for any tapping of telephones that might be required. In 1937, however, the Home Secretary and Postmaster General decided, as a matter of policy, that thenceforward records of telephone conversations should be made by the Post Office and disclosed to the police only on the authority of the Home Secretary. The view was taken that certain statutes which permitted the interception of letters and telegrams on the authority of a Secretary of State were wide enough to cover telephone tapping. . . .

One result of the change in the status of the Post Office in 1969 was that as it was no longer under the direct control of a Minister of the Crown, but had become a corporation with a large measure of independence from the Crown, no assumption could any longer be made that the Post Office would act upon a warrant of the Home Secretary to tap telephones. . . . one aspect of the change was dealt with by section 80 of the Act. This provision . . . runs as follows:

'A requirement to do what is necessary to inform designated persons holding office under the Crown concerning matters and things transmitted or in course of transmission by means of postal or telecommunication services provided by the Post Office may be laid on the Post Office for the like purposes and in the like manner as, at the passing of this Act, a requirement may be laid on the Postmaster General to do what is necessary to inform such persons concerning matters and things transmitted or in course of transmission by means of such services provided by him.' . . .

This, said the Solicitor-General, plainly showed that Parliament intended to provide lawful authority in the changed circumstances for what had previously been done in the old circumstances. The Home Secretary's warrant, which had previously been given under administrative arrangements, now had a statutory function as being a 'requirement' under section 80, and, what is more, as a requirement that statute authorised to be 'laid' on the Post Office. Although the previous arrangements had been merely administrative, they had been set out in the Birkett Report a dozen years earlier, and the section plainly referred to these arrangements; if not, it was difficult to see what the section had in view, and certainly nothing intelligible has been suggested. A warrant was not needed to make the tapping lawful: it was lawful without any warrant. But where the tapping was done under warrant (and that is the only matter before me) the section afforded statutory recognition of the lawfulness of the tapping. In their essentials, these contentions seem to me to be sound.

Section 80 of the Post Office Act 1969 does not stand alone, however; there is also paragraph 1(1) of Schedule 5 to that Act. . . .

This sub-paragraph provides that in proceedings against any person for an offence under these provisions [Telegraph Act 1863 s. 45; Telegraph Act 1868 s. 20; Post Office (Protection) Act 1884 s. 11, which made the improper disclosure, etc, of the contents of telegrams and, as interpreted, telephone conversations a crime.], 'it shall be a defence for him to prove that the act constituting the offence was done in obedience to a warrant under the hand of a Secretary of State.' . . . It is true . . . that Schedule 5 does not in terms empower the Home Secretary to issue a warrant in the way that is done by section 4 (1) of the Official Secrets Act 1920 . . . [Where it appears to a Secretary of State that such a course is expedient in the public interest, he may, by warrant under his hand, require any person who owns or controls any telegraphic cable or wire, or any apparatus for wireless telegraphy, used for the sending or receipt of telegrams to or from any place out of the United Kingdom, to produce to him, or to any person named in the warrant, the originals and transcripts, either of all telegrams, or of telegrams of any specified class or description, or of telegrams sent from or addressed to any specified person or place, sent or received to or from any place out of the United Kingdom by means of any such cable, wire, or apparatus, and all other papers relating to any such telegram as aforesaid . . .]. That, however, does not alter the fact that by the Post Office Act 1969 Parliamentary recognition to such warrants was given. . . .

Third, there is the right of privacy. Here the contention is that although at present no general right of privacy has been recognised by English law, there is a particular right of privacy, namely, the right to hold a telephone conversation in the privacy of one's home without molestation. . . . I am not unduly troubled by the absence of English authority: there has to be a first time for everything, and if the principles of English law, and not least analogies from the existing rules, together with the requirements of justice and common sense, pointed firmly to such a right existing, then I think the court should not be deterred from recognising the right.

On the other hand, it is no function of the courts to legislate in a new field. The extension of the existing laws and principles is one thing, the creation of an altogether new right is another. At times judges must, and do, legislate; but as Holmes J once said, they do so only interstitially, and with molecular rather than molar motions: see *Southern Pacific Co v Jensen* (1917) 244 US 205 at 221, in a dissenting judgment. Anything beyond that must be left for legislation. No new right in the law, fully-fledged with all the appropriate safeguards, can spring from the head of a judge deciding a particular case. . . . The wider and more indefinite the right claimed, the greater the undesirability of holding that such a right exists. Wide and indefinite rights, while conferring an advantage on those who have them, may well gravely impair the position of those who are subject to the rights. To create a right for one person, you have to impose a corresponding duty on another. In the present case, the alleged right to hold a telephone conversation in the privacy of one's own home without molestation is wide and indefinite in its scope, and in any case does not seem to be very apt for covering the plaintiff's grievance. He was not 'molested' in holding his telephone conversations: he held them without 'molestation,' but without their retaining the privacy that he desired. If a man telephones from his own home, but an open window makes it possible for a near neighbour to overhear what is said, and the neighbour, remaining throughout on his own property, listens to the conversation, is he to be a tortfeasor? Is a person who overhears a telephone conversation by reason of a so-called 'crossed line' to be liable in damages? What of an operator of a private switchboard who listens in? Why is the right that is claimed confined to a man's own home, so that it would not apply to private telephone conversations from offices, call boxes or the houses of others? If they were to be included, what of the greater opportunities for deliberate overhearing that they offer? In any case, why is the telephone to be subject to this special right of privacy when there is no general right?

That is not all. Suppose that there is what for brevity I may call a right to telephonic privacy, sounding in tort. What exceptions to it, if any, would there be? Would it be a breach of the right if anyone listened to a telephone conversation in which some act of criminal violence or dishonesty was being planned? Should a listener be restrained by injunction from disclosing to the authorities a conversation that would lead to the release of someone who has been kidnapped? . . .

I turn to *Rhodes v Graham* 37 SW (2d) 46 (1931), the case on private wire-tapping. . . . it would be deplorable if English law gave no remedy to the plaintiff in such a case. . . . It is not easy to see what remedy there would be in English law. If instead of tapping a wire a person uses some form of wireless transmitter in order to obtain information as to the contents, sender or addressee of any message, whether sent by wireless or otherwise, then unless he is duly authorised, he would in England be guilty of an offence under section 5(*b*) of the Wireless Telegraphy Act 1949; and similarly as to disclosing any information so obtained, except in the course of legal proceedings or for the purpose of any report thereof. In short, what is often called 'bugging' appears to be caught by this provision . . . I have not been referred to any corresponding provision for cases where no wireless is used. If some wire or other tapping device is attached to a telephone wire in the airspace over the plaintiff's land, no doubt there would be some remedy in trespass. But if the connection is made to the wire after it has left the plaintiff's land, then whatever remedy the Post Office may have, it is difficult to see how the plaintiff could succeed in trespass. . . . The tort of breach of statutory duty is not discussed, doubtless because section 5 of the Act of 1949, for instance, is framed in terms of simply creating an offence rather than imposing a duty. . . .

Fourth, there is the right of confidentiality. . . . If telephone services were provided under a contract between the telephone subscriber and the Post Office, then it might be contended that there was some implied term in that contract that telephone conversations should remain confidential and be free from tapping. . . .

Mr Ross-Munro conceeded that there was no contract as such between the plaintiff and the Post Office; . . .

The right of confidentiality accordingly falls to be considered apart from any contractual right. In such a case, it has been said that three elements are normally required if a case of breach of confidence is to succeed. First, the information itself, in the words of Lord Greene MR in *Saltman Engineering Co Ltd v Campbell Engineering Co Ltd* (1948) 65 RPC 203 at 215, 'must "have the necessary quality of confidence about it." Secondly, that information must have been imparted in circumstances importing an obligation of confidence. Thirdly, there must be an unauthorised use of that information to the detriment of the party communicating it': see *Coco v A. N. Clark (Engineers) Ltd* [1969] RPC 41 at 47, cited by Lord Widgery CJ in *A-G v Jonathan Cape Ltd* [1976] QB 752 at 769. Of the second requirement, it was said in the *Coco* case, at pp. 47–48:

'However secret and confidential the information, there can be no binding obligation of confidence if that information is blurted out in public or is communicated in other circumstances which negative any duty of holding it confidential.' . . .

It seems to me that a person who utters confidential information must accept the risk of any unknown overhearing that is inherent in the circumstances of communication. Those who exchange confidences on a bus or a train run the risk of a nearby passenger with acute hearing or a more distant passenger who is adept at lip-reading. . . .

When this is applied to telephone conversations, it appears to me that the speaker is taking such risks of being overheard as are inherent in the system. . . . the Younger Report referred to users of the telephone being aware that there were several well-understood possibilities of being overheard, and stated that a realistic person would not rely on the telephone system to protect the confidence of what he says. That comment seems unanswerable. In addition, so much publicity in recent years has been given to instances (real or fictional) of the deliberate tapping of telephones that it is difficult to envisage telephone users who are genuinely unaware of this possibility. No doubt a person who uses a telephone to give confidential information to another may do so in such a way as to impose an obligation of confidence on that other: but I do not see how it could be said that any such obligation is imposed on those who overhear the conversation, whether by means of tapping or otherwise.

Even if any duty of confidentiality were, contrary to my judgment, to be held to bind those who overhear a telephone conversation, there remains the question of the limits to that duty. I have already discussed and accepted the formulation of Lord Denning MR in *Fraser v Evans* [1969] 1 QB 349 at 362, namely, that of 'just cause or excuse for breaking confidence,' as well as his formulation in *Initial Services Ltd v Putterill* [1968] 1 QB 396, based on whether the disclosure is in the public interest. I . . . treat the former as including the latter.

. . . The rights and liberties of a telephone subscriber are indeed important; but so also are the desires of the great bulk of the population not to be the victims of assault, theft or other crimes . . .

If certain requirements are satisfied, then I think that there will plainly be just cause or excuse for what is done by or on behalf of the police. These requirements are, first, that there should be grounds for suspecting that the tapping of the particular telephone will be of material assistance in detecting or preventing crime, or discovering the criminals, or otherwise assisting in the discharge of the functions of the police in relation to crime. Second, no use should be made of any material obtained except for these purposes. Third, any knowledge of information which is not relevant to those purposes should be confined to the minimum number of persons reasonably required to carry out the process of tapping. . . . I am not, of course, saying that nothing else can constitute a just cause or excuse. . . I am not, for instance, saying anything about matters of national security: I speak only of what is before me in the present case, concerning tapping for police purposes in relation to crime.

So far as the evidence goes, it seems to me that the process of tapping, as carried out on behalf of the police in relation to crime fully conforms with these requirements. . . .

Fifth, there is Mr Ross-Munro's second main [contention for the plaintiff] based on the European Convention for the Protection of Human Rights . . . and the *Klass* case. The first limb of this relates to the direct rights conferred by the Convention. Any such right is . . . a direct right in relation to the European Commission of Human Rights and the European Court of Human Rights, and not in relation to the courts of this country; for the Convention is not law here. . . .

Sixth, there is the second limb of Mr Ross-Munro's contentions, based on the Convention and the *Klass* case as assisting the court to determine what English law is on a point on which authority is lacking or uncertain. Can it be said that in this case two courses are reasonably open to the court, one of which is inconsistent with the Convention and the other consonant with it? I refer, of course, to the words of Scarman LJ in the *Pan-American* case [above, p. 5]. I readily accept that if the question before me were one of construing a statute enacted with the purpose of giving effect to obligations imposed by the Convention, the court would readily seek to construe the legislation in a way that would effectuate the Convention rather than frustrate it. However, no relevant legislation of that sort is in existence. It seems to me that where Parliament has abstained from legislating on a point that is plainly suitable for legislation, it is indeed difficult for the court to lay down new rules of common law or equity that will carry out the Crown's treaty obligations, or to discover for the first time that such rules have always existed.

Now the West German system that came under scrutiny in the *Klass* case was laid down by statute, and it contained a number of statutory safeguards. There must be imminent danger: other methods of surveillance must be at least considerably more difficult; both the person making the request for surveillance and the method of making it are limited; the period of surveillance is limited in time, and in any case must cease when the need has passed; the person subjected to surveillance must be notified as soon as this will not jeopardise the purpose of surveillance; no information is made available to the police unless an official qualified for judicial office is satisfied that it is within the safeguards; all other information obtained must be destroyed; the process is supervised by a Parliamentary board on which the opposition is represented; and there is also a supervising commission which may order that surveillance is to cease, or that notification of it is to be given to the person who has been subjected to it. Not a single one of these safeguards is to be found as a matter of established law in England, and only a few corresponding provisions exist as a matter of administrative procedure.

It does not, of course, follow that a system with fewer or different safeguards will fail to satisfy Article 8 in the eyes of the European Court of Human Rights. At the same time, it is impossible to read the judgment in the *Klass* case without its becoming abundantly clear that a system which has no legal safeguards whatever has small chance of satisfying the requirements of that court, whatever administrative provisions there may be. Broadly, the court was concerned to see whether the German legislation provided 'adequate and effective safeguards against abuse.' Though in principle it was desirable that there should be judicial control of tapping, the court was satisfied that the German system provided an adequate substitute in the independence of the board and Commission from the authorities carrying out the surveillance. Further, the provisions for the subsequent notification of the surveillance when this would not frustrate its purpose were also considered to be adequate. In England, on the other hand, the system in operation provides no such independence, and contains no provision whatever for subsequent notification. Even if the system were to be considered adequate in its conditions, it is laid down merely as a matter of administrative procedure, so that it is unenforceable in law, and as a matter of law could at any time be altered without warning or subsequent notification. Certainly in law any 'adequate and effective safeguards against abuse' are wanting. In this respect English law compares most unfavourably with West German law: this is not a subject on which it is possible to feel any pride in English law.

I therefore find it impossible to see how English law could be said to satisfy the requirements of the Convention, as interpreted in the *Klass* case, unless that law not only prohibited all telephone tapping save in suitably limited classes of case, but also laid down detailed restrictions on the exercise of the power in those limited classes. It may perhaps be that the common law is sufficiently fertile to achieve what is required by the first limb of this; possible ways of expressing such a rule may be seen in what I have already said. But I see the greatest difficulty in the common law framing the safeguards required by the second limb. Various institutions or offices would have to be brought into being to exercise various defined functions. The more complex and indefinite the subject matter, the greater the difficulty in the court doing what it is really appropriate, and only appropriate, for the legislature to do. . . .

I would only add that, even if it was not clear before, this case seems to me to make it plain that telephone tapping is a subject which cries out for legislation. . . .

Seventh, there is Mr Ross-Munro's third main contention, based on the absence of any grant of powers to the executive to tap telephones. I have already held that if such tapping can be carried out without committing any breach of the law, it requires no authorisation by statute or common law; it can lawfully be done simply because there is nothing to make it unlawful. Now that I have held that such tapping can indeed be carried out without committing any breach of the law, the contention necessarily fails. I may also say that the statutory recognition given to the Home Secretary's warrant seems to me to point clearly to the same conclusion.

Claim dismissed

NOTES

1. The Privy Councillors' Committee (Report, p. 15) had earlier sum-marised, in somewhat unsatisfactory terms, the legal status of telephone tapping by the Government as follows:

'(*a*) The power to intercept letters has been exercised from the earliest times, and has been recognised in successive Acts of Parliament.
(*b*) This power extends to telegrams.
(*c*) It is difficult to resist the view that if there is a lawful power to intercept communications in the form of letters and telegrams, then it is wide enough to cover telephone communications as well.'

2. The *Klass* case, Eur Court HR, Series A, vol 28, Judgment of 6 September 1978, concerned the West German law applicable in *security* cases. The equivalent West German law in *non-security* cases provides for judicial supervision of interceptions. Cf. the same requirement in the US: *Berger v New York* 388 US 41 (1967). Might this reinforce Sir Robert Megarry VC's conclusion that the purely administrative and internally supervised arrangements in the UK in both security and non-security cases are contrary to the ECHR? Would the 'prescribed by law' requirement in Article 8(2), ECHR be complied with? Note that a person whose telephone is tapped in security or non-security cases in West Germany may challenge its legality in court during and after its occurrence and may claim damages or the destruction or restitution of documents. Could he do so in the UK?

3. Section 5(b) of the Wireless Telegraphy Act 1949, to which Sir Robert Megarry VC refers, provides:

'5. Any person who...
(*b*) otherwise than under the authority of the Postmaster General or in the course of his duty as a servant of the Crown, either—
   (i) uses any wireless telegraphy apparatus with intent to obtain information as to the contents, sender or addressee of any message (whether sent by means of wireless telegraphy or not) which neither the person using the apparatus nor any person on whose behalf he is acting is authorised by the Postmaster General to receive . . .
shall be guilty of an offence under this Act.'

It is also an offence 'to instal or use any apparatus for wireless telegraphy' except under the authority of a Post Office licence (s. 1(1)). 'Wireless telegraphy' is defined (s. 19(1)) so as to exclude devices using wires. The Act therefore covers telephone tapping by means of radio transmitters only (see paras (g) and (h) in the table below). The Younger Committee (Report, p. 300) suggested:

'The tapping of telephone wires which results in the abstraction of electricity might be caught by section 13 of the Theft Act 1968 which creates an offence of dishonestly using or causing electricity to be wasted or diverted without authority. But clearly the provision was not intended for this purpose and there might be difficulty in securing a conviction since no appreciable amount of electricity would be used, though there has been a conviction for making calls without paying the fee.'

It is not theft to 'steal' electricity: *Low v Blease* [1975] Crim LR 513, DC.

4. The Younger Committee (Report, p. 154) listed the technical surveillance devices it had come across. In addition to telephoto lenses, scanners to read the contents of envelopes, and tape recorders, they included the following listening devices:

Device	Capability and other characteristics
(g) microphone using wired link, the wired link either being specially laid or using existing pair of wires or single insulated wire; can also be applied like a stethoscope to listen to sounds on the other side of a wall:	range and sensitivity in effect unlimited depending on size of the microphone; certainly able to be superior to the human ear; a microphone about the size of a match head can pick up a whisper at 20 feet.
(h) microphone using radio link, i.e. a microphone coupled to a radio transmitter; this is the proverbial 'bug', intruded in many ways, e.g. in a cocktail olive, a cuff link, tiepin, telephone, dart shot into a wall:	sensitivity of the microphone as (g) above; size, including battery, of a lump of sugar; practical transmission range about a quarter of a mile.
(i) tap on a telephone line—this can be a metallic contact, but this is not necessary, as an induction device which picks up the pulses in the line is equally effective; these draw an almost undetectable amount of electricity from the telephone wire and give no betraying noises:	reception just as good as the telephone user's; can be applied at any point on the line, indoors or out.
(j) 'infinity transmitter', a device inserted into a telephone handset, which, when activated by dialling the number and giving an ultrasonic note on the last digit, prevents the telephone ringing and transmits over the dialler's telephone line all the sounds in the room where the telephone is situated, whether the handset is on or off the telephone:	can be installed in three minutes; reception just as good as the telephone used properly; but works only on telephones with direct Post Office lines; that is, not through a switchboard.
(k) induction device to pick up telephone conversations from the stray magnetic field of the telephone itself:	must be within about 4 feet of the telephone.
(l) directional (or 'parabolic' or 'telescopic') microphone concentrating a beam of sound from a distance onto a sensitive microphone and so hearing across intervening noises:	range about 25 yards; rather bulky and so difficult to conceal, and background noise can interfere.
(m) invisible light beams for monitoring vibrations, usually spoken of in the context of the laser; the vibrations can be sensed on any object near the speaker, including a window pane if it is coated with an invisible metallic film:	there is a lack of agreement about the capability of these; it does not appear that they yet exist in any marketable form.

For other descriptions of technical surveillance devices, see the Justice Report, Appendix D, and M. Jones (ed) *Privacy* (1974) pp. 26–40. A bugging device found hidden in a cigarette packet behind a painting of Queen Victoria's Jubilee in Burnley Town Hall just before a meeting of the town's ruling Labour group was said by the police to have a transmitting range of about 70 yards and of being capable of being received by any VHF radio. It could have been made for a few pounds and with only a basic knowledge of electronics. It was uncovered after the Labour group had become suspicious about recent 'leaks': *The Times*, 25 May 1978.
5. In *R v Maqsud Ali* [1966] 1 QB 688, CCA, the appellants had been convicted of murder. The evidence against them included tape recordings

of what they had said to each other while unaware that the room in which they were was 'bugged'. The Court of Criminal Appeal rejected an argument that the tape recordings should not have been admitted in evidence Marshall J stated at p. 701:

'Both appellants had come voluntarily to the Town Hall, they were not in custody and no charge was brought against them until June 13 and 15, 1964, respectively. They were left in the room together. They had not, of course, been warned of the presence of the microphone. The police were inquiring into a particularly savage murder and it was a matter of great public concern that those responsible should be traced. There is no question here of being in custody and subject to any Judges' Rules. The criminal does not act according to Queensberry Rules. The method of the informer and of the eavesdropper is commonly used in the detection of crime. The only difference here was that a mechanical device was the eavesdropper. If, in such circumstances and at such a point in the investigations, the appellants by incautious talk provided evidence against themselves, then in the view of this court it would not be unfair to use it against them. The method of taking the recording cannot affect admissibility as a matter of law although it must remain very much a matter for the discretion of the judge.'

Would the appellants have had any remedy in civil law? What difference would it have made on the admissibility point if the appellants were being questioned by the police or were left together in a cell after arrest? Is there any reason why the ruling in *R v Maqsud Ali* should not apply to evidence obtained by the use of any of the technical surveillance devices listed by the Younger Committee? See also *Hopes and Lavery v HM Advocate* 1960 JC 104, 1960 SLT 264, High Court of Justiciary, in which a person being blackmailed was fitted with a 'bug' by the police. Tape recordings of conversations with the black-mailer obtained by means of the 'bug' were held to be admissible.

6. The Younger Committee considered that the use, or abuse, of technical surveillance devices (by which it understood 'electronic and optical extensions of the human senses' (Report, p. 153)) was an area in which the law needed strengthening. It suggested a new criminal offence of surreptitious surveillance by means of a technical device with the following constituents (Report, p. 173):

'a. a technical device;
b. surreptitious use of the device;
c. a person who is, or his possessions which are, the object of surveillance;
d. a set of circumstances in which, were it not for the use of the device, that person would be justified in believing that he had protected himself or his possessions from surveillance whether by overhearing or observation;
e. an intention by the user to render those circumstances ineffective as protection against overhearing or observation; and
f. absence of consent by the victim.'

The Committee also proposed a tort of unlawful surveillance by technical devices. This would have the same elements as the offence but the act would not need to be surreptitious.

6 Computers

Report of the Committee on Data Protection, Chairman: Sir Norman Lindop (Cmnd. 7341 1978)

38.00. We list here our main proposals for a Data Protection Act . . .
38.07. The Act should make it the duty of the DPA [Data Protection Authority] to ensure:—
(1) that, so far as is practicable, the automatic handling of personal data in the United Kingdom is carried on with adequate safeguards for the interests of the data subjects, and in particular for their privacy;

(2) to that end, that persons carrying on or causing to be carried on the automatic handling of personal data in the UK will comply, to the extent which may in all the circumstances of the case appear to the Authority to be necessary or desirable, with the principles set out in the Act; . . .

38.08. The following should be the statutory principles:

(1) Data subjects should know what personal data relating to them are handled, why those data are needed, how they will be used, who will use them, for what purpose, and for how long;

(2) Personal data should be handled only to the extent and for the purposes made known when they are obtained, or subsequently authorised;

(3) Personal data handled should be accurate and complete, and relevant and timely for the purpose for which they are used;

(4) No more personal data should be handled than are necessary for the purposes made known or authorised;

(5) Data subjects should be able to verify compliance with these principles; . . .

38.09. The Act should specifically direct the DPA to take the following criteria into consideration:— . . .

(4) the risks to the interests of the data subjects, and in particular to their privacy, which the handling presents or is likely to present;

(5) the adequacy, in the light of the foregoing considerations, of the safeguards provided by or on behalf of the user against those risks;

(6) the cost to the user of providing additional safeguards; . . .

38.10. "Privacy" should be defined, in relation to any data subject, as his interest to determine for himself what data relating to him shall be known to what other persons, and upon what terms as to the use which those persons may make of those data.

38.11. The DPA should draft Codes of Practice for the different classes of personal data handling applications. . . .

38.14. Each Code of Practice should specify the data handling activities to which it applies and the measures to be taken by users to achieve the levels of compliance with the statutory principles judged necessary in that case.

38.15. The Codes of Practice should take the form of subsidiary legislation and acquire the force of law.

38.16. There should be a scheme of registration, with a degree of discretion for the DPA over its timing and extent.

38.17. The DPA should be required to call in for registration all the personal data handling applications of central and local government.

Until the legislation is in force the Government should republish at least annually an expanded and updated version of Tables 1 and 2 of the White Paper Supplement *Computers: Safeguards for Privacy* (Cmnd. 6354).

38.18. In the industrial and private sectors, the DPA should be able to determine when considering a Code of Practice whether or not the registration of all users whose applications are governed by that Code is necessary or helpful.

38.19. The DPA should be required to compile and maintain a register and to ensure that it is accessible to the public. The register should show sufficient and updated particulars of each registered application, which Code of Practice applies and certain other information.

38.20. The DPA should be empowered to place certain information on a part of the register not open to public inspection, either at the reasonable request of a user or where disclosure could hinder the detection or prevention of crime, or apprehension or prosecution of offenders.

38.21. The DPA should be bound to supply any person on request with copies of entries in the public part of the register upon payment of an appropriate fee. Copies of the DPA's findings at public hearings should also be available. . . .

38.26. Failure to register a registrable activity should be a criminal offence triable only in a magistrates' court at the instance of the DPA.

38.27. Breach of a Code of Practice should be a more serious offence. It should be triable at the instance of the DPA either in a magistrates' court or in the Crown Court.

38.28. As well as providing an appropriate range of penalties, the Act should empower the court to make an order requiring the convicted user to take appropriate steps for complying with his Code of Practice, or in extreme cases to suspend the application altogether. Failure to comply with such a court order should be a serious offence, and a term of imprisonment should be available for those shown to be deliberately and personally responsible.

38.51. Any power of the Secretary of State to grant exemptions from the purview of the DPA should be precisely limited to national security. Police records, including criminal intelligence records, having no bearing on national security should not be exempted.

38.64. There should be a new cause of action for a data subject who has suffered ascertainable damage as a foreseeable result of the automatic handling of personal data about him in breach of a Code of Practice.

NOTES

1. On privacy and computers, see Corbett, (1976) 126 NLJ 556; A. R. Miller, (1969) 67 Mich LR 1091; Norman and Martin, *The Computerised Society* (1973); Roe, (ed.), *Privacy, Computers and You* (1972); P. Sieghart, *Privacy and Computers* (1977); C. Tapper, *Computer Law* (1978) Chap. 5 (for a forceful statement of the view that the privacy problem has been overstated); M. Warner and M. Stone, *The Data Bank Society* (1970); *Confidential: Computers, Records and the Right to Privacy* (NCC L) (1979).
2. The question of safeguarding privacy in the use of computerised data banks containing personal information about individuals in the private sector was considered by the Younger Committee (Report, Chap. 20). The Committee stated that 'of all the forms of invasion of privacy which have been cited in evidence to us that involving the use or misuse of computers has been the least supported in concrete terms' (Report, p. 179). The Committee could not on the evidence before it 'conclude that the computer as used in the private sector is at present a threat to privacy, but we recognise that there is a possibility of such a threat becoming a reality in the future' (Report, p. 191). In recognition of the potential threat, the Committee formulated ten principles (Report, pp. 183–4)—the Younger Principles—which it proposed computer users should adopt at once on a voluntary basis in the handling of personal information. The Committee also proposed that the Government should establish machinery to keep the situation under review. In 1975, the Government published a White Paper (*Computers and Privacy*, Cmnd. 6353) in which it stated that 'the time has come when those who use computers to handle personal information, however responsible they are, can no longer remain the sole judges of whether their own systems adequately safeguard privacy' (Cmnd. 6353, p. 8). The Government therefore proposed (ibid, pp. 8–9)

> 'that the right course is to introduce legislation involving two elements: first the establishment of a set of objectives, to set standards governing the use of computers that handle personal information; and second the establishment of a permanent statutory agency to oversee the use of computers, in both the public and private sectors, to ensure that they are operated with proper regard for privacy and with the necessary safeguards for the personal information which they contain.'

As an interim step, the Government established the Data Protection Committee (the Lindop Committee) which was, inter alia, to advise on the form that the proposed legislation should take. Parliament has yet to debate the Lindop Committee Report.
3. The areas in which computers are used in the *public* sector to store personal information are described in a Supplement to the 1975 White Paper (Cmnd. 6354). Summarizing the *central government* position, the Lindop Committee stated (Report p. 53):

> 6.05. . . . Certainly the government now collects and holds 'a good deal of information' about individuals; indeed, paragraph 10 of the Supplement rightly describes the total list as 'formidable'. There are some huge operations covering large sections of the total population. For example, the Department of Health and Social Security (DHSS) does not have files on every individual, but the systems dealing with National Insurance, Pensions and Child Allowances hold some 48 million records. The Department of National Savings (DNS) handles about 10 million National Savings Bank accounts; the Department of Education and Science (DES) has collected the records of some 3.5 million students for the Further Education Statistical Record (FESR); and the Office of Population Censuses and Surveys (OPCS) aims to collect, for statistical purposes, information about every individual in the country. Many routine tasks in relation to such a volume of information can, for all practical purposes, only be carried out by computer. However, the amount of personal information

held about each individual is usually small, and the operations themselves are straightforward. Often the names and addresses of individuals are not stored on computer files because they are not needed there and some identifier, such as an account number, can be used to link the information held on computer with that held in manual files.

On the use of computers by the *police*, the Lindop Committee stated (Report, pp. 80–84):

8.07. The PNC [Police National Computer] holds five major files: the index to national records in the Criminal Records Office (CRO), a file of vehicle owners, a file of stolen and suspect vehicles, an index to the national fingerprint collection and a file of wanted or missing persons. . . .

8.13. The PNC is connected, by a network of private lines provided by the Post Office, to some 300 wholly dedicated terminals situated in police premises and operated by police forces in Great Britain; thus police information on the PNC is available only within the police service. Local forces can input, alter and delete data on the stolen and suspect vehicles and wanted and missing persons files. The chief officer of a force which receives information from the PNC is responsible for ensuring that it is dealt with in accordance with the practices which apply to police information generally. The Home Office has recently issued notes for the guidance of chief officers of police on privacy precautions in police systems handling personal information; these deal mainly with the security of records.

8.14. The Home Office said in evidence that the PNC has no computer links with any other central government department and that no such links are planned. . . .

8.18. The White Paper Supplement mentioned that 'A computer system is being planned to handle information held by the Metropolitan Police about crime, criminals and their associates. The system will be internal to those branches of the force which now use this information in manually held records and it will not be connected to any other system'. On 14 February 1977, *The Times* carried an article about the new computer. It said 'By 1985 the names and details of up to 1,300,000 'criminals and their associates' will be fed into a secret computerised record system being built up by Scotland Yard. The computer will cover all crime and information on suspected criminals, but Scotland Yard will not say whether that will include records of people suspected of criminal subversion'. . . .

8.19 When witnesses from the Metropolitan Police gave oral evidence to us [they] . . . considered that saying that the information concerned 'crime, criminals and their associates' met the requirement in paragraph 34 of the White Paper that the existence of computer systems should be publicly known. . . .

8.20. The witnesses confirmed that the computer would hold information on named individuals and they said that there was no objection to the public knowing that the computer system had a multi-factor searching capacity (e.g. it could answer the question 'Which red-haired Irishmen on record drive a white Cortina with MR and 6 in the registration'?) because it would be understood that this enabled the police to do their job more quickly. This type of information was already held on manual systems. The witnesses considered that they could properly claim that Parliament had sanctioned the collecting of such information.

An indication of the kind of information stored on the Police National Computer appeared in a report in *The Guardian*, 20 September 1979 on 'jury-vetting'. Information on 19 of the 93 potential jurors in a conspiracy case with political overtones at the Old Bailey was given to the prosecution by the police for 'jury-vetting purposes'. The information identified people who had friends or relations with criminal records, had complained against the police, were squatters, had 'spent' convictions under the Rehabilitation of Offenders Act 1974 or had been the victims of crime. The jurors concerned were not aware that the information was being passed on to the prosecution. Was this a case of information collected for one purpose being used for another purpose? Would you object to information about you being collected and used in this way?

The Lindop Committee also described the use of computers by *local government*, the *nationalised industries* and in *schools* and *higher education*. As far as local government is concerned, the Committee stated (Report, p. 94):

'The conflict between efficiency in the performance of those tasks and respect for the privacy of the individual is, in principle, the same as it is in central government. But it is much more acute because a smaller community is administered, and there is no legal separation of departments which establishes their independence from each other. Departments of State infrequently pass information about identifiable persons between one another; departments of a local authority rely upon such transfers for the proper exercise of their functions. And there is no doubt that local government comes closer to the lives of ordinary people than any other body in the public or private sectors.'

In the *private* sector, the Committee described the use of computers in employment, consumer credit, banking, insurance and direct marketing and by building societies.

4. As the Government White Paper states (Cmnd. 6353, p. 4), 'none of the functions carried out by computers within an information system is different in kind from those which are, or could in principle be, carried out by traditional means'. The reasons why they nonetheless present a problem for the protection of privacy requiring special treatment are stated in the White Paper as follows (Cmnd. 6353, p. 4):

'6. The speed of computers, their capacity to store, combine, retrieve and transfer data, their flexibility, and the low unit cost of the work which they can do have the following practical implications for privacy:
    (1) they facilitate the maintenance of extensive record systems and the retention of data in those systems;
    (2) they can make data easily and quickly accessible from many distant points;
    (3) they make it possible for data to be transferred quickly from one information system to another;
    (4) they make it possible for data to be combined in ways which might not otherwise be practicable;
    (5) because the data are stored, processed and often transmitted in a form which is not directly intelligible, few people may know what is in the records, or what is happening to them.

7. How computers affect people's lives depends on how they are used—or abused. Their actual and potential benefits are great: in the saving of routine clerical work; in the economy, accuracy and speed with which information can be processed; in forecasting, planning, or matching supply to demand; and, in the service of central and local government, in making public administration more responsive to the needs of the individual citizen and his family. It is clearly of the first importance that we should exploit to the full the benefits which computers can offer. It is against those benefits that we must weigh the possible threats. For, like other powerful tools that man has devised, computers have the capacity to do harm if they are misused.
8. The principal potential dangers to privacy come from three main sources:
    (1) inaccurate, incomplete or irrelevant information;
    (2) the possibility of access to information by people who should not or need not have it;
    (3) the use of information in a context or for a purpose other than that for which it was collected.
Any of these dangers can come about either intentionally, or by accident, and properly designed safeguards must therefore provide against both eventualities.'

The storing of inaccurate information results from human error and can be countered by a right of subject access. Cases in which the person about whom inaccurate information is compiled is not made aware of this fact (see, e.g., those in Hewitt, *The Information Gatherers*, 1977, pp. 1–2) present the greatest problems. As far as the other two 'principal potential dangers' to which it refers are concerned, the White Paper states (Cmnd. 6353, pp. 5–6):

'14. The very complexity of computers and their operations creates problems for anyone who tries to gain unauthorised access to them . . .
15. Where data are printed out in human readable form, computer based systems share the security weaknesses of manual systems. . . .
16. Where someone with authorised access to information uses that information for an improper purpose, it is a breach of confidence . . . and our law already provides a number of remedies for it . . . The additional fear that arises from the development of computers is that someone will make improper use of the computer's capacity for storing, processing and

transferring data so as to combine information from a number of sources about individuals without their knowledge and consent. . . .

18. The confidentiality of personal information held in a computer system can of course also be put at risk through accident, carelessness or sheer lack of foresight. In practice, that is the way in which confidentiality—and also accuracy—are most likely to be compromised in the foreseeable future. Any computer system which is properly designed and operated must therefore ensure that risks of this kind have been foreseen, and that adequate safeguards are maintained to obviate them.'

Commenting on the combining and transferring of information, the Lindop Committee (Report, p. 54) noted:

'6.07. The prospect which seems to cause most public alarm is the possibility that the government might, with the aid of computers, collate and centralise all the government-held information about an individual to form a personal dossier. Such a collation and centralisation, for however beneficial a purpose, would, in our view, be thoroughly undesirable. It would give any government too great a potential power over its citizens and it would be dangerous if it fell into the wrong hands. It is therefore important that some independent body should be able to ensure that reasonable limits are placed on the possible collation of information.'

The Committee could see that in some cases the transfer of information from one computer-based information system to another could be justifiable in the public interest. It quoted the following case (Report, p. 55):

6.11. On 17 January 1977, the *Daily Mail* had a story under the heading 'Taxmen Use Driving Licence Computer To Spy' and a version of the same story was also reported in other papers. There was at that time a public outcry over the fact that the Driver and Vehicle Licensing Centre (DVLC) at Swansea, whose records are held on computer, supplied the Inland Revenue with individuals' addresses. This was taken by some to be a new and clandestine scheme, to which the involvement of computers lent Orwellian overtones. In fact, since 1931 the driving and vehicle licence authorities have supplied the IR on request with individuals' current addresses in order to trace tax-evaders. This use of computerised information was noted in the White Paper Supplement, and it involves the transfer of information which the IR needs to carry out its statutory duties and which it has reason to believe is being deliberately withheld.

6.12. There is nothing underhand about this procedure and many regard it as highly desirable. It is a pity, therefore, that it should have given rise to public suspicion.

On the 'statutory principles' recommended by it (para. 38.08, above p. 335) the Lindop Committee stated (Report, pp. 201–2):

'21.10. It will be seen that our set of principles does not spell out expressly some of those to be found in the other sets which have been published in the past, including the objectives recited in paragraph 34 of the White Paper. One example is what is known as the 'principle of publicity', expressed in a report of the US Health, Education and Welfare Department in the form "there must be no personal data record-keeping systems whose very existence is secret". Another is the much debated right of subject access. The reason why we have not spelt them out is that we regard them as means to an end, rather than as ends in themselves. Their proper place is therefore in the detailed rules which would need to be made in order to apply the principles.

21.11. Thus, rules of subject access will often, but not always, be the means by which the DPA will ensure compliance with the statutory principle that data subjects should know what data about them are handled. Likewise, the principle of publicity can in many cases best be met by our recommendations for a public register in paragraph 19.73.'

On the question of exemptions for police and security service information systems, the Committee stated (Report, pp. 218–220):

'23.03. The White Paper claims that exemption from the purview of the DPA would be necessary for at least some of these information systems. . . .

23.04. Our principal aim in recommending that data protection should be implemented by means of Codes of Practice is to ensure that there is enough flexibility to allow for the special needs of different categories of user, and so make statutory exemptions unnecessary. We had hoped that this would mean that the DPA and those responsible for the police and for the security services could, through the normal process of negotiation, arrive at mutually acceptable Codes of Practice. These would inevitably have to allow substantial departures from the general principles about, for example, public knowledge of systems and access by the subject but we thought that the very fact that an independent DPA had helped to set the data protection standards for these systems would help to reassure the public about their methods of operation. . . .

23.05. We put this view to the Home Office. . . .

23.06. . . . they distinguished between data which were matters of fact and of public record, and therefore suitable for the DPA to monitor, and criminal intelligence material and certain other material held for the purposes of national security (which could include criminal and terrorist intelligence data that depend for their value on the protection of the sources of the information held). . . .

23.07. It is clear from this that the present view of the Home Office is that criminal intelligence and the handling of personal data by the security services should not come within the authority of the DPA. If the legislation is to be put forward on this basis we recommend that the Secretary of State's power to grant exemptions in this field should be precisely limited by the statute to national security, and that criminal intelligence records having no bearing on national security should not be exempted.

CHAPTER 8

Freedom of religion

1 Introduction

Freedom of religion includes freedom of worship and expression and freedom to conduct one's life in accordance with one's religious beliefs. Freedom of worship is now virtually complete. Freedom of expression on religious matters is limited only by the remnants of the law of blasphemy. The Christian morality underlying English law means that most Christians have no difficulty in practising their religion in their daily lives. Members of some minority Christian and non-Christian denominations lack the same facility, as the sections in this Chapter on criminal law, employment, religious holy days and immigration show. Immigration from the new Commonwealth since the 1950s has provided new evidence of the link between Christianity and the law. The same development of a more multi-racial society has increased the importance of freedom of religion.

Another element of freedom of religion is freedom from discrimination between religions. The Church of England's status as the established church means some preference in law for it over other denominations, although establishment carries disadvantages too. Religious toleration has reached the point where almost all of the disabilities formerly suffered by dissenters have been removed and atheism is within the policy of the law. In addition to the aid to religion that the establishment of a particular church represents, the state provides support to religion generally or to particular denominations in other ways as well. The provision made for religious education in schools, for Sunday observance, for religious broadcasting and for exemption from taxation are examples. *Private* discrimination on religious grounds is mostly uncontrolled. There is no statute like the Race Relations Act 1976 prohibiting it.

Little has been written on the legal aspects of freedom of religion. See St. J. Robilliard [1978] PL 379 and H. Street, *Freedom, the Individual and the law* (4th edn., 1977) Chap. 7. On freedom of religion in Northern Ireland, which is too large and complex a subject to be considered here, see K. Boyle, T. Hadden, and P. Hillyard, *Law and State: The Case of Northern Ireland*, (1975) Chap. 2, and H. Calvert, *Constitutional Law in Northern Ireland*, (1968) Chap. 14. And see the Fair Employment (NI) Act 1976 and the Prevention of Incitement to Hatred Act (NI) 1970.

2 What is a religion?

R v Registrar General, ex parte Segerdal [1970] 2 QB 697, [1970] 3 All ER 886, [1970] 3 WLR 479, Court of Appeal

The applicants sought mandamus requiring the Registrar General to register the chapel of the Church of Scientology at East Grinstead as a 'place of meeting for religious worship' under the Places of Worship Registration Act 1855. They appealed to the Court of Appeal against the refusal of the Divisional Court to make an order.

Lord Denning MR: . . . This group of persons desire to register this building, which they describe as a chapel, as a 'place of meeting for religious worship.' If it is so registered, they will obtain considerable privileges. They will have taken one step towards getting a licence to celebrate marriages there; they will be outside the jurisdiction of the Charity Commissioners; and the building itself may become exempt from paying rates [General Rate Act 1967 s.39] . . .

The registrar, having considered the matter and made all the inquiries he thought necessary, refused to record this place as a place of meeting for religious worship. . . . In addition to the Sunday afternoon service, Mr Segerdal says there are other religious ceremonies at the chapel, such as christenings, funeral services and wedding ceremonies. He says the chapel is also open at other times for private prayer and meditation.

We have had much discussion on the meaning of the word 'religion' and of the word 'worship,' taken separately, but I think we should take the combined phrase, 'place of meeting for religious worship' as used in the statute of 1855. It connotes to my mind a place of which the principal use is as a place where people come together as a congregation or assembly to do reverence to God. It need not be the God which the Christians worship. It may be another God, or an unknown God, but it must be reverence to a deity. There may be exceptions. For instance, Buddhist temples are properly described as places of meeting for religious worship. But, apart from exceptional cases of that kind, it seems to me the governing idea behind the words 'place of meeting for religious worship' is that it should be a place for the worship of God. I am sure that would be the meaning, attached by those who framed this legislation of 1855.

Turning to the creed of the Church of Scientology, I must say that it seems to me to be more a *philosophy* of the existence of man or of life, rather than a *religion*. Religious worship means reverence or veneration of God or of a Supreme Being. I do not find any such reverence or veneration in the creed of this church, or, indeed, in the affidavit of Mr Segerdal. There is considerable stress on the spirit of man. The adherents of this philosophy believe that man's spirit is everlasting and moves from one human frame to another; but still, so far as I can see, it is the spirit of man and not of God. When I look through the ceremonies and the affidavits, I am left with the feeling that there is nothing in it of reverence for God or a deity, but simply instruction in a philosophy. There may be belief in a spirit of man, but there is no belief in a spirit of God.

This is borne out by the opening words of the book of ceremonies: It says, at p.7:

'In a Scientology Church Service we do not use prayers, attitudes of piety, or threats of damnation. We use the facts, the truths, the understandings that have been discovered in the science of Scientology.'

That seems to me to express the real attitude of this group. When Mr Segerdal in his affidavit uses the word 'prayer' he does not use it in its proper sense, that is, intercession to God. When the creed uses the word 'God' (as it does in two places) it does not use it in any religious sense. There is nothing which carries with it any idea of reverence or veneration of God. The 'sample sermon' has no word of God in it at all. It says that man has a body, mind and spirit. It emphasises man and not God. It seems to me that God does not come into their scheme of things at all.

Winn and **Buckley LJJ** delivered concurring judgments.

Appeal dismissed.

NOTES

1. This is one of the few cases in which a court has considered what is meant by a 'religion', 'religious belief', etc. See also *Cave v Cave*, below, p. 353, and *Goodbody v British Railways Board*, below, p. 353. 'Religion' is defined in the Oxford English Dictionary in a number of ways including 'recognition on the part of man of some higher unseen power having control of his destiny, and as being entitled to obedience, reverence, and worship.' On scientology, see further below, p. 361.

2. The Places of Worship Registration Act 1855 applies to places of worship of all denominations except the Church of England. Registration is not compulsory but it carries with it tax and other advantages, as Lord Denning indicated. A charity need not be registered under the Charities Act 1960 in respect of any place of worship registered under the 1855 Act (Charities Act 1960, s. 4(4) (d)).

3 Church and state

(a) THE ESTABLISHED CHURCH

The Canons of the Church of England (Canons Ecclesiastical promulgated by the Convocations of Canterbury and York in 1964 and 1969)

CANON A 1

The Church of England, established according to the laws of this realm under the Queen's Majesty, BELONGS to the true and Apostolic Church of Christ; . . .

CANON A 7

We acknowledge that the Queen's most excellent Majesty, acting according to the laws of the realm, is the highest power under God in this kingdom, and has supreme authority over all persons in all causes, as well ecclesiastical as civil.

NOTES

1. On establishment, see R. Davies (1976), 7 Cambrian LR 11; C. Garbett, *Church and State in England*, (1950); and E. G. Moore, *An Introduction to English Canon Law* (1967) Chap. II.

2. Although the Church of England had become the established church in England long before the 16th Century, it is with the Reformation statutes of that time, which severed the link with Rome and stated the doctrine of royal supremacy, that one associates the idea of establishment in its present form. See, in particular, the Ecclesiastical Appeals Act 1531; the Submission of the Clergy Act 1533; the Appointment of Bishops Act 1533; the Ecclesiastical Licences Act 1533; and 26 Hen 8 c 2 (Supremacy of the Crown) (1534). None of those statutes, which are now mostly repealed, expressly 'establishes' the Church of England. The above extract from the Canons of the Church of England recognises the fact of establishment as clearly as any other legal source. Canon law is a part of the ecclesiastical law of the Church of England; it is binding upon the clergy of the Church, not the laity. The Church in Wales was disestablished by the Welsh Church Act 1914. On the special status of the Church of Scotland, see F. Lyall, 1976 J R 58, 65.

3. The Sovereign is the head of the Church of England. Canon A 7, Canons of the Church of England, above. The Act of Supremacy 1558, s. 9, now repealed, referred to the Sovereign as 'the Supreme Governor of the Realm in all spiritual and ecclesiastical causes as well as temporal.' The Act of Settlement 1700, s.3, provides that

'whosoever shall hereafter come to the possession of this crown shall join in communion with the Church of England as by law established.'

The same Act (s.2) also provides that

'all and every person and persons who shall or may take or inherit the said crown by virtue of the limitation of this present Act and is are or shall be reconciled to or shall hold communion with the see or church of Rome or shall profess the popish religion or shall marry a papist'

is disqualified from being the Sovereign. In 1978, Prince Michael of Kent renounced his claim to the throne upon marrying a Roman Catholic.

4. The Church of England's position as the established church gives it certain privileges in law. The Archbishops of Canterbury and York, the Bishops of London, Durham and Winchester and 21 other diocesan bishops by seniority in office are members of the House of Lords (*Erskine May* (19th edn., 1976) p. 4). The 1968 Government White Paper on House of Lords reform (Cmnd. 3799, paras. 63–7) accepted that, the presence of the 'lords spiritual' could be defended by reference to the control that Parliament has over Church of England affairs and suggested that they should remain 'at least for the present', although their number should be reduced to 16 in the proposed smaller chamber. The 'lords spiritual' are free to debate and vote on any matter before the House and not only on matters of direct concern to the Church. The ecclesiastical law of the Church of England is a part of the law of the land (*Mackonochie v Lord Penzance* (1881) 6 App Cas 424 at 446, HL) and is enforced by the state. The Sovereign is crowned by the Archbishop of Canterbury.

5. The price that the Church pays for these and other privileges is a certain degree of state involvement in its affairs. The state has control over law-making by the 'parliament' of the Church of England, the General Synod (formerly the National Assembly). *Canons* (which cannot be contrary to the prerogative or statutory or other law of the realm (Submission of the Clergy Act 1533, s.3)) passed by the General Synod require the royal assent to be law (Synodical Government Measure 1969, s.1). *Measures* (which have the force of statute and hence may change any law) passed by it have to be approved by the two Houses of Parliament as well as obtain the royal assent (Church of England (Assembly) Powers Act 1919). In 1927 and 1928, Parliament rejected proposed measures for the revision of the Prayer Book passed by the National Assembly. Archbishops and bishops are appointed by the Crown (see 1 Co Inst 134 and the Appointment of Bishops Act 1533, s.3) on the advice (by convention) of the Prime Minister. As of 1977, the newly established Church of England Crown Appointments Commission puts forward two candidates (in order of preference if it thinks fit) for the Prime Minister's consideration. The understanding is that he will recommend one of these candidates, normally the 'first choice' candidate if there is one. The new arrangement applies only to Archbishops and diocesan bishops; in the case of suffragan bishops, the appointment is made on the basis of recommendation from the diocesan bishop. The Crown is also the patron of a large number of benefices, or livings. Appointments to these are made after consultation with the Church.

6. Is an established church contrary to Article 9 ECHR as read with Article 14, ECHR (above, pp. 19, 20)? Is *any* discrimination between religions (see the section on toleration and aid to religion below) contrary to the ECHR?

(b) TOLERATION OF OTHER DENOMINATIONS

Lord Chancellor (Tenure of Office and Discharge of Ecclesiastical Functions) Act 1974

1. For the avoidance of doubt it is hereby declared that the office of Lord Chancellor is and shall be tenable by an adherent of the Roman Catholic faith.
2. In the event of the office of Lord Chancellor being held by an adherent of the Roman Catholic faith it shall be lawful for Her Majesty in Council to make provision for the exercise of any or all the visitational or the ecclesiastical functions normally performed by the Lord Chancellor, and any patronage to livings normally in the gift of the Lord Chancellor, to be performed by the Prime Minister or any other Minister of the Crown.

NOTES

1. At the time of the Reformation settlement, a consequence of the establishment of one denomination was inevitably the proscription of others. Since then the church has lost most of its temporal power and attitudes have mellowed to the point where it is not illegal to profess or practise any religion and nearly all of the other disabilities to which non-conformists were subject (e.g. exclusion from Parliament) have been removed. (See, mainly the Toleration Act 1688 (protestant non-conformists); the Roman Catholic Relief Acts 1791 and 1829; and Religious Disabilities Act 1846 (Jews)). The Prime Minister may be of any religion or none. So may the Lord Chancellor, as the Lord Chancellor, etc., Act 1974 makes clear. The Act was expressed in terms only of Roman Catholics because there was felt to be no doubt that adherents of other religions were eligible. And at least one Lord Chancellor had been 'a devoutly practising atheist' (352 HL Deb written answers 11 June 1974 col 417). But the Sovereign must, as noted above, be a member of the Church of England and his or her consort may not be a Roman Catholic. Other minor disabilities (mostly affecting Roman Catholics) are listed in Moore, *An Introduction to English Canon Law* (1967) pp. 161–2.
2. Another result of religious toleration is the Oaths Act 1888 which provides (s.1):

'Every person upon objecting to being sworn, and stating, as the ground of such objection, either that he has no religious belief, or that the taking of an oath is contrary to his religious belief, shall be permitted to make his solemn affirmation instead of taking an oath in all places and for all purposes where an oath is or shall be required by law, which affirmation shall be of the same force and effect as if he had taken the oath.'

Bowman v Secular Society [1917] AC 406, House of Lords

The appellants challenged the validity of a testamentary gift to the respondent company on the ground that the latter's objects were illegal so that the gift was for an illegal purpose. Its objects were 'to promote . . . the principle that human conduct should be based upon natural knowledge, and not upon super-natural belief, and that human welfare in this world is the proper end of all thought and action'.
   Lord Sumner: My Lords, the question is whether an anti-Christian society is incapable of claiming a legacy, duly bequeathed to it, merely because it is anti-Christian. . . . is the maxim that Christianity is part of the law of England true, and, if so, in what sense? If Christianity is of the substance of our law, and if a Court of law must, nevertheless, adjudge possession of its property to a company whose every action seeks to subvert Christianity and bring that law to naught, then by such judgment it stultifies the law. . . .
   My Lords, with all respect for the great names of the lawyers who have used it, the phrase 'Christianity is part of the law of England' is really not law; it is rhetoric . . . One asks what part of our law may Christianity be, and what part of Christianity may it be that is part of our law? Best CJ once said in *Bird* v *Holbrook* (1828) 4 Bing 628 at 641 (a case of injury by setting a

spring-gun): 'There is no act which Christianity forbids, that the law will not reach: if it were otherwise, Christianity would not be, as it has always been held to be, part of the law of England'; but this was rhetoric too. Spring-guns, indeed, were got rid of, not by Christianity, but by Act of Parliament. 'Thou shalt not steal' is part of our law. 'Thou shalt not commit adultery' is part of our law, but another part. 'Thou shalt love thy neighbour as thyself' is not part of our law at all. Christianity has tolerated chattel slavery; not so the present law of England. Ours is, and always has been, a Christian State. The English family is built on Christian ideas, and if the national religion is not Christian there is none. English law may well be called a Christian law, but we apply many of its rules and most of its principles, with equal justice and equally good government, in heathen communities, and its sanctions, even in Courts of conscience, are material and not spiritual. . . . In the present day reasonable men do not apprehend the dissolution or the downfall of society because religion is publicly assailed by methods not scandalous . . . Accordingly I am of opinion that acts merely done in furtherance of paragraph 3 (A) and other paragraphs of the respondents' memorandum are not now contrary to the law, and that the appeal should be dismissed.

Lords Dunedin, **Parker of Waddington**, and **Buckmaster** delivered concurring speeches. **Lord Finlay** LC delivered a dissenting speech.

Appeal dismissed.

NOTES

1. *Bowman v Secular Society* was one of two cases decided in the space of three years in which the House of Lords adjusted the policy of the common law to reflect the change in the relationship between church and state that has occurred since the Reformation. The other was *Bourne v Keane* [1919] A C 815, HL, in which it was held (overruling *West v Shuttleworth* (1835) 2 My & K 684) that a trust for the saying of Roman Catholic masses for the dead was valid. In these cases, the old idea that the 'Church must help the State to maintain its authority, and the State must help the Church to punish nonconformists and infidels' (W. Holdsworth, (1920) 36 LQR 339) gave way to one emphasising freedom of conscience instead. Nonetheless, although, in Lord Sumner's famous dictum, it may only be 'rhetoric' to say that 'Christianity is a part of the law of the land', most of English law remains firmly based on Christian moral values. Consequently, members of the main Christian denominations are unlikely to find themselves out of step with the law as they practise their religion in their daily lives. As the cases later in this Chapter show, the same may not be true of members of some of the minority Christian sects (see e.g. *R v Senior*, below, p. 350) or of non-Christian denominations, whether the latter are denominations that have long been well represented in the community (see e.g. *Ostreicher v Secretary of State for the Environment*, below, p. 357) or denominations that are now more common because of recent patterns of immigration (see e.g. *Ahmad v Annex London Education Authority*, below, p. 353). Note also that, despite the general approach taken by the House of Lords in *Bowman v Secular Society*, the offence of blasphemous libel does not apply to an attack upon a religion other than Christianity (see *R v Lemon* [1979] 1 All ER 898, AC 617, HL.

2. In *Cowan v Milbourn* (1867) LR 2 Exch 230, an owner of a room refused to honour a letting when he discovered that it was to be used by the Liverpool Secular Society (not to be confused with the Liverpool Football Club, which is a religious society) for a lecture questioning christian doctrine. The Court of Exchequer Chamber held the refusal to be justified as the intended use was for an unlawful purpose, Christianity being a part of the law of the land. The case was overruled in *Bowman v Secular Society*.

(c) ASSISTANCE TO RELIGION

(i) Education

Education Act 1944

25. General provisions as to religious education in county and in voluntary schools
(1) Subject to the provisions of this section, the school day in every county school and in every voluntary school shall begin with collective worship on the part of all pupils in attendance at the school, and the arrangements made therefor shall provide for a single act of worship attended by all such pupils unless, in the opinion of the local education authority or, in the case of a voluntary school, of the managers or governors thereof, the school premises are such as to make it impracticable to assemble them for that purpose.
(2) Subject to the provisions of this section, religious instruction shall be given in every county school and in every voluntary school. . . .

26. Special provisions as to religious education in county schools
Subject as hereinafter provided, the collective worship required by subsection (1) of the last foregoing section shall not, in any county school, be distinctive of any particular religious denomination, and the religious instruction given to any pupils in attendance at a county school in conformity with the requirements of subsection (2) of the said section shall be given in accordance with an agreed syllabus adopted for the school or for those pupils and shall not include any catechism or formulary which is distinctive of any particular religious denomination . . .

27. Special provisions as to religious education in controlled schools
(1) Where the parents of any pupils in attendance at a controlled school request that they may receive religious instruction in accordance with the provisions of the trust deed relating to the school, or where provision for that purpose is not made by such a deed in accordance with the practice observed in the school before it became a controlled school, the foundation managers or foundation governors shall, unless they are satisfied that owing to special circumstances it would be unreasonable so to do, make arrangements for securing that such religious instruction is given to those pupils at the school during not more than two periods in each week.
(6) Subject to any arrangements made under subsection (1) of this section, the religious instruction given to the pupils in attendance at a controlled school shall be given in accordance with an agreed syllabus adopted for the school or for those pupils.

28. Special provisions as to religious education in aided schools and in special agreement schools
(1) The religious instruction given to the pupils in attendance at an aided school or at a special agreement school shall be under the control of the managers or governors of the school and shall be in accordance with any provisions of the trust deed relating to the school, or, where provision for that purpose is not made by such a deed, in accordance with the practice observed in the school before it became a voluntary school . . .

NOTES

1. See E. Taylor and J. B. Saunders, *The Law of Education* (8th edn., 1976) (see index) and G. R. Barrell, *Teachers and the Law* (5th edn., 1978) Chap 12. The Education Act provisions on religion distinguish between county and voluntary schools. *County* schools are state schools established and maintained by local education authorities (Education Act 1944 s. 9(1)). *Voluntary* schools are schools that have been established privately but that have been voluntarily brought within the state system and as a result are, to varying degrees, maintained by local education authorities and subject to their control (ibid, s. 9(2)). Most of the latter are denominational. There are three categories of voluntary schools: controlled, aided and special agreement schools. Sections 27 and 28 distinguish between religious instruction (but not the collective act of worship) in (1) controlled and (2) aided and special agreement schools, with schools within the latter two categories having the greater freedom in deciding the kind of instruction they provide.

2. *Collective worship.* In county schools, the collective act of worship must not be 'distinctive of any particular religious denomination' (s. 26). In voluntary schools, it may be denominational. It is evident from a recent survey that the traditional act of worship is no longer held in many schools. 'The hymn singing, the joining together in saying the Lord's Prayer, the reading from the Bible have been replaced by folk songs accompanied by pop groups, dramatic happenings and readings from a wide range of sources' (*Religious Education*, Report of a survey conducted by the Assistant Masters Association in 1975). The survey also showed that Jehovah's Witnesses commonly exercised the right of parents under s. 25(4) of the Act to withdraw their children from worship (and instruction) and that the 'number of schools which reported withdrawal of pupils of non-Christian faiths was small' (ibid). Of the 922 county and voluntary schools included in the survey, 'in a little more than one-half of them the pupils cannot assemble in one hall on the school site; and of those where this is possible, only in about one-fifth do the pupils meet daily for a corporate act of worship'. (ibid). In 1976, 'a Sheffield parent and a devout Christian, successfully forced a primary school attended by his five year old daughter . . . to restore morning assemblies after threatening to take the matter to the courts' (*Daily Telegraph*, 9 December 1976). What legal remedy might the parent have obtained?

3. *Religious instruction.* The 'agreed syllabus' referred to in ss. 26–8 is drawn up by a conference convened by the local education authority consisting of representatives of (i) such religious and teachers associations as, in the opinion of the authority, ought, having regard to the circumstances of the area, to be represented; (ii) the Church of England; and (iii) the authority (s. 29 and Sch. 5). Such conferences were held (although the Roman Catholic church did not participate) (Taylor and Saunders, *The Law of Education* (8th edn., 1976) p. 46) and syllabuses adopted. In fact, such syllabuses had commonly existed before the Second World War. They are amended from time to time to keep abreast of changes in attitudes and population. The 'agreed syllabus' (like the collective act of worship) must not be 'distinctive of any particular religious denomination'. The 'law officers of the Crown have decided that the ten commandments, the Lord's Prayer, and the Apostle's Creed are not distinctive and their use is not a violation' of the Act: Barrell, *Teachers and the Law* (5th edn. 1978) p. 246. On the difficulty of providing a satisfactory non-denominational form of religious instruction in a multi-cultural society, see Gates, in Cole (ed), *World Faiths in Education* (1978), Appendix. The survey referred to in the preceding note showed that 'in only 47% of the schools included in this analysis did every pupil have at least one period of RE on his timetable' and that the record of voluntary aided schools was better than that of voluntary controlled and county schools. The law 'was being broken by a large number of schools' and 'schools generally attached little significance' to the 'agreed syllabus'.

4. In 1977, a teacher who was the head of religious studies in a comprehensive school in Hertfordshire was dismissed when he refused to give an undertaking to teach the story of the creation in Genesis as 'myths and legends' which did not conflict with evolutionary theories, as the 'agreed syllabus' required. He lost his claim for unfair dismissal before an industrial tribunal (*Sunday Telegraph*, 25 March 1978).

5. The Education Act provisions on religion in schools are in striking contrast with the law in the United States where the saying of prayers (*Engel v Vitale* 370 US 431 (1962)) and the reading of verses from the bible (*Abingdon School District v Schempp* 374 US 203 (1963)) at the beginning of the school day in state (but not private) schools is an 'establishment of religion' contrary to the First Amendment. Religious instruction classes in state schools during school hours, whether given by state-employed teachers or by teachers provided by religious denominations and allowed a 'right of entry' (cf. s. 26, proviso, Education Act), are likewise unconstitutional (*McCollum v Board of Education* 333 US 203 (1948)).

(ii) Other forms of assistance

Apart from the assistance given in schools, the law aids religion in many other ways. The Sunday Observance Act 1780, as amended, prohibits public entertainments and amusements on Sundays for which an admission charge (as opposed to a charge for a programme or carparking) is made. Its rigours have been reduced somewhat by the Sunday Entertainments Act 1932 (museums, picture galleries, zoological gardens, etc may open) and, more recently, the Sunday Theatre Act 1972 and the Sunday Cinema Act 1972 which permit the opening of theatres and cinemas subject to certain limitations. In 1976, seven people were convicted under the Sunday Observance Act 1780. The Home Office consolidated circular to the police on crime states that it is assumed that the police will take the view that prosecutions under the Act can best be brought by private persons rather than the police: 952 HC Debs written answers 21 June 1978 col 204.

The Shops Act 1950, section 47, requires that shops be closed on Sundays other than for the sale of some items and with certain other exceptions (holiday areas, shopkeepers who observe the Jewish Sabbath). The Crathorne Committee Report (1964) recommended the substantial relaxation of Sunday observance laws, but it has yet to be generally (i.e. beyond theatres and cinemas) implemented.

Religious institutions are exempt from most forms of taxation: see Robilliard, [1978] P L 379, 384. Account is taken of the increased diversity of religions in the United Kingdom by the Matrimonial Causes Act 1973, section 47, by which Parliament changed the policy of the law so that matrimonial relief now is available to a party to a polygamous marriage. Places of religious worship are protected by the criminal law from 'riotous, violent or indecent behaviour' (Ecclesiastical Courts Jurisdiction Act 1860, section 2, interpreted recently in *Abrahams v Cavey*, above, p. 159). It is also an offence to use force to prevent a Minister from celebrating divine service (Offences against the Person Act 1861, section 36). It is doubtful whether a Roman Catholic priest is privileged in the law of evidence in respect of what is said to him in the confessional: Cross, *Evidence* (5th edn, 1979) p. 295 In the Irish Case of *Schlegel v Corcoran and Gross* [1942] IR 19, H Ct Ireland, it was held that consent to the assignment of a lease was not 'unreasonably withheld' by a Roman Catholic widow who refused her consent to the assignment to a Jewish dentist of a tenancy of rooms used for a dental practice in the house which she owned and in which she lived. There is no comparable English case interpreting the same 'consent not to be unreasonably withheld' provision in Landlord and Tenant Act 1927, s. 19(2). Cf. the Race Relations Act 1976, s. 24, below, p. 349. When a parliamentary election is held on a Saturday, provision is made (Representation of the People Act 1949, Sch. 2, Rule 39(1)(b)) for the registration of the votes of Jews unable to vote themselves for religious reasons.

Arrangements exist to hear appeals by members of the regular Armed Forces whose claim for discharge on grounds of conscientious objection has been rejected by the Service authorities. Such appeals go to the Advisory Committee on Conscientious Objectors, an independent, non-statutory body established in 1970 (see 807 HC Deb 2 December 1970 col 423) whose members are appointed by the Lord Chancellor. The Committee, which hears argument in public, has advised acceptance of 8 out of 32 appeals. Its advice is normally followed. For the most recent successful appeal (by an army captain who objected to the British military presence in Northern Ireland), see *The Guardian*, 16 May 1979. Although neither the BBC nor commercial broadcasting are legally obliged to broadcast religious programmes, there is a strong tradition that they should.

On freedom of religion in prisons, see Rules 10–16, Prison Rules, S.I. 1964 No 388 and *A 5947/72* 5 DRECom HR 8 (1976).

4 Religion and the criminal law

R v Senior [1899] 1 QB 283, Court for Crown Cases Reserved

The defendant was a member of a Christian religious sect called the 'Peculiar People'. Following its beliefs, he refused to allow his child, aged 9 months, to be treated by a doctor. The child died and the defendant was convicted of manslaughter for having caused the death by an unlawful act—'wilful neglect'—of a child in his custody contrary to the Prevention of Cruelty to Children Act 1894, section 1. The defendant was the father of 12 children, of whom 7 had died. More than one would appear to have died because of the defendant's religious beliefs. The following extract concerns solely the question whether these beliefs could provide a defence to the charge.

Lord Russell of Killowen CJ: . . . Mr Sutton contended that because the prisoner was proved to be an affectionate parent, and was willing to do all things for the benefit of his child, except the one thing which was necessary in the present case, he ought not to be found guilty of the offence of manslaughter, on the ground that he abstained from providing medical aid for his child in consequence of his peculiar views in the matter; but we cannot shut our eyes to the danger which might arise if we were to accede to that argument, for where is the line to be drawn? In the present case the prisoner is shown to have had an objection to the use of medicine; but other cases might arise, such, for instance, as the case of a child with a broken thigh, where a surgical operation was necessary, which had to be performed with the aid of an anæsthetic; could the father refuse to allow the anæsthetic to be administered? Or take the case of a child that was in danger of suffocation, so that the operation of tracheotomy was necessary in order to save its life, and an anæsthetic was required to be administered. *Conviction affirmed.*

NOTES

1. Before the Suicide Act 1961 (which abolished the offence), a person who refused medical treatment for himself for religious or other reasons with the result that he died was guilty of suicide. A person who aids, abets, counsels or procures another to commit suicide is still guilty of the offence of complicity in suicide (Suicide Act 1961, s. 2).
2. In *R v John* [1974] 1 WLR 624, CA, the Court of Appeal held that a motorist's religious beliefs cannot constitute a 'reasonable excuse' for his failure to provide a specimen of blood contrary to the Road Traffic Act

1972, s. 9(3). The appellant was a Mesmerist and believed that he was possessed of certain faith healing powers derived from the presence in his blood of certain divinely given gifts. The Court followed *R v Lennard* [1973] 1 WLR 483, 487, CA in which it was held that 'no excuse can be adjudged a reasonable one unless the person from whom the specimen is required is physically or mentally unable to provide it or the provision of the specimen would entail a substantial risk to his health'.

3. In 1976, a Moslem Ugandan Asian was fined £20 by Burnham Magistrates for stopping illegally on the hard shoulder of the M 4. He had been found there beside his car at sunset praying as his religion required (*Daily Telegraph*, 7 September 1976).

4. Religious belief is a statutory defence for a Sikh motor-cyclist. It is a principle of his religion that a Sikh wear a turban in public. The wearing of a crash helmet with or without a turban is a breach of this principle. After a series of cases (see e.g. *R v Aylesbury Crown Court, ex parte Chahal* [1976] RTR 489 DC) in which Sikhs were convicted (one more than 30 times) of riding motor-cycles with turbans and without crash-helmets contrary to the Motor Cycle (Wearing of Helmets) Regulations 1973, S.I. 1973 No. 180, the Motor-Cycle Crash-Helmets (Religious Exemption) Act 1976 provided an exemption for 'any follower of the Sikh religion while he is wearing a turban' (s.1). In 1977, Robert Relf was convicted under the Regulations of riding a motor-cycle without a crash helmet because his religion forbad him from wearing any headgear at all: *The Times* 16 September 1977.

5. The Abortion Act 1967, s. 4, provides:

'**4.**—(1) Subject to subsection (2) of this section, no person shall be under any duty, whether by contract or by any statutory or other legal requirement, to participate in any treatment authorised by this Act to which he has a conscientious objection:
   Provided that in any legal proceedings the burden of proof of conscientious objection shall rest on the person claiming to rely on it.
   (2) Nothing in subsection (1) of this section shall affect any duty to participate in treatment which is necessary to save the life or to prevent grave permanent injury to the physical or mental health of a pregnant woman.
   (3) In any proceedings before a court in Scotland, a statement on oath by any person to the effect that he has a conscientious objection to participating in any treatment authorised by this Act shall be sufficient evidence for the purpose of discharging the burden of proof imposed upon him by subsection (1) of this section.'

S. 4(1) offers a defence against criminal liability for a doctor, nurse, etc., who is unable to carry out an abortion for reasons of conscience. Cf. the limitation in s. 4(2) with the summing up by Macnaughten J in *R v Bourne* [1939] 1 KB 687:

'. . . there are people who, from what are said to be religious reasons, object to the operation being performed under any circumstances. That is not the law either. On the contrary, a person who holds such an opinion ought not to be an obstetrical surgeon, for if a case arose where the life of the woman could be saved by performing the operation and the doctor refused to perform it because of his religious opinions and the woman died, he would be in grave peril of being brought before this Court on a charge of manslaughter by negligence. He would have no better defence than a person who, again for some religious reason, refused to call in a doctor to attend his sick child, where a doctor could have been called in and the life of the child could have been saved.'

6. *R v Blaue* [1975] 1 WLR 1411, CA, concerned the religious beliefs of the victim. The question was whether a Jehovah's Witness who had been stabbed by the defendant and who refused a blood transfusion that would have saved her life had broken the chain of causation by her action so that the defendant was not guilty of her manslaughter. The Court of Appeal held that she had not:

'It has long been the policy of the law that those who use violence on other people must take their victims as they find them. This in our judgment means the whole man, not just the physical man. It does not lie in the mouth of the assailant to say that his victim's religious beliefs which inhibited him from accepting certain kinds of treatment were unreasonable. The question for decision is what caused her death. The answer is the stab wound.'

7. See also the Slaughterhouses Act 1974, s. 36(3), and the Slaughter of Poultry Act 1967, s. 1(2), which exempt from the provisions of those Acts the slaughtering of animals and birds by the methods used by Jews and Moslems in the preparation of their food provided that unnecessary suffering is not inflicted.

5 Religion and employment

Saggers v British Railways Board [1977] 1 WLR 1090, [1977] ICR 809, [1977] IRLR 266, Employment Appeal Tribunal

The appellant, a Jehovah's Witness, was dismissed by the defendants for refusing to join a trade union as required by a closed shop agreement. He claimed compensation for unfair dismissal on the basis that his dismissal was contrary to the Trade Union and Labour Relations Act 1974, Schedule 1, para 6(5), as amended, which permitted an employee to refuse to join a trade union despite a closed shop agreement if he 'genuinely objects on grounds of religious belief'. The appellant, who had earlier been a trade unionist and a Jehovah's Witness, agreed that the beliefs of the Jehovah's Witnesses did not prohibit membership and that some Jehovah's Witnesses were union members. But he maintained that the religious convictions that he now held prevented him from being a trade unionist. He appealed against an industrial tribunal's decision rejecting his claim.

Arnold J: . . .'The language which is used [in the Act] is this: "the employee genuinely objects on grounds of religious belief". The objection which has to be taken into consideration quite simply must be the objection of the employee. Then one has to consider upon what that objection is grounded; that is, religious belief. The word "belief", first of all, seems to us to suggest that which is believed by the person whose belief is under consideration; and for that reason it seems to us that the word more naturally describes the content of intellectual acceptance by the person under consideration than an established body of creed or dogma appertaining to himself as well as a number of other persons. In almost every case, no doubt, the two are identical. In many cases it will not be easily credible that a faithful adherent to a particular organisation has developed a body of belief which can truly and accurately be described as religious and which differs from that generally accepted within that body. But it seems to us that if, perhaps in the exceptional case, the tribunal, having considered the evidence of what the body generally believes, and having considered the evidence of what the employee claims to believe, is convinced that in spite of differences between the two the employee's claim is truly and genuinely justified as being that which the tribunal is convinced that he does really and truly believe, then there does not seem to us to be any conceptual impossibility about accepting that that is indeed his religious belief. But, of course, it cannot be sufficiently stressed that these are practical matters to be decided by practical men. A very strong pointer, no doubt, to the question what his religious belief really and truly extends to, will in almost every case be assisted with insight by establishing what is the body of belief commonly held by the sect or denomination to which he belongs.'
Appeal allowed.

NOTES

1. The 'religious belief' exception is now in the Employment Protection (Consolidation) Act 1978, ss.23(6) (action against a non-member by an employer short of dismissal) and 58(3) (dismissal). The wording has not been changed.

2. In *Cave v Cave* [1976] IRLR 400, an industrial tribunal held that it was not necessary for an employee who relied on the 'religious belief' exception, and did so on the basis of the beliefs of the religion to which he belonged, to produce *written rules* to which those beliefs have been reduced showing that they proscribed union membership. On the meaning of 'religious beliefs', the tribunal stated:

'Any attempt to frame a comprehensive definition is more than likely to meet with failure. There will, no doubt, be those cases which are clearly outside the exemption. The self-confessed atheist must fail however deeply felt his conviction against trade unionism. We hazard the opinion that a man will likewise fail if he professes adherence to a purported religion, one or more of the tenets of which are so repugnant to all right thinking people that in truth is to be regarded as wholly anti-social. . . .

But we do not regard Christadelphianism as practised by the father to be tainted in any way. . . . There is a clear recognition of and subjection to superhuman power—in the case of the Christadelphians; recognition of the one God of Christian faith and recognition of Christ and subjection to his commands.'

In *Goodbody v British Railways Board* [1977] IRLR 84, an industrial tribunal stated obiter that a 'religious belief' did not require that 'the holder should be a practising member of a religious community or body.' The tribunal also sought to distinguish 'a religious belief from a political or social belief or some other belief derived from a private or personal ethic other than a religion.'

3. The European Commission of Human Rights has admitted for consideration of their merits two applications (*Young and James v UK*, 9 DREComHR 126 (1978) and *Webster v UK*, 12 ibid. 168 (1978)) brought by former British Rail employees dismissed for not joining a trade union as required by a closed shop agreement, their claims to religious exemption being rejected. The applications rely upon Article 9, ECHR, above, p. 19.

Ahmad v Inner London Education Authority [1978] QB 36, [1977] 3 WLR 396, [1978] 1 All ER 574, Court of Appeal

The appellant, a devout Moslem, was employed as a full-time schoolteacher by the ILEA. From 1968 to 1974, he taught at a school that was too far away from a mosque for it to be necessary for him in accordance with his religion to attend one on Fridays for prayer. Upon being transferred by the ILEA to a school only 20 minutes away from a mosque, he went there for prayers on Fridays as his religion required. This meant that he missed 45 minutes of teaching time, during which his teaching had to be done by someone else. The school's work was to that extent disrupted and his colleagues objected. The ILEA informed the appellant that if he continued to go to the mosque, he would have to give up his full-time post for a part-time one at a lower salary. The appellant thereupon resigned and applied to an industrial tribunal for compensation and for reinstatement on the ground that the ILEA's conduct had forced him to resign and amounted to unfair dismissal contrary to the Trade Union and Labour Relations Act 1974. The tribunal held against him on the ground that the employer had not acted unreasonably so that the dismissal was not unfair. The Employment Appeal Tribunal rejected his appeal. The appellant appealed further to the Court of Appeal. He relied upon section 30 of the Education Act 1944, which reads:

'Subject as hereinafter provided, no person shall be disqualified by reason of his religious opinions, or of his attending or omitting to attend religious worship, from being a teacher in a county school or in any voluntary school, or from being otherwise employed for the purposes of such a school; and no teacher in any such school shall be required to give religious instruction or receive any less emolument or be deprived of, or disqualified for, any promotion or other advantage by reason of the fact that he does or does not give religious instruction or by reason of his religious opinions or of his attending or omitting to attend religious worship: Provided that, save in so far as they require that a teacher shall not receive any less emolument or be deprived of, or disqualified for, any promotion or other advantage by reason of the fact that he gives religious instruction or by reason of his religious opinions or of his attending religious worship, the provisions of this section shall not apply with respect to a teacher in an aided school or with respect to a reserved teacher in any controlled school or special agreement school'.

Lord Denning MR: . . . On the appeal, Mr Ahmad relied much on section 30 of the Education Act 1944. . . . If the words were read literally without qualification, they would entitle Mr Ahmad to take time off every Friday afternoon for his prayers without loss of pay. I cannot think this was ever intended. The school time-table was well known to Mr Ahmad when he applied for the teaching post. It was for the usual teaching hours from Monday to Friday, inclusive. If he wished to have every Friday afternoon off for his prayers, *either* he ought not to have applied for this post: *or* he ought to have made it clear at the outset and entered into a 4½-day engagement only. . . .

I think that section 30 can be applied to the situation perfectly well by reading it as subject to the qualification 'if the school time-table so permits.' . . . It has been so interpreted by the great majority of Muslim teachers in our schools. They do not take time off for their prayers. . . . The industrial tribunal said:. . . none of the other education authorities has ever received such a request from Muslim staff and the problem would seem to be unique to the applicant, Mr Ahmad.' . . .

During the argument Scarman LJ drew attention to article 9 of the European Convention on Human Rights. . . .

The convention is not part of our English law, but . . . we will always have regard to it. We will do our best to see that our decisions are in conformity with it. But it is drawn in such vague terms that it can be used for all sorts of unreasonable claims and provoke all sorts of litigation. As so often happens with high-sounding principles, they have to be brought down to earth. They have to be applied in a work-a-day world. I venture to suggest that it would do the Muslim community no good—or any other minority group no good—if they were to be given preferential treatment over the great majority of the people. If it should happen that, in the name of religious freedom, they were given special privileges or advantages, it would provoke discontent, and even resentment among those with whom they work. As, indeed, it has done in this very case. And so the cause of racial integration would suffer. So, whilst upholding religious freedom to the full, I would suggest that it should be applied with caution, especially having regard to the setting in which it is sought. Applied to our educational system, I think that Mr Ahmad's right to 'manifest his religion in practice and observance' must be subject to the rights of the education authorities under the contract and to the interests of the children whom he is paid to teach. I see nothing in the European Convention to give Mr. Ahmad any right to manifest his religion on Friday afternoons in derogation of his contract of employment: and certainly not on full pay. . . .

I would dismiss the appeal.

Scarman LJ: The true construction of s. 30 is at the heart of this case. . .The reasons for its 30 years of immunity from judicial interpretation are not hard to see. First, and foremost, local education authorities, like the ILEA in this case, have treated it as no more than of negative intent—forbidding discrimination on the ground of religion in the selection and employment of teachers, but not obliging them to ensure that religious minorities are represented amongst their teachers. The ILEA, we have been told, have sought to comply with the section by not asking questions, the theory being that, if you do not know a man's religion, you cannot discriminate against him on that ground. Secondly, there were until recently no substantial religious groupings in our country which fell outside the broad categories of Christian and Jew. So long as there was no discrimination between them, no problem was likely to arise. The five-day school week, of course, takes care of the Sabbath and of Sunday as days of special religious observance. But with the advent of new religious groups in our society section 30 assumes a new importance. . . .

When the section was enacted, the negative approach to its interpretation was, no doubt, sufficient. But society has changed since 1944: so also has the legal background. Religions, such as Islam and Buddhism, have substantial followings among our people. Room has to be found for teachers and pupils of the new religions in the educational system, if discrimination is to be avoided. This calls not for a policy of the blind eye but for one of understanding. The system must be made sufficiently flexible to accommodate their beliefs and their observances: otherwise, they will suffer discrimination—a consequence contrary to the spirit of section 30, whatever the letter of that law. The change in legal background is no less momentous. Since 1944 the United Kingdom has accepted international obligations designed to protect human rights and freedoms, and has enacted a series of statutes designed for the same purpose in certain critical areas of our society. These major statutes include the Trade Union and Labour Relations Act 1974, the Employment Protection Act 1975, the Sex Discrimination Act 1975, and the race relations legislation.

They were enacted after the United Kingdom had ratified the European Convention on Human Rights . . . and in the light of our obligations under the Charter of the United Nations. Today, therefore, we have to construe and apply section 30 not against the background of the law and society of 1944 but in a multi-racial society which has accepted international obligations and enacted statutes designed to eliminate discrimination on grounds of race, religion, colour or sex. Further, it is no longer possible to argue that because the international treaty obligations of the United Kingdom do not become law unless enacted by Parliament our courts pay no regard to our international obligations. They pay very serious regard to them: in particular, they will interpret statutory language and apply common law principles, wherever possible, so as to reach a conclusion consistent with our international obligations. . . .

With these general considerations in mind, I conclude that the present case, properly considered, begins but does not end with the law of contract. It ends with a very difficult problem—the application to the particular circumstances of this appellant of the new law associated with the protection of the individual's human rights and fundamental freedoms. . . .

The ILEA submits that because of its context, coming as it does as a final saving for the position of teachers at the end of a set of sections dealing with religious education in schools, the section is to be read as limited to attending, or omitting to attend worship in school. . . .

Although I see the force of the submission, I reject it; because fundamentally a narrow construction of the section is in conflict with the developments in our society to which I have already referred—developments which are protected by the statutes to which I have also referred. A narrow construction of the section would mean that a Muslim, who took his religious duty seriously, could never accept employment as a full-time teacher, but must be content with the lesser emoluments of part-time service. In modern British society, with its elaborate statutory protection of the individual from discrimination arising from race, colour, religion or sex, and against the background of the European Convention, this is unacceptable, inconsistent with the policy of modern statute law, and almost certainly a breach of our international obligations. Unless, therefore, the language of section 30 forces one to adopt the narrow construction, I would think it wrong to do so. But it does not: the section, linguistically speaking, can be construed broadly or narrowly. No doubt, Parliament in 1944 never addressed its mind to the problem of this case. But, if the section lends itself, as successful human rights or constitutional legislation must lend itself, to judicial interpretation in accordance with the spirit of the age, there is nothing in this point, save for the comment that Parliament by refusing to be too specific was wiser than some of us have subsequently realised. The choice of construction, while it must be exercised judicially, is ours: for the reasons which I have attempted to formulate, the decision must be in favour of the broad construction.

Construed broadly and as part of the teacher's contract for full-time service, the section means that the teacher is not to receive less emoluments by reason only that during school hours he attends religious worship. It is immaterial whether he does so in the school or elsewhere; but the right to go to church, chapel, temple or mosque whether it be inside or outside the school, which the section confers on the teacher, has to be read into his full-time contract. In the context of such a contract the right is to be exercised in such a way as not to conflict with the duty of full-time service. . . .

Nor do I think there is any substance in the point that a broad construction of section 30 imposes an unfair burden upon the teacher's colleagues. . . . If, however, my view of section 30 is correct, all that is necessary is that the authority should make its administrative arrangements on the basis of that view. It may mean employing a few more teachers either part-time or full-time: but, when that cost is compared with the heavy expenditure already committed to the cause of non-discrimination in our society, expense would not in this context appear to be a sound reason for requiring a narrow meaning to be given to the words of the statute. The question, therefore, as to whether Mr Ahmad broke his contract ultimately depends upon an examination of the particular circumstances of his case. . . . I therefore would allow the appeal. . .

Orr LJ delivered a judgment concurring with **Lord Denning MR.**
Appeal dismissed.

NOTES

1. Would it have made any difference if the ECHR were incorporated into English law by a Bill of Rights? Would the 'protection of the rights and freedoms of others' limitation in Article 9(2) apply?

2. British government contracts (unlike Federal government contracts in the United States) do not require that the firm awarded the contract not follow an employment policy that discriminates on religious grounds. See C. Turpin, *Government Contracts* (1972) pp. 257–8.

6 Religious holy days

Case 130/75: Prais v EC Council [1976] ECR 1589, [1976] 2 CMLR 708, European Court of Justice

The plaintiff, a British national, applied for a job in the European Communities as a translator. By a letter of 23 April 1975 she was told that the written examination would be on 16 May 1975. By a letter of 25 April 1975, the plaintiff informed the Council that she was unable to attend on 16 May because she was Jewish and that day was a Jewish holy day. The application form had no place for an applicant's religion and the plaintiff had not otherwise informed the Council of her religion. By a letter of 5 May, the Council replied that the plaintiff could not be given an alternative date for the examination for security and administrative reasons. In her application to the European Court of Justice, the plaintiff sought the annulment of the decisions taken against her and damages.

JUDGMENT OF THE COURT.

The plaintiff claims that Article 27 of the Staff Regulations ['Officials shall be selected without reference to race, creed or sex'.] is to be interpreted in such a manner that the defendant should so arrange the dates of tests for competitions to enter its service as to enable every candidate to take part in the tests, whatever his religious circumstances. Alternatively the right of freedom of religion guaranteed by the European Convention [Article 9, above, p. 19] so requires. . . .
The defendant does not . . . seek to suggest that the right of freedom of religion as embodied in the European Convention does not form part of the fundamental rights recognized in Community law, but says that neither the Staff Regulations nor the European Convention are to be understood as according to the plaintiff the rights she claims.
The defendant submits that such an obligation would force it to set up an elaborate administrative machinery. Article 27 does not limit its application to any particular creeds by enumerating them, and it would be necessary to ascertain the details of all religions practised in any Member State in order to avoid fixing for a test a date or a time which might offend against the tenets of any such religion and make it impossible for a candidate of that religious persuasion to take part in the test. . . .
When the competition [for posts] is on the basis of tests, the principle of equality necessitates that the tests shall be on the same conditions for all candidates, and in the case of written tests the practical difficulties of comparison require that the written tests for all candidates should be the same.
It is therefore of great importance that the date of the written tests should be the same for all candidates.
The interest of participants not to have a date fixed for the test which is unsuitable must be balanced against this necessity.
If a candidate informs the appointing authority that religious reasons make certain dates impossible for him the appointing authority should take this into account in fixing the date for written tests, and endeavour to avoid such dates.

On the other hand if the candidate does not inform the appointing authority in good time of his difficulties, the appointing authority would be justified in refusing to afford an alternative date, particularly if there are other candidates who have been convoked for the test.

If it is desirable that an appointing authority informs itself in a general way of dates which might be unsuitable for religious reasons, and seeks to avoid fixing such dates for tests, nevertheless, for the reasons indicated above, neither the Staff Regulations nor the fundamental rights already referred to can be considered as imposing on the appointing authority a duty to avoid a conflict with a religious requirement of which the authority has not been informed.

In so far as the defendant, if informed of the difficulty in good time, would have been obliged to take reasonable steps to avoid fixing for a test a date which would make it impossible for a person of a particular religious persuasion to undergo the test, it can be said that the defendant in the present case was not informed of the unsuitability of certain days until the date for the test had been fixed, and the defendant was in its discretion entitled to refuse to fix a different date when the other candidates had already been convoked.

Application dismissed

NOTE

In his opinion in the case, the Advocate General (Mr J-P Warner) summarised British practice in regard to examinations:

'It seems to be the invariable practice of professional and academic bodies in the United Kingdom to make, when requested, alternative arrangements for observant Jewish candidates whose examinations fall on Jewish holy days. The letter from the Civil Service Commission shows that its practice is quite different. Under the heading of "Criteria observed when setting examination dates" it states:
"Known factors which could affect particular groups of candidates would be taken into account as far as is possible when constructing the programme. For example, the Board of Directors of British Jews have for many years provided the Commission with a list of dates on which Jewish Holy days are given . . . The Commission expects all candidates to make arrangements to attend the examination on the date(s) set.
(ii) An examination is not deferred, or the date altered, to suit the needs of individual candidates.
(iii) Special separate sittings are not arranged for individuals who cannot attend on the examination dates.'

Ostreicher v Secretary of State for the Environment [1978] 3 All ER 82, [1978] 1 WLR 810, Court of Appeal

The applicant, a devout Jewess, lodged an objection through her surveyor, Mr L, to a compulsory purchase order made by the second respondent, a local authority, which applied to houses which she owned. By a letter of 5 February 1976, Mr L was informed that the inquiry would be held on 21 April 1976. This was one of 11 annual Jewish festival days on which the applicant was forbidden to work or to employ anyone to work for her. On 1 April 1976, Mr L wrote to the first respondent stating that the applicant was unable to attend the hearing for religious reasons.

He did not mention the question of representation. In the letter, Mr L indicated the reasons for the applicant's objection to the order and asked for a special hearing at which they could be put orally in respect of one of the houses. On 7 April, the first respondent rejected this request and suggested that the applicant could be represented at the inquiry. The inquiry was held on the scheduled day and the order confirmed. By notice of motion, the applicant applied under the Housing Act 1957, Schedule 4, para. 2, for the order to be quashed for non-compliance with the rules of natural justice in not giving her an opportunity of being heard by the inspector who held the inquiry. The applicant appealed to the Court of Appeal against an order dismissing her application.

Lord Denning MR: It is one of the elementary principles of natural justice, no matter whether it is in a judicial proceeding or an administrative inquiry, that everything should be done fairly: and that any party or objector should be given a fair opportunity of being heard. . . . Sometimes a refusal of an adjournment is unfair, but quite often it is fair. It depends on the circumstances of each particular case. . . . There is a distinction between an administrative inquiry and judicial proceedings before a court. An administrative inquiry has to be arranged long beforehand. There are many objectors to consider as well as the proponents of the plan. It is a serious matter to put all the arrangements aside on the application of one objector out of many. The proper way to deal with it, if called on to do so, is to continue with the inquiry and hear all the representatives present; and then, if one objector is unavoidably absent, to hear his objections on a later day when he can be there. There is ample power in the rules for the inspector to allow adjournments as and when reasonably required.

. . . it seems to me that the men at the department acted perfectly reasonably in what they did. First, they acted reasonably in arranging the date of 21st April, the Wednesday after Easter Monday. . . . I cannot think that even in Hackney [with its high Jewish population] it would be wrong for the Secretary of State to give that date as a suitable date for the inquiry. Indeed, no objection was ever taken to it by anyone until two or three months later when this letter of 1st April 1976 was written on behalf of Mr and Mrs Ostreicher. In that letter the surveyors do not say that they could not attend themselves or that anyone else could not attend on behalf of Mr and Mrs Ostreicher to look after their interests. Moreover that letter only refers to one house, no 16. . . . The Secretary of State's representative wrote back quite reasonably. He said: 'Should your clients deem it necessary they are open of course to arrange to be represented at the inquiry in their absence.' . . . There was no reply to that letter. If Mr and Mrs Ostreicher or their representative thought that there ought to be a postponement or an adjournment, so far as their houses were concerned, they could have written back and said so. . . .

Second, the inspector acted reasonably in going on with the inquiry as he did. No representative turned up on behalf of Mr and Mrs Ostreicher. It seems to me that the inspector could well have understood from what had happened that they were content to leave the position as it was on the papers. . . . I see no want of natural justice whatever in what the inspector did either at the inquiry and later on in making his report.

. . . I would dismiss the appeal accordingly.

Shaw LJ concurred. **Waller LJ** delivered a concurring judgment.

Appeal dismissed.

NOTE

At first instance, Sir Douglas Frank QC, sitting as a deputy High Court judge, had rejected an argument based upon the freedom of religion guarantee in Article 9, ECHR on the ground that it was 'of little assistance because it does not apply and moreover it is in vague terms' [1978] 1 All ER 591. He also referred to the dictum in *Prais v EC Council*, above, that the administration must be given notice in good time of an objection to a proposed date.

7 Religion and the law of trusts and succession

Re Lysaght [1966] Ch 191 [1965] 3 WLR 391, [1965] 2 All ER 888, Buckley J

By her will, the testatrix established a trust for scholarships tenable at the Royal College of Surgeons. To qualify, a student had to be 'of the male sex and a British born subject and not of the Jewish or Roman Catholic faith'. Buckley J rejected the College's submission that the religious discrimination clause was void for uncertainty. He then considered in the following extract a submission by another beneficiary under the will that the trust as a whole was contrary to public policy.

Buckley J: . . . I accept that racial and religious discrimination is nowadays widely regarded as

deplorable in many respects and I am aware that there is a Bill dealing with racial relations at present under consideration by Parliament, but I think that it is going much too far to say that the endowment of a charity, the beneficiaries of which are to be drawn from a particular faith or are to exclude adherents to a particular faith, is contrary to public policy. The testatrix's desire to exclude persons of the Jewish faith or of the Roman Catholic faith from those eligible for the studentship in the present case appears to me to be unamiable, and I would accept Mr Clauson's suggestion that it is undesirable, but it is not, I think, contrary to public policy. [Buckley J then, after holding that it was an essential part of the testatrix's intention that the College should be the trustee and noting that the College felt itself unable to be such if it discriminated on religious grounds, ordered by way of scheme that the trust should be administered by the College with the offending words omitted.]
Declaration accordingly.

Blathwayt v Baron Cawley [1976] AC 397 [1975] 3 WLR 684, [1975] 3 All ER 625, House of Lords

One question in this case was whether a forfeiture clause in a trust established by will by which a beneficiary forfeited his interest if he 'be or become a Roman Catholic' was invalid for reasons of public policy. The following extract concerns this question only.

Lord Wilberforce: . . . Finally, as to public policy . . . it was said that the law of England was now set against discrimination on a number of grounds including religious grounds, and appeal was made to the Race Relations Act 1968 which does not refer to religion and to the European Convention of Human Rights of 1950 which refers to freedom of religion and to enjoyment of that freedom and other freedoms without discrimination on ground of religion. My Lords, I do not doubt that conceptions of public policy should move with the times and that widely accepted treaties and statutes may point the direction in which such conceptions, as applied by the courts, ought to move. It may well be that conditions such as this are, or at least are becoming inconsistent with standards now widely accepted. But acceptance of this does not persuade me that we are justified, particularly in relation to a will which came into effect as long ago as 1936 and which has twice been the subject of judicial consideration, in introducing for the first time a rule of law which would go far beyond the mere avoidance of discrimination on religious grounds. To do so would bring about a substantial reduction of another freedom, firmly rooted in our law, namely that of testamentary disposition. Discrimination is not the same thing as choice: it operates over a larger and less personal area, and neither by express provision nor by implication has private selection yet become a matter of public policy.
    Lord Cross of Chelsea: . . . Turning to the question of public policy, it is true that it is widely thought nowadays that it is wrong for a government to treat some of its citizens less favourably than others because of differences in their religious beliefs; but it does not follow from that that it is against public policy for an adherent of one religion to distinguish in disposing of his property between adherents of his faith and those of another. So to hold would amount to saying that though it is in order for a man to have a mild preference for one religion as opposed to another it is disreputable for him to be convinced of the importance of holding true religious beliefs and of the fact that his religion beliefs are the true ones.
Lord Simon, **Lord Edmund-Davies** and **Lord Fraser** delivered speeches to the same effect.

NOTES

1. On *Re Lysaght*, see (1965) 29 Conv. 407; (1966) 82 LQR 10.
2. Contrast the refusal of the courts in these cases to find private religious discrimination to be contrary to public policy with the Race Relations Act 1976 which prohibits private racial discrimination on grounds of colour in charitable trusts. See below, p. 393.
3. Trusts for the advancement of religion are valid whatever the religion benefited. See *Bowman v Secular Society*, above, p. 345, and *Bourne v Keane*, above, p. 346. Trusts for the advancement of religion are charitable. *Income Tax Special Purposes Comrs v Pemsel* [1891] AC 531 at 583, HL. This is probably true of all religions, although the cases are as yet limited to

Christianity and the Jewish religion. See M. Chesterman, *Charities, Trusts and Social Welfare* (1979) p. 158. To be charitable (and hence exempt from most forms of taxation) a trust must be for the public benefit. A trust for a Roman Catholic order of strictly cloistered and contemplative nuns is therefore not charitable: *Gilmour v Coats* [1949] AC 426, HL.

8 Religion and immigration

Home Office Policy on Religion and Immigration 424 HC Deb 5 July 1946 Cols 2580–2

Mr Ede (Home Secretary)
I am not prepared to apply religious or political tests to people who desire to come into this country unless it can be established that they desire to come here to carry on subversive propaganda as defined by the Acts concerned with seditious practices. . . .

I desire that the ancient record of this country as a place of free speech, where the flow of ideas from all parts of the world is welcome, may be maintained; and while I will not guarantee that some of the people I admit may not be charlatans, may not . . . even be false prophets on occasion, I desire to impose no censorship other than that which the law entitles me to impose against subversive propaganda on any person who desires to come to this country to meet people of his own persuasion. I am confident of this, that as far as this particular movement is concerned, there are some people in this country who gain spiritual sustenance from it. . . . Therefore I desire to live and let live in this particular matter.

NOTES

1. The 'particular movement' to which the Home Secretary referred was Moral Re-Armament, or the Oxford Group Movement, founded by Dr Buchman, an American evangelist. The statement was made following criticism in Parliament of Mr Ede's decision to admit into the UK a number of aliens who were members of the Movement and who intended to further its cause here. The persons admitted had committed no crime under English law. The criticism was based mainly on the fact that certain leading members of the Group had been Nazi sympathisers.
2. It would seem that the 1946 statement still represents Home Office policy. The Home Secretary's discretionary power to exclude aliens and other non-'patrials' from the United Kingdom is now based upon Immigration Act 1971, s. 3 and is exercised in accordance with Immigration Rules made by him under that section. The Rules provide for the admission of ministers of religion, missionaries and members of religious orders coming to work as such, including those engaged in teaching. Permission to enter in this category is not confined to the Christian religion; it may be extended to any faith provided it is clear that the person is coming solely to do work connected with the furtherance of his religious beliefs. On scientology, see below. On the special position under the Treaty of Rome of Common Market nationals who wish to enter the United Kingdom for employment, see *Van Duyn v Home Office*, below, n. **3.** In 1976, when rumour had it that a Danish film maker, Jens Thorsen, was planning to enter the United Kingdom to make a film portraying the sexual life of Christ, the Under Secretary of State for the Home Department pointed out that were Thorsen, a Common Market national, actually to seek entry into the United Kingdom the question would arise whether he could be excluded under the Treaty of Rome on grounds of 'public policy' (918 HC Deb 26 October 1976 col 239–248).

3. In 1968, the Minister of Health (Mr Robinson) announced (769 HC Deb written answer, 25 July 1968 col 189) that the Government had decided that scientology was 'socially harmful' (although not illegal) and that foreign nationals seeking entry to work or study at scientology establishments in the UK would be refused admission. The Minister described scientology as 'a pseudo-philosophical cult'; he did not refer to it as a religion. It was described by Sir John Foster in his *Enquiry into the Practice and Effects of Scientology*, 1971–72 HC 52, Chap. 9, as a form of psychological medicine or therapy. See also the less kindly assessment in *Hubbard v Vosper*, above, p. 322.

In *Schmidt v Secretary of State for Home Affairs* [1969] 2 Ch 149, CA, the Court of Appeal held that the plaintiffs, who had been refused an extension of their permits to enter the United Kingdom to study at the Hubbard College of Scientology at East Grinstead in accordance with the new policy, had no cause of action in English law; the Home Secretary had acted properly within his power to exclude aliens under the Aliens Order 1953. In Case 41/74: *Van Duyn v Home Office* [1975] Ch 358, ECJ, a Dutch secretary was refused entry into the United Kingdom to work at the same College. The European Court of Justice ruled that the refusal was not contrary to Article 48 of the Treaty of Rome (by which nationals of European Communities countries have, subject to certain limitations, freedom of movement for employment purposes within the Communities; it could be justified as being 'on grounds of public policy' (Article 48(3)). An application to Strasbourg by the Church of Scientology under Article 9, ECHR also failed because it does not protect companies (such as the Church): *Church of X v UK*, 12 YBECHR 306 (1969).

The 1968 policy statement on scientology still applies: 954 HC Deb written answer 26 July 1978 col 727–8. It was criticised by Sir John Foster, *loc. cit.* above, para 3, on the ground that 'the mere fact that someone is a Scientologist is . . . no reason for excluding him . . . when there is nothing in our law to prevent those of his fellows who are citizens of this country from practising Scientology here.' Scientology is the only organisation whose members or followers are controlled in this way. In 1979, a German Baroness was refused entry into the UK when immigration authorities decided that her visit was 'in association with and to promote the interests of the Church of Scientology' (*Daily Telegraph*, 18 September 1979). Mr R. Hubbard, the leader of the Church, is not permitted to enter.

9 Religion and parents' rights

A child's religion and his religious education are matters for the parents to decide until he reaches the age of discretion. The mother has an equal voice with the father in the matter (Guardianship Act 1973, section 1(1)). In the case of an illegitimate child, the matter is one just for the mother (Children Act 1975, section 85(7)). If a dispute concerning the religious upbringing of a child should reach the courts, it must be decided in accordance with the welfare of the child (Guardianship of Minors Act 1971, s. 1). See further P. M. Bromley, *Family Law* (5th edn., 1976) pp. 332–6.

Watt v Kesteven County Council [1955] 1 QB 408 [1955] 1 All ER 473, [1955] 2 WLR 499, Court of Appeal

The defendant Council did not provide a state grammar school for boys. Instead they arranged for boys to go to Stamford School, a public school within its area, at the Council's expense. The plaintiff, a Roman Catholic, did not want his children to go to Stamford School. He sent them instead to a Roman Catholic boarding school outside of the Council's area and asked the Council to pay the fees (which were less than those for Stamford School). The Council agreed to pay only a part of the fees. The plaintiff sought a declaration that the defendants were under a statutory duty to pay the whole of the fees, an order of mandamus directing them to carry out their duty, and the repayment of the fees he had paid.

Denning LJ: . . . I desire to say at the outset that the question in this case does not depend in the least on the religious views of the parent. The question would be the same if a member of the Church of England living in Stamford wished, for some reason or other, to send his boys away to a boarding school in some other part of the country. He might wish to send them there because it was his old school . . . I can find nothing in the Act which compels the county council to pay the fees at any school which the father chooses. . . . They must make schools available for all the pupils in their area. But they can fulfil this duty, not only by maintaining schools themselves, but also by making arrangements with certain other schools. . . .

At the other schools with which they make arrangements, they must provide free places or pay the fees in full. . . . If a father wishes his child to go to yet another school of his own choice, with which the county council have no arrangements, then he cannot claim as of right that the county council shall pay the fees.

[Lord Denning then considered the effect of section 76 Education Act 1944[1]:]

. . . It is obvious that that section cannot stand by itself. It only applies in the exercise of some other power or duty contained in the Act. In this case it was said to apply in the exercise of section 8[2]. It was said that, when there is no maintained or grant-aided school, the county council have a duty under section 8 to make available an independent school and to pay the fees in full: and that, in exercising that duty, they must under section 76 have regard to the general principle that pupils are to be educated in accordance with the wishes of their parents. . . .

I think that that argument is mistaken. It assumes that the duty of the county council under section 8 is to make available for the pupils any of the independent schools over the length and breadth of the country. That is not correct. Their duty is only to make available the particular independent school with which they have made arrangements. . . .

Even if it was the duty of the county council to make available all the independent schools in the country, nevertheless I do not think that section 76 means that every parent has a right to choose any of them he likes. Section 76 does not say that pupils must in all cases be educated in accordance with the wishes of their parents. It only lays down a general principle to which the county council must have regard. This leaves it open to the county council to have regard to other things as well, and also to make exceptions to the general principle if it thinks fit to do so. . . .

This being so . . . there is no need to consider the question, which was much debated before us, whether a breach of section 76 gives rise to a cause of action for damages. . . . I do not think an action lies in this case. It is plain to me that the duty under section 8 (to make schools available) can only be enforced by the Minister under section 99 of the Act and not by action at law. That being so, a breach of section 76 in the exercise of section 8 can also be enforced by the Minister and not by action at law.

In my opinion, therefore, the appeal should be dismissed . . .

Birkett LJ concurred and **Parker LJ** delivered a concurring judgment.

Appeal dismissed.

---

1. Ed. s.76 reads: 'In the exercise and performance of all powers and duties conferred and imposed on them by this Act the Minister and local education authorities shall have regard to the general principle that, so far as is compatible with the provision of efficient instruction and training and the avoidance of unreasonable public expenditure, pupils are to be educated in accordance with the wishes of their parents'.

2. Ed. s.8(1) reads: 'It shall be the duty of every local education authority to secure that there shall be available for their area sufficient schools . . . (b) for providing secondary education . . .'

NOTES

1. Although, as Denning LJ indicated, the decision did not turn upon the religious views of the parents, the Court of Appeal's interpretation of the 'freedom of parental choice' provision in s. 76 is significant for parents who seek to exercise such choice on grounds of religion. The conclusion to be drawn from the case (that s. 76 is of little help) is confirmed by *Cumings v Birkenhead Corpn.* [1972] Ch 12, CA. There the local authority found themselves with more than enough children to fill the places at their non-Roman Catholic schools. In this situation, they sent a circular to parents of children moving from primary to secondary schools stating that all children who had attended Roman Catholic primary schools would be allocated to Roman Catholic secondary schools. Their parents were given no choice in the matter, although a procedure was established to consider exceptional cases. A declaration was sought unsuccessfully by Roman Catholic parents challenging the authority's action as illegal. The authority had not acted unreasonably or beyond their powers. As far as s. 76 was concerned, 'the wishes of the parents are only one thing. There are many other things to which the education authority may have regard and which may outweigh the wishes of the parents'. (per Lord Denning MR). The Court also held that where the allegation is that a local authority has acted unreasonably in the exercise of their powers under the Education Act or failed to exercise a duty thereunder, the remedy is not through the courts but by appeal to the Minister under the Act (ss. 68 and 69). The courts could intervene, however, where the allegation was that the authority had acted beyond their powers.

2. On parental rights to withdraw children from religious education in schools, see the Education Act s. 25, above, p. 363. Parents may also withdraw their children from school 'on any day exclusively set apart for religious observance by the religious body to which his parents belong' (s. 39(2)) (eg. Ascension Day (for members of the Church of England or Roman Catholics) or the Day of Atonement (for Jews)). And see *Marshall v Graham* [1907] 2 KB 112, DC.

3. Mixed sex schools have presented problems for Moslem parents. In 1972, a Moslem parent in Blackburn was convicted of failing to cause his daughter to receive efficient full-time education when he kept her away from a co-educational secondary school because he 'believed that, having regard to the tone of present-day society, she would lose her virtue and become unmarriageable': Barrell, *Teachers and the Law* (5th edn., 1978) p. 27, referring to a report in the *Daily Mail*, 3 November 1972. The parent was fined £5. Similarly, when Peterborough amalgamated two single sex schools in 1973 in the course of local government re-organisation, the parents of Moslem children who were allocated to a co-educational secondary school appealed unsuccessfully to the Minister on the ground their religion forbad mixed schooling. In the same year, a Moslem family in Bradford returned to Pakistan to avoid mixed schooling: *The Times*, 15 December 1973.

CHAPTER 9

Freedom from racial discrimination

1 Introduction

The Race Relations Act 1976 (the 1976 Act) is the third Act of Parliament on racial discrimination. It repeals the Race Relations Act 1968 and what remained of the Race Relations Act 1965. In much of its form and its content, the new Act follows the pattern of the Sex Discrimination Act 1975. Ultimately it is hoped to merge the two.

The common law had only incidentally and exceptionally offered protection against racial discrimination before Parliament acted. See, e.g., *Constantine v Imperial Hotels Ltd*, below, p. 379, and *Scala Ballroom Ltd v Ratcliffe* [1958] 3 All ER 220, CA (officials of Musicians' Union did not commit the tort of conspiracy by refusing to allow members to play in a ballroom with a colour bar to protect livelihood of its coloured members). In the words of Lord Simon in *Applin v Race Relations Board* [1975] AC 259, 286, HL:

> The common law before the making of the first Race Relations Act (1965) was that people could discriminate against others on the ground of colour, etc., to their hearts' content. This unbridled capacity to discriminate was the mischief and defect for which common law did not provide. The remedy Parliament resolved and appointed was to make certain acts of discrimination unlawful. The reason for the remedy must have been that discrimination was thought to be socially divisive (indeed, section 6 of the Act of 1965 [incitement to racial hatred] suggests, potentially subversive of public order) and derogatory to human dignity.

The arrival of immigrants from the West Indies and later India and Pakistan to take jobs in the 1950s and 1960s resulted in friction and discrimination. Racial incidents such as the Notting Hill riots in 1958 and the example of the Civil Rights Act 1964 in the US led Parliament, after much hesitation, to enact the Race Relations Act 1965. This made it illegal to discriminate in certain places of public resort (e.g. pubs and dance halls) and in the disposal of tenancies, and created the offence of incitement to racial hatred. Conciliation procedures operated by the Race Relations Board (RRB) and local conciliation committees were the key to enforcement of the Act, with recourse to the courts by the Attorney General available as a last resort. These modest provisions soon proved insufficient and were replaced or supplemented by those of the Race Relations Act 1968. This was enacted in the light of evidence (see the PEP Report, *Racial Discrimination in Britain* (1967)) that much discrimination existed in areas not covered by the law and that the 1965 Act enforcement procedures needed strengthening. The violent riots in Watts and elsewhere in the US in the mid-1960s also cast their shadow. The 1968 Act, which was influenced by the favourable assessment in the Street Report (H. Street, G. Howe and G. Bindman, *Report on Anti-Discrimination Legislation,* (1967)) of the effectiveness of US race legislation, extended the prohibition of discrimination to include goods, facilities and services generally, employment, housing and advertisements and modified the system of enforcement mainly by allowing the RRB to take cases to court instead of the Attorney General if conciliation failed. The Act also established the Community Relations Commission (CRC) to promote good race relations. The 1968 Act, in its turn, came to be seen as inadequate. The Government White Paper (*Racial Discrimination,* Cmnd. 6234) introducing the present 1976 Act contains the following passages justifying legislation on racial discrimination generally and suggesting the new direction it should take:

4. . . . The Government's proposals are based on a clear recognition of the proposition that the overwhelming majority of the coloured population[1] is here to stay, that a substantial and increasing proportion of that population belongs to this country, and that the time has come for a determined effort by Government, by industry and unions, and by ordinary men and women, to ensure fair and equal treatment for all our people, regardless of their race, colour, or national origins. Racial discrimination, and the remediable disadvantages experienced by sections of the community because of their colour or ethnic origins are not only morally unacceptable, not only individual injustices for which there must be remedies, but also a form of economic and social waste which we as a society cannot afford. . . .

23. Legislation is the essential pre-condition for an effective policy to combat the problems experienced by the coloured minority groups and to promote equality of opportunity and treatment. It is a necessary pre-condition for dealing with explicit discriminatory actions or accumulated disadvantages. Where unfair discrimination is involved, the necessity of a legal remedy is now generally accepted. To fail to provide a remedy against an injustice strikes at the rule of law. To abandon a whole group of people in society without legal redress against unfair discrimination is to leave them with no option but to find their own redress. It is no longer necessary to recite the immense damage, material as well as moral, which ensues when a minority loses faith in the capacity of social institutions to be impartial and fair. . . .

25. Legislation is capable of dealing not only with discriminatory acts but with patterns of discrimination, particularly with patterns which, because of the effects of past discrimination, may not any longer involve explicit acts of discrimination. Legislation, however, is not, and can never be, a sufficient condition for effective progress towards equality of opportunity. A wide range of administrative and voluntary measures are needed to give practical effect to the objectives of the law. But the legislative framework must be right. It must be comprehensive in its scope, and its enforcement provisions must not only be capable of providing redress for the victim of individual injustice but also of detecting and eliminating unfair discriminatory practices. . . .

31. It is not possible to provide a quantifiable measure of the practical impact of the 1968 Act. Generally, the law has had an important declaratory effect and has given support to those who do not wish to discriminate but who would otherwise feel compelled to do so by social pressure. It has also made crude, overt forms of racial discrimination much less common. Discriminatory advertisements and notices have virtually disappeared both from the press and from public advertisement boards. Discriminatory conditions have largely disappeared from the rules governing insurance and other financial matters, and they are being removed from tenancy agreements. It is less common for an employer to refuse to accept any coloured workers and there has been some movement of coloured workers into more desirable jobs. . . .

33. And yet, at the end of the decade, both statutory bodies have forcefully drawn attention to the inability of the legislation to deal with widespread patterns of discrimination, especially in employment and housing, a lack of confidence among minority groups in the effectiveness of the law, and a lack of credibility in the efficacy of the work of the Race Relations Board and the Community Relations Commission themselves. The continuing unequal status of Britain's racial minorities and the extent of the disadvantage from which they suffer provide ample evidence of the inadequacy of existing policies.'

---

1. Ed. The Office of Population Censuses and Surveys estimated that in mid-1977 there were 1,846,000 people of new Commonwealth and Pakistani ethnic origin resident in the UK (i.e. about 3.4 per cent of the population) of whom about 40 per cent had been born here (*The Guardian,* 31 August 1978).

Evidence of the 'continuing unequal status' and 'disadvantage' in employment and other areas had been produced in a series of PEP Reports: D. Smith, *Racial Disadvantage in Employment* (1974); N. McIntosh and D. Smith, *The Extent of Racial Discrimination* (1974); D. Smith and A. Whalley, *Racial Minorities and Public Housing* (1975), and D. Smith, *The Facts of Racial Disadvantage* (1976). The strike by Asian workers in the Mansfield Hosiery Mills in 1972, which revealed that skilled jobs were being reserved exclusively for whites (RRB Report 1972, p. 10), was also important.

The areas covered by the 1976 Act are essentially those covered in 1968 although there are a number of particular changes, including the extension of the law to cover contract workers (section 7), partnerships (section 10) and clubs (section 25). The principle that the law should not apply to 'personal and intimate relationships' is retained (Cmnd. 6234 p. 15). The definition of discrimination is widened to include discrimination on the ground of nationality (section 3) and, in accordance with the new strategy of attacking 'patterns of discrimination' (such as that in the Mansfield Hosiery Mills case) as well as particular 'discriminatory acts', *indirect* discrimination (section 1 (2)) and 'discriminatory practices' (section 28) are prohibited too. The Crown is liable under the Act (section 75).

As in 1968, discrimination is treated as a statutory tort. Apart from the offence of incitement to racial hatred and certain minor offences (e.g. that in the 1976 Act, s.29(5) below, p. 391), the remedies provided by the law remain civil, not criminal. In other respects the enforcement machinery in the 1976 Act differs markedly from that which predated it. The emphasis in the earlier legislation had been on enforcement by conciliation by the RRB following complaints by individuals of particular 'discriminatory acts'. Three major changes have been made. Firstly, conciliation has been largely abandoned; complaints may be taken straight to court instead. Secondly, the decision to take a case to court is in most cases in the hands of the individual complainant; the CRE is there simply to offer him assistance if he wants it. Thirdly, in keeping again with the realisation that underlying 'patterns of discrimination' need to be tackled as well as (and perhaps more than) individual cases of 'discriminatory acts', the CRE is given wide-ranging authority to conduct formal investigations on its own initiative. Armed with a new power to sub-poena evidence, the CRE may investigate 'discriminatory acts' or 'patterns of discrimination' and may issue non-discrimination notices that are binding in law. It is too early yet to say how effective these new procedures will be.

If a Bill of Rights incorporating the ECHR were enacted, the 1976 Act would continue to apply in parallel with the guarantee of freedom from 'degrading treatment' in Article 3, ECHR (which prohibits racial discrimination in immigration at least: *East African Asians* cases, 20 YBECHR 642 1977)) and the guarantees in Article 14, ECHR of Freedom from racial discrimination in the protection of the rights in the convention.

It is sometimes argued that law cannot be effective in an area such as race relations where feelings are high and attitudes are deep rooted. Consider after reading the materials in this Chapter whether the law of the last 15 years or so has changed conduct and might in the long term influence opinions.

On the law of racial discrimination generally, see A. Lester and G. Bindman, *Race and Law* (1972); I. A. MacDonald, *Race Relations—The New Law* (1977) and D. J. Walker and M. J. Redman, *Racial Discrimination* (1977). On the interpretation of race relations legislation, see J. K. Bentil [1973] PL 157.

The remainder of this Chapter deals with most aspects of the 1976 Act, but does not consider in detail the provisions of Part II of the Act on employment and related matters. Although discrimination in employment is of prime importance, it is best seen as an area of employment law and is fully treated in books on that subject (see e.g. B. Hepple and P. O'Higgins, *Employment Law* (3rd edn. 1979) Chap. 11, and B. Hepple, *Race, Jobs and the Law in Britain* (2nd edn. 1970)).

2 The meaning of discrimination

Race Relations Act 1976

1. Racial Discrimination
(1) A person discriminates against another in any circumstances relevant for the purposes of any provision of this Act if—
(*a*) on racial grounds he treats that other less favourably than he treats or would treat other persons; or
(*b*) he applies to that other a requirement or condition which he applies or would apply equally to persons not of the same racial group as that other but—
    (i) which is such that the proportion of persons of the same racial group as that other who can comply with it is considerably smaller than the proportion of persons not of that racial group who can comply with it; and
    (ii) which he cannot show to be justifiable irrespective of the colour, race, nationality or ethnic or national origins of the person to whom it is applied; and
    (iii) which is to the detriment of that other because he cannot comply with it.
(2) It is hereby declared that, for the purposes of this Act, segregating a person from other persons on racial grounds is treating him less favourably than they are treated.

2. Discrimination by way of victimisation
(1) A person ('the discriminator') discriminates against another person ('the person victimised') in any circumstances relevant for the purposes of any provision of this Act if he treats the person victimised less favourably than in those circumstances he treats or would treat other persons, and does so by reason that the person victimised has—
    (*a*) brought proceedings against the discriminator or any other person under this Act; or
    (*b*) given evidence or information in connection with proceedings brought by any person against the discriminator or any other person under this Act; or
    (*c*) otherwise done anything under or by reference to this Act in relation to the discriminator or any other person; or
    (*d*) alleged that the discriminator or any other person has committed an act which (whether or not the allegation so states) would amount to a contravention of this Act,
or by reason that the discriminator knows that the person victimised intends to do any of those things, or suspects that the person victimised has done, or intends to do, any of them.
(2) Subsection (1) does not apply to treatment of a person by reason of any allegation made by him if the allegation was false and not made in good faith.

NOTES

1. Discrimination in any of the three forms prohibited by ss. 1–2 (direct and indirect discrimination and victimisation) is only illegal if it occurs in one of the areas of conduct or activity covered by Part II (employment and related matters), Part III (education; goods, facilities or services; housing; clubs), or Part IV (advertisements) of the 1976 Act. As well as being unlawful to discriminate, it is illegal to instruct someone to discriminate (s. 30, below, p. 371n) or to 'induce or attempt to induce' a breach of Parts II or III of the Act (s. 31). A person who 'knowingly aids another person to do an act made unlawful by this Act shall be treated for the purposes of this Act as himself doing an unlawful act of the like description' (s. 33). Employers and principals are liable vicariously for the acts of their employees and agents (s. 32).

2. *Section 1 (1) (a): direct discrimination.* A single act of discrimination is illegal. S. 1(2) makes it clear that segregation (e.g. in public houses) is illegal. The exception for sleeping cabins on board ship in the 1968 Act has been repealed: see below, p. 379. On the meaning of 'racial grounds', see s. 3, below, p. 372.

3. *Section 1 (1) (b): indirect discrimination.* See G. Bindman, (1979) 129 NLJ 408 and L. Lustgarten [1978] PL 178. The 1976 Act makes indirect discrimination illegal for the first time. The Government White Paper (Cmnd. 6234, pp. 8, 13) explained the reason for this and gave examples:

'One important weakness in the existing legislation is the narrowness of the definition of unlawful discrimination upon which it is based . . . . [I]t is insufficient for the law to deal only with overt discrimination. It should also prohibit practices which are fair in a formal sense but discriminatory in their operation and effect. . . .

The new Bill . . . will, for example, cover the situation where an employer requires applicants to pass an educational test before obtaining employment if (a) it operates to disqualify coloured applicants at a substantially higher rate than white applicants and (b) it cannot be shown to be significantly related to job performance. The employer will be required to stop using such a test. . . . The provision will similarly apply to requirements concerning the clothing worn by employees (e.g. preventing the wearing of turbans or saris) or their minimum height, where such requirements cannot be shown to be justifiable.'

The concept was consciously imported from US law. In *Griggs v Duke Power Co* 401 US 424 (1971), the US Supreme Court used it in the employment context to rule against a requirement for certain jobs in a power station that the occupant have graduated from high school or have passed an intelligence test. The Court stated (p. 431):

'Congress has now provided that tests or criteria for employment or promotion may not provide equality of opportunity merely in the sense of the fabled offer of milk to the stork and the fox. . . . The Act proscribes not only overt discrimination but also practices that are fair in form, but discriminatory in operation. The touchstone is business necessity. If an employment practice which operates to exclude Negroes cannot be shown to be related to job performance, the practice is prohibited.'

Indirect discrimination was introduced into English law in the Sex Discrimination Act 1975 which contains in s.1 (1) (b) the same provision *mutatis mutandis* as the Race Relations Act 1976, s.1 (1) (b). The caselaw that has developed under the Sex Discrimination Act is helpful in interpreting the Race Relations Act. A 'requirement or condition' need not be formally contained in any rules. It is sufficient that it is 'the normal practice': *Steel v Union of Post Office Workers* [1978] 1 WLR 64, EAT. In *Price v Civil Service Commission* [1978] 1 WLR 1417, EAT, the applicant, who was in her 30's, complained that a requirement that a candidate for a post as an executive officer in the civil service should be 'at least 17½ and under 28' was indirect discrimination against women. She contended that the age bar of 28 was more disadvantageous to women than to men because the former tended to drop out of employment in the years leading up to it to have children. Applying the Sex Discrimination Act, s. 1 (1) (b), Kilner Brown J (for the Appeal Tribunal) said:

'In one sense it can be said that any female applicant can comply with the condition. She is not obliged to marry, or to have children, or to mind children; she may find somebody to look after them, and as a last resort she may put them into care. . . . Such a construction appears to us to be wholly out of sympathy with the spirit and intent of the Act. Further, it should be repeated that compliance with sub-paragraph (i) is only a preliminary step, which does not lead to a finding that an act is one of discrimination unless the person acting fails to show that it is justifiable. "Can" is defined (*The Shorter Oxford English Dictionary*, 3rd edn. (1944) p. 255) "To be able; to have the power or capacity." It is a word with many shades of meaning, and we are satisfied that it should not be too narrowly—nor too broadly—construed in its context in section 1 (1) (*b*) (i). It should not be said that a person "can" do something merely because it is theoretically possible for him to do so: it is necessary to see whether he can do so in practice. . . .

Knowledge and experience suggest that a considerable number of women between the mid-twenties and the mid-thirties are engaged in bearing children and in minding children, and that while many find it possible to take up employment many others, while desiring to do so, find it impossible, and that many of the latter as their children get older find that they can follow their wish and seek employment. This knowledge and experience is confirmed by some of the statistical evidence produced to the industrial tribunal. . . . This demonstrates clearly that the economic activity of women with at least one Advanced Level falls off markedly about the age of 23, reaching a bottom at about the age of 33 when it climbs gradually to a plateau at about 45. Basing ourselves on this and other evidence, we should have no hesitation in concluding that our own knowledge and experience is confirmed, and that it is safe to say that the condition is one which it is in practice harder for women to comply with than it is for men. . . . The difficulty is to quantify this in the terms of a "considerably smaller" result. We find that it would be unsafe for us to reach a conclusion without having had the benefit of hearing the statistician give evidence and be subjected to cross-examination upon the proper analysis and inferences to be drawn from the statistics.' [The case was remitted to the industrial tribunal and the claim was upheld].

Can social customs be taken into account in deciding what a person can do 'in practice'? In *Singh v Lyons Maid Ltd* [1975] IRLR 328, an industrial tribunal held that the dismissal of a Sikh for refusing to shave off his beard for work in an ice-cream factory was not unfair for the purpose of employment law. Would the claimant in that case have been able to claim indirect discrimination? Could an Englishman complain if a publican in Wales refused to serve anyone who did not speak Welsh? With whom would his 'racial group' be compared?

In *Meeks v National Union of Agricultural and Allied Workers* [1976] IRLR 198, Ind Trib, a female part-time typist complained that a lower hourly rate of pay for part-time, as opposed to full-time, typing was indirect discrimination under the Sex Discrimination Act. Although rejecting her claim on another ground, the industrial tribunal accepted her contention that the 'considerably smaller' criterion had been fulfilled. It did so on the basis of statistical evidence showing that 97 % of employed men were in *full-time* employment (and hence satisfied the requirement for the higher rate of pay) but that only 68 % of female employees were in such employment. Is statistical evidence conclusive if available and adequate? Is there a particular percentage required, or does it depend upon the facts of each case? What if there is no statistical evidence available?

The 'justification' defence in s. 1 (1)(b) (ii) was accepted in *Panesar v Nestlé Co Ltd* (1979) 129 NLJ 139, CA (justifiable under the Race Relations Act, s.1, for a chocolate factory to refuse to employ a bearded Sikh on grounds of hygiene). It was discussed in *Steel v Union of Post Office Workers* [1978] 1 WLR 64, EAT. In that case the Post Office's 'normal practice' by which a 'walk', or postal round; was allocated on a seniority basis was successfully challenged as indirect sex discrimination. Phillips J stated the correct approach to the defence as follows:

'First, the onus of proof lies upon the party asserting this proposition, in this case the Post Office. Secondly, it is a heavy onus in the sense that at the end of the day the industrial tribunal must be satisfied that the case is a genuine one where it can be said that the requirement or condition is necessary. Thirdly, in deciding whether the employer has discharged the onus the industrial tribunal should take into account all the circumstances, including the discrimi-natory effect of the requirement or condition if it is permitted to continue. Fourthly, it is necessary to weigh the need for the requirement or condition against that effect. Fifthly, it is right to distinguish between a requirement or condition which is necessary and one which is merely convenient, and for this purpose it is relevant to consider whether the employer can find some other and non-discriminatory method of achieving his object.'

In the *Meeks* case, an argument that a requirement was 'justifiable' because it was part of a collective agreement with a trade union was rejected. Could an Indian complain if a job as a nightclub 'bouncer' was reserved for persons over a certain height and weight?

The prohibition of indirect discrimination in s.1 (1) (b) is supplemented by that in s.28. This provides

'—(1) In this section "discriminatory practice" means the application of a requirement or condition which results in an act of discrimination which is unlawful by virtue of any provision of Part II or III taken with section 1(1)(*b*), or which would be likely to result in such an act of discrimination if the persons to whom it is applied included persons of any particular racial group as regards which there has been no occasion for applying it.

(2) A person acts in contravention of this section if and so long as—

(*a*) he applies a discriminatory practice; or

(*b*) he operates practices or other arrangements which in any circumstances would call for the application by him of a discriminatory practice.'

The purpose of s.28 is indicated in the Government White Paper (Cmnd. 6234, p. 13):

'It will also be unlawful to apply a requirement or condition which results or would be likely to result in an act of discrimination as defined above, irrespective of whether the requirement or condition is actually applied to a particular victim. . . . This will, for example, cover the situation where an employer operates recruiting arrangements which result in there being no coloured applicants for job vacancies and thus no act of discrimination against any individual victim.'

Section 28 is enforceable only by a non-discrimination notice issued by the CRE after a formal investigation, see below, p. 398. Thus in the *Barlavington Manor Children's Home* case, Formal Investigation report, April 1979, a private children's home which had made it known that it was not prepared to accept black children from local authorities so that no such children had been sent to it was found to have operated a discriminatory practice contrary to s.28 and a non-discrimination notice was issued.

A person may be found to have acted illegally under s.1 (1) (b) even though his intention is quite innocent. Damages or compensation may not be awarded against the discriminator, however, if there was no 'intention of treating the claimant unfavourably on racial grounds' (the 1976 Act, s. 57 (3), below, p. 402). A declaration or other civil remedy is available. For the meaning of 'racial group', see s.3, below, p. 371.

4. *Section 2: Victimisation.* The fear of victimisation and the absence of any protection from it was identified by the Race Relations Board as one of the reasons why minority groups had been reluctant to complain under the 1968 Act. (RRB Report 1973, p. 14). Section 2 covers victimisation by a third person as well as the person against whom proceedings have been brought, etc. It also protects persons who are not themselves victims of direct or indirect discrimination. For example, s.2 would protect the employee of an employment agency who notified the Race Relations Board of unlawful discrimination that had occurred within the agency under the 1968 Act and was dismissed for doing so (RRB Report 1973, p. 40). And see *Zarczynska v Levy*, below, p. 371.

5. *Reverse discrimination.* Sometimes called 'positive discrimination' or 'affirmative action', reverse discrimination means discrimination in favour of a racial group on the ground that it would be in the public interest to take steps to redress the balance of racial disadvantage from which members of the group have suffered. A protected quota of places in higher education would be an example. In the US, the Supreme Court has upheld affirmative action in an employment case (*United Steel Workers v Weber* 61 L Ed 2d 480 (1979)). But has ruled against a University admissions quota (*Regents of the University of California v Bakke* 438 US 265 (1978)). The Government White Paper (Cmnd. 6234, p.14) was against reverse discrimination and the definition of 'discrimination' in s.1 makes it illegal. If, for example, preference is given to a black applicant for a job because of his colour, then applicants of a different colour are given 'less favourable treatment' on racial grounds. The 1976 Act allows some exceptions. See ss. 35–8. Thus it is not unlawful to afford 'persons of a particular racial group access to facilities or services to meet the special needs of persons of that group in regard to their education, training or welfare, or any ancillary benefit' (s.35) and special training schemes (public or private) to boost the number of members of a racial group in an occupation in which their number is disproportionately low are lawful (ss. 37–8).

Zarczynska v Levy [1979] 1 WLR 125, [1979] 1 All ER 819, Employment Appeal Tribunal

Kilner Brown J (for the appeal tribunal): . . .
On 8 July 1977, the complainant, Miss Zarczynska, obtained employment as a part-time barmaid at a public house where the employer, Mr Peter Levy, was the licensee. Mr Levy and his wife did not want coloured people as customers and they instructed the barman and the barmaids that they were not to serve them. On 25 August the complainant was told that she must not serve some black customers; she insisted that this was not a reasonable or lawful instruction and her employment came to an abrupt end. Whether she resigned or was dismissed is immaterial because, if it was an order in breach of the law, the conduct of the employer would be in breach of the contract of employment entitling her to walk out. Miss Zarczynska reported the matter and the Commission for Racial Equality has taken up the case. The Commission has begun proceedings against the employer in the county court under section 30 of the Race Relations Act 1976[2]. If they succeed, they will obtain a declaration that he has given instructions to his employees which are in contravention of the Race Relations Act 1976 and which discriminate against customers on racial grounds.
But what good is this to the unfortunate and righteous complainant? She has lost her job because she tried to uphold the law. She made a complaint to an industrial tribunal in London North alleging that she was unfairly dismissed and victimised under the Race Relations Act 1976. . . . The industrial tribunal correctly came to the decision that as she had not been employed for sufficient length of time she could not bring what might be called the 'ordinary' proceedings alleging unfair dismissal. The only available complaint had therefore to be brought within the provisions of the Race Relations Act 1976. The industrial tribunal came to the conclusion that the facts fell squarely within the provisions of section 30 and that the scope of that section coupled with sections 54 [allowing individual complaints in employment cases] and 63 [allowing only the CRE to bring proceedings enforcing section 30] was exclusive of all other remedies in any other context and that no remedy was available to the complainant . . .
We . . . consider it most unjust that the complainant should be deprived of any opportunity to obtain compensation for losing her job because she tried to uphold the law which forbids discrimination on racial grounds. It is not easy for us to discover any error of law. But can nothing be done? We turn first to the Court of Appeal decision in *Race Relations Board v Applin* [1973] QB 815 [below, p. 385]. It is not exactly in point but there are passages . . . which afford us help and guidance even though they may be strictly obiter dicta. Thus, Lord Denning MR dealt with the application of the words in section 1 (1) of the Race Relations Act 1968 which are very similar to the words used in the Act of 1976, viz: 'a person discriminates against another if on the grounds of colour . . . he treats that other . . . less favourably that he treats . . . other persons.' Taking the example of two white women coming into a public house with coloured men and who might be barred against entry by the innkeeper, Lord Denning MR concluded at 828, that the innkeeper would be discriminating

---

2. Section 30 reads:
    It is unlawful for a person—
    (*a*) who has authority over another person; or
    (*b*) in accordance with whose wishes that other person is accustomed to act,
to instruct him to do any act which is unlawful by virtue of Part II or III, or procure or attempt to procure the doing by him of any such act.

against the women on the ground of colour. Stephenson LJ added at 831, that if it were necessary for the purposes of his judgment he would agree with and decide as Lord Denning MR that A can discriminate against B on the ground of C's colour, race or ethnic origin. Can it not be said in the instant case that in dismissing the one barmaid because she wanted to serve some coloured men, and not dismissing a barmaid who was prepared to apply the embargo, the employer treated the one less favourably than the other on racial grounds? We recognise that section 1 (1) of the Act of 1976 has to be read in conjunction with the other provisions to which reference has been made and that a broad approach to section 1 (1) may be prevented or delimited by the effect of other provisions. If we could say, however, that such other provisions are explanatory of or provide remedies for instances of breach of the general principle, then the general principle would not be restricted. This might involve reading into section 1 the purposive intent of Parliament to make it a section which overrides subsequent sections which might otherwise be deemed to limit the provisions of that section. If this is not done the strict interpretation of the relevant sections taken as a whole may well create an absurd —or unjust situation which Parliament would not have intended if they had contemplated its possibility.
    . . . We are of opinion here that if Parliament had had pre-knowledge of this unfortunate complainant's predicament they would have made clear that the great civilised principle upon which the Act was based was one which overrode all apparent limitations expressed in other sections which had the effect of denying justice to someone who was victimised.
    [The appeal] is allowed upon the basis that the industrial tribunal erred in finding that there was no contravention of Parts I and II of the Act [ss. 1–16]. Further, there should be read into section 54 words to the effect that the said jurisdiction shall be exercised in addition to the jurisdiction provided for in section 63 of the Act.
    We unanimously conclude that the decision of the industrial tribunal should be set aside and declare that there is jurisdiction to hear and determine the complaint in so far as the complainant claims compensation for victimisation.
Appeal allowed.

NOTES

Was the plaintiff in this case discriminated against contrary to s. 1 or victimisation contrary to s. 2? Or both? Why was the case such a difficult one for the tribunal? Was the plaintiff really trying to enforce s. 30? Would a publican who refused to serve a white customer because he was with a black girlfriend be acting contrary to s. 1? s. 2?

Race Relations Act 1976

3. Meaning of 'racial grounds', 'racial group' etc.
(1) In this Act, unless the context otherwise requires –
'racial grounds' means any of the following grounds, namely colour, race, nationality or ethnic or national origins;
'racial group' means a group of persons defined by reference to colour, race, nationality or ethnic or national origins, and references to a person's racial group refer to any racial group into which he falls.
(2) The fact that a racial group comprises two or more distinct racial groups does not prevent it from constituting a particular racial group for the purposes of this Act.
(3) In this Act –
(a) references to discrimination refer to any discrimination falling within section 1 or 2; and
(b) references to racial discrimination refer to any discrimination falling within section 1, and related expressions shall be construed accordingly.
(4) A comparison of the case of a person of a particular racial group with that of a person not of that group under section 1(1) must be such that the relevant circumstances in the one case are the same, or not materially different, in the other.

NOTES

1. See L. Lustgarten, (1979) 28 ICLQ 221.
2. The term 'national origins' as it appeared in the 1968 Act was examined

by the House of Lords in *Ealing London Borough Council v Race Relations Board* [1972] AC 342, HL. See J. Hucker (1975) 24 ICLQ 284. In that case the appellants had refused to put a person of Polish nationality – a Mr Zesko – on their council housing waiting list because he was not, as their rules required, a British subject. The House of Lords held that discrimination based upon nationality was not discrimination on the ground of 'national origins' and since discrimination on the ground of 'nationality' was not prohibited, the 1968 Act had not been infringed. Lord Simon said (pp. 362–3):

'The Acts of 1965 and 1968 do not provide a complete code against discrimination or socially divisive propaganda. The Acts do not deal at all with discrimination on the grounds of religion or political tenet. It is no offence under the Acts to stir up class hatred. It is, therefore, unquestionably with a limited sort of socially disruptive conduct that the Acts are concerned, and it is, on any reading, within a limited sphere that Parliament put its ameliorative measures into action.

. . . Moreover, "racial" is not a term of art, either legal or, I surmise, scientific. I apprehend that anthropologists would dispute how far the word "race" is biologically at all relevant to the species amusingly called homo sapiens.

This ["colour, race or ethnic or national origins"] is rubbery and elusive language— understandably when the draftsman is dealing with so unprecise a concept as "race" in its popular sense and endeavouring to leave no loophole for evasion.

. . . "Origin," in its ordinary sense, signifies a source, someone or something from which someone or something else has descended. "Nation" and "national," in their popular in contrast to their legal sense, are also vague terms. They do not necessarily imply statehood. For example, there were many submerged nations in the former Hapsburg Empire. Scotland is not a nation in the eye of international law, but Scotsmen constitute a nation by reason of those most powerful elements in the creation of national spirit—tradition, folk memory, a sentiment of community. . . .

. . . To discriminate against Englishmen, Scots or Welsh, as such, would, in my opinion, be to discriminate against them on the ground of their national origins. To have discriminated against Mr Zesko on the ground of his Polish descent would have been to have discriminated against him on the ground of his national origins.

There is another situation which the phrase is apt to cover, namely, where a person of foreign nationality by birth has acquired British nationality or where a person of British nationality by birth is descended from someone of foreign nationality. There are those who are apt to say "The leopard cannot change his spots; once an Erehwonian always an Erehwonian." To discriminate against a British subject on the grounds of his foreign nationality by birth or alien lineage would be to discriminate against him on the ground of his national origins. To have discriminated against Mr Zesko on the ground of Russian nationality by birth (if such was his case, which is not clear) would have been to have discriminated against him on the ground of his national origins. . . .'

Lord Cross said (pp. 365–6):

'There is no definition of "national origins" in the Act and one must interpret the phrase as best one can. To me it suggests a connection subsisting at the time of birth between an individual and one or more groups of people who can be described as a "nation"—whether or not they also constitute a sovereign state. The connection will normally arise because the parents or one of the parents of the individual in question are or is identified by descent with the nation in question, but it may also sometimes arise because the parents have made their home among the people in question. Suppose, for example, that a man of purely French descent marries a woman of purely German descent and that the couple have made their home in England for many years before the birth of the child in question. It could, I think, fairly be said that the child had three "national origins": French through his father, German through his mother and English not because he happened to have been born here but because his parents had made their home here. Of course, in most cases a man has only a single "national origin" which coincides with his nationality at birth in the legal sense and again in most cases his nationality remains unchanged throughout his life. But "national origins" and "nationality" in the legal sense are two quite different conceptions and they may well not coincide or continue to coincide. . . . It is not difficult to see why the legislature in enacting the Race Relations Act 1965 used this new phrase "national origins" and not the word "nationality" which had a well-established meaning in law. It was because "nationality" in the strict sense was quite irrelevant to the problem with which they were faced. Most of the people against whom discrimination was being practised or hatred stirred up were in fact British subjects. The reason why the words "ethnic or national origins" were added to the words "racial grounds" which alone appear in the long title was, I imagine, to prevent argument over the exact meaning of the word "race." For example, a publican who had no objection to West Indians might refuse to serve Pakistanis. He could hardly be said to be discriminating against them on grounds of colour and it might well be argued that Pakistanis do not constitute a single "race." On the other hand, it could hardly be argued that they did not all have the same "national origin."'

What emerges from these speeches is that the terms used in s. 3 are to be understood in their popular rather than their scientific meaning (insofar as there is an agreed scientific meaning for them: see A. Dickey, 1974 JR 282), and to be read as covering, under one head or another, members of all of those minority groups that might popularly be regarded as having a racial character. This approach is in tune with the statement made by the Home Secretary (Sir Frank Soskice) when the 1965 Bill was before Parliament (716 HC Deb 16 July 1965 cols 970–1):

'It is an objective which is of prime importance in the Bill that no grouping of citizens of whom one could, in ordinary English parlance, predicate that they have, or are thought to have, or are merely represented to have, some common features or characteristics or origins that, broadly speaking, one relates to the stem from which they proceed. . . . should be excluded.
　The word "colour" is one which ordinarily would be understood. . . .
　The word "race" is perhaps a little more ambiguous. The words "ethnic or national origin" are deliberately introduced into the Clause to make certain that no one is left out of the description "colour or race". We want to be certain that, because of some accident of language, some ambiguity of outline attaching to the words "colour or race", we do not fail to cover anybody who could possibly have fallen outside the ambit of these two words.
　I put it to the House that the word "ethnic" is not an unsuitable term. . . . stemming as I hope it would be thought to stem in this context, from the Greek word *ethnos*—people, a group—[it] would have the effect of removing any doubt as to whether a particular group fell outside the scope of the other words in the Clause.'

3. Discrimination on the ground of 'nationality' was added by the 1976 Act in the light of *Ealing London Borough Council v Race Relations Board.* The 1976 Act s. 78(1) provides that 'unless the context otherwise requires' " 'nationality' includes citizenship' ". This wording takes account of the two-tier system of nationality within the Commonwealth under the British Nationality Act 1948. Thus discrimination that turned upon the status of a person as a British subject (as in the *Ealing* case) or as a citizen of the UK and Colonies (or as the holder of the local citizenship of any Commonwealth country) would be discrimination on the ground of 'nationality'. Discrimination against aliens by legislation or with legislative authority in areas covered by the Act (e.g. immigrant work permits) is protected by the 1976 Act, s. 41 (which protects all acts done under statutory authority, etc.); other laws (e.g. those preventing an alien from owning a British ship or voting) are not within the Act because of their subject-matter.

4. Discrimination on religious or political grounds is not covered by the Act: see Lord Simon in the *Ealing* case, above. An attempt to include discrimination on religious grounds in the 1976 Act was unsuccessful, the Government arguing that a separate tailor-made bill would be necessary to deal with all of the issues peculiar to religion that would arise and that the Act's prohibition of indirect racial discrimination would (like that of direct discrimination) deal with a lot of cases of religious discrimination.

　The absence of discrimination on religious grounds has raised the question whether Jews are protected by the Act. In the debate on the 1965 Act, the Home Secretary had no doubt (711 HC Deb 3 May 1965 cols 932–3):

'It is certainly the intention of the Government that people of Jewish faith should be covered. The words have to be construed in law according to the ordinary canons of construction, as an ordinary person would read ordinary English language. I would have thought a person of Jewish faith, if not regarded as caught by the word "racial" would undoubtedly be caught by the word "ethnic", but if not caught by the word "ethnic" would certainly be caught by the scope of the word "national", as certainly having a national origin.'

Some members were sceptical, believing that 'the Jewish identity is essentially a religious one' (Mr N. St. John-Stevas, Standing Committee B, col 70, May 27 1965). In its First Report, the RRB sought clarification of the position (i.e. whether covered by the Act or not) of 'groups such as the Jews, the Sikhs, and the Gypsies, which may not be primarily ethnic or racial, but which may be so regarded by those who discriminate against them.' (RRB Report 1966–7, p. 13). Hepple (*Race, Jobs and the Law*, 2nd. edn., 1970, p. 37) suggests that in such a case one should look to the understanding and motive of the discriminator:

> . . . [T]he problem is not really one of definition but of proof . . . it is erroneous to lay down, in the abstract, whether discrimination against Jews or Sikhs is on racial grounds rather than for religious reasons. In each case, . . . the actual relationship of the parties must be examined to determine whether the discriminator believed his victim to be a member of some distinct race and for that reason discriminated against him.'

Cf. Lester and Bindman, *Race and the Law* (1972) p. 157. The RRB looked to the motive of the alleged discriminator in the following case (RRB Report 1970–1, p. 7):

> 'Two complaints dealt with in the field of private education concerned allegations that children had been refused admission to certain schools because of their Jewish ethnic origin. The Act does not deal with discrimination on religious grounds; and it was maintained by the schools complained against that to admit more than a certain proportion of children of the Jewish faith would affect the Christian character of their schools, and that the schools therefore operated Jewish quotas which varied from 25 to 50 per cent. Enquiries showed that one of the schools was established by its charter as an Anglican foundation. The Christian character of the other school was not so apparent, but enquiries showed that the parents of the children concerned had answered "Jewish" to questions on the school's application form which asked for their religious denomination. In both of these cases the Board concluded that the discrimination was religious and not ethnic.'

What if D were to discriminate against V in the belief that V was a French national and for that reason when V was in fact a UK citizen? Would that be direct discrimination? Can one rely on the understanding and motive of the discriminator in respect of *indirect* discrimination? Or is it necessary to decide to what 'racial group' V actually belongs?

As far as gypsies are concerned, the RRB stated in its second report that it had 'been advised that Gypsies should, in general, be regarded as being within the terms of the Race Relations Act' (RRB Report 1967–8, p. 8). In *Mills v Cooper* [1967] 2 QB 459, DC, Lord Parker CJ understood 'gypsy' in the Highways Act 1959 s. 127 (which makes it an offence for a gypsy to encamp, etc., on a highway) in the 'general colloquial' sense of 'a person leading a nomadic life with no, or no fixed, employment and with no fixed abode' and not as a person 'of the Romany race'. In Lord Parker's view, it was 'difficult to think that Parliament intended to subject a man to a penalty in the context of causing litter and obstruction on the highway merely by reason of his race'. He also noted that it would be 'too vague of ascertainment, and impossible to prove' that a person was 'of the Romany race'.

3 Education

Race Relations Act 1976

17. Discrimination by bodies in charge of educational establishments
It is unlawful, in relation to an educational establishment falling within column 1 of the following table [omitted], for a person indicated in relation to the establishment in column 2 (the 'responsible body') to discriminate against a person—
  (a) in the terms on which it offers to admit him to the establishment as a pupil; or
  (b) by refusing or deliberately omitting to accept an application for his admission to the establishment as a pupil; or
  (c) where he is a pupil of the establishment—
      (i) in the way it affords him access to any benefits, facilities or services, or by refusing or deliberately omitting to afford him access to them; or
      (ii) by excluding him from the establishment or subjecting him to any other detriment.

18. Other discrimination by local education authorities
(1) It is unlawful for a local education authority, in carrying out such of its functions under the Education Acts 1944 to 1975 as do not fall under section 17, to do any act which constitutes racial discrimination. . . .

NOTES

1. S.17 applies, by virtue of the Table attached to it, to all state and independent primary and secondary schools in England and Wales, including private schools for handicapped children and private community homes (education). It also applies to most institutions of higher education. Universities, polytechnics, colleges of education, colleges of further education and designated institutions (such as the College of Nursing and the Co-operative College) are within the section. Other non-designated institutions are controlled by s.20, below, p. 378, not s.17.
2. Although the 1968 Act did not contain any provision comparable to s.17 dealing just with discrimination in education, a number of cases arose under the equivalent provision to the 1976 Act s.20, below, p. 378, in respect of educational facilities. A case in which a private preparatory school was found by the RRB to have unlawfully refused to admit a child of Iranian origin (Case 6, RRB Report 1974, p. 36) would now come within s.17(1)(b). For the 'Jewish quota' case, see above, p. 375. The RRB also examined under the 1968 Act the London Borough of Ealing's dispersal policy for immigrant children. By this policy, Asian children were not admitted to local schools in Southall but 'bussed' to schools elsewhere within the Borough's jurisdiction. After obtaining the opinion of an expert assessor, the RRB reported on the policy as follows (RRB Report 1975–76, p. 6):

'30. In his report Professor Kogan explained that dispersal was introduced in Ealing in the mid-1960s. In 1976 nearly 3,000 Asian children of primary school age were sent by coach every day to other parts of the Borough. In the great majority of cases the dispersal was on educational grounds, but there was evidence which suggested that a number of these children were dispersed away from their neighbourhood schools even though their knowledge of the English language was perfectly adequate. The local authority argued that any such Asian children were dispersed because of cultural needs. The Board formed the opinion that such children were being treated less favourably than other children for no other reason than their ethnic origins. Attempts at conciliation failed and the Board determined to bring proceedings.'

After legal proceedings had been instituted against the Borough (see *Race Relations Board v London Borough of Ealing (No 2)* [1978] 1 WLR 112, CA), an out of court settlement was reached (CRE Report 1978, p. 101):

'The central feature of the settlement was that in future no child would be "bussed" except on the basis of educational need, and a special assessment procedure was introduced to enable the language needs of children entering the education system for the first time to be individually defined. Moreover, no additional children would be "bussed" after September 1979 and it was expected that new school building in the Southall area would enable "bussing" to be completely phased out by 1981.'

See also the dispersal case reported in RRB Report 1974, p.6. Pakistani pupils have been 'bussed' in Bradford since 1964 although the policy is to be phased out for pupils over the age of 9. What would have to be proved to establish that 'bussing' in these dispersal cases was direct or indirect discrimination? Note the dictum in *Cumings v Birkenhead Corpn.*, above, p.363, that the allocation of children to particular schools on the basis of the colour of their skin would be unlawful as an 'abuse of power' (quite apart from race relations legislation).

Another issue has been the testing and classificaton of school children as educationally subnormal and their placement in special schools. Following a complaint concerning Haringey, 'the Board noted that West Indian children in the borough concerned, and in a number of other local education authority areas, were over-represented in the group considered to be educationally sub-normal. The evidence suggested that this situation had come about because the intelligence tests in general use do not effectively distinguish the educationally sub-normal from those whose performance is at a similar level as a result of educational or cultural deprivation' (RRB Report 1970–71, p. 7). The RRB did not consider that there had been any unlawful discrimination contrary to the 1968 Act. Might there be *indirect* discrimination under the 1976 Act? Following the Haringey case, the Department of Education and Science decided to reconsider the question of classifying immigrant children with language and other cultural difficulties as educationally subnormal (RRB Report 1971–72, p. 8). In 1979, the CRE decided to conduct a formal investigation into referrals of pupils in Birmingham to the city's specialist education centres and into the suspension and exclusion of pupils from school (*The Guardian*, 26 July 1979).

In another complaint to the RRB it was alleged (but not proven) that a headmaster had discriminated in the protection of school children from assault by other children (Case 5, RRB Report 1972, p. 35). Would this be unlawful discrimination under any part of s.17?

3. Unlike s.17, ss.18 and 19 apply only to 'racial discrimination', which (see s.3(3) above, p. 372) excludes victimisation contrary to s.2. The allocation of local authority grants for higher education is subject to s.18. A three year residence condition for eligibility for such grants was considered by the RRB to work harshly against some immigrant pupils seeking further education but was not thought to be contrary to the 1968 Act (RRB Report 1969–70, p. 9). The CRE, which has stressed 'the extreme importance of education in our total work' (CRE Report 1978, p. 11), has taken up the question with the DES (ibid). Might such a condition be *indirect* discrimination?

4 Goods, facilities and services

Race Relations Act 1976

20. Discrimination in provision of goods, facilities or services
(1) It is unlawful for any person concerned with the provision (for payment or not) of goods, facilities or services to the public or a section of the public to discriminate against a person who seeks to obtain or use those goods, facilities or services—
    (*a*) by refusing or deliberately omitting to provide him with any of them; or
    (*b*) by refusing or deliberately omitting to provide him with goods, facilities or services of the like quality, in the like manner and on the like terms as are normal in the first-mentioned person's case in relation to other members of the public or (where the person so seeking belongs to a section of the public) to other members of that section.

(2) The following are examples of the facilities and services mentioned in subsection (1)—
    (*a*) access to and use of any place which members of the public are permitted to enter;
    (*b*) accommodation in a hotel, boarding house or other similar establishment;
    (*c*) facilities by way of banking or insurance or for grants, loans, credit or finance;
    (*d*) facilities for education;
    (*e*) facilities for entertainment, recreation or refreshment;
    (*f*) facilities for transport or travel;
    (*g*) the services of any profession or trade, or any local or other public authority.

NOTES

1. *Goods, facilities or services.* These terms are not defined in the Act. A. Lester and G. Bindman, *Race and Law* (1972) p. 260, suggest:

'They must be given their ordinary and natural meaning. "Goods" are any movable property, including merchandise or wares. "Facilities" include any opportunity for obtaining some benefit or for doing something. "Services" refer to any conduct tending to the welfare or advantage of other people, especially conduct which supplies their needs. Each of these expressions is deliberately vague and general; taken together, they cover a very wide range of human activity.'

Manufacturers, wholesalers and retailers are all subject to s.20. Thus a wholesaler who refused to supply a retailer (retailers being a 'section of the public') with goods on racial grounds would be in breach of the Act.
2. S.20(2) gives certain examples of 'facilities and services'. Places 'which members of the public are permitted to enter' include shops, banks, public houses, restaurants, public parks, dance halls, and theatres. This first example overlaps with the subsequent ones in that many of the places that come within it (e.g. public houses) provide a 'facility' (e.g. refreshment) listed in another. The place may be publicly or privately owned. There need be no legal right of entry; a licence to enter is sufficient. The test is whether the public or a section of it (e.g. persons over 18) are customarily or on a particular occasion (e.g. garden open to the public one day in the year) 'permitted to enter'. See further Lester and Bindman, *Race and Law*, (1972) pp. 261–2, and I. Brownlie, *The Law relating to Public Order*, (1968) pp 160–2. For one of the many statutes with similar wording referred to by Brownlie, see the Public Order Act 1936, s.9(1), above p. 151. Would the organisers of the meeting in *Thomas v Sawkins*, above, p. 64, have been entitled to exclude a black member of the public from the meeting because of his colour?
3. 'Hotel' in the phrase 'hotel, boarding house or other similar establishment' can be taken to have the meaning that it has in the Hotel Proprietors Act 1956, s.1(3):

'An establishment held out by the proprietor as offering food, drink and if so required sleeping accommodation, without special contract, to any traveller presenting himself who appears able and willing to pay a reasonable sum for the services and facilities provided and who is in a fit state to be received.'

This definition is also that of an inn at common law. An innkeeper is obliged at common law to receive allcomers without discrimination. Thus in the famous case of *Constantine v Imperial Hotels Ltd* [1944] KB 693, QBD, judgment was awarded against an innkeeper for refusing to accommodate a well known black West Indian cricketer (and later a member of the Race Relations Board) during the Second World War for fear of upsetting members of the US armed forces. The case would now fall within the 1976 Act, s.20 and the plaintiff would have to bring proceedings under the Act and not at common law (see the 1976 Act, s.53, below, p. 401). The wording 'boarding house or other similar establishment' includes bed and breakfast establishments and other establishments insofar as they offer *short-term* (see 'similar') residential accommodation for travellers. A holiday camp might qualify; it might also be said to offer facilities for 'recreation'. The longer term 'facilities' offered by private or residential hotels, 'bed-sits', and university halls probably fall within s.21, below, and not s.20. (But note that a *long-term* private children's home was treated by the CRE as being within s.20 in the *Barlavington Manor Children's Home* case, Formal Investigation report, April 1979.) But the examples listed in s.20(2) are not exhaustive and it could be that as far as accommodation is concerned there is some overlap between ss.20 and 21, below. In that case, the generality of the wording of s.20 ('facilities for . . .') might in a few cases make it more useful than the more precise wording of s.21. The 'small premises' exception in s.22, below, applies to both s.20 and s.21.
4. Although s.20 refers to 'facilities for education' without qualification, the 1976 Act s.23(1) provides that s.20 does not apply to discrimination in education rendered unlawful by ss. 17–18, above. As a result, s.20 has only a modest role. It applies to establishments not covered by s.17, such as driving schools, foreign language schools, crammers, and to piano lessons (whether in the pupil's home or that of the teacher).
5. For a case of discrimination by a restaurant ('facilities for refreshment'), see the *Genture Restaurants Ltd* case, below, p. 400.
6. 'Facilities for transport and travel' include sleeping cabins for passengers on board ship. The 1968 Act, s.7(6), permitted the segregation of persons of different 'racial groups' in such cabins as a result of pressure from British shipping companies to protect them from international competition. As with innkeepers, the obligation of the common carrier at common law to accept allcomers is placed upon a statutory basis and any proceedings against him for racial discrimination must be brought under the 1976 Act, s.53 below, p. 401.
7. 'Trade' in the phrase 'the services of any profession or trade or any local or other public authority' includes 'any business' (1976 Act, s.78(1)). Estate agents and accommodation bureaux come within this wording (they *may* be subject to s.21 too, see below). Estate agents are also controlled in respect of racial discrimination by the Estate Agents Act 1979 (not yet in force). An estate agent is defined as 'a person who, by way of profession or trade, provides services for the purpose of finding premises for persons seeking to acquire them or assisting in the disposal of premises' (1976 Act, s.78(1). An estate agent (or accommodation bureau) may rely upon the 'small premises' exception (1976 Act, s.22, below) even if the property does not fall within it if he has taken 'all reasonable steps in the circumstances to ensure that the accommodation with which he is concerned and in respect of which racial stipulations are sought to be imposed falls within' it: *Race*

Relations Board v Furnished Rooms Bureau, Westminster C Ct 1972 RRB
Report p. 38. Normally, 'the agent could be expected in relation to each
property to ascertain and record the specific facts relevant to section 7
[1968 Act, see now the 1976 Act s.22] and would, where any doubt existed,
carry out further investigation to satisfy himself that the criteria in the
section were met' ibid.

The 1976 Act is supplemented by the Consumer Credit Act 1974,
s.25(2)(c), which provides that in determining whether an applicant for a
license to carry on a consumer credit or consumer hire business is a 'fit
person', account must be taken of evidence that he has practised
discrimination on grounds of sex, colour, race or ethnic or national origins
in or in connection with the carrying on of any business.

8. The wording 'local or other public authority' covers discrimination in
the provision of public housing (as does s.21) and other 'services'. The
police are covered only in the few areas where they offer 'services' (e.g.
crime prevention advice); discrimination in the course of their operational
duties is subject not to s.20 of the 1976 Act, but to the police complaints
procedure under the Police Acts (see pp. 118–122, above): cf. 374 HL
Deb 29 September 1976 col 525. The work of other public servants such as
immigration officers, public health inspectors and inland revenue officials
likewise does not constitute a 'service'; cf. ibid.

9. In *Applin v Race Relations Board* [1975] AC 259, HL, Lord Wilberforce,
after studying the examples given in it, drew the following conclusion from
s.2(2) of the 1968 Act (now the 1976 Act s.20(2)):

'What it suggests, in combination with section 2 (1), is that the area in which discrimination is
forbidden is that in which a person is concerned to provide something which in its nature is
generally offered to and needed by the public at large, or a section of it, which is offered
impersonally to all who choose to go through the doors or approach the counter: things which,
in their nature, would be provided to anyone, and the refusal of which to persons of different
colour etc., could only be ascribed to discrimination on grounds of colour etc. Conversely,
they do not extend to matters, the provision of which is a private matter, as to which the
motives of the refusing provider may reasonably have nothing to do with colour etc., at all.'

10. *RRB and CRE practice.* An early problem in cases referred to the RRB
was discrimination in motor and life insurance. A number of
complaints revealed that it was common for insurance companies to refuse
car hire insurance if the applicant was born abroad. The Board took the
view that this was illegal discrimination ('national origins') (RRB Report
1968–69, p. 14) and negotiated an agreement with the Lloyd's Motor
Underwriters' Association by which members of the Association would
replace their 'born abroad' test by one of three years residence together
with appropriate driving experience. (RRB Report 1969–70, p. 50).
Subsequently, the Board noted that some companies still laid down periods
of residence of 'ten or fourteen' years and that this was 'much too long'
(RRB Report 1971–72, p. 8). The Board also intervened in a case of the
refusal of an 'owner only driving exclusion' (and therefore lower premium)
to a man born in India who had lived in this country for 12 years, since the
age of 13 (RRB Report 1968–69, p. 14). In respect of life insurance, the
Board took up a case in which a form used by a life assurance society asked
the proposer to state whether he was 'Caucasian, Negroid or Asian'. The
company agreed to abandon this question and to ask instead about the
proposer's length of residence in the United Kingdom. The Board took the
view that 'dubious anthropological concepts such as caucasian, or negroid,
can have no actuarial relevance to life or sickness assurance' (RRB Report
1971–72, p. 9) and that discrimination based upon them was illegal (RRB

Report 1970–71, p. 9). In 1973, the Board reported that 'discriminatory conditions have largely disappeared from the rules governing insurance. . . .' (RRB Report 1973, p. 13).

A PEP Report in 1974 (McIntosh and Smith, *The Extent of Racial Discrimination* (1974)) showed that discrimination by estate agents against Asians and West Indians house buyers had dropped a lot in the five years since the law was extended to cover housing in 1968. There had been discrimination in 64 % of cases in tests conducted in 1967. In tests in 1973 there was discrimination in one form or another in 17 % of cases. According to one manager of an accommodation agency, '95 per cent of landlords using the agency gave racially discriminatory instructions (RRB Report 1974, pp 12).

Discrimination in pubs may take the form of overcharging (Case 5, RRB Report 1966–67, p. 8), discrimination in the time allowed for drinking *Race Relations Board v Royal Oak Public House, London E. 15*, Westminster C Ct, 1977 CRE Report, p. 118), or refusal or serve *Race Relations Board v White Hart Public House, Kent*, Westminster C Ct, 1973 RRB Report p. 42). In 1973, the RRB reported 'an increase in the number of complaints in which it was alleged that licensees told Asian customers they would only be served if they and their friends talked to each other in English'. The Board stated that 'to refuse any group merely for speaking a language other than English is unreasonable; where the real ground for the refusal is racial, it is also unlawful' (RRB Report 1973, p. 4. See also RRB Report 1974, p. 5). Summarising the effect of the 1968 Act, the RRB stated (RRB Report 1975–76, pp. 5–6):

'We are of the view that the Act has worked well in relation to public houses and that whereas before 1968 members of minorities were never sure whether they would be served, they can now enter the vast majority of public houses reasonably confident that they will be treated in the same way as others. Since 1968 brewers and the National Union of Licensed Victuallers have done a great deal to ensure that licensees are made familiar with the Act and we believe that their work has played an important part in reducing discrimination.'

Even so, the CRE received 80 complaints of discrimination in pubs in 1978 and assisted in two successful county court cases (CRE Report 1978, p. 16).

Complaints about discrimination in dance halls (like some complaints about pubs) have raised the question whether it is lawful for the owner to exclude all persons belonging to a particular 'racial group' because one or more members of that group have caused 'trouble' in the past. In *Race Relations Board v Mecca Ltd (Hammersmith Palais)*, Westminster C Ct 1974 RRB Report, p. 39, at the time that the complainant, a West Indian, was refused admission to the Palais 'a temporary ban had been imposed on West Indians and the Company claimed that the ban was imposed following a disturbance involving some coloured youths'. Judge Ruttle gave judgment for the Board. Repeating what he had said in *Race Relations Board v Morris* (reported in 1973 RRB Report, p. 42, as *Race Relations Board v White Hart Public House, Kent*), he stated

' . . . I think he [the licensee] has to consider them as individuals and not jump to the conclusion because a man happens to come from a particular country that he will be in the gang. He has to bring his judgment to bear upon the individuals as such as distinct from being of a particular colour, race or ethnic origin'.

See also *Race Relations Board v Mecca Ltd (Leicester Palais)*, Nottingham C Ct 1975–1976, RRB Report, p. 54.

There have not been many complaints of discrimination in shops. In *Race Relations Board v Beckton*, Leeds C Ct 1975–1976 RRB Report, p. 52, a declaration was made against a shopkeeper who 'lost his temper and went beyond the bounds of proper behaviour when he shouted at Mrs Robinson and ordered her out of his shop' because 'colour was a matter which played a very large part in the defendant's conduct'. In another case, RRB Report 1970–71, p. 44, a complaint was made against a hairdresser who charged more for cutting 'Asiatic' and 'Negroid' hair. The local conciliation committee appointed an assessor who 'gave it as his opinion that there was no technical difference between the cutting of European and the cutting of Asian hair. Negroid hair required a different technique, but this could be learnt and, once learned, could be carried out as quickly as cutting European hair'. The committee took the view that unlawful discrimination had occurred. 'The respondent gave an assurance against future unlawful discrimination and removed the words "Asiatic" and "Negroid" from his price list.'

In *CRE v Marr, Cleanersweep Ltd*, CRE Report 1977, p. 120, the Newcastle County Court issued a declaration against a chimney sweep who refused to sweep a Pakistani chimney ('we don't deal with you people'). See also *Race Relations Board v Botley, Motor Vehicle Repairs*, Westminster C Ct ibid, p. 118, (declaration against garage for refusal to re-spray car: 'you're coloured and that's enough for me').

Are Irish jokes prohibited by s.20, or any other part of the 1976 Act?

Charter v Race Relations Board [1973] AC 868, [1973] 1 All ER 512 [1973] 2 WLR 299, House of Lords

The complainant was an Indian living in East Ham. He applied for membership of the East Ham South Conservative Club. As a Conservative male of 18 or more, he was eligible for admission. The Club committee rejected his application on the casting vote of the Chairman. The vote was taken after the Chairman had said, in reply to a question from a committee member, that he regarded the applicant's colour as relevant to the decision. The complainant took the matter to the RRB which, after attempting conciliation unsuccessfully, brought legal proceedings alleging discrimination contrary to the 1968 Act and seeking a declaration and damages. The Board relied upon section 2 (1) of the 1968 Act which prohibited discrimination in the provision of 'goods, facilities or services' to 'the public or a section of the public'. The question arose as a preliminary point of law whether the members of the Club constituted a 'section of the public' so that the Act applied. The Court of Appeal, reversing the judgment of the county court, unanimously held that it did. The Club appealed to the House of Lords.

Lord Reid: . . .

Read literally the words ['a section of the public'] denote any two or more persons associated together in any way—perhaps any one person could be a section of the public but I shall assume not. But that cannot be the meaning of those words in this context. The head of a household provides facilities for all members of his household. Suppose he has in his household three servants one of whom is coloured, and, though asked to do so, he refuses to the coloured servant facilities which he provides for the others and says that he does so on the ground of colour. The board admit that that is not within the scope of the Act. Plainly there is discrimination within the meaning of section 1 and the only possible ground for excluding such a case from the operation of the Act is that the household is not a section of the public. Various sections of the Act make it clear that it is not intended to interfere with people's domestic lives and counsel for the board both made it clear that they did not contend otherwise.

So the words 'a section of the public' are words of limitation. If they were not, there would have been no point in inserting in the section the words 'the public or a section of the public.'

The section would read perfectly well without them, but then the case which I have supposed of discrimination within a household would have been within the scope of the Act.

The question, then, is how far does the exception in limitation extend. Counsel for the board contended that it only extends to the purely domestic sphere. For the appellants it was contended that the natural antithesis to public is private.

Before coming to the facts of the case I think it well to consider a few quite possible cases. Suppose that in the absence of a nursery school a woman with some knowledge of children lets it be known among her neighbours that she is willing (whether with or without payment) to take a few children into her house for some hours each day either just to look after them or to conduct some kind of kindergarten or its modern equivalent and she refuses to take the child of a coloured neighbour. Or suppose a small bridge club which meets in the houses of its members and which rejects an application for membership by a coloured person. Or suppose a man let it be known among his friends that he would like to take a congenial party abroad: a coloured friend of his seeks to be included in the party but he says some of the other members of his party would object and therefore he is sorry he cannot include his coloured friend.

Mr Comyn [for the Board] argued that all these cases are within the Act so that the discrimination in all these cases would be actionable. Junior counsel, however, informed us that the board do not want to have to deal with such cases.

Now let me come to clubs. I leave out of account various societies or associations which call themselves clubs but have no premises where members meet for social intercourse. No doubt social clubs vary in character. . . .

I cannot see any reasonable or workable dividing line so long as there is operated a genuine system of personal selection of members. There is no public element where a personally selected group of people meet in private premises and the club which they constitute does not provide facilities or services to the public or any section of the public. So section 2 does not apply.

But a clear dividing line does emerge if entry to a club is no more than a formality. This may be because the club rules do not provide for any true selection or because in practice the rules are disregarded. There are, or at least have been, clubs which are in fact no more difficult to enter than a restaurant. There may be some delay, and there may be entry money and a subscription but that makes no difference. In fact the club services and facilities are provided to any one of the public who wishes to come in, provided that he does not have such obvious disqualification as might cause the manager of, say, a good restaurant to exclude him. And it would make no difference if entry were confined to a particular section of the public— Conservatives or graduates or any other.

The board say that this club falls within the latter class. So we must go to the admission set out in the order for the trial of the preliminary issues. The board found in the admission that at all material times any member of the East Ham Conservative Association who applied and was eligible under the club rules was admitted to membership. But that is qualified by the admission that such admission was by means of the election procedure prescribed by the rules: that must mean that the rules were not disregarded. So we must go to the rules. . . .

So the rules provide for three stages. First and perhaps most important, the applicant must find a proposer and a seconder who will vouch for his respectability and fitness to become a member. There is nothing to suggest that this is a formality or that members asked to propose or second an applicant do not take their responsibilities seriously. Then the nomination form must be posted on the club notice board. And thirdly the committee must consider each application. There is nothing to suggest that this has been a mere formality.

No doubt every applicant who has been vouched for by a proposer and seconder during the material time has been elected. But that by itself is quite inconclusive. Unsuitable aspirants to membership may have taken no steps because they knew they would not succeed, or they may have failed to find proposers and seconders. The most we could infer is that this club is not very exclusive. It cannot be inferred from the facts at which we are entitled to look at this stage that there is no genuine selection of members of this club.

So if the case has to be finally decided on the admissions I would hold . . . that they do not disclose a situation to which section 2 applies. . .

I would therefore allow this appeal . . .

Lords Hodson, **Simon**, and **Cross** delivered concurring speeches. **Lord Morris** delivered a dissenting speech.

NOTES

1. *Charter v Race Relations Board*, which was decided in accordance with the clear intention of Parliament (see e.g. Lord Simon, speaking extra-judicially in 374 HL Deb 29 September 1976 col 549), was the first of three cases (the others being the *Dockers* case and *Applin v Race Relations Board*, below) to reach the House of Lords in rapid succession on the meaning of 'a section of the public' in the 1968 Act, s.2. The phrase is repeated in s.20 and can be taken to have the same meaning there. Clubs, therefore remain outside s.20 because they are not a 'section of the public'. They are, however, brought within the law by the 1976 Act, s.25, below, p. 388, which in effect reverses *Charter v Race Relations Board*. The above is true only of what might be called genuine clubs. A club that does not have a 'genuine system of personal selection of members' (Lord Reid's phrase) falls on the public side of the division between public and private groups that the House of Lords sought to draw. It is thus 'a section of the public' and subject to s.20, not s.25. The RAC (*associate* membership: contrast *full* membership) and the London (and other) Co-operative Societies are examples. They do not under their constitutions apply a 'genuine system of personal selection': they take all motorists or allcomers. A club which provides for 'personal selection' in its rules but in which 'in practice the rules are disregarded' (Lord Reid) is similarly not a genuine club. An example of the latter kind is to be found in the facts of *Panama (Piccadilly) Ltd v Newberry* [1962] 1 WLR 610, DC. The proprietor of the Panama Club appealed against convictions for keeping premises for public dancing, etc., without a licence on the ground that only members and guests were allowed to enter the club. The appeal was rejected because any member of the public was in fact admitted at the door upon payment of a 25s. annual membership fee. Although there was provision for the nomination and seconding of applicants, the procedure was not followed. To Lord Parker CJ's mind, it was 'open to any member of the public to go in, pay 25s. and see the show'. The case was referred to by two members of the House of Lords in *Charter v Race Relations Board* as that of a club that would be 'a section of the public' for the purposes of s.2. For a similar case under the 1968 Act, see *Race Relations Board v Hatherton House Discotheque* 1971–72 RRB Report, p. 51. Although the distinction between genuine and other clubs drawn in *Charter v Race Relations Board* would appear to survive the 1976 Act in law, it is no longer important in view of s.25 (unless the more general wording of s.20 offers a fuller remedy).

2. In *Dockers' Labour Club and Institute Ltd v Race Relations Board* [1976] AC 285, the House of Lords unanimously extended its ruling in *Charter v Race Relations Board* to cover *associate* club members. The complainant, a coloured person, was a member of a working men's club in Preston. The club was a member of the Working Men's Club and Institute Union with the result that he was, upon payment of a small charge, entitled to associate membership of other clubs members of the Union. Taking advantage of this arrangement, the complainant went to another club in Preston for a drink but was asked to leave because that club operated a colour bar. Both clubs involved were genuine clubs in the sense of the *Charter* case. The House of Lords, overruling the Court of Appeal, held that associate members were not a 'section of the public' within the meaning of the 1968 Act, s. 2. Lord Reid said:

In *Charter's* case the House ... did not consider the position of guests, temporary members under reciprocal arrangements with other clubs, or associates of this union—persons selected by some person or body other than the club or its committee.

Here I think it best to go back to the central and most obvious exclusion from the operation of the Act—the private household—because it shows that selection is not the only basis for holding that one is in the private and not the public sphere. A father does not select his children. He selects his own guests and may select his servants. But he need not select his children's guests whom they bring to his house. Yet I do not think that it could possibly be argued that he commits an offence if he discriminates against a guest brought to his house by his child on the ground of colour, race or ethnic or national origin. . . .

On the other hand, the head of the household can go outside the private sphere. If he opens his house to the public on certain occasions I have no doubt that he would commit an offence if he refused admission to anyone on any of the grounds stated in the Act. And I think the same would apply if he opened his house to a section of the public, for example, members of a particular profession.

Similar considerations must I think apply to a club. Discrimination against or between guests of a member of the club would no more be struck at by the Act than discrimination by the father against guests of his children.

Coming nearer to the present case it is common for clubs which exercise a rigorous choice in electing their members to have reciprocal arrangements with other clubs in this country or abroad whereby each will offer hospitality or temporary membership to members of the other club. If either attempted to discriminate against visitors from the other that might have serious consequences but I find it impossible to hold that there could be an offence against the Act.

But again a club can go outside the private sphere. Reference was made to a golf club which might admit members of the public or of some section of the public at particular times in payment of a green fee. There too I would have no doubt that they would commit an offence if they discriminated against anyone wishing to play on any of the grounds stated in the Act.

So I think that the question here is whether a working men's club which belongs to the union goes out of the private into the public sphere in offering admission to associates of the union. I would reserve my opinion about a case when so many non-members habitually attend that the club loses its character of a private meeting place. Here there is nothing of that kind. Associates enter this club frequently but they do not swamp it. It appears that on the day in question about one in 12 of those present was an associate and that that is a normal proportion. There is no suggestion that attendance of associates in any way alters the private character of the club.'

See now, s. 25(3) of the 1976 Act, below, p. 389.

3. In *Race Relations Board v Bradmore Working Men's Club and Institute*, Birmingham C Ct, 1969–70 RRB Report, p. 48, the facts were reported as follows:

'Part of the Bradmore Working Men's Club and Institute, Wolverhampton, was hired for a staff Christmas Party by a member of the staff of the Wolverhampton telephone exchange. All members of the exchange staff, their relatives and friends were eligible to buy tickets for the party. One member of the staff who bought a ticket, a Jamaican-born woman, was subsequently refused admission to the party by the club's officials. The reason given was that coloured people were not allowed to enter the club's premises.'

An action brought by the Board for a declaration was successful for the following reasons:

'The judge found that when the club's hall had been hired for a specific occasion by a group of people, any members of which were entitled to buy tickets for their own use or for use by friends and relations, then so far as the club was concerned those people constituted a section of the public. On such an occasion, therefore, that part of the club's premises which had been hired out could not be covered by the club's normal rules.'

Is the case consistent with the *Dockers' Club* case?

4. In *Applin v Race Relations Board* [1975] AC 259, Mr and Mrs W had for many years fostered children in care of local authorities. They normally had four or five children in their home, each staying for about 3 weeks. About 60 per cent of the children were coloured. The appellant, a member of the National Front, learnt of this and brought pressure to bear upon Mr and Mrs W to stop fostering coloured children. The RRB sought a declaration that the appellant's conduct was incitement to commit an act of unlawful discrimination, contrary to the 1968 Act, s. 12 (now the 1976 Act, s. 31). The House of Lords ruled in favour of the Board on the ground that the fostering of children in care was the provision of facilities or services to a 'section of the public' (children in care) so that the refusal to take in children because of their colour would be unlawful discrimination.

The decision in the case was reversed by the 1976 Act, s. 23(2) which creates an exception to s. 20:

'Section 20(1) does not apply to anything done by a person as a participant in arrangements under which he (for reward or not) takes into his home, and treats as if they were members of his family, children, elderly persons, or persons requiring a special degree of care and attention.'

5 Housing, etc.

Race Relations Act 1976

21. Discrimination in disposal or management of premises
(1) It is unlawful for a person, in relation to premises in Great Britain of which he has power to dispose, to discriminate against another—
  (*a*) in the terms on which he offers him those premises; or
  (*b*) by refusing his application for those premises; or
  (*c*) in his treatment of him in relation to any list of persons in need of premises of that description.

(2) It is unlawful for a person, in relation to premises managed by him, to discriminate against a person occupying the premises—
  (*a*) in the way he affords him access to any benefits or facilities, or by refusing or deliberately omitting to afford him access to them; or
  (*b*) by evicting him, or subjecting him to any other detriment.

(3) Subsection (1) does not apply to a person who owns an estate or interest in the premises and wholly occupies them unless he uses the services of an estate agent for the purposes of the disposal of the premises, or publishes or causes to be published an advertisement in connection with the disposal.

NOTES

1. '*Premises*'. These 'include land of any description' (the 1976 Act s.78(1)). The use (residential, business, recreational, etc.) to which the land is put does not matter, although racial discrimination is mostly a problem of housing. In *Race Relations Board v Haigh & Co*, Leeds C Ct, (1969), *Times*, 11 September, it was held that a builder who refused to sell a house under construction on a housing estate to the complainant because of his colour had acted contrary to the 1968 Act, s.5(a), which prohibited discrimination in the disposal of 'housing accommodation, business premises or other land'. The partly-built house was 'housing accommodation' although not ready for occupation. The case would have the same outcome on this point under the different wording of s.21. After the case, the builder stated that he would 'reluctantly' change his policy and sell to coloured applicants: *The Guardian*, 11 September 1969, quoted in Lester and Bindman, *Race and Law*, (1972) p. 235.
2. *Power of disposal*. A 'power of disposal' includes the granting of a right to occupy the premises' (the 1976 Act, s.78(1)). Generally, the 'disposal' of premises would appear to include the sale of a fee simple, the assignment or granting of a lease or tenancy, and the granting of a licence to occupy premises. Public housing authorities have the 'power to dispose' of housing within their control. An estate agent or accommodation bureau will be subject to s.21 (as well as s.20) if, as is sometimes the case, he or it is given a 'power to dispose'.
3. Would a covenant by which land may not be sold to persons 'not of the caucasian race' (see the facts of *Shelley v Kraemer* 334 US 1 (1948)) be unlawful under s.21? Or at common law on grounds of public policy? See

S. Cretney (1968) 118 NLJ 1094; J. F. Garner, (1972) 35 MLR 478; and Brooke–Taylor, (1978) 42 Conv(ns) 24. And see the public policy cases in Chap. 8, section 7.

4. Section 21(1) does not apply to disposals of property that come within s.21(3). This was an exception that would have been available to the defendant in *Race Relations Board v Relf*, below, p. 391, had he, when selling his house, refrained from advertising it as well as from using an estate agent. Since a 'for sale' or 'vacancies' notice on the premises is an advertisement, the exception is a very narrow one. The 'small premises' exception in s.22, below, also applies to s.21(1).

5. *Management of premises.* A case of discrimination in the management of premises under the 1968 Act that would now come within the 1976 Act, s.21(2) was reported by the RRB as follows (RRB report 1970–71, p. 11):

'During the year the Board formed the opinion that a local authority had acted unlawfully by treating a Cypriot tenant less favourably than other tenants. The complainant received a letter from the local housing manager concerning his children's behaviour which stated that because of his limited residence in the country he was fortunate to have local authority accommodation, and indicated that his tenancy might be terminated if a further complaint were received. No such warning was sent to an English tenant whose children had also been the subject of adverse reports by the same caretaker. The Council apologised to the tenant and gave an assurance against further acts of unlawful discrimination.'

Other examples suggested by Macdonald, *Race Relations – The New Law* (1977), p. 90, are 'separate toilet or bathroom facilities for coloured tenants in a boarding house or the situation where the landlord sends a rent collector to white families but makes the coloured families call in at the rent office'.

6. Examples of discrimination in the terms on which premises are offered (s.21(1) (a)) that occurred under the 1968 Act are the refusal on racial grounds to allow a house purchaser mortgage facilities available to other purchasers (RRB Report 1969–70, p. 13) and insistence upon a coloured house purchaser buying both houses in a two house development (for fear that the other house would otherwise be difficult to sell) when such a requirement would not have been placed upon a white purchaser (Case 7, RRB Report 1974, p. 36). Charging a higher purchase price would be another obvious example. Refusal to renew a lease (*Race Relations Board v Wharton*, 1977 CRE Report, p. 119), to rent a flat (RRB Report 1974, p. 11), or to sell a house (Case 8, RRB Report 1975–76, p. 46) come within s.21(1)(b). Section 21(1)(c) applies to waiting lists kept, for example, by a caravan site owner or a local authority. Local authority waiting list rules were the subject of several investigations by the RRB. Wolverhampton Corporation's 'housing waiting list rule which, broadly speaking, treated people on the waiting list who were born outside the country less favourably than others by applying to them a longer qualifying waiting period' was declared by the RRB to be unlawful and later abandoned by the Corporation (RRB Report 1970–71, p. 11). The rule was replaced by one which applied a residence (as opposed to a place of birth) test, a longer qualifying waiting period being applied to persons who had lived in the United Kingdom for less than 10 years. This rule was dropped after the RRB began an investigation of it (RRB Report 1970–71, p. 10). It was reported in 1975 (Smith and Whalley, *Racial Minorities and Public Housing* (1975) p. 36) that a number of local authorities in the London area required an applicant for council housing to have lived within its area for 5 years. Might such a rule be indirect discrimination (the 1976 Act, s.1(1)(b))? What of a rule by which residence in a borough is effective for waiting list purposes only from the date that the applicant is joined by his family (RRB Report 1969–70, p. 12 and RRB Report 1970–71, p. 11)? On nationality restrictions, see *Ealing London Borough Council v Race Relations Board* and the 1976 Act, s.3, above, pp. 373–4.

7. S.24 makes it illegal (subject to a 'small premises' exception) for a landlord to discriminate in refusing to agree to the assignment of a tenancy. See also the Landlord and Tenant Act 1927, s.19, and *Schegel v Corcoran*, above, p. 349.

Race Relations Act 1976

22. Exceptions from ss.20(1) and 21: small dwellings
(1) Sections 20(1) and 21 do not apply to the provision by a person of accommodation in any premises, or the disposal of premises by him, if –
  (a) that person or a near relative of his ("the relevant occupier") resides, and intends to continue to reside, on the premises; and
  (b) there is on the premises, in addition to the accommodation occupied by the relevant occupier, accommodation (not being storage accommodation or means of access) shared by the relevant occupier with other persons residing on the premises who are not members of his household; and
  (c) the premises are small premises.

(2) Premises shall be treated for the purposes of this section as small premises if –
  (a) in the case of premises comprising residential accommodation for one or more households (under separate letting or similar agreements) in addition to the accommodation occupied by the relevant occupier, there is not normally residential accommodation for more than two such households and only the relevant occupier and any member of his household reside in the accommodation occupied by him;
  (b) in the case of premises not falling within paragraph (a), there is not normally residential accommodation on the premises for more than six persons in addition to the relevant occupier and any members of his household.

NOTE

The exception in s.22 applies to s.21(2) as well as s.21(1), the management of premises being covered by the wording 'the provision by a person of accommodation in any premises'. A person is a near relative of another 'if that person is the wife or husband, a parent or child, a grandparent or grandchild, or a brother or sister of the other (whether of full blood or half blood or by affinity), and "child" includes an illegitimate child and the wife or husband of an illegitimate child' (1976 Act, s.78(1)(5)). 'Accommodation . . . shared' (s.22(1)(b)) includes a bathroom, kitchen, or toilet; it does not include a stairway. Hotels, boarding houses and other similar establishments' that would otherwise be subject to the 1976 Act, s.20 are exempt from it if they can bring themselves within the 'small premises' exception in s.22.

6 Clubs

Race Relations Act 1976

25. Discrimination: associations not within s.11
(1) This section applies to any association of persons (however described, whether corporate or unincorporate, and whether or not its activities are carried on for profit) if –
  (a) it has twenty-five or more members; and

(*b*) admission to membership is regulated by its constitution and is so conducted that the members do not constitute a section of the public within the meaning of section 20(1); and
(*c*) it is not an organisation to which section 11 applies [Trade Unions, etc].

(2) It is unlawful for an association to which this section applies, in the case of a person who is not a member of the association, to discriminate against him –
(*a*) in the terms on which it is prepared to admit him to membership; or
(*b*) by refusing or deliberately omitting to accept his application for membership.

(3) It is unlawful for an association to which this section applies, in the case of a person who is a member or associate of the association, to discriminate against him –
(*a*) in the way it affords him access to any benefits, facilities or services, or by refusing or deliberately omitting to afford him access to them; or
(*b*) in the case of a member, by depriving him of membership, or varying the terms on which he is a member; or
(*c*) in the case of an associate, by depriving him of his rights as an associate, or varying those rights; or
(*d*) in either case, by subjecting him to any other detriment.

(4) For the purposes of this section –
(*a*) a person is a member of an association if he belongs to it by virtue of his admission to any sort of membership provided for by its constitution (and is not merely a person with certain rights under its constitution by virtue of his membership of some other association), and references to membership of an association shall be construed accordingly;
(*b*) a person is an associate of an association to which this section applies if, not being a member of it, he has under its constitution some or all of the rights enjoyed by members (or would have apart from any provision in its constitution authorising the refusal of those rights in particular cases).

26. Exception from s.25 for certain associations
(1)An association to which section 25 applies is within this subsection if the main object of the association is to enable the benefits of membership (whatever they may be) to be enjoyed by persons of a particular racial group defined otherwise than by reference to colour; and in determining whether that is the main object of an association regard shall be had to the essential character of the association and to all relevant circumstances including, in particular, the extent to which the affairs of the association are so conducted that the persons primarily enjoying the benefits of membership are of the racial group in question.

(2) In the case of an association within subsection (1), nothing in section 25 shall render unlawful any act not involving discrimination on the ground of colour.

NOTES

1. As noted earlier, p. 384, in *Charter v Race Relations Board*, it was held that genuine clubs were not subject to the 1968 Act's prohibition of discrimination in the provision of goods, facilities and services. In enacting the 1976 Act, Parliament decided that such clubs should be controlled in this respect. It decided to achieve this result not by amending the section on goods, facilities and services (now the 1976 Act, s.20), but by adding a new section—s.25—specifically dealing with clubs. The Government White Paper explained its reason for wanting to bring clubs within the Act as follows (Cmnd. 6234, p. 18):

'72 . . . Some 4,000 working men's clubs, with a total membership of about 3½ million people, are affiliated to the Club and Institute Union and are not covered by the 1968 Act. In some towns they have replaced public houses as the main providers of facilities for entertainment, recreation and refreshment. In addition, thousands of golf, squash, tennis and other sporting clubs registered as members' clubs are, almost certainly, also outside the 1968 Act, except in so far as they may offer only limited playing facilities to the public generally. Many clubs do not discriminate on racial grounds but at present they may lawfully do so. The Government considers that it is right that all clubs should be allowed to apply a test of personal acceptability to candidates for membership, but it considers that it is against the public interest that they should be entitled to do this on racial grounds. The Government believes that the relationship between members of clubs is no more personal and intimate than is the relationship between people in many situations which are rightly covered by the 1968 Act; for example, the members of a small firm or trade union branch, children at school, or tenants in multi-occupied housing accommodation. In principle it is justifiable to apply the legislation in all these situations because of the inherently unjust and degrading nature of racial discrimination and its potentially grave social consequences. In practice the objectives of the legislation will be seriously undermined if its protection does not extend beyond the work-place and the market-place to enable workers and other members of the public to obtain entertainment, recreation and refreshment together on the basis of equality, irrespective of colour or race.

The Bill will therefore make it unlawful for a club or other voluntary body to discriminate as regards the admission of members or the treatment accorded to members. Subject to this the Bill will not, of course, affect the right of such a body to withhold membership or facilities from someone who does not qualify for them in accordance with its rules. Small voluntary bodies will be exempted from this provision so as to avoid interference with the kind of regular social gathering which is genuinely private and domestic in character. In addition, there will be an exception to enable bona fide social, welfare, political and sporting organisations whose main object is to confer benefits on a particular ethnic or national group to continue to do so.'

Similarly, the Race Relations Board stated (RRB Report 1970–71, p. 7);

'Once a man knows that the colour of his own skin makes him unacceptable in his white workmates' club, then his relations with them must be adversely affected, no matter how good they have hitherto been. The knowledge that he can drink with them in a pub and go to the same cinemas, dance halls and cafes is likely to make exclusion from the club the more unbearable. The truism that the amelioration of some grievances makes those that remain more unacceptable is well demonstrated in this situation.'

A club that is not a genuine club in the sense of the *Charter* case, so that its members are a 'section of the public', is subject to s.20 and not s.25.

2. Section 25(3) reverses *Dockers' Labour Club and Institute Ltd* v *Race Relations Board*, above, p. 384, so that discrimination by a club against an associate member is prohibited by the 1976 Act. The RRB reported in 1974 that there were about 1 million members of working men's clubs who held associate member cards valid in other clubs members of the Working Men's Club and Institute Union. (RRB Report 1974, p. 4). What if a club refuses to admit one of its own member's guests because of his colour? Would that be illegal discrimination against the guest? The member?

3. The exemption for small clubs (s.25(1)) was set at 25 members because that is the minimum number of members that a club must have to qualify for registration under the Licensing Acts. It was suggested in debate in Parliament that there will be few clubs with a list, as opposed to an active, membership of less than 25 (374 HL Deb 29 September 1976 col 538).

4. Section 26 safeguards such clubs as the Caledonian Club, the London Welsh Rugby Club and the Indian Workers Association (see Standing Committee A, Race Relations Bill, 9th Sitting HC Deb col 400, 25 May 1976). It would not allow a person who was otherwise qualified for membership of such a club to be excluded because of his colour. It would, however, allow him to be excluded on 'racial grounds' other than colour.

7 Advertisements

Race Relations Act 1976

29. Discriminatory advertisements
(1) It is unlawful to publish or to cause to be published an advertisement which indicates, or might reasonably be understood as indicating, an intention by a person to do an act of discrimination, whether the doing of that act by him would be lawful or, by virtue of Part II or III, unlawful.

(2) Subsection (1) does not apply to an advertisement –
(*a*) if the intended act would be lawful by virtue of any of sections 5, 6, 7(3) and (4), 10(3), 26, 34(2)(*b*), 35 to 39 and 41; or
(*b*) if the advertisement relates to the services of an employment agency (within the meaning of section 14(1)) and the intended act only concerns employment which the employer could by virtue of section 5, 6 or 7(3) or (4) lawfully refuse to offer to persons against whom the advertisement indicates an intention to discriminate.

(3) Subsection (1) does not apply to an advertisement which indicates that persons of any class defined otherwise than by reference to colour, race or ethnic or national origins are required for employment outside Great Britain.

(4) The publisher of an advertisement made unlawful by sub-section (1) shall not be subject to any liability under that subsection in respect of the publication of the advertisement if he proves –
(*a*) that the advertisement was published in reliance on a statement made to him by the person who caused it to be published to the effect that, by reason of the operation of subsection (2) or (3), the publication would not be unlawful; and
(*b*) that it was reasonable for him to rely on the statement.

(5) A person who knowingly or recklessly makes a statement such as is mentioned in subsection (4)(*a*) which in a material respect is false or misleading commits an offence, and shall be liable on summary conviction to a fine not exceeding £400.

NOTES

1. The number of discriminatory advertisements would appear to have dropped considerably since 1968 when they were first prohibited. In 1973, the RRB reported that 'advertisements and notices indicating an intention to discriminate . . . have virtually disappeared both from the press and from public advertisement boards' (RRB Report 1973, p. 13). Comparing advertisements in one London newspaper in July 1968 and July 1969, the Board noted that it had 18 discriminatory advertisement ('no coloured', 'Europeans wanted', 'coloured only', 'Jew preferred') in 1968 and none a year later (RRB Report 1969–70, p. 53). A similar survey of newsagents noticeboards in 1970 revealed 1 discriminatory accommodation advertisement out of 36: *ibid.* Nonetheless, in 1978 the CRE disposed of complaints about 63 advertisements. 35 were found to be unlawful and the complaint was settled informally in all cases (CRE Report 1978, p. 20).
2. 'Advertisement' is defined very widely. Section 78(1) of the 1976 Act reads:

' "advertisement" includes every form of advertisement or notice, whether to the public or not, and whether in a newspaper or other publication, by television or radio, by display of notices, signs, labels, showcards or goods, by distribution of samples, circulars, catalogues, price lists or other material, by exhibition of pictures, models or films, or in any other way, and references to the publishing of advertisements shall be construed accordingly;'

The display of a 'notice' was the reason for the well publicised case of *Race Relations Board v Relf*, RRB Report 1975–76, p. 56. The RRB report reads:

'The West Midlands Conciliation Committee formed the opinion that Mr Robert Relf contravened Section 6 of the Act [now the 1976 Act, s.29] when he displayed an unlawful notice in the window of his house which was advertised for sale. Conciliation failed and the Board brought proceedings. The Birmingham County Court on 21 November 1975 declared that Mr Robert Relf, by displaying or publishing, or causing to be displayed or published a notice on his property which read: "For Sale to an English Family", acted unlawfully by virtue of Section 6 of the Race Relations Act 1968. The Judge granted an injunction restrainingMr Relf from doing similar acts in the future. The defendant was ordered to pay the costs of the action.
    Notwithstanding the injunction, the notice remained on display. On 7 May, 1976 the Board applied to the Court for Mr Relf to be committed for contempt . . . Judge Sunderland said

that there had been a breach of the injunction and that if the sign was removed from outside Mr Relf's house it would be the end of the proceedings against him. Mr Relf told the court that he would not remove the notice. The Judge then committed Mr Relf to prison.

The Official Solicitor on 27 May 1976 applied to the Court for Mr Relf's release on medical grounds. The hearing was adjourned until 7 June when the Board asked the Court to consider the possibility of ordering the bailiff to remove the notice. Mr Relf told Judge Sunderland that he would rather stay in prison than remove the notice. Judge Sunderland said that Mr Relf had made it manifest that he would not obey the Court's order and that he was guilty of gross deliberate and wanton contempt of Court which could not be ignored. He said he was satisfied there was no immediate danger to Mr Relf's health. The Judge refused the application for Mr Relf's release.

On 21 June 1976, because of Mr Relf's deteriorating health [he had been on hunger strike], the Official Solicitor made another application for Mr Relf's release, and this time it was granted.'

The Official Solicitor has as one of his diverse functions the welfare of persons committed to prison for contempt.

3. The 'Scottish porridge' case also illustrates the wide field of application of s.29. It was reported by the RRB as follows (RRB Report 1969–70, p. 6):

'Here a Scottish doctor living in Eastbourne sought a "daily" able to cook plain Scottish food. But he advertised for a "Scottish daily". There can be few who would regard such a restriction as anything but innocuous, but a member of the public insisted that the Board should investigate a complaint. The regional conciliation committee understandably formed the opinion that the advertisement contravened section 6 of the Act [now the 1976 Act s.29]. Having called the doctor's attention to section 6 of the Act, the committee proposed to do no more.'

Would the doctor have infringed the Act if he had advertised for a 'daily' who could cook plain Scottish food?

4. Partly because of cases like the 'Scottish porridge' case, enforcement of s.29 is placed solely in the hands of the CRE, which may issue a non-discrimination notice after a formal investigation (s.58) or bring legal proceedings for a declaration or an injunction (ss.63, 64). Damages may not be awarded. A discriminatory advertisement may be a part of an employer's recruiting arrangements, in which case an aggrieved individual, exceptionally, may bring a claim before an industrial tribunal for a breach of s.4(1)(a): see *Brindley v Tayside Health Board* [1976] IRLR 364, IT (a sex discrimination case). If an advertisement is published by someone (e.g. a newspaper) other than the advertiser, the publisher is liable under s.29 as well as the advertiser. The publisher has a defence of 'reliance' in such cases (s.29(4)).

5. Section 29 has been criticized for making it illegal, subject to s.29(2), to advertise something that may in itself be perfectly lawful, as in the case of a letting of accommodation exempted from the Act by the 'small premises' exception (s.22). The justification for this in the Government White Paper (Cmnd. 6234, p. 19) was that 'the public display of racial prejudices and preferences is inherently offensive and likely to encourage the spread of discriminatory attitudes and practices'.

6. In *Commission for Racial Equality v Associated Newspapers Group Ltd* [1978] 1 WLR 905, an advertisement in the *Daily Mail* for nurses to work in South Africa read 'all white patients'. Although discrimination in the employment of persons *to work abroad* was not contrary to the 1968 Act (nor is it illegal under the 1976 Act), the advertisement was nonetheless illegal under the 1968 Act if it 'could reasonably be understood as indicating an intention to do an act of discrimination' (see this wording in, now, the 1976 Act s.29(1)), whether that act was lawful or not. The Court of Appeal decided not to disturb the finding of fact of the county court that the words did not carry for a reasonable person the implication that only white nurses would be employed. The advertisement was, therefore, not illegal.

8 Charities

Race Relations Act 1976

34. Charities
(1) A provision which is contained in a charitable instrument (whenever that instrument took or takes effect) and which provides for conferring benefits on persons of a class defined by reference to colour shall have effect for all purposes as if it provided for conferring the like benefits –
    (*a*) on persons of the class which results if the restriction by reference to colour is disregarded; or
    (*b*) where the original class is defined by reference to colour only, on persons generally;
but nothing in this subsection shall be taken to alter the effect of any provision as regards any time before the coming into operation of this subsection.

(2) Nothing in Parts II to IV shall –
    (*a*) be construed as affecting a provision to which this subsection applies; or
    (*b*) render unlawful an act which is done in order to give effect to such a provision.

(3) Subsection (2) applies to any provision which is contained in a charitable instrument (whenever that instrument took or takes effect) and which provides for conferring benefits on persons of a class defined otherwise than by reference to colour (including a class resulting from the operation of subsection (1)). . . .

NOTE

Quite a number of charitable trusts apply in areas covered by the Act, particularly education and housing. Section 34 only concerns those that discriminate on grounds of colour. Others that do so on grounds of race, etc. (see s.3) are not affected, although they may be void at common law for reasons of uncertainty or public policy. As to uncertainty, see, for example, *Clayton v Ramsden* [1943] AC 320 HL, in which a condition subsequent in a will by which a beneficiary was to forfeit a legacy upon marrying a person 'not of Jewish parents and not of Jewish faith' was held void for uncertainty. As to public policy, see *Re Lysaght*, above, p. 358.

9 Incitement to racial hatred

Race Relations Act 1976

70. Incitement to racial hatred
(1) The Public Order Act 1936 shall be amended in accordance with the following provisions of this section.
(2) After section 5 there shall be inserted the following section:—
"5A. Incitement to racial hatred
(1) A person commits an offence if—
    (*a*) he publishes or distributes written matter which is threatening, abusive or insulting; or
    (*b*) he uses in any public place or at any public meeting words which are threatening, abusive or insulting,
in a case where having regard to all the circumstances, hatred is likely to be stirred up against any racial group in Great Britain by the matter or words in question. . . .
(3) In any proceedings for an offence under this section alleged to have been committed by the publication or distribution of any written matter, it shall be a defence for the accused to prove that he was not aware of the content of the written matter in question and neither suspected nor had reason to suspect it of being threatening, abusive or insulting.
(4) Subsection (3) above shall not prejudice any defence which it is open to a person charged with an offence under this section to raise apart from that subsection.
(5) A person guilty of an offence under this section shall be liable—
    (*a*) on summary conviction, to imprisonment for a term not exceeding six months or to a fine not exceeding £1000, or both;

(*b*) on conviction on indictment, to imprisonment for a term not exceeding two years or to a fine, or both;
but no prosecution for such an offence shall be instituted in England and Wales except by or with the consent of the Attorney-General.
(6) In this section—
'publish' and 'distribute' mean publish or distribute to the public at large or to any section of the public not consisting exclusively of members of an association of which the person publishing or distributing is a member;
'racial group' means a group of persons defined by reference to colour, race, nationality or ethnic or national origins, and in this definition 'nationality' includes citizenship; . . .
'written matter' includes any writing, sign or visible representation."

NOTES

1. See on incitement to racial hatred, A. Dickey, [1968] Crim LR 489; Khan, (1978) 122 Sol Jo 256; P. Leopold, [1977] PL 389; D. G. T. Williams, [1966] Crim LR 320. On the situation of Bengalis in East London, see *Brick Lane and Beyond: Inquiry into Racial Strife and Violence in Tower Hamlets*, CRE, (1979).
2. The Public Order Act 1936, s.5A replaces the offence in the Race Relations Act 1965, s.6, which had been left unrepealed by the 1968 Act. Referring to incitement to racial hatred and to the similar offence in section 5 of the Theatres Act 1968, above, p. 232, the Government White Paper explained its reason for moving the former offence from the Race Relations Act to the Public Order Act as follows (Cmnd. 6234, p.30):

'125. These offences are entirely separate from the anti-discrimination provisions of the race relations legislation. They deal with the stirring up of racial hatred rather than with acts of racial discrimination; they are criminal rather than civil; and they are enforced in the criminal courts rather than by the Race Relations Board in the civil courts. In several respects they are similar to the offence under Section 5 of the Public Order Act 1936 of using threatening, abusive or insulting words, in any public place or at any public meeting, with intent to provoke a breach of the peace or whereby a breach of the peace is likely to be occasioned. They are concerned to prevent the stirring up of racial hatred which may beget violence and public disorder.'

3. As defined in the 1965 Act, s.6, the offence of incitement to racial hatred required an 'intent to stir up hatred' against a racial group. As redefined in s.5A of the Public Order Act 1936, it no longer requires this subjective intent. It need only be proved that hatred is likely to be stirred up by the defendant's act. The Government White Paper justified this widening of the offence as follows (Cmnd. 6234, p. 30):

'126. Relatively few prosecutions have been brought under section 6 of the 1965 Act and none has been brought under section 5 of the Theatres Act. However, during the past decade, probably largely as a result of section 6, there has been a decided change in the style of racialist propaganda. It tends to be less blatantly bigoted, to disclaim any intention of stirring up racial hatred, and to purport to make a contribution to public education and debate. Whilst this shift away from crudely racialist propaganda and abuse is welcome, it is not an unmixed benefit. The more apparently rational and moderate is the message, the greater is its probable impact on public opinion. But it is not justifiable in a democratic society to interfere with freedom of expression except where it is necessary to do so for the prevention of disorder or for the protection of other basic freedoms. The present law penalises crude verbal attacks if and only if it is established that they have been made with the deliberate intention of causing groups to be hated because of their racial origins. In the Government's view this is too narrow an approach. It accepts the observation made by Sir Leslie Scarman in his report on the Red Lion Square disorders that section 6 is too restrictively defined to be an effective sanction. It therefore proposes to ensure that it will no longer be necessary to prove a subjective intention to stir up racial hatred.
127. The present law does not, however, penalise the dissemination of ideas based on an assumption of racial superiority or inferiority or facts (whether true or false) which may

encourage racial prejudice or discrimination. It is arguable that false and evil publications of this kind may well be more effectively defeated by public education and debate than by prosecution and that in practice the criminal law would be ineffective to deal with such material. Due regard must also of course be paid to allowing the free expression of opinion. The Government is not therefore at this stage putting forward proposals to extend the criminal law to deal with the dissemination of racialist propaganda in the absence of a likelihood that group hatred will be stirred up by it. It recognises, however, that strong views are held on this important question and will carefully consider any further representations that may be made to it

The reference to the Scarman Report on the Red Lion Square disorders, was to the following passage (Cmnd. 5919, p. 35):

'125. Section 6 of the Race Relations Act is merely an embarrassment to the police. Hedged about with restrictions (proof of intent, requirement of the Attorney-General's consent) it is useless to a policeman on the street . . . . The section needs radical amendment to make it an effective sanction, particularly, I think, in relation to its formulation of the intent to be proved before an offence can be established.'

4. Prosecutions may only be brought 'by or with the consent of' the Attorney-General who, in practice, consults the Director of Public Prosecutions. 24 persons were prosecuted under the 1965 Act, of whom 15 were convicted. *R v Britton*, below, was the first case. Another was *R v Jordan and Pollard*, (1967) *Times*, 26 January in which the defendants were found guilty under s.6 for distributing anti-semitic and anti-coloured immigrant literature. The first defendant, a British national socialist, was sentenced to 18 months imprisonment. In *R v Malik* [1968] 1 WLR 353, CA, a 'black power' leader was sentenced to 12 months imprisonment. In *R v Sawh* (1967) *Times*, 30 November, 4 'black power' speakers at Hyde Park Corner were fined a total of £270. Four members of the white Racial Preservation Society were acquitted at Lewes Assizes in 1968: *The Times*, 29 March 1968. The question whether Enoch Powell might be prosecuted under the 1965 Act was apparently referred to the Attorney General: see *The Times*, 4 May 1968 and 23 November 1968. See, in particular, his 'river of blood' speech in Birmingham on 20 April 1968 (printed in Powell, *Freedom and Reality*, (1969), p. 281ff.). By April 1980, 15 prosecutions under s.5A had been completed, leading to 9 convictions. The most publicised of these was that of Mr Robert Relf who was sentenced to 9 months imprisonment for distributing leaflets with such titles as 'nigger muggers unite' and 'jungle news': see *The Guardian*, 30 January 1979. It may be that despite the elimination of the subjective intent requirement the need to prove that *hatred* is stirred up will prevent many successful prosecutions, especially if the defendant elects for a jury trial. *Quaere* whether the Attorney-General (or a private person in a relator action with his consent) could obtain an injunction to prevent incitement to racial hatred: see *Thorne v British Broadcasting Corporation* [1967] 1 WLR 1104, CA (unsuccessful claim by a private individual for an injunction to prevent broadcasts of anti-German programmes as incitement to racial hatred without obtaining the Attorney-General's consent refused).

5. For the meaning of 'public place' and 'public meeting' in s. 5A, see the Public Order Act 1936 s.9, above, p. 151.

6. The common law offence of sedition, above, p. 291, and s. 5 of the Public Order Act 1936, above, p. 151, also control conduct tending to cause racial hatred. Section 5A has effectively replaced sedition, although the latter may still be of use if it extends to conduct causing hatred against religious groups within society. In *R v Caunt* (1947) (above, p. 293) the jury was directed that an article aimed at Jews could be seditious. Where there is a likelihood of a breach of the peace, a charge under s.5 of the Public Order Act 1936 may be brought with or instead of one under s.5A. A convinction under s.5 may be easier to achieve: see *R v Jones*, (1978) *Times*, 25 July.

R v Britton [1967] 2 QB 51, [1967] 1 All ER 486; [1967] 2 WLR 537, 51 Cr App Rep 107, Court of Appeal, Criminal Division

Lord Parker CJ (for the court): The short facts were that the Member of Parliament for Southall lives at Hayes; he is a Mr Bidwell, and at 10.15 pm he heard a crash of glass, went to the door, found the glass panels broken, saw someone running away whom he chased and with the assistance of his dog caught. The man caught was the defendant whom Mr Bidwell brought back to his porch. When he got there he saw stuck on the door a pamphlet . . . which in large black letters said: 'Blacks not wanted here,' and a big hand pictured on the poster, clearly indicating 'stop'—'stop further immigration' presumably. Underneath was written 'Greater Britain Movement, London, W.C.1.' There was also evidence that four or five similar pamphlets had been left in the porchway, and near by a beer bottle round which had been wrapped another of the leaflets.

Mr Bidwell sent for the police, and various conversations took place. Apparently . . . Mr Bidwell said: 'You are only a little weed' and the defendant replied: 'So was Hitler.'

Finally Police Constable Cargill arrived, the defendant would not answer any questions, and he was taken to the police station, where he complained that the Member of Parliament, Mr Bidwell, was the person responsible for bringing the blacks to Britain. In his pocket, Police Constable Cargill found another leaflet, this time in large letters: 'Do you want a black grandchild?' That, however, had never left his pocket.

. . . The point which has concerned the court in this [prosecution under the Race Relations Act 1965, s.6] . . . is whether there can properly be said to have been distribution within the meaning of section 6.

. . . To take the pamphlet which was put on the door itself, that was a distribution . . . to the Member of Parliament. It is difficult to say that that was a distribution to the public at large, even if one takes into consideration that apparently his wife was in the house, and his son-in-law and daughter. Nor . . . can one say . . . that the Member of Parliament or his family were a section of the public . . . .

As it seems to this court, a 'section of the public not consisting exclusively of members of an association of which the person publishing or distributing is a member' connotes the idea of an identifiable section of the public who, but for those words, might be said not to be members of the public at large, in other words members of a club or of an association. What is then said is:

'Oh, but there were other pamphlets left in the porch, and one on a beer bottle, and that is a distribution, particularly since with the sound of breaking glass, and the commotion, other people came onto the scene, ordinary members of the public, and apparently walked up Mr Bidwell's private garden or drive or pathway to his porch.'

Again, this court finds it quite impossible to say that leaving four or five pamphlets in a porch could be a distribution to the public. It may be that the public would see them if Mr. Bidwell let them come up to his front door, but it seems impossible to treat that as a distribution by the defendant to the public at large.

It may, of course, be that by putting a pamphlet up on the door and scattering pamphlets in the porch, members of the public might see them; there is no suggestion they could here, because it was dark, and this was some distance from the road. But it might amount to a publication to whoever passed along the road if they could see it. But again, this man was not charged with publication, but only with distribution.

However, the court finds it unnecessary to come to any concluded decision as to the circumstances in which it could be said that there was distribution to the public at large, because in the present case that issue was wholly withdrawn from the jury. Before the jury retired, the chairman read to them the particulars of the indictment, and it began: 'On 16 July of this year distributed,' and the Chairman then said: 'There is no contest about that.' In other words, here, even if there was any evidence of distribution, it was withdrawn from the jury.

Finally, the court would like to say that it seems difficult to believe that Parliament ever intended that there should be any distribution within the meaning of section 6 by leaving a pamphlet of this sort with a Member of Parliament with the object of persuading him to change his policy, and fight against allowing immigrants to come into the country. It is difficult to think that, even if technically there was a distribution or a publication to him, it could be said that in those circumstances it was a distribution or publication intended to stir up hatred. It is the distribution which must be intended to stir up hatred, not the words used.

In these circumstances, this court is quite satisfied that this verdict cannot stand and the conviction must be quashed.

Appeal allowed; conviction quashed.

NOTE

Is the Court of Appeal's interpretation of 'section of the public' in s. 6(2) of the 1965 Act (now in s. 70 of the 1976 Act) consistent with the House of Lords understanding of the same phrase in *Charter v Race Relations Board*, above, p. 382, in the different context of s. 2(1) of the 1968 Act (now s. 20(1) of the 1976 Act)? Should it be? If the National Front were to send through the post copies of a 'Go home blacks' pamphlet to the homes just of members of the Indian Workers Association, would s. 5A apply?

10 The Commission for Racial Equality

Race Relations Act 1976

43. Establishment and Duties of Commission
(i) There shall be a body of Commissioners named the Commission for Racial Equality consisting of at least eight but not more than fifteen individuals each appointed by the Secretary of State on a full-time or part-time basis, which shall have the following duties –
    (*a*) to work towards the elimination of discrimination;
    (*b*) to promote equality of opportunity, and good relations, between persons of different racial groups generally; and
    (*c*) to keep under review the working of this Act and, when they are so required by the Secretary of State or otherwise think it necessary, draw up and submit to the Secretary of State proposals for amending it.

NOTES

1. The CRE has its full complement of 15 members. There are two full-time commissioners—the Chairman (Mr David Lane) and one other. Extra commissioners may be appointed *ad hoc* for the purposes of a particular investigation (s. 49(2)). The CRE is a body corporate (1976 Act, Sch. 1). It is wholly independent of the Government. It is 'not an emanation of the Crown, and shall not act or be treated as the servant or agent of the Crown' (ibid.).
2. The CRE replaces and merges the enforcement and promotional functions of the RRB and the CRC. In carrying out the very wide duties listed in s. 43, it is authorised (i) to 'give financial and other assistance to any organisation appearing to the Commission to be concerned with the promotion of equality of opportunity, and good relations, between persons of different racial groups' (s. 44(1)); (ii) to 'undertake or assist (financially or otherwise) the undertaking by other persons of any research and any educational activities, which appear to the Commission necessary or expedient for the purposes of s. 43(1)' (s. 45(1)); (iii) to issue codes of practice aimed at the elimination of discrimination in employment and/or 'the promotion of equality of opportunity in that field between persons of different racial groups' (s. 47(1)) – a code is being prepared; (iv) to give assistance to an individual bringing a claim under the Act (s. 66, and

see below, p. 402), and (v) to conduct formal investigations as to which see below. The CRE's work is summarised in its annual report.

Race Relations Act 1976

48. Power to conduct formal investigations.
(1) Without prejudice to their general power to do anything requisite for the performance of their duties under section 43(1), the Commission may if they think fit, and shall if required by the Secretary of State, conduct a formal investigation for any purpose connected with the carrying out of those duties. . . .

49. (4) Where the terms of reference of the investigation confine it to activities of persons named in them and the Commission in the course of it propose to investigate any act made unlawful by this Act which they believe that a person so named may have done, the Commission shall –
   (*a*) inform that person of their belief and of their proposal to investigate the act in question; and
   (*b*) offer him an opportunity of making oral or written representations with regard to it (or both oral and written representations if he thinks fit);
and a person so named who avails himself of an opportunity under this subsection of making oral representations may be represented –
   (i) by counsel or a solicitor; or
   (ii) by some other person of his choice, not being a person to whom the Commission object on the ground that he is unsuitable. . . .

51. Recommendations and reports on formal investigations.
(1) If in the light of any of their findings in a formal investigation it appears to the Commission necessary or expedient, whether during the course of the investigation or after its conclusion –
   (*a*) to make to any person, with a view to promoting equality of opportunity between persons of different racial groups who are affected by any of his activities, recommendations for changes in his policies or procedures, or as to any other matters; or
   (*b*) to make to the Secretary of State any recommendations, whether for changes in the law or otherwise,
the Commission shall make those recommendations accordingly.
(2) The Commission shall prepare a report of their findings in any formal investigation conducted by them.

58. Issue of non-discrimination notice.
(1) This section applies to –
   (*a*) an unlawful discriminatory act; and
   (*b*) an act contravening section 28 [discriminatory practices]; and
   (*c*) an act contravening section 29 [advertisements], 30 [instructions to discriminate] or 31 [pressure to discriminate],
and so applies whether or not proceedings have been brought in respect of the act.

(2) If in the course of a formal investigation the Commission become satisfied that a person is committing, or has committed, any such acts, the Commission may in the prescribed manner serve on him a notice in the prescribed form ("a non-discrimination notice") requiring him –
   (*a*) not to commit any such acts; and
   (*b*) where compliance with paragraph (*a*) involves changes in any of his practices or other arrangements –
   (i) to inform the Commission that he has effected those changes and what those changes are; and
   (ii) to take such steps as may be reasonably required by the notice for the purpose of affording that information to other persons concerned.

(5) The Commission shall not serve a non-discrimination notice in respect of any person unless they have first –
   (*a*)given him notice that they are minded to issue a non-discrimination notice in his case, specifying the grounds on which they contemplate doing so; and
   (*b*) offered him an opportunity of making oral or written representations in the matter (or both oral and written representations if he thinks fit) within a period of not less than 28 days specified in the notice; and
   (*c*) taken account of any representation so made by him.

59. Appeal against non-discrimination notice.
(1) Not later than six weeks after a non-discrimination notice is served on any person he may appeal against any requirement of the notice –
    (*a*) to an industrial tribunal, so far as the requirement relates to note which are within the jurisdiction of the tribunal;
    (*b*) to a designated county court or a sheriff court, so far as the requirement relates to acts which are within the jurisdiction of the court and are not within the jurisdiction of an industrial tribunal.

(2) Where the tribunal or court considers a requirement in respect of which an appeal is brought under subsection (1) to be unreasonable because it is based on an incorrect finding of fact or for any other reason, the tribunal or court shall quash the requirement.

NOTES

1. The CRE's power to conduct formal investigations is a key part of the strategy of the 1976 Act. An investigation may concern any question of discrimination within the Act. It can be exercised on a very broad front (e.g. the proposed investigation of the immigration service, below, and the pending investigation of employment by the National Bus Company, CRE Report 1978, p. 7) or in respect of a particular complaint (see the *Genture Restaurants Ltd* case, below). The wide-ranging nature of the power, coupled with the powers to subpoena written and oral evidence (s. 50) and to issue non-discrimination notices that are binding in law makes it potentially a much more formidable weapon than the limited investigative power that the RRB had (1968 Act, s. 17).
2. By the end of 1979, five investigations had been completed: the *Genture Restaurants Ltd* case, below; the *Barlavington Manor Children's Home* case, Formal Investigation report, April 1979; *Antwerp Arms Public House* case, Formal Investigation report November 1979; the *Mount Pleasant United Working Men's Club* case, Formal Investigation report, December 1979; the *Woodhouse Recreation Club* case, Formal Investigation report, December 1979. Discrimination was found to have occurred and a non-discrimination notice issued in each of these cases. Over 20 investigations are in progress; more than half concern employment (CRE Report 1978, p. 5). In the preface to its report in the *Genture Restaurants Ltd* case, the CRE commented on its power to conduct formal investigations as follows:

'In order to exercise this power most effectively, the Commission have devised a strategy of investigations and will be examining in depth those areas of activity where, in their view, it is most important that discrimination should be eliminated and equality of opportunity provided. Moreover, in addition to these broad, strategic enquiries the Commission will conduct formal investigations if they receive strong evidence of particular acts of discrimination and it appears that an investigation would be the best way of tackling the matter. These investigations will not generally be extensive but sometimes they will have far reaching consequences and implications. They may, for example, identify unlawful practices which are used throughout the country; or they may bring home to other organisations in the same field of activity the need to ensure as effectively as possible that their practices are free from discrimination.'

Most of the investigations underway are into 'particular acts of discrimination'. It has been suggested that the CRE should concentrate on fewer and more general cases (*A Review of the Race Relations Act 1976*, Runnymede Trust, 1979, p. 91). In 1979, the Attorney-General's Office advised the Home Office that the CRE was not empowered to conduct a formal investigation into racial discrimination in the immigration service. The advice was given after the CRE had indicated that it proposed to conduct such an investigation unless the Home Office conducted its own,

(*The Guardian*, 20 July 1979). One incident which had led the CRE to take this initiative was the disclosure that Asian women had been required to undergo virginity tests before entry into the UK (ibid.). What, if anything, is there in the wording of s. 48 or any other provision of the 1976 Act that could be the basis for the Attorney-General's advice? Is that advice binding upon the CRE, an independent body? Could Commissioners be surcharged or dismissed if they were to go ahead despite the advice?

3. Sections 49(4) and 58(5) provide certain safeguards for a 'fair hearing' for a person (i) when a decision has been taken to investigate his conduct and (ii) when it has been investigated and the CRE is 'minded to' issue a non-discrimination notice against him. He also has a right of appeal against a notice under s. 59(1). The CRE has criticised the s. 49(4) procedure (CRE 1979, p. 6):

'Our progress in formal investigations must inevitably be slow. The issues under enquiry are often very complex, and great care is required in the interests of natural justice. But in our view the procedures laid down by the Act are unnecessarily cumbersome in one major respect. By virtue of Section 49(4) we are obliged to give respondents the opportunity to make representations before we embark on investigations where we believe that those respondents may have committed acts of unlawful discrimination. This sometimes involves delays of several months, and it does not give a respondent any significant extra safeguard because:
  (*a*) we have the power to conduct an investigation even in cases where we have not formed the belief that acts of unlawful discrimination have occurred; and
  (*b*) if we contemplate issuing non-discrimination notices respondents will have the right to make representations before such notices are issued.
Moreover, where we plan to investigate an employer's recruitment practices, and we receive evidence of a single act of discrimination in recruitment by that employer, we are obliged to tell him that we believe he may have discriminated and the grounds for our belief before we can embark on the investigation. This not only wastes time, but puts the investigation on to an unfortunate footing at the very outset.'

The CRE may conduct a further investigation to check whether a notice is being complied with during the 5 years after it has become final (s. 60).

4. A formal investigation report must be published by the Secretary of State if the investigation was one required by him (s. 51(3)). Otherwise, the CRE has the choice of publishing copies of the report or simply making it available for inspection (s. 51(4)). The reports made so far have been published. The CRE is required to keep a register of non-discrimination notices and to make it available for public inspection (s. 61). It is kept in the CRE's library in London.

5. On administrative enforcement of race relations legislation, see J. Jowell, [1965] PL 178.

Genture Restaurants Ltd, Case Report of a formal investigation into certain activities of Genture Restaurants Ltd and its Chairman, Mr J. Weston Edwards, November 1978 (Report published by the CRE)

2. Ms Tranter and Ms Biddle alleged that on 7 July 1977 Mr Weston-Edwards refused to accept a booking from Ms Tranter for a private party to be held at Pollyanna's, a public restaurant owned by Genture Restaurants Ltd, because a large proportion of those attending would be coloured. They also alleged that during their visit to Pollyanna's Mr Weston-Edwards had turned to one of his staff and reminded her of instructions to limit the number of coloured people using Pollyanna's.
3. Ms Hanstock alleged that on 25 July 1977 a member of the staff at Pollyanna's told her in a telephone conversation that Chinese people were not admitted to the restaurant.
4. On the basis of these allegations the Commission decided in September 1977 to conduct a formal investigation under Section 48 of the Race Relations Act 1976, and drew up the following terms of reference:
    The Commission believe that Genture Restaurants Ltd and Mr J. Weston-Edwards, its

Chairman, may have done or may be doing acts of any or all of the following descriptions:
>   (*a*) unlawful discriminatory acts in breach of section 20 of the Race Relations Act 1976;
>   (*b*) contraventions of section 30 of the Race Relations Act 1976[3]. . . .

6. In accordance with section 49(4) of the Act, the Commission notified the respondents of their belief stated in the terms of reference and offered them the opportunity to make written or oral representations, or both. They elected not to make representations, and the Commission decided in October 1977 to embark upon the investigation. . . .

25. Having considered all the evidence the Commission decided to accept the account given by Ms Tranter and Ms Biddle of the discussion that took place at Pollyanna's on 7 July between themselves, Mr Weston-Edwards and Ms Trahearn. They were therefore satisfied that on 7 July 1977 the respondents discriminated unlawfully in breach of section 20 of the Race Relations Act 1976 against Ms Tranter by refusing, on racial grounds, to accept her booking for a private party at Pollyanna's Restaurant. . . .

35. The Commission concluded that Ms Tranter and Ms Biddle had given an accurate account of the discussion in the restaurant and accepted that Mr Weston-Edwards instructed Ms Trahearn to limit the admission of coloured people to the restaurant. They were therefore satisfied that the respondents had contravened section 30 of the Race Relations Act 1976 by instructing an employee of the Company to do unlawful discriminatory acts in breach of section 20 of the Act. . . .

39. In the absence of any evidence other than the statement by Ms Hanstock and the respondents' reply [which denied any recollection of the telephone call], the Commission had to decide whether they believed that the alleged telephone call had been made and the conversation accurately reported by Ms Hanstock and whether the Company had in the course of that conversation refused to admit certain Chinese students to Polyanna's Restaurant on the grounds of their ethnic or national origins. The Commission accepted the evidence of Ms Hanstock and concluded that the Company had refused to admit her Chinese students on the grounds of their ethnic or national origins.

40. The Commission were therefore satisfied that on 25 July 1977 Genture Restaurants Ltd committed an unlawful discriminatory act in breach of section 20 of the Race Relations Act 1976 by refusing or deliberately omitting to admit persons on the grounds of their ethnic or national origins.

NOTE

Having found against them, the CRE, after complying with s. 58(5), issued non-discrimination notices against the respondents, who did not exercise their right of appeal under s. 59(1). The order was complied with after the CRE had initiated court proceedings to enforce it. (s. 58(7)).

11 Enforcement in the courts

Race Relations Act 1976

53. Restriction of proceedings for breach of Act.
(1) Except as provided by this Act no proceedings, whether civil or criminal, shall lie against any person in respect of an act by reason that the act is unlawful by virtue of a provision of this Act.
(2) Subsection (1) does not preclude the making of an order of certiorari, mandamus or prohibition.
[ss. 54–6 provide for remedies in employment and similar (partnerships, trade unions, etc) cases arising under Part II (ss. 4–16) of the Act. A person alleging discrimination against him may take his case directly to an industrial tribunal (s. 54(1)). If conciliation through ACAS

---

3. S. 30 reads:
It is unlawful for a person—
>   (*a*) who has authority over another person; or
>   (*b*) in accordance with those wishes that other person is accustomed to act,
to instruct him to do any act which is unlawful by virtue of Part II or III, or procure or attempt to procure the doing by him of any such act.

(s. 55) proves unsuccessful, the tribunal will hear the case and may make an order declaring that discrimination has occurred, award compensation, or recommend action to rectify the wrong done (s. 56).]

57. Claims under Part III
(1) A claim by any person ('the claimant') that another person ('the respondent') –
  (*a*) has committed an act of discrimination against the claimant which is unlawful by virtue of Part III; or
  (*b*) is by virtue of section 32 [vicarious liability of employers and principals] or 33 [aiding unlawful acts] to be treated as having committed such an act of discrimination against the claimant,
may be made the subject of civil proceedings in like manner as any other claim in tort or (in Scotland) in reparation for breach of statutory duty.
(2) Proceedings under subsection (1) –
  (*a*) shall, in England and Wales, be brought only in a designated county court; and
  (*b*) shall, in Scotland, be brought only in a sheriff court;
but all such remedies shall be obtainable in such proceedings as, apart from this subsection and section 53(1), would be obtainable in the High Court or the Court of Session, as the case may be.
(3) As respects an unlawful act of discrimination falling within section 1(1)(*b*), no award of damages shall be made if the respondent proves that the requirement or condition in question was not applied with the intention of treating the claimant unfavourably on racial grounds.
(4) For the avoidance of doubt it is hereby declared that damages in respect of an unlawful act of discrimination may include compensation for injury to feelings whether or not they include compensation under any other head. . . .

NOTES

1. Section 53 excludes the few common law remedies that might be available, e.g. a claim in tort against an innkeeper (see above, p. 379). The prerogative orders remain available where they apply and may be cheaper and quicker to use in some cases.
2. The Act provides for the first time (except for unfair dismissal cases under the Trade Union and Labour Relations Act 1974, as amended) for direct and immediate access to court for an aggrieved individual to challenge acts of discrimination contrary to the Race Relations Act. Under the 1968 Act, his only remedy was to complain to the RRB which attempted conciliation and took the case to court if conciliation failed. This approach was criticised as 'paternalistic' and an individual may now take a case claiming a breach (either directly or by virtue of ss. 32 or 33) of Part II (employment and related matters) to an industrial tribunal and of Part III (education, goods, facilities, services, housing, and clubs) to a county court (composed for this purpose of a judge and two lay assessors).
3. The limitation period is very short. Cases must be brought within 3 months of the alleged act of discrimination before an industrial tribunal (s. 68(1)) and within 6 months before a county court, except for public sector education cases under ss. 17–18 (8 months) and cases where assistance is sought from the CRE (8 or 9 months) (ss. 68(2)–(4)). The claimant does not have to inform the CRE that he is bringing proceedings, although he will obviously do so if (as in practice he normally has) he seeks the assistance which the CRE can give him (s. 66). In 1978, the CRE considered over 900 applications (i.e. about the number of complaints received annually by the RRB under the 1968 Act). Of those on which decisions were taken

'137 applicants were offered legal representation and 33 were offered representation by the Commission's Legal Officer or Complaints Officers. 334 applicants were offered extensive advice and assistance in preparing their cases. 223 were given only initial advice and assistance in drafting the appropriate documents and questionnaires. 99 were given no assistance. 20 applications were withdrawal and eight were considered to be outside the scope of the Act.' (CRE Report 1978, p. 21).

About two thirds of the applications received during the year concerned employment. Legal aid is available in county court cases. Guidance to local legal aid committees has suggested that legal aid should be given in accordance with the importance of the case to the individual and not the likely amount of damages (which may not be great). Legal aid is not available in industrial tribunal cases, but the 'green form' £25 legal advice scheme applies and trade union representation may be available. In both county court and tribunal cases, the degree of assistance and representation is likely to be important. The CRE 'gave assistance in one form or another in 191 of the 298 cases heard by industrial tribunals in 1978 *and provided representation in 17 of the 20 successful cases*' (CRE Report 1978, p. 22) (Italics added). In *Science Research Council v Nasse* (sex discrimination); *B L Cars Ltd v Vyas* (racial discrimination) [1979] 3 All ER 673, HL, the complainants (who were alleging sex and racial discrimination in promotion and transfer decisions respectively) sought orders of discovery of employers' records about them and their competitors. The House of Lords held that the question of disclosure of confidential documents was for the industrial tribunal to decide in its discretion. In exercising its discretion, the tribunal should, in the words of Lord Wilberforce, act in accordance with the following rules:

> The ultimate test in discrimination (as in other) proceedings is whether discovery is necessary for disposing fairly of the proceedings. If it is, then discovery must be ordered notwithstanding confidentiality. But where the court is impressed with the need to preserve confidentiality in a particular case, it will consider carefully whether the necessary information has been or can be obtained by other means, not involving a breach of confidence.
>
> In order to reach a conclusion whether discovery is necessary notwithstanding confidentiality the tribunal should inspect the documents. It will naturally consider whether justice can be done by special measures such as 'covering up', substituting anonymous references for specific names, or, in rare cases, hearing in camera.

The cases were remitted to the tribunals concerned to inspect the documents.

4. There are special arrangements for the enforcement of the education provisions in ss. 17–19. Ss. 17 and 18 cases arising in the public sector (i.e. excluding universities and independent schools) must be taken first to the Minister for Education (s. 57(5)). They may be referred to a county court if no satisfactory solution has been reached within two months. The general duty in s. 19 is not enforceable under the Act at all, either through the courts or by a non-discrimination notice. It is enforceable instead by the Minister for Education acting under his Education Act 1944 powers (1944 Act, s. 19(4)).

5. The burden of proof in cases arising under the Act is the normal civil law burden of proof upon the balance of probabilities. It falls upon the claimant, although in a case of indirect discrimination the burden of proving that a requirements or condition is 'justifiable' is upon the defendant.

6. The remedies available to an individual in a county court are those available in any tort claim (s. 57(1)). Damages may include damages for injured feelings (s. 57(4)). As noted above, p. 370, no damages may be awarded for indirect discrimination if there is no wrongful intention. In employment cases, a declaration or compensation, including compensation for injured feelings, may be awarded on ordinary tort principles up to £5200 (s. 56(1)). Instead of the power to issue an injunction, there is a power to make a 'recommendation' to take such action as appears to the tribunal to be practicable for the purpose of obviating or reducing the adverse effect of the discrimination (ibid).

7. Enforcement through the CRE by formal investigation and non-discrimination notices has been dealt with in the previous section. Although it lacks the power the RRB had to refer cases in any area covered by the Act arising out of individual complaints to the courts, the CRE retains a limited enforcement role in the courts. As well as giving assistance to claimants bringing their own cases (which has, as noted, been very important so far), the CRE also has the exclusive right to bring legal proceedings before a county court or industrial tribunal to enforce ss. 29 (advertisements), 30 (instructions to discriminate), and 31 (inducement to do so). In each of these cases the tribunal or court may only make a declaration or issue an injunction; no damages or compensation may be awarded (s. 63). See *Zarczynska v Levy*, above, p. 371, on the relationship between claims by the CRE and by individuals. The CRE may also within a five year period obtain an injunction from a county court for 'persistent discrimination' where a non-discrimination notice or an industrial tribunal or county court judgment has been made against a person (s. 62).

8. For differing assessments of the likely effectiveness of the enforcement procedures of the Act, see G. Bindman, (1976) 3 British Journal of Law and Society 110 and M. D. A. Freeman, (1977) 127 NLJ 304. Commenting on the Government White Paper (Cmnd. 6234), the RRB expressed considerable reservation as to the enforcement scheme that has been adopted (RRB Report 1975–76, p. 67):

'On this issue our view remains that the balance of advantage for individuals seeking redress rests strongly with the retention and strengthening of the present conciliation system, combined with the right of complainants to have access to the Courts when they are dissatisfied with the Board's handling of their case.

. . . our objections to the proposals for dealing with complainants . . . mainly concern the difficulties the complainant will meet in formulating his case, the problems of aid and representation for the complainant, and the difficulty he will have in proving discrimination to the satisfaction of a Court or tribunal. We also consider that another major disadvantage is the almost complete separation of the complaints process from the Commission's strategic role. Our strongest reservations, however, relate to the use of County Courts for non-employment complaints. We know from our experience over seven years how reluctant complainants are to face any publicity, and how reluctant judges are to make a finding of discrimination and it is our view that the use of County Courts for non-employment could lead to the Act, outside of the employment field, falling largely into disuse. Even at this late stage we would urge the Government to consider, if not the retention of the present conciliation system, at least the institution of special tribunals to deal with all cases of racial discrimination.'

See also the comments in *A Review of the Race Relations Act 1976*, Runnymede Trust, (1979).

CHAPTER 10

Prisoners' rights

1 Introduction

In 1978, the average daily prison population in England and Wales was 41,796 adults and juveniles (*Report on the Work of the Prison Department 1978*, Cmnd. 7619, p. 3.) The great majority were convicted criminals. The remainder were on remand pending trial, detained prior to deportation or extradition, or in prison for civil contempt. Prisons in England and Wales are administered by the Prison Department of the Home Office. The Secretary of State for Home Affairs is responsible to Parliament for their administration. The law governing the prison system is contained in the Prison Act 1952 and the Prison Rules 1964, S.I. 1964 No. 388, as amended.

Prisons are subject to the supervision of Boards of Visitors. These are independent of the Government and have as their general task that of satisfying themselves as to the state of the prison premises, the administration of the prison and the treatment of the prisoners' (Rule 94(1), Prison Rules). To this end, the full Board normally meets at the prison for which it is responsible once a month (see Rule 93(1)), and at least one of its members must visit the prison between Board meetings (Rule 96(1)). The Board must hear complaints and requests from prisoners and inspect the food (Rule 95(1) (2)). It has access to all prisoners, to all parts of the prison and to prison records (Rule 96(2) (3)). In addition to its supervisory role, a Board also serves as a disciplinary tribunal. Members are appointed by the Home Secretary, usually on the recommendation of the Governor or existing Board members. There are on average 15 members of a Board, of whom about half are magistrates. The effectiveness of a Board of Visitors depends a lot on its own approach to its work and its relationship with the Governor. Zellick ((1974) 24 U of Toronto LJ 331, 338) has expressed doubts about the value of Boards of Visitors as they function at present:

'First, so many of the important decisions are for the Home Office – for example, transfer to another prison – that all the board can do is make a recommendation. They may, however, grant extra visits or letters, for example. Secondly, many of the real complaints about imprisonment – living conditions, diet, overcrowding, type of work, educational facilities – are wholly beyond the scope of the board. Thirdly, prisoners have little confidence in the boards, which they come to identify with the management of the prison, a factor all the more understandable when it is remembered that boards are also a disciplinary tribunal. That is not to say, however, that the board of visitors is not a valuable feature of the English prison system. It does suggest, though, that reform is necessary . . .'.

Concern for prisoners' rights in English law is a recent phenomenon,

echoing earlier developments in the United States where prison adminis-
tration has in the last decade been brought under closer legal control by the
United States courts acting under the US Bill of Rights. See *Prisoners
Rights*, published by the Practising Law Institute, 2 vols (1972) and
T. Emerson, D. Haber and N. Dorsen, *Political and Civil Rights in the
United States*, (4th edn. Vol. 1, 1976) Chap. XVI. On conditions in
American Prisons, see N. Mitford, *The American Prison Business* (1973).
Although the English courts apply the ordinary civil and criminal law to
prisons to protect prisoners and prison staff, the same courts have until
recently regarded the operation of the statutory prison law entirely as an
internal administrative matter. In particular, they have held that a prisoner
may not challenge a breach of the Prison Act or Rules in court. The recent
decision in the *St. Germain* case, below, p. 432, in which it was held that the
courts have jurisdiction to review the proceedings of a Board of Visitors in
disciplinary cases, indicates a departure in one respect from the 'hands off'
doctrine that the courts have previously applied. Legislation over the last
thirty years has brought the prisoner's legal status largely into line with that
of other persons and in the last few years prison practice on such matters as
letters and visits, access to the courts, and disciplinary procedures has been
altered to his advantage also.

Some of these changes in practice have occurred as a result of two
striking developments. First, the Parliamentary Commissioner for
Administration (the Ombudsman), established in 1967, now regularly
investigates prisoners' complaints submitted by Members of Parliament
(who alone can seize him of a case) and his criticisms or comments have led
to the reconsideration of prison practice in some cases and at least revealed
more precisely what that practice is in others. The remedy the
Commissioner offers is a limited one in that he cannot question Prison Rules
and cannot require the prison authorities to take action in a case in which
he finds that maladministration has occurred. The standard outcome of a
case is for the Home Office to apologise or express regret. His Reports for
the parliamentary session 1977–78 include eight prison cases. See the 1st,
5th and 7th Reports, PCA, 1977–78, under the heading 'Home Office'.
These concern such matters as medical treatment, conditions in prison,
access to legal advice, transfer to another prison, parole, and the
notification of a prisoner's illness to his family. The Commissioner found
reason to criticise the prison authorities in a majority of the eight cases. In
one the Home Office agreed to reconsider prison practice.

Secondly, prisoners have since 1966 been able to apply to Strasbourg
under the ECHR. Two cases – the *Golder* and *Knetchl* cases (below, pp. 418
and 422) have led to changes in prison practice. Other prison cases are
pending. Although Strasbourg cases take a long time to be heard (see
above, p. 29), so that the decision may be too late to benefit the applicant
the bringing of the application may cause the Home Office to reconsider a
case while it is pending and a favourable Strasbourg decision will benefit
other prisoners.

The material in this Chapter concentrates upon the position of convicted
adult prisoners, although much of it applies to unconvicted and juvenile
convicted prisoners as well. For reasons of space, many parts of the Prison
Rules (e.g. those concerning medical treatment, clothing, food, religion,
work and parole) are not dealt with. Other topics which can only be
mentioned briefly here are the conditions in prison generally, the use of
drugs and marital rights.

Article 3, ECHR is relevant to the first two of these. In A.6870/75, 10

DRE Com HR 37 (1977), the European Commission of Human Rights declared admissible an application alleging that conditions generally in Broadmoor were contrary to Article 3. Might the overcrowding (in 1977, 4,995 prisoners lived 3 to a cell) (928 HC Deb 18 March 1977 col 793) and other conditions (see the articles by P. Evans in *The Times*, 13, 14, 15 December 1976) in prisons raise the same question. On the 'control units' at Wakefield and Wormwood Scrubs (closed in 1975), see the Fowler Report 1976/77 HC 453, Appendix 15, and (1974) 30 *New Society* 68. An application has been lodged at Strasbourg concerning the conditions in the Maze Prison in Northern Ireland in which IRA prisoners are campaigning for treatment as 'political prisoners' (CE Press Release B (78) 51 18 October 1978). See also *Williams v Home Office*, below, p. 412.

As to the use of drugs, the Home Office has consistently stated that drugs 'are neither prescribed nor given to prisoners for the express purpose of modifying behaviour, but for the restoration of health or the relief of symptoms' (913 HC Deb written answers 21 June 1976 col 312). An editorial in *The Times*, 23 October 1978, refers to an article in the *Prison Medical Journal* which 'describes the experimental use of tranquillizers on prisoners who "show no evidence of formal illness as such", but who present "control problems" and become dangerous or "a nuisance" in the stress of prison conditions.' The six prisoners involved 'were said to have given their consent, but only reluctantly.' A retired prison doctor is reported as stating that hormone treatment has been given to sexual offenders who have consented (despite the possibility of side effects such as the development of female breasts which have to be amputated) in the hope of early release. See *Times* 16 November 1978, p. 5. Might the use of drugs in these cases raise a question of compliance with Article 3, ECHR?

Other questions which have arisen recently at Strasbourg are marriage while in prison and conjugal visits. The Commission has admitted for consideration on the merits the *Hamer* case 10 DRE Com HR 174 (1977) in which the applicant complains that he was refused permission to marry by the Home Office contrary to Article 12, ECHR. When the applicant's case arose, a prisoner was only allowed to marry to legitimise a child. While the decision as to the admissibility of the applicant's case was pending at Strasbourg, the Home Office issued a Circular Instruction whereby, as of 1977, a prisoner with more than 12 months to serve (other than a life sentence prisoner, who will be given permission to marry only when a provisional date for his release has been set) will be given permission to marry, whether to legitimise a child or not (387 HL Deb 1 December 1977 col 1353). The Commission has rejected as inadmissible an application from the UK (*A. 6564/74* 2 DRE Com HR 105 (1975)) in which it was argued that the prohibition of conjugal visits to prisoners was a violation of Article 8 and Article 12, ECHR above, pp. 19 and 20.

On prisoners' rights, see S. Cohen and L. Taylor, *Prison Secrets*, (1976); English, in J. W. Bridge, *et al*, (ed), *Fundamental Rights*, (1973) Chap. 15; and G. Zellick (1974) 24 U of Toronto LJ 331. For accounts of prison life by prisoners, see J. Boyle, *A Sense of Freedom*, (1977), and R. Caird, *A Good and Useful Life* (1974). The author of the latter was imprisoned after *R v Caird*, above, p. 160. Although the recollections of prisoners have a tendency towards exaggeration, they do present the consumer's viewpoint and the above accounts are more reliable than most.

In 1978, the Government set up the May Committee to review the role, grading, structure, pay, conditions of service and operational organisation

of the UK Prison Service. The Committee reported in November 1979:
Report of the Committee of Inquiry into the UK Prison Service, Cmnd. 7673.

2 The application of the ordinary law to prisoners and prisons

A considerable improvement in the legal status of the convicted prisoner has occurred during the last 30 years. Although the Forfeiture Act 1870 repealed the law whereby a felon forfeited his land and chattels, other restrictions upon the private and public law status of persons convicted of felony (including prisoners) remained. These were largely abolished by the Criminal Justice Act 1948, section 70(1), or lapsed with the ending, by the Criminal Law Act 1967, section 1, of the distinction between felonies and misdemeanours. A prisoner may not conduct any business activity in prison but will be allowed reasonable facilities for arranging for its conduct on his behalf (e.g. through a power of attorney)[1]. Subject to the governor's discretion, an inmate may be allowed to sign cheques, make and sign documents (e.g. wills, contracts) and to have such documents witnessed. He will not, however, be allowed to do these things in order to engage in his private business. In public law, a prisoner loses his vote in parliamentary and local government elections during his imprisonment (Representation of the People Act 1969, s. 4) and, if his sentence is imprisonment for life, or a term of 5 years or more or detention during Her Majesty's Pleasure – is disqualified from jury service thereafter (Juries Act 1974, Schedule 1, Part II). A person sentenced to a term of imprisonment of 3 years or more may not have a firearm or ammunition in his possession (Firearms Act 1968, s. 21). The Home Office will not renew the passport of a prisoner while he is in prison, other than at the end of his sentence in time for his release.

The ordinary law of the land, both civil and criminal, applies in prisons. Thus the civil and criminal law of assault applies for the protection of prison officers and prisoners alike. So does the law of negligence.

Ellis v Home Office [1953] 2 All ER 149, Court of Appeal

The Plaintiff was an unconvicted prisoner remanded in custody in Winchester prison pending trial. He was placed in the hospital wing (C. 2 Block) because of a suspected illness. The ordinary practice was for prisoners on the wing to be released from their cells each morning in four small groups to empty their slops. On the day in question, they were all released together because of a shortage of staff. At a time when they were so released and when the only prison officer on duty was, for a reason that was never explained, not in attendance, prisoner H entered the plaintiff's cell and assaulted him with an instrument causing serious injury to his head. H was a convicted prisoner who had been placed in the hospital wing for observation because of a report that he was mentally defective. The plaintiff brought a claim against the Home Office for breach of the Prison Rules (failure to segregate convicted and unconvicted prisoners) and for negligence. The former claim was dismissed. The following extracts concern the appeal to the Court of Appeal against Devlin J's dismissal of the claim in negligence.
Jenkins LJ: . . .

---

1. This, and much of the other information on prison practice was supplied by the Home Office.

There remains the claim for negligence at common law. That claim was pleaded solely on the footing that the defendants knew or ought to have known that Hammill was a man of violent propensities, i.e., a person who might be expected at any moment to make a violent and unprovoked attack on a fellow prisoner. The learned judge, having heard the evidence, and having seen the witnesses (and in particular having heard the evidence of the prison medical officer, Dr Fenton) found, in effect, that, although, admittedly, Hammill was a mental defective, there were no circumstances in his history as then known, and no symptoms of his insanity then observable by reason of which the prison authorities either knew or ought to have known that he was any more violent or dangerous than an ordinary prisoner. In my view, on that finding of fact this claim must fail, and it would be wrong for us sitting in appeal to disturb the conclusion of the learned judge. He held (and, indeed, it was not in dispute) that the common law duty owed by the prison authorities to the plaintiff as an inmate of Winchester Prison was to take reasonable care for the safety of the plaintiff as a person in the custody of the prison authorities. The finding of the learned judge as to what the defendants knew or ought to have known in regard to Hammill's state of mind and his probable conduct absolved the defendants from taking any special precautions to prevent Hammill having access to other prisoners. Once the need for special vigilance based on actual or imputed knowledge of Hammill's dangerous abnormality is out of the way, in my view (though I regard the case as near the line), the conduct of the prison officer, McHugh, in leaving the C.2 block during the period of the slopping-out operation without locking up all the cells, and, in particular, in leaving Hammill's cell door open and the plaintiff's cell door open so that Hammill could have access to the plaintiff, irregular though it may have been, and remiss though McHugh may have been in thus absenting himself, could not have been reasonably expected to result in an attack being made by Hammill on the plaintiff, or (to view the matter more generally) in an attack being made by one or other of the prisoners on one or other of his fellow prisoners, the victim as it happened turning out to be the plaintiff, with Hammill as the aggressor.

...although the plaintiff has not succeeded in fixing the defendants with liability in the particular circumstances of this case, the evidence can hardly be said to have shown that the administration of the prison at the date in question was all that it should have been. No doubt, the authorities have their difficulties in the way of finding suitable staff, and so on, but I cannot regard the course of events on that day as reflecting any credit on the people in charge.

Devlin J, felt grave concern about this case from another point of view. In his judgment he said:

'The plaintiff is in the unfortunate position that he has been quite unable to test that evidence [in regard to Hammill] in any way at all. The facts relating to Hammill's behaviour in prison are known only to the prison authorities. Documents, of course, are brought into existence in relation to that. The hospital officers prepare a daily report in which, of course, it would be their business to note down anything with regard to Hammill which was significant, because he was put in the C.2 wing in order that he might be kept under observation. Those reports, if they were examined, might or might not show something which would lead a medical man to suppose that Hammill's conduct ought to have given rise to a suspicion of violence. Those reports are not before the court because the defendants—who are, of course, also the Crown—have claimed Crown privilege for them, and that claim has not been challenged. Having regard to *Duncan v Cammell Laird & Co Ltd* [1942] AC 624 HL., I suppose it could not be sensibly challenged.

Having stated his conclusion, the learned judge said this:

'But before I leave this case I must express, as I have expressed during the hearing of the case, my uneasy feeling that justice may not have been done because the material before me was not complete, and something more than an uneasy feeling that, whether justice has been done or not, it certainly will not appear to have been done.'

That is a serious thing for a judge to have to say as to the administration of justice in his court.

Morris and **Singleton JJ** delivered concurring judgments.

Appeal dismissed.

NOTES

1. *Ellis v Home Office* confirms that the Home Office owes a duty of care in negligence to prisoners to protect them from assaults by other prisoners. In *Anderson v Home Office* (1965) *Times*, 8 October, the duty was stated as going 'no farther than a duty to take reasonable steps to protect prisoners under their charge against dangers they knew or ought to have known'. As in *Ellis's* case, no breach of duty was found to have occurred on the facts

The plaintiff was badly slashed in the face by another prisoner in the exercise yard and required 25 stitches. No prison officer on duty witnessed the incident and although 'it must have been seen by a considerable number of the prisoners', they 'to a man when interviewed denied having seen anything at all'. That such claims can succeed is shown by *D'Arcy v Prison Comrs* [1956] Crim LR 56, DC, in which the plaintiff was slashed in the face and neck by fellow prisoners and recovered £190 damages in negligence.
2. The common law duty in negligence 'to take reasonable care for the safety of . . . [persons] in the custody of the prison authorities' (Jenkins LJ) extends beyond attacks by other prisoners. In several Commonwealth cases, it has been applied to prison work. In *Morgan v A-G* [1965] NZLR 134, NZ S Ct, the plaintiff was issued with boots that were inadequate for the work of log-cutting to which he was assigned. He was awarded damages for an injury to his foot. In *Danard v R* [1971] FC 417, F Ct Can, in which a prisoner was awarded damages for an injury caused when he was ordered to mow the grass on a slope made slippery by rain, the court emphasised that the plaintiff would have been guilty of a disciplinary offence if he had not obeyed orders. In the English courts, in *Pullen v Prison Comrs* [1957] 3 All ER 470, DC, in which it was held that the Factories Act did not apply to prison workshops, Lord Goddard LCJ would have been prepared to have found in favour of the plaintiff at common law if his tuberculosis could have been shown to have been caused by negligence on the part of the prison authorities in placing him in the workshop where he was sent to work. More recently, in *Ferguson v Home Office* (1977) *Times*, 8 October, Caulfield J awarded damages to a prisoner who was injured while using a circular saw to which he had been assigned without adequate training. The duty to take reasonable care in a work context is distinct from the common law duty to provide a safe system of work. The latter does not apply since a prisoner is not an employee: *Morgan v A-G* [1965] NZLR 134 NZ S Ct. See also *Pullen v Prison Comrs* [1975] 3 All ER 470, DC.
3. For cases in which prison officers were prosecuted in the criminal courts, see those arising out of the Hull Prison Riot of 1976, as to which see the Fowler Report, 1976–77 HC 453. 8 prison officers (out of 12 who were prosecuted) were convicted of conspiracy to assault prisoners. They were given sentences ranging from four to nine months imprisonment suspended for two years. See *The Guardian*, 5 and 6 April 1979.
4. *Forced feeding.* In *Leigh v Gladstone* (1909) 26 TLR 139, a suffragette who had been forcibly fed while on hunger strike in prison failed in her claim for damages for assault. Lord Alverstone CJ said that it was the legal duty 'both under the [Prison] Rules and apart from the Rules, of the officials to preserve the health and lives of the prisoners, who were in the custody of the Crown'. There was, as a result, no liability in tort when forced feeding was necessary for reasons of health and when effected without 'undue violence'. *Leigh v Gladstone* remains the only English case on the legality of forced-feeding. The case has been criticised because the question of a common law duty to force-feed was not argued fully and because such a duty runs counter to the principle of self-determination. Most commentators take the view that the common law rule should be that medical treatment may not be given to an individual who is capable of refusing his consent to it and does so. See e.g. Lord Devlin, *Samples of Lawmaking*, (1962), pp. 91–2; P. D. G. Skegg, (1974) 90 LQR 512, 523–9; and G. Zellick, [1976] PL 153, 170–1. Lord Alverstone's direction to the jury, which goes the other way, is limited in terms to the prison custodial situation. If the general view is correct, is there any reason for treating the

prisoner as an exception so that his refusal of consent is not conclusive? Prison discipline? *In loco parentis*? The political or other embarrassment of a death on hunger strike? The common law criminal offence of suicide was abolished by the Suicide Act 1961. Does this affect the authority of *Leigh v Gladstone*?

In a statement in 1974, the Home Secretary stated that a prison doctor was not required by 'prison practice' (i.e. under Standing Orders or other instructions to employees) to feed a prisoner against his will (877 HC Deb 17 July 1974 col 451). In the same year, the British Medical Association issued an ethical statement in which the decision to feed by force was left to the individual doctor's conscience (1974 British Medical Journal 2, 52). Mr Jenkin's statement arose out of the forced feeding of the Price sisters, convicted IRA bombers who went on hunger strike to obtain their transfer to a prison in Northern Ireland. Two other prisoners were fed by force in 1975. There would appear to have been no case of forced feeding since then, although prisoners still go on hunger strike.

5. *Crown Privilege. Ellis v Home Office* was the high water mark of the old approach to crown privilege. See [1954] CLJ 11; (1953) 69 LQR 449; (1953) 16 MLR 509. Applying *Duncan v Cammell Laird* widely, the courts in the 1950s and early 1960s were prepared to accept without question a claim of crown privilege of the class claim kind made in *Ellis v Home Office* if the Crown submitted an affidavit to the effect that the documents should not be admitted in evidence in the public interest. As a result of the disquiet caused by *Ellis v Home Office* and other cases, the Lord Chancellor (Viscount Kilmuir) made a statement in Parliament (197 HL Deb 6 June 1956 col 741) in which he indicated that in future the Crown would not normally claim privilege in respect of certain kinds of documents, including prison medical reports.

Since then, the courts have become less 'executive-minded' (*Liversidge v Anderson* [1942] AC 206 at 244, HL, per Lord Atkin) and *Conway v Rimmer* [1968] AC 910, HL, suggests that, even if made, the medical report class claim put forward in *Ellis v Home Office* would not be accepted now. The Crown also claimed privilege successfully in *Ellis v Home Office* in respect of another document because it contained the Prison Standing Orders in an appendix. Would such a claim be successful today?

The disclosure of documents concerning 'control units' was ordered in *Williams v Home Office*, below, p. 412.

Arbon v Anderson [1943] KB 252, [1942], All ER 264, 112 LJKB 183 Goddard J

This was an action for breach of statutory duty for alleged breach of the Prison Rules 1933 in the detention of prisoners on remand.

Goddard J: . . . With regard to the Prison Rules, it would be enough to say that there were no breaches, but, in case a higher court should take a different view, I should say that, in my opinion, neither do these rules confer rights on prisoners which can be enforced by action. They are made under the Prison Act 1898, s. 2, for the 'government of prisons.' I think it unnecessary to review the long series of cases which deal with the question whether the breach of a duty imposed by statute confers a right of action on an individual. The question depends on the scope and language of the Act which creates the obligation and on considerations of policy and convenience: per Lord Macnaghten in *Pasmore v Oswaldtwistle Urban Council* [1898] AC 397. Whether the Act provides for a penalty or whether some special tribunal is set up to deal with matters arising under the Act are matters, no doubt, to be taken into account in determining whether a cause of action is also given, and either may be the determining factor, but neither the presence nor the absence of such a provision is conclusive. The real question which falls to be determined is whether it is intended by the statute to confer an individual right. I am clearly of opinion that neither the Prison Act 1898, nor the rules were intended to confer any such right.

. . . it seems to me impossible to say that, if [A prisoner] . . . can prove some departure from the prison rules which caused him inconvenience or detriment, he can maintain an action. It would be fatal to all discipline in prisons if governors and warders had to perform their duty always with the fear of an action before their eyes if they in any way deviated from the rules. The safeguards against abuse are appeals to the governor, to the visiting committee, and finally to the Secretary of State, and those, in my opinion, are the only remedies. *Judgment for defendants.*

NOTES

1. The same approach was taken by the Court of Appeal in *Becker v Home Office* [1972] 2 QB 407. The plaintiff, a prisoner, sought to rely on the Prison Rules 1964 when claiming, inter alia, damages against the Home Office for the wrongful detention of a cheque. In the course of rejecting the claim, Lord Denning MR stated:

'If the courts were to entertain actions by disgruntled prisoners, the governor's life would be made intolerable. The discipline of the prison would be undermined. The Prison Rules are regulatory directions only. Even if they are not observed, they do not give rise to a cause of action.'

In *Silverman v Prison Commissioners* [1955] Crim LR 116, Streatfeild J held that the courts had no jurisdiction to grant a declaration to the effect that a Prison Rule was ultra vires, because the Prison Rules did not confer enforceable legal rights on prisoners.

2. Should a prisoner be allowed a remedy in the courts for some or all breaches of the Prison Rules? Or is the internal complaints procedure (below p. 413) and the possibility of recourse (a) to the Parliamentary Commissioner through a Member of Parliament and (b) to the European Commission of Human Rights (before which he may challenge the Prison Rules themselves as well as breaches of them) sufficient?

3. In the case of some breaches of the Prison Rules – e.g. the use of unnecessary force by a prison officer against a prisoner (Rule 44(1)) – there will be a remedy in tort or in criminal law. The same will not be true in respect of a breach of most of the Rules, e.g. those concerning letters and visits (below, p. 415).

4. In *Williams v Home Office* (1980) *Times* 10 May, pp. 1, 2, a claim for damages for false imprisonment and a declaration in respect of detention in a 'control unit' failed, notwithstanding a breach of the prison rules.

3 Prison law generally

The legal rules applying in prisons are mostly contained in the Prison Act 1952 and the Prison Rules 1964, S.I. 1964, No. 388, as amended by S.I. 1968, No. 440; S.I. 1971, No. 2019; S.I. 1972, No. 1860; S.I. 1974, No. 713; S.I. 1976, No. 503, made under it. The Act establishes the general framework and the Rules fill in some of the details. A booklet containing information about prison taken from the Rules and other sources is made available to prisoners. Rule 7, Prison Rules reads:

'*Information to prisoners* – (1) Every prisoner shall be provided, in his cell or room, with information in writing about those provisions of these Rules and other matters which it is necessary that he should know, including earnings and privileges, and the proper method of making complaints and of petitioning the Secretary of State.

(2) The governor, or an officer deputed by him, shall ensure that every prisoner has as soon as possible after his reception into prison and in any case within 24 hours, read the information so provided or, in the case of a prisoner who cannot read or has difficulty in understanding, had it so explained to him that he can understand his rights and duties.'

'A complete copy of the Rules can be made available upon request' (933 HC Deb written answers, 24 March 1977 col 601). The rules are available to the public as statutory instruments.

The Prison Rules leave a lot of discretion to the prison authorities. This is exercised in accordance with the Prison Standing Orders, Circular Instructions, and other documents, all of which are issued by the Prison Department of the Home Office. Consistently with the very centralised nature of the prison service (much more centralised than the police service), these documents are very detailed. Even so, a lot of discretion still remains to be exercised in particular cases so that practice may vary a lot from one prison to another. Action based upon Standing Orders, etc., is lawful insofar as it is consistent with the Prison Act and Rules. They are 'management instructions issued for official purposes' (384 HL Deb 27 June 1977 Col 994). As such they are not made available to prisoners or the general public, although some of their contents become known through, for example, the booklet given to prisoners, statements in Parliament and the *Reports* of the Parliamentary Commissioner. There are copies of the Standing Orders, available to Members of Parliament, in the House of Commons and House of Lords libraries. Should they and Circular Instructions, etc., be made more generally available to prisoners and the public so far as they concern the treatment of prisoners?

On government secrecy generally, see pp. 272–291 above. As civil servants, prison officers are subject to the Official Secrets Act in what they say about their work. The 1972 Franks Committee Report on Section 2 of the Official Secrets Act 1911 (Cmnd. 5104) proposed that information about prison treatment should be available to the public. This was a matter of public interest and 'Parliament and the people need adequate information to satisfy themselves that proper and effective measures are being taken and proper standards of behaviour are being observed' (para. 172).

4 Complaints and requests

Prison Rules 1964

8. Applications.
(1) Every request by a prisoner to see the governor, a visiting officer of the Secretary of State or a member of the . . . board of visitors shall be recorded by the officer to whom it is made and promptly passed on to the governor.
(2) On every day, other than a Sunday or public holiday, the governor shall hear the applications of prisoners who have asked to see him.
(3) Where a prisoner has asked to see any other such person as aforesaid, the governor shall ensure that that person is told of the request on his next visit to the prison.

NOTES

1. Rule 8 indicates how a prisoner may register a complaint or a request within the prison system. In most cases, a prisoner will apply to the Governor. He may prefer to wait until the next monthly visit of the Board of Visitors or for the visit of a Board member between full Board visits. Or he may wait for the next (probably quarterly) visit of a 'visiting officer of the

Secretary of State' (usually a Regional Director). If he exhausts one of these remedies without success, he is free to try another with the same complaint or request. Another important remedy is the petition to the Home Secretary. The right to make such a petition is not stated in the Prison Rules in general terms (it is implied in, e.g., Rule 34(7) (8), below, p. 415, and Rule 56, below, p. 426) but follows from the constitutional right to petition the Crown. A petition is channelled through the Governor and is usually forwarded with a report and a recommendation attached. In most cases the prisoner will be expected to have his case considered locally before making a petition. In some cases (e.g. a request for remission of a disciplinary award (Rule 56) or a request that a prisoner be allowed to appear in court in, for example, matrimonial proceedings concerning him), the matter is one that can only or can most effectively be dealt with by the Home Office so that a petition may be made at once. The length of time it takes for petitions be dealt with varies a lot. Some are dealt with in a matter of days. Others take longer. In one case the Parliamentary Commissioner concluded that 'the Home Office were at fault for taking more than four months to deal with the petition' (6th Report, PCA 1975–76, p. 167). In another case, a petition was not answered for 13 months (6th Report, PCA 1976–77, p. 186). Under Prison Standing Order 5B12 a prisoner cannot, subject to certain exceptions, submit a second petition while he has one outstanding unless the Governor considers the matter to be of such urgency that it cannot wait, see 1st Report, PCA 1976–77, p. 197. The exceptions are where the second petition concerns his conviction or sentence, parole or deportation.

In 1975, about 11,000 petitions were made to the Home Secretary of which about 20% were successful (908, HC Deb written answers, 1 April 1976 col 559). Reasons are not usually given, at least formally, for refusing a petition. The reply in the *Golder* case (below, p. 418) read:

'The Secretary of State has fully considered your petition but is not prepared to grant you your request for transfer, nor can he find grounds for taking any action in regard to the other matters raised in your petition.'

Should a prisoner be entitled to know the reasons why his petition is refused? Might the Bail Act 1976, which now provides a general right to know why bail is refused, provide a relevant precedent?

2. Under Rule 47, Prison Rules, (below, p. 424), it is a disciplinary offence to make a 'false and malicious allegation against an officer' or to 'repeatedly make groundless complaints.' In the *Kiss* case, (1977) 7 DRE Com HR 55 the applicant lost 80 days remission as a punishment for the former offence. The existence of such offences may prevent a prisoner from complaining. Are they necessary in order to protect prison officers and ensure the good running of the prison?

3. The Home Office has refused to recognise a prisoners' trade union or pressure group which might act for prisoners collectively. Preservation of the Rights of Prisoners (PROP) is the prisoners' unofficial trade union. It has no special standing and is treated like any other unofficial organisation. Any correspondence with PROP is subject to the rules governing prisoners' correspondence generally. This means that a prisoner is not permitted in any letter to PROP (which would be counted against his ordinary entitlement of letters) to discuss crime in general, to write about his treatment in prison, or ask that any proceedings be taken on his behalf. Visits by PROP representatives are not normally permitted.

5 Letters and visits

Prison Rules 1964

33. Letters and visits generally.
(1) The Secretary of State may, with a view to securing discipline and good order or the prevention of crime or in the interests of any persons, impose restrictions, either generally or in a particular case, upon the communications to be permitted between a prisoner and other persons.
(2) Except as provided by statute or these Rules, a prisoner shall not be permitted to communicate with any outside person, or that person with him, without the leave of the Secretary of State.
(3) Except as provided by these Rules, every letter or communication to or from a prisoner [may] be read or examined by the governor or an officer deputed by him, and the governor may, at his discretion, stop any letter or communication on the ground that its contents are objectionable or that it is of inordinate length.
(4) Every visit to a prisoner shall take place within the sight of an officer, unless the Secretary of State otherwise directs.
(5) Except as provided by these Rules, every visit to a prisoner shall take place within the hearing of an officer, unless the Secretary of State otherwise directs.
(6) The Secretary of State may give directions, generally or in relation to any visit or class of visits, concerning the days and times when prisoners may be visited.

34. Personal letters and visits.
(1) An unconvicted prisoner may send and receive as many letters and may receive as many visits as he wishes within such limits and subject to such conditions as the Secretary of State may direct, either generally or in a particular case.
(2) A convicted prisoner shall be entitled—
    (*a*) to send and to receive a letter on his reception into a prison and thereafter once a week; and
    (*b*) to receive a visit once in four weeks. . . .
(3) The governor may allow a prisoner an additional letter or visit where necessary for his welfare or that of his family.
(4) The governor may allow a prisoner entitled to a visit to send and to receive a letter instead.
(5) The governor may defer the right of a prisoner to a visit until the expiration of any period of cellular confinement.
(6) The . . . board of visitors may allow a prisoner an additional letter or visit in special circumstances, and may direct that a visit may extend beyond the normal duration.
(7) The Secretary of State may allow additional letters and visits in relation to any prisoner or class of prisoners.
(8) A prisoner shall not be entitled under this Rule to communicate with any person in connection with any legal or other business, or with any person other than a relative or friend, except with the leave of the Secretary of State.
(9) Any letter or visit under the succeeding provisions of these Rules shall not be counted as a letter or visit for the purposes of this Rule.

37. Legal advisers.
(1) The legal adviser of a prisoner in any legal proceedings, civil or criminal, to which the prisoner is a party shall be afforded reasonable facilities for interviewing him in connection with those proceedings, and may do so out of hearing but in the sight of an officer.
(2) A prisoner's legal adviser may, with the leave of the Secretary of State, interview the prisoner in connection with any other legal business in the sight and hearing of an officer.

37A. Further facilities in connection with legal proceedings.
(1) A prisoner who is a party to any legal proceedings may correspond with his legal adviser in connection with the proceedings and unless the Governor has reason to suppose that any such correspondence contains matter not relating to the proceeding it shall not be read or stopped under Rule 33(3) of these Rules.
(2) A prisoner shall on request be provided with any writing materials necessary for the purposes of paragraph (1) of this Rule.
(3) Subject to any directions given in the particular case by the Secretary of State, a registered medical practitioner selected by or on behalf of such a prisoner as aforesaid shall be afforded reasonable facilities for examining him in connection with the proceedings, and may do so out of hearing but in the sight of an officer.

(4) Subject to any directions of the Secretary of State, a prisoner may correspond with a solicitor for the purpose of obtaining legal advice concerning any cause of action in relation to which the prisoner may become a party to civil proceedings or for the purpose of instructing the solicitor to issue such proceedings.

NOTES

1. *Restrictions on Letters.* There are extensive restrictions, stemming from the above Rules, upon the convicted prisoner's freedom to correspond by letter with the outside world. In particular, there are limitations upon the number of letters, the identity of the prisoner's correspondents, and the contents of the letters. See A. Beaven, (1979) 95 LQR 393, 404–9.

Under Rule 34(2), a prisoner may send out of public funds and receive one letter a week. Under Standing Orders, he may send and receive an extra letter a week provided that, in the case of the outgoing letter, he pays for the stamp himself. Such outgoing letters are known as 'canteen' letters because the stamp is bought (out of earnings) at the prisoners' 'canteen', or shop. More letters are commonly permitted to the extent that there is the staff needed to censor them. Can a limit on the number of letters that a prisoner sends out or receives be justified under Article 8, ECHR? See F. G. Jacobs, *The European Convention on Human Rights* (1975), p. 141, and the *Golder* case, below, p. 418.

Prisoners are not permitted to write to the press or 'to correspond with marriage bureaux or with pen-friends obtained through advertisements in newspapers or magazines' (S.O. 5A23(3), quoted in 4th Report, PCA, 1974–5, p. 115). Letters to the press occasionally avoid detection. Permission to correspond with any person not known to the prisoner before his imprisonment may be refused (See 4th Report, PCA, 1974–5, p. 115), as may permission to correspond with a person who is or has been a convicted prisoner unless that person is closely related to the prisoner (see ibid. p. 122). A prisoner may be prevented from corresponding with a person who has been precluded for any reason from visiting him (see ibid). Are these restrictions consistent with Rules 33 and 34 and with Article 8, ECHR?

As to the contents of letters, Standing Orders do not permit a prisoner to correspond with anyone other than his Member of Parliament about his treatment in prison. In one case, two letters to a prisoner's friend and two others to the NCCL and the Howard League for Penal Reform were stopped on this ground (6th Report, PCA, 1975–6, pp. 144–5). Correspondence with such organisations on matters other than complaints about prison treatment and conditions is permitted. Under Standing Order 5C1 a letter to a Member of Parliament on a matter of prison treatment is only permitted after the internal remedies have been used without success. (See *ibid* and Vol 901 H C Deb written answers, 1 December 1975 col 378). Commenting on this requirement, a Government spokesman agreed that 'many cases take many months to dispose of' internally. (387 H L Deb December 13 1977 col 2102) and see above, p. 414. Should a prisoner only be allowed to correspond with his Member of Parliament about his treatment in prison and then only after internal remedies have been exhausted? Are these restrictions consistent with Rule 33(1), Prison Rules? Or with Article 8, ECHR? See the *Golder* case, below, p. 418. Is the fact that a complaint to a Member of Parliament will lead in any event to an internal investigation to provide an answer for the Member a good reason for requiring the internal complaint procedure to be followed before a prisoner is allowed to write to a Member of Parliament? If a prisoner's letter contains matters relating to his health or medical treatment, the normal practice is to refer it to the prison medical staff before posting it (6th Report, PCA, 1975–76, p. 145). The Parliamentary Commissioner remarked of this last practice that the 'price may be some delay in the posting of prisoner's letters but, provided that is kept to a minimum, it seems to me to be a reasonable price to pay for what could be a useful safeguard' (ibid). Letters which contain threats to anyone or obscene language may be stopped as 'objectionable' (Rule 33(3)).

Does the wording 'with a view to securing discipline', etc., at the beginning of Rule 33(1) control the Governor when deciding whether to stop a letter as 'objectionable' under Rule 33(3)?

A criticism which the Parliamentary Commissioner made in one case was of a lack of consistency in censorship decisions. This, the Commissioner concluded, 'may have caused the complainant to suspect that his correspondence was being dealt with in an arbitrary fashion' (1st Report, PCA, 1976–7, p. 189).

2. *Reading of Letters.* With the exception of legal correspondence under Rule 37A(1), a prisoner's outgoing and incoming correspondence 'may' be read under Rule 33(3), Prison Rules. In practice, it is always read, except that in open prisons 'censorship of correspondence with relatives and friends has been virtually abolished' (387 H L Deb 13 December 1977 col 2104). From July 1975, inmates at open prisons have been able to hand ordinary domestic letters to the prison staff sealed for posting. Incoming post is opened by the censor officer in the inmate's presence, and those which appear to be ordinary domestic letters, with no contraband or cash enclosed, are handed to him unread. The normal rules about the content of letters continue to apply and random checks are made to see that they are complied with.

A prisoner is told if an outgoing letter is stopped and is usually told why. The prisoner will be offered an opportunity to rewrite an outgoing letter where appropriate. The original letter may not be returned to him, but is placed on his file 'to ensure that evidence is available to establish whether the decision to stop a particular letter is justified' (see 1st Report, PCA, 1976–77, p. 198). Prisoners are not normally told of incoming letters that have been stopped.

3. In *Procunier v Martinez* 416 US 396 (1974), the US Supreme Court stated that the First Amendment guarantee of freedom of expression meant that a prisoner's correspondence cannot be censored 'simply to eliminate unflattering or unwelcome opinions or factually inaccurate statements'. Censorship must instead be necessary in furtherance of 'one or more of the substantial governmental interests of security, order, and rehabilitation'. Is this a criterion that English law could adopt? Does it permit censorship of outgoing letters commenting on a prisoner's treatment? Might it be in the interests of a prisoner's rehabilitation in some cases to allow him to write to persons whom he did not know before he entered prison?

4. *Visits.* A prisoner is entitled to a visit once in four weeks (Rule 34(2)(b)). In most prisons, visits are in fact allowed more frequently than this (388 H L Deb 16 February 1978 col 1516). Most visits are within the sight and hearing of a prison officer (Rule 33(2)(3)). Visits by Members of Parliament are conducted out of the hearing of an officer unless there is a security reason to the contrary (901 H L Deb written answers 1 December 1975 col 378). See also the exception in legal cases, below, p. 423. There are restrictions on the persons who visit prisoners so that, for example, a former convicted prisoner may not do so. Nor may a person not a friend of the prisoner before his imprisonment (925 H C Deb written answers, 3 February 1977 col 237). For a description of visits, see Caird, *A Good and Useful Life* (1974) pp. 34–5.

5. *Telephone calls.* Although there are no formal arrangements whereby convicted prisoners are allowed telephone calls, there are exceptional circumstances when such calls are allowed. A governor has discretion to allow calls where urgent domestic problems would be eased by the prisoner contacting his family, or where visits are impracticable either due to the infirmity of the visitor or geographical inaccessibility. These calls would normally be monitored by a prison officer. There is, currently, however, an experiment being conducted in an 'open prison' in the north of England which permits prisoners to use a coin-box telephone to make unmonitored calls at certain times of the day.

Golder case Eur Court HR, Series A, Vol. 18, Judgment of 21 February 1975

The applicant was serving a prison sentence at Parkhurst Prison in 1969 when a serious disturbance occurred in which L, a prison officer, was assaulted. L made a statement which identified the applicant as one of the assailants. L later made a second statement in which he indicated that he might have been mistaken in his identification and another prison officer gave evidence that the applicant had taken no part in the disturbance. Thereupon, disciplinary charges which it had been proposed to bring against the applicant were dropped and the entry in his prison record about the matter was marked 'charges not proceeded with'. The entry was deleted from the record in 1971 during the examination of the case by the European Commission of Human Rights. The applicant understood that L's first statement was still on his record and believed that this was why he had been refused parole. For this reason, he sought permission from the Home Secretary in 1970 to communicate with a solicitor with a view to bringing a libel action against L. Permission was refused under Rule 34(8), Prison Rules. The applicant then applied to Strasbourg in the same year. The case reached the European Court of Human Rights in 1975 when the Court considered whether the refusal to allow the applicant to communicate with a solicitor was a violation of Articles 6 or 8, ECHR (above, p. 19). The applicant had in the meantime been released on parole in 1972. He did not pursue his libel action.

JUDGMENT OF THE COURT

I. On the alleged violation of Article 6(1)

26 . . . Clearly, no one knows whether Golder would have persisted in carrying out his intention to sue Laird if he had been permitted to consult a solicitor. Furthermore, the information supplied to the Court by the Government gives reason to think that a court in England would not dismiss an action brought by a convicted prisoner on the sole ground that he had managed to cause the writ to be issued – through an attorney for instance – without obtaining leave from the Home Secretary under Rules 33 § 2 and 34 § 8 of the Prison Rules 1964, which in any event did not happen in the present case.

The fact nonetheless remains that Golder had made it most clear that he intended 'taking civil action for libel': it was for this purpose that he wished to contact a solicitor, which was a normal preliminary step in itself and in Golder's case probably essential on account of his imprisonment. By forbidding Golder to make such contact, the Home Secretary actually impeded the launching of the contemplated action. Without formally denying Golder his right to institute proceedings before a court, the Home Secretary did in fact prevent him from commencing an action at that time, 1970. Hindrance in fact can contravene the Convention just like a legal impediment.

It is true that – as the Government have emphasised – on obtaining his release Golder would have been in a position to have recourse to the courts at will, but in March and April 1970 this was still rather remote and hindering the effective exercise of a right may amount to a breach of that right, even if the hindrance is of a temporary character. . . .

28 . . . Article 6 § 1 does not state a right of access to the courts or tribunals in express terms. It enunciates rights which are distinct but stem from the same basic idea and which, taken together, make up a single right not specifically defined in the narrower sense of the term. It is the duty of the Court to ascertain, by means of interpretation, whether access to the courts constitutes one factor or aspect of this right. . . .

[After examining the text of the Convention, its object and purpose and also general principles of law, the Court continued:]

36. Taking all the preceding considerations together, it follows that the right of access constitutes an element which is inherent in the right stated by Article 6 § 1. This is not an extensive interpretation forcing new obligations on the Contracting States: it is based on the very terms of the first sentence of Article 6 § 1 read in its context and having regard to the object and purpose of the Convention, a lawmaking treaty (see the *Wemhoff* judgment of 27 June 1968, Series A no. 7, p. 23, § 8), and to general principles of law. . . .

38. The Court considers . . . that the right of access to the courts is not absolute. As this is a right which the Convention sets forth (see Articles 13, 14, 17 and 25) without, in the narrower sense of the term, defining, there is room, apart from the bounds delimiting the very content of any right, for limitations permitted by implication. . . .

39. The Government and the Commission have cited examples of regulations, and especially of limitations, which are to be found in the national law of states in matters of access to the courts, for instance regulations relating to minors and persons of unsound mind. Although it is of less frequent occurrence and of a very different kind, the restriction complained of by Golder constitutes a further example of such a limitation.

It is not the function of the Court to elaborate a general theory of the limitations admissible in the case of convicted prisoners, nor even to rule *in abstracto* on the compatibility of Rules 33 § 2, 34 § 8 and 37 § 2 of the Prison Rules 1964 with the Convention. Seised of a case which has its origin in a petition presented by an individual, the Court is called upon to pronounce itself only on the point whether or not the application of those Rules in the present case violated the Convention to the prejudice of Golder. . . .

40. . . . In petitioning the Home Secretary for leave to consult a solicitor with a view to suing Laird for libel, Golder was seeking to exculpate himself of the charge made against him by that prison officer on 25 October 1969 and which had entailed for him unpleasant consequences, some of which [mainly the entry still in his record and the refusal of parole] still subsisted by 20 March 1970. . . . Furthermore, the contemplated legal proceedings would have concerned an incident which was connected with prison life and had occurred while the applicant was imprisoned. Finally, those proceedings would have been directed against a member of the prison staff who had made the charge in the course of his duties and who was subject to the Home Secretary's authority.

In these circumstances, Golder could justifiably wish to consult a solicitor with a view to instituting legal proceedings. It was not for the Home Secretary himself to appraise the prospects of the action contemplated; it was for an independent and impartial court to rule on any claim that might be brought. In declining to accord the leave which had been requested, the Home Secretary failed to respect, in the person of Golder, the right to go before a court as guaranteed by Article 6 § 1.

II. On the alleged violation of Article 8 . . .

43. The Home Secretary's refusal of the petition of 20 March 1970 had the direct and immediate effect of preventing Golder from contacting a solicitor by any means whatever, including that which in the ordinary way he would have used to begin with, correspondence. While there was certainly neither stopping nor censorship of any message, such as a letter, which Golder would have written to a solicitor – or vice-versa – and which would have been a piece of correspondence within the meaning of paragraph 1 of Article 8, it would be wrong to conclude therefrom, as do the Government, that this text is inapplicable. Impeding someone from even initiating correspondence constitutes the most far-reaching form of 'interference' (paragraph 2 of Article 8) with the exercise of the "right to respect for correspondence"; it is inconceivable that that should fall outside the scope of Article 8 while mere supervision indisputably falls within it. In any event, if Golder had attempted to write to a solicitor notwithstanding the Home Secretary's decision or without requesting the required permission, that correspondence would have been stopped and he could have invoked Article 8; one

would arrive at a paradoxical and hardly equitable result, if it were considered that in complying with the requirements of the Prison Rules 1964 he lost the benefit of the protection of Article 8. . . .

44. In the submission of the Government, the right to respect for correspondence is subject, apart from interference covered by paragraph 2 of Article 8, to implied limitations resulting, *inter alia*, from the terms of Article 5 § 1 (a): a sentence of imprisonment passed after conviction by a competent court inevitably entails consequences affecting the operation of other Articles of the Convention, including Article 8.

. . . that submission conflicts with the explicit text of Article 8. The restrictive formulation used at paragraph 2 ('There shall be no interference . . . except such as . . .') leaves no room for the concept of implied limitations. In this regard, the legal status of the right to respect for correspondence, which is defined by Article 8 with some precision, provides a clear contrast to that of the right to a court (paragraph 38 above).

45. The Government have submitted in the alternative that the interference complained of satisfied the explicit conditions laid down in paragraph 2 of Article 8.

It is beyond doubt that the interference was 'in accordance with the law', that is Rules 33 § 2 and 34§ 8 of the Prison Rules 1964.

The Court accepts, moreover, that the 'necessity' for interference with the exercise of the right of a convicted prisoner to respect for his correspondence must be appreciated having regard to the ordinary and reasonable requirements of imprisonment. The 'prevention of disorder or crime', for example, may justify wider measures of interference in the case of such a prisoner than in that of a person at liberty. To this extent, but to this extent only, lawful deprivation of liberty within the meaning of Article 5 does not fail to impinge on the application of Article 8. . . .

In order to show why the interference complained of by Golder was 'necessary', the Government advanced the prevention of disorder or crime and, up to a certain point, the interests of public safety and the protection of the rights and freedoms of others. Even having regard to the power of appreciation left to the Contracting States, the Court cannot discern how these considerations, as they are understood 'in a democratic society', could oblige the Home Secretary to prevent Golder from corresponding with a solicitor with a view to suing Laird for libel. The Court again lays stress on the fact that Golder was seeking to exculpate himself of a charge made against him by that prison officer acting in the course of his duties and relating to an incident in prison. In these circumstances, Golder could justifiably wish to write to a solicitor. It was not for the Home Secretary himself to appraise – no more than it is for the Court today – the prospects of the action contemplated; it was for a solicitor to advise the applicant on his rights and then for a court to rule on any action that might be brought.

The Home Secretary's decision proves to be all the less 'necessary in a democratic society' in that the applicant's correspondence with a solicitor would have been a preparatory step to the institution of civil legal proceedings and, therefore, to be exercise of a right embodied in another Article of the Convention, that is, Article 6.

The Court thus reaches the conclusion that there has been a violation of Article 8. . . .

For these reasons, the Court,

1. *Holds* by nine votes to three [Judges Verdross (Austrian) Zekia (Cypriot) and Sir Gerald Fitzmaurice (British) dissented] that there has been a breach of Article 6§ 1,
2. *Holds* unanimously that there has been a breach of Article 8; . . .

NOTES

1. See (1975) 38 MLR 683; (1974– 5) 47 BYIL 391; and G. Triggs, (1976) 50 Aust LJ 229. A breach of the right of access to the courts under the Prison Rules as they existed prior to the *Golder* case was also found to have occurred in the *Hilton* case: CM Res DH (79) 3. There are several other applications concerning prisoners letters (to lawyers and others) pending at Strasbourg. See, e.g. *Colne v UK* (1978) 10 DRE Com HR 154.

2. The Court did not make an award of compensation (see above, p. 29): it considered that a declaratory judgment in favour of the applicant was sufficient reparation.

3. The three dissenting judges considered that Article 6 did not guarantee a right of access to the courts. Judge Sir Gerald Fitzmaurice was the only dissenting judge to take the view that, supposing there were a right of access protected by Article 6, it had not been infringed in the applicant's case:

'He had been prevented from consulting a solicitor with a view – possibly – to having recourse to those courts; but this was not in itself a denial of access to them, and could not be since the Home Secretary and the prison authorities had no power *de jure* to forbid it. I might nevertheless be prepared to hold, as the Court evidently does, that there' had been a "constructive" denial if, *de facto*, the act of refusing to allow Golder to consult a solicitor had had the effect of permanently and finally cutting him off from all chances of recourse to the courts for the purpose of the proceedings he wanted to bring. But this was not the case: he would still have been in time to act even if he had served his full term, which he did not do, being soon released on parole.'

4. In order to comply with the *Golder* case, the Home Secretary added Rule 37A(4) to the Prison Rules. (See the statement by the Home Secretary, Mr Jenkins, 897 HC Deb written answers, 5 August 1975 col 147). This abolishes the need to obtain permission before writing to a solicitor to discuss or institute civil proceedings. (The same absence of a need to obtain permission under Rule 34(8) had earlier been established in respect of correspondence with 'legal advisers' concerning *pending* proceedings (civil *or criminal*) with the introduction of Rule 37A(1) in 1972.) The wording 'Subject to any directions of the Secretary of State' in Rule 37A(4) serves to incorporate Circular Instruction 45/75 (text printed in Logan, 74 *Guardian Gazette* 566 (1977)). This indicates that 'civil' proceedings are understood to include divorce proceedings, civil actions arising out of criminal proceedings (e.g. actions against police officers or witnesses under the Police (Property) Act 1897), and applications for a prerogative order. The Circular Instruction allows the prisoner to choose his own solicitor, 'including a solicitor who is employed by an organisation such as NCCL'. It also contains an important limitation on the freedom of access to a solicitor recognised by Rule 37A(4):

'In the case of any proposed civil proceedings by an inmate against the Home Office (or any Minister or servant of the Home Office) arising out of or in connection with his imprisonment, facilities are not to be granted until the inmate has ventilated his complaints through the normal existing internal channels, ie, by petition to the Secretary of State or by application to the Board of Visitors or a visiting officer of the Secretary of State, or under the procedures of CI 88/1961. The purpose of this is to give management an opportunity of investigating the matters complained of (including, for example, a complaint against an adjudication, finding or award) and taking any necessary steps in the interests both of the prisoner and of prison order.'

In a case in which a prisoner who wished to bring an action for assault against a prison officer was refused access to a solicitor because of the above limitation, the Parliamentary Commissioner expressed the opinion that 'provided the prisoner can have access to his legal adviser if he is dissatisfied with the outcome of the Home Office's investigation of his complaints—and the Parliamentary Under-Secretary of State gave the Member an assurance that this was so . . .—it seems to me a reasonable enough line for them to follow' (1st Report, PCA, 1977–78, pp. 150, 153). Whether information obtained from any statement made by the prisoner in the course of ventilating internal procedures will be used by the Home Office in any subsequent court proceedings that the prisoner may bring 'will depend on its relevance to those proceedings', Home Secretary (Mr Rees), HC Deb (942 HC Deb written answers 23 January 1978 col 414). Would a prisoner such as the applicant in the *Golder* case now have to seek an internal remedy before being allowed to take his libel action to court? Can recourse to the internal complaints procedure provide a satisfactory remedy if the prisoner's purpose in seeking to bring court action is to obtain damages? Might the need to have recourse to it (which, as noted above, p. 414, may take a long time) be a 'hindrance' to the right of access to the courts contrary to the *Golder* case?

5. The *Golder* case was preceded at Strasbourg by the *Knetchl* case (13 YBECHR 730 (1970). Decn. Admiss.) in which the applicant challenged Rule 34(8) as it applied to his proposed civil action for negligent medical treatment. In 1967 the applicant had a leg amputated in prison. He applied to the Home Secretary for permission to contact a solicitor in order to bring a claim against the Home Office for allegedly negligent medical treatment which made the amputation necessary. Permission was refused because 'prisoners were not usually allowed to institute legal proceedings against the prison authorities unless they could make out a prima facie case of negligence', and in this case the applicant had, despite requests, not given sufficient details of his complaint to permit the Home Secretary to find that a prima facie case existed. In 1969, the applicant took his case to Strasbourg alleging violations of Articles 6 and 8 of the Convention. He alleged that the United Kingdom had infringed the right of access to a court in civil proceedings that was impliedly protected by Article 6(1) and that it had also violated the right to respect for his correspondence guaranteed by Article 8(1). The European Commission of Human Rights admitted the application in respect of both allegations. In 1972, the case was settled by a 'friendly settlement' by which the applicant accepted £750 as an ex gratia payment from the British Government in full and final satisfaction of his complaint that he was not allowed to communicate with a solicitor while in prison (Report of the European Commission of Human Rights, 24 March 1972). The applicant had earlier taken his case to the Parliamentary Commissioner, who had found no maladministration and hence had not made a recommendation in the applicant's favour. The Commissioner did, however, suggest to the Home Office that it review the rule governing permission to obtain legal advice in cases of the applicant's kind. The Home Office did this but found no need to make any change. Then the House of Commons Select Committee on the Parliamentary Commissioner examined the case and recommended in 1971 that further consideration be given to the question (2nd Report, Select Committee on the PCA, 1970–1, p. xii). Later in the same year, the Home Office announced the following change in prison practice (Cmnd. 4846):

'Instructions have, therefore, been given that with immediate effect if a prisoner has suffered some physical injury or disablement, or impairment of his physical condition, and claims damages for the alleged negligence of the prison authorities or staff, he will be allowed to consult a solicitor and give instructions for the institution of proceedings in accordance with the latter's advice without restriction unless there are overriding considerations of security. This new practice will apply to cases involving alleged medical negligence. It is already the current practice to grant access freely to legal advice and the courts in cases involving industrial injury or other accidents on prison premises.'

Whether the pending proceedings before the European Commission or the recommendation of the Select Committee had more to do with the Home Office's change of mind is unknown. Despite the wording 'without restriction' in Cmnd. 4846, it would seem that a '*Knetchl* case' is subject to the internal remedies limitation that applies under Rule 37A(4).

6. Rule 37A(4) does not remove the need to obtain permission under Rule 34(8) to correspond with a lawyer or any other person about possible criminal proceedings which a prisoner might wish to bring or about legal matters unconnected with possible court proceedings (e.g. the making of a will or the sale of property). With regard to the former, the Home Secretary (Mr Rees) stated:

'A prisoner may not communicate with a solicitor with a view to instituting criminal proceedings. If he has reason to believe that a criminal offence may have been committed by a member of staff he should inform the governor. If the governor is satisfied after investigation that there appears to be any substance to the allegation he will ordinarily seek instructions from Prison Department Headquarters whether the police should be invited to investigate the matter. If so, the question whether criminal proceedings would be instituted would be for the police to decide' HC Deb (940 HC Deb written answers 9 December 1977 col 901).

The police began investigating the allegations against prison officers at Hull Prison after the 1976 riot, see above, p. 410, as a result of a letter which reached them from a prisoner (*The Guardian*, 5 April 1979).

7. Under Rule 37A(1), a prisoner's correspondence with his 'legal adviser' in respect of *pending* proceedings may not be read or stopped under Rule 33(3) unless there is reason to believe that it contains matter not related to the proceedings. Outgoing letters within Rule 37A(1) must be handed in unsealed. Incoming letters from solicitors marked 'Rule 37A(1)' will only be opened if there is reason to believe that they contain extraneous matter. Enclosures with a letter are treated as a part of the letter for this purpose: Home Secretary (Mr Rees), 942 HC Deb written answers 28 January 1978 col 413). No such exception is made for other legal correspondence, including that within Rule 37A(4). Is a Governor's decision that he 'has reason to suppose' that the correspondence contains extraneous matter (which must clearly be based on information obtained other than by a reading of the letter) subject to review in the courts?

8. *Visits on legal matters.* These may be conducted out of the hearing of a prison officer when they concern legal proceedings to which the prisoner is a party. (Rule 37(1)). Otherwise they must be conducted within the hearing of a prison officer. This is so even though they concern possible proceedings against the Home Office or a prison officer.

9. *Applications to Strasbourg.* In compliance with Article 25(1) *in fine*, ECHR, permission under Rule 34(8) is not needed for a prisoner to write a letter to the European Commission of Human Rights making an application under the ECHR or concerning an application which it is proposed to make or has already been made. But the letter is subject to Rule 33(3). As far as the Home Office is concerned, a prisoner need not exhaust internal remedies before applying to Strasbourg. They must be exhausted, however, before an application will be considered by the Commission (Article 26, ECHR).

Article 25(1) *in fine* is supplemented, for prisoners or their legal advisers 'taking part in proceedings instituted before the Commission', by the European Agreement relating to Persons Participating in Proceedings of the European Commission and Court of Human Rights 1969, (Cmnd. 4699), to which the UK is a party, which provides in Article 3(2) and (3):

'(2) As regards persons under detention, the exercise of this right [to correspond freely, with the Commission and the Court] shall in particular imply that:
(a) if their correspondence is examined by the competent authorities, its despatch and delivery shall nevertheless take place without undue delay and without alteration;
(b) such persons shall not be subjected to disciplinary measures in any form on account of any communication sent through the proper channels to the Commission or the Court;
(c) such persons shall have the right to correspond, and consult out of hearing of other persons, with a lawyer qualified to appear before the courts of the country where they are detained in regard to an application to the Commission, or any proceedings resulting therefrom.

(3) In application of the preceding paragraphs, there shall be no interference by a public authority except such as is in accordance with the law and is necessary in a democratic society in the interests of national security, for the detection or prosecution of a criminal offence or for the protection of health.'

A prisoner's correspondence with a solicitor concerning a pending or proposed application to Strasbourg is also regarded as being subject to Rule 33(3) although in practice it will not be read. A prisoner who has lodged an application with the European Commission is not a 'party to any legal proceedings' so that Rule 37A(1) does not apply: *Guilfoyle* case (decided in the High Court by Pain J) *The Guardian* 5 July 1979. A visit by a solicitor in connection with a pending or a proposed application to Strasbourg may be conducted out of the hearing of a prison officer.

6 Prison discipline[2]

Prison Rules 1964

47. Offences against discipline.
A prisoner shall be guilty of an offence against discipline if he—
(1) mutinies or incites another prisoner to mutiny;
(2) does gross personal violence to an officer;
(3) does gross personal violence to any person not being an officer;
(4) commits any assault;
(5) escapes from prison or from legal custody;
(6) absents himself without permission from any place where he is required to be, whether within or outside prison;
(7) has in his cell or room or in his possession any unauthorised article, or attempts to obtain such an article;
(8) delivers to or receives from any person any unauthorised article;
(9) sells or delivers to any other person, without permission, anything he is allowed to have only for his own use;
(10) takes improperly or is in unauthorised possession of any article belonging to another person or to a prison;
(11) wilfully damages or disfigures any part of the prison or any property not his own;
(12) makes any false and malicious allegation against an officer;
(13) treats with disrespect an officer or any person visiting a prison;
(14) uses any abusive, insolent, threatening or other improper language;
(15) is indecent in language, act or gesture;
(16) repeatedly makes groundless complaints;
(17) is idle, careless or negligent at work or, being required to work, refuses to do so;
(18) disobeys any lawful order or refuses or neglects to conform to any rule or regulation of the prison;
(19) attempts to do any of the foregoing things;
(20) in any way offends against good order and discipline; or
(21) does not return to prison when he should have returned after being temporarily released from prison under Rule 6 of these Rules, or does not comply with any condition upon which he was so released.

48. Disciplinary charges.
(1) Where a prisoner is to be charged with an offence against discipline, the charge shall be laid as soon as possible.
(2) A prisoner who is to be charged with an offence against discipline may be kept apart from other prisoners pending adjudication.
(3) Every charge shall be inquired into, in the first instance, by the governor.
(4) Every charge shall be first inquired into not later, save in exceptional circumstances, than the next day, not being a Sunday or public holiday, after it is laid.

49. Rights of prisoners charged.
(1) Where a prisoner is charged with an offence against discipline, he shall be informed of the charge as soon as possible and, in any case, before the time when it is inquired into by the governor.

---

2. Ed. See also s. 47(2). Prison Act 1952: 'Rules made under this section shall make provisions for ensuring that a person who is charged with any offence under the rules shall be given a proper opportunity of presenting his case'.

(2) At any inquiry into a charge against a prisoner he shall be given a full opportunity of hearing what is alleged against him and of presenting his own case.

50. Governor's awards.

Subject to Rules 51 and 52 of these Rules the governor may make any one or more of the following awards for an offence against discipline: —

(*a*) caution;

(*b*) forfeiture for a period not exceeding 28 days of any of the privileges under Rule 4 of these Rules;

(*c*) exclusion from associated work for a period not exceeding 14 days;

(*d*) stoppage of earnings for a period not exceeding 28 days;

(*e*) cellular confinement for a period not exceeding 3 days;

(*f*) forfeiture of remission of a period not exceeding 28 days;

(*g*) forfeiture for any period, in the case of a prisoner otherwise entitled thereto, of any of the following: —

    (i) the right to be supplied with food and drink under Rule 21 (1) of these Rules; and

    (ii) the right under Rule 41 (1) of these Rules to have the articles there mentioned;

(*h*) forfeiture for any period, in the case of a prisoner otherwise entitled thereto who is guilty of escaping or attempting to escape, of the right to wear clothing of his own under Rule 20 (1) of these Rules.

51. Graver offences.

(1) Where a prisoner is charged with any of the following offences against discipline: —

(*a*) escaping or attempting to escape from prison or from legal custody,

(*b*) assaulting an officer, or

(*c*) doing gross personal violence to any person not being an officer,

the governor shall, unless he dismisses the charge, forthwith inform the Secretary of State and shall, unless otherwise directed by him, refer the charge to the board of visitors.

(2) Where a prisoner is charged with any serious or repeated offence against discipline (not being an offence to which Rule 52 of these Rules applies) for which the awards the governor can make seem insufficient, the governor may, after investigation, refer the charge to the board of visitors.

(3) Where a charge is referred to the board of visitors under this Rule, the chairman thereof shall summon a special meeting at which not more than five nor fewer than two members shall be present.

(4) The Board so constituted shall inquire into the charge and, if they find the offence proved, shall make one or more of the following awards: —

(*a*) caution;

(*b*) forfeiture for any period of any of the privileges under Rule 4 of these Rules;

(*c*) exclusion from associated work for a period not exceeding 56 days;

(*d*) stoppage of earnings for a period not exceeding 56 days;

(*e*) cellular confinement for a period not exceeding 56 days;

(*f*) forfeiture of remission of a period not exceeding 180 days;

(*g*) forfeiture for any period, in the case of a prisoner otherwise entitled thereto, of any of the following: —

    (i) the right to be supplied with food and drink under Rule 21 (1) of these Rules; and

    (ii) the right under Rule 41 (1) of these Rules to have the articles there mentioned;

(*h*) forfeiture for any period, in the case of a prisoner otherwise entitled thereto who is guilty of escaping or attempting to escape, of the right to wear clothing of his own under Rule 20 (1) of these Rules.

(5) The Secretary of State may require any charge to which this Rule applies to be referred to him, instead of to the board of visitors, and in that case an officer of the Secretary of State (not being an officer of a prison) shall inquire into the charge and, if he finds the offence proved, make one or more of the awards listed in paragraph (4) of this Rule.

52. Especially grave offences.

(1) Where a prisoner is charged with one of the following offences: —

(*a*) mutiny or incitement to mutiny; or

(*b*) doing gross personal violence to an officer,

the governor shall forthwith inform the Secretary of State and shall, unless otherwise directed by him, refer the charge to the board of visitors.

(2) Where a charge is referred to the board of visitors under this Rule, the chairman thereof shall summon a special meeting at which not more than five nor fewer than three members, at least two being justices of the peace, shall be present.

(3) The board constituted as aforesaid shall inquire into the charges and, if they find the

offence proved, shall make one or more of the awards listed in Rule 51 (4) of these Rules, so
however that, if they make an award of forfeiture of remission, the period forfeited may exceed
180 days.

56. Remission and mitigation of awards.
(1) The Secretary of State may remit a disciplinary award or mitigate it either by reducing it or
by substituting another award which is, in his opinion, less severe.
(2) Subject to any directions of the Secretary of State, the governor may remit or mitigate any
award made by a governor and the board of visitors may remit or mitigate any disciplinary
award.

NOTES

1. See K. Martin, (1974) 27 *New Society* 766.
2. In 1977, there were 22,160 convictions for disciplinary offences. See
Prison Statistics England and Wales 1977, Cmnd. 7286, p. 72. Most of them
were for minor offences such as 'disobedience' (about 1/3rd of the total),
'unauthorised transactions/unauthorised possession', and 'disrespect/im-
propriety'. There were 16 convictions for 'gross personal violence to
officers' and over 1000 for lesser assaults upon officers.
3. Many of the offences in Rule 47 are criminal offences also. The decision
whether to call in the police with a view to prosecution before the ordinary
courts is taken by the prison authorities. The main purpose of referring
'graver offences' (Rule 51) and 'especially grave offences' (Rule 52) to the
Secretary of State is for the Home Office to consider whether the case
should be referred to the police for investigation. In 1974, 77 cases were
referred to the police (*Report of the Home Office Working Party on
Adjudication Procedures in Prisons, 1975*, p. 11).

Should the accused prisoner be entitled to insist upon a case being
referred for trial by the courts? The Jellicoe Committee (*Board of Visitors of
Penal Institutions*, a report of a Committee set up by Justice, the Howard
League for Penal Reform, and the National Association for the Care and
Resettlement of Offenders 1975, p. 71) proposed that the 'especially grave
offences' in Rule 52 should be looked at with a view to their abolition and
the trial of all offenders by the ordinary courts under the equivalent
criminal offences. In their view, it was 'undesirable in principle for it to be
possible for internal adjudication (with its less extensive procedure
guarantees) to result in a loss of remission exceeding one year in total on a
single occasion (whether as single or consecutive awards)'. It is not contrary
to the double jeopardy for disciplinary and criminal proceedings to be
brought in turn on the same facts, but a court should, when sentencing,
take into account any sentence imposed in the disciplinary proceedings: *R v
Hogan* [1960] 2 QB 513, CCA.
4. The sentences listed in Rules 50–52 include the forfeiture of remission.
Under Rule 5, Prison Rules, a prisoner may be granted remission not
exceeding one-third of his sentence 'on the ground of his industry and good
conduct'. This is distinct from parole (for which a prisoner is eligible after
serving one-third of his sentence). Although remission is not a matter of
legal right (see *Hancock v Prison Comrs* [1960] 1 QB 117, Vac Ct), one-third
remission is invariably granted in the absence of a disciplinary award
reducing it. Commenting on loss of remission as a sentence, the Jellicoe
Committee stated (Report, p. 35):

'For most purposes the maximum is 180 days, but it is possible to have consecutive sentences if
there is more than one charge, and several totals of 300 days or more have been reported in
recent years [see e.g. the facts of *ex parte St. Germain*, below, p. 430]. Such periods of course

relate to the actual time to be served and are comparable with court sentences 50 per cent longer because they would normally attract one third remission. For example a loss of 180 days' remission usually has the same practical effect as a court sentence of 9 months, three months of which would be remitted for good conduct.'

In 1977 the most common forms of punishment were stoppage or reduction of earnings, loss of remission, loss of privileges, exclusion from associated work, cautions, and cellular confinement – in that order: *Prison Statistics England and Wales 1977*, Cmnd. 7286, pp. 72–75. Corporal punishment and 'restricted diet' (bread and water) were abolished in 1967 (Criminal Justice Act 1967, s. 65) and 1974 (S I 1974 No 713, Rule 5) respectively.

5. *Procedure before the Governor.* The Home Office Working Party (Report, pp. 12–13) describes the initial procedure as follows:

'30. The prisoner is informed of the charge by the serving on him of a Notice of Report . . . Governors are required to record on the form the date, time and place of the alleged offence; the precise wording of the offence as set out in Rule 47 must be quoted, with the number given to the offence in that Rule; explanatory detail of the offence, sufficient to leave the prisoner in no doubt of, the precise nature of the charge, must be included, and the time of the hearing must also be stated.
31. . . . Unless a charge is laid early in the day, the governor's hearing does not normally take place until the following day, and, in a cellular prison, and particularly when, under Rule 48(2), the prisoner is kept apart from other prisoners pending adjudication, it is customary for the prisoner to be informed of the charge as soon as it is laid. To ensure that the prisoner has a reasonable time to prepare his defence, and especially to cater for those cases where the charge is not served on the prisoner overnight, eg when the charge is laid early in the day, or the prisoner is in an open prison and it is not desirable to serve a charge overnight, governors have been instructed that there should be at least two hours between service of the charge and the hearing of the charge.

The Working Party's Report continues:

'Every charge must in the first instance be the subject of an adjudication by the governor, and most cases will be disposed of by his either finding that the charge has not been proved and dismissing it; or by his making an award with the powers open to him under Rule 50.'

In 1977 approximately 95 % of charges were decided by the Governor. Caird, *A Good and Useful Life*, 1974, p. 54, described the procedure before the Governor as follows:

'The prisoner is given a small slip of paper after he has been 'nicked' saying what the charge is; the Governor invites him to state his case in front of the accusing officer. Predictably, perhaps, most governors are not prepared to admit to a prisoner that they disbelieve one of the officers. . . . Without access to legal advice or witnesses, unable to build up a case on his own behalf, the prisoner has little chance of persuading the Governor to believe him rather than the officer, who begins with the massive advantage of the lawful gaoler accusing the already-convicted criminal. Only in the most exceptional situations is a prisoner acquitted of a charge. Most governors, if they feel doubt about the prisoner's guilt, will merely caution him – thereby saving everyone's face, except that of the prisoner, who still has a finding of guilt placed on his record.'

6. *Adjudication by Boards of Visitors.* In the serious cases covered by Rules 51(1)(2) and 52(1), the Governor may or, in some cases, must refer a charge to the Board of Visitors for adjudication. In 1974, 1944 charges were referred to Boards of Visitors, with the number dealt with by a particular Board ranging greatly from 161 to none. The average figure was 27 charges per Board of Visitors. The prisoner pleaded not guilty in respect of 625 (about ⅓) of the charges brought before a Board of Visitors. 64 charges were not proved (Report of the Home Office Working Party, Annex B). The Working Party's report recommended that the Governor or a senior member of staff should be present at the hearing to make his report and also to keep himself informed on matters affecting the management of the prison. In order to stress the Board's independence, the Governor should be seated 'separately from and at a suitable distance from' the Board and should not be present when the Board reaches its decision.

7. The Working Party's recommendations have been accepted by the Home Office and separate (though basically similar) standard procedures for the conduct of adjudications by Governors and Boards of Visitors 'were promulgated in three recommendations in April 1977' (*Report of the Work of the Prison Department 1977*, Cmnd. 7290, p. 19). The procedures have been incorporated into Standing Orders. For some indication of their content, see the *St. Germain* case, below, p. 430 (Boards of Visitors).

8. The Jellicoe Committee (Report, p. 81) recommended that the disciplinary role of the Board of Visitors should be taken from it and given instead to tribunals composed of professional Chairmen drawn from lawyers of the standing required for appointment as Circuit Judges or Recorders and one, or preferably two, lay members drawn from members of the local magistracy who were not members of the Board. The Committee stressed that it made this proposal not as a criticism of Boards of Visitors but because it considered that they exercised two incompatible functions. Their role as an independent element in the supervision and the running of prisons (which the Committee wished them to retain) involved their having the trust of prisoners who were expected to approach them with requests and complaints and otherwise confide in them. It was difficult for prisoners to feel this trust in a body which they associated with the establishment because of its disciplinary role. The Home Secretary did not accept that the supervisory and disciplinary roles were incompatible and decided not to implement the recommendation (921 HC Deb written answer 7 December 1976 col 114). The May Committee Report (Cmnd. 7673), which was particularly influenced by the possibility of judicial review of Board proceedings since the *St Germain* case, below, p. 430, also recommended that Boards of Visitors should continue to exercise the two roles (Report, p. 280).

Fraser v Mudge [1975] 1 WLR 1132, [1975] 3 All ER 78, Court of Appeal

Lord Denning MR: This is an unusual application on behalf of the plaintiff, Mr. Francis Davidson Fraser. He is at present serving a long sentence of imprisonment and is detained in Her Majesty's Prison at Bristol. It is said that last weekend he assaulted a prison officer. He is charged with an offence against prison discipline. It is to be heard by an adjudication committee of the board of visitors at 2.15 today at Bristol Prison. Now he or someone on his behalf has instructed lawyers. They wish to represent him at the hearing by the board of visitors. . . . [A] writ has been issued today against the three named members of the board of inquiry seeking a declaration that he is entitled to be represented by solicitor and counsel and an injunction restraining the board from inquiring into the charge until he has had an opportunity of appearing by lawyers. Chapman J has refused. . . .

The Prison Act 1952 says that rules are to be made for ensuring that a prisoner who is charged with any offence under the rules shall be given a proper opportunity of presenting his case. Rule 49 (2) of the Prison Rules 1964 . . . is in virtually the same words. The rule applies not only to a charge before the board of visitors, but also to an inquiry made by the governor, and also in addition to an inquiry by an officer appointed by the Secretary of State: see rules 49–52. . . .

Mr Sedley has referred us to *Pett v Greyhound Racing Association Ltd* [1969] 1 QB 125, where a charge was made before the Greyhound Racing Association that dogs had been doped. We indicated that it might well be proper that a legal representation should be allowed. But it seems to me that disciplinary cases fall into a very different category. We all know that, when a man is brought up before his commanding officer for a breach of discipline, whether in the armed forces or in ships at sea, it never has been the practice to allow legal representation.

It is of the first importance that the cases should be decided quickly. If legal representation were allowed, it would mean considerable delay. So also with breaches of prison discipline. They must be heard and decided speedily. Those who hear the cases must, of course, act fairly. They must let the man know the charge and give him a proper opportunity of presenting his case. But that can be done and is done without the matter being held up for legal representation. I do not think we ought to alter the existing practice. We ought not to create a precedent such as to suggest that an individual is entitled to legal representation. There is no real arguable case in support of this application and I would reject it.

Roskill LJ: I entirely agree with the refusal of Chapman J to grant this ex parte injunction and with what Lord Denning MR has said. In so far as reliance is placed upon *Pett v Greyhound Racing Association Ltd* [1969] 1 QB 125, that case is clearly distinguishable, because there was there a contractual or quasi-contractual relationship between the plaintiff and defendant, since the plaintiff held a licence from the defendants which the defendants were intending to revoke. . . . I wish to make it plain that I do not subscribe to the view that in every type of case, irrespective of the nature or jurisdiction of the body in question, justice can neither be done nor be seen to be done without legal representation of the party or parties appearing before that body. . . .

Ormrod LJ concurred.

Appeal dismissed

NOTES

1. The Home Office Working Party (Report, p. 23) considered and rejected the case for the representation of prisoners in disciplinary proceedings:

'. . . [w]e consider that it would be extremely difficult for anyone from outside the establishment to undertake the representation of a prisoner. He could not be expected to be familiar with the circumstances of the establishment and the relevant background to the case, and if it were proposed that hearings should be adjourned to allow someone from outside to make the inquiries necessary to overcome these difficulties, this would inevitably introduce the kind of delays which could only prolong tension in an institutional setting. Equally, we think that since – unlike persons involved in criminal proceedings – prisoners and staff involved in an adjudication have to continue in association and daily contact afterwards, there would be inevitable difficulties about a prisoner or member of staff representing or acting as advocate for a prisoner. (A member of staff could, for example, find himself caught between conflicting loyalties with his wish to do his best for the prisoner inhibited by a natural reluctance to challenge his colleagues.) It is a further consideration that representation for the prisoner would at once raise the question of representation for the reporting officer. With the exception of one member, we therefore think that it should remain the task of the prisoner to present his defence himself.'

But the Party did recommend an experiment in which a prisoner charged with an offence to be heard by a Board of Visitors would be offered the assistance of a prison officer or an assistant governor in preparing his case. This was described in (1975) 33 *New Society* 527 as being 'like offering the accused in a criminal case the helping hand of a policeman'. One member of the Party (note of dissent by Dr J. E. Harris) proposed that assistance to the prisoner in the preparation of an presentation of his case should be given by a member of the Board. The Home Office is conducting an experiment at Pentonville in accordance with the latter proposal.

2. In *Wolff v McDonnell* 418 US 539, 570 (1974), the US Supreme Court ruled that the 'due process' clause in the Constitution did not guarantee the right to counsel in disciplinary proceedings:

'The insertion of counsel into the disciplinary process would inevitably give the proceedings a more adversary cast and tend to reduce their utility as a means to further correctional goals. There would also be delay and very practical problems in providing counsel in sufficient numbers at the time and place where hearings are to be held.'

And see the decisions in Commonwealth courts to the same effect in *Re Armstrong and Whitehead* (1973) 11 CCC 2d 327, Ont CA, and *R v Visiting Justice at HM Prison, Pentridge, ex parte Walker* [1975] VR 883, S Ct Vict.

R v Hull Prison Board of Visitors, ex parte St. Germain (No. 2) [1979] 3 All ER 545, [1979] 1 WLR 1401, Queen's Bench Divisional Court

The Hull Prison Riot in 1976 caused considerable disruption and damage to property. See the Fowler Report, 1976–77 HC 453 and Zellick, 18 BJ Crim 75 (1978). 185 of the 310 Prisoners at the prison were dealt with by the Board of Visitors for offences against prison discipline arising out of the riot. The disciplinary awards made by the Board included loss of privileges, loss of earnings and loss of remission. In the most serious of the cases that led to the present proceedings, the prisoner lost 720 days remission, later reduced by the Home Secretary to 600. In this application for certiorari, seven prisoners punished for breaches of discipline claimed that proceedings before the Board had not complied with the rules of natural justice. After reviewing the law governing proceedings before Board of Visitors (s. 47(2), Prison Act 1952 and Rules 49–56, Prison Rules, above, pp. 424–6), Geoffrey Lane LJ, giving the judgment of the court, (Lord Widgery CJ, Geoffrey Lane LJ and Ackner J) continued:

Geoffrey Lane LJ:
A document entitled 'Explanation of the procedure at adjudications by board of visitors' is provided to every prisoner accused of a disciplinary offence who is to appear before a board of visitors. It sets out the procedure which follows essentially that which would occur in any magistrates' court on summary trial. These paragraphs of this explanation are relevant and we quote from them:

'(5) When a witness has given his evidence you will be told that you may question him if you wish. You may then ask the witness any questions which you think may help your case. Remember just to ask questions and not to argue with the witness. If you want to dispute something he has said you should either ask him another question or explain your point to the Chairman who will help you. . .

'(7) If you want to call witnesses ask the Chairman for permission to do so. Tell him who they are and what you think their evidence will prove. If the Board think that the witnesses may be able to give useful evidence they will hear them. After they have been heard the Board will ask you if you want to say anything further about the case, and you may then comment on all the evidence and point out anything that you think is in your favour.

'(8) If you have pleaded not guilty, but in the end are found guilty, you will be given an opportunity, before punishment is imposed, of giving any reasons why you think you should be dealt with leniently.'

Megaw LJ in his judgment in *R v Hull Prison Board of Visitors, ex parte St. Germain* [[1979] 1 All ER 701 at 713, [1979] 2 WLR 42 at 57] referred to the submissions of counsel that proceedings of boards of visitors for offences against discipline are 'subject to judicial review, at any rate where the allegations are of breaches of the procedure laid down in the Prison Rules and/or rules of fairness and natural justice'. He said:

'I think that is too widely stated. It is certainly not any breach of any procedural rule which would justify or require interference by the courts. Such interference, in my judgment, would only be required, and would only be justified, if there were some failure to act fairly, having regard to all relevant circumstances, and such unfairness could reasonably be regarded as having caused a substantial, as distinct from a trivial or merely technical, injustice which was capable of remedy.'

He further pointed out that which has been frequently stated recently, that it would be fallacious to assume that the requirements of natural justice in one sphere are necessarily identical in a different sphere. In our judgment there is nothing in the procedure as detailed in the written explanation to which any objection can properly be taken.

We turn now to the way in which the case has been presented on behalf of the applicants. . . .

Counsel accepted that it was perfectly proper for a chairman to insist that all questions were put through him where he was of the view that otherwise arguments would break out between the prisoner and the witness, which would make the proceedings difficult to control. There was some suggestion that the chairman should have no discretion to disallow the calling of a witness whose attendance is requested by the prisoner. . . . Those who appear before the board of visitors on charges are, ex hypothesi, those who are serving sentences in prison. Many of such offenders might well seek to render the adjudications by the board of visitors quite impossible if they had the same liberty to conduct their own defences as they would have in an ordinary criminal trial. In our judgment the chairman's discretion is necessary as part of a proper procedure for dealing with alleged offences against discipline by prisoners.

However, that discretion has to be exercised reasonably, in good faith and on proper grounds. It would clearly be wrong if, as has been alleged in one instance before us, the basis for refusal to allow a prisoner to call witnesses was that the chairman considered that there was ample evidence against the accused. It would equally be an improper exercise of the discretion if the refusal was based on an erroneous understanding of the prisoner's defence, for example, that an alibi did not cover the material time or day, whereas in truth and in fact it did.

A more serious question was raised whether the discretion could be validly exercised where it was based on considerable administrative inconvenience being caused if the request to call a witness or witnesses was permitted. Clearly in the proper exercise of his discretion a chairman may limit the number of witnesses, either on the basis that he has good reason for considering that the total number sought to be called is an attempt by the prisoner to render the hearing of the charge virtually impracticable or where quite simply it would be quite unnecessary to call so many witnesses to establish the point at issue. But mere administrative difficulties, simpliciter, are not in our view enough. Convenience and justice are often not on speaking terms. . .

At the outset of his submissions counsel for the board of visitors urged that there was no obligation at all on the board to allow any witnesses to be called. He said, and to this extent we accept his submission, that the written explanation of the procedure at adjudications by boards of visitors has no statutory force. He based his submission on the bald proposition that although natural justice imposes an obligation to hear the party accused, it does not involve any obligation to hear any witnesses whom he wishes to call. . . .

[His lordship discussed *Board of Education v Rice* [1911] AC 179 and *General Medical Council v Spackman* [1943] AC 627 and continued:]

. . . It was in fact in *De Verteuil v Knaggs* [[1918) AC 557 at 560] that the Privy Council stated:
'Their Lordships are of opinion that in making such an inquiry there is, apart from special circumstances, a duty of giving to any person against whom the complaint is made a fair opportunity to make any relevant statement which he may desire to bring forward and a fair opportunity to correct or controvert any relevant statement brought forward to his prejudice.'

These words were quoted with approval in the Privy Council in *University of Ceylon v Fernando* [[1960] 1 All ER 631 at 638, [1960] 1 WLR 223 at 232]. They imply, in our view, that the right to be heard will include, in appropriate cases, the right to call evidence. It would in our judgment be wrong to attempt an exhaustive definition as to what are appropriate cases, but they must include proceedings whose function is to establish the guilt or innocence of a person charged with serious misconduct. In the instant cases, what was being considered was alleged serious disciplinary offences, which, if established, could and did result in a very substantial loss of liberty. In such a situation it would be a mockery to say that an accused had been given a proper opportunity of presenting his case' (s 47(2) of the Prison Act 1952) or 'a full opportunity . . . of presenting his own case' (r 49(2) of the Prison Rules 1964), if he had been denied the opportunity of calling evidence which was likely to assist in establishing the vital facts at issue.

. . . We now turn to the suggestion that hearsay evidence is not permissible in a hearing before a board of visitors.

It is of course common ground that the board of visitors must base their decisions on evidence. But must such evidence be restricted to that which would be admissible in a criminal court of law? Viscount Simon LC, in *General Medical Council v Spackman*, considered there was no such restriction. That was also clearly the view of the Privy Council in *University of Ceylon v Fernando*.

The matter was dealt with in more detail by Diplock LJ in *R v Deputy Industrial Injuries Comr, ex parte Moore* [[1965] 1 All ER 81 at 94, [1965] 1 QB 456 at 488] as follows:
. . . these technical rules of evidence, however, form no part of the rules of natural justice. The requirement that a person exercising quasi-judicial functions must base his decision on evidence means no more than that it must be based on material which tends logically to show the existence or non-existence of facts relevant to the issue to be determined, or to show the likelihood or unlikelihood of the occurrence of some future event the occurrence of which would be relevant. It means that he must not spin a coin or consult an astrologer, but he may take into account any material which, as a matter of reason, has some probative value in the sense mentioned above. . . .

However, it is clear that the entitlement of the board of visitors to admit hearsay evidence is subject to the overriding obligation to provide the accused with a fair hearing. Depending on the facts of the particular case and the nature of the hearsay evidence provided to the board of visitors, the obligation to give the accused a fair chance to exculpate himself, or a fair opportunity to controvert the charge, to quote the phrases used in the cases cited above, or a proper or full opportunity of presenting his case, to quote the language of s 47 or r 49, may oblige the board of visitors not only to inform the accused of the hearsay evidence but also to give the accused a sufficient opportunity to deal with that evidence. Again, depending on the nature of that evidence and the particular circumstances of the case, a sufficient opportunity to deal with the hearsay evidence may well involve the cross-examination of the witness whose evidence is initially before the board in the form of hearsay.

We again take by way of example the case in which the defence is an alibi. The prisoner contends that he was not the man identified on the roof . . . [and] has been mistakenly identified. The evidence of identification given by way of hearsay may be of the 'fleeting glance' type as exemplified by the well-known case of *R v Turnbull* [[1976] 3 All ER 549 [1977] QB 224]. The prisoner may well wish to elicit by way of questions all manner of detail, eg the poorness of the light, the state of confusion, the brevity of the observation, the absence of any contemporaneous record, etc, all designed to show the unreliability of the witness. To deprive him of the opportunity of cross-examination would be tantamount to depriving him of a fair hearing.

We appreciate that there may well be occasions when the burden of calling the witness whose hearsay evidence is readily available may impose a near impossible burden on the board. However, it has not been suggested that hearsay evidence should be resorted to in the total absence of any firsthand evidence. In the instant cases hearsay evidence was only resorted to to supplement the firsthand evidence and this is the usual practice. Accordingly where a prisoner desires to dispute the hearsay evidence and for this purpose to question the witness, and where there are insuperable or very grave difficulties in arranging for his attendance, the board should refuse to admit that evidence, or, if it has already come to their notice, should expressly dismiss it from their consideration. . . .

We now turn to consider the effects of those conclusions on the individual applications which are before us. . . .

[After quashing one conviction because a witness had not been called, but ruling that the Board had not acted incorrectly in refusing to call other witnesses in other cases, His Lordship considered the question of hearsay evidence:]

After the disturbances had subsided all the prison officers involved submitted written reports of their observations, naming such prisoners as they had seen taking part in the riot. A dossier was then prepared in respect of each prisoner so named . . . .

The governor explains in his affidavit, and it can be seen from the record of the proceedings, that from time to time, at the tacit or express invitation of the chairman, the governor would give to the board of visitors information which he derived from the dossiers. To take one example: the applicant Saxton faced a number of charges, one of which was under r 47(10) of the 1964 rules, the particulars being that he had been seen on 'A' wing roof filling bottles with floor polish. The suggestion was that these were to be used as incendiary bombs. Evidence was given by Officer Wooldridge that he had seen through binoculars Saxton and another man, Duffy, filling the bottles. Saxton said he knew nothing about it. The chairman asked him: 'Are all the officers wrong?' whereupon the governor said this: 'Six out of 14 sightings say he was the first man onto the roof—others suggest it was Saxton who carried the bed to smash the windows to get on the roof.' Then the chairman said: 'Case proven.'

It is clear that no opportunity was given to the applicant to examine the evidence to which the governor was referring. He was not told the names of the officers who had allegedly seen him at the material time and place, or from what positions they had observed him. He was not given the opportunity, so far as one can ascertain, to make any comment on what the governor had said.

. . . It seems to us that in the way this hearsay evidence was handled there was a departure from the rule of fairness and that that departure could reasonably be regarded as having caused what Megaw LJ describes as 'a substantial, as distinct from a trivial or merely technical, injustice'.

[His Lordship then dealt with each case in turn and held that 11 convictions, involving 6 of the applicants, should be quashed because hearsay evidence had been improperly admitted].

Orders accordingly.

NOTES

1. In *R v Hull Prison, Board of Visitors, ex parte St. Germain* [1979] 2 WLR 42, the Court of Appeal, in a decision of great importance, had held that the proceedings of a Board of Visitors acting judicially as a disciplinary tribunal were subject to judicial review by way of certiorari. The holding was limited to Boards of Visitors. Megaw LJ stated obiter that certiorari would not lie to disciplinary proceedings before a Governor:

[The function of the board of visitors] is materially different . . . from the function of the governor in dealing with alleged offences against discipline. While the governor hears charges and makes awards, his position in so doing corresponds to that of the commanding officer in military discipline or the schoolmaster in school discipline. His powers of summary discipline are not only of a limited and summary nature but they are also intimately connected with his functions of day-to-day administration. To my mind, both good sense and the practical requirements of public policy make it undesirable that his exercise of that part of his administrative duties should be made subject to certiorari.

Shaw LJ disagreed:

I do not for my part find it easy, if at all possible, to distinguish between disciplinary proceedings conducted by a board of visitors and those carried out by a prison governor. In each case the subject matter may be the same: the relevant fundamental regulations are common to both forms of proceeding. The powers of a governor as to the award he can make (which really means the punishment he can impose) are more restricted than those of a board of visitors in a corresponding situation; but the essential nature of the proceedings as defined by the Prison Rules is the same. So, in nature if not in degree, are the consequences to a prisoner. . . .

Waller LJ reserved his judgment on the question.

2. In holding that prison disciplinary proceedings before a Board of Visitors are subject to judicial review, the Court of Appeal follows recent decisions in other Commonwealth countries. See *Stratton v Parn* (1978) 52 ALJR 330, HC Aust; *Daemar v Hall* [1978] 2 NZLR 594 NZ S Ct; and *Martineau v Matsqui Institution Inmate Disciplinary Board* (*No. 2*) (1978) 40 CCC(2d) 325 S Ct Can. Similarly, the US Supreme Court has held that prison disciplinary proceedings are controlled by the 'due process' clause of the Constitution: *Wolff v McDonnell* 418 US 539 (1974). See further Zellick, (1979) 129 NLJ 309.

3. Should there not at least be the *possiblility* of review of decisions by Governors too?

4. In the *Kiss* case, see above, p. 414, the European Commission of Human Rights held that the 'fair trial' guarantee in Article 6, ECHR did not apply to English prison disciplinary proceedings. In the *Engel* case, Eur Court HR, Series A No 22, Judgment of November 23 1976, the European Court of Human Rights had earlier held that Article 6 applied to certain of the Dutch army disciplinary proceedings before it in the case, mainly because the accused in them could be deprived of their liberty if convicted. The accused soldiers could, therefore, be said to be subject to a 'criminal charge' (Article 6(1)). In the *Kiss* case the Commission held that the possibility of loss of remission as a punishment did not bring prison disciplinary proceedings within Article 6 because there was no legal right to liberty in the form of remission. The decision is an important one because English prison disciplinary proceedings do not comply with Article 6 in several respects.

5. On the *St. Germain* cases see A. M. Tettenborn, [1980] PL 74.

Index

Official secrets—*continued*
enemy—*continued*
meaning 277
foreign agent, communication with 276,
277
Franks Committee 278, 279
mens rea in disclosure of 278
prejudicing safety of State 280–284
statutory provisions—
arrest, power to 274
atomic energy 276
attempt to commit offence 275, 276
documents, misuse of 275
generally 272
harbouring spies, penalty 274
incitement to commit offence 275,
276
information, wrongful communication
of 273
interpretation 274, 275
obstruction of forces or police 276
penalties 276
prohibited place—
definition 273, 274
gaining admission by false pretences
276
prosecution, restriction on 274
search warrants 274
spying, penalties for 273
Open spaces
beaches 141
bye-laws regulating 140, 141
Crown or local authority, resting in 140
generally 140–143
Hyde Park 142
parks and recreation grounds 140
Trafalgar Square 142, 143
Oppression
meaning 116
Order
law and, maintenance of. *See* PUBLIC
ORDER
Organisation
meaning 131
proscribed. *See* NORTHERN IRELAND;
TERRORISM

Parliament
absolute power of 1
disorder within precincts of 145
meeting near—
regulation of 143–145
sessional orders—
enforcement 143, 145
power to give 143
streets to be unobstructed 144
petitions to 144, 145
presentation of addresses to 143, 144
processions near—
police powers 144
prohibition during sittings 144, 145
sovereignty of 15
**Parliamentary Commissioner for Adminis-
tration**
prisoners' complaints to 406

Passing off
tort of 323
Photographs
copyright, breach of 316, 317, 319
indecent 238, 239
publication of—
as contempt of court 248–252
Press Council opinion 308
right to take, general principle 308
trespasser taking 307
Picketing
control of numbers of pickets 175
highway, on 136
obstructing police 175, 176
obstruction of highway 176
peaceful, law as to 176
Police
arrest, powers of, *See* ARREST
assault on—
car, by driving 90, 91
generally 39–41
premature attack 69
statutory penalty 36
boats and vessels, power to search 92, 93
citizens' duty to help 104
complaints against 118–122
computers, use of 337
disadvantages under which working 33
drugs, powers of detention and search for
92, 93
entry, powers of—
common law, at 63–66
generally 63
invitation, by, express on implied 63
public, as members of 64–66
request to leave, effect 68
statutory power, by 63
warrant, by authority of 63, 70 et seq.
execution of duty, acts within 40, 41
firearms, power to search for 90, 93
interrogation by. *See* INTERROGATION
leave and licence to enter garden 69
obstruction of—
active and passive 36
breathalyser test, frustration of 36
enforcement of sessional orders where
145
generally 34
hostility to police 37
meaning 35
prevention of lawful arrest of another
58
refusal to act 36
refusal to follow traffic instruction 37
refusal to move car 57
speed trap, warning of 37
wilful, meaning 35
powers and duties—
arrest 46–63
See also ARREST; ARRESTABLE
OFFENCE
co-operation of citizens, need for 33
documents, seizure of 85, 86, 95, 96
drug offences 51–53
entry 63–70
See also ENTRY